THE
RELATIONS
OF
NATIONS

THIRD EDITION

Frederick H. Hartmann
ALFRED THAYER MAHAN PROFESSOR, NAVAL WAR COLLEGE

THE MACMILLAN COMPANY · New York
COLLIER-MACMILLAN LIMITED · London

TO

Hildegarde Millar

AND

Dorothea and Joseph Kittredge

. . . But we have been insulated . . . in our international life by our long sheltered position behind two oceans. More than this, we have been actually misled by the experience of our two dramatic sorties into the larger world. It has seemed to us that it is our role to intervene in world affairs with sporadic and violent bursts of energy and with decisive and definitive effect —to appear on the scene in the nick of time like a knight errant, rescue the lady, and ride away.

But the experience brought its disillusionment. The lady did not remain as glamorous; she did not even seem particularly grateful; she became demanding. And then, too, there was no secure and serene place to ride to. Our castle walls had crumbled, we found ourselves living on the plain with everyone else. We had the problem of neighbors. And so the occasional challenge of high adventure became the constant and nagging problems of everyday life.

FORMER SECRETARY OF STATE DEAN ACHESON
In the Introduction to Louis J. Halle,
Civilization and Foreign Policy, 1955

Preface to the Third Edition

THE most important function the preface to a third edition can fill is to give an overview of the changes reflected in the revision. Certain chapters have been almost entirely rewritten; few pages stand without at least some minor change. While the format of the previous editions has not been altered except for the consolidation of the material on the foreign policies of the major European powers into one less chapter, the total revision is quite substantial.

The "updating" necessary to integrate five further years of developments goes without much need for special comment. But there is also an increased stress on the "developing nations"—a stress sometimes not completely obvious from the table of contents (but clear enough in the index). Chapters ostensibly on topics such as the United Nations naturally cover much about such areas. One important aspect of the Sino-Soviet dispute, covered in some detail, is over the very point of how revolutionary discontent in the newer nations can be or should be exploited.

Second, I have taken greater pains (I hope, successfully) to spell out theoretical points and linkages. These changes reflect some evolution in my own thinking, but primarily they are designed to make more explicit what was implicit or less explicit. I have made this type of change within self-imposed limits, for it is no service to the undergraduate to lead him into unnecessary complications until he has a good basic grounding.

My own impression of the theory in my book is that it is quite close in most major aspects to much of the thrust of recent emphases in the field. In using the unifying concept of national interests I have always done so within a framework quite clearly different from what is sometimes loosely called the "power struggle–national interest" school. To me, national interests are, as policies, goal inputs into the system. But the systems context has in itself an important effect upon how interests are formulated. Any purely abstract conception of a system (apart from particular roles played by individual nations in it) can be carried only so far (to the limits of uniformities) before distortions creep in. Let me express the point less abstractly. Nations not only show uniformities in behavior but striking differences. This range can, of course, be scaled and nations categorized on such a scale. But we will still need to decide which is what, when we attempt to talk about the behavior of particular nations. I am irreverently reminded of the German soap slogan, "Persil bleibt Persil" (which of course means essentially "Oxydol remains Oxydol"). So too Japan remains Japan. Even if it is changing, it is still uniquely Japanese, before and after. It never quite becomes "China" or "Indonesia." Yet, for certain systems effects, the identity of the nation may be essentially irrelevant. We must be very careful in deciding which is which.

It may be useful to repeat at this point from the preface to the first edition (omitted here): ". . . much of the controversy among scholars in the field of international relations is the result of the attempt to emphasize a single cause for action on the part of nation-states, whether this be characterized as the desire for peace or the struggle for power. There *is* a single theme common to the actions of nation-states in the sense that they follow out in their policies their particular concept of their national interests, but since the particular concept of these interests will vary from state to state, and even for a single state with time and circumstances, this is only a conceptual tool that permits us in a single phrase to deal with what is inherently varied and complex. As such a single phrase it is extremely useful, provided it is kept in mind that its precise and concrete meaning (or context) varies from one sovereign entity to the next. Conversely, the real weakness of characterizing the actions of all states, throughout time, as based on a desire for peace or a struggle for power (as is often done) is that it is too rigid a description for what is so abundantly varied.

". . . the phrase 'national interest' . . . is not being used to describe the 'selfish' actions of individual states, nor to counsel 'selfishness.' Where the actions described are 'selfish,' it will be because the nation's policies are such. But that a nation's concept of national interest may be extremely broad and generous—quite 'unselfish'—we do not for a moment deny or wish to change. Britain's concept of her national interests in terms of the balance of power prior to World War I led her to uphold the independence of small European states (here 'realism' became 'unselfish'); Britain's wish for peace in 1938 led her, however, to sacrifice Czechoslovakia at Munich (here 'idealism' became 'selfish'). Enough has been said for now, we hope, to show that these terms of realism, idealism, selfishness, and unselfishness are in any event misleading. Britain's two quite diverse policies were equally formulations of Britain's interests as she conceived them at the time— however wisely or unwisely."

What I said in part in the preface to the second edition is also still quite pertinent: ". . . a careful combination of theory with historical and other data has been attempted so that the student would be neither adrift in a sea of unstructured fact nor confronted with abstract and bare generalizations of theory which remain disconnected and undigested. It helps, for example, even while making full allowance for the emotionalism with which the United States approaches the Chinese problem, to realize that Chinese intolerance and pride make the combination even worse, and to realize that Chinese arrogance has ancient roots. As Chinese Emperor Ch'ien Lung wrote to King George III of England in 1793: "You, O King, live beyond the confines of many seas; nevertheless, impelled by your humble desire to partake of the benefits of our civilization, you have dispatched a mission respectfully bearing your memorial. . . . I have perused your memorial; the earnest terms in which it is couched reveal a respectful humility on your part which is highly praiseworthy. . . ."

Any text reflects decisions on the relative stress to be placed in what all must agree is a vast field. Some problems continue to be more important than others. I have continued, as before, to doubt that the fundamental arrangements which have characterized the Cold War era in Europe and Asia could remain frozen—a doubt that seems increasingly justified now by the sweep of events.

As I said in the preface to the second edition, one of the real pleasures that comes to someone so brave or foolhardy as to write a textbook on international relations is the letters which come from readers. These reactions are very interesting—and useful. Sometimes they are simple but heartwarming notes of appreciation from a student two thousand miles away. Sometimes they are letters from colleagues in the United States or Switzerland or India who point out minor errors or make suggestions for changes. I have given these suggestions very careful consideration. I look forward to more letters.

Finally, I wish to express my appreciation to those who have helped me in one way or another with this book as it has taken shape in successive editions. It is a very real pleasure to record my debt to Professor Harry R. Warfel, of the Department of English at the University of Florida, who did so much to bring clarity to the original edition; and to Professor Arthur C. Turner, of the University of California at Riverside, for his thorough, detailed, and unusually helpful critique of the original manuscript. Professor Alfred Diamant (Haverford) aided me immeasurably in shaping my ideas for the first edition. I wish to thank also my former colleagues at the University of Florida, such as Manning J. Dauer, Harry Kantor, John Spanier, and Oscar Svarlien. John Brown Mason (California State College at Fullerton) read much of the original manuscript, as did Ross Y. Koen. Many former graduate students or assistants of mine deserve mention. From previous editions I recall again with appreciation the efforts of James Fitzgerald, Jackson Smith, Harry Macy, Wayne Bailey, Troy Parris, Howard H. Symons, and Gail Roemheld. For this present edition I would mention especially Jose Ojeda for his untiring assistance, and Richard Bowman and Stuart Herrington.

I would add in closing that the Naval War College neither necessarily agrees nor disagrees with the views and opinions expressed in this book. In international relations as in other parts of the curriculum here, the emphasis, in the normal academic tradition, is always that "there is no school solution."

F. H. H.

Newport, Rhode Island

Contents

PART THREE
The Relations of States

PART FOUR
Conflict Resolution: The Settlement of Disputes

PART FIVE
The Problem of Power and the Power Patterns

PART SIX

Contemporary International Relations

List of Diagrams, Maps, and Tables

Diagrams

Maps

Tables

PART ONE

The Fundamentals of the State System

CHAPTER I

An Introduction to International Relations

The old order changeth, yielding place to new.
ALFRED, LORD TENNYSON

IN the first years of the last third of the twentieth century mankind possessed in abundance the power literally to destroy civilization. The "small" and scarce atom bomb of 1945 had been supplemented by whole "families of nuclear weapons," while ownership of these means of unprecedented destruction had spread from the United States, first to Russia and to Britain, and then to France and China. More nations would inevitably follow. The conquest of outer space was accelerating, potentially adding a new dimension to warfare. For the first time since the Black Plague of the Middle Ages the contemporary generation had to face the shocking possibility that its days might be numbered far shorter than the ordinary lifespan of mankind—that it might indeed be the last generation of mankind in anything like the numbers or conditions now prevailing. It is a new feeling for man to live, as it were, with a bottle of nitroglycerin in every living-room.

These developments in the technique of warfare have made deliberate resort to a war, with these weapons used in any abundance on both sides, completely pointless so far as achieving "victory" is concerned. Generals are now given custody of stockpiles of arms whose point is to *deter* any enemy from making them use them. These rather brutal facts of life are completely unaffected by the philosophies men live by: communism, however aggressive it is deemed to be, cannot conquer the world by force of arms—since not enough world would be there when they finished; capitalism, however defensive, cannot keep the ramparts of democracy intact against the onslaught —since the ramparts would consist quite quickly of radioactive dust.

Within this framework of a world so deeply torn by friction, and possessed of outlandishly extravagant means of violence which sane men could not desire to unleash, we see immense and unprecedented changes occurring. The participants in international relations, the nation-states, have been multiplying like the ameoba. The United Nations, bulging at the seams with two and a half times the membership with which it began in 1945, was hard put to find seating space.[1]

---

[1] The UN, when the Charter came into force on October 24, 1945, had 51 members. Twenty years later, on October 24, 1965 it had 117 members. On October 24, 1966 it had

Only rarely have these dozens of new members included a state which existed in independence before World War II (such as Japan, admitted in 1956). Most of them are fresh from colonial status—at first from southeast Asia and the Middle East, later from Africa. In a month's time in the fall of 1960, 16 new members were admitted from Africa alone. The impact of this influx is continuing to be felt by the UN and the world at large. Significantly the UN's most ambitious undertakings have been in former colonial areas: "police action" in Korea, an "emergency force" for the Suez area, an "African force" for the Congo, and a pacifying force for Cyprus.

These changes have already revolutionized international relations. As late as the nineteenth century, world affairs meant basically European affairs, and the ramification of the affairs of Europe's powers to the distant areas of the earth. Now the peoples of Asia and Africa speak their hopes and fears for themselves. As a result, there are many more sovereign states able to decide for themselves what they wish to do. There are also more Asian national armed forces available for organized reciprocal violence—as India has come to know well. The keys to the major developments in international relations have correspondingly been more widely scattered and international relations have lost much of their former European-centered character.

In a world of paradox and change one more should be noted: even while new, economically weak, and politically untried states are springing into existence and the "Balkanization" or fragmenting of the world into ever more separate units is continuing, an opposite trend has occurred to some extent among the older communities of power. In Western Europe, the European Community begun with the Coal and Steel Community (Schuman Plan), and continuing with the Common Market, and Euratom, are changing the economics of the third important industrial complex in the world—with important, although still limited, political effects. While in Africa the semblance and substance of sovereignty is being avidly sought after, in Europe some of the jealous prerogatives of that same sovereignty have been waived in the common and greater interest.

The great integrating developments of our time, such as the European Community or the North Atlantic Treaty Organization, likely foreshadow an ultimate trend toward a regionalism superimposed upon essentially sovereign national states, or even toward a more organic union. The world is probably too small and the conditions of separate existence too dangerous and too uneconomic for the trend toward ever larger numbers of individual states to remain unreversed.

Yet the disagreements which have plagued these organizations give fair warning of the difficulties of the process. It is too narrow to attribute these disagreements simply to the stubborn character of a de Gaulle. The European Communist states have encountered parallel problems in the economic sphere

---

121 members. (These figures each count Russia three times, once as herself, once as the Ukrainian S.S.R., and once as the Byelorussian S.S.R.)

in COMECON. The disrupting effect of Germany's division, which entails Europe's division, interferes seriously with these plans for political order-building.

The problems inherent in such supranational organs are well demonstrated by NATO. In its amazing complexity for a peacetime alliance mechanism it has gone well beyond the pre-World War II models. In the nineteenth century, in rare cases an alliance might be cemented through exploratory staff conversations by the military and naval chiefs before the outbreak of war. But detailed defense plans and elaborate depots of supply on a coordinated and interlocking basis in peacetime, as in NATO, are highly modern. In fact, NATO is probably either too modern or not modern enough, for the decisions to use such force must be made, in the nature of things, jointly. But its members remain sovereign (i.e., still capable of separate decisions). De Gaulle did not invent this dilemma. Nor do proposals for a NATO multilateral nuclear force (M.L.F.) resolve it. NATO, like any coalition of the past, still depends upon the continuing support and consensus of individual states.

Complex contemporary mechanisms such as NATO and the United Nations essentially represent coordinating devices for the interests of member states. Until and unless the decisions are no longer taken in the capitals of the members, we must, to be accurate, speak of the evolving forms of interstate relations rather than the replacement of the state system itself.

To keep perspective, we must remember that change in these forms has always been a feature of the system. States over the centuries have *institutionalized* many of their relations—with varying degrees of success.

Realistically, no one can ignore the twin facts that today there are ever more sovereign nation-states (free to try to find their own way to the satisfaction of their wants and interests—or to make war on one another), and that their levels of armaments are rising (although at greatly differing rates). Nor would it be safe to conclude, because of the destructive nature of modern weapons, that nations (especially non-nuclear states) will cease to resort to organized violence for the attainment of their ends. But a more conservative assessment of what is "worth" a war can be anticipated. "Indirect aggressions" are on the increase.

I *National Interests: Common and Opposed*

IN the very broadest sense, the term *international relations* embraces *all* intercourse among states and all movements of peoples, goods, and ideas across national frontiers. However, as a field of study its focus is on the processes by which states adjust their national interests to those of other states. In turn, national interests may be defined in terms of what states seek to protect or achieve vis-à-vis other states.

National interests cover categories of desires on the part of sovereign states that vary enormously from state to state and from time to time. There is an irreducible core for any state at any time. This core consists of the "vital" interests—those for which a state is normally willing to go to war immediately or ultimately.[2] Such vital interests include for all states, as a minimum, the protection of their existing territory and the preservation of their prestige from a massive "loss of face." By contrast, the less-than-vital or secondary interests cover all the myriad desires of individual states which they would like to attain but for which they will not fight.

Taken together, the vital and secondary interests of states are important in international relations, because they form the raw material out of which foreign policy is made. An ideal foreign policy contains a systematic formulation of national interests in which inconsistent interests have been weeded out, the interests have been judged against one another in terms of priorities, and the interests as a whole have been budgeted against the estimated power of the state to achieve those interests.

Once this process of molding national interests into an over-all foreign policy is consummated, the state is presumably ready, in its dealings with other states, to pursue a logical and consistent policy. Of course, there is no magic formula which ensures that the interests and therefore the foreign policies of states will prove compatible. If opposed policies are pursued that prove irreconcilable short of war, and if the states furthering these policies nevertheless persist in them, force is the final resort. This simple truth explains why war and peace have alternated with each other for as long as the multistate system has existed.

Assuming the continued existence of sovereign states, the hope of preventing war must lie either (1) in a willingness of states to formulate mutually compatible foreign policies or (2) in the ability of nations to adjust conflicting policies peacefully, once conflicts are found to exist. Whether the devices and techniques that states utilize for their diplomatic, legal, economic, and organizational relations are adequate to prevent war (or even designed for that purpose) will be considered in later chapters.

In the twentieth century, rapid change, destructive wars, and the competition of ideologies clamoring for the allegiance of the masses have combined to foster extremist and dogmatic points of view. This has drastically reduced, and in some cases even eliminated, the willingness of peoples and states to adjust themselves peacefully to one another. There is a marked inclination toward "black and white" classifications almost to the ridiculous extent of the revolutionary slogan of the animal insurrectionists in George Orwell's *Animal Farm*—"four legs good, two legs bad." In a time of Cold War or high tension, we develop whole hosts of similar slogans which, while perhaps expressing basic truths, oversimplify the issues.

Governments and politicians gathering votes are often tempted to depict the relations of their own nation with others in black and white or otherwise

---

[2] If a nation feels hopelessly outclassed in power, it *may* surrender the interest without a fight; this is, however, rare. Much more usual in such cases is a short but hopeless struggle, ending in a defeat with honor intact.

fixed and absolute terms. The consequences that follow from such rigid and inflexible distinctions can be enormous. Great Britain, from the viewpoint of the United States, is today a basically friendly (i.e., "white") state. Yet Thomas Jefferson once wrote of her (June 12, 1815): "We concur in considering the government of England as totally without morality, insolent beyond bearing, inflated with vanity and ambition, aiming at the exclusive domination of the sea, lost in corruption, of deep-rooted hatred towards us, hostile to liberty wherever it endeavours to show its head, and the eternal disturber of the peace of the world." [3] The Soviet Union, conversely, is basically a rival, quasienemy (i.e., "black") state. Yet the United States continues to find some of its interests opposed to Britain and some common to those of the Soviet Union. And in earlier decades American relations with these two states were almost exactly reversed. This point applies to China, too.

In formulating a foreign policy it is imperative to express what is to be sought in accurate and modest terms. It is often said that American foreign policy is simply "anti-Communist." This is far too simple a formulation to be of real use. It fails to provide for Tito's Communist Yugoslavia, let alone the Sino-Soviet split, and it condemns American foreign policy (if put into practice) to a sterile, negative role of opposition to communism, whether such opposition is actually desirable or not for America in particular instances. Such a formulation of United States foreign policy fails on three grounds: (1) it does not offer any precise indication of how such a vague aim can or should be consummated; (2) it lumps *all* Communist states and *all* Communist movements together; and (3) it creates difficulty in exploiting points where the United States and the Soviet Union actually have common interests. Today, for example, they have common interests in exchanging ambassadors, in carrying on negotiations for conflict resolution, and in participating in the United Nations. That the United States and the Soviet Union seek to use the United Nations for opposed purposes does not alter their common interest in its existence. Politics, as has so frequently been remarked, makes for strange bedfellows. In 1955 both the United States and the Soviet Union (although for very dissimilar reasons) found a common interest in signing the Austrian Peace Treaty, creating a neutral but armed and unoccupied Austria. In 1965 they felt equal concern over the possible escalation of the Viet-Nam War and China's renewed threat to India.

If it is assumed that two states have *no* common interests, possibilities of diplomatic settlement of issues almost automatically evaporate. Concessions are not given, since to give anything, even for equivalents, becomes "appeasement."

Over the centuries individual states have from time to time actually acted on the assumption of completely opposed interests vis-à-vis another state. Cato the Elder, in the Roman Senate, reiterated his insistent injunction,

---

[3] In a letter to Thomas Leiper. Paul L. Ford, ed., *The Works of Thomas Jefferson,* New York: Putnam, 1905, Vol. 11, pp. 475–476.

"censeo Carthaginem esse delendam" ("I declare that Carthage must be destroyed") so convincingly that in 146 B.C., at the end of Carthage's defeat in the Third Punic War, the city was leveled and salt put upon the ruins so that thenceforth nothing would grow there. It is possible that the ultimate question for Western civilization today is who, following a hydrogen war, will sprinkle salt on whose capital. But before such a gloomy view of the future is accepted, it will be well to examine the present crisis in international relations very thoroughly to see whether there are indeed no other feasible alternatives. This is why "meetings at the summit," although so far short in actual accomplishment compared to hopeful expectation, continue to occur (1955) or be attempted (1960).

Even during World War II, the United States and Nazi Germany retained a few common interests. Both were interested (despite violations) in the treatment of prisoners according to the rules of war, the exchange of prisoner-of-war lists and prisoner-of-war mail through Switzerland, and the evacuation and repatriation of enemy diplomats caught in hostile territory. This is not an exhaustive list; it is enough to show that *even in the midst of total war* two enemy states retained some common interests. The primary motive behind the treatment of the prisoners of war was fear of retaliation in kind—a distaste for the consequences that would follow from a policy of complete ruthlessness. Even so, the interests *were* common, and, more often than we might at first be prepared to admit, the common interests of states arise out of a concern over retaliation, or at the very least a fear of inconvenience. That the source of a consensus of interests may be such does not eliminate the reality of that consensus. But these observations do underline the potentially transitory character of both opposed and common interests between any two states. The United States and West Germany are now allies!

Furthermore, the degree to which common interests exist between two nations depends upon the general conditions of international relations and the particular policies of the states in question, at a particular time. The range of common interests between the United States and the Soviet Union in 1944 was immeasurably greater than in 1953; the range of common interests between the United States and Japan in 1944 was immeasurably smaller than in 1953. (See Diagram 1 for a representation of United States–Soviet relations in the twentieth century.) A too great emphasis on, and preoccupation with, the relations of two powers at a given time easily produces a tendency on the part of observers to picture those relations (1) too simply and (2) too statically.

The too simple view not only distorts the objective situation but reduces the opportunity of statesmen to manipulate it by convincing people that nothing can be done. There is then no use in negotiating with the Russians (or Chinese), since they will not make agreements, and even if they make them will not keep them. But agreements between two states may be possible and may be kept for the same reason that both the United States and the Soviet Union support the United Nations: each hopes to gain something from the arrangement. Similarly, Stalin was willing to (and did) divide

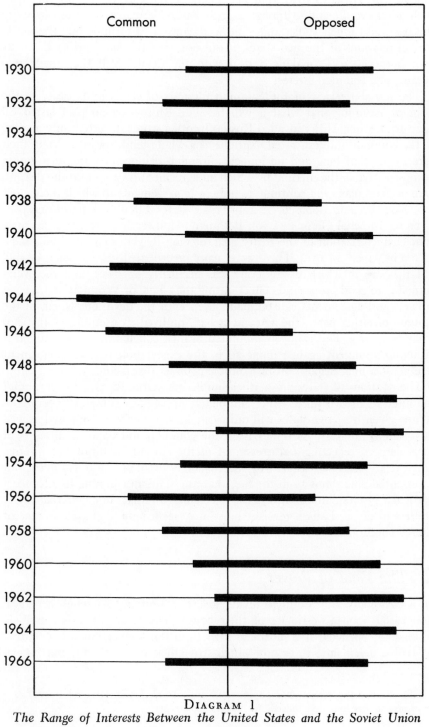

DIAGRAM 1
The Range of Interests Between the United States and the Soviet Union

Poland with Hitler in 1939: they had a common interest in avoiding war with each other over Poland. Although a great Russo-German celebration followed the pact, and much vodka and wine were consumed to underline the newly cordial relations of the two states, it did not alter the fact that each, for its own purposes, was "making a deal with the devil." Still they made it— because of a common interest.

The too static view of the common interests of states leads easily to the error of assuming that what is will be. The Russo-German pact lasted till June 1941, when Hitler invaded Russia. In other words, it lasted only as long as the common interest lasted. Nations as a whole tend toward keeping their agreements that long and no longer,[4] although democracies are, as a group, more sensitive to the method by which an agreement is eased into the discard. Democracies may even continue to adhere to agreements to which their interests have become opposed. Authoritarian states often feel fewer scruples. Even so, Imperial Germany's von Bethmann-Hollweg lived to regret his arrogant characterization of the treaty guaranteeing Belgian neutrality as a mere "scrap of paper" in 1914. There were many precedents for doing what he did, but the way in which it was done was peculiarly offensive, and the Allies turned it to good propaganda effect during the whole of World War I.

Pacts and agreements can be made, even with the devil, but when, in the opinion of either party, the agreement has "outlived its usefulness," it is not likely to survive. This is not an argument against concluding agreements; it is rather an argument against doing so in the expectation that any agreement represents a final disposition of a problem under discussion.

The relations of states are neither simple nor static. Rarely, if ever, are *all* the interests of two states either completely opposed or completely common. At any given time two states will ordinarily have a number of opposed as well as common interests. As time passes, the common and opposed interests of each changes, reflecting a reassessment of the current conditions of international relations. The reasons why these changes occur are quite complex. But an essential clue stems from the fact that any state, in choosing to advance a particular interest, almost always has rejected an alternate or *counterbalancing interest* to do so. Later a reverse choice may seem more desirable in view of altered conditions.

2 *The Role of Power*

IT is customary and useful to divide sovereign units into a rough classification based upon an estimate of their *power*. The term *power* is extremely ambiguous, but what it is meant to refer to in this connection is how strong or weak a given state is, or how much strength it has at its disposal for na-

---

[4] States may also retain common interests, and observe agreements and treaties as a result, over a very long time indeed. See below, Chapter 4.

tional purposes. The estimate of strength inevitably must be made against the yardstick of possible or actual conflict, since as a first principle a state must be concerned with its own preservation in an uncertain world. To preserve itself it may have to fight.

Wars have begun in the nation-state system (between 1480 and 1941) on the average of once every two years.[5] In every war, national independence is to some degree at stake, or, at the very least, territorial integrity. The penalty for losing wars is a matter of everyday knowledge. Power is consequently important to every state, large or small; and although states vary in the amount of power they can amass or exert, they are always preoccupied with power status. This preoccupation expresses itself in the universal use of the classification of states into *small powers, middle powers,* and *great powers.* To this tripartite division has been added, since World War II, yet a fourth category reserved for the two power giants, the United States and the Soviet Union. To them has been given the superlative distinction "super power."

Estimates of national power are difficult to arrive at on any reliable grounds. It is apparent that states vary greatly in *size.* They also vary markedly in population, natural resources, type of terrain, and climate, as well as in factors less easy to measure but equally fundamental, such as the historical experience they have undergone, the type of government they have developed, and their peoples' attitudes toward life, war, and the State—in short, their general philosophy, outlook, and experience. The general philosophy of a people affects power in two ways. It not only makes them stronger or weaker per se, but it determines the use to which, and the circumstances under which, a nation may be prepared to resort to what is euphemistically termed the "verdict of arms."

Nothing is more difficult of interpretation than the underlying attitudes of nations and groups within nations and the value systems that cause them to embark upon or refrain from given actions. A nation such as India, heavily imbued with Gandhian pacifism, may find its own hand stayed by its unwillingness to use force. Or a nation such as France, while not at all pacifistic, may find a considerable portion of its population weary in the face of the Nazi threat and inclined to accept coming defeat. Recognition of the difficulties of assessing such factors and their undoubted effect upon the national power of the state in question will bring a realization that estimates of power are precarious things. Indeed, France collapsed in 1940 with hardly a struggle, although it was generally conceded to have the best army in all Europe. Similarly, the Soviet Union, which was given six weeks by most military observers before it would be crushed by the Nazis in 1941, survived to occupy Berlin. And India took Goa by force in 1961, fought an undeclared war with China in 1962, and another with Pakistan in 1965.

At the same time that states vary tremendously in power, those in similar

---

[5] See especially Quincy Wright, A *Study of War,* Vol. I, Tables 31–41, pp. 641–646. Counting "civil" wars and "indirect aggressions," the rate is about the same today.

power categories often have similar attitudes. Although it would be fallacious to assume that *all* great powers are distinguished from *all* small powers in such attitudes, or that *all* states in a given category have a *similar* attitude, the tendency exists. The great powers are prone to think of the smaller states as elements in a situation that can be manipulated. The small powers, on the other hand, are usually and habitually worried for fear of being manipulated—or worse. In 1945, at the San Francisco Conference on the United Nations, the small powers insisted upon greater restrictions on the use of the veto, while the great and "super" powers (including the United States) stubbornly held to a broad interpretation of the conditions under which they could resort to a veto. Voting "blocs" in the UN, such as the Afro-Asian bloc, exist partly for this same reason of a common fear of being manipulated by the great powers.

Not only, then, are there differences in power among states, but also power status influences national attitudes and behavior. Consequently, states somewhat equal in power tend to develop patterns of behavior and outlook typical of their power group.

3 The Problem of Power

AS we have seen, international relations is concerned with the process by which sovereign states adjust their national interests to one another. Under such a system there is always the possibility of war since the essence of sovereignty is the capacity of a state to make decisions, including the decision to go to war. This generalization does not imply that any state, large or small, will make any decision in a vacuum. It will weigh the probable effects of its decisions on other states, and the possible or probable reactions that will ensue. Nevertheless, in Washington a decision *can* be made that will put the United States at war with another power. In Moscow a similar decision can be made, and so on around the globe. Since there are over 130 sovereign states where such decisions can be taken, it is evident that the absence of war in the world depends ultimately upon the willingness of sovereign states to refrain from declaring or waging war. Similarly, the absence of general or world war depends upon the willingness of most of the great powers to refrain from war. Whether they will so refrain, regardless of any deterrent effects stemming from the international system, can never be certain as long as they retain the sovereign power of declaring war.

Of course, most conflicts of national interest are *not* settled by war. Grayson Kirk has written:

Although we live in a world in which the state is still the highest sovereign entity, it would be false to conclude that most interstate conflicts are settled on a crude power basis. The possibility of a final resort to the arbitrament of force is always in the background of *serious* international differences, but force is too ponderous and costly a weapon to use except when the stakes are so high that national existence demands it. *Most clashes of national interest are settled without using force, or even the threat of force. . . .* Most of them are settled by the routine process of diplomacy and conference.[6]

Clashes of national interest that are not settled through diplomacy and conference may be resolved, if the national interests concerned are not too explosive or dynamic, by legal procedures: resort to arbitration or to the International Court of Justice. Alternately, they may be settled in the halls of the United Nations, short of war, by the mediatory devices available to that body. We shall explore later the diplomatic, legal, economic, and organizational relations of states as they seek mutually to adjust their national interests, the procedures that have been evolved for conflict resolution (especially the mechanisms for the peaceful settlement of disputes), and the military relations of states when war occurs.

Because the cost of war is great in both human and material terms and because its outcome is unpredictable, states do not resort to it lightly. At the same time, just because of its costs and uncertainties, a great deal of the attention of statesmen must be given to preparation for possible armed conflict, since the hazards of war are enormously increased for a state plunged into conflict unprepared.

As we saw when we examined the range of common and opposed interests between states, two states rarely have completely common or opposed interests. To assume otherwise would be to distort the nature of international relations. The picture, as we saw, is more complex than pure black and white. Whether it is *perceived* as more complex is another question. Similarly, it would be a distortion of the nature of international relations to present it either as predominantly a study of war or a study of peace. Rather, it is a study of war *and* peace. These are alternate conditions under which the consummation of national interests is sought by states. Since the state system itself is multiple, the interaction of the interests or policies of two states is from the outset never purely bilateral. Thus the "exterior" environment represented by the system not only affects the choice of policy to begin with, but consistently affects the subsequent interplay at every stage. Peace and war then are the *by-products* of the interplay of the national interests of states, and which of the two results depends upon that interplay.

How is a state to preserve and/or achieve its vital interests and make itself secure in a world where peace hangs upon the slender thread of sovereign states refraining from taking decisions to go to war?

In the first place, security is a relative condition. There can be no absolute security for any one state as long as others continue to exist. The most vital national interest of any state is self-preservation. A state will seek to make itself secure from losses in territory and population. Whether it is large or small, surrounded by mountains or in the midst of open plain, neighbor to traditional and bitter enemy or to firm and proved ally—all these factors will

---

[6] Grayson Kirk, *The Study of International Relations*, p. 13. Italics added.

influence the ways in which security is sought by the nation. All these will affect the success of its security efforts.

In the second place, it is important to keep clearly in mind that states seek security rather than peace per se. Although war has its horrors, dangers, and uncertainties, these will most often be endured by a state rather than surrender any national territory or permit national prestige and honor to be humiliated. The state is willing to go to war rather than suffer the obvious consequences that failure to go to war under such circumstances entails. Normally most states feel more secure under conditions of peace, but their preference for peace is not unqualified. They seek peace but not at the price of security.

If this view is granted, it becomes clear that peace is a by-product of security. Yet frequently the cart is put before the horse when the interrelations of peace and security are examined. This reversal occurs because, as we have remarked, most nations *do* feel more secure under conditions of peace. It happens when means and end become confused—a confusion that disappears rather abruptly in the minds of citizens if there is a Pearl Harbor attack. Once national security is obviously imperiled by an overt attack, there is little disposition to say, "Let us continue to seek peace."

In the third place, it is apparent that what security means for each state varies with that state. Because security is the *sum total of the vital national interests of the state* and because a vital national interest is one for which a nation is willing to go to war either immediately or ultimately, concepts of national security will vary from state to state in proportion to the concept of vital national interests that any given state entertains at any given time. If the realization of German vital interests means recovering territory lost to Poland which Poland wants to keep, the security of Germany is the insecurity of Poland, and vice versa. Similarly, with Alsace and Lorraine, as long as neither France nor Germany became reconciled to allowing these provinces to be permanently incorporated within the other's frontiers, the security of Germany was the insecurity of France, and vice versa.

If France and Germany, and Poland and Germany, had been more concerned with the preservation of peace than with their respective national security—i.e., vital interests—no wars would have been fought over these territories. Yet such wars were fought, and will continue to be fought unless nations either evolve concepts of national security that are compatible one with the other or evolve mechanisms that prevent the incompatibility from disintegrating into open war.

As a result, states are continually attempting in international relations either to pave the way for successful wars or attempting to arrange affairs in such a way that their potential enemies will be deterred from war—all in the name of security.

Since states vary enormously in their *power* (i.e., in their ability in the last analysis to use force), the restraining effect, or lack of one, of the security arrangements of states varies roughly with the power of the states concerned.[7] It is relatively easy for a medium power to counter the ambitions of Guatemala but extremely difficult for it to do the same thing in terms of the United States or the Soviet Union. Nevertheless, while the restraint or lack of restraint depends upon the power of those to be restrained versus the power of the restrainers, and while states may be engaged in attempting either to maintain or to overthrow an existing *status quo, no state can ignore the problem that confronts it as a result of the existence of other potentially hostile states.* In this respect all states are equal, for every one of them has a *power problem* that it must somehow resolve. That the particular nature of the problem will vary from state to state is important. That each state has a power problem is fundamental. The power problems of states are always at the core of their international relations. How each state conceptualizes its power problem will in turn determine its choices of national strategies designed to ensure national security.

4 *The Patterns of Power*

FROM the point of view of organizing a power system, five possible strategies ("solutions" to the power problem) exist. In discussing these strategies and their systems effects, we shall call these collectively the *patterns of power*. While each of these is logically distinct we shall find that states frequently attempt to combine them—with results we shall note later.

First, a nation can depend solely upon its own power, make no alliances, and join in no collective security arrangements. It can deal with the power problem *unilaterally* and "go it alone." Isolationism and neutrality are the most familiar expressions of a unilateral power policy, but unilateralism can take "interventionist" forms as well. The essential requirement for a unilateral policy is that a state pursue it by itself, independently of any alliance ties. Whether unilateralism will prove successful in terms of the security of the state practicing it depends upon many factors. The Swiss, as the most notable example, have chosen neutrality for considerably more than a hundred years.

As a second possibility, a nation may choose to make alliances or to arrive at understandings with friendly states to band together against mutual enemies. This is the classic pattern of *alliances*, which are at the heart of the *balance of power process*. The enemies against which such a coalition is formed may or may not join in a rival coalition at first, although sooner or later this union of strength occurs. The Triple Alliance of Germany, Austria-Hungary, and Italy existed as early as 1882; it was renewed regularly and was in effect in 1914 when hostilities broke out. The opposite coalition of the Triple Entente

---

[7] It varies "roughly" with the power of the states concerned because other states may perceive the power relationship erroneously or judge falsely the capability of one or more states to bring that power to bear effectively.

(Russia, France, and England), on the other hand, did not take its shape until as late as 1907, although Russia and France had entered into a military convention as early as 1892 and into a dual alliance by 1894. In the case of the contemporary NATO alliance, the opposing Communist alliance group had already concluded a network of bilateral treaties when NATO came into existence and effect in 1949; [8] in 1955 the Communist states paralleled NATO with their "Warsaw alliance."

Such balance-of-power alignments and alliances are created in the hope of protecting the security of the participating states by providing each of them with allies in the event of war with rival powers. Whether such arrangements will work depends in a crisis upon the readiness of alliance partners of the state in question to stand by it. No matter how solemnly made, the engagements may not be honored when war threatens.

If the balance works well, war may not result, and peace will be the by-product of the system. Some advocates of the balance-of-power principle have justified the use of such alliance systems on the proposition that the balance will preserve peace. Critics of the balance principle, conversely, have insisted that the balance of power leads inevitably to war because of the race for power that typifies the last or disintegrating stage of such balances. Yet from the point of view of the security of the participating states, the usefulness of a balance does not rest upon whether it ends in war or prevents war per se, but whether it enhances their individual security under conditions of war and/or peace. To say that the balance of power ends in war is not necessarily an argument against the effectiveness of alliances in terms of security, although it is an argument that seems particularly forceful to those who regard peace per se as the goal of states.

World War I proved so destructive, and the shock of its occurrence after a century of general peace was so great, that there was a widespread feeling and demand in 1919 for a more effective method of solving the power problem than that given by the traditional unilateral or balance-of-power devices. The result was *collective security*, the third of the patterns of power.

Collective security is a term which, like so many others in current usage, has tended to lose specific meaning as a result of its being applied to many dissimilar arrangements. Originally it meant (and its original meaning will be adhered to in this book) that *all* nations could be secure if all were guaranteed their "territorial integrity and existing political independence" against "external aggression" [9] by *any* state or states. The idea was basically a mutual insurance plan, membership in which would be either universal or as nearly universal as possible. All the members of the security organization would assist any member attacked (either by another member or members, or from

---

[8] NATO as a balance-of-power arrangement is explored further in Part Five.

[9] These terms were actually used in Article X of the Covenant of the League of Nations. Article X was considered by President Woodrow Wilson to be the "heart" of the Covenant and League system.

outside the organization). The idea rested upon certain assumptions. First, it was rooted in the hope that at the time of crisis such obligations would be honored by the members. Second, and even more fundamental, it assumed that the security interests of most states were fundamentally *compatible*. Third, it assumed that the power of revisionist ("have-not") states, desiring the overthrow of the existing *status quo*, would be so small in comparison to the power of the "law-abiding" states that none would dare war, or, if they did, that they would be defeated in short order and with relatively small effort.

Thus the "shortcomings" of the balance-of-power pattern were to be overcome by the use of a universal or quasi-universal alliance, directed not against a particular state or states (as in the balance of power) but against *any* power that embarked upon aggression.

These three patterns of power—unilateralism, balance of power alliances, and collective security—are the organizational alternative strategies available for coping with the power problem *under the assumption of the continued existence of the nation-state system* in anything like its present form.[10] There is another theoretical possibility—that one state might come to control such a large segment of the earth's resources (although short of complete elimination of all other sovereign entities) that it would feel permanently unchallengeable and secure. In the practical sense, however, its dominance could not be certain while other sovereign states remained in existence. That is why the Romans sprinkled salt upon Carthage.

There are two further possible organizational "solutions" to the power problem. Both of these would involve ending the nation-state system as we know it. One of these is implicit in the theoretical possibility stated in the preceding paragraph. If one state should succeed in destroying *all* other sovereign units, it would successfully resolve the power problem that results from the existence of sovereign entities possessed of power (which can or might be used against other states). The state system would be transformed into a *world empire* through *world conquest*. Rome approached this result, but its final collapse under the pressure of barbarian elements coming from outside the Roman frontiers demonstrates that Rome did not complete the process on which she was well embarked. In more recent times Germany and Japan between them came within striking distance of world conquest. After World War II the possibility of the ultimate unification of the world under communism became a very real fear among the Western nations. It was this very possibility that brought NATO into existence.

The same result of resolving the power problem *on the nation-state level*, by doing away with the nation-states, might conceivably occur through the fifth possibility—*voluntary world federation*. If all the world were to unite,

---

10 "Regional defense pacts," while "collective" arrangements in that they are multilateral, are from a power-alignment point of view, substantially the same as balance-of-power alliances vis-à-vis states outside the arrangement. See below, Part Five,

voluntarily surrendering sovereignty to a world government, this action would resolve the power problem for individual sovereign states. However, if only a portion (even a *large* portion) of the 130 or more sovereign units were to unite, although the union would represent tremendous and impressive power, it would not have resolved the power problem on the level of the nation-state system, since decisions could still be taken by the non-member units (either individually as sovereign states or collectively as an alliance or a rival "world government"). If there were two units, each aspiring to form the world government, the stage would be set for the greatest conflict of recorded history.

These fourth and fifth patterns—world conquest and world government—would not, if they came to pass, eliminate questions of power in the world. Power groups and power rivals *within* the world state would probably continue a struggle for the vast stakes of control of the state. Civil wars might well occur. Even so, the unification of the states into one world state would eliminate the power problem *on the nation-state level* by eliminating the nation-states themselves.

These five patterns of power are mutually exclusive courses of action for any state in terms of a *given problem*. A state cannot at one and the same time choose unilateralism in the form of neutrality as a course of action toward its neighbors *and* participate in a balance-of-power alliance system on the side of one group of its neighbors, directed against the other group. It may, of course, choose two different patterns for two different problems. Whether incompatibility will result will depend upon whether the problems are truly separate. If a state joins a mutual alliance group limited to ten or twenty states, and at the same time is a member of the United Nations collective security organization pledged to repulse aggression by *any* state, and aggression is committed by one of its balance-of-power allies, that state has incompatible obligations unless somewhere in the two sets of arrangements it has been clearly established *which* obligation takes precedence. So-called "neutralist" members of the United Nations can encounter the same problem.

Part Five of this book will be devoted to a detailed examination of these five patterns of power. As long as sovereign states exist, and therefore the power problem that their sovereign existence creates persists, a state must seek its security within the three alternative patterns of unilateralism, balance of power, and collective security. The case studies of Part Five will clothe the bare bones of these ideas with the flesh of specific example.

5   An End and a Beginning

THE student beginning the study of international relations is naturally predominantly concerned with the crisis and tension that form the background of today's headlines. Indeed, it is inevitable and desirable that attention should be focused upon the present stage of development of international relations. The sixth and seventh parts of this book, especially, treat the present crisis in considerable detail.

Even so, we cannot begin with the end. The problem of the present cannot be dealt with as such, and cannot indeed be understood with necessary perspective, until we have mastered the operation of the nation-state system as a whole. We must begin with sovereignty and nationalism, for these are the roots of the system which have given international relations their distinctive character. We must, secondly, explore the problems each individual state must confront in assessing national power and linking it to foreign policy. Thirdly, we must observe how states deal functionally with one another as the interaction of their foreign policies produce diplomatic, legal, economic, organizational, and military relations. Fourthly, we must survey the procedures that have been evolved to settle disputes arising out of these relations. Fifthly, since security is of vital concern to each state and since war is always possible in a sovereign state system, we must explore the alternative patterns of power that states may choose to resolve or cope with the power-security problem which lies at the core of all their relations. And, sixthly, we must see contemporary international relations in the perspective this examination can give us.

This is the plan we shall follow. These are also the major parts into which this book is divided. This chapter will serve its purpose if it makes clear how and why these six parts are in their large outlines interrelated. Proceeding in this sequence in no way implies that international relations are simply the sum total of the relations of individual states added together. The very existence of the multiple state environment within which individual policies are formulated, the very interaction in the system with its feed-back effects on policies, would make such an approach of dubious utility. What we are doing, rather, is proceeding from examining common characteristics of states in their "individual" capacities (power, policy, etc.), to an analysis of their total interactions on a functional basis (legal, political, etc.), followed by a searching look at their most important or security interactions, as a means ultimately to understanding the contemporary scene.

CHAPTER 2

Sovereignty and Nationalism

A portion of mankind may be said to constitute a nationality if they are united among themselves by common sympathies which do not exist between them and any others—which make them cooperate with each other more willingly than with other people, desire to be under the same government, and desire that it should be government by themselves or a portion of themselves exclusively.

JOHN STUART MILL
Considerations on Representative Government

To understand contemporary international relations we must have a thorough knowledge of the operation of the state system. But to understand the state system we must first have a grasp of the fundamental significance of two basic phenomena: sovereignty and nationalism.

Sovereignty may be defined as the ability of a state to make independent decisions. A sovereign nation is one that is, in a legal sense, free to decide to pursue the path of peace or the ways of war as its national interests may dictate. But what imbues the freedom to make decisions with real meaning and power is the will and desire of the people of the nation to implement the sovereign decision with "blood, sweat, and tears," and money and matériel. What holds the people together in common support of national objectives is what we call nationalism.

To understand the role that sovereignty and nationalism play in modern international relations we must see briefly how and why they emerged. Their very existence testified to the passing of the feudal age, just as the advent of feudalism was the sign and token of the disintegration of the Roman Empire. A brief survey of the successive development of Roman Empire into feudal age, and feudal age into modern state system, will provide proper perspective.

1 The Roman Empire

THERE have been empires that have rivaled or exceeded the Roman Empire in size, as did that of Alexander the Great. There have been empires that have lasted over comparably long periods, such as that of the Tartars under Genghis

Khan and his heirs, or the later Ottoman Empire in the Near East and Balkans. But no other empire ever held together so long, governed a contiguous area so vital in the later history of civilization, and controlled that area as effectively as did Rome.

The Roman Empire was and remains the solitary example of the nearest approach to a universal state that the world has known. In its best period, the Roman legions patrolled the well-built roads, the remains of which still exist, bringing peace and stability to the far-flung corners of the domain. At its greatest extent, in the first years after Christ, it extended westward from the borders of India to the site of the future city of Glasgow in Scotland, from the Rhine and the Danube (and even beyond) southward to the hot sands of the Sahara. And while it was not a universal empire covering all the world, it was an empire that embraced the areas from which three of the world's important cultures have sprung. Not only Christianity, but Judaism and Mohammedanism also were born within that area. From within its former frontiers have originated fundamental precepts that have prevailed in the minds of many peoples ever since.

In a very real sense, subsequent history is the story of the impact of the former parts of the Roman Empire upon the rest of the world. The earliest-formed nation-states, those of Western Europe, such as England, Spain, France, and Portugal, were all parts of the Roman Empire before the Middle Ages.

In early modern times they colonized much of the globe, so that the precepts of Western civilization were spread far and wide, even altering in many ways equally ancient cultures such as those of the Far East. The influence of the Roman Empire, therefore, long survived its temporal passing.

2 The Breakdown of Universalism

THE dissolution of the Empire was well under way by the year 410, when the Visigoths under Alaric sacked Rome. By 476 the rule of the last Roman Emperor in the West had come to a close. Rome's temporal power collapsed but the ideas formulated during the Roman Age lived on.

The "universal" state disintegrated into many thousands of feudal units. Imperial rule from one center was replaced by local rule in each locality. Even Charlemagne's great empire in the ninth century never restored the earlier unity. When the Holy Roman Empire was established in 962, it included only the German states, Switzerland, Austria, and northern Italy. Even this comparatively smaller area was not really under the effective control of the emperor (or of the pope). Thus Voltaire's well-known quip that the Holy Roman Empire was "neither Holy nor Roman nor an Empire." Real power remained in the hands of feudal lords or, as in Western Europe, in the kings who had already begun the consolidation of domains that in time would become modern England, France, Spain, and Portugal.

While the political power in practice was no longer concentrated in an emperor, theory lagged behind practice. Already by the early years of the four-teenth century, when Dante Alighieri, famed as a poet, wrote his *De mon-archia* bewailing the passing of the "seamless robe" (i.e., the old Roman Empire) and arguing for a strengthened Holy Roman Empire to end Eu-rope's chaos and disunity, he was a voice lamenting a universalism that was decayed beyond repair. When the modern order emerged in Europe in the sixteenth and seventeenth centuries, it was not to be on the basis of a restored universal state. Instead it was on the comparatively parochial basis of na-tionalism, embodied in the national state.

What was occurring in terms of political power had its counterpart in the religious sphere. The Christian Church was broken in two by the effects of the division of the Roman Empire into East Roman and West Roman Empires in 395. As a result, there was both an Orthodox Catholic Church, whose citadel was Constantinople, and a Roman Catholic Church, focused on Rome. In the sixteenth century came still further divisions. The Protestant Reformation (1517) destroyed the unity of Western European Christendom itself, and Catholic fought Protestant.

Thus universalism of state and church was replaced by the particularism of national states and even national churches. When King Henry VIII declared himself the head of the Church of England, he was merely one of the first to take the step. The unity of Europe even as a theoretical ideal began to dis-appear, as in practice it had done long before. Even so, the memories of that unity formed an ineradicable part of the past of Europe, and the sense of community that once really existed was never after this time entirely lost. Today's familar idea of a "community of nations" sharing common values has its roots in this past, and international law was built upon the moral foundations of the ideas of universal natural law that the Roman Empire left behind as its legacy to the modern world.

3 The Rise of National Particularism

WITH the passing of the centuries, consolidations of feudal units took place through conquest and marriage. This process occurred both within and outside the bounds of the Holy Roman Empire. In Western Europe great areas were subordinated to the rule of certain feudal lords who in time came to govern effectively, taking to themselves the titles of duke, prince, or king. Even though the feudal system continued in this period, the various feudal lords came to acknowledge the common overlordship of the one ruler, duke, or king. The most successful of these newly powerful individuals ultimately succeeded in gaining control of all or a great part of the domains that were to become recognizable as the future nation-states of Western Europe. Between the mid-dle of the fourteenth century and the middle of the sixteenth century, this process was much advanced. Outside the Empire, France, England, and Castile and Aragon (Spain) were already ruled by kings. Even inside the Empire, the Hapsburgs as hereditary rulers of Austria had begun to govern sizable territories. These they controlled effectively, not as Holy Roman Emperors (which they often were as well), but as rulers of the Hapsburg hereditary lands. Kings created dynasties, and son followed father to the throne.

So it happened that the kings of Western Europe consolidated their domains and their personal power. The new trends were clearly discernible in Italy. Already by the twelfth century northern Italy's consolidation into dukedoms had occurred. While Western Europe continued its consolidation into *large* states, northern Italy continued to be divided into small units. The shifting alliances of these states, and their geographical location between papal lands, imperial domains, and French territory exposed them to a triangular struggle for power and made of them the most frequent battleground of all medieval Europe. These factors effectively prevented their union under one king—contrary to what happened farther west. These states—Venice, Genoa, Florence (Tuscany), Parma, Modena, the Papal States, and others, exposed as they were to these rivalries and the natural geographical focus of them, provided an interesting example in miniature of some of the worst features of the early, not yet institutionalized, sovereign state system.

Niccoló Machiavelli (1469–1527), although his primary concern was the unification of Italy, realistically wrote in *The Prince* of how a ruler or sovereign could retain power under the new system of separate states. He accepted the facts of his day without attempting to justify them particularly as right or wrong, or treat them in systematic theoretical terms. The central fact that lay in the background of his advice to princes was that each state in northern Italy was independent of every other state and, therefore, any state at any time might decide to go to war against its neighbors. He saw that control of the destinies of the state had in fact passed into the hands of the rulers of each state, and that the survival of the state depended upon the wisdom of its governors rather than on any universal imperial or spiritual power. The stubborn facts were no longer in accord with the medieval theory of political relationships. With Machiavelli, the doctrines of the old universalism were hastily buried, although the ghost of values superior to the state continued in the next centuries to walk abroad, a disembodied reminder of the earlier unity of the civilized world. Each state, admittedly or not and often with troubled conscience, let its own interests become more and more the center of its own moral universe.

This was the system that Machiavelli observed and described. He left it to others to erect a scaffolding of theory to justify the independence of the state, which he merely took for granted.

To Jean Bodin fell this role of theorist; to him must go the title of founder of the modern doctrine of state sovereignty. In his *Six Books on the State* [1] (1586) he claimed that the King of France ruled by "divine right" as the appointed representative of God for the earthly affairs of France. A ruler held

---

[1] Which he first wrote and published in French in 1576. The edition of 1586 was an enlarged version in Latin.

his power, Bodin asserted, directly from God. To challenge that power through revolution or in any other way was to flout the will of God.

The chaotic conditions of Bodin's day not only inspired but reinforced the power of his idea. Ever since the Protestant Reformation had begun in 1517, Christendom had been torn by a religious strife that dwarfed any previous doctrinal disagreements. Protestant and Catholic vied with each other in attempting to drive out the rival belief by exterminating its adherents.

The strong French king, Henry IV, in the process of re-establishing order also achieved absolute power. It was as a plea for this very kind of centralized, orderly rule that Bodin had brought forth his concept of "divine right." Since the alternative was renewed chaos and conflict, struggle over the throne, and religious strife, the idea received much support in France. It later won the approval of the rising commercial class elsewhere in Western Europe.

Although it was not until the Stuarts that the new idea of "divine right" was brought to England, Henry VIII (who reigned from 1509 to 1547) had grasped the opportunity in the schism of the Reformation to renounce the pope's right to rule the English Church, and had assumed the position of head of the Anglican faith. So it happened that both in Protestant and Catholic states the new absolute or strong monarchs gained effective control not merely of the temporal but of all or some of the spiritual powers as well.

This kingly absolutism was in turn challenged by the religious minorities (by Catholics in a Protestant country, and vice versa) who had nothing to lose and everything to gain by their opposition, since the monarchs generally attempted to establish a single religious faith in their domains through conversion or execution.

The minorities of either faith contended that the power of the king was not and could not be absolute, since it was subject to the laws of God, the laws of nature, and the provisions of the supposed (and mythological) original *contract* of the people with the king. Thus the "contract theory" came into being in this form and gained adherents as a direct consequence of the religious strife. This new formulation was particularly the work of Johannes Althusius. Its importance lay in the fact that it attempted to set limits to the power of the absolute kings by insisting that the original source of power was the people. These had entrusted it to the hands of the king *under certain conditions*. If the king failed to abide by these conditions he could and should be overthrown. In this way revolution was justified and a theoretical basis for republics and other non-monarchical forms of government was established.

Bodin and Althusius, although the former was justifying and the latter opposing absolute monarchy, focused on the distribution of power *within the sovereign state*. The question to which they addressed their attention was: given the fact of sovereignty, who ruled the state? Hugo Grotius, the "father of international law," avoided this internal jurisdictional issue by defining sovereignty as "that power [in a state] whose acts are not subject to the control . . . of any other human will." This might be centered in an individual (as in a monarchy) or in a group (as in a republic). He went on to assert that

every sovereign state's jurisdiction was unchallengeable within its own frontiers but was limited to those frontiers by the fact that other states were also
sovereign in their own territories.

It is significant that the definition of state sovereignty formulated by
Grotius in the early years of the modern state system is equally useful today.

4 *The Growth of Nationalism*

WE have seen how in Western Europe consolidation of feudal domains gradually led to the predominant power of absolute kings. Within the boundaries
of the Holy Roman Empire, although that archaic apparatus lived on still
in senile decay, the real power passed out of the hands of emperor and pope
into the eager fingers of dukes, princes, and kings. The significant difference
between Central and Western Europe in the sixteenth, seventeenth, and
eighteenth centuries is that in the West consolidation took place on what we
now call a *national* basis, while the unit of organization within the Empire
and in the south of Italy was less than national. There were many German
and Italian states; Prussia as one of those states was soon to become a great
power even though still within the Empire, but in the West there came to be
one French state, *one* English state, and *one* Spanish state.

Thus by the time of the French Revolution, France and the Western
European states had been unified and centralized states for several hundreds
of years. A gradual growth in national feeling had resulted, but it had been a
slow and quiet growth of sentiment. Local loyalties had remained, but a
newer, larger concept of loyalty to France (or Spain, or England, etc.) had
grown up. Prior to the revolution, this loyalty had been focused upon the
king, so that Louis XIV could boast with truth: "L'Etat, c'est moi" ("I am
the state"). But with the beheading of Louis XVI, this symbol of unity was
destroyed. The revolutionary leaders had of necessity to rest their newly seized
power on the basis that they were the embodiment of the will of *la nation,* to
which all patriotic Frenchmen owed support—particularly in the light of the
foreign danger. This appeal proved extraordinarily effective, and the French,
utilizing mass citizen armies for the first time in modern history, found them
imbued with a fighting spirit compounded out of love for country and an
awareness that they were fighting in their own interests. This patriotism
energized them to overwhelm their better trained but less spirited adversaries
who put most of their faith in old-fashioned, hired mercenaries.

The nationalism that the French, in the wake of their victories under Napoleon, carried deep into Eastern Europe, awoke a popular awareness of the
political power implicit in large numbers of people living together within a
state. Until this time, by and large, on the continent of Europe the people as
a whole had little interest and no real share in the processes of government. A
fundamental revolution in their ideas and a new political awareness were the
first fruits of the French Revolution, even though farther east in Europe it
took longer for these fruits to mature.

It is significant that, while the French were hailed as liberators from monarchical tyranny and at first were greeted as such, the subdued peoples ultimately considered them new oppressors, and foreign ones at that. The very ideas of nationalism that the French had done so much to spread among other peoples in the end greatly accelerated their own defeat. The Prussians, for example, reorganized their army around Prussian draftees and raised the standard of a national crusade to free their lands from foreign yoke. Similarly in Spain, the Achilles heel of Napoleon, the common people, armed with little more than antiquated muskets and scythes and stones, immobilized entire French armies. In distant Russia, too, the people responded to the peril facing their homeland; they harassed the French on the road both to and from Moscow in 1812. In these movements the people played a part truly revolutionary when compared with their previous relatively inert role. Mercenary armies of hired soldiers (often themselves aliens) everywhere began to be abandoned, and mass armies of nationals on the model of the French example became the rule. This process not only required more mass participation in the armed forces, but led to the gradual awakening in those same masses of the political possibilities inherent in their combined strength. The power of the people was an established fact. Although the monarchs of Europe attempted to "put back the clock" after Napoleon's downfall, they found the task of regaining absolute power almost impossible. They were in the position of plugging one leak in the dike only to have the irresistible pressure open three new leaks as a result.

5   From Liberal to Integral Nationalism

AFTER the French Revolution the feudal idea—that people, like cattle, were the property of the king—could never be effectively revived. It was rapidly replaced in the minds of those who had come into contact with the contagious French ideas by the new *national* principle. This principle of national *self-determination* meant essentially that a people should be citizens of whatever state they wished.

In the course of the nineteenth century, this objective of liberal nationalism triumphed in most of Europe and in the Americas. In the twentieth century it spread to the colonial areas of the world—to the Middle East, to Asia, and to Africa. Everywhere in these areas nationalism became the rallying cry of the people. With the end of World War II these pressures mounted and new states appeared in dozens. Where 815 million of the world's 2.1 billion population prior to World War II were under colonial rule, by 1955 (with world population estimated at 2.5 billion) some 750 million of the former colonial peoples were living in newly established states, and only 170 million were still under colonial administration.[2] Colonial rule today barely exists.

---

[2] Zbigniew Brzezinski, "The Politics of Underdevelopment," *World Politics*, Vol. IX (October 1956).

Liberal nationalism's success was once thought to be virtually a guarantee of a more peaceful world. As people came to be ruled in a manner of their own choosing they would have little desire to resort to war. Certainly they would no longer have to fight to establish their independence. But the stubborn persistence of violence between independent nations has considerably undermined the optimistic former view, and independence is nowadays argued for on the simple basis that it is right and just.

Once peoples become free and have their own state they must face two related questions: how is the state to survive the dangers that threaten it from outside, and who shall control the machinery of state within? That states do not remain automatically democratic is only too obviously true. Are there indeed any limits to the power of the state over its own citizens? Are there spheres of the human personality that are above and beyond the state and its control or not?

Two thousand years ago Jesus Christ tried to suggest a rule of thumb that would mark out the sphere of the state's authority from that of the individual's discretion when he said: "Render therefore unto Caesar the things that are Caesar's, and unto God the things that are God's." But in all states it is a difficult distinction to make and an even more difficult one to preserve in practice.

To cope with the *external* danger, the people of a state may feel that they must render more "unto Caesar" than they would under other and safer conditions. This is especially true in an increasingly industrialized world in which the waging of war becomes ever more complex. It is this factor that above all explains the universal tendency for governments in the twentieth century to exercise greater and greater powers—a tendency that is obviously not restricted to dictatorships. Each government is "strengthened" in power because other governments are. And other governments are so "strengthened" because the external threat is, therefore, even graver. In times of total war (i.e., the world since 1914) this condition becomes chronic. The result is a vicious circle. In the twentieth century individual liberty becomes ever harder to preserve. The demands of nationalism increase and less is left to the discretion of the individual.

The struggle to resolve these dilemmas is at the heart of the political process in the newer nations where traditions of self-government are often weak. In foreign affairs they may take refuge in a precarious neutralism. But internally, since their governments are so often inexperienced and unstable, they may fall prey to a "strong man"—most frequently an army officer who may have behind him in the form of the armed forces the only reliable source of power and support. Such rulers may concentrate exclusively on suppressing opposition. The more sophisticated try for a broader-based political concensus. Turkey's modernization under Ataturk in the 1920's finds a species of imitation in some "tutelary democracies" in Africa today. But pressures in underdeveloped countries for an immediate solution to the problem of raising low living standards may make preservation of civil rights even appear quite secondary or even irrelevant. Industrialization, too, as the prerequisite for military power, may seem worth almost any price since it may appear to be the key both to internal stability and external safety.

Thus *liberal* nationalism, with its democratic connotations, is always in danger of being displaced by the newer and more intolerant form called *integral* or totalitarian nationalism. Where the slogan of liberal nationalism was freedom from foreign rule and a government of one's own choosing, the watchword of integral nationalism is "the exclusive pursuit of national policies, the absolute maintenance of national integrity, and the steady increase of national power—for a nation declines when it loses military might." [3] In the present insecure world, according to the logic of integral nationalism, the nation-state must look first to its safety—that is a basic demand that its citizens make of it. But to be secure, the argument continues, the state must concentrate its energies upon the advancement of its national interests (narrowly defined) [4] and particularly to seek by every means to increase its own power.

While in most nations there is a continuing struggle between these two forms of nationalism, no nation among the older (or now the newer) nation-states can resist succumbing to the logic of integral nationalism *to some extent.* This is so because the analysis that integral nationalists make of the basic problem confronting nations in the present state system is correct. It is only their remedy for the problem that goes too far, so that in the name of the security and national interest of their own state they may attempt to destroy those of others. How far the process of eliminating individual rights at home or turning an aggressive face abroad is carried depends upon the degree of restraint and balance a people feel. It depends upon their sense of security and stability, and how much their inner faith in themselves and the resilience of their institutions is able to triumph over their fears and frustrations. The range of possible internal reactions extends from the one extreme of executions and purges to "witch hunts," and from there to the other extreme of the English tolerance of the Hyde Park "Red." Similarly, the span from the fanatical will-to-conquest of the Nazi legions of World War II to the sturdy determination of the Swiss citizen-soldier to defend himself if attacked covers a great range of possible external reactions. What accounts for the vast differences in reaction to an essentially similar problem is one of the most fascinating aspects of nationalism—national character and the national experience. In the next chapter we shall discuss this point further, as it affects national power and policy.

---

[3] Quoted in C. J. H. Hayes, *The Historical Evolution of Modern Nationalism*, p. 165, from Charles Maurras, who gave the term wide currency. See also pp. 164–166.

[4] See below, Chapter 13, for a discussion of narrowly and broadly defined national interests.

6 *The Elements of Nationalism*

OUT of what is nationalism, whose development we have traced, composed? Renan, the French philosopher, has answered this question by saying: "What constitutes a nation is not speaking the same tongue or belonging to the same ethnic group, but having accomplished great things in common in the past and having the wish to accomplish them in the future." [5] It is for this reason that fighting a war does much to develop nationalism.

For nationalism, there must be a feeling on the part of a people that they possess *group values*, or, as John Stuart Mill expressed it at the head of this chapter, "common sympathies." They must have a *common outlook* at least to this extent: that they agree they are a distinct group who ought to be governed by themselves and as a group. The *form* of government desired may vary infinitely but the feeling of groupness for purposes of government is at the root of nationalism everywhere. This loyalty to the national group is further distinguished from loyalty to other and smaller groups to which the individual may belong, in that whenever *conflicts of loyalty* arise, the difficulty is resolved in favor of the national group. Also, it is not necessary that the national group's ambitions to possess their own state apparatus shall have been fulfilled, so long as they *exist*. Whether the group possesses its own state or not, it feels that it *should*. Scottish nationalism is no less real (insofar as it exists) than Irish nationalism because the former is unconsummated by the erection of a Scottish national state, while the latter has realized part of its ambition in the creation of the Republic of Ireland (Eire).

Other common factors, of whatever kind, *assist* in the growth of nationalism, but no one of these—a common language, or religion, or color, or territorial propinquity—is essential per se.

A few examples will help to make this clear. If we think of Switzerland, where French, German, and Italian are the principal tongues, and where nevertheless a Swiss nationalism has come into being we realize that although in most nation-states there is one common tongue, it is not an indispensable element. If we consider the question of religion, we find that in America there are a multitude of religious faiths, the adherents of which live in harmony with one another. A single religion, too, is not indispensable. Nor is territorial propinquity essential, as the existence of Pakistan demonstrates. Pakistan exists in two pieces, separated one from the other by a thousand miles. In the case of the Jewish people who today inhabit the new state of Israel, the group itself was scattered among a score of countries; they did not even dwell together in one or two territorial areas. Nor is common color an essential prerequisite for nationalism, as the nationalism of the United States and that of the Soviet Union indicate.

It is remarkable how relatively readily the most diverse peoples can be blended, given proper circumstances, into a group with a feeling of common

---

[5] Quoted in Sharp and Kirk, *Contemporary International Politics*, p. 113.

nationalism. In nations created primarily through immigration the degree of mobility and intermixing has important effects upon results. Had the American people remained stratified into geographically concentrated culture groups, as was quite usual in the Middle West between 1870 and 1890, we would today be encountering many of the difficulties the Canadians have been experiencing. Swiss nationalism survived despite several separated cultures but not because of it; deep permanent antagonisms were side-tracked by persistent foreign pressures—a factor not present in Canada's two-culture case.

A way out of this dilemma, if one does not initially build from a two-culture base, is to choose immigrants from cultures most easily assimilable. Australia chose that path—but at the price of a dangerously small present population in an area of the world where population densities are very great. The immigration laws of the United States for a half century until 1965 were based upon the same kind of "national origins" basis, giving pronounced preference to Northern Europeans. Since America attracted large numbers, its population grew to twice or more what it would otherwise have been. Whether restrictive policies prove to be wise or not depends upon the results. But such policies are themselves reflections of nationalistic sentiment.

7   The Symbols of Nationalism

NATIONALISM, once strongly intrenched in a nation, gains momentum and vigor almost of its own accord. It becomes a habit of mind. But its power is also carefully reinforced by the use of symbols.

These symbols frequently represent the future hopes of a people or call attention to past triumphs or glory. Language has symbolic value. Within the old Austro-Hungarian Empire some large areas for centuries used German as the language of culture as well as of shop signs, but in Prague in little over a decade Czech replaced it. This shift in language did not mean that the people of Prague had changed, except in their sentiments. It was a harbinger of the later collapse of that Empire as a consequence of the opportunity presented to the Czechs by World War I. "Unity" is another symbol. The West German government issued in 1952 propaganda stamps showing divided Germany, with the inscription: "Only if these frontiers disappear will Europe find peace." [6] Fifteen years later its maps still portrayed *West* Germany, *Middle* Germany (i.e., *East* Germany), and *East* Germany (i.e., East Prussia and the Silesian and other territories lost to Poland and Russia in the two world wars). These are symbolic representations of the nationalist aspirations of patriotic Germans. The "past" can be a symbol. Mussolini erected on the Via Imperiale in Rome, not far from the busy Piazza Venetia, four marble mosaics. These showed the growth of Rome from a small city-state to an empire at the height of its glory under Augustus and Trajan. The implied com-

---

[6] For further comment see Ernest S. Pisko, "A Progress Report on the Reluctant Warriors: The German Side," *The Christian Science Monitor*, February 16, 1953.

parisons in terms of what could be expected of the new Italian Empire were the more obvious for being omitted.

Nationalistic symbols are familiar in everyday life. The flag, the salute to the flag, the national anthem, the national shrine, all these are to be found everywhere that nationalism as a creed has penetrated. In the United States one can visit Mount Vernon, the home of Washington, and see his tomb as well. In Washington, D.C., the Declaration of Independence and the Constitution are carefully preserved and guarded. In Paris the tomb of Napoleon and the Arc de Triomphe are focal points of nationalist sentiment and glory. Following the French victory of World War I, the place where the armistice was signed was marked with a stone slab bearing the inscription: "Here, on 11 November 1918, succumbed the criminal arrogance of the German Empire that tried to enslave the peoples of Europe." And on that same spot, in retribution, Hitler danced a jig and forced defeated France in 1940 to sign *his* armistice. He also destroyed the stone slab to avenge *German* honor. Such symbols may antedate modern nationalism. Yearly in Geneva the Swiss reenact the 1602 victory over the Duke of Savoy in the pageant of the "Escalade." Every December the populace, dressed in medieval costume, with lances, pikes, and horses, restages the battle successfully brought to a climax by the pouring of hot soup over the enemy as he attempted to scale the city walls.

Popular slogans expressing nationalist sentiments abound in the literature and usage of each people. They call up emotional reactions far more powerful than the words themselves suggest, since they stand for whole attitudes and responses that go far back into national history. A few examples will suffice: "The sun never sets on the British flag"; "Life, liberty, and the pursuit of happiness"; "Liberty, Equality, Fraternity."

By the use of these symbols each nation-state and each people develops its nationalism, its own national views on life. All this is further fostered by the schools. Instruction in the national tradition—the folklore, the ancient ways of the people, the immemorial customs—begins very early for the child. The heroic anecdotes, which are the sacred literature of patriotism, are repeated. In America the story of George Washington and the cherry tree is learned, while over across the deep Pacific, Japanese schoolboys until recently were taught reverence for an emperor descended from the Sun God. While the American child learns the significance of the fifty stars and thirteen stripes and where the colors of red, white, and blue originated, in Japan the red sun ball on the white field is similarly explained.

The learning process itself begins with familiar, everyday things. Next the child learns that his town or city is a part of a larger territory, and gradually he comprehends the fact that he is a member of a nation-state with certain boundaries and frontiers. He is aided in his understanding by maps, prominently displayed, which traditionally show the particular state in question as the center of the world. Rarely does the child stop to realize that maps are made by first choosing a central point and then drawing in the world around it. The choosing of the central point is, after all, quite arbitrary: by choosing Switzerland, India, or any state as the central point, it can be made to appear the center of the universe.

For the individual, where *he* lives is naturally the center of his own personal universe. It is equally natural for him to consider, as he becomes aware of the wide world around him, that his nation, too, is the center of the physical universe. In this process his nation-centered maps assist, and on those maps his own state usually appears in particularly conspicuous colors, further aiding the illusion. As he learns from his geography and history lessons about foreigners, he begins to form a mental picture of other peoples who differ from *his* people in that they wear wooden shoes, or no shoes at all, or no shoes in the house. Or their skin is of a different color. He also gets the impression that although these variations from the norm (i.e., his own nation) may be harmless in most cases, his own ways are greatly to be preferred.

Each nation has its own rose-colored mirror. It is the particular quality of such mirrors to reflect images flatteringly: the harsh lines are removed but the character and beauty shine through! To each nation none is so fair as itself. "Oh, to be in England, Now that April's there." Or as Sir Walter Scott put it: "Breathes there the man, with soul so dead, Who never to himself hath said, *This is my own, my native land!*" Each nation considers (to itself or proclaims aloud, depending upon its temperament and inclination) that it is "God's chosen people" and dwells in "God's country."

There is a curious psychological paradox in these views. Because one's own nation is fairest and best (and therefore different from the others), the difference is usually considered not one so much of kind as of degree. The national traditions and outlooks of one's native land are not normally considered as in complete contrast to those of other nations but rather as a more perfect expression and embodiment of the good, the true, and the ideal of the universe. Rarely does a nation feel that it is apart from all the others in outlook and values but rather that it has brought world values to a higher state of perfection in the flowering of its own society. To be God's chosen people and live in God's country implies, since God is a *universal* God for all peoples and lands, that one's own nation's name, like that of Abou ben Adhem in the fable, *leads all the rest.* For a nation to think itself unique, except in perfection, would be to admit the shadow of suspicion that, since no other nation shares the same values and since other nations have a different set of values, perhaps it is one's own values that are wrong and at fault.

Each nation and each ideology asserts that the values it espouses are *universal* values that it embodies in purest form. Thus nations and ideologies habitually give expression to this underlying belief by pushing forward views and policies couched in terms of universal and eternal principles. Thus President Calvin Coolidge justified American annexations in this way: "The legions which [America] sends forth are armed not with the sword but with the Cross. The higher state to which she seeks the allegiance of all mankind is not of human but of divine origin. She cherishes no purpose save to merit the favors of Almighty God. . . ." [7] Even so, he later admitted that "We extended our domain over distant islands in order to safeguard our own interests," but he justified this action because, in doing so, America "accepted the consequent obligation to bestow opportunity and liberty upon less favored people." [8] Earlier, President McKinley, who had actually made the decision to take the Philippines, had spoken of "Christianizing" the natives. A *Filipino* patriot, some years ago, found occasion to comment:

Catholics may demur to the McKinley proposition, or that part of it about Christianizing the Philippines, on the not unreasonable ground that the Philippines had been a Christian country somewhat longer than the United States, the cross having been planted on the islands before the Pilgrims landed on a rock now commemorated by a well-known make of American automobile; nor were Filipinos exactly savages when the Americans came, saw and conquered; but on one score there is no argument. The Americans educated.[9]

To cite a further example, in the United States the "American way of life" is not only lauded for its own sake but also, when America speaks to the "conscience of the world," it does so, secure in the belief that American principles *are* universal principles. This opinion is considered valid because the *essential* virtue of the American way of life to Americans is that it is believed to be in harmony with the natural inclinations and preferences of mankind and human nature. Thus Americans expect that people not at present subject to Soviet oppression will react in much the same way as Americans do to communism; they are disappointed at the "neutralism" of India, which then becomes inexplicable other than on grounds of ignorance or shortsightedness.

What is true of American actions in this regard is equally true of other nations, some of whom are much more adept and much more arrogant in finding that whatever they wish to do is in reality for the good of the world.

8 *The Results of Nationalism*

THE basic result of nationalism is that each state has become increasingly the center of its own universe. It is itself more and more its own first concern and preoccupation. It fabricates and elaborates a national way of looking at life— what the philosophers call its own "universe of discourse." Words and terms lose objectivity since they take on meanings given to them by nationalistic aspirations and national interests.

What is fairly obvious in terms of the different meanings of the word *democracy* in America and the Soviet Union is no less true of other terms current among nations. At the Disarmament Conference held under the auspices of the League of Nations in the early 1930's, there was general agreement that

---

[7] From the Inaugural Address of Calvin Coolidge, March 4, 1925.

[8] *Ibid.*

[9] Teodoro M. Locasin, "When the Americans Came: The Second Wave," *Philippines Free Press*, December 1, 1951, p. 2.

"offensive" weapons should be prohibited and only "defensive" weapons retained; whereupon the British and the Germans fell into hot dispute over the classification of the submarine. Obviously, said the Germans, this is a defensive weapon (against British surface sea power). Obviously, said the British, the submarine is offensive (in all senses of the term). Further than this they could not go.

The terms used in international relations by states for these reasons often mean (as Lewis Carroll's Humpty-Dumpty said of the words he used) what the states say they mean. It is not enough to know what is said; you must also know who said it if you would ascertain what is really meant by it.

The consequence of the separate universes of discourse is that international morality becomes an extension of national morality. Each national group jealously guards its national values, emphasizing the superior level of perfection attained in its own nation-state, but simultaneously believing that most other nation-states share the same values in less well-realized forms. The net effect is that each state acts on a basis of its particular values while insisting that the particular values are indeed universal values as well. Thus the national values are projected onto the international scene, and the state sees reflected back its own value image and labels it "universal." This process eliminates the logical incompatibility between what a nation wishes to do and what the world might deem right and just (*if* the world *could* judge *as an entity* rather than as a group of nation-states, each with its own values). What the nation values, the world values, and what the world values, the nation values.

Thus, although Western tradition has been expressed in terms of universal values ever since the days when nationalism began back before the French Revolution, values have been consciously or unconsciously "nationalized." They have been given particular interpretations and meanings in each separate and sovereign state community. Only the shell and form of universality are left today: the reality is far different.

Take a reputed universal value: all people hate war—people are peace-loving. Yet, as everyone knows, there are states that force war upon others. Are their people then peace-loving? Of course it may be said that these people are saddled with dictators who embroil them in foreign wars to divert their attention from embarrassing scarcities at home or losses of freedom. Their people may still love peace, but they supposedly have no choice: it is a police state; they will be shot if they resist. Are the people then to be held responsible for the actions of their governments or not? If they are, then the people saddled with a dictatorship that leads them into war cannot truly be peace-loving or they would not permit it, and would not fight if they were unable to prevent it. If they are not to be held responsible, then the assertion that all peoples are peace-loving becomes meaningless verbiage. Unless dictatorship can be prevented, one peace-loving people will continue to fight another and there will be war. Are dictatorships preventable? Who is to prevent them if not the people who are being subjected by a dictator? But they will be shot if they resist. At this point we have come full cycle in the reasoning process.

Actually, no people likes war and all people love peace—in the abstract. Witness the enthusiastic reception given to the Briand-Kellogg Pact. Signed in 1928, it came into effect on July 24, 1929, and was ratified ultimately by the largest number of states ever to accept a multilateral political instrument up to that time. It is one of the shortest treaties on record. The important articles follow:

ARTICLE I

The high contracting parties solemnly declare in the names of their respective peoples that they condemn recourse to war for the solution of international controversies, and renounce it as an instrument of national policy in their relations with one another.

ARTICLE II

The high contracting parties agree that the settlement or solution of all disputes or conflicts, of whatever nature or of whatever origin they may be, which may arise among them, shall never be sought except by pacific means.[10]

When the treaty was debated in the United States Senate, many senators made it clear that they were of the opinion that the greatest sanction (enforcing measure) behind the treaty would be the force of aroused world public opinion.

It is highly significant that almost all the civilized states of the world were able to sign and ratify the treaty. Were they not all peace-loving and against war? In the diplomatic notes exchanged prior to the signing it was made clear, however, by one state after another, that *the right of self-defense would remain unimpaired*. In addition the United States specifically called attention to her commitments under the Monroe Doctrine—these were excepted. Britain called attention to her obligations toward the Dominions and her Empire—and these were excepted. Each nation took care to exempt its vested interests from the confines of the treaty.

Even without these specific exceptions, the unimpaired right of self-defense was an exception of such significance that compared with it the obligation to be peace-loving became exceedingly anemic. What measures are legitimately those of self-defense? If you declare war first, are you acting in self-defense? According to this standard, Great Britain aggressed upon Germany in 1939. Are you an aggressor if you mount the first offensive or probing attack *after* war is declared? According to this interpretation, France aggressed upon Germany in 1939. Clearly the words "self-defense" are elusive and at the same time rather all-inclusive. To defend oneself one must defeat the enemy, but has it not been said that the best defense is a good offense?

In practice, states (and peoples) are prepared to defend what they consider to be their vital national interests (their *security*). How they go about it is a

---

[10] *United States Treaty Series*, No. 796, Washington, 1929. Today the nuclear test-ban treaty has exceeded the Briand-Kellogg Pact's popularity. More that 100 nations have adhered to it.

question of strategy and tactics. Where they draw the line at what is or is not a vital interest depends upon the people and the circumstances. Even though they are peace-loving, *they will defend those interests.* If two peace-loving peoples consider that their vital national interests are at stake and that those interests are incompatible, they may very well resort to war. Each loves peace in general and in the abstract—but they also love what is near and dear to them: homes, families, ways of life, and national objectives enshrined in the immemorial historical past. For the safety of all these they will fight—even though they love peace and love life as well. One is reminded of George Orwell's quip in *Animal Farm:* "All . . . are equal but some are more equal than others." All are peace-loving, but some are more peace-loving than others—depending upon the vital interests at stake.

If the universal love of peace is tempered by the particular national interests of states, it might be contended that all peoples love *justice.* This, upon examination, turns out to be even more ambiguous than the peace-loving nature of peoples. What is justice? To have a universal yardstick against which to measure justice one might assume that there must be one general point of view; a *majority* point of view would then be hardly enough unless it was that of an *overwhelming* majority. Could what 51 per cent consider just be so by mere virtue of that extra 1 or 2 per cent (which might easily shift later to the opposite point of view)? Surely justice is more stable and more solidly capable of definition. There must be universal or quasi-universal agreement. Yet it is difficult to find universal or quasi-universal agreement on any values, other than as pure abstractions. What is actually meant concretely, by states invoking those values in justification of their actions, cannot be determined unless their actions themselves are examined.

The viewpoint of any given nation-state will be rooted in its own interpretation of the universal value at stake. It will not reject the value but rather interpret its own conduct favorably in the light of, and on the basis of, that value. This process need not even be a conscious one. In this way two states may follow contrasting policies and justify them under the identical universal value.

What we call world public opinion is misnamed, and misunderstood, if we think of it as representing a consensus based upon universal values interpreted in a uniform manner and against uniform concepts of what those values mean. "World public opinion" could be more accurately described as a *coalition of national opinions* expressed through a common policy or policies. It is not an organic thing in itself; it is no more nor less than the states (and the opinions of the peoples thereof) who make it up. These opinions and the policies that represent them may be very similar. They may be, for many states, concerted and made identical or almost identical. As a consequence, if the value view of many peoples is substantially the same for the moment or for longer, the policies of many states may be capable of being expressed in a single general policy endorsed by those states. So-called "world public opinion" is founded upon the shifting sands of coincidence of national viewpoints and sufficiently similar conceptions of what a given universal value means in concrete terms; this does not mean that it is unimportant in international relations but only that its *efficacy* as a restraint upon national policies is seriously diminished by the nature of its composition. This also explains why so-called "world opinion" at times seems very potent as a restraint, and at other times appears completely impotent. It depends upon the degree of coincidence of national values and thus upon the ultimate extent to which states are prepared to use power in common for a common objective.

9 *One World—Or Many Worlds?*

NATIONALISM has in many ways forced modern man to attempt to combine the uncombinable. Each national group has its separate existence and admits the differences between itself and other groups, while clinging to the idea that the world is yet one world and all the universe is governed by the same ultimate laws. The reason for this continuing attempt to combine national separateness with universal togetherness is embedded deep in the traditions of Western civilization. The idea that no man (or group of men) can be an island unto himself (or themselves) is rooted in past centuries. Although the tenets and beliefs of Western civilization have never been universal (the wisdom of the Chinese sages, for example, is often at variance with our own precepts), Westerners have always believed in the universality of their ideas. And since much of the world was settled and brought under control from Europe, or at least exposed to Western traditions and ideas, in the modern age Western ideas have been the predominant ideas in the world. All the great powers until the present century have historically had a Western civilization orientation or have assumed a Western veneer. In that tradition the idea and ideal of universality has been a central concept.

At one time, the Western world was in fact substantially one world—under the Roman Empire and later the Roman Church: one world politically, economically, religiously—one world in values. As the centuries passed, the onenesses bifurcated and multiplied into many: instead of one political entity, many; instead of one economic system, many; instead of one religious faith, many; instead of one system of values, many.

While the universal tradition remains, the actions of states have become increasingly particularistic and even parochial. Sovereignty is a precious prerogative and guarded as such; nationalism is a jealous god and must be regarded as such. The displacement of *liberal* nationalist attitudes by *integral* nationalist attitudes, and the corresponding tendency towards separate "universes of discourse" has merely accelerated the accumulations of tensions that nationalism from the first implied in its division of group from group on a basis of loyalty to one nation or state rather than to another. With the world organized into nation-states it is not surprising that national loyalties and values take precedence over universal loyalties to abstract moral values. It would be surprising if this were not so.

Since the rise of international communism as an ideology, many have predicted that *it* would replace nationalism. Unquestionably it has had an effect on nationalism, but it has not either ended it or transformed its basic effects. Indeed, "national communism" is now a well established phenomenon, quite obviously so in the post-Stalin era. (In later chapters we shall examine these developments in depth.)

As a result, the often heralded decline of nationalism, like the reports of Mark Twain's death, has been grossly exaggerated.

Some, in despair, have gone to the root of the trouble and proclaimed that sovereignty has outlived its usefulness and must either be abolished or made to "wither away," that its strength must be sapped by the continued encroachment of supranational organizations, until only the mere shell remains. Perhaps ultimately this will indeed happen. But to remain completely realistic one must face squarely the fact that no matter how many so-called partial surrenders of sovereignty a state makes—whether by joining NATO or the European Community, or both of these at once—until the state reaches a point of no return, when it no longer wishes to withdraw and can no longer decide to withdraw, it still remains as sovereign as ever. The essence of sovereignty is the retention of the ultimate *ability to decide,* and although such supposed "surrenders of sovereignty" may restrict a state's freedom of decision, either that ability is present or it is not. In this ultimate sense, sovereignty is coldly pragmatic. To settle the issue as to whether sovereignty remains in the hands of the former independent parts may take trial by combat. Thus the common uniform for French and German soldiers proposed for the abortive European Defense Community would no more have ensured against a new war between them than did a common schooling at West Point and a common American army uniform prevent General U. S. Grant from fighting General Robert E. Lee.

On the other hand, a common threat and potential enemy is a powerful cement, binding nation to nation. In the face of such a common threat, persisting over a long enough time, common values are often hammered out. This has been the historical path that nationalism itself has taken. The supranational institutions that states have been creating since the end of World War II call for a higher allegiance, if they are to endure and become significant, than the relatively narrow parochialism of modern state nationalism. And this has occurred at the very time when nationalism is even stronger than before, most everywhere. If the older states are to become now multinational (in today's sense of the term "nationalism"), then the values of the former parts must be swallowed up into new and common values for the greater and newer whole. If done geographically, a "Western nationalism" must replace, for example, the present separate French and German nationalisms. If done ideologically, a Communist organic unity must overcome Soviet-Yugoslav-Cuban differences. The great obstacles in the way are obvious. In Africa, conversely, the problem is at the earlier stage of overcoming tribalism on some national basis.

PART TWO

National Power
and Foreign Policy

CHAPTER 3

The Elements
of National Power

Butter makes us fat, but iron makes us strong.
HERMANN GOERING

Walled towns, stored arsenals and armories, goodly races
of horse, chariots of war, elephants, ordnance, artillery,
and the like; all this is but a sheep in a lion's skin, except
the breed and disposition of the people be stout and
warlike. Nay, number itself in armies importeth not much,
where the people is of weak courage; for as Virgil saith:
"It never troubles a wolf how many the sheep be."
FRANCIS BACON
Of the True Greatness of Kingdoms and Estates

POWER, as we briefly defined the term in Chapter 1, means: How
strong or weak is a given state? In a more formal sense, power is the
strength or capacity that a sovereign nation-state can use to achieve its
national interests. The extent to which a state will attempt to bring its power
to bear upon the solution of any problem will vary with time and circumstances.

In one sense, states are ceaselessly using their power against one another.
The very existence of power has an effect. Even when it is not deliberately
capitalized upon, it exists as a possible threat. No state can ignore the possibility that the power of another state will be used. And therefore the power of
that other state is in effect used, and plays some part both in the initial formulation of policies and in the subsequent relations of the states concerned,
even where it is not intentionally put to use. In this sense, the relations of
sovereign states, each possessed of power, are always at root those of "power
politics." Power that may be used is already being used, even though no overt
or willful act by the state possessing that power has occurred. Thus the threat
and possibility of the use of force are always implicit in the multistate system.
Power lurks in the background of all relations between sovereign states.

The degree to which a state will consciously seek to use its power (as distinguished from its inevitable but unconscious *influence*) will vary greatly. It
will vary in terms of what is at stake, and with whom the state is dealing. And
it will vary with the circumstances, the mood of the nation, and the moment.

41

Although power is ever-present in the background, the frequency and extent to which it will consciously be used and intruded into the forefront of international relations is less than might be expected. The relations of states are frequently routine; they are carried out along well-worn, habitual paths, using techniques developed over centuries. Many problems are adjusted by ordinary negotiation or by the application of the rules of international law bearing on the case in point. The great majority of problems arising between and among states can be settled on a basis of custom or mutual convenience and necessity—without power consciously being used by any of the parties to the problem. Influence or reputation plays no small role in avoiding the conscious use of power.

There is a second group of problems where conscious power does enter—but on a willfully limited scale. In these the nations go beyond influence to the use of *pressure*, but there is no intention of using the final degree of conscious power—*force*. There are infinite gradations in the use of pressure. These gradations begin with the first conscious and intended use of power (perhaps a veiled hint or threat) and extend all the way to measures just short of force. In later chapters we shall see many examples of states using pressure on one another.

And, finally, there is a third group of problems where conscious power is used as physical force. The nation declares war, fights an undeclared war, or engages in a "police action."

Obviously, the extent and degree to which power is consciously brought to bear by one state in its relations with another is a decision of great importance and consequence to the states concerned. When consciously to use power, how much power to use, and for what purposes—these are the highest and most intricate problems in formulating a foreign policy. This problem will be dealt with at length in the chapter that follows. In this chapter we shall concern ourselves primarily with exploring the nature and the sources of the national power a state may wield. This somewhat arbitrary division for purposes of analysis cannot be as easily separated in practice. To illustrate, we are asking here what makes a state strong or weak. The answer in part is location. The location of Great Britain off the continent of Europe combines factors of strength and weakness. An element of strength is in her physical isolation from the Continent, because her territory is less exposed to the threat of invasion; still, her dependence on food imported by sea because she is an island kingdom is a factor of weakness. With the one factor weighed against the other, some balance can be struck. Yet there is more to it. The very fact of Britain's location set the mold of her national interests to an enormous extent. It brought in its train a concern for a superior navy, an awareness of extra-European developments far higher in sensitivity than the norm for a continental power, and a certain historical tendency toward aloofness from an integral role in European balance-of-power relationships. In short, Britain's location actually affects her estimate of her national interests and the foreign-policy role she chooses to play as decisively as it affects her total power. Any "black" African state, located in an area still greatly influenced by memories

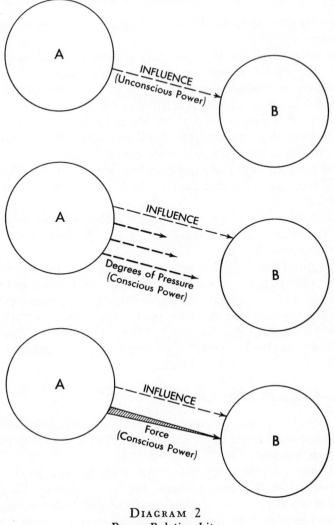

DIAGRAM 2
Power Relationships

of imperialism, and neighbor to others with similar experiences, is as decisively motivated toward neutralism for those reasons as for lack of real power.

Consequently, while the major concern in this chapter is with what are customarily called the elements of national power, it must be remembered that these same elements that determine the strength of a state necessarily and inevitably have much to do with how individual states evolve their own conceptions of their national interests.

The Elements of National Power

WHAT makes a state strong or weak? What are the elements into which the power of a state can be divided for purposes of analysis?

Six elements come to mind. These six elements can be put in the form of six questions:

1. How many people are there, are they growing or declining in number, and what is the population structure (the *demographic* element)?

2. Where do these people live, what is their climate and location, and what is the size of their territory (the *geographic* element)?

3. What are their raw material possessions and resources, what critical and strategic material shortages confront them, and what are their present and projected production rates (the *economic* element)?

4. What has been their past experience as a nation-state, how do they look at life, and how cohesive is their society (the *historical-psychological-sociological* element)?

5. What is their form of government, what is their attitude toward it, how strong do they desire it to be, and how strong and efficient is it (the *organizational-administrative* element)?

6. What armed forces do they possess, what are the relations between the size of the military-age group and the size of the armed forces, and how well-trained, armed, and equipped are those forces (the *military* element)?

Any careful evaluation of the total power of a nation must take each of these six elements (and their interrelationships) into account. Governments wealthy enough to afford it spend huge amounts of money annually collecting such intelligence data on a detailed basis.

2 *The Demographic Element*

THE first element of national power is the demographic: how many people are there, what is the trend of population, and what is the military-age structure of the population?

The first factor is *size*. Every state, large or small, has a population base. Other elements for the moment aside, the more populous the state the greater its power since there are more people to work, more women to bear children, and more men for the armed forces. In terms of population there is an enormous range between the smallest and the largest states. At one extreme we find such tiny states as the Vatican City (with a population of 1,000), or San Marino, Lichtenstein, and Monaco.[1] At the other are those with huge populations such as China (with approximately 775,000,000), or India, the Soviet Union, and the United States.[2] In between are many states of 5 to 15 millions, a group of twenty-one states with between 15 and 35 millions, and above 35 millions only ten states not already mentioned: Indonesia, Pakistan, Japan, Brazil, West Germany, Nigeria, United Kingdom, Italy, France, and Mexico.[3]

---

[1] Respectively, 17,000; 19,000; and 24,000.

[2] Respectively, 492,000,000; 230,500,000; 195,000,000.

[3] Respectively, 107,000,000; 100,762,000; 97,960,000; 82,222,000; 58,819,000; 56,-400,000; 54,066,000; 52,520,000; 48,900,000; 40,913,000.

The states with population greater than 35 millions approximate a listing of the great and medium powers. Obviously this approach is too superficial, since some states of greater total power are eliminated by this method of assessment, and others of lesser power are included. Canada, with about 19.6 millions, is more powerful than Pakistan with 101 millions. Again, Canada, with about two-thirds the population of Spain, is more powerful. More than population statistics go into the total assessment of power. As a beginning point for the evaluation of power, population analyses have their value—provided such qualifications are kept in mind.

After establishing how many people, it is well to ask in what direction the population is moving, and how fast. Is it growing, declining, or remaining stationary? What, to turn to the second factor, is the *trend?*

Trends in gross population growth or decline are not easily or quickly reversed. Sometimes their results over decades are startling. In 1871, when Germany had 41 millions, France had 36 millions. Since this German total included two million inhabitants of Alsace-Lorraine, taken by Germany from France the year before, the relative position at the outbreak of the Franco-Prussian War was more nearly 39 as against 38 millions. Yet in 1955, when Alsace and Lorraine were again part of France, Germany had almost 70 millions while France had 43 millions. Between 1931 and 1955 the net French increase was only one million. India, on the other hand, is presently suffering from a reverse trend—a galloping population growth that continues as in much of Asia to outdistance the increases made in the food supply.[4] The United States itself for more than a decade has been in the midst of an enormous demographic increase. From 145,000,000 in 1948, to 167,000,000 in 1956, to 195,000,000 in 1965 comprises a spurt in America's population that upset prewar estimates entirely.

A third meaningful population factor, this time from a viewpoint of contribution to the military and industrial power of a nation, is to go beyond the gross population figures and consider the military-age structure: the men up to age 34. It is from this source that the armed forces are principally drawn. The table below uses a slightly larger age group in order to show comparisons between those presently below 20 years of age, and those 20 to 39. These figures, in showing comparative trends, allow us to see what will hap-

---

[4] Of the total population of the world (which exceeds 3,336,000,000), Asia (excluding the Soviet Union) has about 56 per cent. China, Japan, and Indonesia together comprise 44 per cent of the population of the world in a land area less than 10 per cent of the world's usable total. Compare total world population now with 1,810,000,000 in 1920, 2,246,-000,000 in 1940 and an estimated 5,965,000,000 in 2000. In 2000 Asia alone is expected to contain about as many people as the present population of the whole world. In 1960 Asia had 1,651,000,000. Comparing other 1960 figures with 2000 estimates, we find Africa going (in millions) from 273 to 768, Europe from 425 to 527, U.S.S.R. from 214 to 353, Latin America from 212 to 624, and U.S.-Canada from 199 to 354. See Jean Bourgeois-Pichat, "Population Growth and Development," *International Conciliation* (January 1966), No. 556, p. 6.

TABLE 1

Manpower of Selected Nations

Nation	Men, Age Groups to 19	Men, Age Groups 20–39
France	7,970,771	6,394,488
United Kingdom	7,348,600	6,131,200
Germany, West *	8,074,500	8,135,900
Germany, East *	2,477,337	1,956,427
Japan	18,497,000	16,003,000
United States	38,442,000	23,658,000
U.S.S.R.	40,473,000	34,410,000

SOURCE: Data compiled from *United Nations Demographic Yearbook, 1964.*
* Excluding Berlin.

pen in the years ahead, as the younger groups in time become the 20–39-year groups. These figures reveal the new vitality of France. They show one meaning of the Berlin Wall in that East Germany now has prospects for increased growth in the very age groups (under 25) which earlier fled to West Germany in disproportionate numbers. (And we can observe the slackening in West Germany's growth which fed on this source.) We see the United States attaining a future near equality in numbers of young men with the Soviet Union, compared to a present substantial numerical lead by the Soviets. When one adds that Russia, because of less efficiency, has had nearly ten times as many people doing farm work as in the United States (52.0 million men and women, versus 5.8 million), the Russian disadvantage increases.

These points are indicative rather than exhaustive.[5] But they show how population factors can be analyzed as they affect national power.

3 *The Geographic Element*

THE second element of national power is the geographic: where do the people live and what climate do they have, how have they been influenced by their geographic location (and in turn affected their geographical environment), and what is the size of their territory?

The view once widely popular that geographic influences determine the nature and achievements of a people must at once be discarded in favor of the more accurate proposition that between people and geographic environment there is a continuing interaction. Even so, geography does influence the people more (and more obviously) than the reverse.

The single most important geographical factor is *climate*. Climate is important, first, in terms of enjoying sufficient heat to grow crops. The portions of the globe excluded from effective habitation because of lack

---

[5] The amount of education, the degree of literacy of the population, and the variety and extent of industrial skills are also important.

of heat are almost entirely in northern Canada, Alaska, and Greenland in the New World; in the north of Asia in the old; and, of course, in Antarctica. Within the remainder of the world's continents a serious limitation on the growing of crops arises from insufficient rainfall. The extent to which this defect can be cured by man's ingenuity in irrigation is a measure of the inter-action of man with his geographical environment. All Egypt is in an area of insufficient rain, but from the time of the Pharaohs the Nile has been used to overcome this deficiency. The natural periodic overflow of the Nile preserved Egyptian civilization from the decline that overtook Babylon and the civiliza-tions of the Arabian Peninsula (where rainfall is also insufficient) once arti-ficial irrigation had broken down. The new Aswan Dam on the upper Nile is designed to add so much new land to cultivation that Egypt's national prod-uct will be doubled. It is to be noted that all the world's present great cen-ters of power lie in zones that have sufficient rain and heat to grow crops.

Climate is also important so far as temperature is concerned. Temperature depends especially upon distance from the equator (from the sun), height above sea level, and such natural phenomena as the Gulf Stream (which has the beneficial effect of raising Northern Europe's temperatures). Without the Gulf Stream, Europe would, because of its location in latitudes similar to those of Canada, be very much colder. From the point of view of human ac-tivity, the temperate zone areas between 20 and 60 degrees north and 20 and 60 degrees south are the most favorable for human activity. It is no accident that the large cities of the world are to be found within these zones. Because the greater part of the land between these latitudes is in the northern hemis-phere, the temperate-zone areas north of the equator have played decisive roles in world history.[6]

This short survey of the effects of climate on the ability to grow food and perform work helps to explain why some locations (to turn to the second factor) are more favorable to a state than others.

Location is important to a nation-state in a dual sense: geographically in terms of the temperate zones, and strategically in terms of its neighbors and its vulnerability to invasion. Location is consequently a primary geographic influence upon foreign policy since it is axiomatic that where the state is must affect directly not only its power but also what it will consider to be its na-tional interests.

So fundamental is the connection between location and foreign policy that it has given birth to geopolitics. Founded as a field of study by Sir Halford Mackinder (who first set forth his theory in 1904), this offspring of the mar-riage of geographic and political concepts has at its best contributed many in-sights.[7] At its worst, as under the Nazi Haushofer school, it disintegrated into

---

[6] About 85 per cent of the land areas of the world (and 75 per cent of the habitable land) lie north of the equator. In these areas dwells nine-tenths of the world's population!

[7] Mackinder's paper was presented before the Royal Geographic Society in London in 1904. In 1919 he followed this with his *Democratic Ideals and Reality*, which is still a

an organic theory of the state. The philosophy at the root of this extreme view rests upon the premise that a state must, like an organism, expand (grow) or eventually decline; that its pattern of growth and the directions and extent of its growth are determined by geography; that the product of its growth will be adequate living space for the nation (*Lebensraum*). German *Geopolitik* was little more than a "scientific" justification for national expansion through aggression.

The insights of the geopolitician have been in danger of being disregarded as a reaction to the extremism of the German school. Yet those insights are in many cases profound. Consider the connection between (1) the development of democracy and civil liberties in both Great Britain and the United States and (2) their relatively secure geographical situation. Britain has not been successfully invaded since 1066; the Americas not since the development of effective United States power after 1815. Again, the Scandinavian nations are noted not only for their democracy but for their social legislation. Here the beneficial effects of relative geographic isolation from the major highways of European invasion have been reinforced by a deliberate policy of avoiding involvement in war. The Swedes have been neutral by policy; the Norwegians by practice insofar as they could.[8] In these cases geography has not determined policy, but it has made a wider choice of policies possible since the peril of invasion has been less immediate.

It is not unreasonable to explain a good deal of Canadian policy on the basis of the fundamental fact that she has a powerful neighbor to the south. In the War of 1812 the United States attempted to invade Canada, and in the middle of the same century claimed portions of what is today western Canada. Under such circumstances there have been powerful motives, aside from sentimental preference, for the continuance of Canada within the Commonwealth: a status with which the large French-speaking elements in Canada were not too sympathetic. One reason for Canada's more independent attitude toward Britain in the twentieth century springs from the Canadian conviction that she no longer needs Britain to protect her from United States aggression.

In a similar fashion almost all the Latin American states participated in the League of Nations despite United States refusal to adhere to the Covenant. As relatively weak states existing under the shadow of the North American Colossus (whose power was not restrained by near and powerful neighbors), they saw in the promises of the Covenant a measure of protection of their independence. Joining the UN is normally among the first sovereign acts of any new African state.

Consider the authoritarianism that for most of modern history has been

---

standard work on geopolitics. Mackinder's central concept was the *Heartland* of Eurasia and its relationship to the rimlands of the Eurasian continent from an historical and military point of view.

[8] Norway is now, however, a member of NATO. She is no longer convinced, after her World War II experience, that her security is best served by aloofness from alliances.

typical of the German and Russian regimes. These two states, for much of the time direct neighbors, lie exposed on the North European plain. Flanked by important military powers, they have no or few natural geographic barriers at their European frontiers. In the whole length of the northern European plain between the Rhine and the Urals there is no natural deterrent to invasion equivalent to the English Channel or the Atlantic Ocean. Both states have been consistently more militarized and less democratic than Britain and the United States.

Or look at Switzerland. Her politics are conditioned by geographical circumstances in a dual sense. Composed, because of her location, of French-, German-, and Italian-speaking peoples, Switzerland has had perforce to choose neutrality to prevent the possible dissolution of the Swiss nation, as a consequence of opposed sympathies among the Swiss people in wartime. In World War I, for example, the Swiss were bitterly divided in their sympathies among the belligerents. In addition, Switzerland is so strategic, containing key routes between France and Italy and between Germany and Italy, that the great powers themselves in 1815 declared Switzerland permanently neutral to guard against such a strategic prize falling into the hands of any one of them. The Swiss, like the Americans, are democratic and enjoy a high standard of living; their welfare is intimately related to their geography. Location of the state is thus extremely important in influencing national policy as well as national power.

The third geographic factor that affects national power is *size*. There is an enormous range in size of states. The smallest is the Vatican with 108.7 acres; the largest by far is the Soviet Union with over 8.6 million square miles. The next biggest are China and Canada with about 3.8 million square miles each, as compared with 3,615,210 for the United States. Only four other states have more than a million square miles: Brazil, Australia, India, and Argentina. Some fifty-four others possess more than 100,000 square miles but less than a million; thirty have more than 40,000 but less than 100,000; thirty have more than 3,000 but less than 40,000; and eleven (including the Vatican) have less than 3,000 square miles.

Of the total of 133 states tabulated—a number constantly changing— Africa contains today the largest group (38), with Asia now in second place (37), and Europe third (34). (Even five years ago, the sequence was: Europe, Africa, Asia.) Of the 62 states with more than 100,000 square miles, Africa with 25 has the largest number while Asia has 17, the Americas have 12, and Europe (with the Soviet Union) has 8. Even in the group between 40,000 and 100,000, Africa and Asia contain 17 of the 30. Since virtually all of Africa and Asia was until recently ruled by Europe, one can see the revolution in world affairs that has occurred.

It is obvious that size by itself does not determine national power. On the other hand size, like location, has an intimate bearing on national power and policy. The very size of the Soviet Union and China makes them difficult to conquer. The 191 square miles of Andorra make that state no conceivable threat to its two neighbors, France and Spain. It is also important to know where the size is located and whether it will support life. Size is inextricably tied into the other geographic factors. A great part of Canada is uninhabitable. This does not mean that northern Canada may not be of strategic or national resource importance, as the recent exploitation of uranium deposits indicates. But since it all cannot support life, the potential power that Canada's size confers on her is limited to that extent in realizable power.

In assessing national power, therefore, so far as the geographic element is concerned, climate, location, and size are basic factors.[9]

4 *The Economic Element*

THE third element of national power is the economic: what are the raw material resources of a people, what critical and strategic material shortages confront them, and what are their present and projected production rates?

At the outset of an examination of the economic element of power, a seeming paradox emerges. Some nations, poor in resources, have developed great economic power; others, richly endowed with resources, have done little or nothing with them. In Asia, relatively poor Japan far outstripped relatively rich China; in Europe, relatively poor Germany far outstripped relatively rich Russia. In an Africa possessing great natural resources, economic progress has been limited. The explanation will not be found through a consideration of economic factors only. It is rather the economic consequence of a historical sociological-political set of circumstances. It is enough here to realize that economic resources do not in themselves mean great economic power. Nor does their lack mean the nation must necessarily be condemned to an inferior economic position. What a nation *has*, and what a nation *does* with what it has, are the two sides of the economic coin.

Countries vary greatly in what they have—in their *natural resources*. The United Kingdom, France, Germany, China, Italy, Japan, and India have either no large oil reserves or none at all. The Arabian Peninsula by contrast, while rich in oil, is poor in iron ore. Rare is the nation that possesses iron, oil, and coal in sizable quantities within its own frontiers. Both the United States and the Soviet Union, almost alone among the states of the world, have them. Other states have one or more of these three vital factors of industrial might within their frontiers; and others like Britain have had them within spheres of influence or areas of control. This is better than not having them all under national control anywhere at all, but it raises a question of transportation.

A nation can transport needed raw materials from abroad, importing them either from its own colonies or from other states. In wartime such sources of supply are uncertain. Britain's historic devotion to a powerful navy, while not solely due to concern over imports in wartime, was very basically tied up with that concern.

---

[9] Other geographical factors such as shape, terrain, river systems, etc., are important too but space precludes their detailed examination.

It is questionable whether any nation, large or small, can be considered self-sufficient today, particularly in terms of the factor of critical and strategic raw materials essential to the making of modern war. The United States and the Soviet Union, while approaching this status more nearly than most, fall short of its attainment. The position of the U.S.S.R. is somewhat more favorable that that of the United States. America was formerly self-sufficient in many minerals now imported, such as copper, zinc, and lead. Of 39 minerals vital to United States industry only nine were supplied entirely in 1964 from domestic sources. All or nearly all industrial diamonds, quartz crystals, and tin were imported, as well as 90 per cent or more of American needs for platinum metal, asbestos, mica, manganese ore, nickel, cobalt, bauxite, and chrome. All or nearly all important non-mineral raw materials such as natural rubber, jute, carpet wool, and shellac, came from abroad. Even the ordinary but indispensable telephone uses 48 imported materials coming from 18 nations.[10]

The United States, once self-sufficient in iron ore, today imports a substantial part of its needs, largely from Canada, Venezuela, Peru, and Sweden. (The U.S. production of crude steel in 1964 was 28 per cent greater than its iron ore production, compared with 18 per cent in 1962.) Every ton of ordinary steel takes about 13 pounds of manganese—98 per cent of it imported. Both manganese and chromite are important in the production of high-grade steel products. When one takes into account the strategic importance of industrial diamonds for the manufacture of machine tools, and of quartz crystals for communication instruments, one begins to see the dimensions of the problem. Not even the most highly armed nation can continue long in war without these materials. The dangers implicit in the situation are graphically revealed by the following table of materials needed to build U.S. missiles:

TABLE 2

*Major Materials Imported for Production
of United States Missiles*

Material	Source
Castor Oil	Brazil
Chrome Ore	Malawi, South Africa
Cobalt	Congo
Columbium	Canada, Brazil, Nigeria
Copper	Chile
Manganese	Brazil, Congo, India
Nickel	Canada
Tantalum	Brazil, Mozambique, Congo
Tin	Malaysia
Tungsten	Bolivia, Korea, Portugal, Argentina

[10] *ABC's of Foreign Trade*, Department of State Publication 7713 (October 1964), pp. 5, 15.

The more the resource deficiencies of the nation, the more it must depend upon the transportation of imports from outside the frontiers. The alternatives to this dependence are two: stock-piling and substitutes. The first of these alternatives is feasible only insofar as stock-piled materials will not deteriorate; the second, only insofar as substitute materials are available. Germany fought longer in World War II because she made oil out of coal, but for the bulk of the war she depended upon the reserves of oil she had stock-piled, together with the production of the Romanian oil fields that she had conquered. United States oil reserves are dangerously low today, and since World War II the United States has become a net importer of petroleum—particularly from Mexico, Venezuela, and the Middle East. Both the Venezuelan and Middle East sources involve vulnerable transportation by sea.

Nations vary greatly, too, in the factor of *production* of goods. The raw materials for what is produced may be available within the frontiers or may need to be imported. Production may be contingent more upon the continued ability to import raw materials than may be at all desirable from the standpoint of national security. The Japanese rate of production during World War II suffered near the end from the exhausting of their prudently accumulated stock-piles and from their inability to replenish them from their rich conquests in the South Pacific because of the efficiency of American submarine warfare.

Comparative production figures for the basic sources of power (coal, oil, electricity) and for basic construction materials (crude steel and cement) are given in Table 3 for principal industrialized nations.

What can we learn from these figures? They show how few countries account for the greater portion of the world's basic production. (If our figures included *all* industrial production, they would show the U.S. presently producing about 44 per cent of the "free" world's industrial output.) The figures show the remarkable industrial growth of Japan, compared to the still quite limited growth of China. Also, if we add the production of the United Kingdom, France, and Germany together, the combined later totals generally approximate Soviet production. Comparing the United States and the U.S.S.R., we find the Soviets still a little behind in coal, substantially behind in oil, even further behind in electricity, not too much behind in steel, and equal in cement. (Cement figures are included because of their importance in terms of pre-stressed concrete construction.)

The comfortable comparisons above, which show the U.S. in the lead, should be weighed against the trends. On coal, the U.S.S.R. increased output between 1955 and 1963 by 50 per cent while U.S. production decreased slightly. On oil, the U.S.S.R. tripled output in those years against a U.S. increase of 10 per cent. On electricity, the U.S.S.R. almost doubled from 1958 to 1963, while the U.S. increased 50 per cent. On steel, comparing 1955 to 1963, the U.S.S.R. almost doubled while the U.S. declined slightly. On cement, comparing 1958 and 1963, the U.S.S.R. doubled; the U.S. increased 10 per cent. The U.S.S.R. is rapidly approaching the mature industrialized status of

TABLE 3

Basic Production
(Millions of Metric Tons)

Commodity	Nation	1948	1955	1958	1960	1963	1964
Coal	World	1,410.7	1,598.5	1,818.6	1,985.3	1,929.0	1,996.9
	U.S.S.R.	150.0	276.6	353.0	374.9	395.1	408.9
	France	43.3	55.3	57.7	56.0	47.8	53.0
	U.K.	212.8	225.2	219.3	196.7	198.9	196.7
	W. Germany	87.3	131.8	133.6⎫	143.3	142.8	142.7
	(Saar)	12.5	17.3	16.4⎭			
	U.S.	592.9	442.4	389.4	391.5	430.5	454.7
	Japan	33.7	42.4	49.7	51.1	52.1	50.9
	China	32.4	98.3	270.2	420.0	—**	—
Oil	World	467.1	771.7	906.5	1,053.9	1,303.5	1,410.1
	U.S.S.R.	29.2	70.8	113.2	147.9	206.1	223.6
	France	.1	.9	1.4	2.0	2.5	2.8
	U.K.	.2	.2	.2	.2	.1	.1
	W. Germany	.6	3.1	4.4	5.5	7.4	7.7
	U.S.	273.0	335.7	331.0	348.0	372.0	376.6
	Japan	.2	.3	.4	.5	.8	.7
	China	.1	1.0	2.3	5.5	—	—
Electricity *	World	809.8	1,544.5	1,908.1	2,301.3	2,849.2	3,104.4
	U.S.S.R.	66.3	170.2	235.4	292.3	412.4	458.9
	France	28.9	49.6	61.6	72.1	88.2	93.8
	U.K.	48.0	94.1	113.4	136.9	173.6	182.8
	W. Germany	32.8	76.5	95.3⎫	116.4	147.3	161.1
	(Saar)	1.3	2.3	3.0⎭			
	U.S.	336.8	629.0	724.8	844.2	1,011.2	1,082.4
	Japan	35.6	65.2	85.4	115.5	160.2	179.6
	China	4.3	12.3	27.5	58.5	—	—
Crude Steel	World	155.8	269.3	273.6	345.6	386.6	424.2
	U.S.S.R.	18.6	45.3	54.9	65.3	80.2	85.0
	France	7.2	12.6	14.6	17.3	17.6	19.8
	U.K.	15.1	20.1	19.9	24.7	22.9	26.7
	W. Germany	5.6	21.3	22.8⎫	34.1	31.6	not available
	(Saar)	1.2	3.2	3.5⎭			
	U.S.	80.4	106.2	77.3	90.1	99.1	115.3
	Japan	1.7	9.4	12.1	22.1	31.5	39.8
	China	—	2.9	11.0	18.4	12.0?	9.5?
Cement	World	103.0	217.0	263.0	317.0	368.0	414.0
	U.S.S.R.	6.5	22.5	33.3	45.5	61.0	64.9
	France	5.8	10.8	13.6	14.3	18.0	21.5
	U.K.	8.7	12.7	11.9	13.5	14.0	17.0

[TABLE 3, Continued]

Commodity	Nation	[1948]	[1955]	[1958]	[1960]	[1963]	[1964]
Cement	W. Germany		18.2	19.4 ⎫	24.9	29.2	33.6
	(Saar)	.2	.3	.4 ⎭			
	U.S.	35.2	53.0	54.8	56.1	61.6	64.4
	Japan	1.9	10.6	15.0	22.5	29.9	33.0
	China	.7	4.5	9.3	13.5	9.0?	10.5?

SOURCE: *United Nations Statistical Yearbook, 1964, 1965.*
* Billion KWH.
** Chinese figures were no longer made available after the failure of the "Great Leap Forward." The 1960 figures are as furnished to the UN, with occasional later figures given from other estimates.

the U.S. The comparative gains of the Soviet Union have been occurring with the advantage of a larger gross labor force but under the handicap of a much greater diversion of labor to agriculture. Since the present Soviet male 10–19 age group totals 16.1 million against 17.7 for the U.S., the Soviets are going to be at a comparative disadvantage in the years just ahead for new inputs into the labor force. One can see why the Soviets are so concerned with the weak agricultural sector.

In human terms, the Soviet worker has not yet been permitted to realize his fair share of the fruits of industrial progress. Although the situation is improving, as late as 1960 an American worker had to labor 23 hours to buy a medium-priced wool suit while his Russian counterpart worked 275 hours; for a pair of men's shoes the figures were 7 hours versus 61. But from a power point of view shoes and suits, and the earning of them, are not direct, major considerations.

One further fact should be kept in mind. The Great Depression before World War II hardly affected Soviet steel production but it drove U.S. production down from 41 to approximately 26 million metric tons. Economic conditions may affect different economic systems in quite contrasting ways.

In assessing national power so far as the economic element is concerned, the factors of raw material resources, critical and strategic material shortages, production rates of basic materials, all help to furnish a rough index of power. Finally, to the extent that depression affects economic power diversely in different states, these effects must also be considered in arriving at realistic estimates.

5   The Historical-Psychological-Sociological Element

THE first three elements of national power have the great merit of being tangible, subject to statistical and mathematical handling. In turning to the fourth element of power we encounter not less important but more elusive factors.

The fourth element of national power is the historical-psychological-sociological: first, what has happened to the nation and state in the past, how do the people tend to think, and what kind of attitudes do they typically have; and, second, what kind of society and structure of society do they possess? The factor of historical experience and national attitude will be examined first.

It is far easier to agree on the importance of the historical factor than to agree upon its contemporary psychological and sociological effects. Yet history is the record of the accumulated experience of past generations, and the present generation is inevitably the product of that experience. The "dead hand of the past" is not really dead; it continues to influence the living. Unless the circumstances in which the nation exists alter radically and permanently, the national outlook is not likely to change significantly.

The existence of a national outlook, of national attitudes, is sometimes questioned. Upon examination these doubts as to the existence of such a thing as a *national character* usually are rooted in the accurate observation that not all Americans, Frenchmen, Italians, etc., think alike or look at life with the same values and approach. Even so, there are typical views and attitudes, expressed by majority sentiment recurring in public pronouncements, which can be both discerned and discussed. The stereotyped ideas as to how Americans behave, or how Englishmen speak, or how Frenchmen make love are exaggerations of national characteristics. Such stereotypes do not spring up entirely without basis, even though, to the extent that they do exaggerate, they are false.

Given diverse historical experiences, two peoples may develop views on life that are very far apart. The Americans and Russians are a case in point. In many ways their experience has been diametrically opposite. Where the scarcity of manpower in America led to a high premium being placed on the worth of the individual, the Russians, under Mongol-Tartar occupation for several centuries, absorbed the Asian concept of the cheapness of human life. Where the dynamic growth and progress of America encouraged an optimistic view of life and hope of wealth, in Russia the poverty of the masses continued generation after generation, engendering fatalism and pessimism. Where land was plentiful and cheap or free in America, the Russian farmer was typically a serf bound to the soil until 1861; even after that time he possessed very little he could call his own. Where American taxation until the present century was light, Russian taxation made the poor poverty-stricken. Where government was predominantly remote in America, in Russia it confronted the peasant at every turn—drafting him into the army, placing him at forced labor on the roads, clapping him into prison for slight offenses. The coming of communism substituted one set of masters for another; the tyranny remained. The only real difference has been in very recent years as the standard of living in the Soviet Union has gone up.

Because of such varying environments, what one people thinks realistic may seem an absurdity to another. Reality is judged against the yardstick of experience. How much is deemed possible is compared in the first instance against what has been possible thus far. The result is that Americans and Russians will attach divergent values to the same facts and circumstances even when they are agreed on what the facts and circumstances are.

Differences in national outlooks are real and have real effects. If the African fears of "neo-colonialism" (by which Western economic control of their means of production and access to markets might replace outright political control) seem almost pathological at times, they are still real fears, producing real consequences.

The failure of the leaders of one nation to grasp how another looks at life and is likely to react often leads to calculations very wide of the intended mark. Adolf Hitler, in his plans to conquer Europe, could never adequately adjust to the contrast between the British and German national characters. Hitler overlooked a prime element in his problem of conquering the European continent when he misjudged British character. In his assessment of that character he was in part penetrating and shrewd. He saw, for example, that the British would make many concessions to preserve peace. Hitler capitalized upon this desire for peace by extorting a series of major concessions for each of which, in return, he gave a promise. Sure of the "shopkeeper" mentality of the English, he drove boldly ahead, making one "final" demand after another upon Neville Chamberlain. But in time Chamberlain came to the angry although reluctant conclusion that he could not do business with Hitler; that he had been made to look foolish. He refused further "bargains." The war began and Hitler overran France, when he was ready, in a few short weeks. As we now know, however, he made no detailed plans for an invasion of the British Isles. German war production was even ordered cut back for a time.

Hitler was convinced that the British had only entered the war half-heartedly, and that they would be happy to have a pretext to make peace once more. In 1940 he considered the British already defeated. After all, at Dunkirk he had defeated the British army and captured almost all their modern and heavy equipment. But what Hitler overlooked was that the British for hundreds of years have lost the initial battles and won the wars. Not since 1066 has Britain been successfully invaded. Secure in their islands, protected by their fleet (and, later, air power), they have licked their wounds and girded themselves for a return in force to the continent. Competent military observers in 1940 may have considered the British defeated, but the British, with this background of experience, did not. Churchill reflected their mood in his fiery declaration: "We shall fight on the beaches, we shall fight on the landing grounds, we shall fight in the fields and in the streets, we shall fight in the hills; we shall never surrender." Since the British would not admit themselves beaten, they were not. And, again, although the odds were closer in World War II, the British ended the war as they had expected—as victors.

Finally, the factor of structure and morale of the national society is important. How torn by cleavages is the national group? What is the state of national *morale?* In 1940 France collapsed with startling rapidity. The French people had become convinced of the truth of the oft-repeated assertion: "*Nous sommes trahis!*"—"We are betrayed!" The will to fight dwindled and died as the people lost faith in their leaders and lost hope for the future. Again, the domestic political deadlock in France in the years after World War II, still reflecting cleavages in French society, shackled French ability to resolve upon a clear-cut and sensible plan for ending the war in Indo-China and the native unrest in North Africa.

A national society torn by cleavages is less able to fight. To the extent that one group hates, fears, and distrusts other groups within the nation more than the foreign rival or enemy nation, the will to fight is sapped. This point is well understood by the Communists, who seek to set class against class within each state.

The national character and outlook of a people, and the structure and morale of a society, as they emerge from the crucible of historical experience, are important factors in the evaluation of national power.

6 *The Organizational-Administrative Element*

THE fifth element of national power is the organizational-administrative: what is the form of government, what is the attitude of the people toward it, how strong do they desire it to be, and how strong and efficient is it? Like the fourth element just considered, this, too, cannot be reduced to statistics or easily measured. Yet it is extremely important. If the government is inadequate and cannot properly bring the potential power of the nation to bear upon a problem, the power might as well not exist. Nor is the answer to this fifth question discernible from a study of statutory arrangements and organizational charts. How well the government operates on paper is not an indication of how well its wheels actually turn.

Nor can an analysis turn upon the type of government a state claims to have. Even the constitution of a state may be misleading in this respect. The Soviet Constitution of 1936, a very democratic-sounding organic law indeed, had little in common with the actual operation of the Soviet regime; the German Weimar Constitution, a model of democratic devices, did not bar Adolf Hitler from reaching power and from creating his own "constitutional law" as he went.

If we examine governments as they actually are, it is immediately apparent that the *form and type of organization* of government is a factor of small importance insofar as it affects state power. Republics are not necessarily weaker or stronger than monarchies; a centralized unitary state may be considerably weaker than a confederation such as the Swiss possess. A monarchy may be constitutional and democratic (as in the United Kingdgom), the façade of a Fascist dictatorship (as in Mussolini's Italy), or even the "front" for a Communist regime (as in Romania for a brief time after World War II).

A government takes the shape it does, and operates the way it does, for very complex reasons. Here the historical-psychological-sociological element again enters into consideration since the government and how it operates reflect the experience of a people and their attitude toward, and expectations of, what the government is to do.

This second factor, *attitude toward government*, is extremely important. The United States Constitution and those of the Third and Fourth French Republics in their provisions deliberately encouraged cumbersomeness. The United States governmental machinery was not designed to operate superbly well from the narrow point of view of efficiency. Too much efficiency might have caused the people to lose control of it—or so they thought—and become robots under the crushing heel of the machinery of state. For this reason the Founding Fathers deliberately made the United States Government inefficient (in the sense of quick, smooth operation) through the well-known "checks and balances." [11] The same fear resulted in the weakness of the French governments after the Franco-Prussian War. The French experience with Bonapartism led them to strengthen the legislature under both the Third and Fourth Republics to a degree that made strong executive leadership almost impossible. The French preferred to suffer the executive weakness rather than run the risks that a strong government would entail. As a result, where the United States had 14 administrations between 1875 and 1940, and the British 20, France had 102. The Fourth French Republic, after World War II, averaged two regimes a year. Yet changing conditions can and do produce changing attitudes. The Fifth French Republic established in 1958 under de Gaulle represented a remarkable contrast. And in the United States the Congress, through legislation and endorsement of presidential "doctrines," has in recent decades widened executive powers greatly.

The British, by contrast, have always had a government in which authority and power are highly centralized. The executive is actually a committee formed from the majority party in the House of Commons. This committee or cabinet system allows a great concentration of power, because the leadership of the executive and legislative branches are one. Although this concentration of power is much nearer the Russian model than that of either France or the United States, Britain remains democratic to the core, and the government limits its own actions to what is permissible within the unwritten rules of the British Constitution. This aggregation of power in the hands of the executive is permitted by the British because they are sure in the light of historical experience of their ability to control it within the framework of British institutions.

Each people, insofar as they are able to control their governmental machinery, must reconcile the demands of abstract efficiency with their ethical demands and beliefs under changing conditions.

Apart from the views of a people on how a government should be operated, turning to the third factor, the problem of actually *operating* government is a

---

[11] This has led, naturally enough, to friction between Congress and President. Theodore Roosevelt berated the Senate for interfering in foreign affairs thus: "When they call the roll in the Senate, the Senators do not know whether to answer 'present' or 'not guilty.'"

problem in bureaucracy. In a government such as that of the United States, one bureau or division or department or council must "clear" with so many others, even within the executive branch, that quick operation is difficult. The Defense Department must clear with the State Department; they must both clear with the Bureau of the Budget and the President; and then there are the Senate and the House (each with their many committees) and the courts still to be considered. On the other hand, quick decisions are not always desirable. The prolonged debate over Secretary of Defense McNamara's decision in 1965 to virtually eliminate army reserve forces had the merit of clarifying the issue. By the time a proposal has run this gantlet from end to end, it ought to be democratic (i.e., reflect the various possible points of view). But it takes time. For authoritarian governments like the Soviet Union, "clearing" must also occur. Coordination is still a problem for them as well. In addition, the haunting fear of a misstep is much greater than in the American bureaucracy. Even so, insofar as operating the machinery of government in any nation-state—democratic or authoritarian—is concerned, the problems of governmental efficiency have a family resemblance. The Soviet complaint, published in their journal, *Soviet State and Law*, that they found they had one hundred forty chiefs in the Russian Soviet Republic's Ministry of Public Utilities for three hundred forty-eight workers, in the first half of 1954, has a familiar ring. The technical board of the same ministry had six chiefs and a chief engineer for seven workers.[12] It is not surprising that governments everywhere are always being reorganized in the search for greater efficiency. This is why organizational charts, when printed, are already obsolescent or obsolete.

Inefficiency in government can cost a nation dearly. The Pearl Harbor disaster of 1941 was in part due to a failure in coordination, not only between the army and the navy, but between Washington and the Hawaiian headquarters. Again, Hitler so organized his armed forces high command that the naval point of view was suppressed. As a result of this one-sidedness and his own ideas on how the British would react to their "defeat," he found himself astride the Channel coast of France with no amphibious operation planned and ready for implementation. Or take the defeat of the Austrians by the Prussians at Sadowa in 1866. The Prussian victory has often been attributed to their needle gun (a breechloader that could be loaded and fired rapidly from a prone position). Yet the needle gun had been invented some thirty years earlier, it had been used by the Prussian army since 1851, and its powers had been demonstrated before Austrian eyes in the joint Austro-Prussian war against the Danes in 1864.[13] The Austrian bureaucracy was notoriously inefficient.

Sometimes the machinery stays the same but the attitudes change. The

---

12 See *The New York Times* (hereafter referred to as NYT), October 24, 1954.

13 See the very informative article by Bernard Brodie, "Military Demonstration and Disclosure of New Weapons," *World Politics*, Vol. 5, No. 3 (April 1953), especially pp. 285–286.

present constitutional arrangement in the United States for the ratification of
treaties is a perennial subject for reform proposals. The constitution provides
that two thirds of the Senators present and voting must concur before Senate
consent to ratification can take place. To reverse this for clarity, one third,
plus one, of the Senators present and voting can defeat a treaty. Under conditions of full attendance by all 100 Senators, thirty-four can block a treaty;
under conditions of less than full attendance this figure of thirty-four drops in
proportion. On occasion, a fourth or less of the Senate can defeat a treaty.
More than one Secretary of State has remarked, in effect, that the Senate
buries treaties rather than consents to their ratification, and that the real
question is whether the interment will be decent or not. Since World War
II, on the other hand, reflecting the tremendous increase in interest in
international affairs in America, and using the same machinery, the Senate
has taken a very liberal view on many of the treaties submitted to it. It agreed
to United States' membership in the United Nations and in NATO, and accepted the Nuclear Test Ban Treaty—to name but a few important treaties.

What the attitude of a people toward their government is, and how well
the government actually operates, will affect, for better or for worse, the nation's power.

7 The Military Element

THE sixth element of national power is the military: what armed forces do a
people possess, what is the relation of the military-age group to the number
of men in uniform and to the population as a whole, and how well armed
and equipped are the forces?

Taking first the *size* of the armed forces, the table below gives a comparison
for the great powers of land, sea, and air components. These figures are constantly changing. It is important to remember that some of the figures shown
in it can change much more rapidly than others. While it takes years to move
from the planning-board stage to production of a modern heavy bomber, the
size of the army may be expanded or contracted within weeks or months. The
table shows only active land forces, although the reserves can be added
quickly in time of war or national emergency.

The figures for land forces deliberately do not cover reserves. While the
quantity of such reserves is sometimes known, the *quality* of their training
and their actual readiness for war are almost impossible to assess. Russia had
9,600,000 reserves in the early 1950's—but that is virtually all that is publicly
known about them. For this reason the military-age group is the second factor
of military power, since it is the manpower reservoir from which the armed
forces are drawn under conditions of full mobilization; where little is known
about effective reserve strength, it is best to concentrate on this figure of the
total potential.

In most great powers the two figures are fairly synonymous. Most of the
powers require men at age eighteen or twenty to serve a year or two in the

armed forces. They then pass into the active reserves for a number of years, and finally into the inactive reserves until they are overage for military duty. For such nations it is the entire prime military-age group that is in fact, whether in name or not, the military reserve.

TABLE 4

Armed Forces of Selected Nations

Country	Military Personnel (in thousands)			Ships		Planes	
	Army	Navy	Air Force	Sub-marines	Destroyers	Bombers	Fighters
U.S.S.R	2,000.0	450.0	510.0	410	220	(4,600)	(6,000) *
France	315.0	72.5	122.5	18	54	18	25 **
United Kingdom	208.0	100.0	132.0	469	71	(500)	(600)
West Germany	278.0	35.0	97.0	12	36	10	4
East Germany	80.0	17.0	15.0	—	4	18	18
United States	970.0	674.1	828.6	150	220	(2,500)	(2,200)
Japan	172.0	35.0	39.0	7	47	—	20
China (Mainland)	2,250.0	95.0	100.0	30	10	60	140
China (Formosa)	380.0	35.0	82.0	—	11	(75)	(200)
India	825.0	16.0	28.0	—	17	13	8
Indonesia	200.0	35.0	20.0	6	10	(75)	(100)
Brazil	210.0	43.0	31.0	4	21	?	?

SOURCE: Adapted from data of Institute for Strategic Studies, London; and *Jane's Fighting Ships, 1964–65*. The data gives a comparison just before the Viet-Nam increases of U.S. forces.
* Numbers
** Squadrons

The United States was for long an exception. After World War I an entire United States generation grew up that was not widely trained in the use of arms. The United States did not practice the European annual age-group conscription described above, but relied instead in both world wars on a draft. The principle of a draft is quite different: the entire military-age group (other than those deferred or rejected) is placed in uniform for the first time as promptly as it is possible to digest them into the mushrooming armed forces. It is basically a "crash" program designed for a sudden emergency. The millions who form the citizen army are thus trained during the war rather than before it. By force of circumstances rather than by design, the United States had approached in effect the European conscription system by the early 1950's. The draft—by virtue of having been used since 1940 on a continuous basis through World War II, the Cold War, and the Korean War—had given essentially the same results. A draft becomes conscription if it is continued to the point where the major source of draftees are those becoming of military age annually. The tapering off of numbers drafted in 1954 and thereafter began once more to make the distinction a valid one, but this trend was in turn reversed in the second half of 1961 due to the Berlin crisis. In 1965 the Viet-Nam crisis again significantly increased draft calls. Whether the United States can afford to rely upon the draft or upon much training *during* hostilities in the nuclear age depends on how much wars continue to be conventional.

A comparison of data already given in Table 1 against figures shown in Table 4 reveals that nations do not in peacetime maintain under arms any standard percentage of the military-age group. West German and French forces were equal (510,000) although there were only three Frenchmen aged 20 to 39 for every four West Germans. The Soviet Union, which on the West German percentage basis, would maintain perhaps 2,200,000 men in uniform, had three-quarter million more than that. The United States, which on the West German basis would have 1,500,000, actually had almost a million more than that under arms. Japan, which on the West German basis would maintain a million men, actually had a quarter of that total. France and the United Kingdom, with almost equal manpower, maintained respectively 510,000 and 440,000.

The percentages in uniform vary with the power problems and armed conflicts of the nations involved. France, some five years earlier than our present data, had about double the armed forces of the United Kingdom: she was fighting a war in Algeria. Japan and Great Britain both maintain far smaller armed forces than they could afford from a manpower standpoint—the British to save money and stabilize the pound, the Japanese because they renounced anything but "self-defense" forces after losing World War II.

In general, however, there is a distinct correlation between how industrialized a state is and how much of its military-age group it can keep on active duty. Thus we see a third factor in evaluating military power. China, with a total population three and a half times greater, is able to keep slightly fewer men in uniform than the United States can. The United States, as the most industrialized nation in the world, tends to have the highest proportion of its military-age group under arms of nations at peace.

This works two ways: first, a highly industrialized nation, because of its high output per man-hour, can permit more of its potential labor force to be put into uniform instead. Second, the more industrialized the state, the more mechanized its armed services will likely be. The more an armed force is mechanized, and the more intricate its weapons and equipment, the larger the forces must be in order to sustain the large overhead in maintenance, processing, and organization, which is necessarily entailed. As a consequence, expressed simply, the more a nation readies itself for "push-button" warfare, the more it needs not only combat personnel but a huge number of push-button servicers—to keep the push buttons operating. Since China is much less industrialized, she cannot in relative terms maintain anything like the armed forces of the United States.

A fourth factor in evaluating military power is *weapons and equipment*. The quantity and quality of a state's weapons and equipment are very important. Here again the lack of reliable data may make evaluation difficult. Table

4 given earlier includes data on the numbers and kinds of naval ships possessed by the leading powers. Their relative performance, however, may be of far more importance than their relative numbers. Quality cannot overcome entirely the advantage in warfare that quantity confers. Even so, a relatively small number of aircraft, with highly skilled pilots, enabled Britain to survive the German attacks with vastly superior numbers in the Battle of Britain in World War II. New, "surprise" weapons may also play an important or even decisive role: radar, proximity-fuse shells that explode when near the target, atomic bombs, atomic cannon, guided missiles, recoilless and portable cannon—the list could be prolonged.

This factor of weapons and equipment is briefly mentioned here as it affects the power of a state; it will receive further attention in the chapter on war and the military relations of states.

8 The Assessment of National Power

THESE then are the elements out of which a nation's power is formed. It is apparent from even this relatively brief survey that the task of making a total estimate of national power is a difficult one. The student who would evaluate national power must keep four points firmly in mind about these six elements.

First, it is obvious that these elements are interrelated. Where the people live will affect what they possess; how many they are will affect how much they possess; what their historical experience has been will influence how they look at life; how they look at life will affect how they organize and govern themselves; and all these elements weighed against the national security problem will influence the nature and size and effectiveness of the armed forces. Therefore, not only must each separate element be weighed and analyzed, but their effect on one another must be considered.

In a fundamental sense, following out this idea, the fifth and sixth elements are the synthesis or outgrowth of the first four. The demographic, geographic, economic, and historical-psychological-sociological elements are the raw materials, the basic human and material stuff out of which the fifth and sixth elements are compounded. The organizational-administrative element and the military element translate potential into realized power. This is the second point to remember. No matter how numerous and skilled the people, nor how imposing their resources, nor how advantageous their location; no matter how fortunate their history, nor how well-balanced their outlook on life and grasp of the realities, unless this potential can be realized by compounding and synthesizing these elements into an effective governmental mechanism and effective armed forces, the state will remain weak because it will not be able to focus and bring to bear its power. Yet how well a nation brings its power to bear upon its security problem is itself an element of national power and, as a consequence, the fifth and sixth elements are power elements themselves.

These six elements therefore are not only interrelated, but the last two are of crucial importance; they are elements of strength and weakness in themselves, and they are also the measure of how successfully the *potential* power of the state can be translated into the concrete and *actual* power to be wielded.

A third consideration relates to the problem of measurement of the elements. The problem concerns the nature and type of the yardstick by which power can be measured. Scientific analysis, as we are accustomed to think of it, consists largely of reducing and relating objective quantities through objective symbols. Before one can assess one must isolate, and once what is to be assessed is isolated, one must tell its weight, its length, its bulk, and its frequency. That is why scientific analysis depends so heavily upon mathematics, since mathematics is the study of the relationship of numbered quantities. Unfortunately, not all the elements of national power can be readily isolated and considered even for the purpose of counting and describing mathematically. Techniques are as yet unavailable that are equivalent in objectivity to arithmetical and mathematical techniques to measure historical experience, social causation, and attitudinal responses and to isolate them one from another without distortion.[14] It is possible to establish with a high degree of accuracy how many people compose a nation, how many are males or females, how many are a given age in a given year, how many are of what profession or trade, and much equally valuable statistical material. It is equally possible to measure statistically how much coal or steel or iron ore is produced in a given year in a given nation, always provided in the case of both population and economic figures that the reliable figures are available. They at least can be available. But what weight is one to give to the status of morale or fighting ability of the armed forces? Size or training of such forces alone is not indicative before the event of how well they will fight. Yet how well they will fight is crucial to the whole question of how strong or weak a nation is. Simply because the measurement is difficult, the proper techniques unavailable, and the results therefore more than normally subject to error does not mean that the whole problem of assessing national power can be shelved until better information is available. The urgency of the problem is more important than the imperfections of its solution. This discussion, therefore, leads not to the judgment that a realistic assessment need not or cannot be made, but rather to the conclusion that the total power estimate will not be as reliable as the estimates of some of the six constituent elements. Roughly the degree of reliability of the answer yielded up by examination of the six elements decreases progressively from element one to element six.

There is yet a fourth point to consider. Nations each day change in both potential and realized power. This is true of all nations, although the rate of change may vary widely from one state to another. Because each nation

---

[14] Although see Quincy Wright, *The Study of International Relations*, 1955, for an important attempt in this direction. Much work in the behavioral sciences is being devoted to these problems.

changes absolutely in terms of power, each also changes relatively to another (except in the highly theoretical case where both nations change to the same extent). Because these changes go on continually, an estimate of national power (and still more an estimate of national power as compared with a foreign state or states) is obsolescent even as the estimate is finished. The greater the rate of change in two states being compared, the greater the obsolescence. Psychologically this can produce a feeling of illusory security based upon confidence in a state of affairs which once existed. The undoubted superiority of the French army that invaded the Ruhr in 1923 over the treaty-limited Reichswehr persisted as an illusion in the West even after the Nazi rearmament program had altered the actual fact, and then in 1938 the actual extent of the change was overestimated. Especially when the rate of change is quick, even if the popular conception of relative power does not fall into the error of lagging behind the fact, it may commit the opposite sin of overestimating the changes which have occurred. It was widely thought in 1941 in Western Europe that the Soviet Red army, previously considered strong, had become much weaker than it was to prove in World War II. The purges of its upper ranks in the late 1930's and its poor showing against Finland of 1939 were overevaluated by Western observers. The obstacles to a correct estimation of changes in power relations arise not only from the errors of evaluating the absolute power of each individual state but also from the comparison of these absolute estimates relative to one another, taking into account the relative changes and the relative rates of change.

To summarize these four points: (1) the elements of power are interrelated, each influencing the other; (2) the elements of organization and efficiency of government, and the fighting ability of the armed forces, are of crucial importance to power since through these elements potential is converted into actual power; (3) the elements are difficult to measure accurately; and (4) the changes in power status of each state in time, and the relative changes in power relations between states that this produces, are even more difficult to measure accurately.

From these considerations emerges the outline of the problem in assessing national power.

CHAPTER 4

Foreign Policy

"I don't see much sense in that," said Rabbit. "No," said Pooh humbly, "there isn't. But there was *going* to be when I began it. It's just that something happened to it on the way."

A. A. MILNE
The House At Pooh Corner

In practical judgments—and diplomacy, when the stakes are life and death, calls for very practical judgments—the criteria are always relative. There is no such thing as absolute power. Whatever the wealth, the power, and the prestige of a nation may be, its means are always limited. The problem of the maker of policy is to select objectives that are limited—not the best that could be desired but the best that can be realized without committing the whole power and the whole wealth and the very existence of the nation.

WALTER LIPPMANN
"The Rivalry of Nations,"
The Atlantic Monthly

A NATION-STATE perennially faces the question: what should the national goals be? The answer to this question we call foreign policy, and it is at once evident that not everything that could conceivably be desired is obtainable. The most obvious limitation on policy is power, and therefore small powers must be more modest in their aspirations than great powers. In the days of the Congress of Vienna in 1815 small powers were actually referred to as "Powers with limited interests."

Yet, as we saw in Chapter 3, national power is limited for great states as well as small. No matter how much a nation has, it is limited both absolutely and relatively. It is limited absolutely, for example, in terms of the annual production of steel, coal, and oil. It is limited relatively in that the national appetite in foreign-policy matters is always bigger than it can afford with the power at its disposal. The list of wants is infinite, and each must be considered against every other. Consequently, the formulation of a realistic foreign policy must always begin with an appraisal of the power reserve upon which it must rest. A nation that overdraws its bank account of power is courting, and often finds itself visited by, disaster. Yet even when a state attempts to keep its policy carefully equated with its power, it encounters at the outset several practical difficulties in following a rational policy.

I *The Abstract Nature of Policy*

THE first difficulty is a result of the fact that foreign-policy objectives are frequently expressed in abstract terms.

The term *foreign policy* suggests a greater degree of rational procedure than is often observable in the way in which states actually proceed toward achieving their long-term objectives. Policy as a term denotes planning. Planning in turn suggests step-by-step procedure toward a known and defined goal. Foreign-policy goals, however, by their very nature, are frequently obviously and painfully abstract. Expressing foreign-policy goals in abstract terms inevitably divorces them one step from concrete reality, because abstractions suppress part of the truth in order to keep sight of the essential idea. Thus the term *democracy* is used with equal enthusiasm by both Washington and Moscow, and both can agree on the need for more of it so long as they refrain from going into detail.

The trouble with abstract goals is that they must constantly be interpreted in terms of immediate, practical circumstances. These immediate circumstances are stubborn and unyielding things. Unless great care is exercised by the guardians of national policy, the abstract goal is lost in the shuffle of the practical situation in which day by day it is given concreteness. As a result, policy may lose direction and, like the fictional knight, go galloping off in all directions.

Decisions must be made to deal with new crises that develop overnight. Only rarely are the nature and future implications of the crisis so clearly defined that the foreign office can make its decision in full and complete confidence that it is a direct step toward the fulfillment of an abstract goal and that it will not appear instead, in the changed perspective of a later time, as a deviation from that goal or even a step backward. The great crises, such as the bombing of Pearl Harbor and the aggression of North Korea, clearly show what must be done; great events reduce a problem to its raw essentials under the brilliant light of dramatic emotion. The lesser crises, which constitute the bulk of times when a path must be chosen, often leave unclear at the moment where one is going. Confronted with the fork in the road, however, one must make a choice, and whether or not progress is being made toward the fulfillment of the abstract goal must often be left to the verdict of history.

At this point the intellectual trap that history sets for the unwary is easily triggered. Having arrived at the goal, one is tempted to look back and divide the correct decisions from the false turns without giving sufficient weight to the fact that the path followed was hard to see at the time it was traveled. Hindsight, indeed, can posture as more perfect than foresight since the claim is in fact true.

The first difficulty in following a rational foreign policy is that the goals are frequently abstract while the choice of alternatives must always be concrete. The result may be the implementation of a policy that in fact does not progress toward the desired goal. The decision may be the product of ignorance of all the facts. Or the pressures of the moment may distort judgment.

2 One Thing Leads to Another

THE second difficulty in following a rational foreign policy stems from the first, since events have a way of taking the bit in their teeth, as it were, and running away with the policy, whereas the process is supposedly just the reverse. This process is cumulative. As George Kennan remarked:

> In the fabric of human events, one thing leads to another. Every mistake is in a sense the product of all the mistakes that have gone before it, from which fact it derives a sort of a cosmic forgiveness; and at the same time every mistake is in a sense the determinant of all the mistakes of the future, from which it derives a sort of a cosmic unforgiveableness. Our action in the field of foreign policy is cumulative; it merges with a swelling stream of other human happenings; and we cannot trace its effects with any exactness once it has entered the fluid substance of history.[1]

Harold Nicolson in the course of one of his books gave trenchant expression to the way in which events may, with a will of their own, shape policy in unanticipated directions:

> Nobody who has not watched "policy" expressing itself in day-to-day action can realize how seldom is the course of events determined by deliberately planned purpose, or how often what in retrospect appears to have been a fully conscious intention was at the time governed and directed by that most potent of all factors— "the chain of circumstance." Few indeed are the occasions on which any statesman sees his objective clearly before him and marches towards it with undeviating stride; numerous indeed are the occasions when a decision or an event, which at the time seemed wholly unimportant, leads almost fortuitously to another decision which is no less incidental, until, little link by link, the chain of circumstances is forged.[2]

This kind of development may also mean that much more power is needed for successful prosecution of the policy than anyone anticipated; in the long run it may force the surrender of other foreign-policy objectives for which power is no longer available, even though such a decision would not have been made if it had been clear beforehand what was going to result.

3 Contradictory or Incompatible Goals

A third difficulty with following a rational policy is that foreign-policy goals may be mutually contradictory. A nation may attempt to achieve two goals that are incompatible with each other. So long as the goals remain abstract,

---

[1] George F. Kennan, *American Diplomacy 1900–1950*, Chicago: University of Chicago Press, 1951, p. 50. Copyright, 1951, by the University of Chicago.

[2] Harold Nicolson, *The Congress of Vienna*, pp. 19–20.

this contradiction may not become serious; but the minute they are given concrete embodiment and implementation, a conflict arises, which, if not resolved, may cause a sort of schizophrenia in the national character. This kind of situation is much more common with abstract than concrete goals, since it is easier to see the discrepancy in the latter case. But a sense of frustration may also arise precisely because only one of two counterbalancing interests can be implemented and these, while leading in incompatible policy directions, are almost equally desirable. Even so, it is the conflict revealed in actual situations between two ideal or abstract goals which is likely to produce the maximum confusion.

It is not unusual for a nation to announce that it seeks both peace and security. The United States, for example, is on record to that effect time and again. These goals are actually compatible, as we saw in Chapter 2, only as long as security can be attained through peace. Given peace, America feels secure. And given security, America feels peaceful. As long as both are obtainable, both are sought. Secretary of State Acheson remarked in March 1950, that while the United States sought peace, it did not seek "peace at any price." Or compare the statement of Russian Ambassador Maisky in London on March 15, 1939: "The foreign policy of the Soviet Government has always been a policy of universal peace. Not a peace at any price, but a peace based on law and order in international affairs."

In other words, upon analysis, it becomes evident that security is the goal, and peace is either the means or a subordinate goal. The reader may indeed agree that this is so, but the point should be clear that America and the other powers continue to announce to the world that each of them seeks peace and security as the twin goals of her foreign policy. The intellectual confusion that results is the direct product of the failure to make the above distinctions clear.

There is a danger that decisions will be made which, while designed to preserve peace, jeopardize security. The classic illustration of modern times is to be found in the actions of British Prime Minister Chamberlain at Munich in 1938. He returned from the conference, he announced, with "Peace in our time," but as it happened he undermined British security in the process. In Winston Churchill's words:

> The subjugation of Czechoslovakia robbed the Allies of the Czech Army of twenty-one regular divisions, fifteen or sixteen second-line divisions already mobilised, and also their mountain fortress line which, in the days of Munich, had required the deployment of thirty German divisions, or the main strength of the mobile and fully trained German Army. According to Generals Halder and Jodl, there were but thirteen German divisions, of which only five were composed of first-line troops, left in the West at the time of the Munich arrangement.

Churchill goes on to point out that, in addition to this loss of some 35 Czech divisions, the Skoda Works, the second most important arsenal in Central Europe whose production between August of 1938 and September of 1939 was almost equal to British arms production during the same time, was subtracted from potential Allied strength and added to that of Germany—a double misfortune. And this was done even though "In 1935, France, unaided by her previous allies, could have invaded and reoccupied Germany almost without serious fighting. In 1936, there could still be no doubt of her over-whelmingly superior strength. We now know, from the German revelations, that this continued in 1938." [3] Ironically, Chamberlain's peace lasted little more than a year.

An unqualified seeking for peace may easily become appeasement; it does become appeasement if national security is put in jeopardy in the process. Thus the third difficulty, where abstract goals are involved, is that one goal may be incompatible with the other at a critical point, and this incompatibility may not be realized. Or it may produce an ill-fated attempt to implement the wrong goal at the expense of the right one, or it may lead to a continued clinging to both when a sharp choice is inevitable and the delaying of that choice is dangerous. The successful execution and implementation of policy is an art demanding skilled practitioners.

4   The Formulation of Policy: Vital Interests

EVEN though the formulation of a rational foreign policy is thus beset with difficulties, a nation must have some clear conception of the policy goals it desires; if its direction is not clear, it is adrift in a whirlpool, at the mercy of the often turbulent currents of international relations. No statement of aims can guarantee that the organization charged with carrying them out will have the wisdom, the skill, and the will to attain them. But if the aims themselves are not defined, national policy disintegrates into mere "playing by ear."

The first task in formulating a foreign policy is to *identify* the goals (i.e., the national interest or interests) to be sought.

What ends might it be desirable for a state to seek to achieve? Since the range of conceivable interests is as broad as the fertile imagination of man-kind, such a list of interests will be long and may include at one end the ab-stractions of "peace" and "security" already mentioned, and, at the other end, such concrete goals as the annexation of an island, a border north instead of south of a given city or river, or a foreign loan to be given or received. Where incompatibilities between potential interests are recognized, choices must be made.

Cutting the list of national interests down to the power thought available to achieve them is the second crucial step in evolving policy. Like the family or national budget, certain items cannot well be cut: they represent fixed obli-gations. These have first priority since they are as vital to the national security as food and shelter to the individual. These vital interests include territorial integrity and independence (freedom from foreign domination). They also often include cherished and historically sanctified policies such as the Monroe

---

[3] Winston S. Churchill, *The Second World War: The Gathering Storm*, pp. 336–337.

Doctrine for the United States. The test of whether an interest is considered vital is simply this: will a nation, unless it feels hopelessly outclassed in terms of power, ultimately go to war to preserve it? If the answer is affirmative, it is considered a vital interest.

It is always possible from an objective viewpoint that a state may mistake what constitutes its vital interests. A nation may choose to fight over what to objective observers is a secondary or even trivial interest. It is not the intrinsic or objective worth of the interest but how much store the people of a state put by its preservation that matters from the standpoint of assessing its importance in a particular foreign policy.[4]

Vital interests are in the first instance predominantly and essentially conservative. That is, they always include things that a state already possesses. While they may also extend to new goals not yet achieved or historically advocated, they are always bound up first and foremost with the preservation of the nation's *status quo*: each nation is determined as a minimum not to lose anything of fundamental importance that it already has.

It should be clear why the vital interests of a state are always strikingly concerned with the wellsprings of its own power. The sources of national power are on the territory of the state itself, and the freedom of its people to use that power for national purposes depends upon their own independence and their undisputed control of their own territory. If they lose these, they lose the possibility of implementing a foreign policy effectively. Therefore, power is linked to policy in two ways: (1) policy rests upon power in the ultimate sense, and (2) policy is concerned always over preserving or increasing that power.

If nations always restricted their views on what constitutes their vital interests to the conservative category mentioned, there would be much less war and threat of war in the world. That this is not the case is obvious. Each nation is the judge of its vital interests. If Germany conceives her vital interests to include (as she did in 1939) the destruction of France's vital interests of independence and territorial integrity, a clash becomes inevitable if Germany puts her views into practice. If Russia conceives her vital interests to include the ultimate extension of communism and Soviet control throughout the world, grave tension is the inevitable by-product. What determines the timing and severity of the clash, as well as who participates in it, depends upon how the vital interest as an objective is translated through diplomacy into an actual political or military problem. A nation which merely professes vital interests that run athwart those of other great powers, even without taking overt action, precipitates tension. The dynamics of statecraft are such that a nation which professes such a vital interest often cannot and does not wish to restrain itself from the realization of its goal. Comparing Nazi Germany and

---

[4] See Chapter 13, Section 2, for a detailed discussion of the wider implications of the national-interest concept, including the problem of whether there are rational general standards against which the nation's accuracy in assessing its interests can be measured.

Soviet Russia in this respect, the main difference to be seen is that Soviet national interests are cloaked in the garments of an international ideology and their views of when the interest must be consummated are more elastic. Hitler considered he must have his war, as he put it, in his prime—in his fifties. The Soviet leaders have always taken a longer view. This was true of Stalin, and Khrushchev spoke of our *grandchildren* being socialists. We might well define an imperialistic or aggressive nation as one which, as a matter of policy, considers that its vital national interests cannot be consummated except at the expense of the vital interests of other powers.

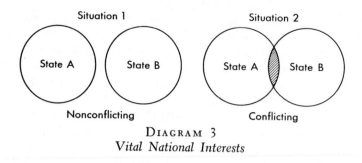

DIAGRAM 3
Vital National Interests

There is no guaranteed way in a sovereign state system of independent nations that the vital interests of states can be kept compatible and that the occurrence of Situation 2, shown in the diagram, can be prevented.

5 *The Formulation of Policy: Secondary Interests*

THE residue of interests beyond the vital interests are termed *secondary* interests. They are the subject matter of the great bulk of diplomatic negotiation, since they are interests that a nation can sacrifice without putting the national security in jeopardy, provided that by and large it receives a *quid pro quo* (something in return).

Every nation is not at all times prepared to give up a particular secondary interest. Although the interest is clearly secondary, the state may feel, for sentimental or economic or historical reasons, that it will not use it as a pawn in diplomatic bargaining. This was true of the American "Open Door" policy toward China in the nineteenth century. It was a secondary interest; yet America was not really prepared to surrender the policy in return for some concession, although she compromised on it from time to time.

Any secondary national interest may temporarily take on in effect the attributes of a vital interest because of a clash of rival powers over it. The most important reason that this happens is that national *prestige* (i.e., both reputation per se and reputation for power) is at stake. Strictly speaking, prestige itself is a vital interest of states, and the secondary interest serves simply as the vehicle for its expression. Thus, in Korea, the American interest was secondary until the 1950 challenge to the United Nations was too flagrant (for

reasons of prestige) to ignore, and because it threatened the precariously maintained balance of power in the Far East. In short, when Korea in 1950 became so vitally important, it was not for its own sake but because of what was
at stake there.[5] Another illustration of this process was the highly dramatic
Fashoda crisis of 1898. Both the British and the French were attempting to
gain title to the Upper Nile (the Sudan). In 1898 the French Marchand mission and the British forces under General Kitchener met at Fashoda. The
British made a poorly veiled threat of war. The French, although much
aroused, decided in the end, because of their naval inferiority and a lack of
support from their Russian allies, to yield. The interest was not sufficiently
vital, and French prestige could still be salvaged.

Thus a nation may or may not be ready to compromise on secondary interests for sentimental, economic, or historical reasons; and secondary interests
may undergo chameleon metamorphoses and become, at least temporarily,
either vital interests or inextricably bound up with vital interests. These qualifications do not alter the general proposition that secondary interests by their
nature provide the pawns that are available in the continuing game of diplomatic "horse-trading" in which all powers constantly engage. The great objective in this game is to receive as good concessions as are given. By giving up
one secondary interest, it may be possible to make another secondary interest
(of more importance to the nation than the one surrendered) attainable and
realizable.

What is sought must be as coherent and consistent as possible. There are
two reasons for this. One is that strength and effort will be dissipated, if the
work of the right hand undoes that of the left. The other is that inconsistency
feeds ammunition for propaganda to opponents. Of course, any action of a
nation may be used by its rivals against it, but propaganda based on proved
inconsistency is particularly effective. This is psychologically interesting in
view of the fact that human beings, either as individuals or groups, so often
are inconsistent. Yet the great emphasis in Western culture on being rational
runs very deep and cannot safely be ignored, even if it were otherwise desirable. Inconsistency can too easily be branded either as weakness (lack of ability to be consistent) or as low cunning (in an intent to deceive).

All the planning as it relates to national interests (the identification of interests, the ranking of interests in order of priority, and the weeding out of
inconsistency) must take place within the power framework mentioned at the
beginning of this chapter. Matching such a list of interests to the power available cannot, however, resemble the exact measurements characteristic of experiments in the natural sciences. Not only is it extremely difficult to measure
available power (as we saw in Chapter 3), but the nature of interests themselves, as should now be clear, is not such that their power costs can be always
accurately assessed. This is particularly true of vital interests where their pursuit may lead to war. Finally, national interests change as the world situation

---

[5] The Korean War is explored at length in Chapter 21.

changes, for they are not only relative to one another and to the available power of a state, but they are also relative to the interests and power of other states as these are perceived by the state formulating its policy.

The dynamic character of national interests within the foreign-policy planning process is what necessitates the continual re-evaluation of foreign policy that is characteristic of modern nation-states. The debate is endless because the task also is endless.

6 *Through the Mill of Public Opinion*

THE debates on foreign policy, which are a familiar spectacle in democracies, occur with less public display in dictatorships. These disputes will occur over the vital interests of the state only where the people remain unconvinced, or incompletely convinced, that the interest is vital. Even if there is agreement on the point of the ends to be sought, there may be acrimonious debate over whether the methods chosen are suitable. The United States decision to resort to force in Korea in 1950 gave rise to a debate over the merits of the action once the idea of "victory" was renounced in the wake of Chinese intervention. Similarly, in 1965–1966, the debate over Viet-Nam waxed strong because many Americans questioned the government's decision that United States vital interests were really involved, while other Americans disputed whether those interests were being advanced by the methods chosen.

One phenomenon is to be observed in these recurrent debates; often the ultimate implications and costs of seeking to achieve certain interests are overlooked or falsely estimated. The whole commitment with all its intricacies can only infrequently be envisaged, because the reactions, interests, and policies of other states can very seldom be established in advance.

This uncertainty, itself a cause of confusion, is responsible for a second phenomenon: the debate is never resumed on the basis of the *status quo ante,* but only on the basis of the *new* situation. Arguments that were in the first instance compelling may seem, in the light of the changed situation, to be specious; and arguments rejected out of hand in the beginning may later be embraced with fervor and deified as "realistic." Thus the process of re-evaluation continues. Frequently the discussion may go far afield from the basic question of whether there is power available for the achievement of the interest. And the typical difficulties inherent in foreign policy may sometimes be passed over too lightly.

It is this second phenomenon which is responsible for much of the heat that often accompanies a foreign-policy debate. Sometimes the discussion tends to be concerned with what, given the present outlook, should have been done at a time when people actually looked at the problem in quite different terms. The perspective and point of view change, and the problem takes on new outlines, but the discussion often proceeds as if the circumstances remained the same.

In post-World-War-II America the Yalta Conference received exactly this type of post-mortem. It was bitterly condemned as an unwarranted act of appeasement in favor of the Soviet Union. Actually, at the time of Yalta, United States policy was actively concerned with bringing Russia into the war with Japan. The Japanese Manchurian Army was to be pinned down by Russia while the United States invaded the home islands of Japan. The United States was willing to pay a price—and paid it.[6] Even with Russian help one million American casualties were anticipated as the cost of the invasion. Moreover, at the time of Yalta, the atomic bomb had not yet been tested and its military capabilities were unknown. The Yalta Conference, considered from the viewpoint of today, however, takes on aspects far different from early 1945. Several of the crucial unknowns of that time have since become known.

Alistair Cooke, an acute British observer, has written of this general phenomenon of judging yesterday in terms of today:

I have said it is a natural thing to want to make the past consistent with the rationale of our present self-respect, or to want to confess an inconsistency when we have confidently outgrown it. This impulse is very strong in America, where people want the best of everything, believe Time is the Siamese twin of Progress, and refuse to let even experience shake them from their belief that happiness is manageable. If we are now baited in every direction by the Russians, it does not satisfy Americans to say that this is the turn of history. It must mean that somebody entrusted with our welfare betrayed us or blundered. A nation with a religious trust in Progress simply cannot admit that even when the best is done, hard times may follow.[7]

What Mr. Cooke has said is true not only of the United States but in some degree of all nations, and this leads us to a third phenomenon in discussions over foreign policy. Not only is the power commitment necessary for the success of a given policy difficult to establish, and not only do changed perspectives often cause the foreign-policy ends of a previous time to seem invalid or worse, but it is also difficult for people to accept failure in their attempts to achieve ends which now, as before, they would like to achieve, although such ends were and are beyond their power. Frustration may result either from a lack of realization of the extent of the difficulty or from the baffling nature of the problem and the enormous power that its resolution would demand. Consider the American debate over the rise of Communist China and the reasons for the failure of Chiang Kai-shek to remain in power. Those who maintain that the United States did not try hard enough, or did not try the right things, will perhaps not be prepared to concede that what America did or did not do vis-à-vis the China problem in the late 1940's could, in the nature of

---

[6] That this was in some respects an unnecessarily high price is perfectly true. The details of the agreement will be considered below, Chapter 22.

[7] Alistair Cooke, A *Generation on Trial*, p. 9. Mr. Cooke became widely known for his work as chief American correspondent of the *Manchester Guardian*. By permission of Alfred A. Knopf, Inc., New York.

things, have little decisive effect one way or the other. Yet this, it would appear, is a dispassionate and substantially correct observation.

Former Secretary of State Dean Acheson once commented acutely on this general problem in these words:

Nobody, I think, says that the Nationalist Government fell because it was confronted by overwhelming military force which it could not resist. Certainly no one in his right mind suggests that. Now, what I ask you to do is to stop looking for a moment under the bed and under the chair and under the rug to find out these reasons, but rather to look at the broad picture and see whether something doesn't suggest itself.

The broad picture is that after the war, Chiang Kai-shek emerged as the undisputed leader of the Chinese people. Only one faction, the Communists, up in the hills, ill-equipped, ragged, a very small military power, was determinedly opposed to his position. He had overwhelming military power, greater military power than any ruler had ever had in the entire history of China. He had tremendous economic and military support and backing from the United States. He had the acceptance of all other foreign countries, whether sincerely or insincerely in the case of the Soviet Union is not really material to this matter. Here he was in this position, and four years later what do we find? We find that his armies have melted away. His support in the country has melted away. His support largely outside the country has melted away, and he is a refugee on a small island off the coast of China with remnants of his forces.

As I said, no one says that vast armies moved out of the hills and defeated him. To attribute this to the inadequacy of American aid is only to point out the depth and power of the forces which were miscalculated or ignored. What has happened in my judgment is that the almost inexhaustible patience of the Chinese people in their misery ended. They did not bother to overthrow this government. There was really nothing to overthrow. They simply ignored it throughout the country.[8]

No nation can control another (particularly one large in area, people, or resources) short of physical occupation—which means war in most cases. It can threaten, it can punish, it can use coercion. It can grant loans and withhold loans. But what it cannot do is decisively to influence a great state, and the people who make it up, to do that which they are not prepared to do and to abstain from doing that which they are determined to do. Consider America's difficulties with Castro's Cuba—and Cuba is a small and weak state! Even the use of military forces for temporary control of small powers may or may not ensure lasting results. From a foreign-policy point of view it may create other difficulties. The United States occupation of the Dominican Republic in 1965 illustrates the complexity of the problem.[9]

There are no magic brews or potent formulas which, prepared when the full moon is high (or any other time), will ensure that a given foreign-policy

---

[8] Dean Acheson, "Crisis in Asia—An Examination of United States Policy," *Department of State Bulletin*, Vol. 22 (January 23, 1950), pp. 112 ff.

[9] See below, Chapter 28, for a fuller discussion.

goal will be crowned by ultimate success. There are always limits to what can be achieved, short of a total *military* effort that may be impossible or undesirable or both. A debate over foreign policy that does not take this factor into proper account fails to be of much use except in the negative way of pointing up the lack of effect of pure exhortation. To will is not enough: the policy must also be feasible in power terms—that is to say, in terms of power available that it is desired to commit for the purpose. Because there always are other commitments, the power for that purpose may not be available and may never have been.

7 Power and Policy: The Process of Adjustment

FOREIGN-POLICY debates serve a useful end if they give impetus to a reappraisal of foreign-policy objectives, and the power available and necessary for their realization.

For all the reasons already mentioned, it is a very difficult accomplishment to keep power and policy in even balance. When it becomes apparent that the two are no longer adequately balanced, a nation has three choices: (1) it can bluff, attempting to create the impression that power and policy are balanced when in fact they are not; (2) it can modify the policy; or (3) it can modify its power.

The last of these three possibilities has already been explored in part in the previous chapter. The problem as outlined there turns on converting potential national power into actual military power—i.e., the realization of further internal power. Power can also be increased externally through new alliances or the revitalization of old and dormant ones. A state may thus increase its power by joining with other states in the defense of common interests.

Winston Churchill, during the last part of World War II, rose in the House of Commons to inform that body of the latest application of a time-honored treaty between Great Britain and Portugal, which increased British power at a crucial moment by revitalizing an old treaty:

I have an announcement to make to the House arising out of the Treaty signed between this country and Portugal in the year 1373 between His Majesty King Edward III and King Ferdinand and Queen Eleanor of Portugal.

This treaty was reinforced in various forms by Treaties of 1386, 1643, 1654, 1660, 1661, 1703, and 1815, and in a secret declaration of 1899. In more modern times the validity of the Old Treaties was recognized in the Treaties of Arbitration concluded with Portugal in 1904 and 1914. Article I of the Treaty of 1373 runs as follows:

"In the first place we settle and covenant that there shall be from this day forward . . . true, faithful, constant, mutual, and perpetual friendship, unions, alliances, and needs of sincere affection, and that as true and faithful friends we shall henceforth, reciprocally, be friends to friends and enemies to enemies, and shall assist, maintain, and uphold each other mutually, by sea and by land, against all men that may live or die."

This engagement has lasted now for nearly six hundred years, and is without parallel in world history. I have now to announce its latest application.[10]

On the other hand, nations may conclude new alliances that are either purely temporary or that may become long-term commitments. An example of the first was the Nazi-Soviet Pact of Nonaggression of 1939, which permitted the Germans to attack Poland and then France in the early days of World War II.

An illustration of a new long-term commitment is the Atlantic Pact and NATO, entered into by the United States and other nations in 1949. The elaborate machinery of organization developed by NATO implied that the alliance commitment was long-term, while the principle adopted of a balanced collective force was an even stronger proof of the same belief. By that principle twelve (later fifteen) nations agreed that primary reliance for air, sea, and land power would be put upon those members of the coalition who were in the best natural position to furnish each type of military power. In the original conception, America was to contribute heavily in air and sea power, as was Britain; France and Belgium, conversely, were to concentrate on land power. No nation is thus willing to depend upon other nations for a well-rounded military force unless it feels convinced that the group will fight as a unit (if war occurs) and that the mutuality of interests is a long-term phenomenon.

It is precisely on this point that de Gaulle, for France, in 1964–1965 expressed skepticism and a desire for change in the alliance structure. The increasing importance of nuclear weapons in NATO defense strategy, the vast stores of such warheads possessed by the United States, and the virtual resignation of Great Britain from independent nuclear power status, all seemed to him to demonstrate an unhealthy reliance of Western Europe upon United States nuclear strength. But what if the United States is not prepared at a time of testing to defend French vital interests? Americans might be willing to die for Paris. But would they die because of Paris? De Gaulle argued that under the circumstances the United States had in effect a veto over French foreign policy. From his point of view, unless France had her own nuclear strike force, however small, and gained "equal" status in NATO's decision-making, the alliance structure had to be revamped into more conventional alliance format. Pursuing these tactics in the face of Western unwillingness to accept his demands, de Gaulle in 1966 served notice of withdrawal from the organized features of NATO (while remaining a nominal member of the alliance itself).

Whether alliances are integrated or not, they provide a mechanism through which a nation may increase its power by pooling it with the power of other states.

Secondly, when power and policy are out of balance, a nation may choose

---

[10] *House of Commons Debates*, Vol. 392, Fifth Series, cols. 716–717 (October 12, 1943).

to modify the policy. It may feel it necessary to cut its commitments. The British Labour Government not only took a liberal view toward what Churchill denounced as the "liquidation" of the British Empire, but was also influenced in its policy in the late 1940's by the need to pare down its obligations in view of the desperate economic situation in the United Kingdom. One indication of this was the British decision (as President Truman expressed it in his speech announcing the Truman Doctrine) that they could "give no further financial or economic aid [to Greece]. . . . Great Britain finds itself under the necessity of reducing or liquidating its commitments in several parts of the world, including Greece." [11] Similar reasons determined the British decision to get out of Palestine.

In terms of national interests this means that the number is reduced in order that the remaining interests can be given an adequate power backing. All nations may from time to time find themselves with such an overload of commitments and interests, often through inertia or unwittingly, and the process of re-evaluation is therefore by design and by necessity a continuous one. It was a question of this sort that was considered by the United States government in 1949–1950 when the President asked the Joint Chiefs of Staff how vital they believed Formosa to be for our national security. The United States had by that time almost by inertia placed itself in a position of underwriting the Chinese Nationalist Government without having undertaken any real re-evaluation of the commitment it involved. A similar question had to be faced by the United States in July 1965, when the erosion of the South Viet-Nam government's military position posed the stark alternative: reinforce or withdraw.

Thirdly, a nation may bluff, following policies which it is aware are not backed by adequate power. An illustration of this is the German reoccupation of the Rhineland in 1936. By the terms of the Versailles Treaty the Rhineland (that part of Germany between the French frontier and the Rhine River) had been demilitarized. This was done as a protection to France, since it removed the German army from the immediate vicinity of the frontier and also made it necessary for the Germans to cross the Rhine as the prelude to any invasion— a process which could hardly allow Germany to launch a surprise attack. In 1936 Hitler ordered his troops into the area, issuing secret orders to his generals that, at the first sign of resistance, they were to retreat as fast as they had advanced. Unfortunately for the Western Powers, the bluff went uncalled and the move succeeded. As a corollary, it weakened the French resolve to stop Hitler, since it made their defense that much more difficult. Ironically, Hitler had only issued the orders for possible retreat because of the fears of his generals. Hitler's success here helped determine conservative opposition in Germany thereafter.

A successful bluff usually augments national power, even if it does not result in tangible and material acquisitions, since it enhances the reputation for

---

[11] *Congressional Record*, Vol. 93, 80th Congress, 1st Session, pp. 1980 ff.

power of the bluffing state. A nation believed to have greater power than it actually has will be accorded the greater deference while deserving (in power terms) the smaller. On the other side of the coin, an unsuccessful bluff is highly dangerous and even disastrous. If the bluff is called and found to be only a bluff, it may be assumed by other nations that the bluffing nation consistently overrates its own power. It may, as a consequence, find it difficult to carry out its policies short of war even though it later has effective power behind them.

Whichever of these methods is adopted, the process of adjusting power and policy must be continuous. For all these reasons, the making of foreign policy remains a difficult and complex art.

In turning next to the five functional relations of states (the diplomatic, legal, economic, military, and world organizational relations) two cautions are in order.

The predisposition is to separate these into "good" relations such as law and organization, leading to "order" or "progress;" and the "bad" relations such as diplomacy or war, leading to "conflict" or "power politics;" with economics occupying a neutral moral ground. (Or possibly diplomacy, too, may be thought of as "good.") But the predisposition is unsound. Factors are at work within the system which foster order or conflict, but they are not coterminous with these functional relations. We may like the interaction of national interests we encounter under the legal heading more than that of war, and we may prefer legal results. But each relation is only a part of all the relations, and each reflects only a partial picture of the interaction of the foreign policies involved. The student must not jump to the conclusion that it is merely a question of "strengthening" one type of relation and phasing out another. Each relation persists for complex reasons.

Parallel with this predisposition is another: to personify a world organization or international law and think of it as an entity existing quite separately from the states who give it life. These relations are the relations of states. While the functioning mechanisms may in turn feed back a behavioral requirement to the participating states (such as a code of behavior in the halls of the UN which Khrushchev violated by banging his shoe), the mechanisms are essentially no more than states seen collectively from a particular functional viewpoint. While law and organization thus in a minor sense help shape the state system, in a major sense they are themselves the product of the state system and derive their characteristics from that system.

PART THREE
The Relations
of States

CHAPTER 5

Diplomacy

The use of deceit in diplomacy is by its very nature limited, since there is no curse that comes quicker to roost than a lie that has been found out . . . it actually does more harm than good to negotiation, since though it may confer success today, it will create an atmosphere of suspicion which tomorrow will make further success impossible.

DE CALLIÈRES

. . . in primitive society all foreigners were regarded as both dangerous and impure. When Justin II sent ambassadors to negotiate with the Seljuk Turks they were first subjected to purification for the purpose of exorcising all harmful influence. The tribal wizards danced round them in a frenzy of ecstasy burning incense, beating tambourines and endeavouring by all known magic to mitigate the dangers of infection. Envoys to the Tartar Khans were also obliged to pass through fire before they could be allowed into the presence, and even the gifts which they had brought with them were similarly sterilized. So late as the fifteenth century the Republic of Venice threatened with banishment, or even death, those Venetians who held intercourse with any member of a foreign legation.

SIR HAROLD NICOLSON
Diplomacy

FOREIGN policy, once formulated, must be put into effect by means of diplomacy. While diplomacy is not the sole functional device by which states mutually attempt to adjust their respective national interests, it is by far the most important. *Diplomacy* as a term customarily refers to the whole process of the political relations of states; by contrast the term *diplomat* has reference especially to the ambassador or minister and his staff abroad. In this chapter we shall consider the machinery by which diplomacy is carried on, and the diplomat in action. We shall then observe how diplomacy is used for state purposes, and the changes in diplomacy and approaches to it that have marked the last decades.

I The Machinery of Diplomacy

THE machinery of diplomacy in a modern state consists of two major parts. First, there is the home establishment: the governmental department, under the chief executive, entrusted with the basic responsibility for the conduct of foreign affairs. Second, there are the diplomatic missions abroad: the embassies and legations and their respective staffs.

Whereas in the United States the governmental department charged with the conduct of foreign affairs is called the Department of State, most other countries prefer to call the equivalent department the Ministry or Department of Foreign Affairs. At the head of this department is the Secretary of State (or Minister of Foreign Affairs) who is supported in his work by various undersecretaries and assistant secretaries. Further down in the administrative framework are offices, divisions, and bureaus, organized along both geographical and functional lines.

As an illustration of this machinery, let us examine briefly the United States Department of State. The undersecretaries and assistant secretaries deal with a great part of the administration of the department. The aim (never quite achieved) is to relieve the secretary from administrative chores so that he may devote himself to policy formulation and coordination. At the top level the Secretary of State is advised by the Policy Planning staffs—an innovation of the postwar period. The intention in creating this committee was to establish an organ for the coordination of policy and also to provide an arrangement by which some high-level officers of the department could be freed from routine tasks and a preoccupation with tactical concerns to concentrate on the strategic or long-range aims of policy.

This new arrangement sought to overcome a difficult organizational problem. It has already been mentioned that the offices and divisions are organized along geographical and functional lines. The reason for having both is that foreign relations are carried on with nations scattered all over the globe, and are simultaneously conducted with international organizations ranging from the United Nations proper to the Universal Postal Union (from a multifunction organization to a single-function organization). There is a need for experts on different nations and areas; there is also a need for economic, legal, and other functional specialists. The area or country expert is expected to be fully familiar with the problems of United States foreign policy in reference to that country. By contrast, the functional specialist concentrates on particular problems (economic, legal, or other) involved in the conduct of relations *irrespective* of the territorial origin or locale of that problem. There is obviously a need for coordination between the two groups, which act, quite inescapably, out of two different frames of reference. This coordination must be done at a high level by officials who are sufficiently free from administrative responsibilities to be able to see and deal with the whole problem. By the same token, shifting administrative burdens from the shoulders of the Secretary of State enables him to meet regularly with the planning committee and work out over-all policy.

One of the reasons that this plan has not worked as well as anticipated is that the Secretary of State is still compelled to appear before innumerable Congressional committees to defend his budget and explain his policy. In addition, in modern times, the Secretary of State has himself participated in high-level negotiation and conferences abroad to an extent unprecedented in earlier times. James F. Byrnes, for example, covered approximately 77,000 miles in his travels to high-level conferences between Yalta in January 1945, and the Paris Peace Conference of July to October 1946. Note that the period covered is *less than two years*. He made all but the Yalta trip as Secretary of State. John Foster Dulles made a traveling record that managed to put Mr. Byrnes's in the shade. In a similar period of time he covered 178,749 miles. While Dean Rusk's record has been of more modest dimensions, these travels remove the Secretary from the focal point of activity in Washington for periods which, added to his duties before Congressional committees, leave him little time for what is ordinarily considered his primary function: formulate policy with the President, coordinate it within the State Department, and administer the Department as a unit of the government. For these reasons, recent Secretaries of State have relied heavily upon the undersecretaries and assistant secretaries for administration, and upon the Planning Staff for the coordination of policy. They have sought to overcome the difficulties that Viscount Grey, British Foreign Secretary at the outbreak of World War I, mentions when he says:

A Minister beset with the administrative work of a great Office must often be astounded to read of the carefully laid plans, the deep, unrevealed motives that critics or admirers attribute to him. Onlookers free from responsibility have time to invent, and they attribute to Ministers many things that Ministers have no time to invent for themselves, even if they are clever enough to be able to do it.[1]

Until 1954 the American practice differed in one important respect from that of the other great powers: there was a rigid distinction between the Foreign Service and the "home" service. Foreign Service officers (F.S.O.'s) manned the legations and embassies overseas, whereas foreign affairs officers (and others with various titles) staffed the Department posts in Washington. Whereas F.S.O.'s were rotated to Washington as occasion presented, the foreign affairs officer remained at home. In the decade after World War II, as the rising demands on American diplomacy hampered rotation, the already existing cleavage in functions between the two groups deepened.

The implementation of the report of the Wriston Committee,[2] following 1954–1955, changed all that. Officers of the home service were brought by "lateral entry" into the Foreign Service. Today there is but one body of State Department officers, rotating from home to abroad, who administer the diplomatic affairs of the United States. There is little doubt that this has increased the overall efficiency with which American foreign relations can be conducted. Still unresolved after the Wriston reform was a related question. The

---

1 Viscount Grey of Fallodon, *Twenty-Five Years*, 1892–1916, Vol. I, p. 6.
2 See Charles E. Saltzman, "The Reorganization of the American Foreign Service," *Department of State Bulletin*, Vol. 31 (September 27, 1954).

United States Information Agency, to name merely one agency dealing abroad with foreign affairs, is not an integral part of the Foreign Service. Even where, as in this case, policy coordination is handled through the Department of State, obvious problems arise. The proliferation of United States foreign aid representatives, military advisory groups, and intelligence personnel abroad, has added another complex dimension to this problem.

Curiously enough, the newer nations have an opposite problem. With trained personnel and money scarce, they can ill afford great diplomatic establishments. This is one reason the newer nations utilize the United Nations so extensively for their serious diplomatic efforts.

2 _Precedence and the Rules of Rank_

SINCE the Congress of Vienna (1815) and Aix-la-Chappelle (1818) evolved rules for the classification of ranks, diplomats have been divided into four categories. They are, in order of rank:

1. Ambassadors extraordinary and plenipotentiary, and papal legates or nuncios, who are accredited to heads of states.

2. Envoys extraordinary and ministers plenipotentiary, similarly accredited to heads of states.

3. Ministers resident, accredited to heads of states (now infrequently used since most states confer the title of (2) upon ministers, whether they are sent for a special mission or for permanent assignment at the foreign post).

4. Chargé d'affaires (the official temporarily in charge in the absence of the ambassador or minister).

These rules of rank are now generally accepted by all states. Seniority at a post establishes precedence in each rank. The senior ambassador is known as the _doyen_ of the diplomatic corps in the particular capital.

The wild absurdities and colorful internecine warfare of the diplomatic corps before such rules of precedence were standardized is difficult to imagine today. On one famous occasion France and Spain came to the brink of war over which state had precedence:

A more serious affair happened in London on September 30, 1661, on the occasion of the state entry of the Swedish ambassador. It was the custom at such "functions" for the resident ambassadors to send their coaches to swell the cortège. The Spanish ambassador de Watteville sent his coach down to the Tower wharf, whence the procession was to set out, with his chaplain and some of his gentlemen inside, and a train of about forty armed servants. The coach of the French ambassador, Comte d'Estrades, with a royal coach for the accommodation of the Swedish ambassador, were also on the spot. In the French coach were the son of d'Estrades with some of his gentlemen, escorted by 150 men, of whom forty carried firearms. After the Swedish ambassador had landed and taken his place in the royal coach, the French coach tried to go next, and on the Spaniards offering resistance, the Frenchmen fell upon them with drawn swords and poured in shot upon them. The Spaniards defended themselves, hamstrung two of the Frenchman's horses, mortally wounded a postillion and dragged the coachman from his box, after which they triumphantly took the place which no one was any longer able to dispute with them.[3]

Shortly before this particular incident the conclusion of peace after the Thirty Years' War (1618–1648) had been repeatedly delayed by squabbles over precedence. The negotiations that began at Cologne in 1636 went on intermittently for twelve years before all the procedural and substantive issues alike had been settled. Before the Protestant Reformation the Pope had (1504), at least theoretically, established the precedence of all Christian rulers. The extreme difficulties just mentioned therefore arose in part out of the breakdown of European-wide Catholicism. Who should enter the room first and leave first? Who should sit at the head of the table? were questions not fully resolved until the time of the same Congress of Vienna that divided diplomats into four ranks. The adoption of the round table eliminated the question of who should sit at its head. At Vienna itself the great conference hall in the Ballhausplatz, where the Congress met in 1815, was equipped with five equal doors so that the reigning monarchs could all enter and depart simultaneously, none yielding precedence to the other. The adoption of alphabetical precedence in the signing of treaties, replacing the round-robin method of signing at the bottom in a circle, removed yet one more vexing problem in diplomacy.[4]

This gradual standardization of the rules of precedence marked a great advance in the institutionalization of diplomacy. Subsequently, the diplomats could avoid unnecessary frictions and could pay more attention to the performance of their substantive functions. Until this had occurred, disputes such as those mentioned above were not at all rare. They did not arise basically out of personal vanity on the part of the ambassador or his king: they were merely the recognition of the importance of prestige to a nation, and precedence was one vital element in prestige.

3 The Functions of Diplomats

THEODORE Roosevelt, whose choice of language was frequently highly flavorsome, once wrote: ". . . there are a large number of well-meaning ambas-

---

[3] Sir Ernest Satow, A Guide to Diplomatic Practice, Vol. I, London: Longmans, Green and Co., Ltd., 1922, pp. 26–27. Sir Harold Nicolson, in his Evolution of Diplomatic Method, London: Constable, 1954, p. 45, mentions another incident that bears repeating. In 1768, at a Court Ball in London, the French Ambassador, seeing that the Russian Ambassador had seated himself in a front seat beside the Austrian Ambassador, climbed over the benches and wedged himself between them. This resulted in a duel in which the Russian was badly wounded.

[4] With the new alternat method, alphabetical precedence was at first as established by the French language. Later English was more and more used. Each nation was customarily accorded the privilege, however, of signing its own copy of the agreement first.

sadors . . . who belong to what I call the pink-tea type." [5] This is, as Americans will quickly recognize, a double-barreled indictment of diplomats, for it is equally as unfortunate to be considered of the "well-meaning" (but inept) type as it is to be classified among the drinkers of pink tea. On the other hand, diplomats have been called worse things. In the popular mind, diplomats frequently are thought of in terms of these two stereotypes: either they are "cooky-pushers" skilled in the art of balancing tea cups and cocktail glasses, or they are "double-dealers" saying anything but the truth; either "social butterflies" or diabolical deceivers. As Sir Henry Wotton wrote in 1604 (and lived to regret it): "An ambassador is an honest man sent to lie abroad for the good of his country."

One reason for these stereotypes is that the diplomat, the ambassador in particular, was and is the representative of the head of state. For several hundreds of years, in an age when republics were exceedingly rare (and even then hardly democratic), this meant that the ambassador represented the *monarch*. The courtesies, privileges, and immunities accorded to ambassadors were those customarily extended to visiting monarchs (or almost so, for of course some distinction had to be made). The ambassador represented the person and power of the king. He also, it need hardly be added, did the king's bidding. Whatever the king was attempting to achieve the ambassador was duty bound to attempt to further. The ambassador was not (and *is* not) expected to speak for himself or follow his own bent, but to carry out the policies of his sovereign. As the reflection of the image of the king (or later of the people), the diplomat was bound to act in accordance with his instructions and faithfully reflect the sovereign's views. The ambassador, in short, was expected to be consistent only in one sense: he was to be consistent with the views of his government. If these views changed overnight, he, too, was to change. Since views, policies, and alliances were habitually shifted with bewildering rapidity in the era of absolutist kings, the diplomat earned a reputation for duplicity.

The second reason for the growth of these stereotypes springs out of the nature of government in the early modern era. Because governments were headed by kings who were absolute, it was necessary for ambassadors to keep a vigilant watch upon the foreign king and the court society in which the king moved, in order to be alert to the currents of opinion and influence that affected the formulating of foreign policy. Today we are so far removed from an era in which the people played no significant role in foreign-policy formulation that it is difficult to remember that in these earlier times, especially between 1500 and 1800, state policy was made by the king and his court. A conscientious ambassador in that day could discharge his duties in a reasonably satisfactory fashion without ever setting foot outside the foreign capital or ever once asking the man in the street what he thought about what was going on, or attempting to influence public opinion in any way. The most important

---

[5] In a letter of January 3, 1905, to R. H. Davis. E. E. Morrison, ed., *The Letters of Theodore Roosevelt*, Vol. 4, Cambridge: Harvard, 1951, p. 1089.

qualification demanded of an ambassador at this time was that he have a thorough knowledge of the intricacies of court society and manners. If he did not have such knowledge, he was handicapped from the outset, and his mission could hardly succeed. Ambassadors in those days were drawn exclusively from noble families, not only because the monarch at home knew them as members of his own court or aristocracy, but also because they were qualified for their diplomatic tasks by virtue of being courtiers. In the prenationalist age foreign diplomats were not infrequently employed. As late as a hundred years ago this was still sometimes done.

With the rise in importance of public opinion in democracy and dictatorship alike, the diplomat today must mend more fences and put his ear to the ground on more levels of society—indeed upon all levels. Even so, the need and ability to mingle with the highest echelons of society have not died away. The instructions of Emperor Napoleon to the Archbishop of Malines, upon the occasion of his appointment as ambassador to London in 1802, have not lost their point: "Above all, do not fail to give good dinners, and to pay attention to the women."

In 1926 the famous French diplomat, Jules Cambon, could still write:

To know a country is to penetrate its spirit, live in the atmosphere of its ideas and be in a position to understand the relations between its external and internal policy. To do so the ambassador will not be content to carry on relations with ministers and political personalities alone. On occasion, conversations frivolous on the surface will teach him much more than discussions of high policy; even the sympathy of distinguished women he meets in society will be valuable to him. In the time of the Directory, to frequent the home of Madame de Staël, and, under the Restoration, to be received by the Princess of Poix, or Madame de Montcalm, meant that one could penetrate the tendencies and play of the parties; and, later on, how could one judge the secret springs of European policy, without being one of the habitués of the salon of the Duchess of Dino, or of the Princess of Lieven? Of course, the importance of the salons is far from being as great today as formerly. I even fear that "high society" is often under singular illusions as to the influence still left to it. But it is none the less true that a "European society" still remains, and that in every circle, intellectual, political and mundane, in the country where the ambassador is expected to exercise his influence, he will do well to create favorable prejudice in his favor.[6]

And if this be the role of a "social butterfly," it can also be very hard work. Walter Hines Page said in a well-known letter of December 22, 1913, commenting upon his job as United States Ambassador in London:

If you think it's all play, you fool yourself; I mean this job. There's no end of the work. It consists of these parts: Receiving people for two hours every day, some on some sort of business, some merely "to pay respects"; attending to a large (and

---

[6] Jules Cambon, *Le Diplomate.* From Chapter 1, pp. 14–15, translated by Professor John B. Whitton, Princeton University. By permission of the translator and the French publisher (Hachette).

exceedingly miscellaneous) mail; going to the Foreign Office on all sorts of errands; looking up the oddest sort of information that you ever heard of; making reports to Washington on all sorts of things; then the so-called social duties— giving dinners, receptions, etc., and attending them. I hear the most important news I get at so-called social functions. Then the court functions; and the meetings and speeches! The American Ambassador must go all over England and explain every American thing. You'd never recover from the shock if you could hear me speak about Education, Agriculture, the observance of Christmas, the Navy, the Anglo-Saxon, Mexico, the Monroe Doctrine, Co-education . . . —just get down the Encyclopaedia and continue the list! I've done this every week-night for a month, hand running, with a few afternoon performances thrown in. I have missed only one engagement in these seven months; and that was merely a private luncheon. . . . Of course, I don't get time to read a book. In fact, I can't get time to keep up with what goes on at home.[7]

Of course, in one important respect aside from the widened sphere of activities and duties, the role of the modern ambassador differs from that of his prototypes. While the modern diplomat must be versatile and expend his energies in ways unknown in earlier times, he has also, by and large, less discretion in carrying out his instructions. There was a time, before the advent of telegraph and telephone, when diplomats with very general instructions, or none at all, had to make vital decisions which deeply committed their government to policies not necessarily approved in advance by those governments. Diplomats in those days often of necessity formulated the policy on the spot and then proceeded to implement it. In the middle of the nineteenth century, British foreign policy on the vital question of the Straits (connecting the Black Sea with the Mediterranean) was on occasion formulated by Lord Stratford de Redcliffe, the British Ambassador at Constantinople. Even as late as the beginning of the nineteenth century, the time needed to travel from London to Rome was almost exactly the time it took a Roman messenger to make the trip over fifteen hundred years before! No wonder, for they used the same method of transportation, changing at posts from one swift horse to another—Pony Express style. The roads were not even as good as Roman roads, which were paved with stones and still endure in places. Until John McAdam (1756–1836), who gave his name to the modern macadamized road, Europe's main roads were often mud tracks.

The advent of railroads, the first telegraphic systems, the radio, and the telephone tremendously altered diplomacy at the end of the nineteenth century from what it had been at the beginning of that hundred years. In the War of 1812 the bloody battle of New Orleans, at which Andrew Jackson rose to fame, took place some fifteen days after the peace treaty had been signed between England and the United States. The news, sent by fast packet, was still en route from Europe when the battlefield dead were buried. Neither the British nor the American forces received word in time to prevent the useless slaughter.

---

[7] Burton J. Hendrick, *The Life and Letters of Walter Hines Page*, Vol. 1, p. 159–160.

Today diplomats may advise their governments that conditions on the spot make a revision of policy necessary or desirable, but customarily they wait upon the answer from home before taking the responsibility of altering the policy themselves. Nowadays the Department of State or foreign office is only minutes or hours away in terms of communication from almost all of its far-flung network of diplomatic posts.

The function of the ambassador has therefore not included the formulation of foreign policy except in an emergency where the communication facilities with his home government have thrust the burden of decision upon him. This kind of emergency is extremely unusual today and in earlier times was the product of necessity rather than design.

Throughout the ages the ambassador has been expected to perform two vital functions, out of which all the tea-drinking, party-giving, and speech-making arise. First, he must keep his government informed on conditions at his post and the policies of the government to which he is accredited. Second, he must implement national foreign policy by carrying out his instructions to the best of his ability, especially in negotiating with the state to which he is assigned.

Since these are the functions of diplomats, and since they must use whatever methods prevail in a given age and must deal with conditions as they find them, the diplomat must be above all else versatile. It is this versatility that has by the same token acquired him his peculiar reputation. In other words, the diplomat should be neither praised nor blamed for the policy of his government. What he deserves praise or blame for is how well he carries out the implementation of his country's policy. The reputation of the diplomat has often been placed in question because of the deeds his country instructed him to do. Inept and dishonest ambassadors have been known to all ages, but the "sins" for which diplomacy has been blamed should in most cases be placed where they belong—upon the foreign policies that states have chosen to follow.

4   *The Art of Negotiation*

THE term "diplomat" (or, in British usage, "diplomatist") came into popular use in the middle of the eighteenth century, arising first in Venice. There were, of course, diplomats before that time—Machiavelli (1469–1527) was one of the best known of these.[8] Callières, whose famous book on diplomacy was published in 1716, never used the word but spoke instead of *"un bon"* or *"un habile, négociateur."* [9] "Negotiator" is the older term. It is also the more accurately descriptive term for one of the most important tasks of the diplomat. The diplomat negotiates. He negotiates whatever matters he is in-

---

[8] It is from Machiavelli's time that the first permanent embassies date. In 1455 the Duke of Milan announced his intention to establish the first permanent embassy abroad.

[9] Quoted by Satow, *op. cit.,* Vol. I, p. 3.

structed to. It may be that he will be commanded to avoid war—on the other hand, he may be told to incite it, even precisely how to provoke it. This is the reason why the diplomat must not, as was commented earlier, be blamed for his instructions, but only for the inept execution of those instructions. This is why, also, Satow has defined diplomacy as a process calling for "the application of intelligence and tact to the conduct of official relations between the governments of independent states" [10]—intelligence in carrying out instructions; tact in avoiding failure because of personal antagonisms and attractions, or lack of skill in human relations. Satow refrains from saying to what use the intelligence and tact will be put, and for what ends—for that is the province of foreign policy and is not at the discretion of the negotiator.

Cambon at one time wrote: "The art of the diplomat stems from the art of governing, for every diplomatic action ends in a negotiation, and whoever says negotiation means, at least in part, compromise." [11] The art of diplomacy, says Cambon, is the art of compromise: to know how and when to compromise is the hallmark of the accomplished negotiator. A good diplomat is always a good compromiser unless the policy of his nation is to prepare the way for war by the extortion of diplomatic concessions—a process Hitler brought to near perfection. To put it another way, provided a state wishes to compromise, one must know when and what and how to compromise on the given issue if the maximum benefit is to accrue to the state making the compromise.[12]

A diplomat, anxious to resolve the difficulty, may make too many and unnecessary compromises to obtain his result: he may pay a higher price than he needs to in terms of the secondary national interests of his nation available for barter. This is one reason why parliamentary politicians, ministers, and cabinet members often make such poor diplomats. Rushing from their domestic concerns to a hastily convened conference, they often want to get to the root of the matter and have done with it without regard for the finer points. Some such "finer points" have led nations subsequently to the brink of war. If statesmen-turned-diplomats avoid the pitfall of too much concession, they are likely to embrace the opposite horn of the dilemma and refuse any significant concession so that public opinion at home will not think that too much of the national interest is being sacrificed. For this reason conferences among politicians serving as diplomats may result in a compromise more apparent than real: finding themselves deadlocked, they may issue a "communiqué." Such a formula is a solution of the problem only in the sense that it obscures the real disagreement, leaving it still unresolved under a camouflage of verbiage.

Negotiation involves a delicate balance between giving what is asked and

---

[10] *Ibid.*, p. 1.

[11] Cambon, *op. cit.*, Chapter 2.

[12] For the rest of this section we shall deal with the more normal conditions under which diplomacy is carried on—where it is not the prelude to armed aggression. In the next, the other possibility will be further explored.

getting what is wanted. To obtain the desired result the negotiator must (especially where he is dealing with an unfriendly state) turn everything to account. Admiral Turner Joy (Chief UN Delegate to the Korean Armistice Conference), speaking of his experience in negotiating with the Chinese Communists, flatly recommends: "Never concede anything to the Communists for nothing, merely to make progress. Make the Communists pay for your acceptance of their point of view. Require an equivalent concession to match yours. . . . To a Communist, your ready acceptance of his proposed solution merely because it is logical and correct is a sign of at least undue haste, indicating a precarious basis on your part." [13]

Diplomacy customarily proceeds essentially like sales of merchandise in oriental bazaars: the asking price at the outset borders on the unreasonable on each side. If a negotiator begins by offering all his concessions or if he reveals initially the level on which he hopes to make final settlement, he is likely in the end to be forced to settle midway between that point and his opponent's demands. He will have given too much because he asked too little to begin with, and he must make concessions if he is not to appear unreasonable and uninterested in resolving the problem. Negotiators must always remain alert if they are to avoid such traps. At the truce negotiations at Panmunjom, to terminate the Korean War, although truce lines usually are drawn along the existing battleline, the Chinese and North Korean negotiators insisted upon a return to the 38th parallel, considerably to the south of most of the actual battleline. Since the fighting was to end, they said, it should end of course where it began. To counter this proposal the UN finally hit upon the expedient of insisting that UN air and sea power effectively controlled large areas of Communist-held territory north of the battleline. Such control would end if an armistice went into effect. The UN then expressed its willingness to settle for the ground battleline as a compromise.

The negotiator, therefore, must begin with demands that are nicely calculated in their excessiveness to match what is considered excessive in the position of his opponent, while making it clear that concessions may be expected. If this is skillfully done, the end result, after concessions are exchanged, is that they will come out near the middle.

Diplomacy designed to effect compromise can fail miserably of its purpose if the psychological results of actions are not borne in mind. Consider the *Panther* incident as discussed in this British diplomatic dispatch:

Sir E. Goschen [British Ambassador to Germany] to
Sir Edward Grey [British Foreign Secretary]
            (Received August 28)
BERLIN,
August 25, 1911.
SIR,—I had to-day some conversation with Herr Zimmermann [of the German Foreign Office] on the subject of Morocco, and particularly on the subject of the

---

[13] Adm. C. Turner Joy, *How Communists Negotiate*, p. 170.

despatch of the [German warship] *Panther* to Agadir [in Morocco on which both Germany and France at this time had designs]. He complained bitterly about Mr. Lloyd George's speech,[14] which, he said, had done untold harm both with regard to German public opinion and the negotiations. I said that for what had done most harm one must go back a little further than Mr. Lloyd George's speech, namely, to the despatch of the German warship to Agadir. He said that he had never understood why public opinion in England had been upset by that event. "When we informed Sir Edward Grey that we were going to send a ship to Agadir—" I here interrupted and said, "You mean that you had sent a ship to Agadir." He acquiesced in my interruption, and continuing, said, "When we informed Sir Edward Grey that we had sent a ship to Agadir he took the news quite quietly, and we had no idea that there was going to be all this trouble about it." I said that it was in my recollection that you had spoken strongly to Count Metternich [the German Ambassador] on the subject. He said, "Well, at all events, we had no idea that public opinion would feel so strongly about it, and Mr. Lloyd George's speech came upon us like a thunderbolt." He added that the whole trouble arose from the fact that it was not recognized in England that the despatch of a ship to Agadir, which had been the Emperor's idea, was really *meant to make it easier* for the French Government to defend any compensation they might be ready to give, and which they had expressed readiness to give, before the French Parliament. *I could not help saying that it seemed to me to be a somewhat dubious method of facilitating the negotiations* . . .[15]

Sometimes the diplomatic process is a very long one, and patience is undoubtedly a foremost diplomatic virtue. At times there is a sudden breaking of the deadlock after each side has reconnoitered the other's position and assessed the strong and weak points. Secretary of State Byrnes wrote of such an experience in the Paris negotiations of 1946. After eleven days of deadlock Mr. Byrnes suggested self-humorously, half-hopefully:

"We should make it a good afternoon and settle the question of the Dodecanese."

To my amazement, Mr. Molotov replied that "the Soviet delegation has no objection to that proposal."

"Did Mr. Molotov say that he agreed the islands should go to Greece?" Mr. Bevin, who had tried repeatedly to settle the issue, asked in disbelief.

The Soviet representative promptly said that he had, and immediately asked that we proceed to the next question.

"Let me have a minute or two to recover," I exclaimed.

Mr. Molotov calmly suggested some other "good agreements" might be made.[16]

This turned out to mean that Russia was prepared to let the UN Assembly settle the vexing question of the Italian colonies. Of course the Soviet Foreign Minister had an end in view—as diplomats usually do under such circum-

---

[14] Lloyd George was at this time the influential Chancellor of the Exchequer.

[15] *British Documents on the Origins of the War, 1898–1914*, Gooch and Temperley, eds., Vol. VII, pp. 487–488. Quoted by permission of the Controller of Her Britannic Majesty's Stationery Office. Italics added.

[16] James F. Byrnes, *Speaking Frankly*, pp. 131–132.

stances. He hoped to have Russia's way, as a *quid pro quo* on some of the explosive issues relating to the Italian Peace Treaty, such as Trieste.

At times success does not come for years if at all, the whole process ending repeatedly in frustration and disagreement because both sides want more than the other is willing to grant. In future conferences on the same issue, this may or may not change. The record of the Korean Truce Conference at Panmunjom on the prisoner-of-war issue was a case in point. Month after month the negotiators met, sometimes for only a minute or two, announced "There is no change in our position," heard the same from the opposite side, and returned to their camps. Negotiations over an Austrian Peace Treaty were finally successfully concluded in 1955 after ten full years of discussions. An equivalent treaty for Germany was still lacking more than twenty years after World War II.

There is nothing intrinsic in the diplomatic process that can assure that a compromise solution can be found: it depends not only on the skill of the diplomats but also on the flexibility of their instructions. If those instructions allow no room for compromise, no settlement is likely unless the other party to the negotiations simply capitulates.

5 *The Limits of Compromise*

COMPROMISE suggests a readiness to be accommodating, to solve a problem by a willingness to make concessions. While compromise is at the roots of normal diplomacy, diplomatic negotiation between the strong and the weak can sometimes disintegrate into a process that is negotiation only in the limited sense of the exchange of views of the holdup man and his victim. Diplomacy is, in the final analysis, the instrument by which national policy is carried into effect, and that policy may be one of pure, unalloyed aggression.

An aggressor nation is far from willing to compromise its quarrel with its intended victim. Aggressors using the diplomatic instrument will purposely refrain from offering any reasonable compromise solution and demand submission—or appeasement. Any such "agreement" between the two states will be an imposition of the wishes of the one upon the other. There will be no negotiation in the sense of finding a middle ground. It would be more correct to describe the process as unconditional or virtually unconditional surrender to the demands of the aggressor state.

Where a state is bent upon aggression, it has excluded compromise with its victims from the realm of possibility, except in the most limited and temporary sense. Granting concessions to an aggressor merely encourages the aggressor to raise his demands, offering in return empty promises of fictional concessions. Here diplomacy takes on the role of advance agent for the military force soon to follow. As Hitler prepared to unleash his armies and completed their training and mobilization, at one crisis after another he repeated his monotonous refrain: "This is the last territorial demand which Germany will make in Europe."

An aggressor nation may be willing for a short time to compromise in its negotiations with other nations who are also eager for territorial expansion, or who might interfere when its attention and forces are preoccupied with its aggression. Hitler's pact with Stalin in 1939 is an excellent example of such a compromise. In the secret protocol attached to the pact it was provided that "In the event of a territorial and political rearrangement of the areas belonging to the Polish state [and this on the eve of the planned invasion] the spheres of influence of Germany and the U.S.S.R. shall be bounded approximately by the line of the rivers Narew, Vistula, and San." [17] Even so, the interests of the two nations continued to be opposed—and within two years after dividing Poland they were locked in a bitter struggle.

Each nation entering upon a diplomatic negotiation must, therefore, determine whether it is dealing with a nation desirous of settling problems or intent upon extorting concessions. This is by no means always easy to decide, either on a short- or long-range basis. One clue is whether the second nation, in full awareness of the significance of her acts, demands concessions that the first considers vital interests. This is not a decisive test in itself of aggressive aims, however. Yet if there is a conflict over vital interests coupled with a past record of aggressive acts and/or an obvious lack of seriousness in avoiding war at the present time, then it is a fairly clear indication that compromise will be of no avail.

In any case where there is a conflict of states over their respective vital interests, whether war is intended by one or not, no compromise possibility exists if the issue is pressed. The only alternative to war (unless one is hopelessly weaker) is to leave the issue unresolved and seek to keep the resultant tensions beneath the boiling point. This obviously takes a modicum of good will on the part of both states which, in such circumstances, is often not forthcoming. Since vital interests are interests that a nation if necessary will go to war to preserve (unless hopelessly outclassed in terms of power), there can be no real compromise. Consider the crisis over Berlin which began in November 1958. Khrushchev threatened to make a separate peace treaty with East Germany unless the West agreed to a precarious "free and demilitarized" West Berlin. When the West, considering Berlin vital, rejected this thinly disguised demand to surrender the city, an uneasy impasse followed.

It is precisely when the vital interests are bartered in return for minor concessions, or none at all, that appeasement has taken place. Appeasement may result from weakness or from ignorance, either from an inability to fight or a misconception of the effects on vital interests. Or it may be the result of both, as at Munich in 1938. At the Munich Conference Prime Minister Chamberlain gave up the Sudeten area of Czechoslovakia, which contained the Little Maginot Line. The remainder being militarily indefensible, it, too, was soon swallowed by Hitler. For such a mistake a country pays dearly—as did England.

A nation must be quite clear as to what is vital and what is secondary. It cannot afford to sacrifice what is vital in the belief that it is secondary. Cham-

---

[17] *Nazi-Soviet Relations, 1939–1941*, Department of State Publication 3023, p. 78.

berlin is reported as having dismissed Czechoslovakia as "a small country, far away," about which Britain knew little (and presumably cared less). On the other hand, it is equally hazardous to regard what is in truth secondary as vital. The need for a clear conception of what interests are secondary stems from the necessity of being clear upon what to defend and what not to defend; it stems also from the need to know what interests may, as secondary interests, be bartered in the diplomatic market place in exchange for equivalent concessions from other states.

The limits of diplomatic negotiation resting upon compromise are the limits of the secondary interests of the state. And when these are bartered, concessions must be received in return. Whether equivalents are received or not is one important difference between appeasement and normal diplomacy.

6 *The Ailments of Contemporary Diplomacy*

CONTEMPORARY diplomacy suffers from three developments that have changed its character in the twentieth century. One development is the shift to "open" diplomacy. A second is the relative inexperience and peculiar approach of the two powers whose attitudes and policies are vital in any contemporary diplomatic problem of importance—the United States and the Soviet Union. The third, for which communism must bear the major responsibility, is the deterioration in good manners. Each of these developments has made for friction and dissension in contemporary diplomacy.

The shift from "secret" to "open" diplomacy followed World War I. It was coincident with the establishment of the League of Nations, but it would have come anyway, and certainly the new "open" diplomacy was not confined to League activities after 1919. Open diplomacy had come into fashion because of widespread popular feeling that the secret intrigues of the Powers, carefully concealed from their own peoples, had led to a war over obligations, promises, and counterclaims that would not have stood the light of public scrutiny. In short, the argument was that the people had been committed to war (or what led to war) without their consent.

There was an element of truth in this assertion. Even in Great Britain, democratic as she was, not even the Parliament was informed on such an important matter as the results of the Franco-British staff conversations in the decade preceding 1914 until the actual eve of war. Even despite this grain of truth, however, the nature of what had occurred was widely misunderstood.

It is true that there were many secret obligations entered into by the Powers before and during World War I that committed them to hard and firm positions on certain matters. It is only fair to add, however, that the most important commitments in these treaties (and particularly in the treaties of alliance) were secret only in the formal sense that they had not been published verbatim. Planned leaks were most often resorted to in order to inform the potential enemy of the coalition ranged against him if he went too far. The reason these leaks occurred was that there was little point in keeping alliance arrangements (except on details) secret, since they could hardly act as a deterrent upon the other party if that party remained in ignorance of their existence. The reason the treaties and agreements were almost always "secret" was not to keep their own people in ignorance but to prevent too much useful information on war plans from being revealed to the enemy. As a matter of fact, even in the subsequent period of open diplomacy, diplomacy was never open in the sense that all secrets were publicly revealed, but only in that the process of negotiation itself became more public.

The post-World-War-I trend toward publishing diplomatic obligations was clearly indicated in the League Covenant. Article 18 required "Every treaty or international engagement . . . by any Member of the League" to be registered "forthwith." The Secretariat would then publish it. No treaty was to be binding "until so registered." The result of this article was that post-1919 treaties tended to be drawn in general terms, leaving the important details and supplementary understandings to be effected through an exchange of diplomatic notes that remained secret. The provisions of Article 18 could hardly, in a practical sense, rob agreements of their binding effect if not registered—they could merely make them unenforceable before the League of Nations, the World Court, or an arbitral body. The logical difficulty in such an arrangement is that one state can hardly force another to carry out an alliance by resorting to a court in any case.

The real changes in diplomacy that resulted from the adoption of "open" methods were to be found in the negotiating process itself, in the attempt to implement the Wilsonian principle of the Fourteen Points that "diplomacy shall proceed always frankly and in the public view." [18] This principle almost wrecked diplomacy on the shoals of impotence. Taken literally (and it was often taken literally), negotiation must then be public.[19] And once negotiation became public, national prestige inevitably became involved.

It is one of the most difficult things in the world for the representative of a great state publicly to change his position and accept less than he started out in demanding. He must consider public opinion and the popular pressure upon the government. Lord Salisbury once compared a foreign minister in a democracy to a man playing a card game while a very noisy "helper" stood behind his chair and loudly called out every card he ought to play. The more democratic the nation, the more severe is the pressure. To be elected, a democratic government must have popular confidence; to have confidence the public must feel that the national interests are being safeguarded. Every time a diplomatic settlement ensues as the result of accepting less than originally demanded, that confidence may be (and often is) put to a strain. Continued strain may easily lead to a loss of confidence in the government.

There are two none-too-simple alternatives for a democratic government participating in public diplomatic negotiation. First, if the public is sophisti-

---

[18] *Congressional Record*, Vol. 56, 65th Congress, 2nd Session, pp. 680 ff.

[19] Wilson's later disclaimer (in a letter to the Senate, 1918) that he had not ruled out "private discussions of delicate matters" had little impact.

cated and educated about the nature of diplomatic negotiation, involving frequently, as it does, compromise, it may proceed with a compromise and recede from its first demands. But even with a sophisticated public, when it is negotiating with a potential enemy, the cry of "appeasement" is sooner or later heard. The people who raise this cry are protesting against concessions made to a potential enemy; the same people are apt to ignore the counterconcessions made in return. So even in this case, public negotiation with a disliked state is apt to run a rocky and uncertain course, even aside from the thorny points specifically at issue.

Second, a democratic government may choose instead to avoid the dangers of publicly receding from the first extreme demands by asking at the outset for only what it is willing to settle for in the end. This has the internal effect that people at home will not cry "appeasement" and that the policy or demand will be deemed "consistent." On the other hand, the nation choosing this alternative is placed in the untenable position of refusing any compromise as *quid pro quo* for the concessions of the other party (which in effect means that soon no concessions will be offered by the other party). This soon brings an end to negotiation and an end to diplomacy. And what is not settled through diplomacy often is settled through war.[20]

This is not to say that a government should keep secret from its people the broad commitments the government has made in their behalf. In a democracy such a policy would be suicidal and self-defeating, for the people ultimately will not back what they do not actually endorse. Even so, much must remain secret for security purposes; the matters to remain secret form a delicate question that can hardly be resolved with a formula or slide rule. In the same way the people are entitled to know the results of a diplomatic negotiation insofar as the publication of those results is consistent with the security of the state. But to demand that diplomats negotiate in public is about as fruitful for progress as insisting that businessmen bargain with one another through advertising in the local press.[21] The negotiating process has correspondingly wilted in the era of open diplomacy.

Indeed a curious new hybrid form of diplomacy is much used today: a combination of private conversation and public spectacle. There was always some element of this technique in diplomacy—elaborate staging for the last meeting, with its ceremonial signings or declarations, was traditional. But today public preformances continue throughout the conference (as at the Geneva Foreign Ministers Meeting in 1959).[22] Even "summit" get-togethers are far from private by the time elaborate news briefings have been given. In

---

[20] There are, of course, methods of settlement *between* diplomacy on the one end and war on the other. Their possibilities are explored in Chapter 11.

[21] Even worse is when the supposedly private remarks of negotiators at a conference are subsequently published officially, as was done, despite British objections and contrary to precedent, by the United States on the Yalta Conference.

[22] See the full account of the formal sessions in *Foreign Ministers Meeting, May–August 1959, Geneva*, Department of State Publication 6882. The verbatim text of the speeches runs to 600 pages.

the United Nations, at the other end of the spectrum of exclusiveness (about which more in later chapters) the private aspect is limited far too much to consultations between groups of states as to the position they will take vis-à-vis other groups at the public debates.

The other related ailment of contemporary diplomacy stems from the relative inexperience in diplomacy of the United States and the Soviet Union, and the attitudes peculiar to those states as they approach and engage in diplomatic negotiation.

Every nation has, of course, its peculiar attitudes—that is, attitudes that are particularly characteristic and representative of that particular state. These attitudes spring out of a variety of background causes, and in the case of the United States and the Soviet Union we shall examine them at length in the latter parts of this book. Both these states approach international problems with attitudes that are not only extremely far apart but also in some respects markedly different from those of other states more experienced in diplomacy. Their conceptions of the world they live in and even of the nature of the diplomatic process are also far, far apart. Both these nations, relatively new as they are to the councils of the great states, tend to approach diplomatic problems from somewhat extreme points of view.

The United States has frequently approached diplomatic problems as though the nation presenting the best argument based on moral principles would win (the implication being that diplomatic concessions are the tributes by opponents to clear consciences impeccably displayed). At the same time, paradoxically, this has been shaded by often obvious misgivings as to whether the rest of the world will not take advantage of American innocence. The Soviet Union, by contrast, while she has often invoked her own "higher morality" of Communist belief, has done so in diplomacy with the air of one not expecting real conversions. Thus diplomacy in the Soviet view becomes a species of political and propaganda warfare between themselves and their mortal enemies (i.e., the "capitalist" states). The first view implies that diplomatic negotiation will be concerned with the translation of universally held moral principles into concrete measures of implementation; the other implies that diplomacy is a series of maneuvers in which the "imperialist" nations are constantly seeking to accomplish the encirclement and defeat of the Soviet Union. A further rigidity, especially in the Stalin era, has stemmed from the frequent reluctance of Soviet diplomats to suggest alterations in the instructions given them.

While such a characterization of these two states oversimplifies a more complex reality, it is nevertheless indicative of the broad differences that have marked their approach to world problems during the greater part of the present century.

George Kennan once expressed very well this American approach when he wrote:

. . . the trouble with the Open Door doctrine and the integrity of China as political principles was simply that these terms were not clear and precise ones which could usefully be made the basis of a foreign policy. To a large extent they were clichés, dangerously inexact and confusing in the associations they provoked in people's minds. It was precisely this aspect of their character which made it difficult for other governments, when summoned by us to stand up and be counted in their feeling about them, to do anything else but reply: "Why, yes, if you put it that way, we agree, of course." These phrases contained too many positive overtones to be safely rejected outright by anyone. It was easier to agree than to try to explain. . . .

Kennan notes that the attempt to achieve American foreign-policy objectives by having other governments agree to professions of high legal and moral principle has had a long history in our diplomatic practice. He links it to the American belief in the ability of public opinion to overrule governments and the "American tendency to transplant legal concepts from the domestic to the international field": the belief that international society can and should be operated on the basis of general contractual obligations. From this is derived a tendency to stress verbal undertaking rather than the concrete political interests involved. Such a habit of approach gave the people an impression of a similarity of outlook among nations, which was actually non-existent, and it created suspicion and bewilderment abroad. "Foreign statesmen were keenly aware of the inadequacy of these general propositions as definitions of any workable agreement or understanding on specific international issues. Assuming, as they must have assumed, that our government was also aware of this, it must have been difficult for them not to suspect our statesmen of holding back and of having ulterior motives in pressing these abstractions upon them as criteria of agreement." [23]

On the other hand, the difficulties that stemmed from the Soviet attitude toward diplomatic negotiation in the decade after World War II are made clear in the following:

In this as in numerous other instances Soviet negotiators, even when under some pressure to reach agreement, have shown that they are in mortal terror of violating any part, minor or major, of their instructions, and are extremely reluctant to report to Moscow that they cannot get every point and every wording in their own drafts. Making recommendations for even slight changes in their instructions exposes them to serious risks. It means that they consider their own superiors slightly less than omniscient. It may mean that they can be accused of giving undue weight to the viewpoint of another government and thus of "falling captive to imperialist insinuations." The result is that, even when, in a given question, the Soviet negotiator is committed to the desirability of achieving agreement, he is unable to take any initiative in finding a reasonable meeting ground of viewpoints and he is usually extremely reluctant even to present to his own government suggestions for compromise or reconciliation of differences which originate in other delegations.[24]

---

[23] George F. Kennan, *American Diplomacy, 1900–1950*, Chicago: University of Chicago Press, 1951, pp. 45–47. Copyright, 1951, by the University of Chicago.

[24] Raymond Dennett and J. E. Johnson, eds., *Negotiating with the Russians*, Boston: World Peace Foundation, 1951, pp. 292–293. This book is a collection of essays written by men who have actually represented the U.S. in negotiations with the Russians.

Khrushchev in 1959 said: "We do not negotiate on the basis of the principle 'concession for concession.' We do not have to make concessions because our proposals have not been made for bartering." [25]

The third development needs the least comment. Illustrations are easily available in the morning newspaper. As Lord Vansittart, a practitioner of the "old school," once observed of the older forms: " 'The rapine underneath' was there, but it was relatively war in lace. Some conventions and ostensible courtesies were preserved." [26] The contemporary invective of Communist China and (until lately) Indonesia has at least this merit: it makes Soviet diplomatic manners seem much better by contrast.

Since the United States and the Soviet Union have approached diplomacy from widely separated extremes, it is not surprising that negotiations that involve them both have often been so unproductive of results. Because contemporary diplomacy has been so largely dominated by these two states and because so much of their negotiations with each other has also been carried out in public, where deliberate resort to invective has become so frequent, it is not remarkable that outstanding diplomatic problems have not been resolved. It is remarkable, rather, that despite these factors so much has been done.

---

[25] In a speech at Tirana, Albania, on May 31, 1959. As quoted in *Foreign Ministers Meeting, May–August 1959, Geneva*, Department of State Publication 6882, p. 307.

[26] See Lord Vansittart, "The Decline in Diplomacy," *Foreign Affairs*, Vol. 28, No. 2 (January 1950), pp. 177–188.

CHAPTER 6

International Law

Law can discover sin, but not remove.

JOHN MILTON
Paradise Lost

The law does not consist in particular instances, though
it is explained by particular instances and rules, but
the law consists of principles which govern specific and
individual cases as they happen to arise.

LORD MANSFIELD
Rex vs. Bembridge, 1783

Lex sempler dabit remedium.
(The law will always furnish a remedy.)

IF it can be said with perfect justice that the role of diplomacy in the
political relations of states is often misunderstood, the same applies with
added emphasis to their legal relations. International law has been both
more eulogized and derided than studied. However, it continues to fulfill a
vital role in international relations. This chapter will be concerned with the
nature of that role as it affects international relations rather than with a detailed study of international law as such. The many principles, rules, and cases
that compose the subject of international law obviously cannot be adequately
examined within the scope of a course on international relations. Therefore,
we shall confine our attention to the origin of international law, the sources
from which it is created, the methods by which legal disputes are settled, and
the vital question of the enforcement of international law.

I *The Origin of International Law*

WE must first inquire as to the *origin* of international law: its historical roots
as well as the nature of the forces which spurred it into existence.

Hugo Grotius by common consent is referred to as "the father of international law." His *De jure belli ac pacis* (*On the Law of War and Peace*), published in 1625, codified international law as it had developed up to that
time. Grotius effectively combined the contributions of the two existing
schools of thought. One school, relying principally upon Roman law (the *jus
gentium* in particular), placed emphasis upon the actual behavior of states;
the second, relying for its basis upon the *jus naturale* (the natural law em-
bodying what was right and just behavior for men and states everywhere),

preoccupied itself with what states ought to do. Grotius set forth both these approaches, pointing out not only what had been done by states but what they should do as well.

What inspired Grotius to that task were the conditions of his day. He wrote during the most savage and prolonged blood-shedding that Western and Central Europe had experienced up to that date in the modern period— the Thirty Years' War (1618–1648). In this war Protestant and Catholic attempted to exterminate each other so rigorously that Grotius observed that throughout the Christian world there was "a lack of restraint in relation to war, such as even barbarous races should be ashamed of; I observed that men rush to arms for slight causes, or no cause at all, and that when arms have once been taken up there is no longer any respect for law, divine or human; it is as if, in accordance with a general decree, frenzy had openly been let loose for the committing of all crimes." [1]

Conditions had deteriorated seriously since medieval times. Consider the contrast with the Papal "Truce of God," especially in the period following 1095, when Pope Urban II had decreed and enforced peace throughout Christendom from Wednesday evening to Monday morning, for the entire forty days of Lent, and for Advent and all other holy days. In the twelfth century, at the height of its power, it left scarcely one fourth of the year for fighting. Grotius was writing in an attempt to bring some order into the chaos of his world, a chaos that in turn had grown out of the revolutionary changes in the structure of European life in the thirteenth, fourteenth, and fifteenth centuries. Not only had political universality broken down with the waning of the imperial Roman authority, but, following the Reformation that began in 1517, the religious universality and spiritual authority of the pope had declined as well. Political and religious power were no longer centered even theoretically in the Emperor of the Holy Roman Empire and the Pope of the Roman Catholic Church. They were no longer even the sole symbols of such power, for kings now ruled effectively over their domains in Western Europe and, with the progress of the religious wars, some of these monarchs even assumed the headship of national churches. In 1534, for example, King Henry VIII of England assumed the title of Supreme Head in Earth of the Church of England. There was no one person or symbol of authority whom all Christendom would respect and obey.

The relations of the newly sovereign states were chaotic enough before the religious wars; when these broke out, conditions became intolerable, as the quotation from Grotius makes clear.

These were the forces that brought about an elaboration of international law and particularly of the rules of war. It is no accident that systematic attempts to formulate international law began in the sixteenth century, for by that time the sovereign-state system that had come into existence was threat-

---

[1] Grotius, *Prolegomena*, Par. 28; translated in *Classics of International Law*, No. 3, Vol. 2, Washington: Carnegie, 1925, p. 20.

ening to destroy itself if some new standards of conduct and behavior were not evolved. From the time of Machiavelli, who noted the same excesses, to that of Grotius, the search for new principles and norms continued—a search that led to the gradual elaboration of international law. The practical focus of that law was at first on methods by which the worst excesses of war could be mitigated or abolished. Neither Grotius nor his successors (until recent times) thought that war itself could be eliminated from international relations. The very title of his book indicates his emphasis on the rules of war. The reason, too, that Grotius spoke in such great detail as to what constituted a "just" war was because of his concern over the immense destruction being caused by indiscriminate warfare. This particular part of his work achieved little practical consequence, but his rules of war became more generally accepted.

The rise of a sovereign-state system actually led logically to the erection of a systematic law of nations, based at first primarily upon the customs and usages that had been evolved among the medieval states. Consider the dilemma of these newly sovereign states, and it will be clear why such a system of law inevitably followed their establishment. Because each was sovereign, each was supreme on its own territory and over its own people; but by the same token it had no authority over other territories and peoples. Nevertheless, each state had relations with the others which, to be effectively carried on, had to be regularized.

Take, for example, the question of the rights and privileges of diplomatic agents. This became a particularly acute question after the midde of the fifteenth century when it became more and more customary for diplomatic missions to be permanently stationed in foreign states. These agents represented the sovereign in states where the sovereign's power did not extend. They could not simply be stationed and left to the mercy of events. They could not carry on their work in such circumstances, even were there no possibility that in such a haphazard situation war might easily develop from some inconvenience or insult (even unintentional) to the sovereign's representative.

Similarly, rules had to be evolved as to the rights and duties of foreign nationals within the state's frontiers, the circumstances under which valid title to territories could be acquired or transferred, the conditions under which treaties came into effect and were terminated, the ways in which treaty provisions in dispute could be interpreted for their meanings, and many other problems. The rules of international law, therefore, had their origin in the need to adjust, on a *reciprocal* basis, the common interests of states who, while fully sovereign at home, could by the nature of things have no sovereignty abroad. Exactly what form these rules took was not so important as that they should exist and be generally recognized as such. Necessity dictated their adoption; convenience shaped their form. What was done was what was convenient and workable. As new states became sovereign powers, they readily adopted these rules, so that in later times it was automatically assumed that new states coming into existence were bound by the customary rules evolved over the centuries. Thus a relatively new state such as the Republic of Indonesia is equally bound by such practices as is Portugal whose present sovereign form goes back hundreds of years. These practices were accepted by the new states for the same reason that had led to their creation in the first place—convenience and the necessity to regularize and systematize certain of their relations with one another that could best be handled on a legal basis.

2   The Sources of International Law

INTERNATIONAL law grew out of the need of nations. Over the centuries its content swelled in volume. What were the *sources* from which this content of international law was created?

These sources are succinctly stated in the Statute of the International Court of Justice (otherwise known as the United Nations Court). Article 38 empowers and directs the Court "whose function is to decide in accordance with international law such disputes as are submitted to it" to apply:

a. international conventions, whether general or particular, establishing rules expressly recognized by the contesting states;

b. international custom, as evidence of a general practice accepted as law;

c. the general principles of law recognized by civilized nations;

d. . . . . judicial decisions and the teachings of the most highly qualified publicists of the various nations, as subsidiary means for the determination of the rules of law.[2]

Thus the Court is to apply (*a*) treaties and agreements, (*b*) custom, (*c*) reason, and (*d*) authority. These sources out of which international law has been created are listed, as it happens, in order of importance today.

Treaties and agreements create rules "expressly recognized" by the contesting nations. In other words, nations are bound by treaties that they have ratified (i.e., accepted as a legal obligation). The obverse of this is equally true and important: no nation is bound by a contractual arrangement that it has not legally accepted.[3]

Treaties as a source of law are as old as the written records of man. Long before Grotius there were treaties; there existed also international rules of legal conduct, however shadowy, before Grotius codified them. There is on record a Hittite-Egyptian treaty that dates back to about 1280 B.C. It provided that if another people were to attack the lands of Rameses, "the great chief of Egypt," and Rameses sent to the "great chief of the Hittites," saying, "Come

---

[2] Complete text of the Statute is given in *United Nations Conference on International Organization: Documents*, Vol. 15, pp. 293 ff.

[3] With one important exception. See below, the following footnote. Up until World War I the *signature* of a treaty was considered the assumption of a definite obligation. Ratification was essentially a formality. The American practice was, however, always different. After World War I the American practice became the rule rather than the exception.

with me with your army against him," the great chief of the Hittites would come and would slay his enemy. The reverse was also to hold true. It was a treaty of alliance concluded (as was customary in that day) "forever."

Treaties are binding between the parties who ratify them and for the period stipulated. For obvious reasons, some thirty-two centuries later the period "forever" is a rarer stipulation in modern treaties.

Treaties may be either "general or particular," that is, they may be multilateral or bilateral. Bilateral treaties have existed in profusion over the centuries, but in the twentieth century a great number of multilateral treaties have also come into existence. The reason for this latter development is to be found not alone in the technological shrinking of the world and the need to cope with the technical problems thus created, but also in the widely shared desire of states to enact new international law which will be in fact world law. Since no state is bound unless it ratifies a treaty, there is no way to extend obligations to most, if not all, states other than through multilateral pacts universally accepted.[4] The Covenant of the League of Nations and the Charter of the United Nations are outstanding examples of multilateral treaties in the last decades, but the difficulties of obtaining universal ratification are underlined by the fact that neither organization so created by treaty has had universal membership.

From the viewpoint of contractual obligations, therefore, the international law binding each state is a matter of its own choosing. This is not as generally realized as it should be. The other three sources of law theoretically apply equally to every state,[5] but treaties apply only to those who accept them through ratification. It is literally true as a result that the rules of international law binding on each state may be (and usually are) different from those binding any other. This is the reason that Charles C. Hyde entitles his three-volume work *International Law Chiefly as Interpreted and Applied by the United States*. A similar volume or set of volumes could be written for each sovereign state—and each would need constant revision.

Because each state is free to accept or reject any proposed treaty—free to bind itself or not as it pleases—the enactment of universal and quasi-universal legislation has been a slow process. It has advanced furthest in the nonpolitical sphere, as we shall see in our later discussion of international organization. But in the political field its greatest achievements to date have undoubtedly been the creation through treaty of the League of Nations and the United

---

[4] Leaving aside, that is, the possibility that a particular obligation may, in time, become customary and therefore binding. It should also be noted that where a multilateral treaty has been very widely adopted this may itself be considered evidence that it is international law and therefore binding on *all* states. On this point international lawyers disagree. But, again, the Statute of the International Court of Justice gives the Court competence only over treaties and conventions "expressly recognized" by the contesting states.

[5] Theoretically for the reasons that will emerge below when the other sources of law are considered.

Nations. Commissions and committees of jurists, working under the direction of these organizations, have from time to time convened conferences to create and ratify further international legislation on topics considered ripe for codification. These efforts, however, have had very limited success.

The second source of law is custom. Over a long period of time, customs and usages, once evolved, acquire legal validity. In the decision in the case of the *Paquete Habana* the pertinent features of customary international law are well set forth. The case itself arose out of an incident in the Spanish-American War involving the capture of fishing vessels by United States warships. The United States Supreme Court commented:

> . . . at the present day, by the general consent of the civilized nations of the world, and independently of any express treaty or other public act, it is an established rule of international law, founded on considerations of humanity to a poor and industrious order of men, and of the mutual convenience of belligerent states, that coast fishing vessels . . . unarmed and honestly pursuing their peaceful calling of catching and bringing in fresh fish, are exempt from capture as prize of war.[6]

Customary law, then, rests upon general consent, independently of any treaty, and such rules of law arise out of the mutual convenience of states. The decision above was made by the United States Supreme Court. Cases in international law may be and often are decided by international courts, but even today the greatest number of international law cases are handled through national courts applying international law. This is particularly true in cases where the status of property of foreign nationals within the jurisdiction of another state is in question. Since an Indian court of last resort, by contrast, might not dispose of a case in exactly the same manner as the United States Supreme Court, even the customary law may be given different interpretations by different national courts. The same point holds true for the courts of all states. This is why it was said above that, treaty apart, the other sources of international law are theoretically equally applicable to all states. The national courts may easily differ with one another on the two remaining sources of law as well.

The third source of international law is reason. This is a necessary source of international law because it may well occur that no treaty provision binding upon the parties in dispute and no customary rule of usage applies to the particular case in point. If courts are to withhold judgment in such cases, they must admit that international law is an incomplete legal system filled with gaps and lacunae. Whatever the theoretical arguments pro and con, it is the fact that they do not so admit—a practice commended by the wording of Article 38 which lists, as a third source of international law, the "general principles of law." As J. L. Brierly has pointed out: ". . . the main cause of uncertainty in any kind of law is the uncertainty of the facts to which it has to

---

[6] 175 U.S. 708.

be applied. Law has necessarily to be stated in the form of general principles, but facts are never general; they are always particular, they are often obscure or disputed, and they were very likely not forseen, and therefore not expressly provided for, at the time when the rule of law received its formulation." [7]

It therefore follows that to apply general principles at all, one must first decide, by a process of reason and logic, which general principles fit the particular case, and what conclusion is reasonable in the light of the principles and facts involved. The process by which a general principle, taken together with the specific facts, is resolved into a decision is through the application of "the corollaries of general principles . . . to find . . . the solution of the problem" as the decision expressed it in the case of the *Eastern Extension*.

In other words, the "general principles" of law, to be applied at all, must be applied in a particular case to specific facts which are the corollaries of those principles. The question asked is: what does the principle mean in this case? The answer is the result of the use of reason. What is the reasonable meaning of the principle for this set of facts? In such a case the process resembles the interpolation familiar to students of mathematical tables: the missing link is supplied through the use of logic, reasoning from the material "given" and already available.

The fourth source of law is authority. The place of authority can be made clear briefly by quoting Mr. Justice Gray in the *Paquete Habana* case referred to earlier: ". . . where there is no treaty . . . resort must be had to the customs and usages . . . and as evidence of these, to the works of jurists and commentators, who by years of labor, research and experience, have made themselves peculiarly well acquainted with the subjects of which they treat." [8] Authority is of importance, therefore, for its elucidation of obscure points.

3 International Courts: Arbitration

WE have seen why international law came into existence and the sources from which it has been derived. We must now consider how an international legal dispute is settled through resort to a judge or court, using one or the other of the two methods of legal settlement—*arbitration* and *adjudication*. Of these two methods, arbitration was evolved many centuries ago whereas adjudication appeared only after World War I. The essential nature of arbitration is made clear in Article 37 of the Hague Convention for the Pacific Settlement of International Disputes (hereafter called simply the Hague Convention), adopted at the First Hague Conference in 1899.

International arbitration has for its object the settlement of disputes between States by judges of their own choice and on the basis of respect for law.

---

[7] J. L. Brierly, *The Outlook for International Law*, p. 16.
[8] 175 U.S. 700.

Recourse to arbitration implies an engagement to submit in good faith to an award.[9]

In arbitration, then: (1) the parties choose their own judges who (2) decide the case on a basis of respect for law, and (3) the decision is *binding*.

Arbitration as an institution was much used in the ancient world. It gained favor in Greek times, and later the pope was frequently chosen to arbitrate disputes between states. It was the pope who drew the famous line of demarcation between the spheres open to Spanish and Portuguese colonial settlement in the New World—a decision, incidentally, based upon faulty maps and, as it happened, one greatly to the advantage of Spain, who received the lion's share.[10] Between the sixteenth and eighteenth centuries arbitration was little used, but in the nineteenth century it again gained favor, stimulated by the famous *Alabama Claims* arbitral settlement between the United States and Great Britain.[11]

In the nineteenth century most resorts to arbitration were on an *ad hoc* basis: that is, states would decide in a particular case to use arbitration. Only a few bilateral treaties providing beforehand for the submission of certain classes of disputes to arbitration had been concluded in the first half of the nineteenth century. By the twentieth century the tricklet became a torrent, and many such treaties were concluded, such as that between Great Britain and France in 1903, which provided that "Differences which may arise of a legal nature or relating to the interpretation of Treaties" were to be settled through arbitration.[12] Such treaties were characterized by broad and elastic provisions exempting from arbitration any disputes that involved questions which states were reluctant to have settled on a legal basis. The usual exemptions, in the words of that same Anglo-French Treaty of Arbitration of 1903, were disputes that involved "vital interests," the independence, or the honor of the two contracting states, and the "interests of third Parties." Secondary national interests "of a legal nature" would be submitted. Nevertheless, even with exceptions of this kind, such treaties marked a step beyond *ad hoc* arbitration. More than two hundred bilateral treaties of arbitration were negotiated in the seventy years preceding World War I. Arbitration was becoming *institutionalized* but until 1899 only on a bilateral treaty basis.

By this time international law had existed for more than two and one half centuries following Grotius' great work, without any central or general court to which legal disputes could be referred. The next step was the institutional-

---

[9] For full text see *Treaties, Conventions, International Acts, Protocols and Agreements between the United States of America and Other Powers, 1776–1909*, Senate Document No. 357, 61st Congress, 2nd Session, pp. 2220 ff.

[10] This is a major reason why in Latin America today only Brazil is Portuguese-speaking.

[11] Between the end of the Napoleonic Wars and 1914 arbitration was used in nearly three hundred international disputes.

[12] Bilateral treaties concluded *after* the establishment of the Hague Court (1899) usually provided (as did this one) for the use of its machinery.

izing of arbitration on a multilateral basis. This came with the establishment of the Permanent Court of Arbitration by the First Hague Peace Conference in 1899 and its revision in 1907 at the Second Hague Conference. The Hague Court still exists, although, as we shall see, in contrast to the later courts of adjudication (the League Court and the United Nations Court), it is a rather primitive type of court. Even so it marked a great advance. Before 1899, parties to a dispute typically first set up a court to handle their disagreement, once they had decided upon a legal solution, and then authorized it to make a decision in the particular case. After that the court was frequently disbanded—an altogether wasteful and time-consuming process.

The Hague Court is not a court in the sense in which the United States Supreme Court is one. Each state upon becoming a member selects four persons whose names are placed upon a general list. The list of names thus created will vary in length with the membership of the court, and indeed two nations may choose to place the same person upon the court. The court has always enjoyed a large membership. On April 29, 1949, there were, for example, forty-five members, and the list of judges at that time, therefore, could not exceed one hundred eighty names.

When two states actually resort to the Hague Court to handle a case, they choose arbitrators from this list. Failing the direct agreement of the parties on the composition of the tribunal, each party appoints two arbitrators. In the words of Article 45, only one of these two can be "its national or chosen from among the persons selected by it as members" of the Hague Court, although each state will naturally attempt to choose as a second arbitrator a person deemed likely to be sympathetic to its case. These four will choose a fifth as umpire. The five arbitrators then hear and decide the case.

Thus an arbitral panel, chosen from the general list, may vary almost infinitely from case to case. Different judges hear different cases. This is the most striking difference between the Hague Court and a court as we are inclined to think of it.

It must be emphasized that resort to the Hague Court is purely voluntary. Article 38 of the Hague Convention says:

> In questions of a legal nature, and especially in the interpretation or application of international conventions, arbitration is recognized by the contracting Powers as the most effective and . . . most equitable means of settling disputes which diplomacy has failed to settle. Consequently it would be desirable that, in disputes about the above-mentioned questions, [the parties should use arbitration] in so far as circumstances permit.[13]

No state is bound actually to use arbitration under the provisions of the Hague Convention: the provisions are there for them to use if they find it convenient and desirable. However, if they do use it, they are bound by the decision.

---

[13] Senate Document No. 357, *op. cit.*

The Hague Court, therefore, although it marks an advance in the institutionalizing of arbitration, adds no feature of compulsory resort to the Court.
Broadly speaking, the bilateral arbitration treaty provides that all disputes will
be settled through arbitration except those that either party does not care to
for reasons of "honor" and the like, while the Hague Court provides for the
settlement by arbitration of only those cases that a state desires to settle
through legal procedures. In the first case all is conceded and then most withdrawn; in the second, nothing is conceded and then something may be given.
From the point of view of compulsory resort to the Court, there is no real
difference, since in neither case does a great power end up by going to court
against its wishes.

Both the obligations of the bilateral treaty of arbitration and those of the
multilateral treaty creating the Hague Court are in any event freely assumed
(or not assumed at all) by states. When great powers accept obligations to
arbitrate, they leave themselves loopholes so that they will not be forced to
arbitrate when they do not so desire; and when they accepted membership in
the Hague Court, they purposely refrained from agreeing to obligations other
than to belong to (not necessarily to use) the Court.

Wherein, then, lies the advantage of institutionalized arbitration on a
multilateral basis, such as the Hague Court, over more primitive types of arbitration?

To answer this question, we must bear in mind the arbitral procedure.
Whether arbitration results as a consequence of an *ad hoc* determination to
resort to it, or as a result of a bilateral or multilateral treaty, and whether or
not the machinery of the Hague Court is used, arbitration in every case is
preceded by what is known as a *compromis*. The *compromis* is a preliminary
agreement or treaty defining the points at issue and arranging any unresolved
procedural aspects of handling the actual dispute.

In the case where no treaty exists at all, and arbitration, if it comes, will be
ad hoc action, the two governments in dispute with one another may, because
of inflamed public opinion at home or because of generally bad relations between them, find it impossible to agree upon such items as the rules of procedure and the method for constituting the court. All this is preliminary and
must be settled before arbitration can even begin. They may never be able to
settle these preliminary points if national tempers have become frayed, and
protracted negotiations may actually worsen relations between them.

Where the dispute arises between two states who already have in force a
bilateral treaty of arbitration, this difficulty is obviated because the procedural
aspects of the arbitration are already basically covered in it. However, even if
a state has negotiated a number of such bilateral treaties, it may easily find
itself in dispute with a state with whom it has none. To avoid this situation, a
state would have to negotiate such a treaty with every other state.

The Hague Court has provided the simplest solution to this problem, resolving both difficulties at once. Not only is the court established by a multilateral treaty, but also the treaty contains the rules for arbitration procedure.

The Hague Convention establishing the Court deals explicitly with arbitral procedure per se and provides a detailed procedure for choosing the judges for the Court.[14] The *compromis* is thus reduced to little more than the formal statement that the powers in question agree to arbitrate the particular dispute between them. Extraneous grounds for disagreement are done away with.

4 *International Courts: Adjudication*

THE next and greatest step forward toward creating a general international court on the model of a national supreme court came with the establishment of the League of Nations. In 1922, as an integral part of the League system, but as an organ separate from the League of Nations proper, the Permanent Court of International Justice was established. This Court, known also as the World Court and the League Court, was replaced, after the demise of the League, by the new International Court of Justice whose Statute forms an integral part of the United Nations Charter. The Statute of this United Nations Court came into effect on October 24, 1945, simultaneously with the other portions of the Charter.

For all practical purposes the League Court and the United Nations Court may be considered together, for the changes in the Statute of the latter from the provisions governing the former are relatively minute. Even the numbering and wording of the articles of the two Statutes is almost identical. Probably the basic reason for establishing a "new" court was the fact that neither the United States nor the Soviet Union had ever been members of the League Court, and in the United States in particular the question of "to join or not to join" had at one time aroused a certain amount of feeling. The setting up of the new court also presented an opportunity for disposing of the rather unfortunate official title of the League Court, which was, it will be recalled, the Permanent Court of International Justice. The suggestion implicit in the title, that there is such a thing as "international" justice, as distinct from justice pure and simple, was thus eliminated.

Both the League and the United Nations Courts are courts of *adjudication* rather than of arbitration. The difference in term has caused some authorities to assert that there is a difference in the type of law upon which the decisions of arbitral panels and those of the League and United Nations Courts are respectively based. The claim has been made that arbitral panels may decide cases not only on a basis of existing international law but also on considerations of equity (what is right and just) as well. Some arbitral panels may well have done so: they have not always given the reasons for their decisions. But so may courts of adjudication, if they will and the parties so agree, since Article 38 of the Statutes of both courts provides for equity decisions (*ex aequo et bono*) if the parties so desire.

The real difference between proceedings in arbitration and adjudication is

---

[14] See Part IV, Chapter III and Chapter II, respectively, of the Convention.

not to be found in the type of law applied, nor in the binding character of decisions (for each kind is equally binding upon the disputants) but in the *composition of the court*. Unlike arbitral panels whose membership may vary almost infinitely, the composition of the court of adjudication remains the same, case after case. The same justices, barring sicknesses, absence on leave, personal disqualification on the part of a justice, or other such usual reservations to such a statement, sit each time.[15]

The advantages over the arbitral type of a court constant in membership can easily be appreciated. Yet until 1922 there was no such international court open to universal membership and resembling closely the usual conception of a court. Why then was it so long delayed, since it is obvious that it eliminates the need to choose judges for each case (which may be difficult), assures continuity in decisions (since judges will tend to decide similar cases similarly), and provides justices well versed and experienced in deciding international legal disputes (despite all their intricacies and complications)?

The answer is to be found by observing the number of justices composing the court. Article 3 of the Statute of the United Nations Court provides that it "shall consist of fifteen members, no two of whom may be nationals of the same state." [16] Even in 1902 there were forty-seven independent states in the world; by 1952 the number had grown to approximately eight-five. Among these, which states were to enjoy the prestige of a seat on the Court? The Hague Conferences of 1899 and 1907 found no solution to so intricate a problem. As we have seen, they finally fell back upon the arbitral panel list, which permitted each state to name four potential justices.

Particularly striking as an illustration of the way in which the past and its practices are bent to the uses of the future was the use of this very list of Hague arbitrators as a first step in resolving the problem. The membership, first of the League Court and now of the United Nations Court, is proposed initially by the members of the Hague list of arbitrators.[17] The list of nominations is then forwarded to the United Nations Security Council and the General Assembly (as formerly it was sent to the League Council and League Assembly), who proceed to vote independently to fill the vacant seats by an absolute majority vote. If a candidate receives such a vote in both bodies, he is elected. If three such sessions fail to fill the vacancies, a joint conference of three members from both the Council and Assembly meets to attempt to agree on who will be elected by a fourth meeting of both organs. If this fails

---

[15] Article 25, Paragraph 3, provides that "a quorum of nine judges shall suffice to constitute the Court."

[16] The text of the Statute may be found in *United Nations Conference on International Organization: Documents*, Vol. 15, pp. 293 ff. The League Court provided for twelve justices and three associate justices, with the same restriction on nationality.

[17] Each "national group" from the Hague Court list (or, for non-Hague Court members, a special equivalent group) may nominate not more than four persons, no more than two of whom may be of their own nationality and in no case more than double the number of seats to be filled on the court of adjudication.

to resolve the deadlock, the members of the Court already elected select the candidates for the remaining vacancies from among those obtaining votes in one or the other of the two organs.

Here, indeed, is ingenuity, based upon a skillful use of the older Hague Court and the major organs of the League of Nations and United Nations. The members of the Court serve for nine-year terms, but it is quite usual for judges to be re-elected. The increase in Afro-Asian states in the United Nations has gradually affected the composition of the Court. Comparing 1950 and 1964, five major and three influential medium powers held seats throughout: the United States, U.S.S.R., United Kingdom, France, and China; Mexico, Poland, and Egypt (United Arab Republic). In 1950 Latin American states held three other seats, but by 1964 only one. El Salvador, Brazil, and Chile had given way to Senegal, Japan, and Peru. Of three remaining seats held by European powers in 1950, only two were still European in 1964. Belgium, Norway, and Yugoslavia had been replaced by Greece, Italy, and Pakistan. Finally, Canada had given way to Australia.

It is obvious that the Court thus represents not only the major legal systems of the world but also the major great powers, the important secondary powers, and various voting blocs as well.

The chief reason that other and smaller states, who stood little chance of a place on the Court, agreed to this system of selection is to be found in the provisions of Article 31 of the Statute. According to Article 31, when a dispute is placed before the Court, "judges of the nationality of each of the parties shall retain their right to sit," and "if the Court includes . . . a judge of the nationality of *one* of the parties, any other party may choose a . . . judge," except where "there be several parties *in the same interest,* they shall . . . be reckoned as one party only," and "if the Court includes . . . *no* judge of the nationality of the parties, *each* . . . may proceed to choose a judge" to sit for that particular case.[18]

In this way every state appearing before the Court can be assured either of having one judge of its own nationality on the bench, or at least of having one judge there to represent its interest. Thus no state goes before the Court in an inferior position vis-à-vis another, and yet the number of judges remains comparatively small. The process of adjudication, therefore, moves further than arbitration in the direction of an "impartial" bench, even though this one concession to the sovereign equality of states is retained. Since the one "national" judge is only one among fifteen or sixteen,[19] he is a small minority. Although the bench of the United Nations Court is not constituted in a completely parallel way to that of a national supreme court, considering the different type of problem in international adjudication, as much progress in

---

18 Italics added.

19 Where only twelve or fourteen judges are sitting in a given case, or where one "national" judge is added to the fifteen permanent judges, there may occur a tie vote. In such cases the President of the Court casts a second and deciding vote.

this direction as is necessary or desirable has now been accomplished. The "weaknesses" of the international judicial process are to be found now not in a lack of adequate courts but in the lack of compulsory jurisdiction on the part of the court.

Arbitration treaties concluded by great powers habitually contain reservations permitting the power to retain discretion as to whether or not to resort to court. The Hague Convention establishing the Hague Court, again merely urged the settlement of legal disputes through that Court and did not even hint at the compulsory use of a court. The same problem had to be faced when the League Court was established: to what extent should it have compulsory jurisdiction?

Article 36 of the Statute of the United Nations Court defining the jurisdiction of the Court is substantially the same as Article 36 of the Statute of the League Court. It provides:

1. The jurisdiction of the Court comprises all cases which the parties refer to it and all matters specially provided for in the Charter of the United Nations or in treaties and conventions in force.
2. The states parties to the present Statute may at any time declare that they recognize as compulsory *ipso facto* and without special agreement in relation to any other state accepting the same obligation, the jurisdiction of the Court in all legal disputes concerning:
     a. the interpretation of a treaty;
     b. any question of international law;
     c. the existence of any fact which, if established, would constitute a breach of an international obligation;
     d. the nature or extent of the reparation to be made for the breach of an international obligation.
3. The declarations referred to above may be made unconditionally or on condition of reciprocity on the part of several or certain states, or for a certain time.

Such declarations have been made under both the League and United Nations Courts. Under the League Court, at one point fifty-six such declarations were in effect. Following the establishment of the United Nations Court, thirty-nine states were bound by the "Optional Clause" of Paragraph 2 as of the end of 1959; but by 1963 the total was only thirty-six. These declarations have included various reservations. Those contained in the declaration of the United States are typical of the reservations made by great powers. It reads:

. . . The United States of America recognizes as compulsory *ipso facto* and without special agreement, in relation to any other state accepting the same obligation, the jurisdiction of the International Court of Justice in all legal disputes hereafter arising concerning [and here follows the *a, b, c* and *d* of Paragraph 2] *Provided,* that this declaration shall not apply to
     a. disputes the solution of which the parties shall entrust to other tribunals by virtue of agreements already in existence or which may be concluded in the future; or
     b. disputes with regard to matters which are essentially within the domestic

jurisdiction of the United States of America as determined by the United States of America; or

c. disputes arising under a multilateral treaty, unless (1) all parties to the treaty affected by the decision are also parties to the case before the Court, or (2) the United States of America specially agrees to jurisdiction . . .[20]

It will be seen at once that reservation b by itself released the United States from the "compulsory jurisdiction" of the Court, since any dispute which the United States unilaterally determines to be a domestic question is excluded automatically from adjudication. The effect of such reservations is similar to the "national honor" clauses of the older bilateral treaties of arbitration: no nation that has "protected" itself with such clauses need go to court *unless it so wishes*. Nor can this situation be altered by the conclusion of a multilateral treaty providing for compulsory jurisdiction unless the very same states that have been so careful to reserve to themselves the decision as to whether or not to resort to court reverse their attitude and ratify such a treaty. Again, no nation is bound by a treaty that it does not ratify.

The decline in popularity of the "Optional Clause" is striking. Not only is there a decrease in absolute numbers but the relative decrease, when contrasted with the growth in numbers of United Nations members, is particularly marked. Only a very few of the newer nations have shown interest in Article 36, Paragraph 2. Not one of the new African states admitted to the United Nations by the end of 1960 was on the list in 1963.

Actual resort to the United Nations Court has shown similar apathy. Taking judgments in contentious cases and advisory opinions [21] together, the League Court between 1922 and 1938 handed down from one to six annually. During that seventeen year period, three times the total reached six and once five. The range in number of judgments and opinions given by the United Nations Court, with up to over twice as many members, has been no greater. Indeed, in only one year did the number reach six during its first seventeen years, and otherwise it never exceeded three. Of the 38 contentious cases on the agenda of the United Nations Court between 1948 and 1962 (some of which involved multiple judgments and some of which were withdrawn by the parties before judgment was rendered), only four or five involved states first created after 1945. The conclusion is inescapable that legal settlement is less popular today, and is not popular at all with the newer nations.

The decision handed down on July 18, 1966 inevitably increased this feeling. The Court by a 7–7 tie, with the President of the Court then casting a second and deciding vote to make it 8 to 7, dismissed the Ethiopian-Liberian complaint that South Africa by her *apartheid* policies, was in violation of her mandate over South West Africa. The Court noted that "the position of a

---

[20] Frederick H. Hartmann, ed., *Basic Documents of International Relations*, p. 221. See also, for text, *Department of State Bulletin*, Vol. 15 (September 8, 1946), pp. 452 ff.

[21] See Chapter 11 for a definition of these terms and for case illustrations of legal settlement in action.

mandatory country caught between the different expressions of view of some 40 or 50 states would [become] untenable. The Court said its duty was "to apply the law as it finds it, not to make it."

5 Law and Change

AT the same time, international law as a body of rules of law, has never grown so rapidly as in the last twenty years. How shall we explain this apparent contradiction?

The growth in numbers of states would alone account for a great increase in the body of laws. Treaties and agreements are the greatest source of new law, and each new state must enter into some with many other states. Furthermore, new problems have appeared which affect new and old states alike, and older problems have taken on changed implications. Outer space transit illustrates the first category, as manned and unmanned vehicles revolve in orbit over the earth. The growth in importance of hitherto neglected polar wastelands, principally for military reasons, illustrates the second category. Such general problems, affecting many or most states, are in principle particularly suitable for handling on a multilateral basis, through treaties specifically designed to codify practice. Yet it is difficult to gain widespread agreement until enough time has elapsed to permit a perspective on the problem. And if there is too much delay, divergent practices become entrenched. Thus the signing of the Outer Space Treaty of December 1966, which prohibited national claims in, or military uses of, outer space, represented exceptional progress.

By contrast, efforts to codify the law of territorial waters illustrate the difficulties which exist on a subject where the layman is apt to suppose that virtual unanimity exists. Not only have states historically claimed sea frontiers of varying widths but even the methods for establishing the shore or off-shore points from which distances shall be measured seaward have been in dispute. Since the decision in the Anglo-Norwegian Fisheries Case of 1951, this question is even less settled than it was presumed to be before. On such questions the newer Afro-Asian states tend as a group to be reluctant to accept more traditional practices. There is a residual suspicion of rules developed by the former colonial powers; there is some feeling that such rules work to the advantage of great maritime powers. While the passage of time and the acquiring of vested interests in new legal rules created by these states will ultimately spark more interest on their part in legal procedures and codification, the divergence of view today still retards progress.

Thus what we are witnessing is more the growth of law through particular, rather than general, agreements. Since international law, as the formalization of the *status quo*, is essentially conservative, reflecting what has been agreed to, its further development on a more general basis must await a greater concensus.

International law is not uniform, universal law. But while the lack of agreement and uniform practice produces difficulties, these are not the kinds of difficulties which generally result in grave tensions between states. Nor are these divergencies of practice responsible for the much-discussed "weaknesses" of international law.

6 *The Enforcement of International Law*

IT is now possible to revert to the question with which this chapter was begun: what is the nature of the role played by international law in international relations? The main outlines of the answer to this question should now be clear. International law is indispensable in the relations of states; still, it fulfills a much more limited role in those relations than might at first have been assumed. It is not so much "weak" as limited in its application to existing international problems. These limitations do not stem from gaps and lacunae in the law, since no legal decision has ever been withheld because the arbitral body or court of adjudication could not find any law that was applicable.

Neither do the limitations of international law stem from a lack of techniques adequate to the formulation of law nor from the inadequacies of existing international courts. It is neither law that is incomplete nor the technical apparatus for making and judging law that is the source of the limitations.

The source is to be found in the states themselves. From the beginning, international law has been the creature of the states, and so it has continued to be. It is the states who have made international law the enduring and respected method for settling disputes within the area of legal domain. They have not willfully disregarded the precepts of their creature, but they have drawn rather definite boundaries around the areas of disagreements and types of problems which they care to have settled through legal procedures. The distinction that states have made between the justiciable and the nonjusticiable have been drawn on a basis of usefulness and convenience to themselves. When they have given a name to the problems they are unwilling to have settled through legal procedures, they have mentioned national honor, independence, vital interests, and the interests of third parties, or problems that are essentially of domestic concern.

Because states have excluded problems of vital interests and power from the domain of legal settlement, most of international law has "enforced itself" in the sense that the question of enforcement has not even arisen. Literally, of course, states must carry out the law, but practically the question of who will make them do so has not often needed consideration. They have not submitted to legal settlements unless they were prepared to accept the decision.

International law, therefore, has been, in general, voluntarily enforced, and the question of coercion has only infrequently arisen. This is not surprising since the states created customary law because it was useful, and accept treaties only as they desire, and in general go to court only when and as they wish. That is why, for example, in the last hundred and fifty years, out of hundreds of cases handled through arbitration or adjudication, the instances of noncompliance with the decision of the Court can be numbered on the fingers of both hands—surely an astounding record!

Where then does the view arise that international law is "weak" and "ineffective"? It is precisely in connection with those problems and disputes that states have not been willing to submit to legal settlement. The "weakness" of international law is discussed almost invariably in connection with the enforcing of some treaty or convention originally imposed by coercion. Where a treaty is forced upon a state, law is made concerning items which that state would not under freer conditions consent to. The most obvious example is a treaty imposed at the end of a war by the victor upon the vanquished.

Treaties imposed upon defeated states as a rule tend to be enforced for as long a period as the victors (and beneficiaries from the treaty) remain able and willing to use force to keep the agreement in effect. An example of this phenomenon was the fate of Articles XI, XIII, and XIV of the Treaty of Paris of 1856. Britain and France had defeated Russia in the Crimean War. One advantage they sought from their victory was the demilitarization of the Black Sea—a point incorporated in the three articles mentioned above. In 1870, it will be recalled, France and Prussia were in the midst of war, Britain stood aloof in neutrality, and Russia was assured of Prussia's good wishes. Accordingly, the Russians moved to break the "shackles" of the treaty. Instructions were sent by the Russian Foreign Minister to the Russian Ambassador in London to take up the point with the British, leaving with them a copy of the note whose text read, in part:

His Imperial Majesty cannot admit, *de facto*, that the security of Russia should depend on a fiction which has not stood the test of time. . . . the Emperor commands you to declare that His Imperial Majesty can not any longer hold himself bound by the stipulations of the Treaty . . . as far as they restrict his Sovereign Rights in the Black Sea.

. . . His Imperial Majesty is convinced that Peace and the Balance of Power will receive a fresh Guarantee if they are based upon a more just and solid foundation than one resulting from a state of things which no Great Power can accept as a normal condition of its existence.[22]

The Treaty of Versailles and its fate at the hands of Hitler is a more recent example. There is almost a classic argument and counterargument that accompanies the process of tearing up an imposed treaty. While the former victors intone *"pacta sunt servanda"* (treaties are binding), the former defeated state qualifies with *"rebus sic stantibus"* (conditions remaining the same—which they have not, or that state would not dare to make its bid for freedom from the treaty). As His Imperial Majesty so aptly put it, the treaty had not stood the test of time.

---

[22] Sir Edward Hertslet, *The Map of Europe by Treaty*, London, 1875, Vol. III, pp. 1894–1895.

Although international law is flexible in the sense that particular rules in a particular case can be deduced from general principles, the law is still fundamentally conservative. The law is not flexible enough to mean tomorrow the reverse of its meaning today. *Law is the formalization of the status quo.* The flexibility inherent in it is a flexibility confined and limited by the boundaries of that *status quo.*[23] In the vast majority of cases, states find mutual advantage in formalizing their legal relationships in treaties that they consider to their mutual advantage. In such cases they are mutually stabilizing their relations on the basis of the *status quo.* But when a treaty is designed by one state to perpetuate a *status quo* distasteful to another whom it can at the moment coerce, the situation is entirely different. Far from the mutual interest in upholding the treaty, there is in the latter case more the relationship of jailer and jailed.

International law, then, is not "weak" except in one restricted sense: it will not, by its mere existence, enforce rules and treaties that affect the vital interests of states but are one-sided in their advantage. States confronted with a situation in which imposed treaties are being challenged have theoretically three alternatives: they can enforce the treaties if they are able and willing to do so, they can revise them on a basis of more mutual advantage to both parties, or they can passively watch as the resurgent power breaks its bonds.

In actual practice, where the first alternative is practicable, one does not hear about the "weaknesses" of international law, for the treaty is being observed—perhaps at bayonet point but still observed. As for the second alternative, the Covenant of the League of Nations, Article 19, provided that: "The Assembly may from time to time advise the reconsideration by Members of the League of treaties which have become inapplicable." The provision remained a dead letter for the obvious reason that states almost never willingly surrendered such advantages as they had gained through war. Therefore, any renegotiation supposedly on a basis of mutual advantage will usually result out of the weakness of the former victor. Once the treaty begins to be revised, the process continues until there is no treaty left in the original sense at all. This is not inevitable, but it is usual, since former victors habitually postpone revision until revision is synonymous with tearing up. And so, when states are too weak to enforce the treaties of coercion they have imposed upon defeated states, the cry is heard that international law is "weak."

Throughout this discussion one major theme can be seen: it is the states who make law, resort to courts, and enforce law. Normally states are prepared to adjust certain of their secondary national interests through legal methods when these interests are the subject of a dispute with another state. But when they are not coerced into signing agreements, they narrowly restrict the problems they are willing to deal with on a legal basis. Although an evolving law is always incomplete, there are no existing problems that states could not handle

---

[23] This point, which is of fundamental importance, will be spelled out further in the case studies of Chapter 11.

on a legal basis if they so wished. But in practice they do not so wish. In effect, they govern their procedure on the basis that legal disputes and problems will be settled legally, and by legal disputes they mean disputes which they are prepared to settle on a legal basis. The distinction that states make between legal and political problems is therefore an arbitrary one having as its basis the attitude of the state toward the *status quo*. Where the state is willing to accept the *status quo* in respect to a given problem, it is prepared to deal with that problem legally: all other problems, *ipso facto*, become for it *political problems*. No amount of exhortation will "strengthen" international law beyond that point. Since it is the creature of the states, it will be what they make it. In the meantime, as before, states will continue to handle "legal" problems legally and without great enforcement difficulty. For "political" problems, especially those involving vital interests, the main resort will continue to be diplomacy and war.

CHAPTER 7

International Economics

One of the purest fallacies is that trade follows the flag. Trade follows the lowest price current. If a dealer in any colony wished to buy Union Jacks he would order them from Britain's worst foe if he could save a sixpence. Trade knows no flag.

ANDREW CARNEGIE

. . . whereas various real and powerful motives of pride, prestige, and pugnacity, together with the more altruistic professions of a civilising mission, figured as causes of imperial expansion, the dominant directive motive was the demand for markets and for profitable investment by the exporting and financial classes within each imperialist regime.

JOHN A. HOBSON
Imperialism

WHEREAS the machinery of government is not only the prime but the sole vehicle for the diplomatic and legal relations of states, much of the content of international economic relations derives from private agreements between individuals. How much freedom is permitted to individuals in such activity varies widely today from state to state. The system as a whole has also fluctuated historically from the one extreme of little regulation to the other of minute prescription. War always accentuates the tendency to regulate.

I International Economics and International Politics

WHILE the Marxists assert that "Wall Street" controls the government, Wall Street simultaneously makes the reverse complaint. Both agree, however, that economics is not "pure," that politics always enters into the "mix." Even a policy of complete external "free trade" is itself a political decision not to regulate.

In international economic relations, therefore, because the states are inescapably involved, the economic process reflects the interaction of state policies even while trade itself is frequently conducted by and through private persons. While the individual is bent on private profit, the state will never act solely on that basis.

We have seen in Chapter 3 that states are dependent upon others for essential imports, frequently of very strategic goods. From this undoubted fact some observers have optimistically concluded that the unity of the world will result. Since virtually no nation is self-sufficient in the complex, modern world, all nations are necessarily interdependent. Because of this interdependence, it is maintained, they will and must be drawn together out of mutual profit and advantage. From a long range point of view, political considerations apart, this is true. But political considerations are anything but apart. There was ample demand for Cuban cigars in the United States in 1965; and Cuba wanted to buy a whole host of American products. But trade between them was almost nil. Trade between Western Europe and Eastern Europe, although increased in the post-Stalin era, remained quite small contrasted with its "natural" possibilities. The controversy a few years ago over selling surplus Western wheat to the grain-hungry Soviet Union illustrates how hard it is to surmount political barriers even when it is a simple matter of food.

Nor does the fact that nations have traded a good deal with each other necessarily overcome political rivalries. Before World War I, Germany and England were respectively among each other's best customers. Germany was actually England's best customer. Before World War II, American-Japanese trade was very important to both nations. Again, Japan and China for the past hundred years have been important customers of each other. They have, nevertheless, fought each other in war after war. The historical evidence tends to show that trade between nations does not assure that their relations will be more peaceful.

What of the effect of so-called "functional loyalties"? Workers, for example, have common problems and interests irrespective of their nationalities. Will not their common interests in time overcome their narrow and parochial nationalisms?

Socialists as a group have put much faith in this idea ever since the first announcement of the slogan of the Communist Manifesto, "Workers of the world, unite; you have nothing to lose but your chains." Others have embraced it in less extreme form. Certainly workers everywhere have a potentially common interest in working conditions everywhere. This is part of the rationale behind the establishment of the International Labor Organization. Yet whether such a potential will be converted into an internationally important political force is open to much doubt; their predominant interest must almost inescapably be focused on home conditions and efforts to improve things within the domestic (i.e., national) framework. The international Socialist movement fell apart in World War I when the various Socialist parties all over Europe forgot their "brotherhood" and soon began backing the war as enthusiastically as anyone else. Nor have Communist advances come about because of the education of the "working masses" to their "Socialist responsibilities." Soviet European successes reflect the adroit exploitation of revolutionary situations existing in the wake of war by Soviet *agents provocateur* who, under the protection of the occupying Red Army, could see their schemes through to success.

More important than functional relationships across frontiers are devices to link whole nations economically, such as the European Common Market. But even such devices can only prepare a basis for political unity; they cannot substitute for it.

Logically, perhaps, the world of contemporary economic cause and effect should be one world, for no nation in it can exist economically by itself. Yet historically the cementing effect of economic interests across state frontiers has been insignificant where it has run athwart politically divergent interests. Economic interests within states have historically bent the policies of those states to their own profit-seeking ends. Conversely, states have, from ancient times, utilized the economic interests of their nationals for purposes of the national interest. Whichever way the process operates, the role played by the state (either through intervention or abstention) has a decisive influence on the economic relations of nations.

2 Mercantilism

IN the last three hundred years or more the degree of overt interference by the state in international economics has varied tremendously from one extreme to the other. In the Middle Ages the Church (then wielding both spiritual and secular power) prescribed in minute detail the conditions under which almost all commercial transactions were to take place. The decline of the power of the Church brought about no real liberalization or increase of trade, because the guilds continued to control production just as minutely. Moreover, Europe was so broken up into customs districts (in Germany alone there were over three hundred fifty as late as the mid-eighteenth century), transportation was so primitive, and the highways so unsafe that there was little incentive for trade to be more than almost purely local. Following the Commercial Revolution, however, two things began to occur that eventually wrought great changes: (1) kings had greatly solidified their domains, and (2) the technical instruments for true world trade, such as the compass (and later the sextant), began to come into use. Both of these developments inspired a great increase in trade, for the "king's men" made the highways safe, uniform royal currencies which began to be used made such trade easier, and the abolition of local tariffs added further stimulant; moreover, the seas— always cheap transportation—could be utilized as never before. The king now issued royal charters and himself prescribed the conditions under which trade was to be carried on, both at home and abroad.

The trade that developed with the Orient in the seventeenth century was both extensive and important. It was, in fact, more important for a long time than intra-European trade. The great difficulty with it was that Europe imported more silks, spices, sugar, coffee, and tea than it was able to pay for with the textiles and other products it sold in return to non-Europeans. The excess of imports over exports had, as a result, to be paid for in precious metal: in gold and silver. Nothing, however, was in greater demand and shorter supply than these metals. The continuing wars in which Western and Central Europe were engaging were a serious drain on the economies of the participating states: gold and silver were needed to pay for the wars continually being fought on the continent, and to pay the men who fought them, for this was before the day of the widespread use of paper currencies.

To meet this situation and conserve gold, the new European states put two remedies ino effect. They regulated trade more drastically than ever before, reducing imports and requiring that goods be transported exclusively in ships owned and operated by nationals of the country. They determined to plant colonies abroad who would supply necessary raw materials to the mother country and accept the mother country's produce in exchange. These remedies formed the doctrine of *mercantilism*. It was hoped to increase stocks of gold and silver and in this way increase national power.

3 *Laissez Faire's Rise and Decline*

THE mercantilist logic contained serious errors that were exposed as early as 1776 with the publication of Adam Smith's *Wealth of Nations*. Smith demonstrated that a nation was not truly more wealthy if it succeeded in selling more than it bought and received gold and silver in payment for the excess. Gold and silver were of little use in themselves; their value came essentially from their ability to command goods and services. A nation with a great stock of gold, which had denuded itself of valuable goods to procure that stock, could, it is true, then use the gold to purchase goods. But unless it did so, it was poorer in the end rather than richer, for there were fewer goods available to consume and enjoy. Smith argued that an excess of imports over exports should no more be considered an "unfavorable" balance of trade (as the mercantilists claimed) than the reverse trend should be considered "favorable." Both were imbalances that would tend to correct themselves automatically if left alone (laissez faire). Thus a great influx of gold into a country tended to raise the price level (more money in circulation would bid prices up); higher prices at home would attract more imports from abroad to take advantage of it; higher costs (because of higher prices) at home would make it harder to export; and therefore soon gold would be exported to pay for the excessive imports, etc. Smith did concede that a nation might out of prudence (although for "uneconomic" reasons) wish to establish "infant industries" and businesses essential to its defense; other than that he saw in world-wide free trade the hope for a glorious and more abundant future.

Despite Smith's forceful writings, mercantilism survived into the nineteenth century as the predominant philosophy of international trade. Then it began to lose ground to the newer ideas, but never completely and never everywhere. At one geographical extreme of Europe, for example, Russia never adopted a low tariff, while England, on the opposite end, following the repeal of the Corn Laws in 1846, inaugurated completely free trade. The rim-land states of Western Europe—England, Belgium, Holland, and France—went furthest in embracing the newer ideas. In Central Europe the German states followed the trend by introducing liberal trade policies and almost abolishing tariffs in the middle of the century. Even in the United States, which never abandoned a protectionist tariff, the duties (especially between 1830 and 1860) were by today's standards extremely low. The general trend was clear: in those countries where industrialization was furthest advanced, completely free trade or nearly free trade tended to be inaugurated because this policy brought the most benefits; in those countries still unindustrialized the high tariff usually continued in effect; and in those nations only semi-industrialized, a half-way policy was most frequently adopted. The choice of policy reflected fairly accurately how strong each nation considered itself to be in terms of competing in world markets and admitting foreign goods to its own. Since newly established ("infant") industries are almost always less efficient than their older competitors, to abandon protection too soon was tantamount to foregoing industrialization.[1] Moreover, foregoing industrialization meant a permanently lower standard of living. Smith's logic applied best to the economic relations of already industrialized states; it was, as a matter of fact, those states who applied it. When free-trade ideas replaced mercantilist concepts, they supplanted them only when and where national conditions and interests made it appropriate.

The Anglo-French Cobden Treaty of 1860 marked the beginning of a twenty-year period in which free-trade policies attained their greatest favor. It is again no coincidence that by this period (1860–1879) the Atlantic states had all progressed substantially along the road to industrialization. In this twenty-year period, out of more than two thousand items in the tariffs of the leading powers in 1860, over half were either reduced or abolished entirely.

For most of these twenty years almost anything produced could be sold. By the last part of the period, though, production began to outrun markets, competition had greatly increased, and enthusiasm for free trade began to evaporate. The businessman who saw his profits dwindle, and the nation that saw its continued economic power in jeopardy, turned toward new protective tariffs once more. Beginning in 1879, Germany under Bismarck commenced high permanent duties on industrial and agricultural products alike. Two years later, in 1881, France followed suit in raising tariffs, at first moderately and then more and more steeply. Across the Atlantic the McKinley Tariff, adopted in 1890, marked the definite abandonment of a low tariff and its replacement by one designed to erect tariff walls too high to be climbed by various goods from abroad. Other states did likewise. Britain almost alone continued to cling to the remnants of free trade until in 1931 it too embraced protectionism.

---

[1] Bismarck commented: "England abolished protection after she had benefited by it to the fullest extent. . . . Free trade is the weapon of the strongest nation." Quoted in W. S. Culbertson, *International Economic Policies*, New York: D. Appleton, 1925, p. 13.

4 Colonial Imperialism

THE last quarter of the nineteenth century was notable in another and connected area of economic policy. It revived an interest in acquiring colonies which had largely expired as a result of the New World's obtaining its freedom and proving that "colonialism did not pay."

While in the period between the Congress of Vienna (1815) and the 1870's industrialization and the growing liberalization of trade had brought profits and prosperity to Europe, the end of the Franco-Prussian War brought the reappearance of economic difficulties. Trade began to slow up. England, for example, was hit by a severe depression in the 1870's. The great outpouring of goods from the factories had to find sales outlets. These economic difficulties were accentuated and made worse by the growing trend, beginning in the German tariff of 1879, toward the abandonment of free or liberal trade policies and the erection of high trade barriers. The solution of Jules Ferry, the French apostle of imperialism, and others began to enjoy sympathetic hearings. Ferry said that "the protectionist system is a steam engine without safety valve if it does not have as correlative and auxiliary a healthy and serious colonial policy." [2]

The new imperialism that began after 1873 made the old look like a mere rehearsal. In thirty years England alone added more than three million square miles (all but one-half million in Africa); the French took even more, claiming an additional four million square miles, with most of this area in Africa too. The gains of the other states were less spectacular. Germany, between 1884 and 1890, acquired nearly a million square miles in Africa, as well as scattered possessions in the Pacific, including a part of New Guinea and a leasehold on Kiaochow in China. Italy managed to obtain Eritrea, Italian Somaliland, and Libya—all in Africa. Belgium acquired the nearly million square miles of the Congo Free State (the Belgian Congo), also in Africa. Japan took Korea from China, and the United States raised its flag over the Philippines and Puerto Rico. Russia's expansion, like that of Austria-Hungary but unlike these others, was continental rather than overseas, but its acquisitions were also impressively extensive.

It can easily be seen that the great bulk of territory taken in this period was in Africa, hitherto almost unexploited because largely unexplored. The secondary area of acquisitions was in the Far East. When the orgy of seizing had expended itself shortly before the outbreak of World War I, very little "uncivilized" territory remained under independent rule. Liberia and Ethiopia remained free in Africa. Other than that virtually no areas were still available for taking save a few "civilized" but weak states such as China.

Imperialism in the latter part of the nineteenth century was justified by essentially economic arguments, even though the movement itself was made

² Jules Ferry, Le Tonkin et la Mère-Patrie, Paris, 1890, as quoted in Parker T. Moon, Imperialism and World Politics, p. 44.

possible through a rather unusual set of political circumstances. But these economic arguments, although they carried much appeal in a century dazzled with the tremendous industrial revolution taking place, and unplagued by the preoccupation of general war, could not by themselves have roused the great powers to such impressive colonial efforts. Nor could they have assured sufficient popular support. As Parker T. Moon says: "Not direct interests, but ideas, not property or profession, but principles, actuate the public at large. The theories spread broadcast by imperialist propaganda are the dynamic factors impelling nations to send out armies, defray expenditures, risk wars, for the conquest of distant colonies and protectorates. It requires ideas, attuned to instinctive emotions, to make modern nations fight." [3] Moon singles out the ideas of "preventive self-defense" (based on fear), worries over "surplus population" (based on self-preservation), "economic nationalism," and "national prestige" (based on gregariousness and self-aggrandizement). To this he adds "aggressive . . . altruism" (based on innate pride). These, as Moon recognizes, are motivations that lie not only behind imperialism but behind war itself. But in the period we have been discussing they found their outlet in imperialism. Consequently the deeper causes for imperialism are inseparable from the deeper causes for conquest and war itself, and we shall continue their study in the next chapter.

Looking back upon the economic arguments advanced to explain imperialism, most contemporary observers have concluded that they were either rationalizations for a desire to expand or else sadly in error. The truth is that the colonies did not pay from an economic standpoint. Almost all the colonies acquired in this period imported more than they exported in the years before World War I. In other words, they absorbed more than they contributed. Individuals, of course, profited, but the mother countries as a whole lost money on their investments. Moreover, the most successful colonial possessions from the standpoint of profit were the British and Dutch colonies, which were also open to other nations for trade on a more or less equal basis with the mother countries. Possession of these colonies per se was therefore of no great economic importance in the sense of exclusive exploitation. After World War I the powers made more of an effort to restrict their colonial trade to their own advantage, but, even so, only the United States and Japan had as much as 50 per cent of their colonies' trade. Moreover, the trade between the United States and Japan was infinitely more important: the United States before World War II had a third of Japan's trade.

There is no doubt that the opening of the new colonial areas of the world to trade had a substantial effect on the world economy as a whole. Regardless of the motives involved or the individual profit to particular states, the new markets and sources of supply undoubtedly gave enormous impetus to international trade. Without the imperialist adventures these areas would still have participated in the new trade because the demand for more and different

---

[3] Parker T. Moon, *Imperialism and World Politics*, p. 67.

types of raw materials was enormous. Their participation, however, would no doubt have been at a much slower rate without the stabilizing and educational effects of European rule and ways of doing things.[4] If participation had been left to the decisions and implementation of the native regimes, solely through the devices of concessions and charters, the development would have been much slower. As it was, world trade leaped ahead before World War I at a swift pace: from a mere $4 billions in 1850 it went by 1870 to $10.6 billions, by 1880 to $14.7 billions, by 1890 to $17.5 billions, and in 1900 to $20.1 billions. By 1910—ten years later—it had risen to $33.6 billions, and in 1913, on the eve of war, it stood at $40.4 billions.

The industrialized states, contrary to the expectations of Jules Ferry, continued to be one another's best customers, but their increased trade with one another rested upon the greatly enhanced sources of raw materials which imperialism had made possible. So, indirectly, imperialism did provide expanded markets, but not in the way anticipated. And this was so despite the protective tariff walls that continued to rise higher and higher around the home countries. At this point World War I intervened, and the weaknesses in the system, of which tariffs were a symbol, were soon revealed.

5 *Post-World-War-I Economic Dislocation*

INTERNATIONAL trade after World War I, and economic relations generally, never fully recovered from the effects of the prolonged conflict.

Before the war, trade rested upon a general acceptance of the gold standard and an almost universal free convertibility of currencies. Each national currency was backed by gold (or gold and silver or, in a rare case primarily in Asia, by silver alone); each dollar or pound or unit of currency was defined in terms of that metal, and the gold itself could be obtained upon demand and freely imported or exported. This automatically tended to fix a definite relationship between each currency and another that was relatively stable. While the worth of gold itself could vary, the ability to convert any currency at will either into gold or into any other currency made it relatively easy to finance world trade. The automatic adjustments of the international market place, as Adam Smith had predicted, worked out fairly well in practice prior to 1914.

The enormous war damage, the tremendous dislocation of world trade, and the great public debts that World War I entailed destroyed this structure. Even though the gold standard began to be resumed (in 1925 by Britain, still at that time the most important financial center, with others following suit), there was a general reluctance to permit the free shipment of gold. Governments and central banks now began to take measures designed to stabilize prices rather than allow them to find their own level. All this took place against a background of war debts and reparations, and higher tariffs than ever before.

---

[4] This is, of course, not to deny the detrimental effects upon native life.

Consider first the enormous war spending. Taking both sides together, the belligerents of World War I spent approximately $270 billions. Approximately two-thirds of this was financed by domestic loans, and another 10 per cent in loans from allies. Thus only about one-fifth of the costs were met out of current taxes. This not only produced inflation at home as the supply of money in circulation increased, but the great bulk of the money spent went into unproductive channels. During the war, gold shipments were prohibited. When the nations attempted to return to the gold standard, they had to do so with currencies that were not worth what they once were and whose value in terms of one another was an open question.[5]

The war debts, the second factor we must consider, were anything but insignificant. The United States alone loaned over $10 billions (not counting interest). When after World War I the United States resorted at first to a deliberate deflationary policy, it made repayment by the borrowers even more difficult.

Between 1923 and 1926 the United States concluded a series of agreements with its debtors. The total arrangement called for the United States to receive $22 billions over a 62-year period. Since Britain alone was owed some $6 billions, the total interallied debts exceeded $28 billions. When the total amount of reparations that Germany, Hungary, and Bulgaria were to pay, as initially fixed, is taken into account, the powers had incurred total obligations running to some $62 billions. Public indebtedness alone in the 1920's called for the transfer of some three-fourths of a billion dollars a year. When private indebtedness is added, about $2.5 billions annually had to be transferred. This at a time when the mechanisms for money and gold transfer were never in worse condition.

Third, there was the reparations factor. At the Peace Conference a Reparations Commission had been established to set the ultimate figure that the Germans were to pay. This Reparations Commission subsequently set the total figure at 132 billion gold marks ($33 billions). When it is remembered that total world trade in 1913 was $40.4 billions, it can readily be seen what a fantastic sum this was, especially considering that Germany's annual share of world trade was about $5.3 billions in 1913. How was she to pay? Only the bitterness of feeling as a result of the war can explain these impossible requirements.

Germany's initial efforts to cope with reparations soon destroyed the mark's value. By the middle of 1922 the mark had fallen to 2,000 to the pound; by its end it was 50,000 to the pound. Germany was declared in default on January 9, 1923, and two days later French and Belgian troops began to occupy the Ruhr, but still the inflation continued until, by the middle of August 1923, the mark stood at 20 million to the pound! Before further reparations could be considered, the German currency had to be re-established. This was done,

---

[5] Britain's resumption of the prewar gold value for the pound seriously overvalued it; France's resumption at one-fifth the old rate for the franc undervalued it. Both moves increased the disequilibrium.

and the Dawes Plan, which came into effect in August 1924, took another look at the reparations problem. It lowered the amount of the annual install-ments, and provided a rising scale of payments (reaching a "normal" 2.5 bil-lion marks in the fifth year), but did not adjust the total due. This soon proved equally impossible; on June 7, 1929, the Young Plan reduced the total debt to $26.5 billions, with payments to extend to 1988. These payments were to increase gradually from 1.7 billion gold marks in 1930–1931, to 2.4 billion gold marks in 1965–1966. They equaled about two-thirds of the payments due each year from the Allies to the United States on their war loans.

Up until the Dawes Plan a good portion of the money paid by Germany came from foreign exchange sent in by speculators in the mark. Later, be-tween 1924 and 1932, Germany borrowed two to three times more in private loans than she paid in reparations. By 1932 German borrowing stood at more than $7 billions, much too much of it in short-term loans subject to abrupt recall. Of this borrowing over half came from the United States. As a result the United States alone loaned Germany more than she paid in reparations. This flow of loans came to an abrupt end with the coming of the Great De-pression. As a consequence Germany could no longer pay, and the Hoover Moratorium on all debts and reparations, which was announced as an emer-gency measure for one year beginning in June 1931, was the actual end of reparations for all practical purposes.

It can easily be seen that what had occurred was that American capital had been loaned to Germany, that from this the Germans paid reparations, that with the reparations the Allies paid their war debts to the United States, and then the cycle began again with the Germans financing their ever-increasing interest load by heavier and heavier borrowing—making new loans to pay off old ones. So it went until the Depression crumpled this fragile financial balloon. It was not a very sound way of doing things but how else were pay-ments to be made?

Theoretically these World War I international obligations could have been met either by the shipment of goods and giving of services, or by the ship-ment of gold (or acceptable currency). The first solution presupposed two things: (1) that tariff barriers would not be interposed to prevent this and (2) that enough goods could be produced and made available for export. Not only were tariffs raised even higher after World War I; it was also difficult to produce great surpluses in the immediate aftermath of the war, and equally difficult to earmark such enormous quantities of goods for export in the face of domestic need.

The obligations again might have been met by the shipment of gold (or acceptable currency). But to ship gold presupposed having gold to ship, and in large enough quantities. This method actually was resorted to but it could not continue long. Already by 1929 the United States held 38 per cent of all the gold in the world; by 1940 the figure was 80 per cent.

In 1929 when the United States had 38 per cent of all the world's gold, all Europe put together had only 41 per cent. In these circumstances, although gold was still shipped in 1932 and 1933 from Europe to the United States as war-debt payments, the process could not continue. Indeed, following 1933, only Finland continued to pay the United States its war debt.

Acceptable currency, the final possibility, was no real alternative. A nation could always furnish its own currency. But unless the nation that would receive it wished to use it to pay for imports from that country, or could convert it into gold or another more useful money, it would have no use for it. If the debtor nation's currency could be converted into gold, unless that nation correspondingly increased its exports, its gold supply dwindled; the same limitations held true for converting into another currency. So ultimately it was either gold or goods and services, and under post-World-War-I circumstances, neither proved sufficient.

The whole financial system was unstable. Credit was enormously overexpanded in the boom years between 1924 and 1928. Overinflated, the system began to crumble following the stock-market panic in Wall Street in October–November 1929. In one day (October 23) stocks depreciated more than $4 billions. As the American credit structure collapsed, short-term loans abroad were hastily called in. Since the German economy was substantially based upon American loans, and since the Germans held interests in turn in Austria which they hurriedly began to liquidate at the same time as the French, for political reasons, withdrew assets from Austria, the first sign of acute distress in Europe appeared there. In the spring of 1931 the great Kredit-Anstalt of Vienna collapsed. Since most European currencies at this time were on a "gold exchange" [6] basis (pegged for the most part to the British pound) rather than the free gold convertibility standard of pre-1914 days, the contractions that ensued soon produced a drain of gold from London, still at that time the financial center of Europe. In September 1931, Britain was forced to go off the gold standard. Country after country followed suit until by 1936 not a state in the world had its currency on a freely convertible gold basis. Nation after nation depreciated its currency, most often between 30 and 40 per cent. Where currencies were henceforth allowed to be freely bought and sold (which became increasingly rare), they sought their own level in terms of one another rather than in terms of gold. But after 1931 states on the whole manipulated their currencies to counteract this—some more, some less. This is still true today.

6 Economic Nationalism After World War I

IN the 1930's, as nation after nation abandoned the gold standard, it was as though link after link of an invisible chain broke. States turned their attention inward as foreign trade declined drastically and depression set in at home. Each began to try to pull its own economy out of the mud uni-

---

[6] A "gold exchange" basis meant that a currency, while not directly itself convertible into gold, could freely be converted into a currency that was.

laterally. All they succeeded in doing was to scatter the mud more widely and mire themselves deeper.

The devices of economic nationalism to which states resorted were not particularly new, but their persistent large-scale, widespread use in the nineteenth and twentieth centuries was. Immediately after World War I, in the first years of disequilibrium, import quotas and other restrictive devices had come into use. But in the more promising years between 1925 and 1929 there had been a movement back toward freer trade. We have seen how, in this period, the gold standard was readopted. Then, after the Wall Street crash, economic nationalism set in with a vengeance.

Tariffs were, as always, one of the main devices used. It is well to remember that they had been rising steadily since 1879. Between 1913 and 1925 alone, taking the average ad valorem duties assessed by sixteen of the leading industrial states, tariffs increased by a third. In the years 1925–1929, when a return to a semblance of normalcy occurred, there was no great downward revision of these tariffs. After 1921, even the British assessed a 33⅓ per cent duty on certain items. Although the United States conversion to the unconditional form of the "most-favored-nation" clause [7] in 1923, and the incorporation of the clause in the same form in the Franco-German Commercial Treaty of 1927, offered some signs of hope, the prevailing trend was not in that direction. After the Wall Street crash the enactment of the Smoot-Hawley Tariff (1930) by the United States, raising the general ad valorem level to 41.5 per cent, dealt the deathblow to any real hopes of generally lowered tariffs. As other nations resorted to retaliatory measures, tariff walls rose even higher. As a consequence American exports, which had stood at $2.62 billions in the first half of 1929, had fallen to $.84 billion by the same period in 1932. In the same two years the new United States tariff succeeded in cutting United States imports by a drastic 62.1 per cent. These effects were not exclusively the results of the tariffs, of course, since business between 1929 and 1931 was already on shaky credit foundations, but the tariffs undoubtedly made the plunge into deep depression inescapable.

It is amazing, in view of this sharp decline and the restrictions hurriedly adopted everywhere, that world trade by 1937 had substantially recovered (in terms of real values) to the predepression levels. But, in the light of the long-range trend in export expansion, recovery even to the previous level meant in reality much smaller trade than there should have been.

Even high tariffs did not sufficiently funnel trade into the directions desired by the states. Accordingly, other devices were utilized. Import quotas and im-

---

[7] The "most-favored-nation" clause in a commercial treaty has this effect: suppose the treaty is concluded by A and B, and then A grants a concession to C. In such case B is extended the same concession—in return for some equivalent if the clause is conditional, or without any *quid pro quo* if it is unconditional. Until this time the United States had used the conditional form. The virtue of the unconditional form is that it multilateralizes bilateral concessions without the need for, and avoiding the difficulties and dangers of, holding a multilateral conference.

port licenses were among the most important of these. The lead by France and Belgium in this direction in 1931 was shortly followed by many others. The great advantage of import quotas to a state was that they set an absolute maximum on what could be imported. Some nations also used export bonuses or "bounties" which in effect defrayed some of the costs involved in meeting foreign tariffs by their own exporters. Hungary not only paid export bonuses but levied special surtaxes on commodities imported from countries whose trade was not considered desirable.

Currencies, too, were now "managed" by the state in whatever way was thought advantageous. The American dollar's value, set by the President on January 31, 1934, at slightly less than 60 per cent of its former gold value, was later reduced further to 50 per cent. Each nation thus arbitrarily fixed the "worth" of its currency, inflating or deflating the supply of money in circulation and producing higher or lower domestic prices that did not reflect world prices necessarily at all. Since states frequently also established direct control over foreign exchange, so that it became illegal to buy or sell such exchange other than at officially determined rates, trade lagged.

The Germans under Hitler isolated their domestic economy entirely from the world market by creating special marks selling at a 20 to 35 per cent discount, and making them available to particular states for purchases from Germany. By using "blocked" marks, the Germans succeeded in harnessing much of Central Europe's economy to their preparations for war. They would, for example, import wheat from Bulgaria and pay into Bulgaria's account in Germany in blocked marks that were good only for purposes of buying German goods (and therefore could not be converted). They would then license Bulgaria to import specified goods which were nonessential to Germany's war effort or in great surplus. In this way Germany flooded Central Europe with gigantic supplies of aspirin, cuckoo clocks, and harmonicas.

In effect these procedures reduced international trade to a primitive barter system. Once a state became entangled in this net it was difficult to withdraw. Not only were other markets scarce, but unless new exports to Germany were permitted, no blocked marks would be made available, or licenses granted to use them, on what was already owed.

Such restrictive devices encouraged the growing bilateralization of trade. Quotas and special and blocked currencies vitiated the effect of unconditional most-favored-nation clauses. It was soon necessary, because of the general difficulties of converting currencies, for nations to conclude clearing agreements and establish clearinghouses. Through these clearinghouses, which were repositories for foreign exchange, nation A's debts to B could be balanced off against B's to A's. Since it was unwise for nation A to develop too large a surplus of B's currency while needing more, let us say, than could readily be attained of nation C's (unless C would accept B's from A in payment of A's debts—which it might or might not), this encouraged bilateralism still more. In 1937 there were 170 clearing agreements in effect—an indication both of distress in the international economy and of the attempt to find a way out through economic nationalism.

7 Economic Recovery After World War II: The First Phase

IT was clear even during the preoccupation of fighting World War II that a new and greater effort would be needed in the postwar period if the economic aftermath were not to be even more unfortunate than after World War I. The devices of economic nationalism, although tenaciously clung to and utilized, had not brought any promise of real improvement. At no time following the Great Depression had these devices been widely abandoned, and the experience of 1919–1924 amply demonstrated that even if they had been allowed to lapse prior to World War II, they would inevitably be reintroduced. And so they were.

Some lessons were learned from previous experience. Although the Germans had been responsible for World War II in a way far beyond their part in causing World War I, reparations were relatively small and for the most part to be made in the return by Germany of assets seized abroad, and in goods to be sent over a period of years to those nations whose lands she had devastated.[8] The reparations from the other Axis Powers were handled in similarly moderate fashion. The German currency was re-established on a firm footing in 1948 in their zones by the United States, Britain, and France, and the West German economy was allowed to revive. The same held true for Italy and Japan.

The question of war debts was avoided from the beginning by the use of the Lend-Lease device by the United States. The money and supplies made available by the United States to its allies after the enactment of Lend-Lease in 1941 were, for all practical purposes, to be regarded as an American contribution toward the winning of the war, and any repayments were to be on such terms as would not interfere with the revival of world trade.

Despite these improvements over the previous handling of reparations and war debts, economic recovery continued to be a formidable problem. For one thing, although America emerged from the war with an intact and expanded industrial plant, Europe's productive resources were in a shambles. The physical destruction to industry of World War II had not been more or less restricted to the north of France and Belgium as in World War I. The bombs and rockets rained on England, and the saturation bombing of Germany, together with the fighting across Italy and France, had produced much worse chaos. Not only was Europe's plant so much destroyed but the immediate postwar policy of the Western Allies in Germany compounded the problem. Many remaining German industrial plants in the Ruhr and elsewhere were

---

[8] In the Soviet Zone of Germany a much more ruthless policy was, however, put into effect.

dismantled or demolished in the name of eliminating German war capacity.

This policy was soon reversed, beginning with the realization on the part of the United States that the alternative to a revival of German industry was the continued drain of American tax dollars to support the German population. It also became evident that Western Europe's industrial complex could not be restored to vigor if a major (German) part of it was artificially kept down. Some other way of ensuring that German warmaking potential would not again be mobilized against the West had to be found. In time this approach led to the European Community institutions of the present day.

Complications in restoring European economic health also stemmed from Britain's precarious financial situation right after World War II. Once the banker of the world, Britain had been forced to liquidate the greater part of her investments to finance the war. This meant she had to increase exports to compensate for the foreign interest payments no longer coming in. It also meant, since many of her investments were in the United States, that she suffered from a shortage of dollars. This led her to currency controls and import quotas, both of them dampers on international trade. The effects of these restrictions were compounded since she remained the financial leader of the "sterling bloc."

The immediate need was for pump-priming—or, even more basically, for providing some pumps to prime. Europe could not be restored to industrial and financial health without American aid. This aid came in the Marshall Plan—about $15 billions of it when the program ended in June 1952. It represented a massive infusion of American aid to stimulate European productivity and bridge the "dollar shortage" (i.e., the lack of dollars in European hands to purchase their needs). By 1959–1960 this program and its successors had successfully bridged the gap. Throughout the 1949–1959 decade unilateral dollar payments by the United States for its military establishment abroad and for nonmilitary grant aid was kept fairly constant at $4 to $5 billions a year. At the price of the United States' incurring a deficit of about $1.5 billions a year in its balance of payments,[9] Europe's production was reaching healthy limits and her dollar and gold reserves were restored to safe levels.

Increased production logically involved an ultimate expansion of world trade. United States measures in this direction brought a further liberalization of the Reciprocal Trade Agreement program inaugurated in 1934. By 1945 the United States had concluded bilateral agreements with thirty states, lowering rates from the Smoot-Hawley tariff base in return for equivalent concessions. All such agreements included the most-favored-nation clause. Amendments in 1945 and 1949 permitted a tariff level at 12.5 per cent of the basic 41.5 per cent Smoot-Hawley ad valorem rate.

---

[9] The balance of payments should not be confused with the balance of trade. The latter is the measure of exports against imports, for the United States or for any other nation. The former measures the total flow of dollars (or gold), for whatever reasons, in and out of the country in a given year. Consequently the balance of payments includes trade, investments, services, etc.

Full concessions were not made in every case, so that the actual effect was more limited. Import quotas on agricultural imports also continued. This was no easy problem. When Denmark in 1953 complained about her import quota of 200 thousand pounds of butter a year, the United States countered by saying that 279 million pounds of United States butter were then in storage.

The General Agreement on Tariffs and Trade (GATT), which came into effect in 1948, marked the beginnings of an international solution to the trade problem which went beyond unilateral dollar grants and credits and bilateral trade agreements. This multilateral convention brought together the results of 123 simultaneous negotiations of 23 states in 1947, covering 45,000 items. By virtue of the most-favored-nation clause the bilateral concessions granted were in many cases multilateralized. This was the first of five tariff negotiation conferences held up to 1961. There were 37 contracting parties in mid-1961, responsible for over 80 per cent of international trade. Their tariff agreements under GATT probably affected more than 50 per cent of their trade even though import quotas and other non-tariff restrictions on their trade were not fully overcome by any means.[10]

GATT was intended as a stop-gap arrangement until a more elaborate international trade organization, as a specialized organ under the UN, was ratified and came into effect. But no such organization came about and GATT in effect filled the gap.

Restoration of Europe's industrial facilities, temporary infusions of outright United States aid, liberalization of United States tariffs, the creation of GATT, all assisted the recovery process. But the struggle to establish free convertibility of the major world currencies lasted until 1958.

So long as Europe's currencies were not freely convertible into each other (let alone into gold), complications remained formidable in making economic gains on an international basis. Western European nations, loath to allow convertibility, at first set their own values on their currencies, with detrimental effects. The "proper" level for an internal price structure in many cases proved an improper level for carrying on international trade. If a country whose currency had been inflated by war loans during the war set the price of its currency lower than real values made necessary, it encouraged further inflation at home. If it set the price higher than real values it discouraged its foreign trade: imports would tend to be maintained because their currency would buy more than with a realistic exchange rate; but exports would slow down because of their excessive cost to foreigners.

Of course, nations have not been unaware of it when, especially for internal reasons, they have pegged currency values at artificial levels. There is not only the evidence of the effect on trade but also the day-by-day reports from the free money markets which are clues too. And if a state lifts some or all restric-

---

[10] See *The Activities of GATT, 1959/60*, General Agreement on Tariffs and Trade, Geneva, May 1960.

tions on an artificially high currency there is an immediate drain on gold and foreign exchange reserves. When Britain in July of 1947 freed the pound, its holder could (under certain conditions) go to the bank and draw $4.03 in dollars. Since the pound at the time was selling for $2.55 to $2.65 in the free money market this meant a clear profit of the difference plus having funds in a "harder" currency. Britain lost gold and dollars so drastically that in August 1947, she had to restrict convertibility once more.

Because of both the dollar shortage and the obvious overvaluing of most other currencies in terms of the dollar, in September of 1949 the United Kingdom devalued the pound sterling from $4.03 to $2.80. Many countries followed suit. France had even earlier (late in 1947) devalued the franc from 119 to the dollar down to 214 as the basic rate, with special, even more attractive rates being offered in foreign trade transactions.

These moves brought controlled values closer to free market values but there were still gaps. In October 1953, the French franc was going for slightly under 400 to the dollar in Geneva. In 1947–1948, it was selling for around 330. For comparison, in October 1953, the British pound was selling for about $2.62; in 1947–1948 it had been worth about 10¢ less. So it can be seen that although the nominal Anglo-French exchange rates for each other's currencies remained the same after 1949, their actual values changed greatly. The effect on trade can easily be understood.

The establishment of the European Payments Union (EPU) in July 1950, helped considerably toward making European currencies convertible, although still in a definitely controlled manner. The EPU acted in effect as a clearinghouse for the central banks of the member states to balance off accounts with one another. It helped to resolve the fundamental difficulty of bilateralism: one nation rarely buys and sells equally from and to another. It also helped provide a substitute for the loss of the gold standard. But it could not do away with fundamental long-continued disequilibrium.

The overcoming of the "dollar shortage" resulted toward the end of 1958 in the restoration of external convertibility by the major European nations; this marked a real step forward. In effect, today, despite certain restrictions, European currencies, including pounds sterling, can be freely converted into dollars (and dollars have a fixed relationship to gold). While this is not the gold standard, it will do. The EPU, no longer needed, was phased out in 1958 and replaced by the broader European Monetary Agreement (EMA).

8 Economic Recovery After World War II: The Second Phase

BY 1958–1959 recovery was in full swing. The great trading nations of the world moved into the contemporary phase. Production was no longer the great problem. Attention now was focused on further rationalization of international trade, especially in view of the impact of the European Free

Trade Association (EFTA) and the European Common Market (or European Economic Community—the newest organ of the "European Community").

The European Common Market and Euratom treaties signed in Rome on March 25, 1957, by France, West Germany, Italy, Belgium, the Netherlands, and Luxembourg, considerably extended the basic concepts of the European Coal and Steel Community founded by those same nations in 1952. The principle of a common external tariff on coal and steel, coupled with no tariffs on such products *within* the Community, was now extended to other goods. By the end of 1961 progressive tariff cuts within the Common Market had already reduced tariffs by forty per cent. By January 1, 1966, the European Economic Community (EEC) had succeeded, ahead of schedule, in bringing the common external tariff into effect. The new timetable called for the abolition of all internal tariffs on industrial goods by January 1, 1967. Only in the important agricultural sphere was there still a question mark. The crisis in the EEC which began with de Gaulle's veto of plans in this area on July 1, 1965, will deserve further attention later.

Confronted by this establishment of the community of the "inner six," an "outer seven" (Austria, Denmark, Norway, Portugal, Sweden, Switzerland, and the United Kingdom—with Finland joining as an "associate") formed the EFTA in 1960. The EFTA program envisaged the elimination of customs barriers among the member states but the continuation of separate national customs for the goods of non-members, together with provisions to prevent imports into low-custom EFTA nations followed by re-exports within EFTA. Full realization of these goals, including abolition of import quotas, was scheduled for the end of 1966.

One may well ask: why *two* West European trade organizations? The reasons are essentially although not entirely political. Those nations who belong to the EFTA are not enthusiastic about the European Community goals of economic-political unity. They wish a looser association.[11] Even so, the United Kingdom in mid-1961 requested discussions looking to joining the Common Market—a move vetoed finally by de Gaulle on January 14, 1963. The British request had been followed by the request of other states to join the Common Market. Failure to achieve agreement meant that the EFTA and EEC went their own respective paths. As a consequence traditional European trade patterns are undergoing grave distortions. Austria's trade is a good example. So is Switzerland's. By mid-1965 EFTA's exports to the EEC had almost ceased to grow. While the EFTA nations were highly disturbed, the EEC nations pointed instead to the growth of *intra*-community trade by 168 per cent between 1958 and 1964.

The EEC's effects on trade have been felt as well by the United States and other major trade nations such as Japan. These effects would be of serious

---

[11] See below, Chapter 27, for further discussion of these political aspects of European development.

enough dimensions even if the problems were confined to what has already been stated. But the EEC, like the EFTA, also has "associate" members. The list of these associates is constantly growing but its dimensions are well illustrated by the EEC's Second Development Fund for 1963–1968. Of the $730 million to be spent, $666 million is earmarked for 17 already associated African states, plus Madagascar. In mid-1965 the EEC was negotiating associated status with Tunis and Morocco while Nigeria had just accepted associated status.

In 1962, responding to these problems, the United States replaced the old Reciprocal Trade Agreement Act with the new Trade Expansion Act authorizing a further fifty per cent reciprocal reduction in tariffs. This led directly to the "Kennedy Round" of negotiations within GATT, beginning officially in May 1964. Since these negotiations were now so complicated they continued through 1965 and 1966 without result. The expectation was for some tariff reductions beginning in 1967, but the great problem of relating EFTA and the EEC more effectively, remained.

Concurrently with these efforts to further rationalize international trade came concern over the "gold drain" from the United States which in turn led to preliminary discussions on a more far-reaching international financial stabilization agreement.

The "gold drain" which caused some alarm by 1960–1961 was a direct reflection of Europe's regained economic health. The outpouring of dollars had generated an increase of United States merchandise exports of 64 per cent between 1950 and 1958, as compared to an increase of 44 per cent in merchandise imports. But between 1955 and 1959 exports increased only 14 per cent and imports increased 33 per cent, narrowing the excess of exports over imports from $2.9 to $1.1 billions. Net dollar holdings abroad were correspondingly increased and the effect was compounded by the $4 to $5 billions spent or given abroad for the military establishment and grant aid, and by the $2 billions increase in new foreign investment by the United States. The greater flow of dollars abroad in 1958 and 1959, plus the conversion of dollars by nations increasing their gold reserves, produced a net loss of $3.3 billions in United States monetary gold. But in 1959 gold purchases were already slackening, compared to 1958, even though the net outflow from the United States of gold *and* dollars increased from $3.4 billions to $3.7 billions.[12] The net outflow of capital in 1964 was $8.1 billion, although the U.S. gold loss was only $125 million. The net gold loss in 1965 was $1.65 billions, partly reflecting France's policy of converting her substantial dollar holdings to gold in order to make the franc a true world currency.

The problem was not as great as it seemed but it implied an increase in United States exports or a decrease in the flow of dollars abroad if the United States balance of payments was to be equalized. Because of the role of the

---

12 Data taken from *Exports, Imports, and the United States Balance of International Payments*, Senate Document No. 105, 86th Congress, 2d Session, April 1960.

dollar as a world reserve currency, however, full equalization was not readily attainable or desirable.

In considering the balance of payments one must not overlook the balance of trade within it. In all the years since the outbreak of World War I the United States has not had an import surplus.[13] In 1958 merchandise imports were $13.0 billions and exports were $16.3 billions; in 1959 imports were $15.3 billions and exports, $16.3 billions. If United States spending for the military establishment and grant aid abroad were sharply curtailed and the average import-export balance remained the same, a dollar shortage could reassert itself. The export surplus in 1964 amounted to $6.7 billion, $2.6 billion above 1963. But the 1964 export surplus was still $1.4 billion below the 1964 net capital outflow. Since the 1965 export surplus was down to $4.8 billion, and the deficits continued, the U.S. imposed "voluntary" restrictions on private capital movements.

The gold drain is thus the product both of the United States balance of payments and the use by other nations of dollars as liquid reserves. If the dollar is to be used as an international standard, it must be available in large amounts to other states. If these nations then convert dollars, the United States loses gold. The answer being sought must keep dollars available while reducing by agreement the amplitude and frequency of surprise "raids" upon the United States supply of gold.

9 The Emerging Nations and Developmental Aid

so far we have considered contemporary international economic problems primarily in terms of the major financial and industrial powers, who are also the great consumer nations. While trade is most abundant between already industrialized nations, another important world economic relationship is between those nations and the vast majority of "newly developing" nations who generally consume much less but who produce the bulk of the raw materials converted by the industrial giants into finished products. Just as within the United States the direct rewards to the farmers for their produce represent a surprisingly small amount of the cost of the processed food products, so too, in the world as a whole, the suppliers of raw materials enjoy much less of the prosperity (and defense capabilities) which their position as initial suppliers might seem to imply. A quick glance back at Table 2, as to the sources of major materials imported by the United States in its missile program, and a look at the living standards of almost all of the suppliers, will confirm this statement. Only Canada, South Africa, and Portugal are exceptions, and these are all "Western" nations.

---

[13] See Walther Lederer, Samuel Pizer, and Evelyn M. Parrish, "The U.S. Balance of International Payments: First Quarter 1966," *Survey of Current Business*, June 1966, for complete data on U.S. balance of payments from 1946 through 1965.

If we take the figures for basic production already presented earlier (in Table 3) and combine the 1963 production of only six nations (the Soviet Union, France, the United Kingdom, West Germany, the United States, and Japan), and then subtract this total from world production, we reach some startling conclusions. For coal, we find that the entire rest of the world produces only one third of the supply (661.8 of the total 1929.0 millions of metric tons). Electricity figures are approximately in the same ratio (856.3 out of 2,849.2 billions of kilowatt hours). Crude steel figures show an even further disproportion for the rest of the world (103.7 out of 386.6 millions of tons). Even the cement figures show the same imbalance (154.3 of 368.0 millions of tons). Finally, for oil—in which Western Europe is notably deficient —the rest of the world produces slightly less than half the total (614.6 out of 1303.5 million barrels). These figures dramatize the gulf between the new nations and the fully industrialized powers. They go far toward explaining what some have called the "North-South axis" of world politics which cuts across the "East-West" rivalries of the Cold War. They explain much about the poverty of the new nations, about their concern over what they call "neo-colonialism." For although the former colonial areas are now free, they remain still poor and very dependent economically upon the rich nations. This is especially true where they are heavily oriented to "one crop" or "one commodity" production (see especially Chapter 28).

Thus the passing of colonial imperialism, while it has snapped the political bonds formerly holding much of the world in subjection, has not severed the economic umbilical cord which ties these states to a highly dependent status mitigated only partially by the possibility of attempting to play East off against West. Thus we see an important reason for the ambivalence of the "Afro-Asian bloc" of states in their behavior both inside and outside the United Nations. The continued existence of the Commonwealth of Nations of former British colonies and their participation in the "Colombo Plan" of development, and the marked tendency of the French-speaking African nations to cultivate a continued close economic association with France in the EEC, each illustrate one strong trend among the newly developing nations. The opposite strong trend by such members of the Afro-Asian bloc as the United Arab Republic, Ghana, and Guinea, has been to induce the ideologically-opposed industrial giants to bid for their favor while leaning more in the Soviet direction. This tactical disagreement shows up very strongly in Afro-Asian voting in the UN and in the variety of conferences held and organizations created by these states.

Within this context the dimensions of the problem of foreign or "developmental" aid take on their full meaning. The problem quite naturally is viewed very differently by the various participants, although to both the economically weak and strong it has not only economic but political-military features. Even if ideological competition did not enter into the picture, both the West and the Soviet Union would be concerned with the problem simply because of their mutual although unequal need for the expansion of world trade. Since ideological and political considerations do enter in, certain distortions in what has been done in the name of foreign aid appear.

In the United States program in the 1950's there was a distinct tendency to weight the "aid program" heavily in the direction of military aid to friendly states, with much smaller amounts going for truly economic aid. (In 1955, 66 per cent went to military aid; in 1965, 66 per cent went to economic aid.) In later years the United States programs have placed great stress on agricultural, medical, educational, and "infrastructure" (access roads, communications, etc.) development. Some tactical changes can also be noted. The United States program is no longer so indiscriminate and "gift-oriented"; the concepts of selectivity and "self-help" are now fundamental. For the fiscal year beginning July 1, 1966, the United States plan was to concentrate 92 per cent of direct country assistance on twenty of seventy nations who would receive aid, with 84 per cent of developmental aid going to eight essentially friendly, relatively important states (Brazil, Chile, Colombia, India, Korea, Nigeria, Pakistan, and Turkey).[14] Because of the U.S. balance of payments problem there has been a further shift in how such funds can be spent. Beginning in 1959, aid funds were limited, when feasible, to the purchase of *American* goods and services. As a consequence the percentage of Agency for International Development (AID) funds spent for U.S. goods and services rose. It was 42 per cent in 1960; the planning figure for 1967 was 88 per cent.

Other non-Communist programs have become important. In 1965, Canada, Western Europe, and Japan provided over $2 billion in economic assistance to Asia, Africa, and Latin America. Added to this is the impact of multilateral institutions such as the World Bank and the new Asian Development Bank. The World Bank's loans by June 30, 1965, had reached the impressive total of $8,772,000,000 in 424 loans for one thousand projects in 77 countries, two-thirds of it for the development of improved electric power and transportation facilities. Even so, in almost half of the 80 less developed nations who belong to the World Bank, per capita income stood at $120 per year and the percentage improvement in the recent past has been one per cent or less.

One dismal aspect of the problem is food. Pressures on food supplies in the emerging nations have been increasing. In Chapter 3 we saw how fast population is expanding in these areas, faster than increases in the availability of food. India, who successfully increased food production twenty per cent between 1955 and 1965, experienced near-famine in 1964–1965 as a result of bad weather. Taking the UN Food and Agricultural Organization standard of 2,360 calories a day, in 1959–1960 Japan just met this figure, while Oceania had 123 per cent of the minimum. The 1959–1961 levels for Communist Asia stood at 76 percent, while East Africa was at 97 percent of the standard.

These figures show the complexity of the problem. Although the newer na-

---

14 Figures taken from the speech by David E. Bell, Administrator of the U.S. Agency for International Development, Memphis, Tennessee, February 21, 1966.

tions aspire to industrialize, their immediate and primary economic problem is actually the less glamorous task of not going hungry. Compounding this problem by 1967 was the fact that U.S. grain reserves (on which India, for example, had come to depend) were no longer large.

The Communist aid programs have been of smaller proportions. Much of their aid has also been military in character, the total between 1956 and 1963 being estimated at three billion dollars as compared with an estimated total for economic aid credits of five billion. The Soviet economic aid program, heavily oriented at first toward impressive but frequently nonproductive facilities, has more lately been pointed toward the creation of industry and such works as the Aswan Dam. Initially because buildings, airports, and paved streets appealed to prestige-conscious new nations in a hurry, the Soviet program (financed through very low interest, long-term loans) enjoyed considerable political success. Lately, however, as the true dimensions of the problem have appeared, and especially in the light of Soviet weakness in the agricultural sector, the glamour of such programs has diminished greatly. Soviet aid (and Communist aid generally) has always been more focused, especially toward certain nations in Africa and Asia. Communist economic aid commitments have fluctuated: the 1964 commitments were something over a billion dollars (compared to the U.S. figure of $3.25 billion appropriated); in 1963 the figure was only a fourth as large; and a couple of years before that, it was roughly at the 1964 level. The Communist one billion dollars ($700 million from the Soviets) went mostly toward new steel plants ($280 million to the United Arab Republic, $150 million to Algeria, $200 million for India). The Chinese efforts in the foreign aid field are obviously politically motivated in the highest degree since their own economic needs are so pressing. (In the later chapters we shall see the competition between the Soviet and Chinese programs, especially in Africa.)

The contemporary problems of international economics remain, as before, complex and far-reaching, especially in view of the growth in institutionalization in Europe. It is apparent, twenty years or more after World War II, that unlike twenty years after World War I, the economic system enjoys considerable health if we restrict our observations to the major industrialized nations. Their problems arise not from stagnation but from growth. In the newly emerging nations, by contrast, despite strenuous efforts to reach economic viability, the gains are still limited and the problems very formidable.

CHAPTER 8

War

It is not the object of war to annihilate those who have given provocation for it, but to cause them to mend their ways.

POLYBIUS
Histories

Till the world comes to an end, the ultimate decision will rest with the sword.

KAISER WILHELM II

T HE acuteness of the problem of war in our time needs no particular stressing; it is apparent to all. Especially when the effects of nuclear weapons are considered, the dangers from fallout alone reach staggering levels—affecting neutrals along with belligerents, for the winds do not recognize national frontiers. The rational assessment of these dangers has not resulted either in the destruction of stocks of arms or their effective control (see Chapter 14). The levels of armaments, both qualitatively and quantitatively, are now greater than ever before. At the same time resort to the classic practice of interstate war has been quite modest since 1945, especially in view of the great growth in the number of actors in the system (the number of sovereign states who each dispose of some armed forces).

Wars fought since 1945 have continued to be conventional despite the availability of nuclear arms to at least some of the participants (as in the case of the United States in the Korean War). The deterrent and restraining effects of nuclear weapons have without doubt played a significant role in keeping recurrent areas of conflict such as Berlin from becoming the cause for war. Under these conditions resort to actions involving grave risks of war (and especially nuclear war) are actions of enormous consequence not to be taken without the most restrained and careful consideration. Yet great powers do at times take such risks, as the Cuban Missile Crisis of 1962 (see Chapter 11) indicates. And the marked increase since 1945 in resort to internal and civil wars may reflect as much the instability of many of the newer nations as it represents a conscious or premeditated avoidance of conventional war. Many of them have not reached a stage in development where resort to war with their neighbors is really likely.

It is true, however, that participation in war via "indirect aggression" has become marked and is a striking feature of post-World-War-II warfare. Intervention with armed forces, either without overt acknowledgment of the action, or without a formal declaration of war, is a contemporary characteristic of warfare. The Viet-Nam War is like the Korean War in this respect. So is the Indian-Chinese border war. Such undeclared or unadmitted wars are both easier to limit and easier to terminate: factors of great utility under present conditions.

I The Causes of War

NOT every nation fighting a war is doing so because it desires war per se, any more than hold-up victims freely choose to be robbed. If a nation is attacked it must either give in or fight. So much is at least logically clear. Normally nations that are attacked do chose to fight. Admitting that the nominal attacker may not bear the entire guilt for the conflict, and that the nation attacked may not be entirely blameless,[1] we are still able to conclude on the most elemental level that wars occur because one sovereign nation decides to attack another. But *why* does one nation attack the other?

Whole libraries have been written to answer this question. Quincy Wright's monumental two-volume *A Study of War* is only one readily available illustration of the exhaustive and painstaking scholarly work in this field. When Andrew Carnegie established the Endowment for International Peace in 1910, he instructed the trustees to devote their efforts to accomplishing "the speedy abolition of international war between so-called civilized nations." Then they were to use his millions on the "next most degrading remaining evil." [2] It need hardly be added that the money is still being spent on doing away with war. Nobel's millions have gone, somewhat similarly, for "peace prizes" that have not yet been any more successful in revealing the way to abolish war. Naturally, the search has continued, and a great number of suggestions have been forthcoming.

These suggestions on the causes of war fall into two categories: the simple (or unifactor) and the complex (or multifactor). Each of these two types can be used in an attempt to explain war in general, or a given war in particular.

Taking particular wars first, it can be asked, for example, what caused the Korean War? The answer on the simple level is that North Korea committed aggression. This is perfectly true insofar as it goes, but it is merely the prelude to a more searching question: why did North Korea commit aggression? Those who pursue the inquiry this far often receive a simple answer: the Russians told them to (which may or may not be true). But then one must ask, why did the Russians want them to? And again the simple answer is: they

---

[1] It is often most difficult to decide *who* is the attacker. Aggression and what constitutes aggression have never been very satisfactorily defined—at least in any way that a large number of states was prepared to accept as legally binding. See the chapters on collective security.

[2] See Holmes Welch, "Philanthropy Uninhibited: The Ford Foundation," *The Reporter*, March 17, 1953, p. 22.

want to communize the globe. But to seek further, why do the Russians want to communize the globe? Because they want power, is the most frequent simple answer. Why do they want power?—because it is human nature to want to dominate. In that case, why is human nature what it is?

Superficialities must be put aside if the question is really to be answered, for here we have at last reached something basically complex. We know that people are what they are because they are the product of their heredity and their environment. Unfortunately there are as many different "heredities" and "environments" as there are people, even though each person has much in common with the others: all people are human. Yet as an explanation of the Korean War, an ultimate simple answer that people are human leaves a faintly unsatisfied feeling.

The alternative is to embark upon the complex labor of determining why the particular national groups reacted as they did. We can search at the outset for the more complex causes: the revulsion of Asians against the remnants of Western imperialism; the rising tide of nationalism in Asia; the frustrated historical experience of the Korean people, always either divided or dominated; the distortion of the natural (or at least former) flow of trade in the area; and the galvanizing effect and example of Communist China's blustering new independence: they threw the Western "foreign devils" out.

These complex explanations, although they have a more solid ring, fail to explain why at a particular moment in 1950 all this culminated in North Korea's attack upon South Korea. What led the government in power to choose that course of action just then? What internal conflicts of view existed within the administration, and why did those who advocated attack gain the upper hand at that time? These questions are rarely answered in any trustworthy way: the memoirs of statesmen are frequently too distorted with bias, and many facts are never known at all.

Sometimes the trend of events and causation is so obvious that the coming of war can be predicted with reasonable sureness (as with World War II), but *when* is either guess, clairvoyance, or access to highly classified and reliable intelligence data. At other times wars either burst upon a startled world (the Korean War), or else fail to occur although expected (the World War III predicted by many in 1948–1949). Once a war has in fact occurred, some explanation for its occurrence can be found. Yet this approach does not help much in regard to the many wars for which impressive causes can (or could) be found, and whose happening could be very adequately explained, but which have never occurred at all! As a matter of fact, explaining a given war either on a simple or complex basis tends often to be ex post facto reasoning.

Explaining individual wars with any accuracy is extremely difficult; explaining wars as *phenomena* is somewhat easier (and perhaps more profitable as a subject for study), although any answers given or hypotheses advanced are necessarily in terms of generalities. Here again war as an institution can be explained either on the simple, unifactor level or the complex, multifactor level.

Lenin chose a simple explanation when he asserted that wars are caused by the stresses and strains of monopolistic capitalism. Speaking of colonial imperialism in particular, he asserted that wars occur under capitalism because private business, finding itself soon in danger of oversupplying its own domestic market, must continually expand to find new markets and sources of raw materials, and new possibilities for the more lucrative investment of profits. Lenin concluded that this leads in the first stage to the colonial conquests by the capitalistic powers described in the previous chapter. But after all the available lands have been expropriated and exploited, the incessant demand for more leads to wars among the capitalist powers themselves. In Lenin's view, capitalism caused wars. It followed that with the destruction of private capitalism wars would no longer occur.[3]

The Nye (Munitions) Committee of the United States Senate (1934–1936) took a second simple approach to the causes of war—what Charles A. Beard called "the devil theory of war." [4] They sought to find the explanation for America's participation in World War I by ferreting out the ways in which they believed the "international bankers" and the "munitions makers" had sought to make profits out of the shedding of American blood. It followed that, if their guilt could be shown and their future activities carefully shackled, America would be drawn into no further wars. While the committee did unearth evidences of actual war-promoting activity, the results of their probe were not very useful as a basic explanation of war.

A third simple explanation for war as a phenomenon is to regard its occurrence as the work of evil men in positions of political power. The demand to "Hang the Kaiser!" was a logical sequel to the belief that Wilhelm the Sabre-Rattler had unleashed "his" war upon an innocent and unsuspecting world. With somewhat more justice various of the Nuremberg Trial defendants were dispatched via the hangman's noose as penalty for their connivance in aggressive war. Yet, although they were undoubtedly the human instruments through which the aggression was committed, to call them—or even Hitler himself—the "cause" of World War II would be a drastic over-simplification.

As a fourth simple explanation there is the contention that wars are caused by propagandists who poison the minds of men and the relations of nations, causing them to regard one another with a suspicion which soon becomes open hostility. It was asserted in the United States, for instance, in the period between the two world wars that British propagandists, who had (because of their control of the international cables) an ample opportunity to slant war news published in the United States in their favor, played the decisive role in causing American belligerency. Yet if national interests had not already inclined their listeners toward a sympathetic hearing and acceptance, it is extremely doubtful that the propaganda alone would have achieved this result.

[3] V. I. Lenin, *Imperialism: The Highest Stage of Capitalism.*
[4] The name Beard gave to one of his books.

A fifth simple explanation for war as a phenomenon is that it is caused by the lust of men for power. This is a highly plausible contention, particularly because of the rather implausible nature of the four simple "causes" already enumerated. It is especially plausible because the assertion is with difficulty subjected to empirical or logical analysis. A lust for power is by nature boundless, irrational, and illogical. The wish to dominate cannot be logically explained other than in terms of itself: i.e., the wish to dominate. If one accepts the will to power as a characteristic of man, and of men in groups, and if one admits its basically irrational character, it is difficult to reject or refute it as *the* cause for war.

2   *The Will to Power as a Cause of War*

RARELY does the leader of a nation (or the people of that nation) announce that he or they are going to war because of their desire to conquer and dominate. He states what is sought through and in war in nice-sounding phrases, such as "justice," "honor," and "duty" (to oneself or one's allies). His choice of phrases may arise from feelings of delicacy or prudence or from unconscious self-deception. Observers of this phenomenon have often concluded that the leaders are really fighting because they *want power*. But since it is unwise to confess a lust for power lest one prematurely stir up too formidable opposition, the leaders are alleged to disguise the will to power for public inspection in more appetizing and "respectable" dress. As Machiavelli pointed out, the vulgar (the many) see the appearance of the thing rather than the thing itself.

There is a great deal of shrewd insight in the view just presented. But it is likely that, applied in the great majority of cases, it is too shrewd—at least where the deception practiced is considered to be so very often deliberate. What historical evidence is available on the motivations of leaders and peoples who resorted to war indicates that most often they believed what they said. Anyone, for example, reading British Foreign Secretary Grey's memoirs [5] cannot help feeling that Grey was honestly persuaded of the truth of what he wrote. For that matter, although Adolf Hitler's *Mein Kampf* is filled with sound and fury and running over with redundancies, a certain ferocious sincerity shines through. While Hitler did not refrain from fabricating border incidents to justify his aggressions, he can hardly be charged with deliberately and knowingly frustrating German national interests as he conceived them to be, and subordinating them consciously to his personal craving for power per se. Actually, when we explain the actions of other nations in terms of a search for, or will to, power, we really mean either that (1) we are opposed to their actions, (2) we disagree with their intentions, or (3) we fail to see any ultimate sense in what they are doing. *Their* values being irrational by *our* stand-

---

[5] See Viscount Grey of Fallodon, *Twenty-Five Years, 1892–1916.*

ards, we describe their actions with an irrational term—the will to power.

There can be less quarrel with the assertion that nations and their leaders deceive themselves by rationalizing their will to power unconsciously behind a respectable façade. But even here a serious qualification needs to be made. Can we be so sure that it is a will to power per se that is being rationalized, or is it more accurate to say that certain national interests that are achievable only through war, and that are the actual incentives to war, are hidden behind a smoke screen (deliberately or unconsciously) of values and attitudes to which all nations give abstract assent? We saw in Chapter 2 how, to use the phraseology we used there, "national" values are "internationalized." Whether this smoke-screen process is truly a resort to deception depends more on whether the particular nation convinces itself of what it asserts, or feels that its position is false, rather than on any objective criteria as such. To say that a nation distorts the truth presupposes the existence of universally agreed truths to begin with.

From both the theoretical and the practical standpoints the view that war is caused by a will to power and a desire to dominate presents difficulties.

From the theoretical standpoint the proposition has the weakness referred to in the beginning—namely, it is unanalyzable other than as a whole. It resists further breakdown, classification, and analysis by parts. A will to power is a will to power; there is not much more that can be said other than that it brings war in its train. The disease has no remedy, for it is born in man. To say that this proposition is unanalyzable other than as a whole is not to say that it is untrue. But does the will to power serve as an adequate explanation of the causes of war? Here we touch upon the more fundamental weakness, for if the will to power fundamentally explained war it would follow that wars would be indulged in by all states, large or small, and as often as possible. But if this is not so, in fact if some states fight not at all, or hardly at all, then obviously other factors not described by the omnibus phrase, "a will to power," are at work in causing or failing to cause wars.

This leads us to the practical difficulty with the view. If the will to power, operating among all peoples and all states, nevertheless causes war sometimes and not always, then it is more correct and more practical to reduce the view to the proposition that man has pugnacious as well as peaceful tendencies, and when he is sufficiently aroused over something he will, under certain conditions, fight. By contrast, his wish to dominate is, under other circumstances, carefully restrained. In the end the assertion that men and nations have a will to power may say little more than the obvious and yet much less than is useful or helpful in making any progress. It is very much like saying that, as a general rule, men who are alive desire to stay alive and will devote their energies to it. As a correct statement of a fundamental truth this is unexceptional. Yet it serves as little more than a take-off point for further investigation. The investigation must center on what it is that men become aroused over, and what conditions normally need to be present for this arousal to produce open conflict.

3 National Interests as a Cause of War

IT might at first seem that the assertion that nations resort to war because they seek the consummation of their national interests is merely a new simple explanation of war to replace the other simple ones previously advanced. But it is actually more than that, for national interests are *different* for each state, and, therefore, produce greatly varying foreign policies, whereas the will to power must be considered a substantially identical trait in all men (and states), potentially inclining them all in the *same* degree to basically similar policies.

Not all nations resort to war to achieve their national interests. Many national interests for particular states are such that they do not have to resort to war. If they were attacked, they might have to, but so long as they are not the victims of aggression, will to power or no will to power, they remain at peace. Whether they do fight or not depends upon the nature of those interests in a given case and upon the objective conditions in the world at large that impinge upon those interests.

In a sovereign-state system it can hardly be overemphasized that war and peace depend upon the decisions of each and every state. War is always potential in such a system. What converts potential into actual strife is an incompatibility between the vital interests of two or more states that is pushed to a point where one or more of the nations involved decide to use force. The "cause" of the war is that one nation cannot obtain what it desires without fighting. What it is that is considered worth bloodshed by a given state may seem trivial or inexcusable by others. It may even be, from an objective viewpoint, entirely trivial. Whether what is fought over is worth the fighting is, however, beside the point. It has only *to be considered to be worth fighting over*, and only by one of the combatants. The others may merely fight because they have been attacked and their security has been imperiled. The decision of the attacker to resort to war may have come as a surprise to the nation attacked, the latter not having understood how far the deterioration of relations had gone. Although the United States realized in December 1941, that relations with Japan had entered a critical phase, the actual attack came as a great surprise. The nation attacked might even, under certain conditions where its prestige was not already in jeopardy, have been prepared to sacrifice whatever it was that led to the attack. More frequently this is not the case, but it can occur.

This is why in one fundamental sense the cause or causes of war, no matter how laboriously analyzed in particular cases, are of so little predictive value for future conflicts. Wars have been fought, especially several hundred years ago, over trade and commercial advantages. Other wars have been fought and still are fought for pieces of land, and yet others because of insults given to or received by the heads of states. Whether any one of these "causes" will trigger off a war depends on which states are involved and what their concept of their interests, and their attitudes toward the interests of others, happen to be. What causes war in one case completely fails to ignite a spark in another.

It is for this reason that astute observers, recognizing the callowness of most simple-causation approaches, such as the "devil theory," either embrace the simple proposition that wars are caused by a will to power or assert the complex proposition that wars are touched off by whole series of factors, including economic rivalries, psychological misunderstandings, and historical enmities and disputes. The simple will-to-power explanation, because it is so all-embracing, is wide enough to include any conflict at any time. It therefore seems adequate to explain all wars—at least those that did occur even if not those that somehow failed to occur. Alternately, the complex economic-psychological-historical theory, by including everything conceivable, manages to include the right reasons for the war by its very exhaustiveness. Any uneasiness over a failure to ascribe the right amount of causation to each of these factors can be resolved merely by saying that "each played a part."

It is true that a will to power exists to some extent wherever human life is found. It is true that the complex omnibus causation theory is basically correct in its insistence upon a multifactor explanation of the causes of war. But it is still more appropriate to analyze the causes of conflicts through the theoretical instrument of the concept of national interests applied to war as a whole, and to particular cases. For the national-interest approach not only makes it convenient and clear to distinguish for any given war (provided enough facts are known) the causes of conflict. At the same time, through the process of analysis itself, it leads to the vital realization that it is not the economic, or historical, or psychological factors in the dispute alone that cause the war. Rather these formed the stuff of dissension between the states in conflict because of *the attitude toward those factors taken by those states*— namely, *their view* of their national interests.

This is not a trivial point. Many proposed solutions to international problems are advanced every day which, by curing some particular evil such as the discrimination of one nation against another in terms of access to raw materials or restrictive immigration policies directed against Orientals, hope to resolve the problem of war in the world as a whole. Such efforts may achieve real good, and may be very useful in diminishing particular international tensions. This will be so where the solution advanced is accurately geared to a situation existing among two or more states that does appear to incline them toward conflict with one another. But no amount of discrimination, or, conversely, the complete absence of it makes war either more or less likely unless the attitude of the states involved is really one of active irritation over it. Thus, in attempting to alleviate tensions that cause wars among states, it is ultimately at least as important to study the peculiarities of the patient as it is to determine the nature of diseases and antibodies from which they may suffer. We already know, as one sign of progress, much about how a stable balance of power is produced; this does not do away with the difficulty of getting particular states to produce it.

These observations are, of course, somewhat theoretical, but they can and later will be applied. They lead to this final point: the basic cause for war in the multistate system is that individual states decide for themselves when they have cause for war. Any cause is enough cause if a state thinks it is. Some states are restrained from finding causes for war with great frequency and regularity only because of the opposition they will surely encounter; others because they are too small or weak to run grave risks; and still others because it is their nature and national character to practice a great measure of self-restraint. The causes of war are thus individual by states as well as functional by types. The study of neither can be neglected.

4   The Increasing Intensity of Warfare

VIEWED especially against the background of the nineteenth and even the eighteenth century, the twentieth century has been notoriously an Age of Bloodshed. In absolute terms this is easy to demonstrate: World War I took more than eight and a half million lives in *direct* casualties, the British alone having sixty thousand casualties in *one day* during the Battle of the Somme (1916); World War II cost around fifteen million lives. Counting war-connected, civilian deaths, the figures reached forty millions for World War I and an even greater total for World War II. By contrast, the total military dead in all wars between 1790 and 1914 is estimated at only about four and a half millions, around two millions of these being French Revolutionary and Napoleonic War victims. Thus there were only some two and a half million war dead in the *whole hundred years* after Waterloo.

Following World War II the Korean War and Viet-Nam War tolls raised the totals even further. Korea cost more than three million dead, wounded, and missing. Thus the total war dead since 1914 reaches the staggering and unprecedented figure of more than 100 million people, counting both direct and indirect deaths. Should an atomic-hydrogen war occur, the casualties would defy imagination. Secretary McNamara estimated American fatalities in such a general war, provided there was one hour's warning, at 122 million.[6] The problems of survival in a war-wracked world are indeed formidable in our times.

Yet the very extensiveness of twentieth-century bloodshed can easily obscure the fact that periods of great slaughter and prolonged wars have occurred before. We have already mentioned the two million war dead of the French Revolutionary and Napoleonic Wars. In the Thirty Years' War it has been conservatively estimated that the population of Germany (the main battle-field) was reduced from twenty-one millions to thirteen and a half millions.[7] Other estimates are much more drastic. In addition, France and the other

---

6 See his testimony to Congress, NYT, February 19, 1965.

7 C. V. Wedgwood, *The Thirty Years' War*, New Haven: Yale, 1939, p. 516.

participants lost heavily too. Since the population of the world was much smaller in those days, the losses of these two earlier periods of general and prolonged war were also, on a relative basis, extremely severe. Even so, the record of the twentieth century is appallingly impressive. Total post-1914 deaths divided by the number of years since 1914 yields an average *annual* death figure which approximates the *entire* 1815–1914 costs.

Throughout modern times the proportion of casualties to total population has tended to rise constantly (with the major exception of the hundred years between Waterloo and Sarajevo). It has been estimated that for every thousand French deaths in the seventeenth century, eleven died in active military service; in the eighteenth, twenty-seven; in the nineteenth, thirty; and in the twentieth—*not* taking into account World War II—sixty-three. The corresponding figures for England are fifteen, fourteen, six, and forty-eight.[8] The war losses of France, as the main contender in the French Revolutionary and Napoleonic Wars, are higher than those of England for both the eighteenth and nineteenth centuries, but, especially in the nineteenth century, the British figures are more typical of the European powers. The figures for the United States, on the other hand, because of the more than six hundred thousand military dead of the American Civil War, show a steady upward trend from the eighteenth century on.

The increase in bloodshed is not due to an increase in the number of wars in Europe (where the wars of greatest bloodshed have occurred, taking the last four centuries as a whole), since although there were over fifty European wars in the sixteenth and seventeenth centuries, there were only half as many in the eighteenth and nineteenth centuries, and only twelve so far in the twentieth. It is due rather to five factors: the greater size of armies involved, the greater number and duration of battles in modern wars, the greater casualties among civilians, the exceptionally long participation by states in twentieth-century wars, and the superlative efficiency of modern instruments of destruction.

Armies have increased as the population has grown and as the technological means to sustain them have improved. Beginning with the French Revolutionary Wars, the average size was increased enormously by the introduction of conscription (as in the French *levée en masse* of 1793 which raised 770,000 men and was copied later by the Prussians). The substitution of the "nation in arms" for the old-style mercenary army also tended to increase the ferocity of wars, although this point can be overstressed.[9] Some mercenary troops in Machiavelli's time fought wars without managing to spill much if any blood, and wars in the eighteenth century, preoccupied as they were with maneuver

---

[8] Quincy Wright, A *Study of War*, Vol. I, p. 243. Many of the figures in this section are drawn from this invaluable study.

[9] The famous stone statue of the "Lion of Lucerne" in Switzerland is a memorial to the Swiss mercenary guards of Louis XVI who died defending the king from the Paris mobs in 1792.

and position, often produced relatively few casualties.[10] Nevertheless, it was not uncommon in the sixteenth century for 40 per cent of the defeated side to be killed or wounded, and perhaps 10 per cent of the victors. The defeated army was sometimes cut down as it ran from the field. This casualty rate compares with 30 to 50 per cent in the Middle Ages and about 60 per cent for the forces mobilized in World War I and World War II.

How much the success of Napoleon's conscripts was due to any greater willingness on their part to fight, as compared with mercenaries, is difficult to assess. Napoleon's superior generalship and tactics and the larger forces he could thus mobilize and deploy were highly important factors in his victories. In any event, once conscription was adopted by one of the belligerents, its ultimate adoption by all to secure the same advantages was inevitable. Thus wars since Napoleon have been fought by "citizen armies."

In the Thirty Years' War nineteen thousand men was the normal size of the army. By the time of Louis XIV, however, forty thousand was usual. In Frederick the Great's wars the average was forty-seven thousand. The beginnings of the Industrial Revolution brought a sharp upward surge by Napoleon's time, and the normal army in his wars reached eighty-four thousand. Average army size declined somewhat in the mid-nineteenth century (seventy thousand in the Franco-Prussian War). By the time of the Russo-Japanese War, however, the figure was one hundred ten thousand.

These figures should not be taken to mean that armies were never larger than just indicated. Even in the sixteenth century, mercenary armies on occasion reached twenty thousand to thirty thousand. In the seventeenth century, armies of fifty to sixty thousand were often assembled. While eighteenth-century armies did not go beyond eighty to ninety thousand, Napoleon had as many as two hundred thousand troops in some battles. Although armies tended down between 1815 and 1870, before the end of the nineteenth century *peacetime* standing armies (and navies) for the eight great powers averaged five hundred thousand apiece, and by 1914 they were around six hundred thousand. Present-day standing forces, as we saw in Chapter 3, are much larger: some three million each for the United States and the Soviet Union, and two and a half million for China as of 1966.

In the seventeenth century, following mobilization, approximately three in a thousand of population was under arms (one third of 1 per cent); by the late nineteenth and early twentieth centuries some five in a thousand were in peacetime standing armies, and full mobilization put as many as 14 per cent of the population into uniform. The percentage of population mobilized went, in the hundred years or so, from perhaps 5 per cent for Napoleon to the 14 per cent of World War I. The tendency in World War II was, however, down, and was nearer 10 per cent because of the increased ratio of workers in

---

[10] One of the typical wars of the eighteenth century was the War of the Bavarian Succession. The war consisted entirely of maneuver and not a battle was fought. See Walter Goerlitz, *History of the German General Staff, 1657–1945,* Chapter 1.

the factories to soldiers in the field necessitated by mechanized warfare. In absolute terms, over sixty-five millions were mobilized during the course of World War I, and more than seventy millions in World War II. These figures indicate one significant reason why bloodshed has increased.

Moreover, the duration and number of battles during a war has increased. In the seventeenth century 96 per cent of the battles lasted only a day or less.[11] By the twentieth century the figure was only 40 per cent. In the sixteenth century the number of important battles in a war averaged less than two; by the next century this had doubled, and by the eighteenth and nineteenth centuries had reached about twenty. By the twentieth century it surpassed sixty.

The third factor in the increasing bloodshed has been the growing number of civilians killed. It is sometimes uncritically thought that the slaughter of noncombatants is only a modern phenomenon in the wars of Western civilization. It is well to remember that the atomic bombing of Hiroshima at the end of World War II, which snuffed out seventy-eight thousand lives out of over three hundred thousand inhabitants, was proportionately less destructive than the massacre of twenty-five of the thirty thousand civilians living in Magdeburg during its sacking in the Thirty Years' War. The population loss of Germany during that same struggle was, as we have seen, one out of three—the vast majority, civilians.

Nevertheless, with the significant exception of the Thirty Years' War and to some extent the French Revolutionary and Napoleonic Wars, there was on the whole a tendency in warfare previous to World War I to spare the civilian and safeguard him as much as possible not only through the rules of war but also in the practice of war. In the seventeenth and especially in the eighteenth centuries wars were fought by professional armies who maneuvered while the people in general carried on with their activities largely unhindered. Moreover, the people were usually prepared to accept whatever peace might be made if "their" side lost. Nationalism was still inarticulate. The victor and new sovereign, for his part, was not anxious to destroy valuable human and material property.

After the French Revolution the indifference of the people as to who ruled them evaporated, and the wars of national liberation of the nineteenth century, especially those in the Balkans, tended to be fierce and fanatic. Since the wars of central and western Europe were relatively short during that century, and since they were fought for limited ends, the full fury of nationalistic feeling in Europe was not revealed until World Wars I and II. In World War II guerrilla armies harassed the rear of the Nazi forces even after the regular forces had retreated or surrendered.

The invention of weapons of mass destruction played an even greater part in pyramiding the figures for civilian casualties. The air bombardments of

---

[11] In the eighteenth century it had fallen to 93 per cent, and in the nineteenth to 84 per cent.

World War II, even counting only the "conventional" high explosive and fire-bomb raids, caused enormous losses of life. The hearts of entire cities such as Cologne, Berlin, London, and Tokyo were destroyed. Beginning with World War I the civilian was exposed to bodily risk in a fashion at least comparable to that of the man at the front. The safe existence of the American civilian was unique—and almost certainly for the last time.

The exceptionally long participation of the powers in the wars of the twentieth century has also increased bloodshed. Modern great power wars are not longer than the average war between 1450 and 1930 (for some 278 wars, an average length of 4.4 years) but the average duration of participation by the powers has climbed from 2.5 years in the fifteenth through the eighteenth centuries, through a low 1.4 in the nineteenth to 4.0 in the twentieth. In the twentieth century, nations have tended to become involved in wars at their outset and stay in them until their conclusion, whereas in previous centuries this was uncommon.

Finally, modern technology has made of war an all-season activity, as well as equipping the armies involved with efficient automatic weapons. Gone are the days when armies withdrew to winter quarters, like General Washington's to Valley Forge. There, while the war technically continued, and although the soldiers might die from privation or exposure, they were at least not shot. In the Middle Ages nine out of every ten battles occurred between April and November (inclusive); in the twentieth century active fighting continues all year. The Ardennes Forest ("Battle of the Bulge") campaign, a crucial battle of World War II, was fought in the Christmas-season snows.

At the same time as modern medical techniques have continually improved the chances of wounded surviving, and have done away once and for all with the terrible conditions that at one time ensured that as little as 10 per cent or less of casualties came from enemy fire, and the rest from the ravages of disease, modern automatic weapons have cut down thousands and millions with such bloody efficiency that it is not an exaggeration to speak of the "lost generation" of World War I. The gaps in the British, French, and German populations left by the ravages of the machine gun in World War I alone were never overcome. It is one reason why the leaders of these nations following World War II tended to be men in their seventies.

All these reasons combined together explain the growing intensity of modern warfare.

5 *Weapons Development and Changing Tactics*

THE new weapons, and the resultant tactical changes they have brought about in warfare deserve more detailed analysis.

All through history advantage has shifted, with the development of new weapons, from the defensive to the offensive, and back again. Every new weapon has tended to produce a new counterweapon. Sometimes the process has been slow; at other times extremely rapid.

For long centuries the process was slow; the main weapon available against fortified positions was starvation. During the early Middle Ages, defense, as it had for centuries, held the upper hand for as long as supplies lasted or the siege was not raised by outside allies. For this reason antiquity had preferred fortified positions. The Great Wall of China and the Great Wall of Nineveh (built before 2000 B.C.) were only the most spectacular of man's efforts in this direction. In Europe today one can still see the ancient towns, built upon hilltops or raised positions to withstand siege, some with the remnants of walls still standing. It is not a very great exaggeration to say that the medieval unit of government consisted of a strategic terrain position on which a fortification could be erected, plus enough surrounding land to keep the inhabitants supplied with the essentials of life. By the early fifteenth century, this way of life was passing away because crude artillery, even if its firepower failed to realize gunpowder's modern potentialities, easily destroyed once impregnable fortresses.

Roman siege machines threw stones weighing up to six hundred pounds as far as a thousand yards; and the Turks' great and clumsy guns used against Constantinople in the fifteenth century shot missiles weighing eight hundred pounds about a mile in the general direction at which the gun was aimed. No great improvement really occurred in fifteen hundred years. Even though artillery gradually became better, especially after more modest-sized shot (the nine-pounder shot, for example) came into use, the effective range of cannon until Napoleon's time was less than that of muskets.

Napoleon capitalized upon improved cannon which, while still smooth-bore and muzzle-loading, could fire "case shot" for an effective range of four hundred yards.[12] Against the musket that could fire less than three hundred yards, this was a highly formidable weapon. Keeping out of musket range, Napoleon's cannon could destroy the enemy with ease.

When the musket had first come into general use in the second half of the seventeenth century, its effective range (about two out of five times) had been no greater than about a hundred yards; at two hundred yards it was not accurate at all.[13] To overcome this deficiency in accuracy it was necessary to fire volleys. This in turn called for close-order tactics in order to maneuver sufficient men into a compact position from which the volley could be fired.

The improvements in cannon range forced the abandonment of close-order tactics using closed ranks. Loose ranks and open squares replaced them, but it was not until the development of conical bullets that rifles were able to fire effectively at six hundred fifty yards. At this point the cannons, in turn, were outranged.

Following 1850 small arms and cannons began to come into general use that were both breech-loaded and rifled in their barrels. The shell gun had

---

[12] Ralph Turner, "Technology and Geo-Politics," *Military Affairs*, Spring 1943, pp. 5–15.

[13] *Ibid.*

been introduced as early as 1824; now, by using trajectory firing, cannon could fire shells fairly effectively for more than two thousand yards. Thereafter range increased rapidly, and with the invention of the recoil cylinder for artillery in 1898, guns became both very much bigger and very much more powerful. Rifles were similarly improved, while the first really workable metal cartridge came in 1846. With the invention of the breech-loading needle gun in 1836 [14] and its adoption by the Prussians in 1851, for the first time a man could fire a shot each minute. Breech-loading made rapid loading and firing from a prone position possible—an event that revolutionized tactics. The rifle had a range of over two thousand yards. Thereafter, firepower and range both increased steadily until on the eve of World War I it had become ten shots a minute per man for double the range of the early needle gun.

In a tactical sense, the nineteenth century had thus wrought great changes. The earlier reliance upon fortifications was discarded and emphasis was placed upon open fighting and firing from prone positions rather than close-order maneuvers in full view of the enemy. Mobility of forces replaced the earlier concepts of stationary warfare. In this connection, the harnessing of railways to military purposes created a tactical revolution. In the United States Civil War the technique was first used to advantage, more by the North than the South (for the former had more railways), and it played a part in the ultimate Union victory. The earlier von Moltke, noting the United States' example, rode Prussia to victory on rails in both the Seven Weeks' War and the Franco-Prussian War. Troops that could be quickly shifted from front to front gave the greater advantage to offense.

Important developments occurred too in naval warfare, and again increased firepower and mobility were among the keynotes of the changes, although armor (unlike land warfare) was not neglected. The unwieldy galleons of the Spanish Armada did not differ essentially from Columbus' tiny ships; in the sixteenth century the "broadside battleship," like those used by Nelson in the Napoleonic Wars, began to come into use. In the seventeenth century wooden ships reached their limit in size; for more than two hundred fifty years there was little change.

In the last half of the nineteenth century, as had been the case with land warfare, great changes occurred. After 1850 the technological devices born out of the Industrial Revolution were harnessed to the uses of warfare. The application of steam power for propulsion, the development of the screw propeller, the use of iron (and later steel) for hulls and armor, all constituted tremendous advances.

The first modern "iron-clads" were wooden-hulled vessels with iron-plated sides and ramming prongs.[15] Because of their wooden hulls and the compara-

---

[14] The same year in which the Colt revolver was patented in the United States.

[15] Korean Admiral Yi Sun Sin built a famous "Turtle"—a 120-foot long, 30-foot wide ironclad with which he destroyed the Japanese invasion force off Pusan in 1592. Propelled by twenty oars, with its iron sides spiked to prevent boarding, and fairly impervious to the fire arrows of the enemy, it was a marvelous weapon.

tive crudity of their machinery and ordnance devices, they were still rather limited in their effectiveness compared to modern men of war, but in the American Civil War where their first famous clash occurred they marked the inevitable ultimate displacement of wooden combat ships. The battle between the Union iron ship *Monitor* ("the cheesebox on a raft"—named so for its revolving gun turret) and the Confederate ironclad *Virginia* (ex-*Merrimac*) on March 9, 1862, was eventually to revolutionize both naval construction and tactics. The first really modern warship, the British *Dreadnought* (which name came to be a synonym for "battleship"), was constructed in 1906. Its displacement of 17,900 tons—eight times that of eighteenth-century capital ships—has since come to appear small indeed when contrasted with the 45,000 tons of the USS *Missouri*, the 64,000 tons of the Japanese *Yamato*, and the 77,000 tons of the USS *America*.

Bernard Brodie comments on this aspect of the mid-Victorian Age:

During the thirty years between 1855 and 1885, guns and warship design were changing at a greater rate than has characterized any comparable period before or since. Battleships changed during that time from wooden, unarmored, broadside, sail-driven vessels to iron and steel steam-driven, heavily armored, turreted monsters. . . . In the implements of land warfare . . . the same period practically spans the change from muzzle-loading muskets to breech-loading rifles, from smooth-bore field guns of bronze or cast iron to rifled, breech-loading pieces made of steel, and covers also the introduction of rather effective machine guns.[16]

Submarines and especially the machine gun, although they were hardly "surprise" weapons, changed entirely the character of World War I from all previous wars. At sea, the first effective naval submarine, ordered in 1886, was launched in 1888.[17] In World War I, armed with the torpedo, its successors destroyed ships at sea in unprecedented fashion. The unseen prowler of the depths had to be "listened for," only the intermittent faint clue of its periscope giving visual evidence of its presence. Luckily for Britain the German underseas fleet was small at the beginning of the war, and submarines could not then operate at sea for very long periods of time. Threatened even so with starvation, England resorted to convoy tactics virtually unused since the Napoleonic Wars. Counterweapons were gradually found to mitigate the submarine menace.

On land, the first primitive machine gun (the "Gatling gun") had been enormously improved by 1914. It mowed down line after charging line with impersonal precision. Troops dug in, crawling down into the earth to escape the deadly spray of machine-delivered lead, emerging only occasionally for often fruitless and hopeless charges against the enemy positions across "no-man's-land."

---

[16] Bernard Brodie, "Military Demonstration and Disclosure of New Weapons," *World Politics*, Vol. V, No. 3 (April 1953), p. 285. The entire article is well worth careful reading.

[17] *The Gymnote* (French).

No effective counterweapon for the machine gun appeared until September 15, 1916, when the British first used tanks in the Battle of the Somme.[18] But because the military had been hostile to their use they were committed only half-heartedly and in small numbers (only 14 taking part in the action). Nevertheless the German line quickly broke as the iron monsters heaved their way across, crushing all beneath their treads.

The tank came too late in the war, in too small numbers, and with too many defects not ironed out, to change the basic character of World War I. The potential revolutionary effect on the tactics of the next war, by restoring mobility to warfare, was not widely grasped. Charles de Gaulle, then a relatively obscure French officer, put his ideas on tank warfare to paper but, unfortunately for France, it was the Germans (and the Russians) who realized the correctness of de Gaulle's tactical concepts. France was already committed to the Maginot Line and a basically defensive, stationary-war concept before the new, universal-service German Army under Hitler had come into being. The very delay in unlimited rearmament enforced upon the Germans by the Treaty of Versailles made it possible for them, once they did rearm on a full-scale basis, to incorporate all the newest technological and tactical improvements.[19]

World War II fully justified the advocates of the tank as a counter to the machine gun. Tanks became enormously heavier than their early counterparts, with heavy armor and heavy weapons. The Germans on invading Russia found to their chagrin that qualitatively the Russian tanks were superior to their own, just as the United States initially had to counter the qualitative superiority of the German tank over its tank by resort to quantity.

Not only improved versions of earlier weapons but also a whole host of new weapons made their appearance—many of which created tactical surprises when they were revealed in action. As a matter of fact World War II probably unveiled more "secret weapons" than any other war in modern history.[20] Although the German 11 inch and 16.5 inch howitzers came as a tactical surprise in World War I, World War II early brought such developments as the Japanese oxygen-driven torpedo (which surpassed the older air-propelled types in both speed and range), and British search radar (used in the Battle of

---

[18] The German use of poison gas was followed by effective retaliation too soon to turn the tide. Besides, it was a very unwieldly weapon at best.

[19] The Germans had for the last hundred years based their strategy upon mobility. From Bismarck through Hitler, German plans turned upon movement.

[20] Until the early twentieth century, nations made no particular efforts to safeguard the secrecy of new advances in weapons—perhaps because improvements were coming so rapidly that they stood to fall behind more in obsolescence than they stood to gain by secrecy. Brodie (*op. cit.*, pp. 287–288) mentions the unusual policy of secrecy adopted by the French in 1898 in respect to the recoil mechanism of their 75 mm. gun, and the similar policy of the British with the *Dreadnought* in 1906. When one recalls that the *Monitor* was constructed in New York without any real attempt at secrecy while the United States was actually at war, one sees how much change has occurred.

Britain in 1940 to the discomfort and surprise of the Germans). Before the war was over, rockets, jet planes, bazookas, recoilless cannon, VT (proximity) fuses, snorkel submarines, and atomic bombs were put into use. Each of these was revolutionary in its effects. The American VT fuse, perhaps the least publicized of these developments, possessed the remarkable quality of exploding a shell when it passed into the vicinity of the target. It was used only at sea against air targets until the Battle of the Bulge in December 1944, in order to preserve its secret by preventing an intact specimen from falling into enemy hands.[21] This development alone constituted the most important advance in the history of artillery use for most of a century. Comparable in terms of sea warfare was the appearance of the snorkel submarines. Simple as an idea, but difficult to execute technically, the snorkel is a steel breathing tube through which fresh oxygen is carried down into the submarine and engine fumes, etc., can be expelled into the air above the ocean surface. By allowing submarines to stay at periscope depth below the surface, operating on diesels instead of quickly exhausted batteries, it serves to reduce greatly the danger to a submarine of being caught recharging batteries on the surface in enemy waters, a position in which it is peculiarly vulnerable.

Most of these new weapons appeared late in the war, just as with the tank in World War I. As a result, although the Korean War presented an opportunity for battlefield tests for both the United States and the Russians, the full capabilities of many of them (especially those not used in Korea, like the nuclear weapons) are still being explored. Their effects on tactics and strategy continue to be the subject of intensive debate in military circles around the world.

Since the end of World War II the advances in weapons have continued at a pace which is comparable in modern times only to 1855–1885. In 1966 four nations had stocks of atomic-hydrogen weapons: the United States, Russia, Great Britain, and France. Communist China, who exploded her first nuclear device on October 16, 1964, was slated to be fifth. There will in time be more. In the nuclear field the early atomic bomb has developed into a whole "family of atomic weapons" of all sizes. Atomic tactical weapons are at one end of the scale. The 280 mm.-atomic cannon has a death-dealing radius of only a mile; even smaller weapons are coming. At the other end of the scale are the hydrogen bombs (which operate on the principle of fusion instead of fission—as in atomic blasts). The first hydrogen bomb exploded by the United States in the Marshall Islands (November 1952) destroyed an entire atoll, making a crater roughly a mile in diameter which sloped down to a maximum depth of 175 feet (the equivalent of a seventeen-story building). The bomb caused complete destruction over a three-mile radius, moderate damage out to seven miles, and light damage as far as ten miles. The surface H-bomb explosion of March 1954, had sufficient power to wreck homes with earthquake shock at

---

[21] *Ibid.*, p. 295.

least 20 miles from the target center, bringing brick walls down on the inhabitants. The Soviet tests in the fall of 1961 were in the 50 and 100 megaton range—a range considered superfluous by the U.S.

Atomic power has also gone to sea. The first atomic submarine, the *Nautilus*, had a full submerged speed of at least 20 knots. This means it could overtake most merchant vessels now afloat while remaining under water—a feat previous submarines were completely incapable of. A whole fleet of atomic subs, equipped with Polaris nuclear missiles, is operational. They need only rare refueling, and can cruise submerged indefinitely (thus reducing their own vulnerability tremendously). In 1964 a United States nuclear surface task force completed a 30,000 mile cruise without refueling.

In air warfare and in missiles giant leaps forward continue. The new jet interceptor-pursuit planes carry tactical atomic bombs. Their speed is well in excess of sound and is being steadily revised upward. Both the United States and Russia possess operational missiles of 8,000 and 9,000-mile range. These ballistic missiles are reasonably accurate provided the target location is accurately known.[22] The filling-in of the cartographic data needed to make such weapons fully effective is a highly important aspect of the Soviet and American space probes. A second help in this respect is a United States radar system, made public in 1960, which can pinpoint key military targets and map streets and other features of great cities hundreds of miles inside the Iron Curtain. In addition, the high degree of sophistication in the development of nuclear war-heads has provided an ease of interchangeability between delivery vehicles, whether bombers, missiles, submarines, or artillery pieces.

Reduction of the vulnerability of these missiles to enemy destruction is also a key continuing activity. The Polaris missile, launched from submarines from beneath the seas, is one such answer. The Polaris, when it became operational in 1960, had a range of 1,380 miles. Later versions doubled its range. The Minuteman, like the Polaris a solid-fuel missile, and thus much more compact than first-generation liquid-fuel missiles, has intercontinental range. Minuteman missile complexes, each containing 150 missiles in deep, concrete-lined, underground "silos," now exist in quantity. An interesting military feature of the Viet-Nam War is the first extensive use of ground-to-air and air-to-air missiles, plus anti-missile systems.

These developments continue further the modern revolution in tactics that

---

[22] Lt. Gen. James M. Gavin, in *War and Peace in the Space Age*, New York: Harper, 1958, on pp. 221–222 remarked about the situation a decade ago that there was no way "to give information to a missile in the United States that will cause it to arrive with accuracy at a specific geographic point in the Soviet Union. This is because the exact relation of specific points in the Soviet Union to the United States is not known except in the case of the few observatories that were in existence prior to the Red Revolution. . . . Existing cartographic data is [are] simply not [sufficiently] accurate, in fact for some areas of the USSR it is virtually non-existent. Even close to home, in the West Indies, for example, we found major errors in the assumed location of some of the islands when we first surveyed the Cape Canaveral missile range."

began with the Napoleonic Wars. The eighteenth-century concept of small, well-trained professional armies, using close-order drill in wars of maneuver revolving around fixed and fortified positions, gave way before mass armies, loosely organized and loosely linked to their bases. Movement has been the keynote, with the exception of World War I, when the temporary superiority of weapons of defense (the machine gun) initiated once more a positional —in this case, trench—warfare. The advent of the tank restored mobility once more in World War II, and the tactical adoption of atomic weapons bids fair to continue it along with a greater emphasis on dispersion than ever before. The use of helicopters has extended both mobility and dispersion. From the stage of armies who stood still facing each other to fire and who could see the whites of the enemies' eyes, we have moved to greatly dispersed forces fighting unseen enemies far away with the aid of modern communication apparatus, some of it operating from outer space.

Our survey indicates that in the last decade more "progress" has been made in producing new, death-dealing weapons than ever before in the history of the world. The effect of these tremendous developments has been to stimulate discussion as to their strategic effects, as well as to redouble the efforts of nations to find a practical path to disarmament. We shall discuss these strategic effects next, leaving the examination of the disarmament problem until Chapter 14.

6 Strategic Implications

THE tremendous advances in weapons pose three types of interlocking problems.

The first problem is one of finances. Even a rich nation cannot afford everything. There is a real temptation, given limited funds, for the armed services within a given nation to argue for priority for their own "wonder" weapon. Each such argument implies, of course, a strategic view. If one believes in 1947 that wars will be fought exclusively with huge bombers equipped with nuclear bombs, an army and a navy seem expensive luxuries. If by 1967 mutual hydrogen missile deterrence appears to be a fact of life but limited wars using infantry and carrier-based air power have continued to occur, the argument changes dimensions. It is difficult to know how to spend defense moneys for wars whose nature is now so various and so debatable.

Thus the second problem is one of strategy: What kinds of wars should a nation prepare for? If a general war occurs between nuclear powers, will it begin and end abruptly with a thermonuclear exchange? Or will conventional weapons be supplemented by "nucs" only if the war continues for some time? Might it begin with mutual nuclear destruction and then continue in "broken-back" fashion for year after year? Or will wars be limited entirely to conventional weapons? If nuclear weapons are resorted to, will they be used only against the offensive nuclear capability of the enemy, against his vulnerable cities, or for both types of targets? Suppose each power has "invulnerable, second-strike" capacity (such as Polaris type submarines secreted in the seas), what effects will follow as to priorities in targeting and on the nature and tempo of hostilities? The answers to such questions are not agreed upon among military services around the world. Even if they agreed, they could be wrong.

The third problem is one of deployment and tactics. Massing troops for an offensive would make them an extremely inviting nuclear target. But if troops are dispersed to avoid offering a target for nuclear weapons they can hardly offer a conventional defense to a conventional assault. If one disperses, is one not then already committed to a nuclear defense? What then is the proper organization of an army division? For a fleet at sea?

The types of problems sketched above are not new but never before has so much of past military experience been of questionable relevance to a future war. Never before have virtually all important aspects been so simultaneously uncertain. Yet, the past offers some guidance. Perhaps its most important lesson is the danger of relying heavily or exclusively on one weapon, on one arm of the services, or on one plan of defense.

France's Maginot Line is the best known illustration. Too much of France's military energies went into that wall of steel and concrete; not enough into mobile, armored forces. Who needed much armor with a Maginot Line? In that same World War II Germany slighted its surface navy so that, once France fell, the Germans found themselves on the shores of the English Channel with no way across except to swim. Only after the British "illogically" refused to surrender as anticipated did the Germans build amphibious craft in large quantity. But it came too late. Within the United States Army prior to World War II the development of an adequate heavy tank was long slighted and armored forces generally were neglected. In the Air Force the concentration on the heavy bomber may have been responsible for the lack of first-rate tactical aircraft. Certain it is that in the early part of the Korean War the American jet pursuit planes were able to cope with the Soviet jets more through better training of the pilots than because of a superior airplane. The American pursuits were at first inferior, just as the early World War II United States pursuits and interceptors were inferior to the Japanese "Zero." The United States Navy for long gave undue priority to the battleship over the carrier. Each of these tendencies proved to be unwise once battle had begun. But the United States was better prepared than if it had chosen the narrower path taken by the French or the Germans.

When World War II began, air power enthusiasts made large claims. The post-mortems on the effectiveness of air bombardment in that war revealed that, although it caused considerable damage and undoubtedly helped to bring the enemy to his knees, it was not as effective as was claimed at the time. Japanese battleships, claimed as sunk through air action, showed up later still afloat.

The Germans, battered as they were from the air, still managed to increase production until the summer of 1944. The Japanese economy was throttled in the end by shipping losses and the great majority of these stemmed from submarine torpedoing. One of General MacArthur's headquarters reports from Japan tells the story: in 1943 a peak wartime production of steel ingots within the Japanese Empire was reached. Approximately 9.6 million tons were produced. Two years later the rate was a mere 120,000 tons a year. The report credited 1.8 million tons decrease to bombing; the other 7.68 million tons was the result of naval blockade. Again, while in 1941 a total of 4 million tons of iron ore was needed by Japanese industry, only a fifth of it was produced within the home islands. The other 3 million and more tons came by sea. By 1944 imported ores had fallen to less than 30 per cent of the 1941 figure. The Germans, despite the slowdowns after mid-1944, fought on for a year against the massive land forces flung at them from the Normandy bridgehead. It might be added, on the other hand, that neither the British evacuation from Dunkirk nor the Normandy landings would have been possible without local command of the air over the beaches. This is, therefore, not an argument against air power; it is only a reminder that it took army, navy, and air force —all three—to win the war against the Axis.

Today, in the midst of the second great military-technological revolution of modern times, the proper balance of forces and selection of weapons is more difficult than ever before. Every weapon has limitations, just as every target is vulnerable if hit squarely with enough force. Precisely because the nature of any future war is so difficult to foresee, a concentration of available resources upon one branch or weapon can hardly be anything but reckless. This was always true; it is truer now. Each weapon has a use, and nothing is so sure about warfare but that the greater the variety of weapons the better the chance not to be caught napping. For not only is a too-narrow range of armament dangerously open to technical obsolescence by enemy leaps ahead, but it also simplifies the enemy's job in finding out where to concentrate his efforts.

The advent of nuclear weapons has not necessarily made conventional weapons obsolete. The same caution given earlier applies here. Although the immense and unprecedented destructive powers of nuclear weapons is indisputable, it would be a naïve nation indeed which concluded that (1) they would never be used (especially since they *were* already used in World War II) or (2) that no more battles between conventional forces would occur (especially in view of the conventional character of both the Korean and Viet-Nam wars).

Short of a weapon which, once used, would bring the enemy immediately to the point of surrender, there is no "absolute weapon" (as the atomic bomb was first termed). Even with hydrogen bombs and missiles, that weapon has not necessarily appeared. This is not meant to underrate the power of hydrogen weapons. The question is not whether these weapons would destroy urban life if used on cities—they undoubtedly would. The question rather is whether a nation so attacked, or two nations so crippled through reciprocal attacks, would continue to fight. It is conceivable that, after such reciprocal damage (for it is not likely that only one nation would suffer all the casualties), it would be harder than ever to bring such a war to a conclusion if surrender did not occur immediately. It would be so much more difficult to bring land forces to bear upon the enemy once the industrial apparatus that nurtures and supports them had been destroyed. Japan surrendered in 1945 before she was physically occupied, but in the certain knowledge of forthcoming one-sided destruction. If two nations virtually destroyed one another, how would they determine who had "won"?

Atomic and hydrogen weapons make it possible to achieve the devastation wrought earlier by conventional weapons much more quickly, and to increase the damage and casualties beyond what was hitherto feasible. They make war much more deadly just as the machine gun did, and before it the use of gunpowder in war did. Urban living may as a result be made obsolete, but wars may continue to occur under the circumstances already described.

It is also quite possible that these fearful new weapons may lead nations to avoid their strategic use in favor of tactical applications. There may be a reluctance to use these weapons for bombing cities out of a fear of retaliation. If this happens, atomic weapons may be used only for tactical results—or conceivably not at all. It may be, finally, that the advent of these weapons may force a return to the concept of limited wars fought on more or less conventional lines—or even to a shrinking from war by the great powers altogether.

What is needed in the light of these revolutionary developments and the unpredictable factors which they bring into being is more than ever a careful blend of conservative refusal to gamble on untested weapons or "one shot" arsenals, and an open-minded acceptance of the quickly changing methods and tactics that these developments make necessary. A nation unprepared for all the alternative types of wars that are conceivable may find itself in extreme danger. It is this logic which leads to the doctrine of "flexible response."

Because of the destructiveness of the new nuclear weapons there is no question but that nations are being forced to appraise the extent of their vital interests more conservatively than ever before. Moreover, the very rapidity and sweep of the arms revolution, and the complex tactical and strategical problems raised, induce caution. No one is completely sure how a new large-scale war would be fought and great nations find it difficult, so long as developments occur so rapidly, to standardize and stock-pile on the scale desirable for any deliberate resort to war. Impressive as the Atlas missile, for example, was, it represented only the Model-T stage in missiles. Its more foolproof and warworthy successors represent missiles which will be modified or replaced at a much slower pace. On the one hand, the arms revolution is slowing down; on the other, the problems it raised are far from answered.

It is worth pondering the fact that World War I did not come until some years after the first prolonged military-technological revolution of modern times had come to an end. A time of stockpiling and re-thinking intervened. Conversely, the shortest period of general peace in modern times, 1919–1939, was marked by few weapons innovations other than the production of more effective versions of existing weapons. To attribute the acceleration or retarding of the onset of World War II to this factor alone would be obviously untenable, but there is certainly a connection. Perhaps the post-1945, or second great military-technological revolution has been, ironically, a factor working to postpone deliberate wide-scale war, even while it has generated greater tensions.

7 Espionage and Intelligence

THE practice of espionage is as old as recorded history but it is pursued even more vigorously nowadays. With the present tremendous pace of weapons development it is vital to know quickly how and what the enemy is doing. One must know, for example, how his war plans are being adjusted to the growing abundance of missiles. How alert and effective are his electronic warning devices? To wait for war to find out the enemy's plans and equipment is foolhardy. Consequently espionage is an activity which goes on during both peace and war but with important differences in method and intensity.

In wartime everyone assumes that spying will go on and nations shoot spies they catch and boast (afterwards) about the success of their own spying activities. A Nathan Hale is publicly acclaimed, quite rightly, as a hero. Only double agents, selling information to both sides for commercial gain, are despised. The emphasis in war is on order-of-battle data, but no information is scorned. In peacetime the problem is somewhat different. Certain conventions are customarily observed, the most important of which is that nations do not *admit* to spying. The reason is not too hard to find: spying implies enmity where enmity is not officially admitted; it is aimed at breaching the target nation's security, which is itself a hostile act.

In May 1960, this problem came into the world spotlight after the spectacular capture by the Russians of an American spy who was flying across the Soviet Union in a U-2 plane. The "cover story" was given out that an American weather observation plane was overdue from its Turkish base and that the pilot had reported oxygen trouble. This implied that the pilot might black-out and "inadvertently" violate Soviet air space. But when the Russians then revealed that Powers (the pilot) had been shot down (so they claimed) near Sverdlovsk, some 1,200 miles inside Russia, the fat was in the fire. That is a long way indeed to fly blacked-out!

President Eisenhower decided, in the wake of conflicting further explanations by various United States authorities, to take the "honest" way out. In an unprecedented act he admitted that the United States had ordered the violation of Russian air space. He explained that we had to have such information and that we would, in effect, keep making such flights. (He later amended that to say we would cease the flights.) Khrushchev, perhaps happy to avoid a showdown on the Berlin crisis, then went into a tirade at the Paris Summit Meeting, and everyone went home angry. Not quite so unprecedented but nonetheless shocking was Powers' failure to destroy his plane and equipment.

In cases of this sort the invariable rule has been to either admit nothing or else claim that the spy was engaged in an unauthorized flight or had deserted, taking his plane with him. Although some Americans reacted to the episode by feeling pleased that we had been doing so boldly and well in espionage, the predominant reaction was that America had placed herself unnecessarily in an embarrassed position.

Espionage, which is a part of intelligence activity, is also the more glamorous and dangerous part. Intelligence gathering is not predominantly spectacular at all. Basically it is akin to ordinary research—the patient accumulation and collation of data, most of which is publicly available in print. The Nazis, for example, accurately estimated United States aircraft production in World War II on the basis of material in the New York Public Library! The technique they used was a simple one of collation of data similar to the one used by the American press in 1956 when the new CIA office building hearings were being held. Allen Dulles of CIA testified that he could not, under law, reveal the number of CIA employees. He then, a few days later, said that he needed "net office space of 98.5 square feet per person" (printed on p. 743 of the hearings). On p. 724 the total space needed is given as 1,135,000 square feet. Result—as the press pointed out: 11,522 CIA employees.

The air waves are also a prime source of materials, for radio broadcasts can be intercepted: the principle of the ordinary radio receiver. When the Germans, under Hindenburg and Ludendorff, hurled back the Russian hordes in East Prussia in 1914 they capitalized upon the fact that the Russians had naïvely broadcast portions of their battle plans in plain language. Similarly, as the Germans revealed after World War II, Rommel's early successes in North Africa owed a great deal to radio code-breaking activities.

Espionage and intelligence, basic as they are to the preparation and conduct of war, will undoubtedly continue to be of prime importance in the future as in the past.

8   *The Object and Future of War*

THE waging of war offers more dangers to a nation's well-being than any other activity in which it engages. Once hostilities begin, new and even unexpected enemies may appear. Not only must a nation count on physical losses but it must gamble its future and perhaps its very existence. War, also, inevitably brings great changes in its wake, and unless a nation is very alert it may emerge victorious in the armed struggle and yet lose much of the potential gains implicit in the postwar situation.

Even a nation which desires no increase in territory cannot be impervious to the gains of others. The power problem vis-à-vis the newly defeated enemies is always succeeded after the war by a power problem with new outlines and with other potential enemies (and former "friends") as its center. No amount of hopeful optimism can alter its occurrence unless the state system itself disappears. This is not the same as saying that the victors must quarrel with one another, or that they will fight one another later (although they may do both). Even if all their relations with one another were for a time eminently friendly—which past historical experience warns us is unlikely—it is not wise statesmanship to base the national security solely or even predominantly upon the most congenial possibility. The real point is not to fight a war as though winning it were all that really mattered.

The object of war in the large sense goes well beyond its definition in the United States Rules of Land Warfare of 1914. Article 10 of these rules says: "the object of war is to bring about the complete submission of the enemy as soon as possible by means of regulated violence." This may be the function of warfare from a military point of view, but it is not the object of war. Clausewitz more accurately places the narrower aim within the wider context when he says: "War is not merely a political act, but also a political instrument, a continuation of political relations, a carrying out of the same by other means." [23] Clausewitz was not saying that politics are war, but that war is also politics. What he is warning against is the tendency of statesmen to lose sight of the purpose of war in the excitement of the process of war. A war begun or carried on because the national interests require it, should be fought to its conclusion with the national interests ever in mind. [24]

Lord Vansittart once wrote that the purpose of the "old" diplomacy (pre-1914 style) was the preservation of peaceful relations between states. Once war came, the diplomats packed their bags and went home. Many diplomatic memoirs convey the same impression. Leaving aside whether Vansittart's view of the purpose of diplomacy is accurate (for we have already discussed this point in Chapter 5), the impression created by such statements and memoirs reinforces the popular tendency to draw a line between peace and war with the remark that "where the diplomats leave off, the generals begin." The unfortunate nation that takes this literally is courting disaster. If diplomacy is really suspended for the duration, there is no judging where "military necessity," narrowly conceived, may lead the nation. War is not simply a military activity fought for simply military ends.

Although no nation does take this quite literally, it may, with almost equally bad results, do so in effect by directing the grand strategy of the war solely in terms of "getting there firstest with the mostest" and smashing through to victory. This, while often sound military strategy, may or may not be desirable in a given instance from an over-all point of view. The military

---

[23] Karl von Clausewitz, *Vom Kriege.*

[24] The evident confusion in the United States in 1951–1952 over what to do about ending the Korean War is an example of what happens when the national interests are not clearly perceived and agreed upon by the great majority of the people, and therefore what happens when the national interests are not kept ever in mind.

object of war is victory through the use of violence; the political objective is national security through the use of diplomacy capitalizing upon the military possibilities.

It is perfectly conceivable that on some occasions it is more desirable from the standpoint of national security not to fight a war to victory. Both the War of 1812 and the Korean War ended for the United States in a negotiated settlement essentially characterized by a return to the territorial prewar *status quo*. This is not the same thing as saying that there was a return to the strategic-diplomatic-political *status quo*. Far from it, for in both cases the postwar situation differed fundamentally from the prewar.

The significance of the War of 1812 was that it finally convinced the British of the tremendous price they would have to pay either to reconquer their former colonies or continue to treat them without the respect due a truly independent nation. The end of British impressment of American seamen was an outward indication of this change in viewpoint; it marked the beginning of a British policy of refraining from running athwart America's vital interests.[25] The cost of winning a true military victory by either side in the War of 1812 would have been prohibitive and was also unnecessary. The war reflected more a mutual testing of strength than a bitter struggle to the end.

Because we are still so close to the emotional turmoil of the Korean War, it is more difficult to see it coldly and objectively. Yet here again the war was fundamentally a test of whether clear-cut, premeditated aggression could be committed with impunity. The military stalemate which followed the entry of Communist Chinese "volunteer" forces was not broken because Communist China could not, by defeating the United States on the American mainland, break the United States' will to resist; and the United States in turn was unwilling to commit herself to a great struggle on the Asian mainland while Soviet Russian forces were left free to do with Europe what they pleased. The cost of military victory was prohibitive for both sides. Yet at the same time the Communist aggressive designs on South Korea were frustrated and international relations following 1950 were fundamentally influenced by the demonstrated willingness of America to oppose clear-cut aggression with force. This in itself was an important United States security objective, since its deterrent effect (even if it should later prove insufficient) could not be questioned.

How such thoughts apply to the Viet-Nam War will be considered later.

Because war is not a game played for its own sake, and despite the fact that the twentieth century has witnessed more total wars in every sense than ever before in the history of Western civilization, the day of limited war for limited ends is not over. Wars as a rule reflect in their ferocity, duration, and method the over-all objectives of their participants. The war the Germans

---

25 The British ship seizures of United States vessels between 1914 and 1917 were a reluctant departure from this policy whose unpleasant repercussions they tried very hard to counteract. They resorted to the policy only because their own vital interests were in jeopardy.

fought against the Slavs between 1941 and 1945 was in many respects more ruthless than the war they fought against the West. The war in the East was much more a war of extermination waged to destroy or cripple once and for all more numerous peoples, while the war in the West was waged more for the prizes, the booty, and the strategic gains that conquest could bring. A war reflects the purpose for which it is fought. Where wars occur in the future that by design or necessity are limited in their objectives, those conflicts too will be limited wars; where (and if) they are fought for total stakes, for the victory of one way of life over another, they can, because of the developments we have seen in this chapter, be more cataclysmic than anything the world has ever known. The prudent nation will be prepared.

CHAPTER 9

International Organization

A majority, of course, is a majority. Arithmetic is arithmetic. But no arithmetic can solve questions pertaining to
matters very far removed from arithmetical problems.
ANDREI VYSHINSKY
UN General Assembly, 1950

I NTERNATIONAL organizations such as the United Nations, since
they so directly reflect man's hopes for peace and progress, frequently
arouse strongly ambivalent and fluctuating emotions. In the mid-1940's,
when there was no record yet by which the UN could be judged, the expectations were almost uniformly extravagant and Utopian. By the early 1950's,
after the disappointments over the Korean "police action," the UN was often
shrugged off with the damning phrase, "debating society." By the mid-1960's,
the new enthusiasm generated in the early stages of the Congo operation
faded into pessimism and jibes as the United Nations struggled to resolve its
financial and constitutional deadlocks.

The mixed reactions to the United Nations in its first twenty years reflected
in part a misunderstanding of its fundamental nature and capabilities. International organizations, like other functional relations of states, often have
more narrowly circumscribed roles in international relations than is commonly assumed. Their part in the affairs of nations is essentially determined
by the nature of the state system itself. As part of the institutionalized
mechanisms states create for handling mutual problems, they must be
expected also to reflect the nature and content of those problems. This can
best be illustrated by comparing the United Nations to the League of Nations
which it replaced. In this chapter we shall be concerned with gaining a clear
understanding of the origin, structure, and machinery; in the next, with an
analysis of the organizations and the causes of their successes and failures.

1 The Origin of International Organization

THE United Nations, when it came into existence in 1945, was built quite
deliberately upon the general pattern of the League of Nations (1920–1939).
Certain changes were made, as we shall note, to "strengthen" the UN and
avoid the weaknesses of the League. But the League itself did not represent
a total innovation. Its major organs, the small Council and the large Assembly, each had roots in previous experience with international organization.

The primitive forerunner of the Council (Security Council in the UN) was what was known in the nineteenth century as "The Concert of Europe"—a system of intermittent conferences (or "congresses" as they were then called) of Europe's great powers to deal with pressing international problems. The Concert normally confined its membership exclusively to great powers. It had no permanent organization.

The system originated in the collaboration of Great Britain, Austria, Prussia, and Russia against France in the Napoleonic Wars. The Quadruple Alliance of 1815 provided for "Meetings at fixed periods, either under the immediate auspices of the Sovereigns themselves, or by their respective Ministers, for the purpose of consulting upon their common interests." The Congresses never became "fixed" in the sense of regularly scheduled sessions, and the four powers soon began to disagree with one another on what was to be done in post-Napoleonic Europe. Originally they were to preserve the Allied victory of 1815 against France. But increasingly they found their main preoccupation in the suppression of revolts against monarchical authority in Europe. Great Britain ceased attending the Congresses after 1822, whereas France, at first excluded, became an active and equal member in 1818. The Holy Alliance, which had come into being in 1815, after this time used the Concert as its instrument. In the Treaty of the Holy Alliance (1815) the contracting monarchs (the rulers of Austria, Prussia, and Russia) had agreed upon "the necessity of establishing the course to be followed by the Powers, in their mutual relations, upon the sublime truths which the eternal Religion of our Saviour teaches to us." [1] What this meant in practice was a mandate to Austria at the Laibach Congress of 1821 to suppress the revolts in Italy and a similar mandate to France at the Congress of Verona in 1822 to do likewise in Spain. The absolute monarchs were attempting to maintain themselves absolutely. This process the British would not and could not support in view of their own interests and the constitutional character of the British monarchy.

The Holy Alliance, and its championship of absolutism, dissolved in the wake of the revolutions of 1830 and 1848 which swept most of Western and Central Europe, but the Concert system itself was salvaged for subsequent use. Britain resumed its participation in the conferences, which had altered their aim from suppression of revolt to the settlement of problems arising out of revolts and the growing nationalism. In 1829 the Powers, acting together, jointly recognized the independence of Greece, and in 1832 British and French forces intervened in Holland to support Belgian independence.[2] In the Belgian case a standing committee of the great powers met from time to time in London over a nine-year period to deal with the ramifications of the crisis. In this committee we see clearly the embryo of the later League and

---

[1] Preamble, *British and Foreign State Papers*, Vol. 3, pp. 211 ff. Author's translation.

[2] France in 1830 had become a constitutional monarchy, and Britain had been one throughout this period.

United Nations Councils. The Congress of Berlin of 1878 managed for a time to settle the Eastern Question (the future of the disintegrating Ottoman Empire), but the Congress system did not always avert war. It did not prevent the Crimean War. In 1870 Count Beust of Austria, failing in his efforts to convene a conference to avoid the Franco-Prussian War, had to exclaim in exasperation: "I cannot find Europe!" In 1914 Sir Edward Grey, British Foreign Secretary, was similarly disappointed by his failure to convoke a conference to prevent World War I.

These acts of the great powers had established important precedents prior to the outbreak of World War I. Thus, creation of the League Council did not mark an abrupt break with tradition. Instead, it reflected the formalization and further institutionalization of a method for dealing with problems affecting international peace and security that had long roots in the Concert system of diplomatic conferences.

Similarly, the roots of the League Assembly (General Assembly in the UN) can be traced back to the experience of great numbers of nations meeting together in specialized organizations (in periodic plenary sessions serviced by a permanent secretariat) to handle common technical problems. Of these, the Universal Postal Union (UPU) is probably the best known. Created in the 1870's, it continues today to supervise effectively the carrying of billions of pieces of mail. At the end of 1964 it had 127 members. This type of functional cooperation by states has been extended progressively during the last hundred years into many fields. By the late 1950's, there were 136 intergovernment organizations, including some less-known ones with more restricted memberships, such as the International Tin Study group and the Central Commission for the Navigation of the Rhine. With the creation of the League, new interest was spurred. Probably the best known specialized agency created in League times is the International Labor Organization, which strives to improve working conditions through international treaties. By the time of the UN, the process of creating new technical organizations, affiliated with the UN, had gone into high gear. Among the major specialized organizations of today, not mentioned so far, are eight of special importance: FAO (Food and Agriculture Organization) works to increase the output of farmlands, forests, and fisheries, as well as to raise nutrition levels. UNESCO (United Nations Educational, Scientific, and Cultural Organization) seeks through programs of cultural and intellectual cooperation to achieve universal literacy and a lessening of tensions that cause war. ICAO (International Civil Aviation Organization) encourages the use of safety measures, tries to gain the adoption of uniform regulations for the operations of international air services, and encourages simpler customs, immigration, and public health procedures at international airports. The International Bank for Reconstruction and Development makes loans for reconstruction and economic development. It works in conjunction with the International Monetary Fund, which is concerned with international monetary problems related to currency conversion and stabilization. WHO (World Health Organization) strives to prevent the spread of disease internationally, and works to stamp out widespread diseases such as tuberculosis and malaria. The ITU (International Telecommunications Union) allocates radio frequencies for the world's radio communication services and promotes cooperation on telegraph and telephone services. WMO (World Meteorological Organization) develops weather-forecasting services and exchanges weather information. This list could be extended almost indefinitely. Each of these organizations performs either a single function (UPU) or a closely related series of functions (ITU). Each tends to include all nations affected by its activities. The eight above as of September 30, 1965, had between 103 and 125 members. All of them so far mentioned are alike in that they were created by the nation-states to facilitate their dealings with one another on specialized functional or technical problems, such as the exchange of mail or allocation of radio wave lengths. Hence the name given to such organizations in the United Nations system today: the Specialized Agencies.

Under the UN the functional treatment of problems has been continued and expanded on an impressive scale. A brief mention must suffice. One outstanding new program has been the extension through the UN of technical skills to underdeveloped peoples. More than forty-five hundred experts, from some seventy different nationalities, participated in this program in the first five years. The United Nations High Commissioner for Refugees has been concerned with the problem of aiding over two million persons and resettling great numbers of homeless in new lands. UNICEF (the United Nations Children's Fund) was working in 1960 in one hundred four countries and territories on 367 projects. The trusteeship system, concerned with the well-being and progress toward self-government of the peoples of the UN trust territories, had its first "graduates" in 1960 when three of the eleven territories were admitted to the UN as full members.

So we see that public specialized organizations not only created precedents useful in establishing the Assembly and General Assembly but that the process has been interacting. Aside from the multiplication of such specialized agencies and the ever-growing extension of their activities, the new feature that has been added to international organization in the twentieth century is the establishment, a quarter century apart, of two general international organizations theoretically competent to deal with *any* international problem, whether technical, legal, or political.

Both the League of Nations (established in 1920) and the United Nations (established in 1945) have been built around a core of three organs: a council and an assembly, plus a court (whose roots were traced in Chapter 6), and a permanent secretariat. The resemblance to the familiar three functional organs of domestic or national government, though deliberate, is misleading in its implications. In both these organizations there was established an "executive" branch (the council being in both cases a small body varying from eight to as many as fifteen states under the League and a steady eleven states for the first twenty years of the United Nations), a "legislative" branch (the assembly's membership being equal to the number of states belonging), and a "judicial" branch. Both headed the "bureaucracy" with a Secretary-General.

The League, according to the Covenant, was designed to "promote international co-operation and to achieve international peace and security," [3] while the United Nations, according to its Charter, was to "maintain international peace and security," "develop friendly relations among nations," and "achieve international co-operation." [4] The strikingly identical aims of the organizations included the handling of unforeseen problems that might conceivably arise between and among states. That this is the intention the member states of both organizations had in mind is made abundantly clear in the remainder of the Covenant and Charter respectively. The League and the United Nations were not to deal merely with the distribution of mail or the control of infectious diseases (although they might through their affiliated organs do this too) but with any and all international problems that might threaten the peace of the world. And not only were they to have this wider authority but they were to exercise it through regular and frequent meetings.

2   The Creation of the League System

THE Covenant of the League of Nations, which formed Part I of the Treaty of Versailles, was signed on June 28, 1919, and came into effect on January 10, 1920.[5] The origin of the name "League of Nations" is obscure [6] but the intention of the founders at the Versailles Conference is clear. In a plenary resolution of the Versailles Conference on January 25, 1919, it was resolved that "a League of Nations be created to promote international co-operation, to ensure the fulfillment of accepted international obligations and to provide safeguards against war." Further, "The members of the League should *periodically meet* in international conference, and *should have a permanent organization and secretariat*." [7] The League, when it was made a living thing, faithfully reflected this intention.

The League's action, according to Article 2 of the Covenant, was to "be effected through the instrumentality of an Assembly and of a Council, with a permanent Secretariat." There were also to be certain permanent commissions, one to advise the Council on military questions and disarmament, and another to do the same for matters relating to the Mandates.[8] In Article 24 it provided that "all international bureaus already established by general

---

[3] From the Preamble of the Covenant of the League of Nations.

[4] From Article 1 of the Charter of the United Nations.

[5] The Covenant was also incorporated into the treaties of peace separately concluded by the World War I allies with the other defeated states.

[6] See F. P. Walters, *A History of the League of Nations.* Vol. I, p. 18.

[7] *Ibid.*, p. 32. Italics added.

[8] The former possessions of the defeated powers in the Pacific, in Africa, and in the Near East were given to the victorious powers for administration as "mandates" pending the time when these mandates might "stand by themselves under the strenuous conditions of the modern world." (Article 22 of the Covenant.)

treaties" be placed under the League's "direction," "if the parties to such treaties consent." All new specialized international organizations (for this is what was meant by the words "international bureaus") would be placed under League direction from the outset.

From these arrangements emerges a clear picture of what was intended by the creation of the League. The League was first to direct the activities of specialized international organizations and to coordinate them ("to promote international co-operation"). This is a logical outgrowth of the nineteenth-century proliferation of such agencies. Some degree of coordination had become necessary to avoid an overlapping of responsibility and unnecessary duplication of staff. Even if the League had not been created with other functions, this alone would have justified the existence of some such centralized organ.

The League was also to see, secondly, that international obligations to settle disputes peacefully were fulfilled and, thirdly, that safeguards were provided against aggression and war. This would be accomplished by means of periodic international conferences within the context of a permanent organization and secretariat. To put it another way, the mechanism of the Concert of Europe was to be reinstituted, with slight modifications, in the Council. Further, the democratic principle that all nations should have some voice (such as they already had in existing technical organizations) would be implemented through an Assembly open to all. Both organs were to meet in periodic conferences. Finally, the whole organization was to be held together on a continuing basis with the aid of a permanent secretariat. This is the Concert of Europe, with democratic additions and with a permanently organized basis. It was also the intention and expectation of the League's founders that the Council would be the main organ of the organization.

It should now be apparent why the League of Nations did not represent in its actual functions an abrupt break with tradition.[9] Rather it represented the institutionalization of the well-accepted diplomatic technique of the international conference, although on a much broader basis than ever before. Instead of *ad hoc* sessions which might not be convened because of the stubbornness and pride of a single power, such as had hampered the work of the Concert, conferences were to be on a permanent basis which would "meet from time to time as occasion" required but "at least once a year," usually "at the Seat of the League" in Geneva, Switzerland. At these meetings the Council could deal "with any matter within the sphere of action of the League or affecting the peace of the world." [10] Similar provisions were made for the meetings of the Assembly, and it was given a similar grant of authority.[11]

The League was essentially a development in harmony with earlier precedents, both diplomatic and technical, except that it went further along already clearly marked-out paths. It brought together under the aegis of one

---

[9] It *did* represent a great break in its underlying ideas as represented in particular by President Wilson.

[10] Article 4.

[11] Article 3.

general organization the hitherto scattered and separate technical organizations and provided for a two-organ permanent international diplomatic conference. Thus was realized the "general association of nations" that President Wilson had called for in the last of his Fourteen Points; in that association diplomacy was henceforth to proceed more or less under the dictum laid down in the first of those same Fourteen Points—that is, "frankly and in the public view." Here a real innovation was introduced, for in the League, and even more so in the United Nations, open diplomacy came into widespread use.

3 *The United Nations*

BEFORE examining the nature of the rocks on which the League of Nations at length came to grief and which today also threaten the United Nations, it will be useful to consider how the United Nations developed from the League, just as we have already noted how the League itself grew out of earlier precedents.

The United Nations, like the League, is a general organization embracing technical as well as diplomatic and legal organs. The number and variety of the specialized agencies has mushroomed under the United Nations. In addition, the number of major organs of the United Nations proper has been increased beyond the bare Council and Assembly of League days. The new and successor Council is now known as the Security Council, and the Assembly of the League has been transformed into the General Assembly of the United Nations.[12] There are now added two new Councils, the Economic and Social Council (ECOSOC) and the Trusteeship Council. Although these new Councils (and the International Court) are all termed *principal organs* of the United Nations, and therefore presumably of equal importance with the Security Council and General Assembly, actually both the ECOSOC and the Trusteeship Council report to the General Assembly, just as under the League the permanent commissions reported to the major organs. Although the structure is more elaborate under the United Nations than it was at first under the League, it basically reflects the *de facto* changes that came about during the League's existence. That is, the United Nations basically incorporated the administrative advances pioneered by the League, and its more elaborate structure does not represent so much a departure from the League system as it does an improved administrative version of the League.[13]

In its essence the United Nations is, so far as its vital functions are concerned, an "improved"[14] version of the League. It provides under one organizational roof for the coordination of a multitude of technical functions and

---

12 The student will do well to fix these terms in mind since they will be used repeatedly in this chapter.

13 This is basically true, although a detailed analysis of the trusteeship system would reveal some striking contrasts to the League Mandates system, etc.

14 Whether it is really an improvement will be considered below.

for the transaction of diplomatic business affecting peace and war through the League (and Concert) device of the international conference on a permanent and continuing basis served by a secretariat.

4 The United Nations: Organs, Composition, and Power

TURNING to the major organs of the United Nations which are in fact the basic organs, the Security Council and the General Assembly,[15] we find some important differences when we compare them with their equivalent organs under the League.

The Charter of the United Nations, signed on June 26, 1945, and coming into force on October 24, 1945, initially provided for a Security Council of eleven members (Article 23), five of whom were stipulated by name: the Republic of China, France, the U.S.S.R., the United Kingdom, and the United States of America. The General Assembly was given the power to "elect six other Members of the United Nations to be non-permanent members of the Security Council" for two-year terms (Article 23). They were not immediately eligible for re-election.

By comparison, the League Council's size was more flexible. While the initial provisions named five permanent powers, the Assembly could add others and could raise the number of non-permanent seats.

During the course of the League's history, Germany was given a permanent seat (1926); when Japan resigned, Russia received one. Italy withdrew in the wake of the Ethiopian crisis. The United States never belonged. While the permanent seats fluctuated, the number of non-permanent seats was altered, too. To generalize, the number of permanent seats tended to diminish between 1920 and 1939, and the number of non-permanent seats to increase (six in 1922, nine in 1926, ten in 1933, and eleven in 1936). Because the United States never accepted her seat, the League Council, designed originally as an executive body with the great powers in a majority, began its existence with eight states, four great and four small or medium powers. The progressive preponderance of the small over the great powers increased with the passing years. By 1936, when there were eleven non-permanent seats, there were only the United Kingdom, France, and the U.S.S.R. occupying permanent seats (and on December 14, 1939, the Soviet Union was expelled). By 1936 the great powers were a small minority on the Council; this fact explains in part the growing impotence of the Council in the mid-1930's.

In the United Nations, by contrast, short of revision of the Charter, this type of development cannot occur, since the seats are fixed by number and by state. This rigidity meant that the Security Council was unable to adjust to fluctuations in the status of nations as great powers. In 1945 all the nations

---

[15] The International Court is a basic organ, too. It has already been considered in detail in the chapter on international law.

capable of exerting really significant force were granted permanent seats on the Council. By 1955 Germany and Japan had regained great power status. But Germany was not admitted to the UN at all and Japan, when it gained membership in 1956, obtained no permanent Security Council seat. This has weakened the all-great-power character of the Security Council. India, although a United Nations member, has no permanent Security Council seat. While China has had a seat on the Council from the beginning, since 1949 the seat has been held by the Nationalist Government on Formosa. To summarize, in 1945 all the then significant powers had seats: four out of four (France, Britain, United States, U.S.S.R.). By a decade later, out of the eight or nine significant powers in the world, only four had seats. The first amendment to the Charter, which came into effect on August 31, 1965, enlarged the Security Council to 15 by adding four non-permanent members. It did not enlarge the permanent seats, nor did it allow the General Assembly discretion to add seats on its own initiative.[16] Thus the trend in the United Nations is identical to that of the League, although for different reasons.

The General Assembly of the United Nations was originally composed of fifty-one nations and by the end of 1950 had attained a membership of sixty. East-West deadlock in the Security Council, and the use of the veto, then held membership constant for over five years. In December 1955, a compromise brought in sixteen new members (12 non-Communist, 4 Communist). In 1956 four more states were admitted (total of 80); in 1957–1958 three more; and in 1960, seventeen—all but one of these last from Africa. The number of members increased five in 1961; six in 1962; and three more in each of the next three years. Eleven of these twenty were African states. In 1965, Indonesia became the first member to withdraw. The total at the end of 1965 was 117.[17] Optimists hailed the virtual all-inclusiveness of the new UN as a mark of progress—which it was. But Indonesia's withdrawal was a danger signal. And the fact that Germany and Communist China, each the center of grave international tensions, remained outside was a source of deep-reaching and continuing weakness. While Indonesia resumed her seat in 1966, the other problems remained.

There are differences in the authority given to the United Nations organs, compared with their League equivalents. It will be remembered that both the League Council and League Assembly were given identical mandates to "deal with any matter . . . affecting the peace of the world." [18] The anticipation

---

[16] The resolution containing the amendment called for the ten non-permanent seats to be allocated by geographic area: five to Africa and Asia; one to East Europe; two to Latin America; two to Western Europe and others. The same amendment added nine new members to ECOSOC. In December 1965, the first elections on the new basis were held.

[17] Syria lost her separate seat in 1958 when she formed the United Arab Republic with Egypt. When this broke up in 1961 Syria was again counted separately. In 1964 Tanganyika and Zanzibar merged to form Tanzania. These changes explain why admission numbers and totals diverge. UN membership in December 1966 reached 122.

[18] Article 3, Paragraph 3 and Article 4, Paragraph 4, for the Assembly and Council respectively.

in 1920 that the Council would be the more important body of the two did not stem from any difference in the basic grant of authority but from the assumption that the smaller body, containing the planned great power majority, would do the primary work because it would be less unwieldy in size and because of its great-power character. In practice the Assembly began to be of progressively greater importance; in the end it virtually supplanted the Council as the major decision-making organ. Since the Council was soon heavily weighted in favor of small and medium powers, the only basic difference between the Council and the Assembly became size. It was soon considered an advantage to have the entire membership assume responsibility for actions taken, by having the decisions made in the Assembly. The relatively small size of the Council, from this standpoint, became a liability.

When the United Nations was created, it was assumed that this League trend, from a power standpoint, was a cause rather than a symptom of the weakness of the organ. Such a trend was to be prevented in two ways. First, the membership of the Security Council would be specified so that each of the great powers would have a seat; this design failed, because its very inflexibility ruled out adjustment to changes in great-power status over the years. Second, the Security Council would be granted greater powers than those bestowed upon the General Assembly.

The Security Council began life with the "primary responsibility" in the United Nations "for the maintenance of international peace and security"; the other members of the United Nations agreed that, in carrying out its duties under this responsibility, the Security Council should act on their behalf (Article 24). Moreover, according to Article 25, "The Members of the United Nations agree to accept and carry out the *decisions* of the Security Council." [19] To emphasize further the preponderant role of the Security Council, Article 12 provided that "While the Security Council is exercising in respect of any dispute or situation the functions assigned to it . . . the General Assembly shall not make any recommendations with regard to that dispute or situation unless the Security Council so requests." By contrast, the League Assembly suffered under no such restriction, and could act concurrently with the League Council.

How these provisions were frustrated in their purpose by subsequent events will be explored in Sections 7 and 8 below.

5 The United Nations: Voting

IN both the League of Nations and United Nations, provision had to be made for the transaction of ordinary, routine business. The arrangements in both organizations were much the same. Under the League (Article 5) "All matters of procedure at meetings of the Assembly or of the Council . . .

---

[19] Italics added. "Decisions" in this sense means actions by the Security Council, under Chapter VII of the Charter, to enforce peace.

may be decided by a majority of the Members of the League represented at the meeting." Under the United Nations the General Assembly's "Decisions on other [than important] questions . . . shall be made by a majority of the members present and voting." (Article 18.) The Security Council was, however, to take votes "on procedural matters . . . by an affirmative vote of seven [out of eleven] members" (Article 27), which is slightly more than a simple majority. The Charter amendment made this 9 out of 15.

On procedural questions all members in both the League and United Nations were and are considered bound by the group decision. They were expected either to comply or withdraw. Such procedural matters were and are normally issues of secondary importance, such as questions of when to meet and when to adjourn, and what agenda items to consider and in what order. All "important" issues were reserved for a different handling altogether.

For important questions under the League, the general rule (Article 5) was that "decisions at any meeting of the Assembly or of the Council shall require the agreement of all the Members of the League represented at the meeting." This was the so-called "rule of unanimity." Under it any one state could block a decision in either body on any important issue. There were important exceptions, and the article just quoted begins with the limiting words "Except where otherwise expressly provided. . . ." In the United Nations Assembly important questions are handled by two-thirds vote and in the Security Council by "an affirmative vote of seven [now nine] members including the concurrent votes of the permanent members." [20]

In general, the United Nations voting provisions on important questions are more liberal. No single state can block Security Council decisions unless it has a veto (U.S., U.S.S.R., Britain, France, and China); under the League Council any one state had a veto. As far as the Assembly is concerned, there is not as great a change, since it was "expressly provided" in several places in the Covenant that on certain specified matters such as the election of non-permanent members to the League Council, a two-thirds vote would suffice. Indeed, in the vital peace machinery as set up in Article 15 there is a provision for a simple majority vote by the Assembly.[21] Since there are no unanimous votes required in the General Assembly, it represents a more liberal arrangement than prevailed under the League.

6 The United Nations: Peace Machinery

THE most important aspect today of the peace machinery of the League is not so much its precise provisions as what happened to it. In Articles 13 through 15 of the Covenant a logical procedure was laid down by which members in dispute were to choose either legal settlement or group mediation

---

[20] The article (27) goes on to say: "provided that, in decisions under Chapter VI, and under Paragraph 3 of Article 52, a party to a dispute shall abstain from voting."

[21] Which was, however, to be coupled to a unanimous vote in the League Council (less the parties to the dispute).

by the Council. Members were obligated to do the one or the other; they were also pledged to refrain from making war on any other party which accepted the court's decision. If the group mediation by the Council was chosen, and the Council decided unanimously (less the parties to the dispute), the parties were pledged not to "go to war with any party to the dispute which complies with the recommendation" of the Council. In case of a split Council vote the obligation of the disputing states was not to go to war for three months. This was the so-called "gap in the Covenant," which allowed war to remain legal under such conditions. Penalties for violation of the Covenant were enumerated in the key Article 16.

According to Article 16, if any member should "resort to war in disregard of its covenants under Articles 12, 13, or 15, it shall *ipso facto* be deemed to have committed an act of war against all other Members of the League." [22]

Sanctions would then be imposed, and the "severance of all trade or financial relations" with the transgressor was to be followed by the Council's recommending "what effective military, naval, or air force the Members of the League shall severally contribute to the armed forces to be used to protect the covenants of the League." [23]

The gaps notwithstanding, the League Covenant promised important safeguards to its members. There was the promise in Article 10 (which Wilson considered to be the "heart" of the Covenant) that "The Members of the League undertake to respect and preserve as against external aggression the territorial integrity and existing political independence of all Members of the League." In case of violation, or even the threat of aggression, the Council was to "advise upon the means by which this obligation" would be fulfilled. There was the promise of immediate and automatic economic sanctions under Article 16 to be used against those resorting to war in disregard of Articles 12, 13, or 15. Supplementing this would be the recommendation to the Members from the Council as to what armed forces they were to "severally contribute . . . to protect the covenants of the League."

The League had hardly commenced functioning before both Articles 10 and 16 were "interpreted."

In 1921 the three Scandinavian nations of Denmark, Norway, and Sweden were disturbed by the prospect of being called upon to shoulder a burden of economic sanctions out of proportion to their strength if Article 16 should be invoked against Germany. They sponsored a set of interpretative resolutions on the "meaning" of that article. The Second League Assembly unanimously agreed that:

---

[22] The article went on to provide that the members would in such case "undertake immediately to subject it to the severance of all trade or financial relations, the prohibition of all intercourse between their nationals and the nationals of the covenant-breaking State, and the prevention of all financial, commercial or personal intercourse between the nationals of the covenant-breaking State and the nationals of any other State, whether a Member of the League or not."

[23] Article 16, Paragraph 2.

3. *The unilateral action of the defaulting State cannot create a state of war: it merely entitles the other Members of the League to resort to acts of war* or to declare themselves in a state of war with the Covenant-breaking State; but it is in accordance with the spirit of the Covenant that the League of Nations should attempt, at least at the outset, to avoid war, and to restore peace by economic pressure.

4. *It is the duty of each Member of the League to decide for itself whether a breach of the Covenant has been committed. . . .*[24]

8. The Council shall recommend the date on which the enforcement of economic pressure . . . is to be begun. . . .

9. All States must be treated alike as regards the application of the measures of economic pressure, with the following reservations:

   (a) It may be necessary to recommend the execution of special measures by certain States.
   (b) If it is thought desirable to postpone, wholly or partially, in the case of certain States, the effective application of economic sanctions laid down in Article 16, such postponement shall not be permitted except in so far as it is desirable for the success of the common plan of action, or reduces to a minimum the losses and embarrassments which may be entailed.[25]

By these interpretations the "teeth" were removed from Article 16. Far from sanctions automatically following a breach of the Covenant, each state would *decide for itself* whether it considered the Covenant breached. If it wished, it was "entitled" to resort to acts of war; but it was in accord "with the spirit of the Covenant" that the League should try to avoid war and restore peace by economic sanctions, provided these could be put into effect without too many "losses and embarrassments"! The freedom of the decision as to whether or not to oppose aggression was then returned to the individual states. That these "interpretations" actually altered the meaning of Article 16 can hardly be doubted when it is remembered that the text of Article 16 as originally proposed at Versailles provided that a Member of the League that resorted to war in violation of the Covenant would automatically be considered in a state of war with the other Members. This was altered to "it shall *ipso facto* be deemed to have committed an act of war against all other Members of the League, which hereby undertake *immediately* to subject it to the severance of all trade or financial relations." This alteration was made because the United States Constitution provides that only Congress has the power to declare war.[26] After these interpretations no immediate economic sanctions could be firmly anticipated. Indeed, unless the states individually decided that

---

[24] This was followed by the injunction that "The fulfillment of their duties under Article 16 is required from Members of the League by the express terms of the Covenant, and they cannot neglect them without breach of their Treaty obligations." Nevertheless, they were to *decide for themselves.*

[25] For the complete text see *League of Nations Official Journal,* Special Supplement No. 6 (October 1921), pp. 24 ff. Italics added.

[26] See F. P. Walters, *A History of the League of Nations,* Vol. I, p. 53, for a discussion of the originally proposed provision.

a breach of the Covenant had occurred, no sanctions of any kind could be expected.

In 1923 at the Fourth League Assembly, Article 10 was "interpreted." Fearing the implications of this article while the United States remained outside the League, Canada sponsored the following interpretation:

1. It is in conformity with the spirit of Article 10 that, in the event of the Council considering it to be its duty to recommend the application of military measures in consequence of an aggression, or danger or threat of aggression, *the Council shall be bound to take account, more particularly, of the geographical situation and of the special conditions of each state.*

2. *It is for the constitutional authorities of each Member to decide,* in reference to the obligation of preserving the independence and the integrity of the territory of Members, *in what degree the Member is bound to assure the execution of this* obligation by employment of its military forces.[27]

"The recommendation made by the Council" was to be regarded as of the "highest importance," but each state was to *decide for itself* whether or not it would do anything to oppose aggression.

This second set of resolutions, sponsored by Canada, failed to gain a unanimous vote (twenty-nine for, twenty-two abstaining, one against). The lone vote of Persia prevented its adoption. But it was another indication of League sentiment. It was perfectly clear that some three-fifths of the Members wanted to retain complete discretion over when and how and whether to participate in sanctions.

Even so, as we shall see in Chapter 20, collective security in the Ethiopian Case was frustrated neither by the "gaps" nor by these wholesale invitations to shirk responsibility in the face of aggression. The fundamental weaknesses of the League were not so much constitutional as the weaknesses of the constitution were a reflection of more fundamental difficulties.

When the United Nations Charter was written, it was intended that such "gaps" would be eliminated and that there would be no doubt of the organization's "teeth." The new security machinery was designed to eliminate loopholes. Just as the heart of the League's machinery for handling disputes was found in four articles, so, too, the heart of the United Nations' machinery is concentrated in a small part of the Charter—specifically in Chapters VI and VII.

Chapter VI, entitled "Pacific Settlement of Disputes," is roughly equivalent to Articles 12, 13, and 15 of the Covenant. In it the parties to any dispute "likely to endanger the maintenance of international peace and security" pledge "first of all, [to] seek a solution by negotiation, enquiry, mediation, conciliation, arbitration, judicial settlement, resort to regional agencies or arrangements, or other peaceful means of their own choice." [28] In short they are to settle the dispute peacefully either by use of a legal or political method.

---

[27] For the complete text see *League of Nations Official Journal,* Special Supplement No. 14 (September 1923), p. 27. Italics added.

[28] Article 33.

The Security Council "may investigate any dispute" [29] and may "at any stage of a dispute . . . recommend appropriate procedures or methods of adjustment." [30] If the parties fail to settle their dispute otherwise (using either political or legal methods), "they shall refer it to the Security Council." [31]

If the Security Council is unable to settle the dispute peacefully, it may use its powers under Chapter VII, which is entitled "Action with Respect to Threats to the Peace, Breaches of the Peace, and Acts of Aggression."

Once the Security Council is convinced that no peaceful solution of the problem is possible, it may decide to use sanctions. Such sanctions are provided for in Articles 41 and 42. Article 41 stipulates that the Security Council "may decide what measures not involving the use of armed force are to be employed to give effect to its decisions, and it may call upon the Members . . . to apply such measures. These may include complete or partial interruption of economic relations and of rail, sea, air, postal, telegraphic, radio, and other means of communication, and the severance of diplomatic relations." If the Security Council considers these measures "inadequate," under Article 42 "it may take such action by air, sea, or land forces as may be necessary to maintain or restore international peace and security. Such action may include demonstrations, blockade, and other operations by air, sea, or land forces of Members of the United Nations." [32] The forces to be so used were to be furnished to the Security Council by prior agreements made by the various members with the Security Council under Article 43. The agreements, to be made "as soon as possible," were "to make available to the Security Council, on its call . . . armed forces, assistance, and facilities, including rights of passage . . ."

This grant of power to the Security Council was far wider than the power given to either the League Council or League Assembly, or to both of them jointly. No loopholes were left whereby parties to a dispute could go to war (other than in self-defense) without violating the Charter. Of course, the Security Council might fail to act, but it was granted the power in Articles 41 and 42 to use any of the means listed, from persuasion and mediation all the way to armed force, if it deemed it necessary. The effective use of such measures depended upon two things in particular: that agreements would be made under Article 43, and that sufficient great-power unanimity would exist to permit their use. But to date no such agreements have been made; and the great powers have not often been unanimous. Which brings us to the veto.

7   The Veto in the Security Council

WE have already made clear the difference in the voting arrangements of the League Council and the United Nations Security Council: on pro-

---

[29] Article 34.
[30] Article 36.
[31] Article 37.
[32] Article 42.

cedural matters they are very similar; on important substantive questions the League Council required unanimity (less the parties to a dispute), and the UN Security Council required seven (now nine) out of eleven (now fifteen) affirmative votes (including the concurring votes of the Big Five). Although the Security Council is freer to act than was the League Council, the provisions are still very similar in that, under both organs, it was taken for granted that, unless the great powers were in substantial agreement, nothing effective in the way of enforcement action could or should follow. Note also that no permanent Security Council member who is a party to a dispute can veto action against itself under Chapter VI, although it can veto the sanctions provided under Chapter VII.[33] This is a step backward from the League machinery in that a Big Five aggressor can veto enforcement action against itself while under the League such an aggressor was excluded from judging its own case.

Although Article 27 of the Charter prescribes, for substantive questions, that the nine affirmative votes should include the "concurring" votes of the Big Five, one great step forward was taken by the Security Council when, in practice, it proceeded to consider that a Big Five abstention was not a veto. This liberalization of the Charter has kept the number of vetoes from being even larger. A permanent member now has three kinds of votes it can cast: affirmative, negative, or abstaining. In circumstances similar to those in which a number of the Soviet Union's vetoes have been cast where she did not oppose the *principle* of what was proposed but wanted the resolution even stronger (as in condemning Franco Spain), she may now choose abstention instead.

The real use and value of abstentions is on issues where a nation does not really wish to be committed either pro or con. Many issues may be forced to a vote that are not ripe for settlement but might be ripe somewhat later. In such cases premature affirmative or negative votes serve no good purpose. The disposition to take a vote anyhow is encouraged by the pseudo-parliamentary machinery of the United Nations. Since the votes reflect national policies and since these policies are rooted in national interests and values, a sharply split vote does no more in the long run than register the disagreement for posterity. Whereas national parliamentary votes are followed by the concrete implementation of the policies adopted by the vote, in a permanent diplomatic conference such as the United Nations a sharply split vote merely records the unwillingness of the negative voters to implement the policy favored by the majority. Particularly where the vote is taken on an important issue, expectations are aroused that are doomed to disappointment. Because in the last analysis the members of the United Nations are sovereign states, the real implementation of policies adopted by the United Nations rests basically on each one of them. Where cooperation in a case is not vital to what is contemplated, it is not important if a state is outvoted. But it is a *reductio ad*

---

[33] See Article 27 of the Charter.

absurdum, for example, for the United Nations solemnly to vote down a Soviet plan for disarmament (by reducing national armed forces by a flat one third), adopt a United States plan that was opposed to it in basic principle, and then expect any concrete results. What has been overlooked in such a case is the elementary consideration that no Western power will disarm unless the Soviet Union does, and if the Soviets will not disarm according to the American plan (or vice versa), there is little point in going through with the solemn farce of voting the one plan in and the other plan out.

Since it was considered in 1945 that the Security Council would be the heart of the United Nations, and since the above argument about the futility of votes under such circumstances was considered valid, the veto was incorporated into the structure. That a Big Five member committing aggression can veto enforcement action against itself under Chapter VII was justified on the basis that collective security, unless supported by all the Big Five, would be futile. This questionable reasoning we shall consider in Chapters 20 and 21 in connection with case studies of collective security. But, in general, the veto was a sensible idea provided its use could be kept within bounds.

The veto was at first used extensively, but later with declining frequency. As of December 19, 1947 (after a little more than two years), some twenty-three vetoes had been cast.[34] By contrast, as of January 1951 a total of only forty-eight vetoes had been recorded. Ten years later still, of a total of 99 vetoes, 92 had been cast by the Soviet Union (and the rest by China, the United Kingdom, and France). By December 1964, the total was only 111, with Russia's share 103. The greatest number of Soviet vetoes was directed in early years at keeping pro-Western states outside the UN membership or at protecting Communist "satellites" from investigation by the Security Council (as, for example, Hungary in 1956).

The Soviets, thus applying the veto, received severe criticism. In turn, they pointed to the "hidden veto" being used by the Western bloc. A proposal, as they said, was as much defeated if it failed to muster the required affirmative votes as it was if it did and was then vetoed. Since the Western bloc has "controlled" sufficient votes, proposals could be (and were) defeated without much use of the veto. The Soviet contention is correct, and it is one-sided to point merely to Russian obstructionism. But it is still valid to observe that the veto as used by the Soviet Union went beyond what was considered sound when the organization was founded.

The decline in resort to the veto stems from three factors. First, the battles over allowing new members no longer occur much since the 1955 deadlock was broken. Second, sufficient precedent and experience has accumulated after twenty years to make it obvious where a veto will be made if the issue is pressed, and the United States has concluded that forcing the Soviet Union to make additional vetoes has limited advantages. Third, and most important,

---

[34] Norman J. Padelford, "The Use of the Veto," *International Organization*, Vol. 2, No. 2 (June 1948), pp. 227–246. This article is an excellent analysis of the problem.

after 1950, much of the important business of the UN began to be transacted instead in the General Assembly where the veto does not apply. Either the Security Council was simply by-passed, or else the issue was removed from its agenda by a procedural vote once deadlock was obvious.

8 The Changed Role of the General Assembly

THE deadlock among the great powers was foreshadowed early in the United Nations' history by their failure to implement Article 43 of the Charter. From a legal viewpoint the United Nations' security apparatus has never really been implemented in the contemplated form. Article 106 of the Charter provided that "Pending the coming into force of such special agreements referred to in Article 43 as in the opinion of the Security Council enable it to begin the exercise of its responsibilities under Article 42" (which permits the Security Council to use armed force), the five permanent powers are to take "such joint action on behalf of the Organization as may be necessary for the purpose of maintaining international peace and security."

Legally, the Security Council has not yet "begun the exercise of its responsibilities" by declaring itself of the opinion that it is ready to use armed force. The Council has functioned, but the Big Five have been the responsible caretakers on an ad interim basis. And these have disagreed with one another. Under such circumstances the United Nations has possessed no pledged armed forces that the Security Council could decide to order into action. It has relied in theory upon the armies of the Big Five and in practice upon forces volunteered.

The Security Council, hampered by the veto, lacking any forces at its command, saddled with a highly restricted and unrepresentative membership, and claiming as permanent members only half the great powers, has lost its originally intended star role. Where, as in the Congo, it has still occasionally begun strong action, the spotlight of attention soon shifts to the Assembly— for at least equal billing.

The move toward "strengthening" the General Assembly began as soon as the early pattern of Security Council behavior had been revealed. A climax came in the wake of North Korea's aggression when, following Secretary Acheson's presentation of the "Uniting for Peace" Resolution to the General Assembly, that body adopted its main provisions on November 3, 1950, by a vote of fifty-two for, five against, and two abstentions. The adoption of this resolution did not mean that the majority of United Nations members had lost all hope of the Security Council's functioning effectively, but it did record their determination to have the Assembly fill the vacuum insofar as and for as long as the Security Council remained deadlocked. The General Assembly recommended that each member "maintain within its national armed forces elements so trained, organized, and equipped that they could promptly be made available . . . for service as a United Nations unit or units." Thus the lack of "earmarked" armed forces was to be remedied, although each member still retained full discretion as to whether and when and how to use such forces. In addition, a "Collective Measures Committee" was to formulate plans for the application of sanctions as needed. It is significant that the fourteen members of this committee included no representatives from the Soviet bloc. The larger role of the General Assembly was emphasized in the resolution which provided that "if the Security Council, because of lack of unanimity of the permanent members, fails to exercise its primary responsibility . . . in any case where there appears to be a threat to the peace, breach of the peace, or act of aggression, the General Assembly shall consider the matter immediately with a view to making appropriate recommendations to Members for collective measures, including in the case

TABLE 5

Meetings of the General Assembly and the
Security Council, 1946–1965

Year	Security Council	General Assembly
	(Total Number of Meetings Held)	(Total Number of Plenary Meetings Held)
1946	88	67
1947	137	61
1948	171	59
1949	62	89
1950	72	50
1951	39	31
1952	42	54
1953	43	60
1954	32	44
1955	23	45
1956	50	72
1957	49	99
1958	36	61
1959	5	65
1960	71	103
1961	68	127
1962	38	115
1963	59	83
1964	104 *	29 *
1965	81 *	94 *

* The figures in these years reflect the deadlock over UN finances which hampered the General Assembly's functioning (see Chapter 10).

of a breach of the peace or act of aggression the use of armed forces when necessary." The General Assembly was henceforth to be summoned in such circumstances on twenty-four hours' notice. These measures were intended to be an organizational improvement over the purely *ad hoc* measures used in the Korean Case. But here, too, the earmarking of forces occurred only on a limited and tentative basis. No great power responded. Ironically, when the resolution was first used in November 1956, in the Middle East crisis, with the dispatch of UN troops to Egypt to supervise the cease-fire, it was again pure *ad hoc* improvisation.

The increased importance of the General Assembly can be seen in quantitative terms.

The relative frequency of meetings is only broadly indicative. More significant in assessing the importance of the change are the data given in the next table. Note how the Assembly has shared or taken over the leading role from the Council. Of course, quantitative data of this kind is worth only so much, for it does not show the comparative importance of issues. And certain issues (such as Kashmir) turn up to be counted every year since they stay on the agenda. Still more significant is to note below who handled the critical fighting stages in the Congo operation.

TABLE 6

Political and Security Questions in the
*United Nations, 1946–1965 **

Year	General Assembly Only	Security Council Only	Both the Assembly and Council
	(Plenary Meetings)		
1946	8	7	2
1947	7	9	1
1948	6	8	3
1949	9	8	5
1950	17	4	4
1951	9	8	3
1952	14	6	2
1953	13	2	2
1954	11	3	2
1955	11	2	2
1956	5	4	1
1957	18	8	2
1958	13	4	1
1959	12	2	0
1960	7	8	2
1961	11	4	4
1962	15	6	1
1963	10	8	3
1964	**	11	—
1965	3	4	—

* Both because UN official records are so slow, and to enhance comparability, this tabulation follows the listing in the quarterly *International Organization*. Issues discussed more than once in any one year are counted once.

** The budget deadlock year. The Secretary General announced the understanding that issues involving objections would not be raised. (See Chapter 10).

9 *The UN: A Preliminary Balance-Sheet*

THE major reason for the UN's existence is its role in peace and security matters. The frequent failure of the Security Council to act decisively, and its increasing lack of important great powers as permanent members, has thrown more responsibility to the General Assembly. The General Assembly may be unwieldy but at least India and Japan are regularly represented there (even if Germany and Communist China are not). Moreover the intensity of the East-West quarrels and the failure to earmark forces reduces expectations of the joint use of force so that the resort to the power of numbers is increasingly tempting. Where the Security Council does not have all the great powers anyhow, and where those that are there disagree and stymie decisions with vetoes, the General Assembly is much freer to act: it has all the great powers represented who are in the UN; it has everybody else too; and there is no veto. If the criterion is force, it has that potentially in its membership; and if the standard is a "representative cross-section of mankind" (world public opinion) then it has that in much greater abundance than the Security Council can hope to have.

So the General Assembly continues to spread its wings; even where action nowadays originates in the Security Council, it is the General Assembly which tends to see it through—at least on issues where concensus is forthcoming. Out of the fact of its increased size and role come other problems—which we shall consider in Chapter 10.

The UN not only became bigger but it also began to think bigger. Later on (in Chapters 12 and 28) we shall examine its contribution to the pacific settlement of disputes. We shall see that in many cases where right and wrong are not clearly distinguishable, and where resort to force has occurred in a fashion not easily definable as "aggression," the UN has, quite sensibly, tended to focus its efforts on ways of bringing hostilities to a close. In its later efforts to do this it has taken the novel step of recruiting armed forces whose primary aim (in contrast to collective security action as in Korea) is not to shoot anyone but to aid in preventing further bloodshed. These peace-keeping forces represent essentially a further elaboration of peaceful settlement techniques.

The first tentative UN efforts along this line came in the Palestine War in 1947–1949 (see Chapter 12); the next development came with the dispatch of the 6,000-man UN Emergency Force from ten nations, to aid in the separation of the belligerents of the Suez War in 1956 (see Chapter 12). In 1958 some 190 military observers from fifteen nations, plus 60 pilots and specialists, were sent to Lebanon as a UN Observation Group.[35] The UN Congo Force (which began with some 10,000 men from nine nations, most of them

---

[35] See Lincoln P. Bloomfield, *The United Nations and U.S. Foreign Policy*, Boston: Little, Brown, 1960, pp. 67–68.

African), dispatched to the Congo in 1960, represented one further and rather revolutionary change. In the other cases the task of these forces was clearly oriented toward preventing further clashes between regular or irregular armed forces of different nationalities, on or near a frontier. In the Congo case the main mission was *internal*: to take over the police function and restore civil tranquility in order to pave the way for a progressive development of still embryonic organs of self-government. Here the Security Council took the initiative (although it did not meet in the later stages of the Congo question to handle the fighting there of December 1961, or December 1962).

Although the Congo operation (see Chapter 28) was certainly in part the result of Western fears of Communist infiltration in the Congo, it was still a remarkable venture—especially for an organization whose Charter imposes the strict rule of non-intervention in internal affairs. This action was precedent-shattering. It led directly to the UN crisis of 1964–1965 examined in the next chapter. Equally precedent-shattering (for much the same reasons, plus the fact that it had no forces to fall back upon) was the Security Council's imposition of "mandatory" economic sanctions against Rhodesia in December 1966. By a vote of 11 to 0, with Russia, France, Bulgaria, and Mali abstaining, 12 of Rhodesia's chief exports were banned and supplies of oil were to be withheld. But, significantly, African amendments requiring the use of naval blockade were voted down. Clearly, the General Assembly would come to play a role in this, too.

10   *The Major Trends*

THIS chapter has shown that in important respects the United Nations is far more like the League than was generally assumed in 1945. Indeed, the development of the organizations show strong parallels, even though the much greater size of the UN, its naturally more ambitious program, and the increased institutionalization of today, also make for significant differences in the UN's scope. Two major common trends should be noted. One is the degree to which the small organ or council has yielded its power to, or shared its power with, the large organ or assembly. The second is the striking fact that under the League the "teeth" of enforcement action were pulled by "interpretation." Similarly in the United Nations the planned-for "teeth" have failed to grow, because the states have failed to provide armed forces automatically available to the Security Council. The states have tended to retain or regain discretion over when and where they will resort to force on behalf of the UN. Both these trends are significant surface symptoms of more deeply hidden difficulties—as the next chapter shows.

CHAPTER 10

International Organization:
An Appraisal

We are trying to make a society instead of a set of barbarians out of the governments of the world.
WOODROW WILSON

D
URING the 19th Session, from December 1, 1964, until February 24,
1965, the United Nations General Assembly functioned only by avoiding all formal votes and taking actions by unanimous consent. What
was at stake was the United States demand that Article 19 be implemented
and the Soviet Union and twelve other nations be deprived of their votes for
being two years in arrears on payment of assessments. So long as no votes were
held the issue remained moot. Albania's demand for a vote led to a roll-call
in February on adjournment which the United States termed at the time
procedural, but which foreshadowed its admission at the 20th Session that it
could not find sufficient support.

I The Nature of the UN Crisis

THE deadlock over finances stemmed from the extraordinary expenditures
caused by the UNEF and ONUC operations. Both these operations had been
very expensive, but each had initially been greeted with great enthusiasm by
the newer members of the UN—especially the Afro-Asian "bloc." As is so
often true in politics, the decisions to establish peace-keeping forces of this
kind gained support for a variety of reasons. To the newer nations they represented primarily blows struck against imperialism: in the Suez case against
Great Britain and France, in the Congo case against the Belgians and other
powers who might potentially intervene unilaterally. To the Soviet Union
they represented opportunities to weaken Western solidarity. To the United
States they represented "order-building" in the "international community."
The Soviet Union in particular, by consenting *de facto* to these operations,
found itself in a quandary. In the UNEF case, since the General Assembly
took the initiative, the dilemma for the Soviets was less pressing; but in creating the ONUC through sponsorship in the Security Council, the Soviets were
directly involved. They agreed to it even though the General Assembly as-

sessed the costs. But the Soviets subsequently refused to pay their share on the grounds that the General Assembly had no authority to apportion the costs of what they insisted were peace *enforcement* operations. France, Belgium, and South Africa refused to pay for ONUC for other reasons. One might argue against the Soviet interpretation on the grounds the UNEF and ONUC were not collective security (i.e., "enforcement") operations. The International Court of Justice, in its advisory opinion of July 20, 1962, by 9 votes to 5, held that the ONUC and UNEF costs were legitimate peace-keeping (but non-enforcement) expenses of the UN, within the meaning of Article 17, paragraph 2 of the Charter.[1] But we are concerned more directly here with the larger implications of the crisis.

The real focus of the crisis relates to the role of the UN itself. The Security Council deadlock, symbolized especially in the early years by the frequent use of the veto, seemed largely irrelevant to the newer nations who ballooned the UN's size in the 1950's. They were impatient with the Cold War and they were largely unrepresented on the small organ. The thrust of their concern could find expression only in the General Assembly where for a time the predominant issues were frequently concerned with beating a dying horse to death: the colonial issue. As membership of these new nations increased drastically in a short span, the General Assembly seemed almost to be suffering from inability to handle anything non-colonial. Both the large numbers which by then made up the General Assembly, and their relative inexperience, combined in a curious way with the unsuitability of the Security Council to play the part, led to the assumption by the Secretary-General of a greatly enlarged role. This was especially true once UNEF and ONUC began, for such complicated operations had necessarily to be directed by a small executive-administrative group such as the Secretary-General and his staff. Such a solution also suited both the super powers who wanted something done but who could not agree on much more than to let the staff handle it. This is the period, in the early 1960's, when Dag Hammarskjold came to virtually personify the UN. His personal and dramatic interventions in the Congo operation put the world spotlight upon him until his tragic death in a plane crash in Africa en route to the Congo on September 18, 1961. His successor, U Thant of Burma (elected initially on November 3, 1961), has played a much less prominent role—partly because ONUC has been phased out. These changes of public focus have led some observers to characterize the UN as successively passing through periods of predominance by the Security Council, then of the General Assembly, and finally of the Secretary-General. Whether this characterization proves essentially correct depends largely upon whether the UN goes in for more collectively financed peace-keeping activities à la the UNEF

---

[1] See, for a readily available source, the summary of the decision given in the *United Nations Review*, August 1962, p. 12. The ICJ opinion said specifically that "the operations known as UNEF and ONUC were not enforcement actions within the compass of Chapter VII of the Charter . . ." See International Court of Justice, *Certain Expenses of the United Nations*, Advisory Opinion of 20 July 1962, ICJ Reports, 1962, p. 166.

and the ONUC. It is clear since ONUC, that the members are much less willing to pay collectively. In 1962, the costs of the UN Temporary Executive Authority in West New Guinea (UNTEA) were paid by the two nations involved, the Netherlands and Indonesia. In 1963, the costs of the UN Observer group in Yemen were borne by Egypt and Saudi Arabia. In 1964, the UN Peace Force sent to Cyprus was financed entirely by voluntary contributions.

Here we come to the deeper issue, the real focus of the crisis. The question can be put simply although such answers as are available are complicated. What do the nations of the world want from the UN? And what will come of it if the many nations of small resources wish to direct UN energies other than to where the few nations of great resources agree? Put another way, the question is how to resolve the conflicting desire of all members to see the UN function effectively while retaining the right to count themselves out where they individually do not wish to pay the price. This is the deeper issue. It can be discussed in terms of vetoes in the Security Council, in terms of weighted voting in the General Assembly, in terms of enlarging the Security Council, in terms of Khrushchev's 1960 demands for a revision of the Secretary-General's office along "troika" lines of equal powers for the East-West blocs and the neutrals, or in terms of whether to create a permanent UN force. But it is always the same basic issue. To the extent that the UN's actions have become less manageable by the United States there is even some common ground with the Soviet Union: both fear a UN of expanded powers which neither effectively controls. But the issue is too simply construed if it is seen as one solely dividing great from small powers. The point is rather than no bloc in the UN, neutral or otherwise, is quite sure of control today, just at a time when the UN has taken on expanded functions. Thus the crisis in the UN goes deeper than how to organize it more effectively or pay for it; the heart of the question is whether more positive agreement will be forthcoming on how to use it if it is to do more, or whether the nations will decide on the conservative side by having it do less.

These issues are not really new; they had already risen in fundamental form during the League. But they are today posed in a new way. There is a great temptation, when examining a League or UN, to assume that its very existence reflects fundamental agreement on the part of its members over everything important connected with it. But such an organization, if it comes into existence at all, and if it manages to survive, need not reflect more than a minimal consensus. The nations may agree that they need a League or UN, create it, and then disagree on what to do with it. Indeed, they may agree they need a League or UN in the first place for quite different reasons. This was in fact the case.

2   Underlying Assumptions and Divergent Interests

THE initial form in which the League and later the UN took shape was each time primarily a reflection of American attitudes, assumptions, and interests.

Not that British and other contributions were insignificant, but the American contribution more than any other set the framework.

Woodrow Wilson was in a real sense the "father" of the League. What were his views and assumptions?

Wilson put these views explicitly on record on January 22, 1917, when he addressed the American Senate on the theme, "World League for Peace." [2] After stating his conviction that "some definite concert of power" must be established "which will make it virtually impossible that any such catastrophe should ever overwhelm us again," he went on to urge the need for a "peace between equals" that would create "the right state of mind" for the settlement of "vexed questions." He then stated his basic assumptions as to what should be done:

I am proposing that all nations henceforth avoid entangling alliances which would draw them into competition of power, catch them in a net of intrigue and selfish rivalry, and disturb their own affairs with influences intruded from without. There is no entangling alliance in a concert of power. When all unite to act in the same sense and with the same purpose, all act in the common interest and are free to live their own lives under a common protection.

On February 14, 1919, these ideas, incorporated into the tentative draft of the League Covenant, were greeted by Wilson with the words, "A living thing is born, and we must see to it what clothes we put on it." Speaking of the draft, he went on to say:

Armed force is in the background in this program, but it *is* in the background, and if the moral force of the world will not suffice, the physical force of the world shall. But that is the last resort, because this is intended as a constitution of peace, not as a league for war. And yet, while it is elastic, while it is general in its terms, it is definite in the one thing we are called upon to make definite. It is a definite guarantee of peace. It is a definite guarantee by word against aggression. [3]

Also it was not to be "merely a league to secure the peace of the world," but "a league that can be used for cooperation in any international matter."

General Smuts, Prime Minister of South Africa and an eminent statesman, became Wilson's welcome collaborator. Since, in the end, the actual League reflected many of Smuts's ideas as well as Wilson's, it is significant that Smuts was determined through the League to achieve, "an inner transformation of international conditions and institutions" of far-reaching proportions. In other words, Smuts and Wilson both assumed that international relations could be reformed through the League. Wilson in particular was convinced that the lack of collective mechanisms for handling collective problems forced nations to adopt selfish attitudes far from their true inclinations.

The original British draft had not proposed any meeting of members except when this was needed to deal with particular disputes. The British idea was to

---

[2] *Congressional Record*, Senate, January 22, 1917. Reprinted in "Official Documents Looking toward Peace, Series II," *International Conciliation*, No. 111 (February 1917), p. 62.

[3] NYT, February 15, 1919.

provide an improved version of the "Concert of Europe" device, which could be depended upon to meet when called and which would take effective action when the powers were in agreement that something must be done. The French, making a different emphasis, produced a first draft that went into great detail on the sanctions machinery which would be used against covenant-breaking states, even providing for a commander-in-chief with a permanent general staff.[4] From these sources came the basic suggestions. The Germans were not consulted. The drafting of the Covenant was an integral part of the Versailles Peace Conference at which the Germans were permitted to appear only during the last days to sign the treaty that the Allies had produced. (Indeed, the Covenant of the League formed Part I of the completed Treaty of Versailles, so that Germany was forced to acknowledge its existence while neither permitted to become a member nor to suggest the form its structure should take.) Nor did the Russians participate, preoccupied as they were with the vast problems and forces unleashed in 1917 by their revolution.

It is apparent that the British approached the League on the assumption that it would be an improved version of the traditional diplomatic instrument of the "Concert of Europe," that the French emphasized its potentialities as an alliance against covenant-breaking states (i.e., Germany), and that the Wilson-Smuts approach was based upon the hope of a thorough-going "reform" of international relations through the League.[5]

The other great powers played little direct or influential part. Accordingly, the final structure in some measure adjusted each of these principal approaches in the machinery that we noted in the last chapter, while leaving to the League proper the problem of which approach to emphasize. Since the United States never joined the League, from the beginning the major influence in the organization was exerted by the British and the French. Ironically, neither of these nations was predominately concerned with the reform of international relations that Wilson had considered of first importance. Accordingly, they bent the machinery to their own diverse needs.

Although Woodrow Wilson's assumptions about the nature of international relations and the sources of tensions among nations was highly idealistic, his appraisal of American national interests in relation to the proposed international organization was far from unrealistic. By force of circumstances, the United States throughout a good part of the nineteenth century had needed no foreign policy other than one that preserved our territorial integrity and the Monroe Doctrine for the Western Hemisphere. Then came World War I, and in 1917 America was drawn into the struggle.

---

[4] Yet neither Great Britain nor France placed the kind of emphasis on the League that America did. Neither Britain nor France was represented on the League drafting commission by either their prime ministers or their foreign ministers. See Alfred Zimmern, *The American Road to World Peace*, New York: E. P. Dutton, 1953, p. 83, for further comment.

[5] All three contemplated the use of sanctions in the event of violation of the Covenant.

What was the national interest of America at the Versailles Conference? It was to restore the happy conditions of the prewar period. In order to do this the conditions that were believed to have brought on World War I would need elimination: these included the balance of power, "entangling alliances," and "secret diplomacy." The United States wished war to be avoided—*any* war that led to the United States being drawn again into a world conflict. The United States was not concerned primarily with the prevention of any particular war or threat of war but with the prevention of war as an institution.

Contrast this attitude with that of the other powers. France was not worried about war in general but about war by Germany on France in particular. The United Kingdom was (in the early 1920's) concerned about French predominance on the continent and the fear that France might be able to keep Germany too weak for the balance-of-power principle to operate. The British were concerned about a particular war, too; their philosophy of the balance of power led them to concentrate their attention on France as the most likely disturber of peace in the early years.

To Wilson an aggressor was an aggressor—no matter who. But the other nations were more typically concerned about particular potential aggressions. These attitudes account for the difference in the responses made by the League to the three aggressor nations and their aggressions in the period between World War I and World War II. The large powers did not welcome the thought of fighting "somebody else's" aggressor while their "own" aggressor was not disarmed.

Since various nations came to League meetings with particular interests that were often divergent, it is not surprising that there were differences of opinion over the purposes for which the machinery was to be used.

When, in 1945, the United Nations was founded, the United States had, if anything, an even deeper commitment to the fundamental Wilsonian ideas. Our basic interest was still the avoidance of a new general war through collective security. Americans had a sense of guilt about the League, whose failure they assessed as partly due to their own nonparticipation. The guiding ideas of the League had failed, in the predominant American view, basically because they had never been put into effect. A stronger instrument was needed, with more forthright obligations. A sense of prudence, and an awareness of the revolutionary nature of the commitment, led the United States to agree with the Soviets on the need for the veto. But the United States also assumed an underlying basic community of interest with the Soviet Union. When the reality of the Cold War could not be denied, the United States set about utilizing the UN for national purposes which it continued to assume (in great part correctly and at least for a time) were widely shared by the other members. Later, as already indicated, it found itself no longer so automatically supported. The more universal the UN became, the more it became apparent that there are typically multiple points of view within the UN.

3 *The Functions of International Security Organizations*

THE difficulties the League and United Nations have encountered in their operations have their roots in these divergent assumptions and interests of their members. Such organizations try to fulfill major political functions that are potentially *incompatible* on any assumptions other than those of Wilson.

The logic of the Wilsonian assumptions, so fundamental in shaping both structure and functions of the League and the UN, assumed that clashes of national interests would be mitigated by cooperative efforts by the members in technical fields, and largely assuaged by the objective contributions of collective third parties to the settlement of disputes. The first assumption proved valid; the second, partially valid. But Wilson made a third (and quite invalid) assumption: that resort to force by states was the ultimate consequence of a chain of entangling alliances which states forged in the absence of a more rational instrument providing a common protection against aggression.

In Chapter 5 we developed the proposition that national security is more important to a state than peace if a state finds itself in the unpleasant position of having to choose between the two. For this reason a state may defy an international organization and perpetrate aggression. On the other hand, peace for a nation not bent upon aggression often means enhanced national security, and that security may be imperiled by its assistance in collective action against an aggressor. Let us now add the proposition that states as members of a League or United Nations continue to be moved basically by the same interests they had prior to membership. The great majority of the individual nations usually are more concerned with their immediate national security than with the ultimate theoretical benefits of collective security. This is especially true if they are required by the dictates of collective security to put their national security in immediate, obvious jeopardy. At the same time aggressors usually are states which feel that to continue at peace must mean to continue to be insecure. Thus, while peace is rejected by the aggressor, it tends to be sought after by all those who are not the direct victims of that aggression.

Wilson disagreed. He rejected the fundamental postulate that the state, as a member of the international organization, would continue to be animated by the same interests and concerns and by a "selfish" preoccupation with its own security. Wilson described the state's behavior prior to the creation of the League as centering in "entangling alliances" that drew them into a "competition of power." This focus created "a net of intrigue and selfish rivalry" that periodically culminated, in his view, in the spectacle of an arms race, the collapse of the balance of power, and war. But if all would band together in one all-inclusive alliance to help one another and to oppose any state that might be tempted along the path of aggression, the interests of all (except, of course, the aggressor) would be the same—to prove that aggression does.not pay. Because of the overwhelming power at the disposal of this grandest of all alliances, the collective security alliance, aggression would be so obviously futile that it would rarely, if ever, be attempted. This is why he considered that the League was "a constitution of peace" rather than a "league for war." Peace would be practically assured because of the concerted power pledged to oppose aggression. He was prepared to see armed force used if "the moral force of the world" did not succeed in keeping the peace—but he did not think physical force would be much needed.

This is a perfectly logical set of conclusions, provided Wilson's initial assumptions are correct. There were four assumptions. First, nations resorted to opposing alliance groups because of the non-existence of a collective security scheme. Second, the opposing interests of states arose from the balance-of-power alliances that ranged groups of nations against each other. The alliance group acquired, as it were, a vested interest in the competitive power status of its group versus the opposing group. Third, a League or United Nations would provide the mechanism whereby all could and would act "in the same sense . . . with the same purpose . . . [and] in the common interest." In other words, the third assumption was that states would have a common purpose in making the organization a success. This common interest would be more vital to them than any separate interests they might once have had. Fourth, the common vital interest that would unite these states was peace. This was conceived as the motive bringing them together in the first place. If there could be peace, all could be secure.

Four difficulties with these assumptions stand out. First, states do not wish peace if the price of peace is too great. Most states normally desire peace most of the time because their vital interests (or what they call their vital interests) are not being endangered under conditions of peace. But if their immediate security is threatened, they will if necessary fight. Second, a particular *status quo* is more advantageous to some states than to others. The vital interests of some states are secure in a particular *status quo*, while for other states that *status quo* is itself the symbol of their unfulfilled and frustrated interests. For Germany, after World War I, the *status quo* meant the continued acceptance of the loss of her former territories, both European and colonial. While the vital interests of France and Poland, who had received the European territories of Germany, remained intact as long as peace was preserved, the opposite was true for Germany unless France and Poland could be persuaded to surrender the former German possessions without war. Third, as a corollary to the second point, the interests of all or even most states are not necessarily "common," as Wilson thought. In some cases, as in the example quoted, they are basically opposed. Fourth, it is the very fact that various states have opposing interests that has historically led to the creation of opposing alliance groups.

It was no small accomplishment both under the League and the United Nations to create better machinery for the settlement of disputes. But no matter how elaborate and permanent, the machinery could not produce common interests where the raw material of the dispute was composed of opposing interests.

This is the reason that the League and the United Nations failed to fulfill

Wilson's dream. Since his basic assumptions were unrealistic in these respects, the organizations were charged with functions that were incompatible. The incompatibility revealed itself in two main ways: (1) the difficulty of at one and the same time preserving the *status quo* and altering it; (2) the difficulty of getting an organization, designed to preserve peace, to engage in war.

4 *Incompatibilities*

INEVITABLY, since both the League and the United Nations began life as the coalition of victors of World War I and World War II respectively, and since they were to preserve peace and security, the peace and security of the victorious coalition was their main concern. Both the League and the United Nations had to begin life that way, or there would have been an obvious disagreement at the outset among the member nations as to what particular peace to preserve. The victorious nations, unless they had utterly refrained from seizing the fruits of victory, could hardly have expected the defeated states to be enthusiastic over the new *status quo*.

Neither World War I nor World War II ended with a mutually satisfactory adjustment of the interests of the defeated and victorious nations vis-à-vis each other as groups or among the members of the victorious coalition. The victorious powers, who were at first united in securing the fruits of victory from the defeated powers, soon were quarreling among themselves as to the disposition of the spoils. Even so, most of the settlements that marked the end of both world wars resembled an imposed peace.

Thus both League and United Nations when they came into existence served initially as the coalition instrument of the victorious powers to maintain the *status quo* (i.e., their imposed settlement). If inner conflicts after 1919 and 1945 destroyed the unanimity of the winning sides, as did happen, it still remained true that the *status quo* they had created was not such as to appeal to the defeated powers.

Once the winning group no longer agreed (after 1919 and again after 1945) on the particular *status quo* to be preserved, the stage was set for the defeated powers to undermine it. And in both cases this has occurred. As a result, a double conflict has arisen within these organizations, one between the upholders of the broad results of the world war and those defeated in the war (i.e., one between the organization and powers not originally in it) and another between the beneficiaries of the victory (i.e., among the powers within the organization as originally constituted). In the UN even a third dimension of conflict has been added which was largely unknown to the League. The new "have-not" nations demand a greater share in the material progress of the world, and a greater influence than their power warrants.

Increasing dissension resulted in both organizations as to the desirability of maintaining the original *status quo*. The inability of the victorious coalition to remain unified in purpose has led the individual victorious powers to court the defeated and even (under both the League and United Nations) to sponsor their admission to the organization. Once this dissension occurs, the split over the desirability of the original *status quo* becomes even more open, and the common basis for the organization, insofar as enforcing the *status quo* is concerned, is virtually destroyed. The organization instead of being, as at first, the citadel of the "haves" versus the "have-nots" becomes the center of their dissensions, as in the League. Alternately, as under the United Nations, the aims of the dominant powers (the United States and the Soviet Union) are so opposed even from the beginning that the common basis for action to preserve the *status quo* disappears even before the admission of the major defeated powers.[6] In the UN both super powers have reached out for support to the former colonial nations who continue to have little interest in being pawns to either side.

The machinery for peace and security of both the League and United Nations is based upon the presumption of an irreducible minimum of agreement among the powers that have dominated these organizations. The increasing inability of both organizations to take a firm stand in preserving peace through collective action and sanctions arises out of this disagreement over *what* to preserve. The willingness of the former colonial nations to allow India to take Goa by force but to demand in 1966 that the Security Council invoke Articles 41 and 42 against Rhodesia for internal racial discrimination is a case in point. This is one reason that in the whole history of the League and thus far in the history of the United Nations only twice have serious sanctions been attempted before 1966 and in both cases with mixed results.

Wilson anticipated that the creation of such organizations would produce common interests. He did not foresee that the nations would bring their conflicting and opposing interests into the organization with them, and that the typical struggles of nations with one another would be resumed and continued through the new organizational apparatus. Wilson's failure to foresee this result stemmed from his belief that most nations wanted peace above all else.

Ironically, Wilson was basically correct that most nations want peace at any given time. Since the majority of states are small and prey to potential aggressors, and since they do not possess the power potential upon which great national ambitions must rest if they are conceivably to be fulfilled, they are, as he saw, "peace-loving" and want to avoid bloodshed (particularly their own).

The "peace-loving" character of small states is what, in addition to the conflicting ambitions and interests of the great powers, leads to the second incompatibility of function—the difficulty of getting an organization designed to ensure peace to engage in war.

Collective sanctions (other than against Rhodesia in 1966) have not been

---

[6] The British-French conflict of views in the early 1920's was an example of the same tendency, but it would not be accurate to say that the conflict had the same intensity. That it was a conflict over the nature of the *status quo* is true.

resorted to under the League and United Nations only twice because only twice have such sanctions been called for by determined efforts at aggression. Far from it. Yet the reluctance of these organizations to implement sanctions cannot be fully explained by great-power dissensions. Here we come face to face with incongruity. Great and small powers alike want to see peace "enforced," but they may not want actually to enforce it.[7] In fact, it was the obviously disdainful character of Italy's aggression against Ethiopia and North Korea's against South Korea that played so large a part in mustering majority support for sanctions. The obvious trammeling of the authority of the organization (and therefore the prestige of its individual members) was sufficient to overcome in these two cases the more normal division of the organization into two or more camps, for great and small powers alike, over any really vital problem. If collective sanctions are used when there is little consensus, "police action" may easily develop into a general war. Yet it is the prospect of being free from general war that is supposed to induce both great and small powers to join such organizations in the first place. Thus the second incompatibility: peace was to be preserved by a willingness to resort to war, but the concern for peace is itself an indication of an unwillingness to use force. Peace and war are discussed and provided for, the one after the other, in both Covenant and Charter, and the presumption was that lawbreakers would have to be punished if they violated the law. The basic purpose was peace, but war is not peace even when it is a "police action." Here we see why the Covenant was interpreted and the Charter provisions on forces went unmet. The members could not with grace repudiate their obligations. But they could and did retain discretion over their individual involvement.

Because of these two sets of potentially incompatible assumptions, difficulties soon developed in both the League and United Nations. It was (and is) difficult (other than in the most flagrant cases of aggression) to muster the support of an overwhelming majority of peace-loving and peace-seeking states for a policy of sanctions (i.e., war). In turn the need for such sanctions typically arises out of the unfulfilled ambitions of certain powers who are more interested in creating a new *status quo*, advantageous to them, than in maintaining the existing *status quo*. In order to meet such a situation there are only two basic alternatives: (1) be ready to use sanctions to restrain those states or (2) make concessions to these "unsatiated" powers so that they will not resort to aggression. The first course is difficult for the very reason that most states desire peace (because they are or feel more secure under such conditions). The second alternative is difficult, because to "satiate" an "unsatiated" state some power must make concessions to its own disadvantage. In an earlier period, and even as late as the early twentieth century, this disagreeable problem was often solved by the "have" state giving the "have-not" state

---

[7] Further evidence for this view is given in detail in later chapters. Note that the UN troops sent to Egypt in 1956 were not sent as sanctions to punish an aggressor. Their task was to preserve the precarious cease-fire already existing rather than themselves to fight a war.

something that belonged to a third (but weak) power. Or the two would each take something from the third. Thus Maria Theresa wept as she accepted her share of Poland in the eighteenth century; in such a way Britain and France managed to resolve their differences in 1904 by agreeing that, in effect, Britain would rule Egypt, and France would have Morocco. Neither Egypt nor Morocco, as it happened, *belonged* to either of these powers. But by the time the League had been created, not only was there a scarcity of such "available" territory, but it had also come to be considered immoral to make this type of settlement. By the time of the UN such procedures had also become politically impossible. Since this was so, in the post-1919 period, concessions to "have-not" powers had by and large to be concessions made by "have" powers out of their *own* possessions. Not only were the "have" powers hardly disposed to make such concessions but, secondly, even if they did, they still might not satisfy the ambitious "have-not" state which might strive to make any concession merely the first of many.

In short, neither the League nor the UN could function without costs of some sort to someone. All agree the price must be paid—preferably by someone else. The League or the UN could have been as successful as Wilson hoped only on the assumption that their very existence with a wide membership would reform international political behavior per se. That neither organization could or did succeed at this task does not mean that they were (1) useless or (2) without great influence on the course of international relations after 1919.

5 *Twenty Years After*

THE UN which began its twenty-first year on October 25, 1965, was a study in contrasts.

The most obvious contrast was its achievement of near universality of membership (so far as lists of states were concerned) while representing only two-thirds of the population of the world. From a population point of view the UN of 1945, with less than half the membership, had been *more* representative. The withdrawal of Indonesia and the exclusion of Germany alone accounted for 170 million people; Communist China accounted for 700 million more. Could a UN which did not include such significant states with so much population continue to represent "mankind"? Indonesia's return in 1966 helped some, but China and Germany were still outside. This automatically tended to keep two of the major problems of the world largely off the UN's agenda.

The UN Charter does not say the organization must be universal. Article 4 says membership "is open to all . . . peace-loving states" who are willing, in the words of the Preamble, "to practice toleration and live together in peace with one another as good neighbors," refusing to use armed force "save in the common interest." By this standard, applied literally, the seats of many of its present members might well be jeopardized. In this literal view a state might not be morally acceptable as a UN member and might not be morally "qualified" (to use John Foster Dulles' term) to associate with other states within the UN. It might not, for example, be "peace-loving" enough. Yet the UN's greatest reason for being, as we shall see in Chapter 12, is as a multilateral vehicle for peaceful settlement. The more universal its membership, the higher the chances of its fulfilling that function. The UN is an agency for the punishment of sins only as a last and unpleasant resort. This pragmatic observation implies logically that a state is "qualified" to be a member of a universal international organization *if it is sovereign and therefore able to cause trouble to other states,* always assuming that it wishes membership, is prepared to bear its share of the expenses, and is not currently the object of collective security sanctions by the organization. The history of international organization demonstrates that troublemaking states tend to be much greater nuisances when they are not inside the organization. When they are outside they feel freer to be defiant—as were Italy, Germany, and Japan before World War II, and Communist China after it.

It is highly ironic that the issue in the UN was most acutely posed over Communist China, for "China" is a charter member and the Chinese have technically always been represented in the organization. The question recurrently voted on is not whether to "admit" Communist China, but whether to seat her delegation instead of the Nationalist Chinese of Formosa. Adding still further irony to this situation is the fact that even Formosa, with its 12 million people, contains a larger population (as U.S. Ambassador Arthur J. Goldberg pointed out in the 1965 debate) than 85 of the then 117 members of the UN. Unless a "two China" policy were adopted, the 12 million Formosans would be unrepresented once the Communist Chinese were seated.

In the more than fifteen years this issue was unresolved, the vote on it was predominantly over the preliminary stage of whether to actually debate the question. No debate on the question itself was conducted after 1950 until 1961. The table below gives the voting results by years, including both types of votes. Some distortion in these votes must be allowed for, since the pro-Chinese Communist vote would have been higher if the form of the debated question had allowed nations to express preferences for *two* Chinas in the UN.

In 1961, 1965, and 1966, after debates, a vote was also taken on whether the seating of Communist China in the General Assembly should be considered an important question, requiring an affirmative vote of two-thirds of those present and voting yes and no. (Establishing this point requires a simple majority vote.) On all three occasions it was decided that it was an "important" question: in 1961, by 61 to 34 with seven abstentions, and in 1965, by 56 to 49 with 11 abstentions. The 1966 vote was 66 to 48 with 7 abstentions, but a simple majority can reverse.

It was apparent that resolving this question by seating Communist China in the General Assembly was only a matter of time. This raised the additional question of what would happen in the Security Council. Contrary to what

Secretary of State Dulles once claimed, it is highly unlikely that a veto could apply to the question of which Chinese delegation should be seated. Since the Security Council is competent to decide this procedural issue for itself, it is even theoretically possible although unlikely that a different China could be seated in each of the two major organs. Advocates of a two-China policy (i.e., seating both Chinas in the General Assembly) had to face the hard fact that a Communist veto could block Nationalist China's *admission* as Formosa, but that a Western veto could not stay the *seating* of a Communist Chinese delegation. A two-China solution would be practical only by prearrangement.

TABLE 7

UN *General Assembly Vote on Seating Communist China*

Year	Against	For	Abstentions	Total Voting (Absentees eliminated)
1951	37	11	4	52
1952	42	7	11	60
1953	44	10	2	56
1954	43	11	6	60
1955	42	12	6	60
1956	47	24	8	79
1957	47	27	7	81
1958	44	28	9	81
1959	44	29	4	77
1960	42	34	22	98
1961	48	37	19	104
1962	56	42	12	110
1963	57	41	12	110
1964 *	—	—	—	—
1965	47	47	20	114
1966	57	46	17	120

* No votes taken. See above, this chapter, on deadlock.

The second great contrast was the comparison of voting strengths in the UN compared with financial contributions. In 1965 the U.S., with one vote, was paying 37 per cent of the total UN assessments. More than four-fifths of the other 116 members were assessed at less than one per cent each. Of these, more than one third were assessed at less than four-tenths of one per cent. There is a close parallel here with what has already been said of the great number of members with populations smaller than Formosa. Well over a two-thirds majority of the UN represent only a relatively small part of the world's population and pay only a relatively small part of the UN's expenses. Yet they are in a position to vote the expenditure of UN funds.

So long as these many small nations were voting to use their own contributions (along with the larger contributions of the more powerful nations) for the regular expenses of the UN, no unbridgeable schism arose. Indeed the growth in the regular expenses of the UN between 1948 and 1964 (from $38,387,531 in 1948 to $102,948,977 in 1964) was not excessively disproportionate to the UN's growth in numbers. Until 1956, expenses for peaceful settlement operations through peace-keeping (non-fighting) forces were taken directly out of the regular budget. They cost 11.5 per cent in 1948, but only 5.8 per cent in 1950, and 3.4 per cent in 1952 for observation and truce supervision groups in the Balkans, Indonesia, India-Pakistan, and Palestine. In 1952, with the Balkan and Indonesian operations liquidated, the ratio fell to 2.4 per cent. But the UNEF venture in 1956 and after, and the much more expensive ONUC operation in 1960 and after, were financed outside of the regular budget through special assessments which departed from the regular scales. The comparison of regular expenses to UNEF and ONUC expenditures respectively, illustrates the financial effects: 1960, $65,264,181, $19,095,945, $48,432,153; 1962, $84,452,350, $19,490,863, $119,992,482; 1964, $102,948,977, $17,748,402, $19,299,938. By 1958, total peace-keeping expenses (part of it financed from the regular budget) were 48.2 per cent of the regular expenses; by 1960, 106.6 per cent; by 1962, 179.6 per cent; by 1964, 53.2 per cent.

The table below gives three selected five-year periods in which peace-keeping expenses were significant.

TABLE 8 *
UN *Peace-keeping Expenses*

Selected Periods	Regular Expenses	Total Peace-keeping Expenses	Peace-keeping Expenses as a Per cent of Regular Expenses
1948–1952	$223,607,699	$ 15,800,533	7.1
1955–1959	$276,080,029	$ 84,944,024	30.8
1960–1964	$415,957,766	$539,513,898	129.7

* Data from unpublished Ph.D dissertation, by Joan S. Carver, *The Non-Fighting Forces of the United Nations: An Instrument for the Pacific Settlement of Disputes,* University of Florida, 1965.

It was expenditures on this scale which led to the UN financial crisis and voting deadlock of 1964–1965. Whether the UN would be able to balance its accounts ultimately depended on whether it avoided new and extensive expenses outside of the regular budget (perhaps by having non-fighting forces paid for by the belligerents or through voluntary contributions). But it was obviously a serious weakness for the UN to be committed to major ventures and expenditures on the basis of votes representing so little of the population and financial power (let alone military power) of the world. Proposals for voting reform were plentiful but they contradicted the concept of sovereign equality (one nation, one vote). What was most obviously wrong, of course, was the ill-considered haste with which so many new nations had been brought into existence with an inadequate material base. It is difficult to see how the UN can reform this situation other than by either (1) a change to some system of weighted voting or (2) a frank acceptance of the principle that those who are willing and able to pay for a venture must have the freedom to initiate it, control it, and terminate it.

6 The Over-All Effects of the League and United Nations

THE Western world since 1919 has tended to alternate wild hopes and gloomy despair toward the League and United Nations. The League was hailed in 1919 as the beginning of a new day. By 1923, at the height of the Franco-British crisis over the French occupation of the Ruhr, the League seemed weak. Then from 1924 to 1929 hopes revived: the great "era of Locarno" with its prospects of permanent accord between France and Germany seemed to herald a better day again. Later, in the 1930's, hopes once more rose and faded as the Ethiopian-sanctions episode at first encouraged and then discouraged people everywhere. In 1945 a new enthusiasm was given to the League's "tougher" and "more realistic" successor, the United Nations. By 1948 gloom was again the prevailing mood. Then came 1950 and the stand against North Korean aggression. Hopes were again revived. By 1953 the failure of the United Nations to bring the Korean conflict to a satisfactory conclusion had once more lowered popular hopes and expectations of the United Nations. But in 1955, at the 10th anniversary session in San Francisco, the conciliatory attitude of both Russia and the United States once more revived hopes. By 1965, gloom again predominated because of financial troubles.

In part this alternation of mood was inevitable, since it reflected popular hopes for peace and fears of war. These hopes and fears fluctuated with the improving or worsening of the international "climate," and presumably would have done so, too, if League and United Nations had not been born. But because the League and United Nations did exist, extravagant expectations arose, grounded in the belief that these organizations would transform international relations into something far higher and better than had typified them earlier. The Wilsonian reformist view had taken deep root in the hearts of the peoples of the West. As a consequence, the alternating feelings of hope and despair over these organizations were much deeper and more thorough-going. Too great enthusiasm tended to be followed by no enthusiasm at all.

Yet while neither the League nor United Nations has succeeded in reforming international relations, *they have been far from useless.* From the very first the quasi-parliamentary structure of these organizations has distorted ap-preciation of what they have done, while encouraging a popular belief that the democratic precept of some form of majority rule could be made to work among many nations on issues both trivial and important. The League and

United Nations look so similar in structure and appearance to a national legislature that it has been easy for people to forget that these organizations were
basically multilateral diplomatic conferences on a permanent basis. In a national legislature, a law is passed by a majority and is binding upon all citizens, including those who opposed the law. The police power of the state is at
the disposal of the national government and can be used against violators. But
the same principle cannot be made to work as readily with sovereign states
each possessing its own police power. Under both the League and United Nations, sanctions, if they were to be applied, had to be applied by states. In
other words, the very instruments of law enforcement were and are the states
themselves, and it was and is hardly reasonable to expect that states who do
not wish to invoke sanctions, and states who do not wish certain "laws"
passed, will in general be prepared to help implement them. The more important the issue, the truer this becomes. On relatively trivial issues states may
acquiesce in decisions they oppose, but they will not do so on matters that
run athwart what they conceive to be their national interests in any important
respects.

The façade and machinery of both the League and United Nations have
made this point often easy to overlook until a difficult situation arises that
makes it obvious. At the same time, the very real contributions of these organizations to the settlement of disputes by multilateral discussions of a multilateral problem have, equally frequently, been overlooked or discounted. The
contributions of the United Nations to the settlement of the Palestine problem, the Indonesian independence problem, and the Soviet-troops-in-Iran
issue are but more recent illustrations of what was true under the League as
well. The existence of such organizations does not result in the automatic settlement of such issues, since settlement depends upon finding an arrangement
satisfactory to most if not all the states concerned. But they do provide the
meeting place at which any such problems may be presented for attempted
settlement. Many problems involve so many states that, if the League or
United Nations had not existed, *ad hoc* conferences would have to be convened to deal with particular issues. It is much more satisfactory to have such
a conference in permanent existence for reasons explained earlier. The real
problem with the United Nations, as with the League before it, is one of
using it correctly. It provides needed and suitable diplomatic machinery for
the consideration of multilateral disputes that was not so readily available
prior to 1919. But no more than any diplomatic machinery can it resolve a
problem that the states who use the machinery are not willing to resolve.

Secondly, in regard to the over-all effects, the League and United Nations
have had great influence upon the course of international relations since 1919.
At first glance this might appear to be a contradiction of the earlier statement
that Wilson's hopes that such organizations would reform international relations were not to be realized—since, in one sense, these organizations have
"reformed" international relations. The crux of the matter is this: while nations have entered such organizations, bringing with them particular interests

that were often opposed to those of other members, the atmosphere and method of functioning of the organizations have modified the way in which states have attempted to realize their interests and have even to a minor extent changed the nature of their interests. The success of such organizations as organizations has become an interest of the members, more strongly felt by some states, of course, than by others. In addition, the rules of the organization, like the rules of a gentleman's club, have influenced the conduct of the members in many cases, causing them to act other than they might have if such organizations had not existed. How far this influence has gone is, by its very nature, a difficult factor to assess, particularly in terms of the conduct of states.[8] But that these organizations and their existence and success as organizations have come to a certain extent to be interests of the members cannot be denied. It is indeed arguable that without a League and United Nations the entire history of the Ethiopian and Korean affairs would have been vastly different.[9] While it is profoundly true that the United Nations, like the League before it, has been the instrument and servant of its members and unable to rise above the level demanded by the more important interests the members have had at stake, it is also true that the very experience by so many states of working together has produced changes for the better in international relations. If the UN can survive its present crisis and time permits the newer members to gain a more subtle understanding of UN functioning and international reality, the ultimate prospects are promising. Results still fall far short of the Wilsonian dream, but they do mark at least a modest step forward—and one not to be despised.

---

[8] See F.P. Walters, *A History of the League of Nations*, Vol. I, pp. 296–297, for an appraisal of the League of Nations in this respect.

[9] See below, Chapters 20 and 21.

PART FOUR

Conflict Resolution: The Settlement of Disputes

CHAPTER II

Case Studies in
the Settlement of Disputes

With a view to obviating as far as possible recourse to force in the relations between States, the contracting Powers agree to use their best efforts to insure the pacific settlement of international differences.

Article 1, Hague Convention for the
Pacific Settlement of International Disputes

ALL states alike have diplomatic, legal, economic, military, and organizational relations with others. But the peculiar or unique quality and content found in the relations of any two states arises out of the particular national interest concepts they hold. Nations customarily exchange ministers or ambassadors, but whether they will utilize them to consolidate the peace or spur on a war depends on their fears and suspicions and their mutual attitude toward each other. As a result, while states have invented and perfected an array of techniques for resolving disputes, the choice of technique and its ultimate success or failure depends upon the purpose, skill, and interests of the disputants. In this chapter we shall survey those techniques and, through the use of selected case studies, examine how they are used and why they are effective or ineffective in particular cases.

I Methods for Settling Disputes

IF a problem is to be settled, it can be done only on a basis of one of three logical possibilities or methods: (1) it can be negotiated (using essentially political techniques) until a mutually acceptable solution is found; (2) it can be arbitrated or adjudicated (using legal techniques) to find out who has the law on his side; or (3) it can be settled by the test of war (using the techniques of force).

Not every dispute or disagreement that arises needs to be "settled." Many settle themselves, especially if they are let alone. But where popular passions become continually more inflamed, and especially where the object of the dispute is a matter of great importance to one or both nations, a policy of drift may in time become a policy of war. War may even be the preferred "solution" of one or both parties. In such cases the failure to resort to peaceful settlement techniques, and the allowing of tension to grow to the breaking point, may be quite deliberate.

Even so, in most cases where tension is growing and where there is no immediate or only a fumbling attempt at peaceful settlement techniques, the explanation is to be found not in a will to war but in terms of national prestige. One or both are unwilling to appear too anxious to avoid a verdict of arms. This unwillingness stems from two causes: (1) the people, once stirred up, may turn their wrath against their own government and "throw the rascals out" for their timidity or moderation; and (2) a too apparent desire to find a peaceful solution may mean that a stiffer price will have to be given for a settlement.

Thus we arrive often at a paradox: the more pressing and important the issue, and the more real the desire on the part of both parties to find a peaceful way out, the harder it may be to find a solution. In such cases appearances are of extreme importance. Not only must the substantive core of the problem be satisfactorily resolved, but the manner in which this is done must be mutually acceptable as well. The graver the problem, the more prestige is involved. Until the prestige issue is properly handled, the substantive problem cannot be either. In preparing for the Berlin Conference of the Foreign Ministers in 1954 (the first such meeting in years), a week of preliminary conversations had to be devoted to the question of how many meetings would be held in West vs. East Berlin. Until a formula provided for the first and third weeks in West Berlin, and the second week in East Berlin, with subsequent meetings (if any) to be settled by the foreign ministers themselves, the conference proper could not meet at all.

The issue of prestige arose again in the Korean War armistice negotiations. The military stalemate implied a cessation of the fighting on or around the existing battle line and the reciprocal exchange of prisoners of war. Since neither had won, neither side could demand extraordinary concessions. Once unconventional demands had been made (in this case that prisoners should be free to return or not), both the UN coalition and the Communist coalition had to pay great attention to avoiding any impression of giving too much. As a consequence the negotiations were greatly prolonged.

An important substantive dispute between essentially friendly nations can be resolved with much less attention to prestige. Concessions to friendly states are much easier to justify than equivalents granted (even in return for equal concessions) to quasi-enemy or hostile states. Yet even here great delicacy is necessary. Secretary of State Dulles' blunt warning in December 1953 to the French that they must ratify the European Defense Community Treaty or else the United States might have to make an "agonizing reappraisal" of its basic policies toward Europe could not avoid injuring French pride. The pressure backfired; the treaty was rejected. Luckily, a more acceptable device replaced it.

Between quasi-enemies the problem of settling differences or disputes is even more difficult because the inevitable introduction of the prestige aspect on top of the array of opposed interests between the negotiating states raises constant popular suspicions on both sides of the "sincerity" of the other. Negotiations between them may have positive results, provided that vital concessions are not made, that secondary concessions are not given without compensations, and that prestige remains unimpaired. But to meet all these conditions is extremely difficult, and it is not surprising that positive progress is so slow and halting.

Thus there is more to differences between states than merely whether there is enough common substantive ground between them to resolve the dispute. If relations are good enough it may sometimes be possible (or, if bad enough, desirable), *not* to attempt to resolve the question for a time or at all. It all depends on whether the problem is postponable. And this is often extremely difficult to judge.

From a minimum point of view the settlement of disputes involves (1) choosing an appropriate technique, (2) avoiding as much as possible prestige complications, and (3) finding sufficient common ground to reconcile the divergent national interests at issue.

2 *Political Techniques*

TECHNIQUES for the settlement of disputes that rest upon negotiation (and therefore ultimately on some type of compromise) comprise the political method. While there are many varieties of such techniques, they can be classified into three groups: (1) diplomatic techniques, (2) good offices and mediation, and (3) inquiry and conciliation.

Diplomatic techniques are by far the most frequently resorted-to devices for the settlement of disputes. Such techniques include at one end of the spectrum direct consultations through existing accredited representatives; and at the other end of the spectrum, organized multilateral conferences. The most frequently used (and the oldest) diplomatic technique is direct consultation, usually on a bilateral basis. Through their ambassadors accredited to each other, two states discuss and perhaps settle a dispute between them. This discussion may entail an extensive exchange of notes, prolonged negotiation, the dispatching of personal representatives of the executive (such as Harry Hopkins' mission in 1945 to Stalin to find a way to break the American-Soviet deadlock over the proposed role of the UN General Assembly), and even a meeting between two foreign secretaries or the two heads of state themselves. Alternately, if the problem is a simple one, a single oral statement or note, delivered by the ambassador of one power to the foreign secretary of the other, together with the foreign secretary's response, may dispose of an issue altogether.

Multilateral conference diplomacy, although an extremely old device, has been used extensively in the nineteenth and especially in the twentieth centuries. Foreign ministers' conferences of three or more powers, the meetings of several heads of state, or the utilization of the sessions of such bodies as the

United Nations Security Council and General Assembly for the discussion by the parties of a dispute involving many states, are all illustrations of the use of this method. The advantage is the ease of exchange of views among all directly interested parties. A dispute that concerns more than two states can frequently not be settled (or only very laboriously) by bilateral conferences proceeding independently, whereas a conference of all parties to the dispute may be able to make good progress with a minimum of organizational difficulties. But the fact that it is multilateral does not of itself guarantee a settlement. As in bilateral negotiation, the ultimate settlement of the dispute rests upon willingness to grant acceptable concessions on the part of the participants.

Whatever the scale of participation, the problems of settlement are basically the same, although the greater the number of parties to the dispute, the greater the potential difficulty in reaching acceptable compromises. This is especially true if sudden actions are taken without advance agreement, the deadlock is public, and positions become intrenched.

The "Trieste Question" of 1953 illustrates. After World War II, the city of Trieste and its hinterland was given a special status under the UN as a "free territory." Claimed by both Italy and Yugoslavia, it was divided into two zones, with "Zone A" occupied by British and American troops, and "Zone B" under Yugoslav authority. When, on October 8, the United States and Britain suddenly announced plans to turn Zone A over to Italy, Yugoslavia reacted violently with an immediate protest. When this failed to produce results, Tito moved troops into Zone B, where they took up positions on the border of Zone A. Italian troops meantime prepared to advance into Zone A. Yugoslavia announced her intention to defend her "rights and national interests with all available means." [1] Within a week Yugoslavia supplemented this statement with a clear warning that it would send armed forces into Zone A if Italy were to move in occupying troops. Tension was now at breaking point.

On October 18 Vice-President Pijade, one of Tito's four top-ranking lieutenants, in a speech to over a hundred thousand people, spelled out the Yugoslav decision in clear terms:

In the event of an unjust decision . . . we know what we will do. . . . Will America and Britain decide to place their soldiers in Trieste as a wall between ourselves and the Italians when we move into Zone A to prevent the implementation of this disgraceful and illegal decision? Such an attitude of the Allies will have terrible consequences. We will not fire at the American and British soldiers, but something else will explode that will in no way be repairable.

He went on to say that if this occurred "the shattered vase" of Allied-Yugoslav friendship might be mended, but it would always "have a crack in it and will only be able to lie in a glass case in the museum." [2]

---

[1] For text see *New York Herald Tribune* European Edition (hereafter cited as *NYHT* EE), and *NYT*, October 13, 1953.

[2] *NYHT* (EE), October 19, 1953.

Once the Yugoslavs had made it clear they would fire *only* on the Italians but that they *would* do that, the tension was slowly dissipated. The United States and Britain, not directly threatened, could now afford to negotiate; Italy, convinced of Yugoslavia's intention to oppose her with force, became more willing to talk the question over, too. After further moves and counter-moves, at the beginning of December both Italian and Yugoslav troops were simultaneously withdrawn from their advanced positions. The way was now open for a conference. After prolonged negotiations the essentials of the Allied plan, with some minor adjustments of the zonal frontier, were accepted by both Italy and Yugoslavia.

The most important conclusion that can be drawn from this case is that sudden, bold moves in diplomacy, intended to cut Gordian knots, may easily bring unintended war, even where the proposal made is a reasonable compromise. When nations become aroused, it is never certain what will happen. In diplomacy, because of the prestige aspect, it is almost always better to move very slowly than very fast.[3]

Good offices and mediation, the second group of political techniques, are frequently resorted to when the disputants (whether they be two or more than two) have become deadlocked in their diplomatic dealings. At this point a third state may offer its services. Article 3 of the Hague Convention of 1899 provided that "Powers strangers to the dispute have the right to offer good offices or mediation even during the course of hostilities." Furthermore, "The exercise of this right can never be regarded by either of the parties in dispute as an unfriendly act." The offer of good offices is an offer that any party to a dispute (or war) can refuse at will. The point of the offer is to permit contact to be resumed between the disputants with the third state acting as go-between. If both or all accept the offer, negotiations proceed through the third party. The fact that the offer has been accepted means nothing more than that the disputants are willing to make another attempt to settle their dispute by peaceful means. They may do this to avoid an impending war; or to conclude hostilities already going on; or simply to settle a question which, although its continuance unresolved does not threaten them with war, makes their relations worse than they wish them to be. During both world wars, prior to becoming a belligerent, the United States offered its good offices to the contending powers, but without result. The Swiss successfully used good offices to arrange an end to hostilities between the United States and Japan in 1945, transmitting the offers and counteroffers of the two warring states to one another.

Once an offer of good offices has been made and accepted, the third state may confine its activities purely to carrying messages, or it may attempt mediation. Good offices frequently become mediation, but whether this occurs depends upon whether suggestions from the third state are invited or

---

[3] For an opposing argument that it was necessary "to increase the immediate danger to win a lasting agreement," see *Full Circle: The Memoirs of Sir Anthony Eden*, London: Cassell, 1960, pp. 175–188.

welcomed. When they are, the third state may itself make proposals designed to be acceptable to the disputants. The role of the mediator is to reconcile "the opposing claims" and appease "the feelings of resentment which may have arisen between the States at variance." [4] To accomplish this not only is tact necessary, but also a formula must be found which will actually express a suitable compromise for the disputants. To be successful such a formula must make use of the common interests of the opposed parties—perhaps their common interests in bringing a mutually unprofitable war to an end, if hostilities are in progress; perhaps in finding a common ground for the powers involved that they were either unwilling or unable to find for themselves in their earlier efforts at diplomatic settlement. The initial success of mediation thus depends upon the skill with which the mediator proceeds, but its ultimate success depends upon the willingness of the disputants to relinquish their extreme demands or positions and accept, via third party negotiations, some sort of compromise.

Probably the most famous use of good offices, followed by successful mediation, occurred at the end of the Russo-Japanese War in 1905. In this war, which began with a Japanese "Pearl Harbor" attack on the Russian Far Eastern Fleet at Port Arthur, the Japanese also won impressive victories in Korea. When Russian naval reinforcements arrived from Europe, these too were destroyed. Russia, fighting at the far end of the long, overland, single-track Trans-Siberian Railroad, was now severely handicapped. Unrest, long-smoldering in Russia, soon broke out into strikes and mutinies. Since Japan, although successful in the Far East, was too weak to press home her attack across Siberia to European Russia, her victory remained incomplete. Thus both Japan and Russia saw an advantage in ending a war that neither could really win. When President Theodore Roosevelt offered to mediate, both accepted; the conference that met at Portsmouth, New Hampshire, on August 5, 1905, ended a month later with a treaty of peace. Russia acknowledged Japan's pre-eminence in Korea, ceded the southern half of Sakhalin Island to Japan, and made other concessions. Both Japan and Russia agreed to evacuate Manchuria and restore it to China, and Russia refused to pay the indemnity the Japanese wanted. These terms, while much more favorable to Japan than to Russia, were obviously far short of total Japanese victory. Thus was concluded through mediation a war that had no further point.

The third group of political techniques, inquiry and conciliation, can also be used where diplomatic negotiations have become deadlocked. The essential idea is to refer the dispute to a group. It may be one already in existence (such as the League Council or the UN Security Council) or to be appointed. Its duties are to make an impartial investigation and (in conciliation) offer suggestions for some settlement. Such groups, when specially appointed for the dispute, either by the parties acting in concert or by the League Council or UN Security Council where these bodies set up special

---

[4] Hague Convention of 1899, Article 4.

groups for the purposes of particular cases, are usually called either commissions of inquiry or commissions of conciliation.

Although the use of commissions for purposes of inquiry and conciliation did not begin with the incorporation of the commission-of-inquiry device in the Hague Convention for Peaceful Settlement, this was its first institutionalization. It was intended for use "In disputes . . . involving neither honor nor vital interests" [5] and envisaged the parties themselves naming such a commission for a particular dispute between them. The commission would then operate according to the rules laid down in the Convention. The report of the commission was to be "limited to a statement of facts," and was to have "in no way the character of an [arbitral] award. It leaves to the parties entire freedom as to the effect to be given to the statement." [6]

The famous use of this device in the Dogger Bank episode came under exceptionally dramatic circumstances. In 1904, when their Far Eastern Fleet was bottled up in Port Arthur by the Japanese "Pearl Harbor" attack, the Russians, desperately needing naval forces at the scene of war, decided to send their poorly trained Baltic Fleet to the Pacific. At this point the war was confined to Russia and Japan, but a general involvement of the powers was distinctly possible. Great Britain had a treaty of alliance with Japan which would become operative if Japan found herself at war with *two* powers. France was already allied to Russia in Europe. Anglo-Russian relations were tense, with war already narrowly avoided in 1875, 1885, and 1898. Yet France, fearful of the rising power of Germany, had also drawn nearer to Britain by concluding the Anglo-French Entente on April 8, 1904. She thus had a foot in both camps. In these delicate circumstances the Russian Baltic Fleet, passing through the Dogger Bank fishing area on October 21, 1904, and fearful of interception by Japanese "torpedo boats" (destroyers), mistook some British fishing trawlers for Japanese. The Russians, after sinking one trawler and damaging others, proceeded south at full speed. When news reached London, the British fleet was ordered to stop the Russians off Gibraltar, using force if necessary.

France, in a dilemma, suggested the way out—a proposal which was acceptable to the British once they realized what had really happened. The Russians, already in difficulties fighting only one enemy, were anxious to pacify Britain provided complete humiliation could be avoided. The commission of inquiry of five naval officers from Britain, Russia, the United States, France, and Austria-Hungary, which reported on February 25, 1905, diplomatically but clearly laid the blame on Russia while stressing her lack of hostile intent. Subsequently, Russia paid damages. The value of the commission of inquiry technique in this case was not really that it established facts not already known. The value was that these facts, established through an impartial agency, became less injurious to national prestige.

---

[5] *Ibid.*, Article 9.
[6] *Ibid.*, Article 35.

Although the commission device was incorporated subsequently in many bilateral treaties, it was little used. Deadlocked states are seldom able to agree even on such limited matters as the appointment of a commission. The so-called Bryan "cooling-off" treaties that the United States negotiated, of which twenty-one came into effect just before the outbreak of World War I, attempted to solve this difficulty. They provided for the appointment of permanent commissions ahead of time by the two states involved, to which every kind of dispute was to be referred. These were never used, primarily because their function was taken over by the League after the war. Even in these treaties, although the parties promised to refrain from war for a year while the commission labored, it was left to the discretion of the parties what use to make (if any) of the report when rendered. The later use of the commission device by the League and UN, in which the organization itself appointed the commission, was much more successful and also much more convenient since the commission was available to all without special action and in the absence of treaty.

The term *conciliation* is frequently used very loosely today. A formal commission of conciliation does not need to be convened or appointed for conciliation to occur. In practice, since the end of World War I, most efforts at conciliation have been carried out by the League Council or UN Security Council, or by commissions and organs appointed by those bodies. Roughly, conciliation may be thought of as *group mediation*. Conciliation as a device differs from mediation in three respects: (1) it is normally carried on by a group or organization that appoints as its agent a committee, or council, or commission, rather than by a single state, monarch, or individual; (2) its proposals may frequently carry more weight inasmuch as the group (especially where it is the League or UN Council) may be the agent of an important bloc of powers; and (3) it is a more formal proceeding, resembling that of a judicial body but without being bound by the rules of law or its findings binding as law on others.

Formal commissions most frequently consist of five members, and voting is by majority. Theoretically a commission of inquiry differs from a commission of conciliation in that the purpose of the first is to resolve "a difference of opinion on points of fact" [7] while the function of the second is to go beyond this and formulate terms of settlement that the parties may be willing to accept. But this is a rather artificial distinction. The terms are used fairly interchangeably. In present practice, commissions, however styled, normally include proposals for a solution of the dispute in their reports; in earlier times this was left to the parties (even though the report obviously implied what needed to be done). To illustrate the interchangeability of the two terms, in 1946 in the Greek Question, the United Nations appointed a "commission of investigation" (or inquiry) that was to consist of all the nations then mem-

---

[7] *Ibid.*, Article 9.

bers of the Security Council and was not only to report the facts as to violations of the Greek frontier, but was also to make proposals for settling the disputes. The most famous commission ever appointed by the League (the Lytton Commission of the Manchurian Case, discussed below) was called a "commission of inquiry" although it was expected to and did propose a settlement of the issue.

The success of both inquiry and conciliation depends ultimately, just as in mediation, upon the willingness of the disputants to utilize the "facts" established as a basis for settlement or to accept the proposals made by the conciliatory body. As in all the political methods, the national interests at stake determine whether a suitable compromise can be found.

Nowhere was this method more clearly illustrated than in 1927 when the League Council itself acted as a conciliation agent in a dispute between France and Germany. Germany had been admitted to the League the year before; the French and the German governments were both actively seeking to lessen their friction with each other. France's position in the German-inhabited Saarland (a coal-rich German territory, technically administered by the League as war reparations, but actually policed by France) was becoming a source of serious dispute. The German press was vocal with demands that the "disguised military occupation" end; the French papers asserted that the heavy police forces there were necessary in view of the "turbulent population." When the question came before the Council, it was already understood by both the German and French delegations that, unless a settlement could be found, Germany might leave the League and the French government might fall. Very little room was left for elasticity, despite the fact that neither government wished to go to extremes. Specifically the Germans demanded that the French troops be reduced from 800 to not more than 500 men. The French insisted that they could not yield. In the inflamed state of public opinion a simple compromise on, say, 650 was out of the question. Yet short of a suitable compromise both Germany and France would be faced by extremely unpleasant developments.

The deadlock was finally broken by an extremely shrewd formula, put forward by the Italian delegate. France would keep its 800 police, but Germany's wishes would be respected by France never showing more than 500 of her 800 at any one time! This formula was accepted with relief by both parties. This Saar police question demonstrates again the importance of prestige to the parties in a dispute. It also shows that even when, as in this case, both parties wish to avoid an open break, it may still be extremely difficult to arrange.

The efforts of disputants to settle their problem—through direct bilateral or multilateral diplomacy, through the acceptance of good offices and mediation, through their use of facts established by commissions of inquiry or their receptiveness to the proposals of commissions of conciliation—stand or fall in the end upon whether the negotations thus directly or indirectly carried on result in a proposal acceptable to the parties. As a consequence, except in rare cases where a threat of extreme measures thinly disguised behind the façade of peaceful settlement procedures produces the agreement, the solution of such disputes inevitably entails compromise.

It should not be thought that the second and third groups of political devices must be used one after the other in any given sequence. Which devices are used, and how many of them, and in what order, depends upon the needs of the case. Initially and customarily, disputes are handled through diplomatic channels; if this form of negotiation fails and further political efforts are made, the next step varies from case to case. The very diversity of these methods results from the pressing need of deadlocked states to find an avenue of escape from their problem. They all rest upon finding a suitable compromise; which way it is found is of lesser importance. Thus all the techniques that comprise the political method of settling disputes stand or fall upon these same points. Success stems from a common willingness to settle an issue, coupled with an adequate face-saving formula and an acceptable basis for compromise.

3   Case Studies in Political Settlement: Diplomacy

THE case which follows illustrates in more detail the circumstances in which such political devices (in this case *diplomacy*) are put to use.

CASE I: THE CUBAN MISSILE CRISIS

(1) Background

President John F. Kennedy was barely settled in the White House after his inauguration in January 1961 when he was confronted with a major decision on Cuba: whether to permit the scheduled "Bay of Pigs" invasion to proceed. With his consent the CIA-organized and equipped Cuban refugee force made the assault. It culminated in a humiliating fiasco, with the CIA part in it quickly revealed.

These events had a prelude—and a postlude. In 1958, a major attempt by the Cuban dictator, Fulgencio Batista, to stamp out Fidel Castro's "26th of July" movement, failed. On January 1, 1959, Batista fled and Castro took power. Within a week the United States recognized the new regime, but relations between the two states deteriorated as Castro suppressed civil liberties and executed many of his former opponents. The refugees from Castro's oppression, given sanctuary in the United States, were ultimately the source of the cadres for the ill-fated "Bay of Pigs" venture. In its wake Castro announced himself as a convinced Marxist-Leninist and in the summer of 1962 his brother Raúl, the Foreign Minister, and Che Guevara, the Finance Minister, journeyed to Moscow to negotiate supplies of arms and arrange for Soviet technicians in Cuba. On September 11, TASS announced that "defensive" arms were being sent. It added explicitly that Soviet nuclear rockets were so powerful in range that there was no need for sending any to bases outside the Soviet Union. But forty-two medium and intermediate-range ballistic missiles were actually then in or en route to Cuba. Within the United States political demands were simultaneously being expressed to end the Communist foothold in the New World. Kennedy resolutely opposed a new invasion although he promised "to watch what happens in Cuba with the closest attention." A U-2 flight over western Cuba on October 14 resulted in pictures indicating a medium-range missile base in the San Cristóbal area. This first news, reported to the President, and supplemented by later verifications of five other MRBM (1,100 mile) and three IRBM (2,200 mile) sites led quickly to a dramatic confrontation between the two foremost nuclear powers.

(2) The Dispute

On October 18, Kennedy met Gromyko, the Soviet Foreign Minister, for a talk already scheduled before the discovery of the Soviet missile bases. Gromyko reiterated Khrushchev's earlier statement that the Berlin question (which had produced a severe crisis in 1959 and again in 1961 when Western rights to access were threatened) would not be re-activated until after the American November 6 elections. Gromyko then said twice that if no agreement on Berlin was reached in the aftermath of the elections, the Soviets would be "compelled" to sign a separate peace treaty with East Germany which would end Western rights in Berlin. On Cuba, Gromyko repeated that Soviet missiles *in Cuban hands* were purely defensive. Kennedy, reflecting on Khrushchev's solicitude in postponing the new Berlin crisis until after November 6, and with the evidence from new photos of the rate at which the Soviet missiles were becoming operational, concluded (correctly) that the timing was deliberate. The Soviet intention was to reveal the threat from Cuba at the height of a new Berlin crisis, hoping by so doing to attain a maximum psychological impact. Americans would feel outflanked, caught in a potential cross-fire.

On October 22, in a television speech Kennedy grasped the initiative, which thereafter was always in American hands. His speech was quiet, very firm, and to the point. "Good evening, my fellow citizens. This Government, as promised, has maintained the closest surveillance of the Soviet military build-up on the island of Cuba. Within the past week unmistakable evidence has established the fact that a series of offensive missiles is now in preparation. . . . The purpose of these bases can be none other than to provide a nuclear strike capacity against the Western Hemisphere." This "sudden, clandestine decision to station strategic weapons for the first time outside of Soviet soil, is a deliberately provocative and unjustified change in the *status quo* which cannot be accepted by this country, if our courage and our commitments are ever to be trusted again by either friend or foe." A selective naval "quarantine" (blockade) against the further shipment of "offensive weapons" would be imposed. "It shall be the policy of this nation to regard any nuclear missile launched from Cuba against any nation in the Western Hemisphere as an attack by the Soviet Union on the United States, requiring a full retaliatory response upon the Soviet Union."

The next days were hectic. The twenty members of the Organization of American states (OAS) met and gave support in a unanimous, broad, authorizing resolution backing the quarantine. (Some later actually participated with their ships.) On Wednesday, October 24, the blockade went into effect. The moment of truth was indeed inevitably coming. On Thursday Adlai Stevenson, U.S. Ambassador to the UN, with photos at hand, cross-examined an ill-prepared Soviet Ambassador Zorin in the Security Council. "Do you . . . deny that the U.S.S.R. has placed and is placing medium-and intermediate-range missiles and sites in Cuba? Yes or no. Don't wait for the translation. Yes or no." Zorin responded angrily: "I am not in an American courtroom, sir." Stevenson interrupted, "You are in the court of world opinion right now!" Zorin went on: "In due course, sir, you will have your reply." Stevenson rapped back: "I am prepared to wait for my answer until Hell freezes over, if that's your decision." Gradually the initial chill of fear which was spreading around the world began to be supplemented by a feeling on the part of other nations that the U.S. had some reason for its actions.

(3) The Outcome

Wednesday all the world waited as eighteen Soviet dry cargo ships plowed on toward the quarantine line. Reports came in of a half-dozen Soviet submarines having arrived to escort these ships. Then the Soviet ships nearest Cuba appeared to slow down. On Thursday a Soviet tanker (tankers were not interdicted) was hailed by a U.S. ship and then allowed to proceed. On Friday a Lebanese-registered freighter under Soviet charter was boarded, inspected, and allowed to pass. By that day sixteen of the eighteen Soviet cargo ships, including all five with large hatches, had turned around. But work on the Soviet missile sites already in Cuba was being pressed forward. News came in of the first downing of a U.S. U-2 over Cuba by a Soviet surface-to-air (SAM) missile. A small gain had been made but the U.S. objective was still not reached.

During these days an exchange of letters (telegrams) continued between Kennedy and Khrushchev. A critical point in the exchange came with the delivery of two Khrushchev letters, one on Friday at 9 P.M., October 26, and a second the next day. The Friday (private) letter, meandering, polemical, and long, seemed to be saying that, inasmuch as Soviet missiles had been placed in Cuba to defend the island from U.S. invasion, they could be withdrawn under UN inspection if the U.S. promised no invasion. (This is the telegram, never made public, which is rumored to have been virtually hysterical in places. Perhaps "frustrated ranting" might be as accurate.) But the Saturday (public) letter, more carefully drafted, seemed to take a harder line, demanding the withdrawal of Jupiter missiles from Turkey in exchange. On Saturday evening, October 27, Kennedy, ignoring the Saturday letter, responded that "the key elements of your [Friday] proposals . . . seem generally acceptable as I understand them." These were:

1. You would agree to remove these weapons systems from Cuba under appropriate United Nations observation and supervision; and undertake, with suitable safeguards, to halt the further introduction of such weapons systems into Cuba. 2. We, on our part, would agree [assuming such effective UN agreements] (a) to remove promptly the quarantine measures now in effect and (b) to give assurances against an invasion of Cuba.

Robert Kennedy delivered a copy of this letter to the Soviet Ambassador with the verbal addition that the U.S. was at the point where strong additional measures would have to be taken unless the President "received immediate notice that the missiles would be withdrawn." [8] On Sunday morning, October 28, the Soviet answer came, announced first over Moscow radio. A new Soviet note was on its way (the fifth since Tuesday) which said: "In order to eliminate as rapidly as possible the conflict . . . the Soviet Government . . . has given a new order to dismantle the arms which you describe as offensive and to crate them and return them to the Soviet Union." The Soviets were "prepared to reach agreement to enable representatives to verify the dismantling. . ."

In the sequel, Castro frustrated the agreed means of verification, refusing to allow a UN team on Soviet soil. Mikoyan, sent by Khrushchev to pressure Castro, argued with Castro for nearly four weeks before giving up. The U.S. tacitly accepted the deadlock and verified for itself by aerial photography that the missiles were being removed. Later complications over withdrawal of Soviet bombers and the more gradual withdrawal of 23,000 Soviet troops were ultimately resolved.

(4) Significance

Kennedy's actions in October 1962 were taken within the framework of a threat by Khrushchev at Vienna in June 1961 that the Soviets would sign a peace treaty with East Germany, ending Western rights in Berlin, and fight if the U.S. contested it. The postponement of this threat did not remove it. Gromyko in October 1962 specifically promised in effect a new Berlin Crisis for late 1962 or early 1963—at a time when the Soviet missiles in Cuba would be operational. As we shall see in a later chapter, Khrushchev after *sputnik* was pressing hard in the confident belief that he could shatter Western unity and make great gains. If the Cuban gambit succeeded he would press even harder with the game of nuclear blackmail as the West fell into greater disarray. But Kennedy drew the line—convincingly.

The subtlety of Kennedy's crisis management had a good deal to do with its success. Destruction of the Soviet missiles in Cuba from the air was at first glance more direct and appealing. But it entailed direct violence against Soviet personnel. Resorting instead to a "quarantine" (for a blockade, too, is an act of war), Kennedy posed the initial and lesser question of *additional*

---

[8] See Theodore C. Sorenson, *Kennedy* (New York: Harper and Row, 1965) p. 715.

missiles for Cuba to the Soviets in a form which allowed at least a couple of days for reflection. It, in effect, was a tacit but not overt ultimatum in the sense that the Soviets' own actions would put it into effect only if their ships kept coming. Having won the first gambit as the Soviets held up a confrontation, he gained the psychological initiative for the second: to get those missiles already in Cuba, out. Prepared to do it with U.S. armed forces, he still extended the Soviets the latitude of deciding to do it themselves. At the same time he made it clear that the time for a Soviet decision was running short. Seizing on Khrushchev's celebrated unpublished Friday letter, he avoided demanding more than he really wanted and gave the Soviet leader a way out without undue humiliation. (Khrushchev was later to justify his actions to the Communist Chinese on the basis that the American pledge not to invade Cuba made the missiles unnecessary.) If instead Kennedy had decided to use force to eliminate the Castro regime, the prestige of the Soviet Union would have been severely jeopardized and the results probably quite different.

In this case study we see a correct use of technique, a classic handling of the prestige complication, and a careful (although not equal) compromise of the divergent national interests at stake.

4   *Legal Techniques*

ALTHOUGH some form of compromise is of the very essence in each of the techniques that comprise the political method, the legal method by its very nature must operate on a basis of law and exclude compromise. The distinguishing feature of the use of legal techniques is that they enable the dispute to be settled on the grounds of legal right. Both legal techniques—arbitration and adjudication—are alike in this feature.[9]

The legal method presents both advantages and disadvantages to states casting about for a means of settling their dispute. It has numerous advantages. First, the case is out of the hands of the parties once they have presented the evidence and made their arguments. The judge or judges have the burden of rendering the decision, and deadlock is ruled out. Second, the verdict of the judges is a decision that the parties have obligated themselves beforehand to accept. A definite disposition of the problem, once and for all, is achieved. Third, the prestige aspect is largely avoided for both parties. The loser has not yielded to pressure or threat of force, but is instead observing the law (which is commendable). Legal solutions are, after all, *ipso facto* "just," and their use may divert popular wrath (on occasion a result of negotiated settlements) from the governments who resort to it.

The disadvantages of the legal method include, most importantly, the consideration that a legal verdict characteristically awards all to one disputant and nothing to the other (since one is "right," and the other is "wrong"). In complex cases involving more than one issue, some points may be decided in

---

[9] For a detailed description of how these techniques operate see above, Chapter 6 (International Law).

favor of each disputant; but, for any single issue, one wins and the other loses. In complex cases all points may consequently be lost or won. For the loser this may entail too great a sacrifice of national interests. The more crucial the issue, the greater the likelihood that both parties will not be equally eager for legal settlement. Even where each feels sure of its case, prudence may well deter them from a gamble in the courts. With the political method, it is always possible in the end, up to the very moment of signature or ratification, to draw back from the bargain, finding some "previously unsuspected complication;" with the legal method, a failure to honor the decision of the court is *ipso facto* evidence of illegal conduct and intent, and cannot fail to injure national prestige.

Since states, unless they have accepted an obligation to go to court under given circumstances, remain free to decide whether or not to seek a legal judgment in a particular case, it is not surprising, in view of these disadvantages, that the usual court case is rather unspectacular and uncluttered with questions of vital interest. On the other hand, the legal method is perfectly adapted to the solution of vexing issues which, while not vital in themselves, plague the relations of two powers. In such cases there is much to be gained for each party, whether it technically loses or wins the case. Questions settled by courts of adjudication under their normal (contentious) jurisdiction include whether the holders of certain Serbian loans issued in France had a right to receive payment in gold, and whether the Colombian Ambassador in Peru, who had given asylum to a Peruvian refugee, could require the Peruvian government to allow the refugee safe-conduct out of Peru. These cases are typical and illustrative of this point.

The case study in adjudication that follows is not typical of such proceedings. It is deliberately chosen for its spectacular character. Its unusual nature delineates not only the uses of legal settlement but, even more important, the limitations.

5 *Case Studies in Legal Settlement: Adjudication*

PROPERLY speaking, the Austro-German Customs Union Case was not a case in the ordinary sense at all. Rather it was disposed of by the Court under what is called an "advisory opinion."

In both the League Court and the UN Court two types of jurisdiction had been provided for: contentious and advisory. Contentious jurisdiction is the normal process by which two states, in agreement as to the desirability of a legal settlement, go to court and present their case for a decision. By the provisions of the Covenant and the Charter, both the League and UN Courts were also given the duty of advising the Council (or Assembly) on the merits of the legal issues involved in a case brought before the political organs for political settlement.[10] The Court was to act as lawyer for the Council, giving legal advice upon request.

---

[10] The Council and Assembly of the League were given this discretion under Article 14 of the Covenant; the Security Council and General Assembly of the United Nations,

Properly used, the advisory opinion device can be extremely helpful to the political organ. The advisory opinion, as advice, can be disregarded if the organ sees fit. Yet the Court, in order to render its advice, often must investigate a dispute to an extent and in a way scarcely to be distinguished from its exercise of contentious jurisdiction. This creates a strong emotional pressure to accept the advice as a judgment (decision). It is obvious that, were the Court to hear the case in its contentious capacity, it would have to render a decision squarely in accord with its advice. As a result, the advice, while technically not binding either on the organ or the disputants, is hard to brush aside.

Because the giving of advice, where a dispute between states is at issue, is tantamount in practical (but not legal) terms, in view of the emotional consequences, to rendering a decision, the League Court in the Status of Eastern Carelia Case refused in 1923 to give advice. It held that while Finland was prepared to accept the Court's opinion, Russia, not then a member of the League, was not, and that "answering the question would be substantially equivalent to deciding the dispute between the parties" without both parties having freely accepted the Court's jurisdiction.[11]

In the Austro-German Customs Union Case of 1931, given below, this result in effect (although not technically) occurred. The Germans did not want a legal settlement of the entire issue. They were maneuvered into agreeing in the Council that one possibly doubtful legal point might need looking into: was the proposed customs union incompatible with Austria's international obligations to maintain her independence? The German attitude did not oppose a legal opinion on this point. But it is perfectly plain from the Council debate that the Germans did not at first grasp that the Court would go beyond an advice on the single technical point, narrowly construed, to an opinion in effect on the broad and future merits of the customs proposal itself. They did not contemplate the full-scale trial that actually occurred. It must be remembered that a European crisis had followed the announcement of the proposed customs union. The German delegate on the Council was greatly concerned with avoiding the impending debate on the proposition that the customs union was a threat to international peace. As a means to that end the "cooling-off" period that would result from seeking legal advice was welcome to Germany. And it seemed an appropriate way to avoid possible French recourse to force—which Germany could not in 1931 have repulsed. The resulting "opinion," for reasons we shall examine shortly, shook faith in the Court's impartiality and undermined its prestige. Where usually the peculiar virtue of the Court has been to still dissensions, in this case, where an unwanted legal settlement was foisted upon Germany, it created still more.

---

under Article 96 of the Charter. In the latter case requests for opinions were to be on "any legal question." Although the phrase in the Charter is more restrictive than that of the Covenant, it consititutes (as we saw in Chapter 6) no real restriction, since any question can be treated on its legal merits.

[11] *Permanent Court of International Justice*, Series B, No. 5.

CASE II: THE AUSTRO-GERMAN CUSTOMS UNION CASE

(1) *Background*

By the terms of the World-War-I settlements, Austria was reduced from a proud empire to a tiny, landlocked state with pressing economic problems. Germany, too, was stripped of territory—most notably, Silesia and the Polish Corridor, as well as Alsace and Lorraine. Defeated and reduced in prestige and power, both German-speaking nations looked upon eventual union as a means of reasserting Teutonic importance and playing a significant part in European affairs. Political union was explicitly prohibited by the peace treaties, but an economic union, as perhaps a first step toward the eventual goal, seemed a possibility. Following secret negotiations, it was announced to a startled Europe on March 21, 1931, that a treaty had been signed by the two states providing for a customs union. To the French and their East European allies (whose territories were largely former portions of the German and Austrian Empires) the prospect was alarming. From a political viewpoint, France was determined to prevent it.

(2) *The Dispute*

Legally the situation turned upon the Treaty of Saint-Germain (the equivalent for Austria of what the Treaty of Versailles was for Germany), which forbade *Anschluss* or union of the two states. Furthermore, the Geneva (Financial) Protocol of 1922, as a condition of economic aid extended to Austria, required her to take no step that would compromise her independence. The dispute was placed by France before the League Council. The Council in May 1931, decided unanimously to ask the Permanent Court of International Justice for an advisory opinion on the legality of the customs union.

(3) *The Outcome*

In September the Court, having heard voluminous testimony, handed down its opinion. By a vote of eight to seven the judges were of the opinion that the customs union was incompatible with the 1922 Protocol. This close vote came from the following situation: seven judges found the union *incompatible* with both the Treaty of Saint-Germain and the 1922 Protocol; seven found the union *compatible* with both; one found it compatible with the treaty but incompatible with the protocol—thus, eight to seven. On the majority side were the French, Italian, Polish, and Romanian judges (France and its allies, plus Italy, which feared *Anschluss*); on the dissenting side were the United States, Chinese, British, and German judges (powers peripheral to the continent, plus Germany who was of course in favor). It is difficult to escape the conclusion that the decision was made according to political attitude rather than legal right.

(4) *Significance*

Judge Anzilotti (Italy), in a separate but concurring opinion, appraised the situation entirely realistically when he wrote: "Everything points to the fact that the answer depends upon considerations which are for the most part, if not entirely, of a political and economic kind." [12] The difficulties involved in handling it legally stemmed from the types of questions that the Court undertook to answer. The question was, Will the customs union constitute *Anschluss?* The answer actually was, Not in itself, but it might easily lead to it. The question was, Will the customs union compromise Austrian independence? The answer was, in all probability, before very long, yes. Thus the real questions turned not only upon immediate consequences but upon ultimate probabilities. A customs union, once in effect, is a living thing that may easily grow beyond its original functions—especially this customs union might. As Judge Anzilotti also said, it was not *a* customs union that was being considered, but *this* customs union in *this* case. At any given later point, assuming the customs union had gone into effect, the Court could have rendered an effective opinion as to whether, at that moment, the customs union had violated the treaty or the protocol. If the customs union had been permitted to begin existence, an adverse opinion at a subsequent date would have run against not a proposed project but a functioning, daily operation. To kill the plan stillborn was relatively easy; later it would be otherwise. This consideration could not be pushed from the minds of the judges.

This case required legal judgment precisely at the point where such judgments stand on their weakest ground—where they come to involve issues not of present fact but of ultimate probability. Where there is a law against robbing banks, it is much easier to determine that A did or did not rob a certain bank than to determine whether, if A (who is suspected of bank-robbing tendencies) is permitted to enter the bank, he will or will not rob it. Measuring temptation and estimating future behavior call not for legal calipers but for psychological-political insight. Here we reach one definite boundary of legal settlement. This is what Judge Anzilotti's words actually point to. This is also why the judges, as it were, voted politically.

There is a further conclusion. In 1931, some two days before the rendering of the opinion, Austria and Germany chose to abandon their project. Their decision was the result of coercion as surely as if troops had been used. In 1938 Hitlerite Germany annexed Austria and set the Court, the treaty, and the protocol all at naught. The moral to be drawn is simple—unless a state really is resorting to Court by its complete free will, it may, if it is strong enough, later have its way by force or threat of force to gain what earlier is denied to it legally. In such cases where states are in Court because of coercion, the legal process is merely a façade behind which the bayonets are only half concealed. Here we reach the other important limitation on the efficacy of the legal method.

The United Nations Security Council, profiting from these dissensions of the past, carefully refrained from requesting an advisory opinion in the Corfu

---

[12] See *ibid.*, Series A/B, No. 41, pp. 68–69 for the opinion of Anzilotti.

Channel Case. Instead, the Council recommended to the parties that they take the case (involving the sinking of British destroyers by Albanian mines) to Court. At this point the British proceeded unilaterally to apply to the Court. They argued that Albania *must* come to Court, since Article 25 of the Charter required that "decisions" of the Security Council must be obeyed and the Council had made a *decision*—namely, *to recommend* that they both go to Court. Of course the Council can make "decisions" in the sense of Article 25 *only* under Chapter VII of the Charter; even there its power is really restricted to decisions to use economic and/or military sanctions.[13] Its "recommendations" are quite another thing (and no more legally binding than those of the Assembly).[14] If the British interpretation were allowed to gain acceptance, the Council could, among its other such vastly increased powers, hand the parties over to the Court whenever it wished. This procedure would go far beyond the advisory opinion technique as used in the Customs Union Case, and go far toward destroying the freedom of states to go or not to go to Court as they please. Albania, while objecting to the British argument and the unilateral application to the Court, expressed herself willing (July 2, 1947) to accept the Court's jurisdiction. The Court, in a preliminary hearing, avoided a direct ruling on the British contention by holding that a case could come before the Court by separate expressions of willingness on the part of both states rather than solely by the more usual joint request. The Court then went on to the merits of the dispute proper, deciding basically in Britain's favor. Albania failed to comply with the verdict.

The cases and examples given above illustrate the use of political and legal techniques in settling disputes. One factor is common to them all. The success or failure of the techniques rests upon the willingness of the state involved either to negotiate a compromise (even a rather one-sided compromise) or to accept as binding and final the decision of judges. The techniques for achieving peaceful settlements are both many and varied, as are the possibilities implicit in them. Therefore, if a dispute cannot be settled by the use of one or more of them, the source of the failure is not likely to be due to a lack of technical devices. It will be found in the ineptness of the parties in handling the prestige issue, or in their unwillingness to adjust their national interests.

---

13 And even there technically non-existent because of its lack of forces.

14 The confusion comes from the loose use of the term *decision* in the Charter. In Article 27 the term *decision* is used as a synonym for *voting*. But in Chapter VII, Article 41, where the Security Council "may *decide* what measures are to be employed" to enforce its will on an aggressor state, the term means that the Council can incur obligations for the members which those states *must honor*. (Italics added.) Thus, to simplify, in Chapter VI the Security Council may decide on recommendations; in Chapter VII it can also decide on decisions.

CHAPTER 12

International Organization and the Settlement of Disputes

> . . . The proper timing and synchronization of orders has to be carefully planned. In Palestine, seven governments had to act simultaneously and orders had to go down through the military hierarchy of as many armies to the front commanders. Some confusion also resulted from the fact that Arabs and Israelis were divided by a difference of time. The parties were therefore made to accept Greenwich Mean Time as a compromise. Further divergencies arose over the proper hours for a cease-fire order. In the Middle East rifle shooting seems to reach its climax at night . . . for that reason the lull of the early morning was held to be the most suitable moment for inaugurating a truce.
>
> PAUL MOHN
> "Problems of Truce Supervision,"
> *International Conciliation*, February 1952

I N the previous chapter, even where the League and United Nations have been involved, the discussion has focused primarily on the roles and viewpoints of the parties to the dispute. Consequently it may not be fully realized how revolutionary the use of conciliation by these organizations actually is. Conciliation is a group device. When conciliation is used by a world organization, the group involved is the world itself, and no problem is peripheral to its concern; rather the reverse. Where formerly the degree of initiative of either the parties to the dispute or some third state offering good offices governed the extent of the use to which all these devices might be put, conciliation as used by the League and United Nations provides third parties almost automatically—indeed the world itself is one. It is almost axiomatic that some effort will actually be made to settle every serious dispute anywhere in the world, even where that dispute is between non-members of the organization.[1] Institutional handling of disputes is available as a supplement to *ad hoc* procedures.

The machinery by which the League and the United Nations have sought

---

[1] See Article 11 of the League Covenant and Article 2 of the UN Charter, each of which makes it clear that non-member disputes are also of concern to the organizations. However, where such non-members are also great powers, the difficulties of handling the cases effectively, drastically increases.

to discharge this obligation has already been outlined in Chapter 9; it now remains to analyze the effects of these efforts upon the settlement of disputes.

I The Role of International Organizations in the Settlement of Disputes

ONE distinction is immediately necessary. What the League and the United Nations have accomplished in the handling of disputes (aside from the use of force by the organization itself in collective security) is conventionally called their "record of peaceful settlement." As soon as this record is examined, it immediately becomes obvious that some very bloody disputes are a part of it. This would appear to be a contradiction in terms. Why the term "peaceful" is applied to the Palestine War becomes clear only if it is remembered that by it is meant, not that force has not been used by the parties in some cases, but that economic or military sanctions have not been used by the organization to bring about the settlement. Under this definition fall all but one of the disputes handled by the League during its lifetime, and two dealt with by the United Nations. The Ethiopian Sanctions Case of the League and the Korean Sanctions Case of the United Nations are the sole proceedings in formal enforcement actions prior to the Rhodesian Case; the handling of all other disputes constitute this "record of peaceful settlement."

The word "peaceful" describes the role of the organization rather than the course of the dispute and its ultimate disposition. This is a highly important point, for on it rests much potential misunderstanding of the usual part played by such an organization during a dispute. As a conciliatory agency the organization is primarily interested in preserving or restoring peace rather than inspiring further bloodshed. The organization and its members must preserve self-respect (collective prestige) and ensure that heed is paid to its counsels. To accomplish this end, it must more often than not move warily, making it as easy as possible for the disputants to comply with its requests and proposals, without loss of face to either organization or disputants, for where its will is flagrantly disregarded and a clear and obvious aggression is committed in direct defiance of the organization, there is no choice but to institute sanctions or allow the organization to disintegrate.

Of the great number of disputes dealt with by the League of Nations and United Nations under their peaceful settlement procedures,[2] in a large number of instances some force was used by one or both parties to the dispute at some stage in its development. The force exerted varied from the firing of a few shots across a tense frontier in a single day, all the way to full-scale warfare over a period of months and years. From the point of view of force exerted and the number of belligerents, the Palestine War easily outranks the Italo-Ethiopian War in its importance. Yet in the former case no

---

[2] Articles 10, 11, 12, 13, 15 of the Covenant; Chapter VI of the Charter. See above, Chapter 9, for discussion of their operation.

aggressor was named or sanctions instituted against him, while in the latter it occurred. Again, the Japanese adventure which began in Manchuria in 1931 compares, as an example of warfare, to the later Korean War. Yet here too the same observation holds true. One must conclude that *it is not the amount or duration of force used by the parties* that distinguishes the situation where the organization does use sanctions from one in which it does not. The distinction arises instead from (1) the presence or absence of obvious intent of the parties to commit aggression across a well-defined frontier in defiance of the organization and (2) the particular circumstances of the case.

Aggression is such a simple-sounding term that the difficulties of determining when and if it has occurred can easily be overlooked. Later on, when we examine the case studies in collective security, there will be an opportunity to study the term further. Here it is enough to realize that disputes rarely can be reduced to the classic theoretical form where A clearly and with aggressive intent crosses B's well-established frontier, with B the innocent and unprovocative victim. Not the least of the reasons is that the frontiers often are not well-established. Yet once this clear-cut case is left behind, one encounters all kinds of complexities. This is in part why the formula "Aggression having been committed, sanctions must be applied" has been so rarely used. It is in part the reason that all but three disputes coming before the League and United Nations have been handled under peaceful settlement procedures. These points can be best illustrated through a study of actual cases, but before turning to cases one further distinction is needed.

A great number of classifications have been applied to the cases coming before the League and United Nations, often with the hope of determining where these organizations have been "effective." The most usual approach has been to distinguish cases involving a great power from those involving small powers. The difficulties with satisfactorily settling the first group are obviously inherently greater. Yet, as a matter of fact, when two relatively small states are bent upon ignoring the efforts of the organization, the results can be equally frustrating for the organization. In the Gran Chaco War, Bolivia and Paraguay fought on despite the League's best efforts to bring the war to a halt. Again, one must consider the intent of the parties and the particular circumstances of the case.

To take both these factors into account, it will be useful to consider peaceful settlement cases, for both League and United Nations, in two categories, arbitrarily classifying them as Category I and Category II:

Category I embraces those cases where both parties to a dispute desire a settlement short of the intentional use of armed force, or are not prepared to risk the almost certain condemnation as aggressors that would in the circumstances of the case follow the intentional and continued use of force.

Category II includes those cases where one or more of the parties to a dispute desire to use organized force, and do so on a continuing basis, but without committing what the League or United Nations deems aggression to be punished by the use of collective security sanctions.

In Category I there is either no intent to use force (even though it may be used), or at least no intent to commit actions which, if persisted in because of the circumstances, will cause a party definitely to risk being met with the use of sanctions. The circumstances in these cases are such that an aggression is too obvious and clear-cut. Although Category I as defined includes two types of cases, (1) where there is no intent to use force and (2) where there may be such intent but there is no willingness to risk very probable sanctions, from an analytical viewpoint the results in these two types are similar—the organization's will is carried out. In Category II, this is not the case. In Category II, by contrast, the intent of one or more parties is to use organized force, but the circumstances are such that the organization cannot readily determine the commission of aggression. Both these categories apply irrespective of whether there are great or small powers involved, and although, for obvious reasons, cases in Category II involving great powers are fraught with more dangerous consequences to all involved, the difficulties of bringing the dispute to an ultimate solution do not vary in any really significant way with the power per se of the states involved.

2 Case Studies in Organized Peaceful Settlement: Category I

TWO cases will be examined under Category I.

CASE III: THE RUSSIAN-ARMY-IN-IRAN CASE

(1) Background

During World War II, Iran was occupied by Soviet as well as by American and British troops. After the war all withdrew except the Russians. On March 2, 1946, the day set for withdrawal, the Soviets were still in occupation of northern Iran.

(2) The Dispute

The dispute began over other issues. In January 1946, Iran placed its dispute with Russia upon the agenda of the United Nations Security Council. She charged the Russians with attempting by coercion to obtain oil concessions and with fostering an independence movement in the Azerbaijan area on the Soviet frontier. On March 19 Iran further charged the Soviets with staying beyond the agreed date for departure. On March 24 Moscow claimed that Russian forces had begun withdrawal on March 2 and that it would be complete in five or six weeks "if nothing unforeseen occurs."

(3) The Outcome

The Council, after discussing the issue when it first came up (before the occupation issue per se), retained it on its agenda while the parties prepared to come to a direct settlement. It kept the issue there even after the Russian announcement of withdrawal and after Iran in April requested its deletion in view of the alleged progress in the direct conversations. By

May 6 the Soviet troops were fully withdrawn (after Iran promised to consider an oil lease—which ultimately came to naught) and the issue lapsed.

(4) Significance

Undoubtedly Russia was exerting great pressure upon Iran for oil leases and to detach Azerbaijan. In such circumstances, where pressure is used but not force, it is peculiarly difficult for other individual states to render aid. Nor did Iran then have allies in the West; yet her territorial integrity was of great (perhaps vital) interest to the Western nations. Placing the dispute before the United Nations was an effective counterstroke to Russian pressure since it put Iran in a far stronger position to resist. If Russia were to go too far, it would be under the spotlight of world attention, and the issue was before a forum that might always decide on concerted action. The very fact that Russia exerted her pressures before the deadline for withdrawal, sufficiently to cause alarm in Iran, indicated a Russian sense of urgency. The imminence of the deadline explains this. Since the Russians were publicly committed to withdrawal as of a given date, their protracted stay after that time would expose the Soviets to the risk of being condemned for aggression—having troops on the wrong side of a clearly defined frontier, with no right to have them there, is a relatively clear and easy test. Had the issue not been so clear, they might have gone on with it; as it was, they withdrew. (The fact that the U.S.S.R. was then without nuclear weapons no doubt also was a factor.)

CASE IV: THE SUEZ 1956 CRISIS CASE

(1) Background

The partition of Palestine (see Case VI) did not end Arab-Israeli tension. Egypt, humiliated by her poor showing in the Palestine War, was determined to even the score. After an internal coup in 1952, Nasser came to power in Egypt. Partly due to his ambitious policies, partly due to unsettled problems in the area, tension steadily increased in the Middle East. Nasser's intentions to unify the Arab world under his leadership and drive the Israelis into the sea ran seriously athwart the major interests of the Western powers in the area who wanted peace and stability, a secure defensive bulwark against the Soviet Union, and a shutting out of Communist influences. In 1955, the creation of the Baghdad Pact, with the important Arab state of Iraq as a member, posed the threat of an end to Nasser's dreams of one great United Arab Republic under his leadership. Nasser turned to the Soviet bloc for arms which were forthcoming in great quantity. This in turn upset (especially potentially) the delicate arms balance between Arab and Jew. Nasser's assistance to the Algerian rebels further upset his relations with France. Similarly he exhausted the patience of Secretary of State Dulles by using East against West in bids for aid. When Dulles, in July 1956, angrily withdrew offers of financing the cherished Egyptian dream of the

Aswan Dam, Nasser in retaliation nationalized the Suez Canal Company (July 26). The British and French, as principal stockholders, were outraged. But their anger was not merely sparked by endangered property rights. The greater concern was the threatened change of the Suez Canal from an international waterway into an instrument of Egyptian foreign policy.[3] The issue quickly became highly charged emotionally. To Israel, France, and Great Britain, Nasser seemed to be engaged in a successful plan striking at vital interests; to many of the newer nations it seemed only a belated redressing of old scores.

(2) The Dispute

Britain and France, prepared to use force, were persuaded by American pressure to try diplomacy first. Dulles, arrived in London, told Eden that Eisenhower "was emphatic upon the importance of negotiation. The President did not rule out the use of force. . . . But he felt that every possibility of peaceful settlement must be exhausted before this was done." Dulles, speaking for himself to Eden, said that Nasser must be made "to disgorge" the canal.[4]

Tedious and prolonged negotiations followed in the next months. All came to naught, foundering on the rock of Egypt's unwillingness to agree to any form of international administration of the canal. Britain and France pushed ahead with military preparations but the first overt military action was launched by Israel on October 29. As Israeli forces swept toward the canal, the British and French issued an ultimatum to both Israel and Egypt to cease fighting within twelve hours and withdraw all troops within a ten-mile radius of the canal. Anglo-French forces would occupy Port Said, Ismailia, and Suez temporarily. Egypt rejected the ultimatum and Anglo-French air attacks on military targets in Egypt began on October 31 as a prelude to landings.

(3) The Outcome

The UN Security Council, blocked by Anglo-French vetoes from action on American and Soviet cease-fire resolutions, was soon deadlocked. The General Assembly, acting under the "Uniting for Peace" Resolution, met in special, emergency session from November 1 to November 10. It called for a cease-fire. The idea of an "emergency force" (UNEF) was proposed by Lester Pearson of Canada as it quickly became apparent that the United States was not willing to back the Anglo-French action. Meanwhile, the Soviets were threatening to send "volunteer" forces to aid Egypt, and talking of bombing London and Paris with rocket missiles. On November 6, Britain yielded; France followed suit; and Israel then reluctantly withdrew. By November 10, the first UNEF troops (authorized by a vote of 64–0–12 on November 7) were at a staging area in Italy. On November 15, they landed in Egypt with Egyptian consent. Just under 6,000 men, drawn from ten small or medium

---

[3] In 1955 almost one out of every three ships using the Canal was British. Out of 108 million tons which went through as cargo, 68 million consisted of oil.

[4] *Full Circle: The Memoirs of Sir Anthony Eden*, London: 1960, pp. 436–437.

powers (out of twenty-four nations who offered troops), constituted this UNEF.[5] Their function was not to fire on any party, but to separate all parties in order that hostilities would end.

(4) Significance

The initial assault by Israel followed a long series of raids from Egyptian territory and the acquisition by Egypt of large quantities of arms to be used against Israel. Moreover, Egypt had for years closed the Suez Canal to Israeli shipping. Britain and France had other grounds for complaint. Their property had been seized and the status of an international canal unilaterally altered. France and Britain saw in Nasser's act the abrogation of the International Convention of Constantinople of 1888 which specifically provided that "the Suez Maritime Canal shall always be free and open, in time of war as in time of peace, to every vessel of commerce or of war without distinction of flag." They feared that Egypt would now decide unilaterally whose ships should be allowed passage, as in the case of Israel. When the three nations resorted to force against Egypt, it was not unprovoked—whether or not it was actually justified.

For the UN, under such circumstances, to have condemned the three nations for aggression, quite apart from the consideration that Britain and France were great powers, would have been unwarranted. The Anglo-French action was explicitly based upon the protection of the canal; and there was obviously no intention to retain Egyptian territory. Given the Soviet threats, the situation was also potentially capable of escalation. However, once the UN had decided to intervene to settle the dispute, a defiance of the organization would have posed the real threat of Britain and France being judged as aggressors. Dismayed in any event by the lack of American support, the British and French accepted the inevitable. Ultimately, under UN supervision, an arrangement was reached under which Egypt guaranteed free passage of the canal (except to Israel) and compensated the stockholders of the canal company.

These two cases have a common feature: at the critical moment, persistence by one or more of the parties in their activities would, almost certainly, have exposed them to a clear risk of being condemned for aggression, since the circumstances in which the persistence would have occurred would have been too clear-cut a defiance of generally accepted standards of right and justice. Once a dispute is resolved down to a simple, uncluttered question such as whether an army of occupation is remaining past the agreed date of departure, or whether a nation is complying with a cease-fire or continuing an offensive across a known and established frontier on the other side of which

---

[5] Brazil, Canada, Colombia, Denmark, Finland, India, Indonesia, Norway, Sweden, and Yugoslavia. The force initially was approximately 6,000 men. In 1964, it was 5,100. Finnish and Indonesian forces withdrew in 1957 and the Colombian unit in 1958. India increased her contribution.

they have no right to be, the nation that persists in thwarting the will of an international organization, such as the League or United Nations, runs a grave risk.

3 Case Studies in Organized Peaceful Settlement: Category II

THE two cases that follow are among the most important ever to come before the League or United Nations. They are cases in which, contrary to the previous examples, organized force was used and persisted in, and in which nonetheless the parties did not commit acts which were punished by collective security sanctions.

CASE V: THE MANCHURIAN AFFAIR

(1) Background

In 1905, as a result of the Russo-Japanese War, Japan became heir to the special position that Russia had held in Manchuria. One token of this position was Japanese control over the South Manchurian Railway. By treaty with China, Japan had a right to garrison the railway and ensure its security. It was out of this situation that the immediate dispute occurred. Its roots go much further back: for years China had been in the turmoil of civil war. By 1930–1931 the Kuomintang government appeared to be strengthening its hold over North China; in 1928 the Kuomintang had occupied Peking, the traditional capital of China. Manchuria might easily be the next item on China's agenda of national regeneration. Semi-autonomous, it was a rich prize, and Japan feared the growing strength of China might entail its loss. Shortly before the incident to be related, a militarist government had come to power in Japan. All these factors, and more, created tension.

(2) The Dispute

On the night of September 18, 1931, an explosion occurred—at least according to the Japanese. It seems to be fairly well established that some individuals did set off some explosion in the vicinity of the railway a few miles north of Mukden. The Japanese claimed that it was the work of Chinese troops attempting to destroy the railroad, and that a Japanese patrol was fired upon when they rushed up. The Japanese in retaliation occupied Mukden, overwhelming the 10,000-man Chinese garrison. Operations continued, and within four days Japanese control had been pushed to a 200-mile radius north of Mukden. By November all northern Manchuria was in Japanese hands.

According to the Chinese version, they had not provoked an incident. They pointed out that the southbound train from Changchun had passed over the presumably wrecked tracks at the scene of the explosion and arrived safely at Mukden. They also pointed out that the Chinese garrison in Mukden was not alert and ready for fighting, which it would have been under the circumstances the Japanese claimed.

(3) The Outcome

The detailed claims and counterclaims were not all immediately known. The Chinese on September 21 protested to the Council. The Council asked the Japanese to give assurances that they had no territorial designs on Manchuria per se and that Japan would withdraw her troops to the railway zone as soon as possible. On September 30, with the Japanese delegate agreeing, the Council, having been reassured on this point by Japan, adopted a resolution asking both parties to restore normal relations and keep the Council informed.

The Japanese resorted to stalling tactics while continuing military operations. On November 21 Japan proposed that a commission of inquiry be sent by the League to the scene. This was done. The commission did not reach Japan until the end of February 1932, and did not submit its report until September of that year. In the meantime all Manchuria was occupied and a puppet state of Manchukuo created.

In January 1932, Japan attacked Shanghai, allegedly as reprisal for the killing of five Japanese monks by Chinese rioters, and to protect Japanese nationals and property there. The Assembly (to whom the dispute had now gone) urged the cessation of hostilities early in March, and after two months of further negotiations the Japanese and Chinese signed an armistice and the Japanese withdrew from Shanghai. The Assembly unanimously agreed (China and Japan abstaining) that they would not recognize any territorial changes brought about by force, and sat back to await the commission's report. The report urged China and Japan to settle their differences through negotiation and to this the League agreed. In the sequel, the League went no further than urging "non-recognition;" another clash early in 1933 came to an end in May with the Truce of Tangku. The Chinese agreed to demilitarize five thousand square miles on the Chinese side of the Great Wall. Japan withdrew from the League.

(4) Significance

Until 1931 Japan was considered a highly reliable League member. It was difficult for the League to believe at first that Japan intended large-scale aggression. Moreover, the case was complicated by many factors that made its handling far from simple. It was difficult for a long time to be sure that clear aggression was being committed. To quote from the report of the commission of inquiry—the *Lytton Commission*, as it was known:

> This is not a case in which one country has declared war on another country without previously exhausting the opportunities for conciliation provided in the Covenant of the League of Nations. Neither is it a simple case of the violation of the frontier of one country by the armed forces of a neighbouring country, because in Manchuria there are many features without an exact parallel in other parts of the world.

The *Report* then continued:

The dispute has arisen between two States, both Members of the League, concerning a territory the size of France and Germany combined, in which both claim to have rights and interests, only some of which are clearly defined by international law; a territory which, although legally an integral part of China, had a sufficiently autonomous character to carry on direct negotiations with Japan on the matters which lay at the root of this conflict.

Japan controls a railway and a strip of territory running from the sea right up into the heart of Manchuria, and she maintains for the protection of that property a force of about 10,000 soldiers, which she claims the right by treaty to increase, if necessary, up to 15,000. She also exercises the rights of jurisdiction over all her subjects in Manchuria and maintains consular police throughout the country.[6]

After examining these special factors, the *Report* noted that "a large area of what was indisputably the Chinese territory has been forcibly seized and . . . separated from and declared independent of the rest of China." [7] This was not done until February 1932, so that it had not occurred at the time of the early consideration of the dispute by the League. The *Report* went on to say that Japan had consistently claimed she was acting under her treaty rights, that in Japan's opinion "all the military operations have been legitimate acts of self-defense," [8] and that the proclaimed independence of Manchukuo was "a spontaneous assertion" of their wishes by "the local population." [9]

The commission also reported that:

An explosion undoubtedly occurred . . . but the damage . . . was not in itself sufficient to justify military action. The military actions of the Japanese troops during this night . . . cannot be regarded as measures of legitimate self-defence. In saying this, the Commission does not exclude the hypothesis that the officers on the spot may have thought they were acting in self-defence.[10]

After all, Japan had not overtly defied the League; on the contrary, she had made promises of compliance as soon as conditions permitted; she had herself proposed the sending of the commission of inquiry.

The circumstances in the case were complex; the way in which the dispute developed made for added difficulty. First, in a broad sense Japan had a right to act as she did *at first*, provided she was sincere in her claims—which at first was at least not unlikely. By treaty she had the right to use her forces in Manchuria (where Chinese central government control was very weak) to protect Japanese lives and property—even beyond the confines of the railway zone. A League cease-fire order, which had worked so well in the Greco-Bulgarian dispute of 1925, presupposed an established frontier to which to return and beyond which there was no good excuse for being. Japan, however, had rights in a sense all over Manchuria. Second, when what she did at first

---

[6] The [*Lytton*] *Commission of Inquiry*, League of Nations, Political Publications, 1932, VII, 12, pp. 126–127.

[7] *Ibid.*, p. 127.

[8] *Ibid.*

[9] *Ibid.*

[10] *Ibid.*, p. 71.

"legitimately" became something else again was difficult to establish. When does a reprisal in self-defense become a conqueror's march? The answer to such a question depends upon subjective values rather than objective standards. Each member of the League had of necessity to draw his own conclusions. Third, nations at times do lose sight of their limited purpose in the excitement of pursuing an adventure; nations engaged in punitive expeditions have been known to go farther than they should before coming to their senses. Fourth, the location of the dispute halfway around the world, and the difficulty of establishing from a distance what was going on, played its part too. Communications in 1931–1932 were far less developed.

Looking back over two decades and more when "the story of Axis aggression" has attained the familiarity of a fairy story (together with a few of such a tale's exaggerations), it is easy to indict the League and overlook these points. It is true that the United States and Russia, non-members of the League, were unprepared to aid with serious sanctions, and that neither England nor France desired a costly involvement in the Far East. Even so, the initial reaction of the League seems to have stemmed from the factors enumerated above; later on, when Japan continued to swallow territory, the points just made played a major role. But by this time the League was in a compromised position. Having allowed Japan to get away with so much already, it was tempting to note the lesson involved and act more wisely next time. If a major power, a member of the League and willing to act, had felt menaced by Japan's actions, the inertia might have been overcome soon enough.

The Manchurian Affair demonstrates that, where the intent to commit aggression is not definitely established soon, and where the circumstances in which the case develops are so complex that it is difficult immediately to designate one state as a wrong-doer, the reaction of the international organization is likely to be, as the Lytton *Report* urged, an attempt "to settle the dispute consistently with the honour, dignity, and national interest of both the contending parties. Criticism alone will not accomplish this: there must also be practical efforts at conciliation." [11]

CASE VI: THE PALESTINE WAR

(1) *Background*

After World War I the disintegrated Turkish Empire was reformed into a series of territories. Among these was the Palestine Mandate, given to Great Britain. Within this mandate, the British fostered, as they had promised in the Balfour Declaration, "a national home for the Jewish people, . . . it being clearly understood that nothing shall be done which may prejudice the civil and religious rights of existing non-Jewish communities in Palestine." This was a clear expression of a very ambiguous intention, to which the British nevertheless attempted to adhere. When the mandate began, some eighty-

---

[11] *Ibid.*, p. 127.

four thousand Jews and approximately six hundred thousand Arabs inhabited the land; by the time of World War II, while the Arabs had increased to about a million, the Jewish population reached almost six hundred thousand. It was clear that events were heading toward a crisis.

(2) *The Dispute*

The dispute really began with the British decision in 1939 (as a result of Arab pressure) to limit Jewish immigration to seventy-five thousand annually for five years, and then to prohibit it entirely (unless the Arabs agreed otherwise). In the aftermath of World War II, as Jewish displaced persons sought to leave Europe, a crisis quickly developed. Illegal or not, the Jews came. The British rounded them up as best they could and sent them out again, but Britain's political and moral position was weak; the situation was obviously one that could not endure indefinitely. Caught between United States and Jewish pressure on the one hand, and Arab pressure on the other, Britain sought a way out by placing the issue before the United Nations in 1947.

(3) *The Outcome*

The UN Assembly met in special session in April 1947, and appointed a special Committee on Palestine. On November 29, 1947, having heard the report, the Assembly voted (33 to 13, with 10 abstentions) in favor of the partition of Palestine into Jewish and Arab states, with an international regime for Jerusalem. Both the United States and the Soviet Union voted affirmatively, Britain abstained, and the measure barely passed by the necessary two-thirds vote. The Jews were pleased, the Arabs angered. Fighting now broke out in Palestine. By May 15, 1948, the British had withdrawn; the Republic of Israel had begun its official existence, and the United States had given it *de facto* recognition.

In April, shortly before, the United Nations had created the office of UN Mediator for Palestine. Count Bernadotte of Sweden, as mediator, attempted to bring the parties together. In April and May the war continued, with the Egyptian army invading Palestine from the south. A cease-fire order on May 29 from the Security Council brought a truce of four weeks. Fighting then began again; the Israelis now began not only to hold the front against the Arab forces but to push them back. On July 15 another cease-fire order from the Security Council, hinting at possible sanctions, brought a truce until October. Despite further United Nations efforts in November, fighting continued off and on until early 1949. At this time Israel and the Arabs ceased hostilities and began negotiations through the United Nations agency in Palestine that had become a Conciliation Commission in December 1948. With Dr. Ralph Bunche, who had succeeded to the office of mediator following Bernadotte's assassination on September 18, 1948, acting as go-between (since the Arabs refused direct conversations), four armistice agreements were signed, the last of them on July 20, 1949. Since then an uneasy peace has generally prevailed, but no peace treaties have been ratified by the belligerents.

Technically (and sometimes actually—as in late 1955, 1956, and 1966), the war continues. As a final result of the fighting, because of Jewish successes in battle, the territory of the State of Israel was greater and more cohesive than that envisaged in the Assembly's partition plan.

(4) Significance

When the United Nations Assembly recommended partition in November 1947, it requested the Security Council to consider "any attempt to alter by force the settlement envisaged by this resolution" [12] as an act calling for sanctions. By the time the Security Council met on February 24, 1948, to act upon the Assembly resolution, war in Palestine was an actual fact. The Security Council thereafter never went beyond a threat that a refusal to cease fire would necessitate the Council's considering the use of sanctions. Nor did the Assembly attempt more than mediation and conciliation. Teams were provided to assist the belligerents in keeping the truces, but there was no real idea of enforcing the partition. Britain continued military aid to the Arab states. The United States, having abandoned the idea (which she had previously supported) of enforced partition after war broke out, by March 1948 was proposing a temporary United Nations trusteeship for Palestine. These actions created crosscurrents that helped to destroy any serious possibility of enforcement action.

Yet the role to which the United Nations restricted itself is to be explained on more general grounds. If Palestine were to be divided into two states, what should be the frontiers? This was the root problem before the United Nations in 1947. The partition plan attempted to place the Jewish and Arab populations as much as possible within their own states.

But the resulting frontiers represented a political impossibility and a military monstrosity. Each state was to be divided into three pieces (six pieces in all), meeting at intersections (a sort of "four corners") in two different places. Each state would consequently have an exposed backbone, easily broken in two places. Although the Jewish side welcomed partition and the endorsement of their hoped-for Jewish state, it is difficult to visualize either Jew or Arab resting content with the arrangement even if fighting had not then broken out. The fact that the Assembly ever went so far as to endorse the idea of these frontiers and propose that they be enforced in the first place is surprising; their subsequent reluctance to attempt to enforce them is much more easily understandable.

The United Nations' specific proposal for division was inept although the idea of division per se was not. Obviously, two states was the only answer. But the acceptability of the frontiers of those states rested in a practical sense with the parties to the dispute. Only those states could in the end determine which particular frontiers they would consider "just." Since they were prepared to use force, of what use would it have been for an additional army or armies to have gone to Palestine, representing the United Nations, to shed further

---

[12] UN Document A/516.

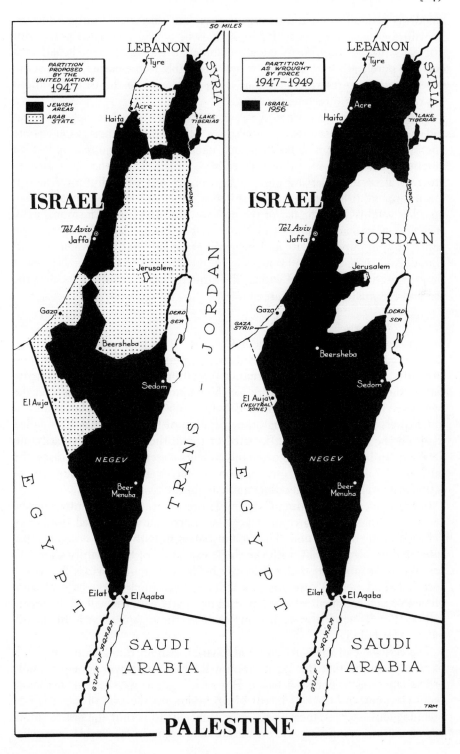

PARTITION
PROPOSED
BY THE
UNITED NATIONS
1947

JEWISH
AREAS
ARAB
STATE

LEBANON
Tyre
SYRIA
Acre
Haifa
LAKE
TIBERIAS

ISRAEL

Tel Aviv
Jaffa

Jerusalem

JORDAN

Gaza
DEAD
SEA

Beersheba

Sedom

El Auja

NEGEV

TRANS - JORDAN

Beer
Menuha

EGYPT

Eilat · El Aqaba

GULF OF AQABA

SAUDI
ARABIA

PARTITION
AS WROUGHT
BY FORCE
1947-1949

ISRAEL
1956

LEBANON
Tyre
SYRIA
Acre
Haifa
LAKE
TIBERIAS

ISRAEL

Tel Aviv
Jaffa

JORDAN

Jerusalem

Gaza
DEAD
SEA

GAZA
STRIP

Beersheba

Sedom

El Auja
(NEUTRAL
ZONE)

NEGEV

Beer
Menuha

EGYPT

Eilat · El Aqaba

GULF OF AQABA

SAUDI
ARABIA

TRM

50 MILES

PALESTINE

blood? Where an international organization can draw new frontiers and see its will done without a need for force, it is obviously a gain for peace. But where its intervention serves merely to broaden the conflict on behalf of a new and purely arbitrary line that is not acceptable to the parties, it is wiser to conciliate than to resort to sanctions. This conclusion of the United Nations was reflected in its subsequent actions.

In the Palestine Case, once the mandate terminated, there were no clear and established frontiers, advances across which constituted aggression against one of the parties. It is difficult in such circumstances to muster support for sanctions to enforce something which was in the first instance created in order to assist in preserving peace. The frontier was not a historical fact; it was a proposal to be brought into existence. Since the frontiers involved had no other validity than the fiat of the organization, and had no historical existence or common acceptance by all the parties but were merely lines drawn on paper, it was impossible to find general agreement that aggression had occurred. And since the circumstances were so complex and the issue far from a simple question of right and wrong, the United Nations chose to localize the war and eventually bring it to an end.

The cases examined earlier under Category I are examples of an international organization performing its role of peaceful settlement smoothly and efficiently. To the student of international relations they show how the organization should work and does work for the majority of disputes. Again, in the two cases where sanctions were used before 1966 (which will be examined in Chapters 20 and 21), although the operation of the device may have failed to attain the ideal standard anticipated of them, they are similarly easily understood. In both Category I cases and collective security sanctions cases, the purpose and actions of the organization are relatively clear. But the type of action least well understood occurs normally in Category II cases.

In the two cases illustrating Category II there was no obvious intent of one or more of the parties to commit aggression across a well-defined frontier in defiance of the organization. The circumstances in both cases were so complicated and ambiguous that, with the single exception of the Security Council's one threat of sanctions if the Palestine belligerents did not cease fire at the specified time, neither case was ever reduced to a simple, clear basis of compliance or non-compliance on the part of one party with the will of the organization. For its actions in such complex cases the organization is frequently indicted for failure.

The very logic of the Covenant and Charter, examined in Chapter 10, leads to an expectation that the organization will either see its will done peacefully or use sanctions to punish defiance. But such logic, as we saw earlier, presupposes clear-cut and obvious intent of aggression on the part of a party, and unambiguous circumstances in the case sufficient to permit the greater number of nations composing the organization to come to agreement over what has actually occurred and what must consequently be done. Even where this clarity and agreement are present, the national interests of the member states may still incline them to refrain from decisive actions; where clarity is lacking, enforcement action cannot be expected. In such cases the organization typically attempts to limit the number of belligerents involved, keep hostilities within bounds, bring the fighting to an early conclusion, and conciliate the dispute at the first opportunity. To expect an international organization, composed of sovereign states, to do more than the members consider desirable and necessary under the circumstances confronting them, is to expect too much. Where the intent and circumstances of the case are muddled and there is no clear consensus based on the national interests of the members of the international organization, the resort to limitation of the war and conciliation of it at the earliest opportunity is to be expected. When India in December 1961, took Goa from Portugal (who had held it since 1504) many Afro-Asian nations, despite the fact of an established frontier, considered that Portugal's right to a piece of "India" was colonial and therefore ambiguous in the first place! Since the use of force was also short, India virtually escaped censure. But confidence in the UN's impartiality was undermined.

4 Conclusions

IN international relations, disputes between states are normal occurrences. In order to see such disputes in perspective one must keep in mind that the number of disputes that sovereign states could potentially have with one another are infinite; their actual disputes are, by comparison, few. In these relatively few cases the conflict of interests may, for an even smaller number, be of such a vital nature that they cannot be settled short of force. Formulas for compromise are then of no use, and resort to legal settlement is ruled out by the nature of the interests involved.

To meet the normal needs of states for devices with which to settle their disputes short of force, the variety of techniques examined in this chapter and the last have been evolved. Where there is truly a will to settle short of force, one or more of these devices can be expected to work. The greatest weakness in the arsenal of techniques until the advent of the League was the lack of an institutional procedure designed to ensure that every dispute would have some opportunity to be settled peacefully. The existence of this conciliatory technique, which is at the heart of the League and United Nations non-sanctions procedure, could not in and of itself peacefully settle disputes in which a party or parties were willing to use force in obvious aggression across a well-defined frontier, despite the organization. To such cases, sanctions were and are the only answer the organization can make, if it remains true to its professed aims. Nor could the technique of conciliation in and of itself ensure that in ambiguous cases, such as Category II, the use of force could be averted. Here the potential availability of sanctions also means little since it is extremely unlikely that they will be used.

One must conclude that for the greatest number of disputes the problem is to find the proper technique and a suitable basis for peaceful adjustment. In the relatively fewer number of cases where organized force is resorted to on the part of a party, unless the action is a clear and unambiguous case of deliberate aggression, the problem is to localize hostilities and bring them to an end as soon as possible. From this point of view the outcome of the Greco-Bulgarian dispute, hailed as a great success of the League, does not differ fundamentally from the outcome of the Palestine War, considered by many a failure of the United Nations. There was only a difference (although an important difference in terms of bloodshed) in the time it took to end the conflict. Neither war was fought to a conclusion because of the role that the international organization played.

Finally, the institutionalization of a third-party presence in every dispute which automatically came about in principle with the League, and the further sophistication in the UN of preliminary measures designed to end hostilities with a view to allowing these techniques to function, is a definite gain. The UNEF, built upon the earlier experience with truce observers in Palestine, represented a novel and important step forward. Through such non-fighting forces, *properly used*, much progress is possible. In the Congo Case, which we can assess more usefully within its African context, this question of valid use became highly important.

PART FIVE

The Problem of Power and the Power Patterns

CHAPTER 13

Security

SECURITY. The quality or condition of being secure. Freedom from exposure to danger; protection; safety or a
place of safety. Feeling of or assurance of safety or
certainty; freedom from anxiety or doubt. That which
secures a means of protection, defense, etc.

Webster's Collegiate Dictionary

UP to this point, the theoretical propositions which lie behind our approach to international relations have not been stressed. Definitions
have been given and relationships described to permit an orderly examination of the fundamentals of the state system, the roles of national
power and foreign policy, the functional relations of states which arise from
interacting foreign policies, and the settlement of disputes occurring as a result of those relations. We have surveyed all of this from a national interests
point of view. It is now time (before proceeding to the core of these relations
as they center on problems of power, security, and the organization of a
power system) to look more explicitly at why we have taken a national interests approach. How does such an approach offer advantages in overcoming
difficulties implicit in earlier approaches? Why were such earlier approaches
taken to the subject? We must also see what difficulties arise from the national interests concept itself.

I Security and the Power Problem

THE first half of the twentieth century was an age of great international tension and violence. The twenty years of general peace between 1919 and 1939
was a lull between major storms, marked by symptoms of recurrent crisis.
Yet, surprisingly enough, it was at first a time of hope and only later a time
of fear and tension. It was a time at first of Wilsonian Utopianism and the
"spirit of Locarno," and only later of the cruel neorealism of the gas chamber
utilized for reasons of state. In such a period it happened that the study of
international relations as an organized discipline first became widespread.
With it came generalizations—also at first those of hope; later those of despair. In a coherent world (or at least one that it is hoped will prove coherent)
generalizations tend toward optimism; in a world torn by conflict and fear
and the expectation of more, they tend toward pessimism. Thus the study
of international relations began in the 1920's with generalizations of hope,

of the brotherhood of man, the rule of law, the community of nations, the banishment of the evils of imperialism, and the abolition of war itself. It continued, as pessimism set in with the 1930's, with emphasis on power, the role of force, the egotism of nations, the recurrence of violence, and the conflicts and disputes of states.

The idea that the end goal of nations is peace was rudely shattered in the 1930's as it became ever more apparent that war was approaching. World War II lacked in its coming the element of blind fate, rushing the great nations of the world involuntarily toward the abyss, which characterized the final crisis in 1914 that began World War I. World War II came with terrifying deliberateness. The signals were the strident invective of Hitler, the posing and chest-thumping of Mussolini, and the ruthless militarism of Japan. The nations that wanted peace and the men of good will who guided their policies were confronted with an unmistakable lust for dominance by the Axis realms. And when it came to the final choice, the men of good will, too, chose war in self-defense, in preference to peace. Clearly the nations who had done most to launch the war, as well as those who had striven hardest to avert it, agreed that there were things more sacred, more desirable than peace per se.

The idea that nations above all sought peace was replaced by the idea that nations above all sought power. In this new view, the difference between the democracies and the dictatorships sprang from their respective power positions and their method of approach to problems, rather than from any basic difference in goals. All nations, it was asserted, sought power. The democracies were attempting to preserve their hegemonic power positions against those who would replace them, but since their philosophy of life excluded their frank recognition and admission of their equally zestful participation in the struggle for power, they instead formulated (and disguised) their aims in moral phrases. Underneath, it was now held, the struggle for power continued.

This formulation had grave defects. The assertion that nations were engaged in an ever-continuing attempt to accumulate power might well illuminate many aspects of the relations of nations by focusing attention upon a problem common to all—survival in an uncertain world. As a guide to the foreign policy of the Maldive Islands or Switzerland, it was of little value. To say that the Swiss were engaged in a struggle for power would certainly be a distorted rendition of their problems and aims. In the nature of things, Swiss power is clearly limited, and a struggle for power more or less impossible. Their choice of a policy of neutrality is clearly indicative of the fact that they place their reliance upon the hope of remaining above the power struggle. Where the Soviet Union or the United States clearly, in the Cold War, were engaged in a power struggle, and their policies and actions could be understood to a large extent within the confines of such a concept, the idea was of much less value when applied to a postwar France engaged in a desperate effort to re-establish national unity and find security. Applied to India's policy since her independence, or to the foreign policy of Britain in the postwar period, the idea was also of limited use. Applied to the way in which nations settle many of their disputes on a basis of mutual convenience and accommodation, often almost completely divorced from power-accumulation considerations, the idea is also of little value. All these criticisms apply if the idea of nations "struggling" for power in an overt, aggressive sense is to be taken literally. If, on the other hand, it is assumed that the term conveys merely the idea that while one nation actively strives to increase its power by aggressive conquest, another may be content merely to muster the power deemed necessary for normal defense purposes, while a third reduces its power by surrendering possessions or cutting back its armaments, then the term "struggle" is, at the very least, misleading.

From a long-range viewpoint both sets of generalizations portrayed only two sides of a single coin, each to some extent rejecting the validity of the other. One, to oversimplify, portrayed nations on their "good" behavior, desiring "good" goals; the other, on their "bad" behavior, desiring "bad" goals. If it were necessary to reduce each set of generalizations to a single word, the good behavior word would be *peace*, and the bad behavior word, *power*. As goals of national activity, each purported to describe what states sought in international relations. Both were and are correct descriptions of at least some of the aims of many states in many instances. Where they failed was in their overly inclusive description of national goals and state behavior as relatively uniform for all or most states at all or most times. Some behavior is uniform (i.e., all states have a concept of what they consider vital, each participates in world affairs to defend or advance its policies). But some behavior is highly individual (i.e., while all states pursue foreign policies, some states have very minimum goals and policies in comparison with others). What is needed in view of both the uniformity and the diversity is a set of generalizations which permits distinctions on exactly those grounds. It must take into account the behavior of a very large number of very diverse states in periods characterized by varying levels of world tension. It must be operationally valid so that it classifies behavior as it actually is. Consequently the generalizations must describe both the uniformities and diversities of state behavior.

It is here that the national interests view offers great advantages. We can classify vital as against secondary interests for any single state, according to that state's own determination. We can compare interests between states as common and opposed. We can introduce counterbalancing interest considerations in determining individual or joint behavior. Consequently, we are equipped with a method which simultaneously embraces the desire for peace and the will to power within the perspective of a still wider whole. Yet it also allows fairly precise descriptions of the parts. We are able to describe what is true of all states (such as interests to protect or advance) while remaining free to distinguish the varying nature of content of those interests from state to state and time to time. More accurate categorization of behavior is possible.

The real virtue of the emphasis on power that began in the 1930's was to focus attention on the problem power creates by its very existence in the hands of sovereign states. In the very broadest sense all nations are involved in a power problem which they cannot escape by an act of will. Regardless of which of the infinite variety of policies they elect to follow in international relations, and even if they follow the most peaceable policy conceivable, each must live in an atmosphere and in a set of circumstances where its involvement in armed struggle cannot be ruled out of the realm of possibility. The ability to decide to make war is an attribute of sovereignty. It applies not only to one's own nation but to all the rest as well. States may vary infinitely from extremely aggressive to completely unaggressive, they may vary from very great in power to very small, but in one respect they are equal: each must fear that it may be attacked or involved in war. The most powerful state is no more immune from this concern, this problem, than the most humble. Every state must at all times reckon with this power problem, even though the intensity of its concern and the precise content or focus of its problem, will vary.

From all that has been said, two things stand out as of primary importance. The first is that nations, in their time, play many parts. There is a vast range of possible policies they may elect to follow, a vast range of possible interests they can seek to preserve or achieve. The will to peace and the desire for power are pieces in this jig saw of possibilities, and how these pieces, with others, will ultimately be combined to form a pattern of foreign policy will depend upon many things. Each nation will approach the world as it thinks best, and its approach will in turn be revealed by its conception of its national interests. Second, regardless of the pattern of policy evolved, regardless of the national-interests concept with which a state approaches international relations, it must come to terms with the problem of power—how to deal with the power of other states which may be used against it.

2 Implications of the National-Interests Concept

BOTH these points need further consideration. In this section the implications of the national-interests concept will be further explored, and in the next, the security problem that the threat of power raises. Then in the following chapters we shall examine the "solutions" to the power problem, both as idea and practice.

The idea that nations attempt to preserve and achieve national interests, rather than strive for peace or engage in a struggle for power per se, advances us beyond the rigidities and difficulties of the earlier views. At the same time the concept of national interests is not itself without difficulties.

The foreign policy of a nation represents its judgment of its national interests. A foreign policy is a systematic statement of deliberately selected national interests. The fact that such interests are selected does not imply universal popular agreement within the nation as to the desirability and wisdom of the selection. In the earlier discussion on foreign policy the point was made that, although there is popular agreement in a nation as to most of its vital interests, there is frequently very much disagreement over how to implement those interests and over what secondary interests to achieve or implement. Although such disagreements are aired more publicly in some states than in others, in every state the subject matter of foreign policy is a question for controversy. Behind the Iron Curtain as in front of it, these matters are the focus of bitter and prolonged debate. It is merely easier to observe the debate in a nation like the United States. One hears arguments and counterarguments over whether the United States would be engaging in "appeasement" if it should recognize Communist China or increase trade with Communist nations. One also hears statements that America's action in making peace in Korea in 1953 was a wise (or alternately, a disastrous) thing to do. These disagreements often continue long after the die is cast and one of two alternative interests chosen and achieved or implemented. If a nation were to wait upon the resolution of all such disagreements before implementing a policy, no policies would ever be implemented.

Thus a further distinction is necessary. One must distinguish between the interests chosen for implementation, and the variety of alternatives possible for each such interest. When it is said that nations in international relations attempt to adjust their national interests to each other, what is meant is that they do so on a basis of the interests they have selected for implementation. The choice may be wise or unwise for any particular state at any particular time. The choice may lead it to great successes or to the brink of catastrophe —as Hitler led Germany, Mussolini led Italy, and Sukarno, Indonesia.

This choice inevitably represents a subjective judgment, made not as the result of a dispassionate study of all the relevant facts (which are hardly ever known in any case at the time), but as the consequence of attempted reasoned analysis blended with and distorted by national bias, strong emotion, internal political pressures and a sometimes highly partial evaluation of the interests and goals of other states. For all practical purposes *the foreign policy of any state can be considered as a subjective formulation approximating to a greater or lesser extent its objective national interest.*[1] It is the nation's own estimate—true or false—of what it is best for it to do, as put into effect by the government and permitted to remain in effect by the people.

How closely the subjective interest approximates in any given case the objective interest is sometimes obvious to the trained observer of international affairs. Where emotion, bias, and pressure have throttled the reasonable conclusions that can be drawn from the available evidence, it may be clear that the nation is committing folly. Even so, in a world where the future is always obscure and the ramifications of events frequently unforeseen, it is only with great circumspection and in relatively rare instances that one can predict with certainty that the particular subjective concept of the national

---

[1] "Objective" as used here means detached, impersonal, unprejudiced. The term is not used in its philosophical sense of existing independent of mind. The distinction is introduced purely for the purpose of facilitating comparison of the content of a foreign policy being implemented, with the wisdom or desirability of that policy.

interest being implemented by a people is unwise. In most instances one can deal only with likelihoods by judging probabilities. As a result, the objective national interest can in many cases be established only by port-mortem evaluation many years later.

These difficulties neither invalidate the concept of national interests nor make its application in analysis impossible. They merely make it harder. For general international-relations purposes (as contrasted to the study of a particular nation per se, with all the forces, pressures, and circumstances acting upon it and the mutually interacting effects of domestic and foreign problems and policies), it is sufficient in the first instance to understand the particular subjective concept of the national interest actually being implemented through its foreign policy. Next, one must note changes in this concept as they occur, so that one does not fall into the error of believing the concept and policy to be what it once was rather than what it now is. From a practical standpoint, whether those policies are objective formulations of the national interest or not, they are the policies being followed; as such they will determine the character of the international relations.

Since nations formulate policy subjectively, they may conceive a very broad or very narrow policy (or anywhere in between), depending on whether the nation keeps its commitments and actions within the very smallest range of possibilities or not. Because the policy is subjective does not necessarily mean that it must be narrow. While a nation attempts through policy to safeguard and achieve its interests, it may well consider that those interests cannot be achieved short of mutual cooperation on a generous basis with other states. In other words, the fact that a state acts out of what it conceives its interests to be does not mean that it will necessarily act selfishly, concerned only with the immediate realization of its own desires. In order to realize its interests it may even be led to go to war on behalf of another state or states. Alliances, after all, rest upon the belief of the parties that they must be willing to defend one another if they would be secure themselves.

Extremely narrow or broad interpretations of the national interest are likely to mean that the policy being followed by a state is far from its true and objective interests. An extremely broad interpretation and policy may dissipate national resources and power by involving the nation in struggles of little or remote importance, or in tasks far beyond the national strength, to the ultimate detriment of national security. Too narrow a policy may allow the natural allies of a nation to be destroyed piecemeal, leaving the first nation at last alone to fight overwhelming odds. It is usually best for a nation to avoid either extreme, but that it will do so can never be assumed as certain. Hitler's decision to invade Russia was based on too extreme a policy—it was too broad for Germany's power to support. On the other hand, a sufficiently broad (but not extreme) concept of national interests led Britain to go to war in 1914 over the invasion of Belgium, even though she was not herself attacked and had no iron-clad treaty obligation to do so. A realistically broad interpretation of national interests similarly led the United States in 1950 to fight the Korean War, although not herself attacked. At the other extreme, a very narrow policy may be followed. In 1938 Britain, in allowing the destruction of Czechoslovakia, failed to see that her own security would be jeopardized by the result. Similarly, in the late 1930's, the United States did not act effectively to discourage Japan from adventures in China—an experience that encouraged the growth of Japanese ambitions and helped to bring on World War II.

From all that has been said in this section it follows that, acting from the same initial point of departure, i.e., the national interest, states may embark upon the most diverse foreign policies imaginable. Although nations often follow substantially identical foreign policies vis-à-vis given problems over long periods of time, especially where the problem and its surrounding circumstances remain basically constant, there is little that is more striking among the phenomena of international relations than the enormous diversity of policies implemented by states over a long period. A France feared for its aggressive policies in time becomes a France fearful of the aggressions of others and still later a France intent on leading an independent Europe. A United States devoted to eschewing "entangling" alliances concludes a network of treaties across a great area of the globe. An England busy with the accumulation of empire embarks as vigorously upon its dismantling and reconstitution.

All these many policies are followed because they seem advantageous at the time to the state in question. Its policy may be extremely broad or narrow. Its form and content may develop out of an extremely accurate or distorted perception of the policies of other states. It also may be conceived in what the world regards as offensive or defensive terms. Yet whatever the ultimate judgment of the "community of nations" and its eventual effects, the immediate action is always at the discretion of the individual sovereign state. Were it otherwise, the state would not be sovereign, for sovereignty, while it does not mean freedom from the ultimate consequences of actions, does mean the initial ability to order national power into action—foolishly or wisely.

The existence of many sovereign entities, each of which is the immediate judge of its own actions and desires, means inevitably that disputes will arise between them. As we saw in the preceding chapters, these are most readily adjustable when they involve disagreements over secondary national interests on the part of both parties. When they center on a persistent clash of vital interests, the dispute may easily ripen into war; vital interests are those that nations normally consider it worthwhile to fight for. There is no guarantee that any state will revise its concept of its vital interests where these interests prove incompatible with those of other states, let alone formulate a modest view of its own interests in the first place. No technique for the peaceful settlement of disputes is proof against this contingency. When opposition is encountered, the state must decide whether and how to press forward. Should it offer some equivalent concession as a means of gaining the interests, or achieve them through the use of its own power, or modify or withdraw them entirely?

Beyond a certain basic initial agreement on what constitutes vital national interests, states vary greatly in their views as to what is worth fighting for. There is general willingness on the part of states to fight to preserve their existing territorial integrity and political independence, as well as their prestige (or "honor"), if massively involved. Beyond that, generalizations cannot be made.

Since the term *security*, as used by states, means the preservation of whatever they conceive their vital interests to be, the term has a defensive connotation only in the sense that each nation is prepared to defend those interests against interference by the use of force. Tito in 1953, in the name of Yugoslav security, was willing to fight Italy if necessary to prevent her occupying Zone A of the Trieste Free Territory. If this armed conflict had actually happened, Italy would have fought back in the name of Italian security. Depending upon the nature of the security concept, a state's actions may appear to the world at large either defensive or offensive. But to the state involved the actions are *ipso facto* defensive—i.e., defensive of the vital interests involved. Thus the assurance of one state to another that it will only act "defensively," and only to safeguard "national security," is reassuring to the other state only to the extent that other factors in the situation make the likelihood of attack remote.

From a fundamental point of view, the security problem of one state arises out of what it seeks in international relations, plus what other states seek. Since there is no way to insure against the possibility that other states may seek interests incompatible with one's own vital interests, the security of one state is potentially jeopardized by the very existence of others.

3 *The Threat of Power: Two Responses*

WHILE what has just been said is perfectly true from a fundamental and theoretical standpoint, in practice the security problem of any given state is made less difficult by two factors: *capability* and *intention*.

Capability, the first of these factors, refers to physical ability to wage warfare on a significant scale. Any sovereign entity, except perhaps the tiniest, possesses capability versus some others. Paraguay, while too small in capability to be a threat to the powerful and remote United States, is not too small to be one to its neighbors, even though they are larger in territory and power. It is not necessary for one state to be equal in power to another to do it significant harm—and this is the criterion. Italy, in 1940, although unequal in power to France, ensured French surrender to the Axis by attacking in the rear at a time when France was desperately engaged in the north. On the basis of this criterion, a combination of states, each relatively harmless in itself, might pose a serious power threat, mitigated only by the loss in efficiency that is inevitably a part of coalition warfare. Where coalitions exist or could be formed on relatively short notice, they pose a potential threat for this reason.

Merely on the basis of capability, the list of states (from the standpoint of any particular nation) whose power needs to be reckoned with is small compared to the number of sovereign entities in the world. For almost any state the gravest threats arise from its own immediate neighbors, especially those with whom it shares a land frontier. Switzerland, landlocked as it is, has under normal circumstances a problem limited basically to France, Germany, Italy, and Austria. Where the borders of a nation give it access to the sea, that nation must also fear those whose power enables them to cross the seas. Italy, in addition to fearing attack from Yugoslavia, must reckon with France, Switzerland, and Austria across land frontiers, and with the great powers possessing sea power as well, because its coasts are long and exposed.

In an age of air power and of mass-destruction weapons deliverable at long range and by remote control, it might be argued that every state must fear any other that possesses such formidable striking power. Switzerland needs to fear the American and Russian hydrogen missiles, for instance. To a certain extent this danger exists, for a nation must fear any state that can attack it in significant fashion—and atomic and hydrogen missiles are anything but insignificant. If a World War III were to break out in Europe, Russia might use missiles against Switzerland to destroy valuable communication and travel facilities through the Alps between Germany and Italy, in order to hamper NATO's strategy. This action might occur despite rigid Swiss neutrality. However, even in an age of missile power, this kind of possibility needs to be feared most under circumstances where war has brought about the transformation of an immediate neighbor's territory into a battleground. A nation in this unlucky position is always in grave danger, for in the sweep of the fighting it too may be converted into a battleground. It is only under these circumstances that attack from the air needs to be greatly feared by a state such as Switzerland or Burma or Afghanistan.

It need hardly be added that every great power must fear every other. Unless the title "great power" is bestowed upon a state through courtesy (as in the case of Nationalist China during World War II), or upon a state once powerful but now no longer a real threat by itself (such as Italy), or upon a state temporarily weak (such as the Japan of 1953), the very designation means that the state is able to exert greatly significant power relative to other states. By this criterion it was not necessary for pre-1941 Japan to be capable of defeating the United States in order to be feared as a great power—it was only necessary that it be able to inflict significant harm upon America. In this respect, speaking for the moment solely in power-capability terms, Britain, France, the United States, China, and Russia must each fear the others.

Intention, the second factor, refers to the likelihood of attack on a significant scale. From among those states who possess the necessary capability to attack, there are many that are not likely under any foreseeable circumstances to do so. Although Canada possesses capability vis-à-vis the United States, the likelihood of Canadian attack upon the United States is so small as to be virtually non-existent. The reverse is also true. In a war between the two states, Canada could in the end no doubt be conquered by the United States. Yet their long frontier devoid of fortifications is not the result of Canadian despair over effectively defending herself—it is rather a symbol of a mutual conviction that the need will not arise.

Such a conviction may arise out of historical experience or present circumstance. Where two states are at the same time allies against a third, unless one fears defection on the part of the other, the likelihood of one ally attacking the other is so small that it can almost always be ruled out of the picture. The United States, Britain, and France have not, as alliance partners in NATO, capability notwithstanding, feared one another. France's withdrawal from the integrated arrangements of NATO has not changed this.

Among the other states possessing capability vis-à-vis one's own, where there is a certain likelihood of attack, the degree of tension in international relations that arises as a consequence will be in direct proportion to the degree of likelihood. Where the likelihood is considered very great (as it was in the United States in 1961–1962 in terms of a Russian thrust), tension will also be very great. Where it is considered small (as in the same set of relations in 1966), tension will also be less. The best that can be hoped for in terms of the relations of two potential enemies, where there is always some likelihood of attack, plus capability, is that tension will be kept within bounds, so that fear will not itself produce a war. Their mutual concern over still a third state, such as Communist China, will also be a factor.

There are two basic responses a state can make to the resulting power problem. One response every state *must* make by choosing how to fit itself *organizationally* into the power system. It must decide on which patterns of power it will utilize in an effort to resolve the power threat that confronts it— whether to refrain from alliances and embrace unilateralism, follow the balance of power by joining alliances, pursue collective security through a League or United Nations, attempt to form a world government, or set out on world conquest. It must adopt one or more of these "solutions" to meet the power threat. The other response to the power problem, which we shall consider in detail in the next chapter, is to seek to reduce tension between it and its potential enemies, and diminish the danger of surprise attack by accomplishing the mutual control of armaments.

How states handle these two basic responses will, taken as a whole, determine the tension level in the world at a given time. Handled well, the tension level will be decreased to the minimum level possible so long as a multistate system exists (i.e., the inescapable residual tension caused by the very existence of those states). Handled poorly, the tension level will rise to peril points where, psychologically, it can hardly be controlled at all and becomes extremely difficult to reverse. The escalation of tensions, moreover, is more natural to the system itself, since suspicion and fear are always residual. Consequently, it takes intelligent and sustained effort to move the tension level down and keep it down; its normal tendency, left to itself, is up. While this is a somber thought it nonetheless directs attention to the real dimensions of the problem.

CHAPTER 14

Disarmament
and Arms Control

And they shall beat their swords into plowshares,
And their spears into pruning hooks;
Nation shall not lift up sword against nation,
Neither shall they learn war any more.

ISAIAH

EVEN if disarmament could conceivably be made total, it would not eliminate the power problem so long as separate sovereign states continue to exist. Potential national power, resting on the fundamentals of an organized pool of manpower and basic economic resources, could again be transformed into eventual actual military power at the whim of individual nations. It would take time before an attack could be launched, but launched eventually it could be.

These remarks point up the role that disarmament fills in the relations of states. That role is twofold. First, the reduction of armaments, either generally or with reference to specific weapons, can curtail the ability of states to initiate sudden, sustained attacks. Second, this curtailment can diminish international tension and bring into being a more favorable atmosphere for the mutual adjustment of national interests.

It is on this practical problem of eliminating the possibility of a sustained surprise attack, rather than on a utopian hope of ending war entirely, that disarmament attempts or arms control agreements have been particularly focused. States have normally sought (1) a total weapons ratio that would discourage hopes of quick victories through lightning assaults or (2) a set of safeguards to warn them of a looming threat of attack.

Here we arrive at a seeming paradox, for even an arms control agreement that does not drastically reduce the general level of armaments may be successful—provided it lessens the likelihood of sudden, sustained armed attack. The goal of arms control is not necessarily to disarm as such; the goal is to mitigate the effects of whatever armaments do exist.

I Enforced Disarmament

ATTEMPTS at disarmament have historically occurred under two very different sets of conditions. Under one, disarmament has been imposed as a penalty following loss of a war; under the other, it has been sought by nations under mutually acceptable conditions. Disarmament achieved under the first condition may become later (at least tacitly) a problem for mutual negotiation. German disarmament, imposed after World War I, became a question for mutual negotiation with the opening of the World Disarmament Conference in 1932. The continuance of German disarmament following the opening of the conference would necessarily have been under conditions very different from those that led up to it. The breakdown of the attempt contributed in the sequel to Germany's casting off all restrictions, in direct defiance of the Treaty of Versailles.

With rather remarkable persistence in the last few decades, victors have imposed disarmament upon vanquished states. In previous centuries it was not so frequently utilized as a device to restrain the defeated. Sometimes the disarmament has been substantially complete, as with Japan and Germany after World War II; most often it has been qualified by provisions allowing the retention of comparatively small and innocuous forces. After Napoleon's humiliating defeat of Prussia in 1806, he permitted her an army of forty-two thousand men. By the terms of the Treaty of Versailles, Germany, defeated once again, was allowed a hundred thousand. The armies of her World War I allies were also limited (except for Turkey, which defied the Allies successfully). In the peace treaty with Italy after World War II, her forces were limited, as were the armies of Hitler's Balkan allies.

The failure of such provisions to have any permanent effects has likewise been remarkable. The Prussians, restricted in numbers, shortened their period of conscript service, and rushed great masses of men through and into the reserves. When the moment of revenge came after Napoleon's disastrous adventure in Russia in 1812, the Prussian Army, fully mobilized, far exceeded the treaty limits. At Versailles, with previous German use of this "escape clause" in mind, the Allies determined that German forces must not only be limited to the hundred thousand men, but that their term of service must be twelve years. Furthermore, certain weapons were to be prohibited to her entirely. Although not openly violating these terms until the 1930's, Germany early resorted to the establishment of arms factories and training grounds on Soviet Russian soil.[1] Also, the long enlistment period required by the Allies itself boomeranged. When restrictions were openly discarded by the Nazis, the nucleus for quick, large-scale enlargement of the army was readily available. The Wehrmacht of the 1920's has been called the "army of sergeants" for good reason. Confined to a small number of men, the Germans had chosen men capable of high non-commissioned rank to serve initially as privates in the limited force.

The trouble with enforced disarmament has always been that, to keep it effective, a constant supervision by the victors and a willingness to act in con-

---

[1] See E. H. Carr, *German-Soviet Relations Between the Two World Wars, 1919–1939*, Baltimore: John Hopkins Press, 1951, and Hans W. Gatzke, *Stresemann and the Rearmament of Germany*, Johns Hopkins Press, 1954.

cert to suppress violations are necessary. Unless the victors remain in occupation and enforce their will by armed coercion on the soil of the defeated, this may mean a reoccupation. To remain indefinitely in occupation and yet permit a national army owing allegiance to the occupied state is a contradiction in terms. Yet once the defeated state has been evacuated, it becomes extremely difficult to be sure that the limitations are being observed. With weapons difficult to conceal, such as tanks (where none are permitted) and ships (which are easy to count), the problem is simplest. Also where, as with Germany after World War I, all aviation, civil and military, was prohibited, violation is relatively obvious. But with machine guns, small arms, and the number of men under arms, where some of each are allowed, and each permitted weapon or soldier looks very much like one not allowed, as well as vice versa, the problem becomes extremely serious. Yet to reoccupy, if resistance is encountered, means a new war. The very secrecy in which violations of the limitations are customarily carried out means that it is hard to be sure that actual violations have occurred and therefore reoccupation justified. At the same time it may mean, if large-scale violations have occurred, that the resistance to reoccupation will be formidable.

Seldom do the allies have to decide this dilemma in concert, since rarely does their wartime solidarity persist into the postwar period. The rearmament and increase in power of the defeated usually goes on simultaneously with the falling out of the allies with one another. This usually takes very little time.

After each of the last three general wars such dissensions among the victors have appeared very quickly. Even before Napoleon's return from Elba, and his attempt to retrieve power that ended with Waterloo, Austria and Britain had entered into a secret treaty to resist Russo-Prussian demands at the peace settlement in Vienna by force if necessary.[2] Tsar Alexander's decision to make concessions averted a war, allowing the four powers to fight Napoleon once more. Yet by 1818 France had been readmitted into the councils of the powers on a basis of equality, and by 1820 Britain stood in fundamental opposition to the policies of her former continental allies. After World War I the disagreements between England and France never became as serious. Yet the French decision to occupy the German Ruhr in 1923 (over a question of reparations) was made in the face of intense British opposition. Russia, who had fought on the allied side in World War I until revolution at home destroyed her capability to fight Germany further, was subjected in 1918 to military expeditions by her former allies. That these maneuvers were designed to put down the Soviets so that Russia would resume the war does not alter the fact that, since the Soviets won, it marked the falling out of the wartime alliance partners. By 1926 Germany had regained substantial recognition as a great power on an increasingly equal footing with the former allies. Following World War II, the early rise of tension between the western allies and Russia led first to the re-establishment of Italy as a power, and then to the revival of German and Japanese armament. In all three cases the disagreements be-

---

[2] The treaty was signed January 3, 1815.

tween the victors either permitted or actually assisted in the resurrection of the power of the defeated. With this, any attempted enforced disarmament went by the board.

The rearmament of the disarmed, once the coalition of victors has lost its unity, is never too difficult. Although the men have been taken out of uniform and the arms destroyed, there still remain men to put back into uniform and new (and more modern) arms that can be manufactured. To disarm a nation thoroughly in modern times one would have to destroy its industrial capacity. Although the United States considered such a policy toward Germany following World War II (the "Morgenthau Plan" for the pastoralization of the Reich), the Allies never went beyond the provisions of the Potsdam Agreement reducing the level of permitted heavy industrial production. Why they did not go further is easy to see and is not to be explained merely on grounds of disagreement over policy. A ruthless policy of forced deindustrialization in a modern state produces chaos. Into this economic disturbance, with its far-reaching complications and consequences, other industrial states are inevitably drawn. The pauperization of Germany could not be accomplished without at the same time destroying the chance of the West for industrial recovery from the war. The disruption of Germany's economy, by the inflation of the 1920's and the reparations policies of the allies, each played their part in bringing on the Great Depression of the 1930's. How much more the evil and havoc that deindustrialization would produce!

But if the industrial base remains, the potential for rearmament remains too. Faced with this dilemma the risk has been run, and with the dissolution of the coalition the rearmament has occurred. All this is a quite natural development, for despite the protestations of Japanese and German leaders after World War II that they did not want to rearm, no nation is long prepared to remain disarmed in an armed camp. Neither Japan nor Germany could for long feel that their security interests were adequately taken care of by alien nations, no matter how much surface unity of interests appeared to exist. The instinctive, almost reflexive tendency to rearm does not necessarily stem from a policy of revenge or renewed aggression. Although the new force may later be used for aggressive purposes, its establishment springs in the first instance from the conservative need to have sufficient armed might to preserve national prestige and the most elementary of vital interests—independence and territorial integrity.

2 Voluntary Disarmament: The Hague Conferences

IF the record of enforced disarmament is one of rather consistent failure, the history of voluntary disarmament attempts is not much less melancholy. Such attempts have sometimes been made on a local, bilateral basis covering a restricted area. Almost always such efforts have had transitory effects. The Rush-Bagot Agreement of 1817 between the United States and Great Britain stands in great contrast by virtue of its longevity: it is still in effect. Originally it provided that the naval forces permitted to each side on the Great Lakes would be limited to three vessels, each force to be of equal tonnage and armament. It was revised during World War II to allow naval construction on the Lakes in the interests of both the United States and Canada. Yet even the Rush-Bagot Agreement has been more important for its symbolic meaning than for its practical effect during most of its life. Originally it served to demilitarize to a great extent the primary theater of war and path of invasion between the United States and Canada. With the coming of railroads and improved highways, giving adequate alternative access, the agreement became essentially symbolic.

From the standpoint of general international relations, it is the voluntary multilateral attempts at disarmament that are most instructive, for at such times what is contemplated is not merely a small and local partial disarmament but one on a great scale, embracing most of if not all the powers. Although proposals for general disarmament, such as that made by Gladstone's government in 1870 shortly before the Franco-Prussian War, were occasionally made by one state or another in the nineteenth century, the first conference actually held for the purpose came in 1899.

The First Hague Conference, in which twenty-eight nations took part, agreed unanimously "That the limitation of military charges, which at present weigh down the world, is greatly to be desired for the increase of the material and moral welfare of humanity." But because of what the President of the Conference called "technical difficulties," it was unable to go beyond a pious hope that the various powers would examine the possibility of an agreement.[3] The Conference adjourned with the expectation of reconvening. An American attempt to reconvene it in 1904 failed because of Russo-Japanese tension, so that the second conference did not meet until 1907. Here it was apparent that nothing constructive had been accomplished in the interval. Indeed, military budgets had almost universally increased. Although forty-four nations attended the Second Hague Conference, their progress on disarmament was no greater. It went no further than urging the governments to "resume the serious examination of this question." [4] Plans were made for a third conference to be held in another eight years or so—but by that time World War I was in full course.

3 Voluntary Disarmament: The Naval Conferences After World War I

THE next general disarmament conference, the Washington Naval Conference, came in 1921. The war had changed the situation in Asia—Japan had

---

[3] James Brown Scott, ed., *The Reports to the Hague Conferences of 1899 and 1907,* p. 12.

[4] *Ibid.,* p. 216. The Hague Conferences did make progress in the field of institutionalizing peaceful settlement procedures. See above, Chapter 11.

inherited the German possessions. Russia, hitherto the strong check on Nip-ponese aspirations, had disintegrated into civil war. Japanese and United States relations could, under such circumstances, become dangerously tense (as they actually did in 1941). Yet neither wanted war at this time with the other. This situation provided the nucleus for a settlement.

What brought about the conference in 1921, however, were two other factors. One was the naval competition between the United States and Britain. It had been settled British policy up to this point to maintain a navy equal in strength to the combined forces of the next two largest navies. With the great expansion of the American fleet, which continued as wartime-ordered units were delivered and commissioned following the close of hostilities, the retention of that standard was beyond British capabilities—at least in the light of the evident American determination to achieve equality.

The second factor was the Anglo-Japanese Alliance. Originally concluded in 1902, it had been renewed in 1905 and altered to provide that an attack upon either party by *one* other power (the 1902 version had covered only attacks by *two* other powers), would be a *casus belli* (cause of war) for both states. Renewed again for ten years in 1911, the alliance was to continue indefinitely after that time, subject to abrogation by either party on one year's notice. After World War I this treaty was causing great alarm in the British Dominions. Canada, in particular, worried for fear its operation might conceivably some day bring her into a war on the side of Japan and against the United States, for although the treaty was strictly between Japan and Britain, the Dominions traditionally fought when Britain did. The inclusion of a provision at the 1911 renewal that neither party was to be drawn into a war with a nation with whom it had a general arbitration treaty, and the existence in effect of such a treaty between the United States and Britain actually made this possibility remote. Nevertheless, the United States, too, desired to see the treaty terminated to weaken Japan's position.[5]

The Washington Conference was attended by the United States, Great Britain, Japan, France, Italy, China, Belgium, Portugal, and the Netherlands (all of whom had interests in the Far East). It convened in November 1921, under the chairmanship of Secretary of State Hughes. In his opening speech Hughes proposed a formula for controlling naval armaments that reflected closely the existing forces of the United States, Great Britain, Japan, France, and Italy.[6] This formula, providing for a ratio of 5: 5: 3: 1.67: 1.67 in tonnage strength for the five nations was formally embodied in the Washington Treaty of 1922, but it was to apply only to battleships and battle cruisers because of the inability of the nations to agree on submarines, cruisers, and

---

[5] Also United States opinion continued to be extremely sensitive about this alliance despite the fact than in Great Britain several authoritative declarations had been made in 1920–1921 calling attention to the exclusion of the United States from hostile action by Britain by virtue of this escape clause.

[6] German naval forces were, of course, already controlled under the Treaty of Versailles.

destroyers. Aircraft-carrier tonnage was limited on a somewhat different basis to 135,000 tons for the United States and Britain; 81,000 for Japan; and 60,000 each for France and Italy.

For ten years no new capital ships (defined in the treaty as a vessel of war, not an aircraft carrier, whose displacement exceeds ten thousand tons or whose gun caliber exceeds eight inches) were to be constructed or acquired, except a few replacement units designated specifically in the treaty. Existing forces were to be stabilized close to the formula by the scrapping of certain ships and the abandonment of building plans for others. In an interim period, 1922–1931, the actual battleship forces, because of the difficulties of bringing such a mathematical ratio immediately into effect, in all cases except Japan, were somewhat in excess of the post-1931 goal. This was by agreement.

These proposals provided for the scrapping of seventy-eight units as of 1922. Initially the United States scrapped fifteen in-service ships (none newer than thirteen years old and most of them seventeen years old) with two more twelve-year-olds to go in 1922 when replaced by new thirty-five-thousand-tonners. Britain scrapped initially twenty completed ships, a couple only seven years old, but most of them nine to twelve years old. The Japanese initially scrapped ten in-service ships, two of them twenty years old, two of them sixteen years old, and the rest eleven to twelve years old. The remainder of units scrapped was composed of ships laid down but not completed, or planned units not yet laid down.

Battleship replacement construction, following 1931, would permit the United States and Britain five hundred twenty-five thousand tons, Japan three hundred fifteen thousand tons, and France and Italy one hundred seventy-five thousand tons each. No other warships exceeding ten thousand tons were to be built at all other than as replacement tonnage in the battleship and aircraft carrier categories, except that each nation might construct two aircraft carriers of not more than thirty-three thousand tons within its overall tonnage limit.

By Article XIX of the Washington Treaty, the United States, Great Britain, and Japan agreed that the existing "status quo . . . with regard to fortifications and naval bases, shall be maintained . . ." in the Pacific, with certain exceptions. The Hawaiian Islands and United States possessions adjacent to the American West Coast (not including the Aleutians) were excepted as were Canada's West Coast, Australia, and New Zealand. Japan promised by the same token to leave the Kuriles, the Bonins, the Loochoos, Anami-Oshima, Formosa, and the Pescadores as they were.[7] No new bases were to be built; the old ones might be maintained.[8]

The Nine-Power Treaty of 1922 and the Four-Power Treaty completed the arrangements of the Washington Conference. The first promised to "respect the sovereignty, the independence, and the territorial and adminis-

---

[7] The League-mandated Carolines and Marianas, which (except for Guam) were in Japanese hands, were not to be fortified under the terms of the mandates.

[8] *United States Treaty Series*, No. 671, Washington, 1923.

trative integrity of China," [9] and the second provided for full and frank communication between the United States, the British Empire, France, and Japan "to arrive at an understanding" as to what to do "jointly or separately" [10] if a "controversy" over "any Pacific question" should arise.[11] By Article IV the terminated Japanese alliance was replaced by this broader (and more innocuous) arrangement.

All three treaties were essential to the settlement thus accomplished. The arms control rested upon a stabilization of the *status quo* going beyond mere battleship strength. The particular formula of limitation, plus the decision to prevent the establishment of further bases and the improvement of existing bases in the Far East, were the symbolization of the more far-reaching and apparent willingness of the parties to maintain the political *status quo*. The agreement to leave China alone was an evidence of this. The ratio chosen for capital ships (the essential nucleus for offensive action in fleet doctrines of the time) is another evidence. The treaties in effect made it possible for the United States to be supreme in the Eastern Pacific, and Japan in the Western Pacific—that is to say, in their respective "home" waters. With only three-fifths of United States battleship and carrier strength, Japan could not carry aggression into the Eastern Pacific; even if the United States kept only a little more than half its total forces there, it would more than balance a Japanese fleet operating at a great distance from home. On the other hand, if the entire American fleet (even in the extremely unlikely event that the Atlantic approaches of the United States would be denuded) were sent to the Far Pacific, it would hardly be sufficient—because of lack of adequate bases and the fact that the Japanese fleet would be based on their home islands—to carry an offensive into Japanese waters. The weakness in the arrangement was that the Philippines were left exposed in tempting fashion to the Japanese, and the whole scheme depended upon Japanese forbearance there and vis-à-vis China. The scheme would have fallen through entirely by Japanese refusal to participate if the United States had attempted to attain a naval position adequate to this purpose, since it would have meant the insecurity of Japan. Every scheme, somewhere, has a weakness.

The Washington Conference was thus but a qualified success. It brought not so much disarmament (for almost all the scrapped units would have been scrapped within seven or eight years anyhow) as stabilization. The mutual decision to scrap planned or uncompleted units meant a halt to further capital-ship competition.

Since the conference had failed to resolve the problem of limiting cruisers, destroyers, and submarines, new conferences were held. At the London Naval Conference of 1930, agreements on maximum tonnage limitations for cruisers, destroyers, and submarines were reached by the United States, Great Britain, and Japan. But the agreed levels tended even more than in 1922 to stabilize

[9] *Ibid.*, No. 723, Washington, 1937, Article I.
[10] *Ibid.*, No. 669, Washington, 1923, Article II.
[11] *Ibid.*, Article I.

rather than reduce naval armaments. A new conference was to be held in 1935.

By the time of this Second London Naval Conference two events had occurred that foredoomed it to failure. The Japanese had announced their intention to terminate the 1922 treaty; the British had concluded a treaty with Nazi Germany permitting the Germans 35 per cent of British naval tonnage, including parity in submarines with the British Empire. The second London Conference met to hear Japan's demand for equality in all categories of naval armaments. Refused, Japan withdrew from the conference. Restrictions on total tonnage now went by the board.

In retrospect the first naval conference was the only really successful conference; it was successful not so much because it brought disarmament but because it stabilized armaments and established a *modus vivendi* in the Pacific. By 1934, however, after Japan had embarked upon her adventures in Manchuria, the whole basis on which the 1922 agreement had been made was gone. Japan's insistence on parity and her withdrawal in the face of Anglo-American opposition were the surface symbols of deep-set disagreement. They were the harbingers of approaching war. Since effective, successful disarmament, in the naval field as on land, depends upon prospects for peace, the purely nominal limitations of the 1930's were already a reflection of the general lack of hope.

4 Voluntary Disarmament: The World Disarmament Conference

GERMANY'S enforced disarmament after World War I, according to the Treaty of Versailles, had been willed as a first step toward the "general limitation of the armaments of *all* nations." [12] But not until December 1925, did the League Council create a Preparatory Commission for a Disarmament Conference. Progress was extremely slow. Almost a year of effort failed to yield up a definition of "armaments." The powers were unable to define what they hoped to reduce! After starts and stops, in December 1930, a skeleton draft convention was created, with alternative texts on those points where agreement had not been reached, and blank spaces where actual figures were to be inserted by the conference itself. The result of five years' work was a paper containing blanks. Even this was done within a framework of French insistence that the arms restrictions of the Versailles Treaty be reserved.

The World Disarmament Conference, which finally met in Geneva on February 2, 1932, after another year's delay, was attended at the outset by the accredited representatives of fifty-nine nations. Theoretically the laboriously prepared draft convention was the point of discussion; from the first, new and dramatic proposals pushed it aside. Some of these are worth mentioning, although all of them in the end came to naught. Premier Tardieu of France

---

[12] Introduction to Part V; italics added.

moved on February 5 to establish an international police force under the League that would also have a monopoly of bombers. Arbitration was to be compulsory, and aggression would be rigidly punished. This scheme perpetuated the Versailles *Diktat* by its insistence on an ultimate legal judgment for any unsettled international dispute; it was completely unacceptable to Germany.

The French plan envisaged "offensive" weapons, such as battleships and large submarines, big guns, and heavy tanks, being placed at the disposal of the League. But there was fundamental disagreement over what constituted an "offensive" as distinguished from a "defensive" weapon. The United States and Britain considered that battleships were "defensive" and that submarines were the only distinctively "offensive" or aggressive naval weapon. By contrast, some of the nations whose main reliance was on land power considered that this description should be reversed. Japan took still another view, arguing that both the battleship and the submarine were defensive but that aircraft carriers were aggressive. Germany considered the ten-thousand-ton "pocket" battleships allowed her by the Versailles Treaty to be defensive but larger naval weapons (prohibited to her) offensive. France and Italy could not agree that the submarine was aggressive in itself, although Italy was willing to prohibit submarines if the battleships were done away with, too. In short, there could hardly have been less agreement on specifics, although all present were in agreement that "offensive" weapons most certainly should be banned.

When it came to land weapons, the same play was re-enacted with different stage properties. As to tanks, the British agreed with the French that large tanks were "offensive"; others, including Italy, Germany, Hungary, and Russia, felt that all tanks were offensive. On artillery the nations were able to agree that all cannon could be used for offensive or defensive purposes, but that their offensive capacity increased with their effectiveness! Nor could the powers agree on a formula for judging the number of military "effectives" (trained military personnel).

In fact, taking all the categories of weapons and manpower considered, virtually the sole item of general agreement involved the offensive nature of chemical and biological weapons. The qualitative approach, distinguishing weapons by the use to which they could be put, was virtually a complete failure. When Germany, who had been denied certain weapons by the Versailles Treaty in order that she could not perpetrate aggression, urged that these prohibited weapons should be considered "offensive" and abolished for all, the proposal met with stony resistance.

The quantitative approach was no more successful. The dramatic proposal of Maxim Litvinov, representing Soviet Russia, calling for total disarmament, caused a stir but nothing more. On June 22, 1932, President Hoover combined both approaches by suggesting that all land forces in excess of Germany's army of a hundred thousand should be immediately reduced by one-third. Bombing planes, large mobile guns, and all tanks were to be abolished, and naval forces should be cut by one-third the existing tonnage for battleships and submarines. This, like the French and Russian proposals, got nowhere.

The really fundamental point at issue in the conference was the inability of France and Germany to come to an agreement.[13] Germany was no longer content to accept the restrictions of the Versailles Treaty, but France could not bring herself to accept the German demand for "equality." From the beginning the French insistence on "security" virtually ruled out any possibility of agreement. Outweighed by Germany in manpower and resources, France by accepting an equality of forces with Germany would inevitably have given the Germans the military advantage. Under conditions of full mobilization the Germans, starting from an army equal in size to the French, could expand more quickly and to a much larger ultimate size than the French could hope to. The superior industrial resources of Germany would further have turned the scales against France. Unless a fully effective collective security scheme were to be put into effect that would aid France if Germany attacked, the French could not grant equality (which meant for them inequality), and the Germans were not prepared to accept anything less.

On this fundamental rock of disagreement the conference came to grief. On September 16, 1932, the Germans withdrew to await a change in the situation. The end was now in sight although the play was not yet ended. In December the French agreed to recognition of equality for Germany in principle, provided that an adequate security system was established. Although nominally a concession, this of course meant nothing in practice. By the end of 1932 a really effective collective security system was no longer likely. The coming of the Nazis to power on January 30, 1933, froze even this nominal sign of progress in its tracks as French fears quickly increased; negotiations deadlocked.

Yet a fourth (and final) dramatic proposal was now made, this time by Britain. Ramsay MacDonald in March 1933, laid a plan before the Conference by which, over a five-year period, European armies would be reduced to two hundred thousand men each for Germany, France, Italy, and Poland. Russia would be allowed five hundred thousand (to counterbalance the Franco-Polish alliance), and in addition France was to be allowed another two hundred thousand stationed in her colonies, and Italy, fifty thousand for the same purpose. This fourth proposal, strictly quantitative, had merits which the other three had lacked: it was simple; it took into account Germany's demand for equality by permitting her to have an army in Europe equal to France's; it put an end to the "indignity" of Germany's enforced inferior position; at the same time, by giving France another force in the colonies equally as large as that at home, it counterbalanced the larger German manpower and industrial resources. Of course, it could not entirely meet the French demand for security (to do so would have been possible only by the disappearance of Germany or the erection of an iron-clad collective security

---

[13] Although in the background there were also fears among the Western nations over future Soviet foreign policy.

system—neither of which was feasible), nor could it entirely meet the German demand for equality (other than in Europe—but this would have been enough, possibly, to meet the minimum German prestige needs). Had the government of Germany in 1933 been that of Stresemann instead of Hitler, this plan might have stood a chance of adoption (although it must not be forgotten how shaky Stresemann's domestic political position was). Or if the plan had come ten years earlier, and France had been able to foresee what was to come, she might have considered it reasonable. The irony and classical tragedy of the situation is that France had waited until her hegemony was seriously in peril. And by that time it was too late.

Even the MacDonald proposals called for a transitional period. The Nazis would settle for nothing less than immediate action. More months went by but the deadlock was complete. On October 14, 1933, Germany announced her definitive withdrawal from the Conference, followed one week later by her withdrawal from the League. On March 16, 1935 Germany openly repudiated the disarmament clauses of the Versailles Treaty. The curtain was rising on a new war.

5 Naval and Land Disarmament Problems Compared

THE relative success of naval disarmament (especially in the Washington Conference of 1922) and the discouraging failure of land disarmament (particularly in the World Disarmament Conference of 1932) make a startling contrast. One is led to consider whether the success of the one and the failure of the other was due to the timing of the conferences and the political-strategic situation at that time, or to the nature of the disarmament problem in sea as opposed to land warfare. The answer is a bit of both.

If the World Disarmament Conference had been held in 1924, when Franco-German *rapprochement*, however limited in time, had become a reality, it would have had much better chances of success. Especially if Germany had *not* already been disarmed so that France and Germany either had to disarm mutually or not at all, the prospects would have been better. The very procrastination, the very extraordinary leisureliness of the Preparatory Commission, was evidence that in the 1920's France was not too concerned about world disarmament other than as a theoretical problem. Her major enemy was already disarmed. Correspondingly in the 1930's it was her major enemy who threatened to rearm. Disarmament came consequently to mean to the French the finding of a formula whereby German disarmament could be maintained at the least French armaments sacrifice. France was not really going to disarm if she was not secure, and how is one land power ever to be secure against a neighbor—immediately on the other side of an easily-crossed frontier—who has more industry and more manpower, once that neighbor is no longer willing to bear the yoke tamely? Disarmament in such cases cannot effectively remove the fuse from the bomb.

Consider by contrast the results of the Washington Naval Conference and the reasons for its success. Japan had no immediate ambitions to overthrow the *status quo* in 1922. Ultimate ambitions, yes, but she had received great gains in the Pacific. Time for consolidation was needed. It would not have been a propitious time to press a challenge, and Japan was not ready to fight the United States. Moreover, it was not essential to agree to disarm to avoid war with the United States, even if it is assumed that Japan could not stand the competitive pace of naval building. Disarmament was not necessary— merely a stabilization *maintaining the same ratio*. This last was of great importance, for we have already seen that this ratio meant that neither Japan nor the United States could then effectively attack the other in her home waters. In 1922 any effective attack of Japan on the United States or vice versa had to come by sea. Such an agreement could provide a reasonable measure of mutual security in contrast to the Franco-German situation circa 1932–1933.

Time and distance (or lack of it) played important roles in both cases. The postwar period of the 1920's, too, was better suited to disarmament or stabilization of armaments than the prewar period of the 1930's. Naval disarmament also ran into great difficulties in the 1930's and was in effect abandoned. But the distance factor also helped to make the Pacific arrangement possible and prevent the realization of one in Western Europe. It is one thing to have a cushion of thousands of miles of open ocean between potential enemies; it is quite another to be cheek by jowl within Europe's narrow confines.

The type of disarmament—naval vs. land—also played a part. It is revealing that a mathematical formula (5: 5: 3: 1.67: 1.67) provided the key to success at Washington but left the Geneva Conference entirely unmoved from any practical standpoint. Long before Hoover proposed his one-third reduction in existing land forces, Lord Esher, a member of the Temporary Commission (the forerunner of the Preparatory Commission), had suggested that European armies be allowed specified units of thirty thousand men each. France would have six; Italy and Poland, four; Great Britain, Spain, and Yugoslavia, three; and so on—a 6: 4: 4: 3: 3: 3 ratio. Even in the face of the successful use of the same kind of device that same year at the Washington Conference, the plan was never seriously considered. Neither the 6: 4: 4: 3 idea nor the straight one-third slash gained favor.

There are several reasons for this. First, a battleship or carrier is peculiarly difficult to hide or disguise. Bulky and distinctive, with few ports of rest, it is rather easy to spy out. The same considerations apply to building it in the first place. Second, a capital ship cannot be built in less than three years; sudden, very great expansion is ruled out. Finally, the number of units involved is small. Even over the whole twenty-year program covered by the Washington Treaty, the number of battleships and heavy carriers involved after the initial scrapping, including replacement tonnage, did not number more than a relatively few score.

With land armaments, by contrast, the existing forces in uniform are, like the iceberg's tip above water, only the part of military power that shows. The number of trained and ready reserves is vital.[14] Even raw recruits can, in less than the space of a year, under emergency conditions be converted into quite serviceable forces. Nor is it easy to detect deception and duplicity. If regimental and divisional insignia are suppressed and if the uniform is the same for all divisions, it is exceedingly hard to be sure that the permitted number of men under arms is being observed. The device of the "Black Emperor," Toussaint L'Ouverture of Haiti, who, to impress others with his military strength, had his troops march by, change uniforms, and march by again masquerading as new troops, can be worked as well in reverse. The difficulties of accurate comparative measurement of such factors as the condition of the railways and highways, and the convertibility of civilian production for war, hinder confident mutual disarmament.

On these grounds naval disarmament is easier to achieve than land disarmament. When this difference is added to the previous points made as to time and distance, the relative success of Washington and the relative failure of Geneva become reasonably clear.

6 Voluntary Disarmament: Nuclear Weapons, the First Phase

THE advent of atomic weapons in the closing days of World War II added a new dimension and a new urgency to the problems of arms control. Advances in biological warfare, equally fantastic, came in for less public attention; disease we have always with us, but atomic holocausts were something new.

On the United States, as the temporary sole custodian of the new fearful weapon, fell the responsibility for making a proposal. Before the newly created (January 24, 1946) UN Atomic Energy Commission, Bernard Baruch presented a plan on June 14, 1946. His plan, based on the proposals of the Acheson-Lilienthal Report, envisaged the establishment, under the United Nations Security Council, of an international authority that would control all phases of atomic energy production and use. It would possess monopoly ownership and exercise exclusive control over all aspects of atomic energy suitable for war purposes, wherever situated. Such facilities would be relatively few and quite large. The authority would be allowed free inspection throughout the territories of UN members in order to assure itself that no clandestine operations were being carried on. (But since they would necessarily be large facilities, they could not be easily concealed.) Moreover, when and if reported violations were made to the Security Council, the vote in that body would not be subject to veto. By stages, as inspection and control became effective, the United States would reveal its atomic information; and when the process of control was complete, it would destroy its stockpile of atomic bombs. This

---

[14] The author once saw in Geneva a regiment of the Swiss army materialize almost out of thin air. As civilians the men went to their homes at midday, but within an hour they were assembling in full uniform carrying their rifles, which they keep with them at home.

plan Baruch introduced at the first session of the Commission with the prophecy: "We are here to make a choice between the quick and the dead. . . . If we fail, then we have damned every man to be the slave of Fear. . . . We must elect World Peace or World Destruction." [15]

Despite the majority approval that the plan quickly received, it foundered on the shoals of Soviet opposition. Russia wanted to outlaw the production and use of the bomb first, followed by the destruction of atomic stockpiles. She would then be prepared to permit limited inspection of certain plants at certain times, but unlimited inspection, let alone monopoly ownership and operation of facilities by an international authority, she would not agree to. Deliberations in the Security Council on reported violations would under the Soviet plan remain subject to veto.

The Baruch Plan was based upon two assumptions, both of which seemed warranted. One, the United States monopoly could only be temporary. Two, the United States could not trust the mere word of the Soviets and destroy the atomic stockpile before international control and inspection had become a reality. This control, which was to come by stages marked by an increasing exchange of confidential information, had to be established first—then the bombs would be destroyed. The United States feared that if the bombs were destroyed first, as the Soviets insisted, control might never really come; the Russians might find pretext after pretext for delaying it indefinitely. Conversely, the Soviets were afraid that control would be established and Soviet secrets laid bare, but that the United States would find reasons for postponing indefinitely the destruction of the stockpile. If the first situation came to pass and the Soviets had a secret stockpile, the United States would have placed herself in severe jeopardy. If the second situation occurred the Soviets, assuming United States resort to infinite delays, would have exposed themselves to the same danger.

Secretary of State Acheson in the General Assembly supported the Anglo-French-United States view that the reduction of *all* weapons (including atomic arms) must be by stages, with arms inventories verified by an international count, and the completion of each stage fully certified before the next began: ". . . in a world charged as ours is with suspicions and dangers, our peoples want the safeguards that disclosure and verification can provide . . . [as] we move from stage to stage we would have increasing evidence of good faith and honesty. We could not go forward without that evidence." The Soviet Union's representative, Vyshinsky, in the Assembly on November 16, 1951, quoted Acheson and then went on to say:

This way of stating the issue can only mean one thing: that the transition from one stage to the next . . . will be directly dependent on whether those states possessing the most powerful, dangerous, and threatening weapons, on which information has to be published and made known at succeeding stages, will be prepared to accept as satisfactory the results of submitting the required information at the

[15] *The First Report of the United Nations Atomic Energy Commission to the Security Council*, Department of State Publication 2737, December 31, 1946, p. 81.

first stage. This can only mean that the fate of the whole plan for collecting data on armaments will reside in the hands of the possessors of the more powerful and dangerous weapons. This, finally, may well mean that the decision as regards the transition from one stage to the next will be entirely up to those same powers, which will decide in accordance with their interests.[16]

In other words, the security of the one was the insecurity of the other. The Soviets could find no grounds for reassurance in the fact that the UN control would be not that of the United States but of an international body. The history of voting in the UN testified to the soundness of Russia's expectation that an atomic control commission, voting by majority vote, and a Security Council weighing atomic security matters without vetoes, would vote fairly consistently for the United States and against the Soviet Union. In the meantime the U.S.S.R., which had fought its way to sovereignty over its own territories between 1918 and 1922 against the efforts of almost all the great powers, was being asked to allow an organization she could not control to exercise sovereign functions on her soil. It is not surprising that the Soviet Union chose to push ahead instead with the development of its own bomb. This is not to say that the United States proposal was ungenerous or unrealistic—she could hardly have offered more; it is to say that the two powers had too little confidence in each other, and their interests in this particular case were too opposed, for either to run any greater risks than their mutually opposed plans envisaged.

While the fruitless discussion went on, the Soviets indeed ended the American monopoly of atomic weapons—and sooner than had been expected. The Soviets claimed definite possession of the bomb in 1949. The United States later verified the occurrence of an atomic explosion in Russia. This the United States was able to do by virtue of the continuous watch she maintains on the atmosphere of the earth with delicate, radiation-detecting instruments. The unexpected quickness of the Soviets to explode a bomb was later partially explained when it was discovered that one Harry Gold received sketches of the basic mechanism of the bomb from David Greenglass, an employee at Los Alamos atomic project, and transmitted them via Soviet agents to Moscow *two months before* the first bomb was dropped on Japan.[17] While the United States could still, even after the Soviet bomb, console herself that she had a long lead in production, this was hardly the same as a monopoly. Work was now pressed forward on an American hydrogen bomb, which was successfully tested in the Pacific proving grounds in 1952. On August 12, 1953, the United States announced that this monopoly, too, had been broken by the Soviet explosion of a hydrogen "device." In that same year a series of United States announcements revealed that tactical atomic weapons had become a reality. The increasing reliance of the United States on such weapons was un-

---

16 UN General Assembly, *Official Records*, 6th Session, 348th Plenary Meeting, November 16, 1951.

17 See Michael Amrine, "A Tale of the Steps to Hiroshima—and Beyond," *The Reporter*, January 5, 1954, pp. 7–12, for an atomic development and espionage chronology.

derscored by the budget proposals and explanations of President Eisenhower in January 1954. Only a couple of months later the British budget revealed that atomic weapons, British-produced, were on their way to the armed forces. Thus at least three nations had nuclear weapons by early 1954.

So between 1949 and 1954, the problem of nuclear disarmament changed in two important respects: (1) nuclear weapons were no longer confined to a single nation, and (2) nuclear weapons were proliferating in kind and number. It was no longer a "battleship" type problem (as the Baruch Plan had visualized it prior to the manufacture of hundreds of warheads which *could* be concealed in sheds) but a "rifle or machine-gun" type problem.

The emphasis in disarmament discussions in this period naturally changed too. Where "the bomb" had at first received the lion's share of attention, the interrelations of all weapons systems was now reasserted—a point of view subsequently reinforced by the extension of nuclear power to tactical battlefield use. The UN merged the Atomic Energy Commission and the Commission for Conventional Armaments into a new Disarmament Commission on January 11, 1952, giving it power to survey the entire problem. As with the former commissions, the new organ consisted of all of the members of the Security Council and Canada (if she was not on the Council). Despite the continuing disagreements in the new commission, which it could not overcome merely because it was a new organ, the change was highly desirable. It permitted a fresh start. It also marked a more realistic approach in recognizing that disarmament by individual classes of weapons, no matter how formidable these were, was not likely to be achieved, divorced from the over-all armaments relations of the great powers. The one undoubtedly affected the other and vice versa. The factors that had made the limitation of battleships relatively easy in 1922, leaving cruisers and submarines unlimited, did not apply here.

As in the earlier commissions, the American and Soviet proposals conflicted in the new, with the former generally receiving majority support, and the latter usually mustering a small minority vote. Yet since American and Russian agreement on how to proceed remained a fundamental prerequisite to disarmament, overwhelming votes in the United Nations the one way or the other meant very little unless both nations voted on the same side. Both states brought their proposals for disarmament of conventional forces before the new commission. In the fall of 1948, even before the new commission came into existence, the Soviet Union began proposing a one-third reduction of armed forces by the great powers. Although the Soviet proposal was substantially that of former President Hoover in 1932, this time the United States steadfastly opposed it. To adopt it would mean a much greater reduction for the Western forces, *each* of which would have to be reduced one-third. Instead the United States urged in mid-1952 that absolute figures be set for the armed forces. The American proposal was for the United States and the Soviet Union and China each to have one-and-a-half million men; France, eight hundred thousand; Britain, seven hundred thousand; and the other nations smaller forces. Under this plan the major Communist forces and the major Western forces would balance one another—three million Russians and Chinese against three million Americans, French, and British. The Soviets in turn opposed this. In any event it was extremely improbable that any numerical limitation agreement on conventional forces could be reached while the future of Germany remained unsettled. It would have been like building a triumphal arch on the understanding that the central keystone would be inserted later. German power, thrown one way or the other, made too much difference.

7 Voluntary Disarmament: Nuclear Weapons, the Second Phase

DEADLOCK in the UN, added to the changing nature of the nuclear problem, led to a fresh and direct approach by the major powers at the "summit" meeting of 1955. These new efforts were not aimed directly at disarmament, but rather at decreasing the tensions implicit in the existence of threateningly large United States and Soviet military forces. The new approach admitted by implication that a method had not been found actually to disarm; yet paradoxically, if tension could be reduced, the way might be prepared for voluntary scaling down of armaments on a significant scale.

Two important proposals were made. President Eisenhower proposed a reciprocal aerial ("open skies") inspection of security installations by the United States and the Soviet Union, together with a complete exchange of blueprints and pinpointed data on such installations. Here the idea of complete inspection was carried far toward its logical limits. But since it was open to the same objections basically as was the Baruch proposal for atomic inspection, the Russian reaction was unenthusiastic. The Soviets, led then by Bulganin, proposed an alternative "crossroads" inspection plan. The heart of the new Soviet approach was the idea of inspection by foreign commissioners of the transportation and communication facilites vital to war preparation, so that there would be warning if mobilization were being attempted secretly for a surprise attack. The United States was equally unenthusiastic about this proposal, primarily because of its limited nature.

As before, neither the United States nor the U.S.S.R. trusted each other sufficiently to institute nuclear or conventional disarmament on a basis of good faith, without guarantees. The problem was what feasible guarantees could be given short of free inspection? If full and free inspection were to be instituted, international inspection teams could probe at will anywhere in the world at any time. There could literally be no more military secrets; no area could be blocked off as not "suitable" for inspection. Whether the United States itself would ultimately agree to such a program, whether the United States Senate would ratify a treaty including such provisions, is very much in doubt. It can be assumed that the likelihood of Russia's doing so is extremely remote. The stabilization of nuclear arsenals at an agreed ratio, without thoroughgoing inspection, is equally improbable. Especially now that atomic tactical weapons have been developed, and atomic "bombs" take the shape of artillery shells and can be numbered in the thousands, the chances for successful duplicity are great. The advent of hydrogen missiles concealed at sea increased the complexity of the problem.

The inability of the nuclear powers to agree on abolishing nuclear weapons had led them by 1955 to explore the possibility of merely inspecting such armaments as each side decided to possess. As such, 1955 already registered one step in retreat from the original (but idealistic) goal. In 1958, attention began to focus on proposals for achieving a nuclear test ban. Considerable world opinion feared the ever-rising radioactivity in the atmosphere resulting from tests. Moreover, the atomic "have" powers had a certain mutual interest in encouraging the cessation of nuclear testing before such devices became more widespread among nations. While nuclear "have-not" powers could not by such an agreement be prohibited from testing, it would make any testing program by them more difficult to defend. While the idea had obvious merit in preventing further pollution of the atmosphere, and some potential for preventing further nuclear proliferation, it represented a second step back from the original goal.

Even this limited proposal had a checkered career. Unilateral suspensions of tests had been announced by the United States, the Soviet Union, and the United Kingdom in 1958 following a technical conference in Geneva on the detection of nuclear blasts. This conference having concluded that an effective control system could be devised to police a test ban, a political conference began its work on October 31, 1958. By late 1960 the political conference (involving the United States, the Soviet Union, and the United Kingdom) had evolved a draft treaty which, while incomplete, represented substantial progress. The Control Organization envisaged was to have joint teams which would monitor blasts from stations around the world. Most importantly, they would be granted access "to the site of any element of the System or any area where an on-site inspection is to be conducted." [18] While the number of such permitted inspections proposed by Russia on July 26, 1960, was in the U.S. view inadequate (only three), this proposal represented the first time the Soviet Union had gone so far as to give a figure.

Progress in the next two years was interrupted by new crises centering on Berlin and Cuba. The abrupt breaking-off of the negotiations and the large-scale resumption of testing by the Soviets in October 1961, culminating in their 50 megaton explosion, shocked public opinion the world around. The United States later also resumed testing.

In the aftermath of the two crises, a sober Khrushchev indicated new interest in an agreement to ban tests. In December 1962, secret conversations were initiated, but the Soviets were still unwilling to permit more than two or three "on-site" inspections, while the minimum U.S. figure was eight or

---

[18] For a full account see *Geneva Conference on the Discontinuance of Nuclear Weapon Tests*, Department of State Publication 7090, as reprinted from the Department of State *Bulletin*, of September 26, 1960.

seven. Since U.S. insistence on its figure stemmed from the difficulty of distinguishing underground blasts from seismic disturbances, and since underground testing has only limited military advantages and does not pollute the atmosphere, the deadlock was overcome by divorcing the two categories of tests.[19] The U.S. was confident that U.S. monitoring systems were adequate to detect all above-ground blasts. The negotiations of mid-1963 thereupon went forward rapidly, the issue of inspections was shelved, and the treaty banning atmospheric tests was signed on August 5, 1963, and ratified by the U.S. Senate by 80-19 on September 4.[20] By the end of 1963, 113 nations had signed or acceded to the treaty. Some 336 nuclear explosions in the atmosphere over a thirteen year period by the United States, the Soviet Union, and Great Britain were now ended. Both France and Communist China refused to sign or be bound by the Nuclear Test Ban Treaty. Their explosions continue.

8 The Disarmament Riddle

THE point was made at the outset of our consideration of disarmament that nations attempt it to bring about a distinct result: to reduce the mobilized and actual military power of their potential enemies and thus to diminish the danger of sudden attack. The limitation of armaments, whether enforced or voluntary, cannot of itself do away with the threat of ultimate attack. The potential power of the possible enemy is the inevitable product of its resources and manpower. Short of dismemberment and its loss of sovereignty, the feared state retains the potential for rearmament or an increase of existing armaments. Because increases are possible despite agreements to the contrary, it follows that successful arms control agreements occur under conditions where the nature of the weapons makes prohibited increases fairly obvious, or the time needed for substantial violation of the agreements would be long, or the likelihood of war is especially remote at the time when controls are attempted.

Ironically, but quite naturally, where the second and third of these possibilities are involved, there is no real will to achieve disarmament or control because the threat is relatively remote. Where there is no great fear, there is usually no feeling of urgency. Conversely, and yet more ironically, the greater the tension and the more the conviction that war is in the offing, the greater the difficulties in reaching agreement to disarm. In 1899 the world was still a relatively peaceful planet; moreover, the idea of a general disarmament was so

---

[19] See Theodore C. Sorenson, *Kennedy*, pp. 728–730.

[20] For text of the treaty see Department of State *Bulletin*, XLIX (August 12, 1963), pp. 239–240. Article I prohibits any nuclear explosions in the atmosphere, in outer space, or under water, plus any underground explosions which would cause "radioactive debris" to carry outside of the territory of the state involved. The treaty's duration is "unlimited."

new that it is not surprising that the First Hague Conference did not achieve disarmament. Alternately, by 1907 and the Second Conference, Europe was rolling down the slope in growing fear toward war. If 1899 was too early, 1907 was too late. The conferences of the 1930's also came too late even though the Locarno Era (1924–1929), when France and Germany had reached a *rapprochement*, offered hope. But then France felt no need. Later the atomic control attempts reflected a sense of need, but the tension was too great. Moreover, effective nuclear disarmament means an unprecedented surrender of national sovereignty. And, especially in Russia's case, it meant a surrender of sovereignty into the hands of an organization dominated by a hostile or quasi-hostile majority. Today, much of the same logic applies to nuclear-armed China. But her nonparticipation in the UN disarmament talks cannot help but give them some air of futility.

In the end one must conclude that the Washington Conference with its relative success in stabilizing a weapons ratio was truly exceptional. The weapons problem it dealt with was by nature susceptible of treatment—battleships and carriers are relatively few, hard to hide, and a long time in building. Even at that it is unlikely that agreement would have been reached if Britain's intention to terminate the Japanese alliance had not been evident. Since none of the three great sea powers wanted war, and since stabilization of capital units in 1922 meant a balance of naval armaments that served to limit the possibilities of successful attack, and since the attack of any one state on others had to come principally and ultimately by sea, and since the weapons involved could not be easily, quickly, or secretly produced, agreement was reached.

It is quite conceivable that stabilization of naval armaments would in this case have come before too long even without an agreement, provided the alliance had been terminated. Once it was clear that Japan was not on the brink of adventures in China, the United States Republican administration would have been tempted to reduce naval expenditures, just as in the relatively untense years between 1945 and 1948 the United States and Britain both substantially cut back their armed forces. In this period British forces were reduced from 5,220,000 men to 850,000, while the United States Army dropped from 8,266,000 to 552,000 men (1,359,131 in army, air force, and navy combined as of June 30, 1948). This was done without any formal agreement and in the face of Russian abstention from wholesale reductions. It reflected in part the faith of the United States in her atomic bomb monopoly. Once Russia had the bomb (although the increasing tension between 1948 and 1952 was certainly not due alone to the Soviet bomb), the minimum forces proposed by the United States for herself (and Russia) were, as we saw earlier, one-and-a-half million each. By 1952 United States forces were double this latter figure—reflecting the changed situation. The point still remains that armed forces were reduced under the proposed level without any agreements whatsoever at a time of relatively little tension. Even formal agreements, in a time of relatively greater tension, did not propose to restore those low levels. Greater armies may increase tension but greater tension undoubtedly increases armies.

By late 1955, again without formal agreement but again reflecting the reduction of tension that followed the conclusion of the Korean and Indo-Chinese wars and diplomatic progress on other outstanding problems, there had been reductions once more. American forces then stood at 2.9 million (as against 3.5 million two years earlier), while the Soviet Union had announced her intention of reducing her forces by 640,000 men by the end of that year. Subsequently she announced further substantial cuts. And, again reflecting increased tensions, the figures on both sides were revised upwards in 1961 because of the Berlin crisis. Thus 1961's tensions brought greater arms and the breaking-off of test ban negotiations—and still more tensions. By 1966, after new cuts following the Test Ban Treaty, figures were again up because of Viet-Nam tensions.

It can be concluded that disarmament agreements on weapons or troop ratios are most likely to be reached under conditions where stabilization or cutback would probably ultimately occur in the absence of such agreements, and that they are highly unlikely under reverse conditions. This is not to say that this type of agreement has no value. If reductions are mutually embarked upon in agreed fashion, results can be achieved with less suspicion and in a more organized fashion which itself diminishes tension still further. Such agreements are also most likely when they form part of or follow an over-all stabilization of a *status quo* that the participants mutually wish to preserve. And agreements are most readily reached under such conditions where they deal with weapons easily controllable per se with a minimum of supervision and inspection. Unfortunately for the peace of the world, such circumstances have been relatively rare in the twentieth century.

At the same time, the picture is not altogether bleak. The Nuclear Test Ban is a step forward. Scientific and technical advances progressively did away with the necessity for on-site inspections, so far as atmospheric tests were concerned, and even the measurement and detection of underground blasts is becoming more precise. Scientific-technical advances wrought other important changes. Eisenhower's "open skies" proposal would have entailed highly complicated and mutually agreed aerial inspections. Yet the same results are now being achieved by inspection and photography from U.S. and Soviet satellites in outer space, without the necessity of overt agreement. The Soviet "crossroads" inspection proposal has also received new attention lately. An agreement along these lines would have considerable merit as a supplement to satellite vehicle inspection. The fact that the Soviets proposed such a plan, and went so far in terms of the nuclear explosion ban inspection as to accept three on-site visits, indicates that the Soviets are willing to accept the concept of limited inspections. Such limited agreements are extremely useful even if military bases remain closed to foreign inspectors, for they can guarantee a continuing appraisal of whether overt preparations are being made for war in the areas of transportation and communication. If radio reports from the foreign inspection team suddenly ceased, the implications would be clear.

The merits of a "crossroads" agreement may appear dubious to those who visualize a World War III as mainly involving a decision by an aggressor to fire missiles without making any other obvious preparations for war. But a nation which thus gained the surprise would inevitably also have its own people equally surprised by the retaliatory blow. It is extremely unlikely that war would begin without detectable and lengthy preparations unless one nation erroneously *thought* it was about to be attacked and attempted to retaliate before it had been physically assaulted—a highly unlikely circumstance, however much its dramatic fascination.

U.S.-Soviet agreement in December 1966 led to another useful step when the UN Committee on the Peaceful Uses of Outer Space completed a draft treaty. By Article 4, parties agreed "not to place in orbit around the earth any objects carrying nuclear weapons . . ." Work continued on a nuclear proliferation ban (with the troublesome question unanswered as to how to convince certain nations without nuclear weapons to remain so). In January 1967 plans were at an advanced stage to de-nuclearize Latin America (where U.S. weapons offered sufficient reliable security).

To return to the beginning: Under present conditions important agreements on weapons ratios are extremely unlikely. But the creation of a set of safeguards to warn of a looming threat of attack is feasible. Such an agreement would lower tension and would no doubt also lead to a lower overall level of armaments. In the nuclear age, that is not much. But it is something.

CHAPTER 15

The Patterns of Power:
Unilateralism and One World

. . . The problem of peace in our time is the establishment of a legal order to regulate relations among men,
beyond and above the nation-states.

EMERY REVES
The Anatomy of Peace

WHILE states are generally free to disarm or not to disarm as seems best to them, the other basic response to the power problem is obligatory and inescapable. Each state, simply because it exists within a multipower system, must react to its power problem and play a part in the organization of that power system one way or another. Each plays a part by virtue of the alliances it makes or fails to make; each plays a part by its own conception of the role it is to play, the end to be obtained, and most particularly by its efforts (or lack of efforts) in shaping the development of the power system. In the end the organization of the power system, and its effects on the world's tension level, is the net result of the interaction of these concepts and efforts. How the power system will be organized and what patterns of power will be formed will depend upon which of the possible lines of approach to the power problem the states take.

I The Patterns of Power

FIVE possible lines of approach to the organization of a power system exist. They are the logical alternatives open to states in their search for security. We have termed these five possibilities the "patterns of power": unilateralism, balance of power, collective security, world government, and world conquest.

The first three are concerned with security solutions *within* the multistate system; the last two, with security solutions which ultimately involve *replac-* two possibilities (i.e., the conquest or forcible union of the world under one state, or its voluntary union in a world federation) were to be achieved, a world state would exist. But so long as the power of the world remains divided among great states, no one of which is supreme over the rest, and so long as there is no voluntary world government, regardless of whether the

288

ultimate intention is the replacement of the state system itself, nations must choose for immediate purposes among the first three patterns.

(1) Unilateralism   (2) Balance of Power   (3) Collective
                           Alignments   Security

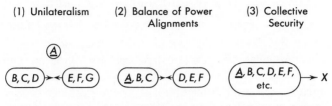

Note A's varying positions. X=aggressor (who may really be B, C, etc.)

DIAGRAM 4
Patterns of Power within Multistate System

Using the first of these three patterns, a state relies on its own power, makes no alliances, and has no obligations to defend others; on the other hand, no other state has any responsibility for aiding it—this "lone wolf" approach we call *unilateralism*.[1] Using the second of the three approaches, a state merges its security interests in an alliance with one or more other states with whom its vital interests are for the time being compatible, with the whole of the group thus formed being ready to take collective action against opposing alliance coalitions as necessary—this "gang vs. gang" approach we call *balance of power alignments*. Both of these first two approaches can be used by states who desire either the perpetuation of the existing multistate system or its ultimate disintegration and supplanting. Resort to these approaches implies no guarantee in itself as to the aggressive or non-aggressive aims of the participants. Or, using the third of the three approaches, a state joins in a universal collective security scheme in which *every* member assumes an obligation to go to the aid of *any* member against whom aggression is committed —this "universal mutual protection" approach we call *collective security*. Participation in such a scheme by an individual nation is no guarantee of aggressive or non-aggressive aims. Non-participation may be indiscreet or unwise. But the aim of the scheme in this case is the preservation of all existing states from unprovoked attack within their existing frontiers. States following either of the first two approaches promise no such thing. Nations embracing unilateralism are concerned with their *own* frontiers; states entering balance of power alignments extend that concern to those of their allies—but that is as far as it goes.

---

[1] A term coined by the author to relate what has been called *isolationism, neoisolationism* (to "go it alone"), and the traditional term of *neutrality* to one another in a meaningful way. See Frederick H. Hartmann, "Away With Unilateralism!" *The Antioch Review*, Vol. 11, No. 1 (Spring 1951), pp. 3–9. While we are using the term here to indicate a choice of pattern, the term can also usefully describe a state of mind in approaching foreign policy problems. The British unilateral disarmament movement illustrates. They wish to "go it alone" in nuclear disarmament, destroying British warheads whether others follow suit or not.

2 *Unilateralism, Balance of Power, and Collective Security: Preliminary Observations*

UNILATERALISM and balance of power have long histories. Both have been practiced since the dawn of the nation-state system. Collective security, on the other hand, is relatively new and has been attempted on a universal or quasi-universal scale only since World War I.

One source of confusion, brought about by the existence of this third pattern (collective security), needs clarification immediately. The second and third possibilities involve a *collective* approach. To the casual observer each might seem as appropriately described by calling it "collective security," because each involves a collective grouping for security purposes. Indeed, the term *collective security* has been used from time to time by members of balance-of-power coalitions such as NATO to describe their alliance arrangements. Yet while NATO is undeniably collective, it is also *exclusive and less than universal* or even quasi-universal, and is therefore not collective security in the established sense as used in this book.

Each of these three patterns, taken in pure form, excludes the others. A state cannot choose unilateralism and hold aloof from alliances and at the same time participate in an alliance system as an avowed member of one or another of the coalitions. Self-imposed isolation, or a policy of neutrality, both familiar expressions of the unilateralist pattern, preclude alliances. Yet it is conceivable that a state can choose to follow both a unilateralist and balance-of-power-alignment approach simultaneously with respect to different areas of the world or different problems.

To illustrate, the United States as a world power has chosen to join in NATO (a balance-of-power alliance) to resolve its power-security problem in geographical area covering the North Atlantic Ocean, Western Europe, and most of the northern shore of the Mediterranean. At the same time the United States has made separate alliances in the Far East with New Zealand and Australia, the Philippines, Japan, Nationalist China (Formosa), and South Korea. All these treaties are also geographically limited to attacks on the territories of the states named. But in those areas of the Far East not covered by alliance provisions, including most importantly the Chinese mainland, the United States has pursued a unilateralist pattern. In 1949–1955, and again after 1963, when United States–Chinese Communist tension was at a peak, it was conceivable that the United States would find herself engaged in a war with China in a fashion that would relieve any of her world-wide allies from any obligation to come to her aid. Whether other alliance partners of the United States could and would stand aloof, although technically free from commitment, is a question in itself. For a state that pursues thoroughgoing unilateralism, such as neutral Sweden, this dilemma is eliminated. But once a state enters into an alliance system, no matter how technically limited its obligations, the ramifications of that system may easily tend to limit its actual freedom to pursue a unilateralist policy elsewhere.

In the same way both unilateralism and balance-of-power alignment as patterns exclude *in pure form* collective security. This principle is easiest to see in the case of unilateralism and collective security. If a state has not joined a world organization nor promised to aid any state attacked, there is no incompatibility in its obligations. Switzerland, wedded to her traditional neutrality, has refused membership in the UN precisely because to honor her obligations to aid in the enforcement of collective security would be incompatible with her neutral status.

Where a state has alliances with other states and has joined a League or United Nations dedicated to collective security action, a similar incompatibility is potential. The potental incompatibility has thus far been little realized in complications in actual cases, because neither the League nor the United Nations has placed a thoroughgoing collective security scheme into operation directly against an aggressor having allies among the international organization's membership. Constitutional loopholes under the League and the veto in the United Nations have also served to limit the theoretical obligations of collective security incumbent upon the members to greatly diminished proportions. Even so, Russia was placed in an awkward situation by North Korea's assault on South Korea in 1950, just as was the United States by Britain and France's war on Egypt in 1956.

So-called "regional arrangements" such as NATO, the Rio Pact system (covering Latin America and the United States), the Russian–East European alliance system, and the Arab League, although permitted by the UN Charter under Articles 51, 52, and 53, and although theoretically subordinate to the UN and even available to the UN for regional enforcement action, actually may come to serve purposes directly opposed to those professed by the general international organization. The claim of all these groupings that they are purely defensive is no guarantee against incompatibility, since aggression remains such an ambiguous and uncertain term in international relations.

Ultimately any alliance less inclusive than the membership of the UN is potentially incompatible with the moral obligations of UN membership. The universal claims of all regional pacts to be compatible with the spirit of the obligations of the UN Charter are valid only so long as the pact members, where they become involved in armed struggle, are in every sense the innocent victims of aggression.

Few Afro-Asian members of the UN are involved in alliances. These "neutralist" states are nominally not following a unilateralist policy since their UN membership in theory at least commits them to collective security. Most do not face any potential conflicting obligations if the UN decides on enforcement action. But it is also obvious that they have little desire to see this happen. The question in their case is whether they could or would discharge their collective obligation. Their characteristic behavior is as a "third force," constituting a sort of group neutrality in any East-West dispute. To cope with any non-colonial issue, their instinct is to attempt group mediation. Their real purpose in joining the UN is to gain a voice in an important diplomatic forum.

3 World Government and World Conquest: Preliminary Observations

ALL five patterns of power represent arrangements to deal with power in the hands of potential enemies. The first three, discussed above, attempt to cope with power under circumstances where power continues to be scattered into the hands of many sovereign units (i.e., the multistate system now in existence). The fourth and fifth patterns, so far barely mentioned, would cope with the power problem of the multistate system by doing away with the source of the power threat—the many separate sovereign states—replacing them with a world state either compulsorily formed or voluntarily created.

If such a world state should come into existence, irrespective of whether it were the product of coercion or of choice, it could not and would not eliminate power problems in the world, but it would end them in their present (i.e., externalized) multistate form. Since power, as we have seen, is implicit in any political organization of men possessing material resources, regardless of whether such potential power has at the moment been converted into actual or military power, any political unit created by men, even if it is worldwide, will still continue to encounter power problems.

The practical significance of this observation is that, even within a voluntary world government, problems of power would continue to pose important questions. The problem would become internalized, but the problem itself would continue to exist. The ever-present possibility of international war would be replaced by an ever-present possibility of civil war. Yet, as we shall see later in this chapter, advocates of world government have often discussed their goal as though its very consummation would end the troublesome impact of power problems on the affairs of mankind. Even a successful world conqueror would continue to face internalized power problems.

Turning to "world conquest" proper, we must begin by recognizing that world conquest in the literal sense has never occurred. It has been approached —in ancient days, for example, by Alexander the Great and Kublai Khan, not to mention the Roman Empire. In modern times, Napoleonic and, even more, the Hitlerian and Nipponese conquests, if not checked, might have developed into world empires, although these, too, failed in the end to achieve such a result. In our own day, the fear has existed that the giant Communist powers may set out to conquer the world by force.

If a power, embarked upon conquest, succeeds in destroying its major greatpower adversaries, whether or not it exercises direct control in all the areas of the world is not so important as the fact that from its position of dominance it can overwhelm any further opposition in time. If Germany and Japan in World War II had held on to the territories they conquered and had brought Britain to her knees before American aid had been effective, they would together have exercised mastery over such a great percentage of the world's material resources that in time they might well have been able to invade and conquer the Americas. If the two conquerors had preserved unity through this point, it is conceivable that an ultimate struggle between the two of them might have ended with one power dominant over the entire world.

From an analytical point of view the ultimate intentions of the successful conqueror are immaterial. Whether or not he *intends* the conquest of the entire world, the successful conquest of large areas embracing former sovereign units means that the security of all other states is in deadly jeopardy. Unless the still existing opposition is able to combine and ultimately defeat the conqueror, they, too, in time will pass into his orbit of control. They will be so outclassed in power that there will be no solution to their power problem. At that point the multistate system would have passed away in the form in which it has existed through recent centuries.

To accomplish world conquest, however, or to attain a hegemonic position short of it in the fashion just described, the conqueror must work toward that position within the three patterns of power possible in the multistate system that exists at the outset of his conquests. Collective security is obviously not suited to his needs (although it may fit those of the coalition formed against him). The would-be conqueror must proceed either unilaterally or in concert with alliance partners. Since the power opposition to be overcome is formidable, he will choose if possible to accomplish his aims with allies, using them as tools and subordinating them later, when he is triumphant, to a lesser position. In this way Hitler used Mussolini to destroy the potential Anglo-French-Italian bloc in the West, and later reduced him to the status of a lackey, and Italy's troops to the status of expendable cannon fodder. In this way Hitler obtained Russia's aid in the despoilment of Poland in 1939, and by the same token destroyed all chance of an effective coalition against him for the time being. Napoleon in 1807, by his arrangements with Tsar Alexander of Russia, had put the same principle into effect.

Since conquerors thus may enter into balance-of-power alliances in order to alter the power *status quo* ("overthrow the balance"), while other states may make alliances to maintain it, the balance-of-power pattern can be followed by states with very diverse ends in mind. To this highly significant point we shall revert again in later chapters.

With these preliminary observations in mind we shall turn to a more detailed analysis, together with case studies, of the patterns of power in operation. Since a study of the pattern of world conquest necessarily involves an understanding of the operations of the balance of power, we shall explore them together. In the remainder of this chapter we shall consider *unilateralism* and *world government* in detail, and in the following chapters, the balance of power and collective security.

4 *The Pattern of Unilateralism*

IN early modern times unilateralism was more practiced and more successful. Before the world shrank under the impact of a technological revolution that has made each nation more militarily accessible to others, it was feasible for states to refrain from alliances and alignments, often for long periods of time. Even where alliances were entered into, marking the temporary abandonment of unilateralism, they tended to be for short periods of time, and alliance might follow alliance, interspersed with or preceded or followed by periods of aloofness from entanglements. The idea of a fifty-year treaty was a radical and theoretical concept in the nineteenth century; in the eighteenth and seventeenth it would have been even more so. Yet in the twentieth century fifty-year treaties appeared with increasing frequency in the proposals of statesmen. The first important multilateral alliance covering such a period —the Western Union of Belgium, the Netherlands, Luxembourg, Great Britain, and France, of March 17, 1948—entered into force on August 25, 1948.

In the seventeenth and eighteenth centuries, alliances were most characteristically made for a war either imminent or already in progress. Even during the course of a war the alliance might be terminated or alliance partners switched. By the nineteenth century, as can be seen in such treaties as the Quadruple Alliance of 1815 of Prussia, Austria, Russia, and Britain, a twenty-year treaty to extend beyond the war and through a peacetime era had made its appearance. In the latter half of the nineteenth and early twentieth centuries, treaties covering a period of years were sometimes repeatedly renewed, as was the case with the Triple Alliance of Germany, Austria-Hungary, and Italy. Originally signed in 1882, it was renewed in 1887, 1891, 1902, and 1912, and was in effect when World War I broke out—a period of thirty-two years. In the aftermath of World War II we find treaties such as the NATO pact which, denounceable on one year's notice after a twenty-year period, early built up an organizational structure designed to be semi-permanent. Insofar as the Soviet Union is able to see to it, the same can be said of the Soviet alliance system.

In the next chapter we shall explore further the results of these changes in alliance patterns. At the moment we are more concerned with the reverse point: in earlier times alliances were for shorter periods and had more of a temporary emergency character than today. Unilateralism was more universally practiced; it was resorted to much oftener and for longer periods of time than has become customary (especially for great powers) in the last hundred years.

Even with the vast technological advances in warfare made in the last twenty years, certain wars still remain relatively unlikely because of the formidable natural obstacles involved. As examples under present conditions we can cite a war fought by the United States in Tibet or an overland war by China in central India. Other wars are today ruled out by a lack of physical facilities presently in the hands of the nations involved, as, for instance, a war fought by the Soviet Union on the American mainland or a full-fledged war fought by Britain on the Chinese mainland. Before modern developments and the revolution in communication and transportation that they brought in their wake, natural obstacles and physical facilities together limited the number of feasible wars.

States that were blessed with a degree of natural isolation were especially able to capitalize upon this situation. Japan for centuries isolated herself from virtually all intercourse with the rest of the world—a period brought to an end with Perry's visit in 1853. His warships and their advanced technological design were properly assessed by the Japanese: they meant that a policy of seclusion could no longer suffice. Modern means of defense had to be acquired. Even so Japan did not abandon a unilateralist policy until the Anglo-Japanese Alliance of 1902. China could also fairly well afford to ignore the outside world over a period of centuries. Tenuously connected with Western Asia only by long and arduous caravan routes, in a time when Japan was in self-imposed isolation and the sea powers unable (because of technological limitations) to bring great forces to bear even upon the coast, the Chinese government was able to pursue this pattern. Not until the central government had become weak and decayed did the Western powers begin imperialism in China. The British victories in the Opium Wars between 1839 and 1860 demonstrated more the military inertia and internal and governmental weaknesses of China than British ability to wage war on a formidable scale far from home. It is highly questionable whether the British, even with command of the seas, could have fought so successfully such relatively large-scale wars (for the time) as the American Revolutionary War and the campaigns in India in the eighteenth century without substantial assistance from the Loyalists in America and the native princes and native troops in India. Against a strong China they would have made little progress. The crucial surrender of General Cornwallis to Washington at Yorktown in 1781, which involved only seven thousand British troops, is an eloquent commentary on the technological limitations of that day.

Britain herself has not been successfully invaded since William the Conqueror's time in 1066. Twenty miles of English Channel proved a formidable barrier even to Nazi Germany with most of a continent prostrate under her feet. It proved even more insurmountable in the nineteenth century, when the airplane was still in the future and Britain took good care to have a great navy. While it is true that no general war occurred in the period from 1815 to 1914 into which Britain would surely have been drawn, it is still remarkable that Britain during most of these hundred years was able to hold aloof from alliances and alignments, and pursue a unilateralist policy self-described as "splendid isolation." After the treaty of 1815, not until 1902 (in Asia) and 1904 (in Europe) did Britain enter into alliances and alignments other than on a temporary basis.

The United States, with three thousand miles of ocean on one side and something like twice that on the other, and with no formidable neighbors, was able to exist between 1815 and 1917 without fighting a non-American power (except Spain) [2] and without consummating a single alliance. For more than a hundred years unilateralism was the steadfast and accepted policy of the United States, and it was both feasible and practical.

States on the peripheral peninsulas of Europe, situated away from the great strategic crossroads, were able to follow a policy of unilateralism during the same period even when unprotected by great navies. Sweden remained neutral in both world wars and still maintains that policy today. Norway, which followed a similar policy in World War I and before, has, after her experience of being invaded in World War II, become a member of NATO.

5 *Unilateralism and the Balance of Power*

IN the examples of unilateralism so far given, natural isolation under the existing historical-technological conditions was initially the predominant factor in their success. Nineteenth-century technological advances altered these conditions. A number of events between 1898 and 1904 reflected the great changes that had occurred. They were all signs that the world had shrunk. Japan formed an alliance with Britain; China was the scene of punitive expeditions in retaliation for the Boxer anti-foreigner uprising (while Manchuria was simultaneously occupied by a hundred thousand Russian troops); the United States fought a war with a European power (Spain) and acquired Far Eastern territories which thenceforth made isolation from the mainstream of international politics impossible; and Britain fought the Boer War in South Africa under the threat of a joint European intervention which, while it did not eventuate, convinced the British it was time to conclude an alliance with the Japanese and an entente with the French. By approximately 1900 a unilateralist policy, made possible predominantly by virtue of natural factors, was a luxury limited to very few states.

The events just recounted at the turn of the century, so far as technological factors were concerned, might have occurred even earlier. Any time after the beginning of the American Civil War the technological stage was set for the end of natural isolation for most states. What delayed its coming was the astounding stability of the balance-of-power mechanism in Europe until rigidity set in at the close of the century. Even after the protection of natural factors had actually disappeared, unilateralism continued to be feasible for most of these states (with the notable exception of China), until increasing tension and a growing rigidity in the balance-of-power mechanism began to nullify its war-restraining influence—a process which, properly speaking, began in 1890, but whose full effects were only appearing a decade and even more later.

---

[2] And even the Spanish-American War came about because of Spanish colonial possessions in the Americas.

Unilateralism is, of course, most feasible when the world is substantially at peace. Once war flares up, it is very much harder to refrain from taking sides. Because of the relatively primitive state of technology prior to the American Civil War, there had been no world wars on the scale of the great wars of 1914–1918 and 1939–1945, which drew the world literally into a holocaust and drenched tropical coral rock and snow-covered plains alike in blood. The fighting in the Napoleonic Wars and in the wars of the eighteenth century was not confined to the European continent; but the campaigns in America and India were semi-divorced wars in themselves, and the scale of the fighting was entirely different from that of World Wars I and II.

In the period between 1815 and 1914 when there was no general war, a state in the middle of Europe and astride major lines of communication—Switzerland—was able to escape involvement in war and pursue a unilateralist policy. Switzerland, it is true, is to some extent protected from invasion by natural barriers. The configuration of the Alps makes invasion from Italy extremely difficult. Nor would it be an easy matter for France to sweep in from the west, for the Jura range meets the Alps in the vicinity of Geneva and leaves only the extremely small gap of the Rhone Valley. But to the north and east the long Lake Constance is a relatively inviting path of invasion. Moreover, it forms part of the Swiss-German border, and since the Germans in the last hundred years have been the most likely to invade Switzerland, this lake has inescapably constituted a weak defense flank. Nevertheless, although Switzerland is a strategic prize (with its passes between Italy and Germany and between Italy and France), each of her neighbors has normally been so determined not to see her territory come under the control of others that she has been in little danger except at times when all her neighbors have been at war with one another.

When such general wars do occur, the obvious merits of unilateralism become tempered by the equally obvious perils. By refusing to enter alliances, a state obtains certain advantages and entails certain risks. Although both Sweden and Switzerland, holding fast to their roles as permanently neutral states, escaped involvement in both world wars, the escape in the second war was very narrow. They were spared bloodshed, destruction, and a depreciated currency, but if they had lost their security gamble, they would have been crushed at a time convenient for the aggressor when no other state could or would go to their aid. Had Hitler's thrust through France in June 1940 been blunted, Germany was poised to push through Switzerland to attack France on the flank. A German army of three hundred thousand stood massed below Munich waiting for the word. Against this use of their country as a highway for invasion, the Swiss could not have countered effectively. Their plans called for harassing the German flank from a fortified position in the heart of the Swiss Alps. Nor by that late date could the French have been any aid—it would have been over far too soon. The Belgians retained faith in neutrality, although they were without any natural barriers, in spite of their World-War-I experience. They denounced their alliance with France in 1936 in the hope of escaping embroilment in a new war. When they appealed for help as the Nazi hordes crossed the frontier in 1940, it was much too late. The off-balance position of the Allies, who hurriedly advanced into Belgium in an attempt to aid, led only to Dunkirk, British evacuation of the continent, and the prolongation of the war.

American neutrality in the first years of World War II, while it spared the United States for a time, ultimately cost dearly. If the United States had not abandoned true neutrality long before entering the war, given Britain arms and destroyers out of its own reserves, convoyed Allied shipping, and fired on sight on Axis submarines—all while technically at peace—Britain might not have survived at all. In such a case, America would have been in deadly peril.

6 The Decline of Unilateralism

UNILATERALISM as a pattern of power in modern times has been decreasing in use. Natural barriers have tended to disappear and lose their effectiveness in the wake of technological advance. The failure of the balance of power to prevent two world wars has compounded the trend. Since the feasibility of unilateralism as neutrality depends so largely upon the continuance of the balance, the increase in world wars has made unilateralism both less feasible and less practical.

Three other factors that have contributed to the decline of unilateralism must be mentioned. One is the result of the same technological progress that has weakened the protective quality of natural barriers. As war has become increasingly mechanized, the basis for war power has similarly become increasingly industrial. Yet since no nation is truly self-sufficient, and especially not during a war when goods and materials are consumed at rates that stagger the imagination, each must endeavor to strengthen itself by imports from other states. Among these imports it is now almost impossible (and was already so by World War I) to distinguish between neutral goods and contraband of war. There is virtually nothing that can be imported which cannot in some measure contribute to the waging of modern war. This has led quite naturally to a blurring-over of the traditional distinctions that once made it possible for international trade to continue during warfare to the profit of neutrals. Even during a relatively limited war, such as that which broke out in Korea in 1950, all sorts of pressures are brought to bear by the belligerents upon neutrals to refrain from giving aid to the enemy. Once a state was considered neutral if it was willing to sell to both sides; now it is becoming more and more the rule that trade with belligerents is *ipso facto* considered as verging upon, if not actually constituting, an unneutral act. Especially is this so when there are many belligerents and the war is world-wide, or the limited war is fought by the United Nations as an international coalition against an aggressor. In the middle of the twentieth century more and more wars fitted into one of these two categories.

This brings us to our second factor. The very emergence of the concept of universal collective security, and its operations (however imperfect), have tended to undermine and destroy the older ideas of unilateralism in the form of neutrality. Before the creation of the League an important and detailed portion of international law was devoted to the rights and duties of neutral states in time of war. To the extent that the League became universal in its membership, and the United Nations becomes so, it is questionable whether these laws are not becoming obsolete. This may be either a good or a bad thing, but it is undoubtedly an inseparable result of post-1918 world organization. It has been forcibly argued by some [3] that collective security represents a *backward* step precisely because, insofar as it is effective in drawing in nations who would otherwise be neutral, it tends to convert any limited war into a general conflict. Backward step or not, it has undeniably occurred, and the process is still continuing.

The third factor that has led to the decline of unilateralism is the increasing duration, inclusiveness, and semi-permanence of modern alliances referred to earlier in this chapter. Taking these three factors together, and adding to them the advance of military technology and the relative instability of the twentieth-century balance of power, it is undeniable that unilateralism in our age has declined as a pattern of power actually adopted by states to resolve the perennial problems of power. States have turned instead to alliances (especially in the form of "regional arrangements"), or have sought security in the halls of the United Nations. It is here that the (perhaps excusable) double standard of the newer nations is most obvious, for they come not to protect but to be protected.

7 The Pattern of World Government

OF all the patterns of power, that of world government is distinguished by being the sole pattern to remain completely theoretical and untried in practice. Perhaps this is not surprising in view of its fundamentally revolutionary character. If it came to pass, it would mean the end of the world as we have known it—whether into something better or worse is in dispute.

Even at the height of public interest in the proposal there was almost no prospect that it would come to pass. Public opinion polls indicated that those in the United States who favored a world government were also decidedly in favor of arrangements that would either ensure United States predominance in the world state or else the retention by the United States of sufficient armed power in one way or another to ensure American security. While contradictory, this dual view was not surprising; and while natural, it was not appealing to other states.

But even if world government has never approached very near to realization, it deserves examination, not only because it is a possible solution to the problem and could some day conceivably come to pass, but also because the

---

[3] See, for example, Edwin Borchard, "The Impracticability of 'Enforcing' Peace," *The Yale Law Journal*, Vol. 55 (August 1946), pp. 966–973.

arguments involved, pro and con, reveal a great deal about international relations and about public attitudes toward international relations.

The basic appeal of the idea of world government, as well as its greatest weakness, lies in its very comprehensiveness. If implemented on a thoroughgoing scale, it would at one stroke resolve the problems of international relations. It would do so by eliminating *inter*national relations. There would be no sovereign states and therefore no quarrels among them. All power would be concentrated in one sovereign entity.

As a matter of historical fact the world has never known this type of sudden, thoroughgoing, and revolutionary alteration of the *status quo*. Changes have occurred in profusion, many of them sudden, some of them thoroughgoing, and an occasional one of them revolutionary, but none of them has ever remade the entire world into something profoundly different between one day and the next—or one year and the next—or even one decade and the next. With a true world government, either it would exist or it would not. A quasi-world government, a world government less than universal, is fundamentally a contradiction in terms.

Not all who have supported the general idea of world government would agree to this observation. On the question of timing, on the rate at which transformation must be brought about, and the degree of initial inclusiveness —all states or only some—a division of opinion occurred. The "Atlantic Union" idea built its plan upon a core of Western democracies.[4] The "World Federalists" recommended a gradual strengthening of the United Nations, seeing in it at least a potential embryo world government. These groups might be called evolutionary world-government advocates. They were content with a gradual development toward world government.

The others, who might be termed revolutionary world-government advocates,[5] were convinced of the impossibility of proceeding by halves. Emery Reves in his *Anatomy of Peace*, a book of wide influence in the middle 1940's, argued persuasively that Russia and America, together with the others, must join together in the federation at the outset. Many taking this position considered that the creation of two world governments, one with Russia and one with America, rather than one with both, would set the stage for an inevitable third world war. And to wait, in this view, for an international organization gradually to become strong enough to serve as the core of a world government would be to risk losing the main chance. This revolutionist view was at its peak just before the end of the war, just before postwar disillusionment with Russia set in.

The evolutionists were correct in recognizing the virtual impossibility of moving in one step from the discords and conflicts of contemporary international relations into the (supposed) harmony of the world federal state, as it were, overnight. They realized, as we have seen in our earlier discussion of the

---

[4] A modification of Clarence Streit's *Union Now* proposal.

[5] The term does not, of course, imply a resort to subversive techniques or violence; it simply indicates the sweeping nature of the changes advocated.

origins and comparison of the organs of the League and UN, that the League was not so revolutionary, nor the UN such an abrupt change from the League, as many people have thought. Yet it must also be said that the revolutionists were correct in foreseeing that a partial world government of the democracies, as in the Atlantic Union plan, or of the Communist states for that matter, or even a close and semi-permanent alliance system among each of the two groups, would not lead to greater prospects for a peaceful world, whatever they might or might not contribute in the realm of national security to the states who took part. Such a development would merely set two blocs against each other, with serious effects upon the flexibility of the balance of power. Properly speaking, the Atlantic Union plan, whatever its merits, is not a world-government proposal at all. The idea that the obvious great strength of such a new unit would attract the rest of the world to unite with it ignores the operation of the balance-of-power mechanism.

Among the evolutionists the position of the World Federalists has been most moderate. Realizing that the world cannot be rushed into a single federal state, they have urged the gradual transformation of the UN to serve as the nucleus. They also have favored a federal form for the world government.

There is a major weakness in each of these two proposals. The first is that the true nature of the UN is misunderstood if one sees it basically as much more than the instrument of nation-states, dependent in every way upon them. This should be especially obvious in view of the deadlocks in the Security Council and the fact that the General Assembly can do nothing more than recommend to the members what should be done. Execution of these recommendations by the states is purely discretionary. Any revision of the Charter to give the organization greater supranational powers is highly unlikely for reasons examined earlier.

The second weakness stems from the form of the proposed world state.

The proposal that the world government should be federal in form arises out of the sound observation that the world is too diverse, culturally and politically, to fit easily into the mold of a single universal, centralized state; that despite the technological shrinking of the world, it would be extremely difficult and extremely costly in human and social values to attempt full and detailed government from a single center. But at the same time the proposal overlooks or unduly minimizes the difficulties of establishing and then retaining the federal structure if it once came into operation.

Constitutional proposals for a world federal state have been forthcoming in profusion.[6] These aim at giving certain essential powers of government into the hands of the over-all center of power and leaving on the local (i.e., nation-state) level the residue. The models that have inspired this idea of a division of powers are most often the governments of Switzerland and the United States. It is also the actual historical formation of these two federal states in the first place that provided inspiration, and convinced the world federal-

_____

[6] See, for example, the *Preliminary Draft of a World Constitution*, Chicago: University of Chicago Press, 1948.

ists [7] that the same development can be brought to pass on a world basis. Since these are the models, they are worth study.

In the case of the United States, the original thirteen colonies experimented with the Articles of Confederation (which gave them roughly what we would call a League or UN structure). Then in 1787 they created the Constitution establishing a federal state. The world federalists, who look upon this as a precedent applicable to the whole world, disregard the fact that the predominant cultural influence in all the colonies was the same; the people were basically British colonials, shaped and tempered by the environment of the New World. Their grievances against Britain were also common, and chief among them was the conviction that they were being deprived of their rights as British freemen. They were, as colonies, not actually without a common central government; but that central government was in London and beyond immediate colonial control.

The first Continental Congress came into existence because of the need to coordinate (however roughly) the common efforts of the colonies against British domination. The Articles of Confederation of 1777, which set up a confederacy to be known as "The United States of America," were inadequate to overcome diversive tendencies once the spur of a common enemy was lost; a critical choice had to be made. The Constitution produced a "more perfect Union" by establishing a single government in American hands. This bold and forward-looking step was made possible by the common history, culture, and experiences of the American people. This is not to deny the reality of state loyalty at the time of its adoption, but if it had really been stronger than "national" loyalties, there would have been no Constitution. The American Civil War showed that that Constitution was to survive and that American unity would remain a living thing.

The case of Switzerland reveals basic similarities as well as some differences. Switzerland, unlike the United States, existed for centuries as a confederation on the basis of thirteen German-speaking cantons. She became a multilingual federal state, including the French-speaking cantons in the west and the Italian-speaking area in the south, as a result of the Napoleonic Wars and the decision of the Congress of Vienna in 1815.[8] Since the world federalists have been especially impressed by the multicultural and multilingual nature of the Swiss state, it is well to bear in mind that Switzerland came to have that form because the great powers, in order to preserve the existing distribution of power in Europe and unable to agree on other solutions, wished to place the

---

[7] Using the term in the broad sense of including all those who advocate world federalism, whether "World Federalists" or not.

[8] The Swiss Confederation of thirteen German-speaking cantons became independent of the Holy Roman Empire at the Peace of Westphalia (1648). It remained so until its subjugation by France in 1798, when it became the Helvetic Republic. In 1803, in the Act of Mediation, Napoleon added six new cantons, chiefly French- and Italian-speaking. In 1815 three French-speaking cantons were added, completing Switzerland's evolution into a multilingual state.

strategic crossroads, which Switzerland represents, beyond the boundaries of all of them. In other words, multilingual Switzerland was the product of great power rivalries rather than the result of "natural," centralizing forces.[9]

Switzerland, too, has had its civil war. In the War of the Sonderbund in 1847 the federation prevailed against the diversive forces inspired by a conflict over the religious question. From then on, the federal structure represented an expression of the political philosophy of the Swiss rather than an evidence of the ability of the individual cantons to defy the federal government.

These two examples show that federation, when it occurs, is likely to reflect a long historical community of interests, perhaps supplemented, as in the Swiss case, by factors from outside which, to a degree, force federation. They also show that it is not unusual within a federation to settle by force the issue of whether the units shall prevail against the whole.

These examples are not very encouraging for the advocates of world government. Federations are historically based upon already existing communities of interest and sentiment. Once established, the initial division of powers, in view of the sooner or later demonstrated superiority of force of the *federal* government, tends ultimately to depend upon the political philosophy of the people concerned. In the world of today this initial community, insofar as it exists at all, is a community of fear. It rests upon a common fear of atomic destruction. This common fear has not drawn all together but has set one bloc against another. Even if the great impediments to the creation of a world federal state were to be overcome, it is apparent from these examples that there tends sooner or later to ensue a civil struggle to test the powers of the units vis-à-vis that of the whole. Could such a struggle be avoided in a world federal state?

8 World Federation, Cultural Tensions, and the Danger of Dictatorship

WHETHER civil struggles would actually occur cannot be known. The friction implicit in bringing together alien cultures, which give rise to tensions in the world of nation-states, might be enormously intensified by the greater number of points of contact in a world federal state. The culture tensions might well increase distrust and hatred among national cultural groups far above their present level.

In the United States the "melting pot" has mellowed and obscured national origins and produced second-generation citizens who are in speech, manner, and dress "typically American," for the immigrants' children, once they find in school that their parents' ways are "foreign," cast them off. So the United States federation proved workable, even with enormous immigration.

---

[9] It is true that before 1798 the nine non-German-speaking cantons had been allied to, protected by, or subjected to the Swiss Confederation. But this relationship is hardly an encouragement to world government advocates.

From many, as the American motto proudly proclaims, one—and it is no idle boast. In Canada and Switzerland, both also federal states, cultural blocs distinct from each other, and geographically separate rather than intermingled and absorbed into the dominant culture, have remained and have posed the kind of problem that would be much more typical of that of a world federal state. In both these states two or three cultural groups have, out of necessity and especially under the pressure of outside forces, created a common nationhood while retaining the cultural diversity indicated, for example, by the two or more languages that continue to be spoken. In both these states it is fair to say that the arrangement has historically produced considerably more tension than the "melting pot" technique of the United States. In Switzerland, World War I brought a very severe strain, for the sympathies of the French-speaking and German-speaking groups were completely and violently opposed. Because Nazi excesses alienated the latter group in World War II, the strain was not as bad between 1939 and 1945. In Canada, because of the French-speaking bloc's opposition, conscription was at first permitted only for troops who were to be stationed in Canada for strictly Canadian defense. Because of the great width of the ocean and the many centuries of geographical and political isolation of these French-speaking groups, their differences with the English-speaking bloc took the form of isolationism. They did not feel a great tie to France, and they retained very few of the sentimental ties of the English-speaking Canadians to the Crown. Pressures from French-speaking Quebec Province were a leading factor in the controversy in 1963–1964, which led to the adoption of a new "Maple Leaf" Canadian flag devoid of British symbolism.

Cultural tensions in the United States have, of course, existed in the form of hostility toward "foreigners" (i.e., immigrants), but racial tensions (white vs. black and white vs. yellow) and the cultural dissimilarity of the North and South prior to the Civil War were far more important and far-reaching. This comparison between Switzerland and Canada on the one hand, and the United States on the other, is not meant to show the superiority of either in the practice of toleration. It does indicate that a grouping of diverse cultures is at best less desirable, from the standpoint of tensions inescapably involved, than a mingling. It is exactly at the point where mingling was not socially feasible —the racial groupings in the United States—that tension has been greatest.

A world federal state would have to use the method of grouping rather than mingling cultures as its major device. Immigrants to the United States were absorbed into the way of life prevailing there because, no matter how large their numbers, they were always a minority within, at any given time, a majority—and they were, in culture and race, assimilable. A world federation today, even were free migration permitted and encouraged, would take a millennium to produce a single world culture. Yet many persons who have advocated a world federal state have done so precisely on the grounds that in this way cultural diversity could be maintained while at the same time avoiding the recurrent scourge of war.

It is often said that closer cultural contacts enrich each of the participants, giving them an understanding of each other. In a sense this is true. But where opposing values are discovered in such contacts, the result may be grave discord. Where two distinct cultures remain there is always more room for tension than where there is but one. The American Civil War came about, in large part, because two geographically distinct cultures had emerged in the United States by the middle of the nineteenth century—one based upon slavery, the other not. The more each understood the nature of the other's culture, the less tolerant of it each became. Inasmuch as a world federal state would, for centuries (if it endured), persist without the elimination of diverse cultures, but with their enforced closer contact, the increased tensions might well spill over into civil wars.

From the standpoint of possibly increased culture tension, causes for wars might be more easily found in a world federal state than they are even within the existing multistate system. How feasible such wars would be would depend mostly upon the arrangements made in such a world state for the armed forces.

A number of possible constitutional arrangements for a world federal state are conceivable. Without denying the importance of such an instrument to the peaceful and useful functioning of the federation, the major danger in such a state would not stem from the constitution but from those who might successfully set it aside by trickery or by force.

In the present nation-state system, the great majority of states at any one time are "peace-loving;" the aggressors are relatively few. The sovereign power of decision in the hands of a would-be aggressor nation facilitates resort to war, but such a decision taken in itself would not mean war without the backing of the population involved. A people bent upon war, who also are a nation, are sovereign, and possess a state, can proceed to go to war in a more orderly and efficient manner. But any large group of people, even less than a nation, even without sovereignty, even without control of a state, can go to war if it desires war strongly enough. Such "civil" wars would therefore remain possible within a world federal state.

From a mechanical standpoint, attempts to avoid this danger would logically have to be through concentration of armed force into one world army. A world federation in which present national armies continued to exist would be a contradiction in terms. It would vitiate the very appeal of the idea. If everyone has arms, all can use them; if no one has arms, everyone can still fight with bare hands. The proposed solution consequently looks toward a world federal army exercising a monopoly of armed power. In such a proposal lurk grave dangers.

Coups d'état within nation-states seek control of the armed forces as the first and most vital concern. Where part of the army is "reliable" (i.e., friendly to the cause of the coup) and part not, the technique is if possible to surprise and disarm the unfriendly forces. Failing that, the issue may have to be fought out or the coup abandoned. Instances of this technique exist by the hundreds. One illustration is the coup in Egypt early in 1954 when General Naguib was ousted by Colonel Nasser, only to be reinstated when the cavalry continued to support him. Later, when the balance of forces changed, he was again ousted. In the abortive Communist coup in Indonesia in 1965, the first attention was given to killing anti-Communist generals. In the Middle East and in Latin America further illustrations occur with frequency.

In a world state the temptations to the power-hungry, or to idealists longing for an end to the tensions forecast in the preceding pages, might well be irresistible. To gain control of the world for "good" or for "evil," one would have to gain control of the army. If this could not be done by deceit and trickery, one part of the army might well fight the other. If one group were to make themselves secure over the rest by trickery, or if at the end of a bloody civil conflict one part obtained victory over the other, the stage would be set for dictatorship on a world scale. If the dictator actually once obtained a virtual monopoly over weapons of mass destruction ranging from machine guns and tanks to nuclear weapons, the prospects for future successful revolts might be very dim. The possibility is by no means remote that a world federal state might eventually be converted into a world dictatorship which, if it survived dissensions among the inner ruling group, could successfully suppress periodic "civil" revolts and continue indefinitely.

9 Regional Arrangements

In the both more dangerous and more interdependent world of the twentieth century, the possible advantages of unilateralism have declined while its obvious dangers have increased. World government, even if it could be brought about, is not without its own built-in problems. Consequently, states have turned to alliances and to the UN as major solutions to their power problems.

Their efforts to achieve security arrangements on a less than universal basis has been the basic force behind the growth of regional arrangements, although other considerations, such as economic interdependence or similar cultural outlooks, have also played a part. These regional developments vary greatly in their characteristics as well as in the degree of unity of action or policy that they develop or enhance. Normally the strongest and most successful of these arrangements have represented common accord on the nature of the power problem facing each member. In these cases members tend to define their individual power problem in much the same way. So they are able to enter into an alliance as the core around which other institutional features are created. At the other end of the spectrum, where weak regional arrangements persist, the source of the weakness is the much more partial agreement on the nature of a common power problem.

The range in degree of cohesiveness in these regional arrangements is quite large. The most cohesive development so far is in Western Europe, in the "European Community," where supranational economic controls have been institutionalized by six of NATO's members. Next in cohesiveness is NATO itself. Third on the spectrum is the Organization of American States (OAS), which is built around the core of the Rio Treaty. Fourth and fifth (and difficult to assign in any clear order) come the Arab League and the Organization of African Unity (OAU). Both these organizations show a great deal of unity on certain problems but there is not sufficient agreement on the overall power problem to say that a really hard and fast alliance exists at the core. Other developments, sometimes termed "regional arrangements," include SEATO and CENTO but in both cases they represent more loose alliance groupings with few real institutional features other than holding meetings with some regularity.

The strong arrangements typically include elaborate techniques for the peaceful settlement of disputes among the members since the implication of the existence of the organization is that these nations are agreed on refraining from war with each other. In the European Community there is an actual "European Court" for the purpose of settling disputes, with very distinct powers in the economic realm over the members. In NATO the Council functions to conciliate disputes but has no legal powers. In the OAS a variety of organs function for this general purpose and the "Organ of Consultation" has met frequently as has its Council (which sits in Washington and acts as the "provisional Organ of Consultation" until the foreign ministers can assemble). By contrast, the equivalent features in the other regional arrangements are far less institutionalized.

These regional arrangements are called by that name because their membership is usually clustered in some geographical area. But the range of geographical inclusiveness varies considerably and not one of them is confined to a true geographical region. Even the European Community has "associate members," most notably in Eastern Europe and Africa. NATO extends from the United States to Turkey. The OAS covers a great part of an entire hemisphere. And the OAU has members over a vast continent with widely divergent orientations north and south of the Sahara. It is precisely because political, military, and economic problems confronting the members of these arrangements extend beyond the geographical areas involved, and because geographical propinquity does not necessarily assure a common outlook on problems, that regional arrangements vary so greatly in their effectiveness.

For this reason, while it is necessary to note the existence of regional arrangements at this point, we will wait until later chapters to examine their operations.

We turn now to the wider context of the power-security problem as it has led nations on a regional or non-regional basis to embrace alliances and follow the pattern of the balance of power.

CHAPTER 16

The Balance of Power

History shows that the danger threatening the independence of this or that nation has generally arisen, at least in part, out of the momentary predominance of a neighboring State at once militarily powerful, economically efficient, and ambitious to extend its frontiers or spread its influence. . . . The only check on the abuse of political predominance derived from such a position has always consisted in the opposition of an equally formidable rival, or of a combination of several countries forming leagues of defence. The equilibrium established by such a grouping of forces is technically known as the balance of power, and it has become almost an historical truism to identify England's secular policy with the maintenance of this balance by throwing her weight now in this scale and now in that, but ever on the side opposed to the political dictatorship of the strongest single State or group at a given time.

SIR EYRE CROWE
"Memorandum," *British Documents*
on the Outbreak of the War

T HE concept of the "balance of power" is one of the oldest in international relations. Like diplomacy, it was practiced well before it had its modern name. Thucydides was versed in the idea, although he did not use our term for it. As "balance of power," it has now been continuously discussed for more than two hundred years and, as an inevitable consequence, the term has accumulated a number of meanings, some of them mutually contradictory. The concept has also accumulated a number of arguments, some of them quite important in their implications.

I Ambiguities

THE ambiguities of the term are least evident in describing (1) actions taken or contemplated; and most marked in describing (2) the intention or goal of states taking actions (especially if a common goal is assumed for all or most of the states involved), and (3) the operational results which flow from resort to this pattern.

Actions taken under the balance of power invariably center on decisions to make alignments (alliances, and understandings of a less formal sort), to change alignments, or to hold aloof from alignments. The action is designed to affect the power equilibrium which the alignments signify, either to change it or to maintain it. So much is common ground in all discussions of the balance of power. The ambiguities appear in two respects. First, when assertions are made that the intention or goal of states, in making such alliance decisions, is to maintain the power equilibrium which actually exists, or restore it to "balance" if the equilibrium has been impaired. Such ambiguities are clustered around the presumption that the actions of these many states have an implicitly common purpose. Second, ambiguities appear when it is maintained that the operational consequences of making alliances are predictable from the fact of the alliance itself. For example, if it is argued that a stable equilibrium inevitably tends to be produced, or that rigidity and war inescapably result.

Our previous analysis of the power problem and successive schools of thought on international relations has equipped us to understand the difficulties which these kinds of assertions always involve. We have already seen that states are concerned with a solution of their own power problems (i.e., achieving national security) and that their individual approach to the organization of a power system will necessarily reflect the nature of their individual power problem. To say that a state enters an alliance (follows the pattern of the balance of power) is simply another way of saying that it institutionalizes its belief that its power problem is similar to that of its alliance partner. If several join together, it implies that they all agree on the compatibility or identity of their own vital interests with each other, agree on the essential nature of the common threat, and wish to counter the power of the rival nation or group. In this way, two or more hostile blocs may emerge, each concerned with deterring the opposing grouping from successful resort to force. Each group has a *similar* interest in restraining the other; but the *common* interest is essentially restricted to the members of one's own bloc. Each bloc forms in relation to the other, but certainly not with its approval.

It is also possible to conceive of a major power holding aloof from two blocs, ready to swing its support to whichever becomes weaker, with the intention of keeping either bloc from gaining predominance. A state attempting this role (the technical term is "balancer") would be convinced that either bloc, if unrestrained, would represent an equal power problem. Such a balancer may, if neither bloc gains a sufficient margin of power over the other to challenge, not *enter* any alliance. Technically a balancer refraining from alliances is actually following the pattern of unilateralism even though its actions may be decisive for those states following the pattern of balance of power alliances. Britain, whose "splendid isolation" from almost all alignments for nearly a hundred years after Waterloo ended with the Anglo-Japanese Alliance, played a great part in the continental balance of power during the whole period—as the headnote to this chapter indicates. To the extent that she was uncommitted to either bloc, she was in theory able to shift her weight as need arose to the weaker side to balance the stronger. She was *of* the balance but not *in* it—as is the case with every unilateralist state.

The intentions of a balancer are presumably known. There exist, too, other unilateralist states whose motivation in choosing this pattern is not immediately evident (except that they believe their choice best enhances their security) who also affect the equilibrium of the balance of power. A state may remain aloof from alliances because it is relatively indifferent to whatever blocs emerge, or because it feels powerless to influence the actions of such blocs, or because it is determined to have the decisive influence over such blocs. We would have to weigh any policy pronouncements and then observe the actual behavior of a unilateralist state before concluding which she is doing. Similarly, we can conclude that a state making an alliance considers its power problem substantially common to its alliance partners but we cannot deduce from the mere choice of pattern how it will attempt operationally to manipulate the resulting power relationships. We cannot know from the fact that the alliance exists, whether any bloc will maneuver for predominance or rest content with simple deterrence. And we cannot know from what has so far been said, whether they will both be content with mere deterrence. They may or may not.

To be even more precise, we can observe the choice of pattern made and feel confident that it reflects an organizational reaction to a power problem. But the choice of pattern does not per se reveal, except in a very general sense, the nature of the operational maneuvers which will ensue. The goal of each state is security, but we still know almost nothing of what they intend to do about it beyond the mere fact of their organizational choice, unless it is to be argued that the bare choice of pattern in and of itself produces a certain foreordained result, irrespective of initial motivation.

Contrary to the above, traditional definitions of the balance of power have often asserted that the balance is a system in which either (1) the participants have the common purpose of achieving a stable power relationship and restraining aggression, or (2) that in any event it works out that way operationally as pressures are equalized by natural counter-pressures. Thus Vattel, an eminent authority on international law in the eighteenth century, defined the "famous scheme of the political equilibrium or balance of power; by which is understood such a disposition of things as no power is able absolutely to predominate, or to prescribe laws to others." [1] Talleyrand, who in his time had helped as a diplomat to make Napoleon and France dominant on the continent of Europe, spoke of the balance as:

A combination of the rights, interests, and the relations of the Powers among themselves, by which Europe seeks to obtain—

First, that the rights and possessions of a Power shall not be attacked by one or several other Powers;

Secondly, that one or several other Powers shall never attain to domination over Europe;

Thirdly, that the combination adopted shall render a rupture of the established order and of the tranquility of Europe difficult or impossible.[2]

---

[1] *The Law of Nations,* Book 3, Chapter 3, Philadelphia, 1829, p. 378.

[2] *The Correspondence of Prince Talleyrand and King Louis XVIII during the Congress of Vienna,* New York, 1881, pp. xv–xvi.

In the twentieth century Quincy Wright has called the balance of power "a system designed to maintain a continuous conviction in every state that, if it attempted aggression, it would encounter an invincible combination of the others." [3]

It is true that no state that participates in such an alliance grouping does intend to be "dominated" (Vattel and Talleyrand's term) or aggressed upon (as Wright expresses it) if it can help it, even if it is itself planning aggression on others. It is also true that one alliance bloc tends to call into existence a second grouping designed to frustrate the ambitions of the first, and that this second group tends to grow by the accession of formerly uncommitted states to the extent that the first group is not truly checked and appears on the brink of successful, thoroughgoing conquest. These alignments are characteristic of the actual workings of the balance in its advanced or later stages.

But to say, with Talleyrand, that "*Europe* seeks" through the balance to see "that the rights and possessions of a Power shall not be attacked by one or several other Powers" is to give an extremely limited definition of what is involved, and, moreover, is to invent a fictitious third party with fictitious interests. It is inexact and misleading because, properly speaking, the balance of power is just as much a method whereby aggressive states act to commit aggression upon their enemies. The balance of power is the product of rival alliance blocs and their relative strength in terms of one another. It is only to the potential aggressees that it is an arrangement for the frustration of aggression. It would be most nearly exact to say that the alliances of any one bloc are designed to see that their own aims are implemented and their own interests safeguarded, and that because other groups who oppose these aims and interests may come into existence, the one group may be checked by the other as a result. To the extent that this process operates effectively, as Vattel and Wright point out, a balance of opposing forces results and the *de facto* distribution of power tends to remain unchanged. But does such a result automatically ensue?

The balance of power is not a "system" in the sense that the states involved necessarily have the common end in mind of preserving the independence of the rival participants, but only in the sense that, since the creation of one power grouping tends to beget another, it is relatively rare to find the one long existing without the other, and a network of alliances (or system) results.

Further, the balance of power, insofar as a "balance" is created between the opposing blocs, is almost entirely an accidental by-product of the existence of two alliance groupings, each formed to counter the power and ambitions of the other. Neither group is particularly interested in "balancing" the other as such, but each is determined to counter the other. This can best be done by mustering a little more power than that of the opposing group. Since power is difficult to estimate, and since mistakes in underestimating potential or actual enemies may be extremely serious, it is almost inevitable that this effort to have a little more power turns into an effort to have a lot more. This urge is common to both sides. On each side there will be a steady concern with the

[3] Quincy Wright, A *Study of War*, Vol. I, p. 254.

interests of the member states, as the group participates in international relations; on neither side will there be concern to establish a balance other than in the negative sense that neither will wish to remain clearly inferior in power to the other. From this contest equilibrium may or may not result.

This observable tendency of each bloc to overbalance, and the equally observable fact that would-be aggressors resort to the balance in order to destroy it, disposes of any validity in the assumption of a common purpose or motivation for all participants. It does not finally dispose of the argument that equilibrium and therefore peace will ensue because each pressure will be met by an equal counter-pressure. The only way to decide this point is to examine case histories (which we shall do in Chapters 18 and 19). The case in logic is equally good either way.

Twentieth century critics of the balance of power concept have argued against it on the grounds that it not only fails to maintain peace but actually brings on war. Woodrow Wilson in 1917 said: "There must be, not a balance of power, but a community of power." He castigated "entangling alliances," as we saw earlier, because he was convinced that they drew nations "into competition of power" and produced "a net of intrigue and selfish rivalry" which ended in war. Alliances brought not peace, but a sword.

But even if the existence of a balance of power actually made war more likely, it does not mean that states will reject it as a pattern. They form the alliances in any event for the ultimate purpose of having pooled power if war comes. States do not dissolve alliances, even where the agreed purpose is simple deterrence, once war comes; they utilize them as operational vehicles for waging war in common. Even if states believed alliances caused wars they would still choose to make them unless they also believed that a more suitable solution of their power problems was to be found in resorting to a different pattern of power. It may be argued that in contemporary times the balance of power, like national sovereignty, is obsolete (and this may or may not be true); but it cannot be argued that it does not actually exist so long as alliances continue to be made.

We are now able to sum up. The essential confusion about the balance of power does not arise out of the pattern as such: the making of alliances. It arises out of arguments over why nations make alliances and what operational consequences follow from their existence, about the *process* which utilization of this pattern produces. Since the term "balance of power" is often used indiscriminately for both pattern and process, ambiguities are bound to appear.

To speak of the balance process is ultimately to view the patterns of power from a particular perspective. Earlier (Chapters 1 and 15) we defined the patterns of power as representing alternatives for organizing a *power system*. We used power system to mean the net or total power relations of all states brought about as the result of the separate power pattern choices of individual states and the resulting interaction. Any power system, whatever its "mix" of patterns, can be diagramed to show the power-organization choices made. A pure system might consist solely of states choosing unilateralism, or relying exclusively on collective security, or depending upon alliances for security. But mixed systems, in which some resort to each pattern occurs, is normally the case. If mixed systems are adopted, then we will have to see how each affects the other. Each such system can also be thought of as a process (i.e., be considered from the point of view of the effects of the mixture on any particular pattern). So if alliances exist on any consequential scale, we are warranted in examining the balance of power process. From this special perspective we note the effects of unilateralist or collective security choices on the alliances which are the hard core of the process. It is similarly possible to focus attention on the collective security process and include any distractive or disruptive effects on such arrangements stemming from alliances. In short, "power system" is a term taking account of all pattern choices, while "balance of power process" is a term for analyzing alliance-centered effects and "balance of power pattern" means simply the making of alignments (i.e., alliances and understandings). While the making of a particular alignment will have a purpose, the balance of power as a process can have no over-all purpose: it is merely a net effect. The variety of behavior, and consequences from such behavior, can be examined in "models" abstracted from case studies.

When we say that between even two states roughly equal in power there will be a certain balance and counterbalance, although rigid, we are discussing the balance of power as a process. We are referring to their rival power relationship rather than to an alliance which links them together on the same side. With three or more states the possibilities become more varied, and the power structure more flexible. There is more opportunity for shifting and re-grouping; there is greater room for adjustments in the strength of rival blocs. This very flexibility may save the balance for long periods of time from disintegrating into war. Even when war comes, the balancing process is not at an end, but, unless the end of the war leaves the prewar basic power of the opposing blocs unchanged—a relatively rare although not unknown possibility—a new balance emerges from the ashes of the war. The changed power status as a result of the decisions of the battlefield and the victory or defeat that has come to each belligerent makes for a new postwar balance. Thus we customarily reckon the duration of a general (i.e., system-wide) balance from war to war.

Since the balance periodically disintegrates into war the charge has been made, as we saw, that the pursuit of the balance causes war. It would be more accurate to say that the inept handling of a balance pattern may bring war about. But this is true of the use of other patterns as well. It is obvious at even the most casual glance that the duration of a general balance of power has varied widely in modern times. When we come to our studies of the balance of power in action, we shall be especially concerned to note the conditions under which the peace disintegrates and a new balance is wrought in the flame of war. We shall also be concerned to establish, if possible, why the length of particular balances has varied so from the maximum of one hundred years without a general war (between 1815 and 1914) to a minimum of twenty years (between 1919 and 1939). If any given general balance is doomed to ultimate disintegration in the crucible of war, it does not follow that its end could not by deliberate measures be postponed almost indefinitely. It depends upon the particular model of the balance of power process used.

2 Alliances and Understandings

THE pattern of balance-of-power alignments as a "solution" to the power problem is very ancient. The idea of a state banding together with a friendly state or states to check or restrain the ambitions of a rival state or coalition found expression as early as the treaty of 1281 B.C. between Rameses II of Egypt and Hattushilish III of the Hittites, directed against the Assyrians. By Greek times alliance systems were well developed, and the present-day annual NATO meetings had their primitive (or, at least, early) counterpart in the conferences of the Peloponnesian League in the fifth century B.C. Although in Roman times, because of the imperial supremacy, the system fell into disuse, it was quickly revived with the re-emergence of a multistate system. From Machiavelli's day to our own, many hundreds of such alliances have been made.

It is relatively clear why any given alliance or understanding is made. The North Atlantic Pact is designed to restrain Russia just as the Sino-Russian Alliance of 1950 is directed against the contingency of "attack" by the Japanese alone or by the Japanese acting in concert with America. The Nazi-Soviet Treaty of Non-Aggression of 1939 was an understanding for the purpose of making Germany's back secure while she fought in the West, and was an alliance in the limited sense and for the limited purpose of providing for the joint despoilment of Poland.

Sometimes understandings have been used in cases where formal alliances are for some reason not considered feasible. Although a degree of support is implied, the obligation is much vaguer and more ambiguous than that of an alliance. Such was the case in 1939 when the common decision to go to war by England and France was based not upon a common treaty but upon a mutual concerting of policy and a close cooperation.

Britain has often preferred to rely upon understandings concluded when the need was apparent and something had to be done. Foreign Secretary Palmerston [4] once explained this predilection in a letter to the British Ambassador in Russia:

It is not usual for England to enter into engagements with reference to cases which have not actually arisen, or which are not immediately in prospect; and this for a plain reason. All formal engagements of the Crown, which involve the questions of peace and war, must be submitted to Parliament; and Parliament might

---

[4] Palmerston held that office between 1830 and 1851, except for a break between 1841 and 1846—certainly a long tenure compared to what is usual today.

probably not approve of an engagement which should bind England prospectively to take up arms in a contingency which could not as yet be foreseen.[5]

Sometimes this predilection has led to great uncertainty over Britain's commitments (or lack of them).

Early in 1906 Sir Edward Grey, British Foreign Secretary, in view of Germany's actions, authorized conversations between French and British naval and military experts "on the distinct understanding that it left the hands of the [British] Government free whenever the crisis arose." Such conversations led in September 1912, to the signing of a British-French naval convention which provided that the French Third Battle Squadron would join the other two in the Mediterranean. The British Malta Squadron was greatly reduced, while the British forces in the North Sea were reinforced. The arrangement clearly envisaged a division of naval responsibility in the event that both found themselves at war with Germany. Sir Edward, in a letter of November 22, 1912, to French Ambassador Cambon, "clarified" these arrangements:

We have agreed that consultation between experts is not, and ought not to be, regarded as an engagement that commits either Government to action in a contingency that has not arisen and may never arise. The disposition, for instance, of the French and British fleets respectively at the present moment *is not based upon an engagement to co-operate in war*.[6]

Nevertheless it was a moral commitment. When war broke out, Grey promised two days before the British declaration of war, which came on August 4, 1914, to protect the North French coast from German bombardment. Needless to say, the French would have preferred all along a concrete treaty with clear obligations such as the one they had with Russia following 1892 which, with admirable directness, provided in Article I: "If France is attacked by Germany, or by Italy supported by Germany, Russia shall employ all her available forces in order to attack Germany." [7]

Understandings that are in effect equivalent to alliances but which lack the precise obligations of such treaties have certain conceivable advantages by way of restraining the ally from precipitous action, but they are also much more dangerous in their potentialities. They give some promise of joint action without the certainty that it will be forthcoming; as such they may fail to restrain the common potential enemy. Certainly Germany was not sure in 1914 that England intended to come in on the opposite side (although it does not follow that Germany would necessarily have acted differently anyhow). Because of this factor of uncertainty in "understandings" which may turn out to be misunderstandings, the balance-of-power *alliance* has been the preferred method for concluding alignments.

---

[5] Quoted in Harold Nicolson, *Diplomacy*, 2d ed., p. 136.

[6] Text of the letter, and the French agreement that this was so, appear in Viscount Grey of Fallodon, *Twenty-Five Years, 1892–1916*, Vol. 1, p. 95. Italics added.

[7] *Documents diplomatiques français* (1871–1914), First Series (1871–1900), Vol. 9, pp. 643 ff.

3 The Balance of Power—Basic Development and Operation

THE balance-of-power process (or effect) can be observed in operation from the lowest or local level (involving two or three states) to the grand level of the general or world balance (involving all the great powers in rival coalitions). Wherever a more or less fixed set of rival power relationships between two or more states is in existence, a core for a balance-of-power system exists, whether or not it becomes fully articulated through the apparatus of great alliance blocs. Each set of fixed or semi-fixed relationships arising out of the power problems of particular states is a local nucleus around which a general alignment system can be created. Whether a general alignment system results quickly or at all depends upon whether the multitude of individual power problems are largely reduced by the pressure of events into over-all power problems—that of bloc A in the light of bloc B's existence, and vice versa.

Local fixed relationships may endure for very long periods of time. Victor Hugo, speaking of the results of the Franco-Prussian War, correctly foresaw that Franco-German relations would be fixed for many years to come by the results of that conflict: "Henceforth there are in Europe two nations which will be formidable—the one because it is victorious, the other because it is vanquished." [8] Franco-German enmity was one set of permanent relations between 1870 and 1914 (and, of course, beyond). On the other side of Europe, between the end of the Crimean War and the outbreak of World War I, Austro-Russian rivalry and hostility over the disposition of the Balkan territories, which one by one were falling from the weak hands of the Turks, furnished another. When Sir Austen Chamberlain, in a speech in the British House of Commons on March 24, 1925, said, "All our greatest wars have been fought to prevent one great military power dominating Europe, *and at the same time dominating the coasts of the Channel* and the ports of the Low Countries," [9] he was referring to still a third.

Because the tsars of Russia found the very thought of an alliance with democratic France distasteful, because Britain hoped to keep the Channel approaches free from domination without entering alliances, because Britain and France and Britain and Russia were serious rivals in the colonial areas of the world, these three sets of fixed relations, or local balances, existed semi-independently of one another for a long period of time before the general alignments of the Triple Entente (Britain, Russia, France) and the Triple Alliance (Germany, Austria-Hungary, Italy) were evolved shortly before World War I. These fixed relationships produced some treaties of alliance such as that between Germany and Austria of 1879 (thereafter carefully renewed continuously), but they continued to be focuses of local rivalries and

---

8 Quoted from Grant and Temperley, *Europe in the Nineteenth and Twentieth Centuries, 1789–1939*, p. 354.

9 *House of Common Debates*, 5th series, Vol. 182, p. 315. Italics added.

local balances of power for many years before Europe settled down into two armed rival camps and the local rivalries were fitted into an over-all rivalry of great-power bloc versus great-power bloc. This is not to say that each set of relationships was unaffected by the existence of the others, but only that the various local relationships had not been fitted into an over-all European relationship.

Taking this period as a point of reference, we can look back to an earlier period when such fixed relationships could create local (in this case less than European) balances of power in which the alternation of war and peace in Western and Eastern Europe proceeded almost entirely independently of each other, and ahead to a later period when the general balance of power had become so world-wide that disturbances of local balances such as the attack of North Korea on South Korea in 1950 almost immediately threatened the entire world with general war.

Up to at least the Peace of Utrecht in 1713, Spain, France, Austria, and Britain in Western Europe, and Sweden, Prussia, Poland, Russia, and Austria in Eastern Europe, carried on relations with one another in local balances with hardly anything but the almost accidental connection of Austria between them. Even the great wars were not general wars in the sense of involving all these powers simultaneously. But by the time of the French Revolutionary and Napoleonic Wars, before Napoleon had passed into final exile at St. Helena, every one of these states had been drawn at one time or another into the common conflict that extended for more than twenty years. Following the Congress of Vienna in 1815, local wars and local balances of power continued to occur, as they have ever since; but thereafter in any general war involving the general balance of power, all the great powers were inevitably drawn in; and characteristically, during the last year or two of the war, all the great powers would be fighting simultaneously.

By the time of the next general war, which was World War I, the United States had attained the stature of a great power. In that conflict, in which Japan also participated, the list of belligerent great powers for the first time included non-European states. Practically since the first settlements by European states in the Americas, India, and elsewhere in various colonies, these non-European areas had served as battlegrounds for European powers as occasion and opportunity demanded. World War I consequently was not the first general war in which battles were fought all over the world, but it was the first in which powers situated *outside* of Europe played a prominent role in the disputes *of Europe in their own right*. The Spanish-American War of 1898, which extended United States territory into the Far East, the Anglo-Japanese Alliance of 1902, and President Theodore Roosevelt's active role in ending the Russo-Japanese War in 1905 and in the Algeciras (or First Moroccan) Crisis in 1906, were all harbingers of revolutionary change.

If it was possible to some extent to ignore this fundamental change in the nature of the general balance between the world wars because of America's return to unilateralism and Japan's preoccupation with her own plans in the peripheral areas of the Far East, the end of World War II made it obvious that the day when the general balance could be manipulated strictly by European powers had passed, never to return. In the immediate postwar years, the obvious predominance of the "super powers"—the United States and Russia —and the temporary weakness of all the strictly European powers, defeated and victorious alike, led to a situation where the general balance was actually in the hands of these two gigantic states, one of which lies entirely separate from the European continent, and the other of which is territorially based more on Asia than Europe. From a condition where the non-European states were pawns in a balance manipulated by European great powers, the relationship had become reversed.

The nature and duration of this spectacular change can easily be (and was) both overestimated and overstated. While it is obvious that the general balance is world-wide in nature and that the super powers play the primary role, it is easy to underestimate the importance of the other powers. Special, and in many cases transitory, circumstances had drained these great powers of much of their former strength: France, fighting year after year in Indo-China; England, confronted with a precarious economic situation; Italy, torn by a seeming inability to improve the lot of its poor and thus stabilize itself internally; Germany, divided between East and West and battered into ruins and inflation; Japan, stripped of armed forces and only beginning to rearm. All appeared weaker and were weaker in the first decade or so after World War II than they subsequently became. The great increase in French power and influence, illustrates. The enormous importance of Germany as the key to the balance of power in Europe has been amply attested to by the continuing struggle of the two super powers to attach it firmly to their respective camps. Europe, while no longer by itself the balance, remains inescapably the focus of a world-wide balance of power. Its great over-all resources, both human and material, continue to have vital and decisive importance in the ultimate outcome of any world-power struggle.

Not only have the older great powers, especially of Europe, recovered strength, but newer great powers have entered the world balance in their own right as important factors. India, completely self-governing, and China, for the first time in modern history a military power unpreoccupied by civil and foreign wars on her own soil, have assumed important roles.

Thus from an over-all point of view the general balance of power has become steadily enlarged in its geographical or territorial basis, from a less-than-European coverage in the seventeenth and eighteenth centuries to a truly world-wide coverage in the present age. Former colonial areas, once the battlegrounds of rival European imperialisms, have entered the world balance as important factors in their own right. Powers largely or entirely non-European, such as the United States and the Soviet Union, have come to play roles of first importance. For a few fleeting years the super powers *were* practically the world balance. Now, with the coming of age of other non-European great powers, and the recovery of older European great states, this role has become more limited but is still enormously important. Their initial monopoly of hydrogen weapons underlined that importance.

Side by side with the general balance through the centuries, local balances have continued to exist, now separate from, now forming the core for, and now subordinated into the general balance. Swallowed up within the larger general balance, they re-emerge after a war or when the danger of a war recedes, just as French distrust of a rearmed Germany was once again very much a factor in the early 1950's and continued to be such even after France had reluctantly ratified having West Germany in NATO. Similarly, the Indian-Pakistani quarrel focused over Kashmir has been a factor in the balance in the Far East—an apparently permanent feature, with fluctuating effects. The extent to which most of the local balances remain stubbornly unintegrated into a general balance is indicative of the relative lack of expectation of general war, just as their subordination within a general balance is a clear sign of increasing tension. When all the nations have been forced or induced to subordinate the whole complex of their relations with various other states into the simple alignment of Camp A vs. Camp B (as France did do in the tense years 1948–1953), the world is nearing—certainly in anticipation and perhaps in fact—a new general war. Conversely, when (as in 1965–1967) "polycentrism" in the East and "Gaullism" in the West, erode alliances, the world is moving away from any imminent expectation of world war.

In its basic operation every balance of power—local or general—implies a power competition and a struggle for relative advantage. With local balances this struggle is carried on within a limited context; otherwise it ceases to be local and becomes general. With general balances, of which any local balance can form the core, the context is potentially as wide at present as the world itself, but the competition may be carried on more or less vigorously, depending upon a number of considerations. The chief of these is the degree to which all other local balances can be integrated within the general balance.

In all cases the struggle for power position is carried on in both absolute and relative terms. Internally this struggle may be expressed in the raising of the armed forces to higher levels, either to gain upon the opposing bloc, or merely to keep even. Externally this struggle for power advantage may take the form of the use of one or more of four techniques that we shall explore in the next chapter.

CHAPTER 17

Techniques of the Balance

The Parties agree that an armed attack against one or more of them in Europe or North America shall be considered an attack against them all; and consequently they agree that, if such an armed attack occurs, each of them, in exercise of the right of individual or collective self-defense recognized by Article 51 of the Charter of the United Nations, will assist the Party or Parties so attacked by taking forthwith, individually and in concert with the other Parties, such action as it deems necessary, including the use of armed force, to restore and maintain the security of the North Atlantic area.

North Atlantic Treaty, Article 5

FOUR techniques have traditionally been used by states in competing for power advantage. Since these techniques are at the heart of the balance-of-power process we shall term them the techniques of the balance of power. They are: (1) the acquisition of allies, (2) the acquisition of territories, (3) the erection of buffer states, and (4) the undermining of the potential (or actual) enemy's strength. The first two are designed especially to increase absolute strength; the third to allow for the disposition (often through neutralization) by mutual consent of a strategic zone which neither power (or bloc) can afford to allow the other to occupy; and the fourth to increase one's own relative strength by decreasing the absolute strength of the enemy. We shall examine each of these four techniques in turn.

I   The Acquisition of Allies

THE most obvious and easiest means of increasing power externally is to acquire allies. If the two nations involved in a local balance of power are able to add many allies to their side, they convert their local balance into a general one.

Of course the process may be and is often carried only part way so that, while the local balance is overthrown, a general balance is not created. This is almost always followed by a limited war. Before 1902 Japan and Russia formed a local balance, each eyeing the other jealously over Korea and Manchuria. Neither had an ally in the Far East although Russia, because of her alliance with France against Germany, was assured of a degree of support in Asia as well. In that year the Anglo-Japanese Alliance destroyed this uneasy equilibrium. With Britain's promise of armed support if Japan were confronted by two powers in a Far Eastern war, the threat of Russia's receiving aid from France was neutralized and the war that followed was limited, for France did not wish war with England.

In the diplomatic maneuvers preceding the Seven Weeks' War of Prussia against Austria in 1866, Bismarck secured an alliance with Italy while Austria was unsuccessful in enlisting France on her side. Since Bismarck had also taken care to earn Russia's benevolent neutrality,[1] in the ensuing war Prussia and Italy easily defeated isolated Austria.

Where, on the other hand, the process is carried through to its logical conclusion by involving all the great powers in two rival blocs, the war, if and when it comes, will be a general war. To illustrate, there had often been friction in Europe after 1870. In 1886–1888 there had been danger of war between Russia and Austria-Hungary. In 1875 and then again in 1885 and 1898, Russia and Great Britain had approached conflict. The same was true of Germany and France in 1875, 1887, and 1905; and of England and France in 1898. But whereas before the Algeciras Conference of 1906 (by which time rival blocs had begun to take definite shape) the two rivals had usually been reconciled by a united Europe intervening as umpire, after 1906 the great powers themselves took sides even where they were not directly involved. To express it in the terms already used, before 1906 the local balances were the focuses of tension; after that time all the powers mentioned had actively entered into one over-all alignment system. As a result there were no unilateralist great powers left in Europe after 1906.

2   The Acquisition of Territory

POWER may also be increased externally by acquiring additional territory, either contiguous to the existing frontier or in colonial (i.e., non-contiguous) areas.

In the eighteenth century Frederick the Great of Prussia, who reigned between 1740 and 1786, was a master of contiguous acquisition. During his reign he added the territory known in modern times as the Polish Corridor, linking East Prussia to Prussia proper; he took the rich Silesian area that until World War II formed an arm hugging Bohemia (the "head" of contemporary, tadpole-shaped Czechoslovakia) on the northeast. The state he passed on to his successors was double the size he had himself inherited.

Such territorial accretions may be accomplished at times in concert with, and at other times at the expense of, rival powers. In the example just given, Prussia took Silesia from Austria by force, but the Polish territories that were gained by the First Partition of Poland in 1772 were shared by Prussia, Austria, and Russia. In this case Prussia's share was more modest in size than that of either of the other two. It is said that Maria Theresa, Archduchess of

---

[1] See below, Section 5.

Austria, wept as she helped despoil Poland, much as Lewis Carroll's walrus who, with tears streaming down his face, consumed his friends, the oysters. Frederick the Great, who was a man not without wit, caused the triumphal arch of the Brandenburger Tor in Berlin to be surmounted by the figures of three women pulling the Prussian chariot of state. Among these three who had aided him one way or another in the expansion of his empire, Maria Theresa of Austria was given an honored place. In 1793 Prussia and Russia took a second and larger bite of Poland, and in 1795, having developed a taste for Polish acquisitions, together with Austria they took the rest.

In the twentieth century, Poland, and this time the Baltic area as well, was again divided between Germany and Russia, the Nazi-Soviet Treaty of Non-Aggression providing (in a secret protocol) that: "the spheres of influence of Germany and the U.S.S.R. shall be bounded approximately by the line of the rivers Narew, Vistula, and San." [2]

Acquiring contiguous territories in Europe has usually been a great deal of trouble and accomplished with more bloodshed and longer wars than those just mentioned. Louis XIV, the great king of France, for all his wars, was not in the end an extraordinary success when measured in terms of real estate. Soviet Russia after 1945 must conversely be ranked among the outstanding successes. Although she has added only slightly to the pre-World-War-I territories of the Russian tsars in terms of land directly incorporated—the little tail of Czechoslovakia and a slice of East Prussia—she regained her large World War I losses. In addition she was able to dominate and occupy much of the Balkans, all of Poland, half of Germany, and a piece of Austria (since evacuated). Hitler and Napoleon were each highly successful for a time. Hitler far surpassed Napoleon's accomplishments until 1939, for the return of the Saar, the re-establishment of full control over the Rhineland, the acquisition of Austria, and the incorporation of the Sudetenland of Czechoslovakia were all accomplished without war. Sometimes rather small areas have been the sought-after territorial prizes in European wars. Alsace and Lorraine, and the Saar, have played enormously—even extraordinarily—important roles in this regard.

It is only the United States and Russia in modern times that have been able to expand literally across continents against relatively inconsequential opposition, annexing huge blocks of land half the size of Europe or more to their own contiguous territories. With the defeat of Japan in 1945 each continued the process in terms of territories in the Pacific, the Soviet Union acquiring the Kuriles, and the United States a vast network of islands extending over an area thousands of miles in width.

Perhaps because the United States and Russia have had such rich contiguous opportunities close at hand, neither went in for the acquisition of colonial (non-contiguous) areas on a large scale. It has already been related in Chapter 7 how vast domains were added to Britain, France, Germany, Italy, Portu-

---

[2] See for text, *Nazi-Soviet Relations, 1939–1941*, Department of State Publication 3023, pp. 76 ff.

gal, the Netherlands, and Belgium by this process. As with acquisitions in Europe this has sometimes been done on a *quid pro quo*, compensatory basis by the powers interested, and sometimes on a purely "catch as catch can—the race is to the quickest and the strongest" basis.

Until the Fashoda crisis of 1898, England and France took territories more or less independently of each other—there was more than enough for both. When most of Africa had been taken by them and the other colonial powers, the struggle for the Sudan culminated at Fashoda. France was forced to yield, renouncing all territory along the Nile in return for some worthless districts in the Sahara Desert. This was nominally a compensatory arrangement but in reality a complete victory for Britain.

By contrast, the Anglo-French Entente (understanding) of April 8, 1904, represented a thoroughgoing *quid pro quo*. The net effect was to grant to England a free hand in Egypt and to France one in Morocco. Neither Egypt nor Morocco belonged to either France or England—a fact that no doubt served to facilitate the arrangement. England was already in occupation of Egypt; but Morocco, because the French held only a foot in the door and German opposition was certain, could not be granted outright to France. Secret articles in the entente promised British diplomatic support when Moroccan independence broke down. Spain was to get a piece too in order to ensure her support. Conflicts of interests between Britain and France—extending from fishing rights on the shores of Newfoundland to questions involving Madagascar (off Africa) and Siam (in the Far East)—were adjusted at the same time. There was to be free passage of the Suez and no fortifications opposite Gibraltar.

The Anglo-Russian Entente of August 31, 1907, represented an equivalent compensatory arrangement, not quite so far-reaching, but also between two ancient enemies. It divided Persia (Iran)—which again belonged to neither Britain nor Russia—into three spheres of influence. The north was to be under Russian control, the south under that of the British, and the middle zone, neutral. The role of Afghanistan as a buffer state under a certain amount of British influence was affirmed, and both governments recognized Chinese sovereignty over Tibet and agreed to respect its territorial integrity.

These colonial adventures of the great powers had an effect upon the balance of power that went far beyond the actual power increases brought about by the acquisitions of territories as such. We shall examine this further in the next chapter.

3   *The Erection of Buffer States*

THE purpose of the third balance-of-power technique is to allow for the disposition (often through neutralization), by mutual consent, of a strategic zone that neither power (or bloc) can afford to allow the other to occupy unilaterally and permanently.

Afghanistan has played such a role ever since British power was expanded up to her southern borders in India and the Russians established a common frontier with the Afghans on the north. There is an old Afghan saying that defines mountainous Afghanistan as "this goat separating the lion from the bear." In 1885 Russian local forces fought with the Afghans and occupied part of the border. For a time it seemed likely that the balance was to be upset by Russian ambitions. Prime Minister Gladstone asked Parliament for eleven million pounds with which to fight. But, after being on the verge of war, the two powers smoothed over the incident. In 1891 Russia turned her attention away from India toward China, and began the construction of the Trans-Siberian Railroad with French money. This new course eventually brought her into rivalry with Japan, but it preserved the buffer status of Afghanistan. In the 1907 Anglo-Russian Entente, as we saw, this status was confirmed. British predominance was assured, but the territory was to remain free from occupation. In contemporary times, although both the Soviet Union and the United States have given economic aid to Afghanistan, her buffer role continues.

Korea, a natural buffer state, has often played that role; more infrequently she has been an occupied possession of China, Japan, or Russia. After the Koreans were defeated by the Manchus in 1637, they recognized Chinese suzerainty although Japan retained similar claims. For over two hundred years Korea was isolated entirely from the world at large. This came to an end in 1876 when Japan recognized Korea as independent. China did not make any immediate protest. Between 1882 and 1885 Japan and China struggled politically for control, both of them withdrawing troops in the latter year. In 1894–1895 the Sino-Japanese War was fought over Korea. By it Japan forced China to recognize Korean independence, but almost immediately Japanese influence there was challenged by Russian penetration. This led to the Russo-Japanese War of 1904–1905 and to Japanese predominance in Korea. Even so, not until 1910 did Japan formally annex Korea. After Japan's defeat in World War II and Korea's partition between Russian and United States occupation forces at the 38th Parallel she again became a pawn in the power struggle. It is Korea's tragedy in modern times that, while she is a natural buffer between China, Japan, Russia, and America, the great powers have been unable to agree on giving her that status and underwriting it on a permanent, international basis, as they did in 1815 with Switzerland.

In Europe, Belgium and Holland have been buffer states between France and Germany. Following Napoleon, and until 1830, Belgium was part of Holland—the two together being known as the Kingdom of the Netherlands. In 1830 Belgium revolted, and by Article VII of the Treaty of 1839 the great powers recognized and collectively guaranteed Belgium as an "independent and perpetually neutral" state. Bismarck was wise enough to plan to observe this treaty and avoid British ire when he went to war with France in the Franco-Prussian War. In early August 1870, after the outbreak of the war, to further reassure the British, and upon their suggestion, new treaties were concluded by England and Prussia and by England and France re-guaranteeing

Belgian neutrality in view of the hostilities. It was the earlier treaty of 1839 that the German war plans made it necessary to violate in 1914, and which Bethmann-Hollweg ineptly characterized as a "scrap of paper." Belgium, failing to find security from her special status, resumed freedom of action following her experience in World War I.

Switzerland is another buffer state whose neutral status was proclaimed by the great powers themselves at the Congress of Vienna in 1815. She has served successfully ever since as a buffer between Austria, Italy, France, and Germany, as we have described elsewhere.

4 Undermining Enemy Strength: The Detachment of Actual Allies

THE fourth and most important technique is aimed at producing or exploiting a weakening of the strength of the potential or actual enemy. This may be accomplished through the use of diplomacy or propaganda, or a combination of the two. It has two major aims: the first, which we shall examine in this section, is to weaken the coalition of the prospective or actual enemy by detaching or semi-detaching one or more of its members from the group. The second, which we shall examine in the next section, is to destroy the enemy's hopes of gaining new allies from uncommitted states, by keeping them neutral.

The first aim is to destroy the enemy coalition or exploit any diversive tendencies in it.

Any coalition is a precarious thing, for it rests upon the effective suppression of divisive tendencies. If an alliance by definition reflects a recognition of a common power problem, it will still be unlikely that the power problem will be considered by all allies at all times as identical. But those areas of national interest not identical may logically be better fostered through alternative policy choices. In such cases, counterbalancing interests will be involved. Where the peril is simple to comprehend, and substantially equal in danger to all the vital interests of all the members of the bloc, the coalition is extremely hard to dissolve. But these circumstances are rarely all present over a long period of time; especially where the blocs are numerically large, as they are today, their unity is very hard to preserve. Beginning in September 1955, tension between Greece and Turkey (and later Greece and Britain) grew as Britain negotiated the future of Cyprus—a British possession with a Greco-Turkish population. All three were members of NATO. In March 1964, a UN peace-keeping force had to be installed on Cyprus to end civil fighting and prevent Greek or Turkish invasion. While NATO survived these tensions without losses, the difficulties encountered illustrate the point. The existence of NATO did not entail the ending of a Greek-Turkish local balance, but merely its subordination in view of a greater common threat. In both 1955 and 1964, Greek-Turkish fears of Soviet aggression were not great and rivalries were reasserted in terms of counterbalancing interests.

This type of trouble is not new in alliances and often has the more far-reaching consequences of one of the members actually severing its relationship. In 1882 Italy, angry at French opposition and thwarted in her ambitions for colonial expansion in Africa, joined Austria-Hungary and Germany in the Triple Alliance. She then took the precaution of issuing a Ministerial Declaration that the alliance could, so far as she was concerned, not be considered as directed against Britain, who at the time was still pursuing her policy of "splendid isolation." After 1907 when England had understandings with both France and Russia, and the latter two were in alliance against Germany and Austria-Hungary, this declaration remained in effect. It served notice that Italy was not anxious to fight a coalition that included England. In 1902, Italian relations with France having improved, the two reached an understanding, exchanging secret assurances that, should the other be the object of "a direct or indirect aggression," or, if either of them after "direct provocation" went to war with a third power, the other would remain neutral. Italy thus assured the French that even if they were to *attack* Germany (providing, of course, that they were directly "provoked"—a circumstance never difficult to arrange in international relations), she would remain neutral. After this, Italian membership in the Triple Alliance was, to say the least, purely nominal. The subsequent Italian declaration of neutrality when war occurred in 1914, and the later decision of Italy to join the conflict on the side of the allies, was already foreshadowed in the arrangements of 1902.

It can easily be seen that Italy's attachment to the Triple Alliance was never thoroughgoing and firm. She joined the alliance out of irritation with the French over colonial matters, and out of a past successful partnership with Germany in the wars of national unity. Yet in the long run her major European ambitions were inescapably frustrated by this course of action, for it made her an ally of the state who held the *Italia irredenta*—Austria-Hungary. While it was theoretically conceivable that Austria-Hungary might, out of gratitude to her ally, someday deliver these territories to Italy, in practice this hope was purely illusory. Any state that covets the territory of another is much more likely to see its hopes realized by fighting and winning a war *against* that state rather than on its side. "To the victors belong the spoils," and victors, conversely, are rarely in a mood to share their own territories with their allies—especially their less powerful allies. Italy much more realistically reassessed the situation when she ultimately went to war against Austria, gaining the desired areas in 1919 as a result.

The lesson is clear: Italy was "detachable" because she had entered a coalition that could not readily serve her most basic interests and yet which at the same time exposed her to the possibility of being subjected to the full force of British sea power if Britain ultimately joined France (as she did). That this situation was adroitly manipulated by the Allies of World War I is undeniable, but, without the basic interests at stake being what and where they were, all the Allied entreaties would have fallen on deaf ears. Adroit diplomacy and clever propaganda are wasted on barren ground.

A second illustration is the detachment of Yugoslavia from the Communist bloc, first made public on June 28, 1948. The actual detachment was not the work of the NATO powers, but they exploited its possibilities in a very shrewd and successful way. By the end of the war Yugoslavia had largely freed itself of Axis occupation troops. Its partisan activity had been marked and successful. It also lay to the side of the advance of the main southern Russian army into Central Europe. Consequently Yugoslavia was not subjected to a large, semi-permanent Russian occupation as was the case with Romania, Hungary, and Bulgaria. Moreover the Yugoslavs had a long history of striving for independence—both against the Ottoman Turks and the Austro-Hungarians. These conditions combined, under circumstances where Moscow was attempting thoroughgoing control of the sovietization of the Balkan states, to create "Titoism"—a refusal to accept Moscow dictation.

In this new bid for independence Yugoslavia had certain weak points against her, and certain strong ones in her favor. She had her own strong army, loyal to Tito, plus a terrain favoring defensive tactics. She was on the extreme fringe of the Communist sphere with borders giving access to NATO and non-Communist states, as well as ports and coastline opening on the Mediterranean and thus accessible to the West from the sea. But, conversely, she broke from the Communist bloc without renouncing communism, and with not the slightest assurance of Western support should Russia attack her.

Although the West had been denouncing all Communists with equal disfavor, once the break came they were quick to make distinctions. While they disapproved of communism anywhere and everywhere, they were opposed to Russian hegemony over other states still more. From there things moved relatively quickly. Overtures toward the West from Yugoslavia were not repulsed, and trade and economic agreements were followed by some military assistance. In 1950 the American Import-Export Bank made available credits of $20 millions; more than twice that amount was given to Yugoslavia for food for her army and people. By November 1951, the United States was supplying military assistance and Britain and France soon afterward joined the United States in aiding Yugoslav industrialization. Already in October 1951, Tito declared that, if Russian aggression caused a third world war, Yugoslavia would fight on the side of the West. In 1953–1954, Yugoslavia even entered a "Little Balkan" Entente with Greece and Turkey, both members of NATO. Since 1959 Yugoslavia, while retaining ties with the West, has moved toward "positive neutralism." But she remains outside the Warsaw Alliance.

In this second illustration, as in the first, an alliance contrary to basic interests of the state involved did not endure. Subservience to Russian dictation was not in Yugoslavia's interests; she, unlike the other Balkan states, was in a position to act in her own interests.

A third example illustrates the reverse process from the second—the case of China, which after World War II shifted *into* the Communist bloc. The reinforcement to the Soviet bloc was very welcome but evidently almost as unexpected as Tito's break with them. In fact, according to Marshal Tito, when

Mao Tse-tung visited Moscow in 1948, Stalin strongly urged him to conclude peace with the Nationalist Chinese and accept a coalition government, rather than risk the entire destruction of the Chinese Communist power. If this account is to be believed (and there are no reasons especially to doubt it) Stalin falsely estimated the possibilities and Mao, while silently nodding assent, returned to China and set his grand offensive in full motion ahead—with overwhelming success.

The signature of the Russo-Chinese Treaty of Alliance, which marked the change in alignment status, came on February 14, 1950. It provided that Soviet Russia and Communist China would cooperate "to prevent any repetition of aggression and violation of peace on the part of Japan or any other state which directly or indirectly would unite with Japan in acts of aggression." If either Russia or Communist China were to be attacked "by Japan or any state allied with her, thus finding itself in a state of war," the other party would "immediately render military or other aid with all means at its disposal." Since the United States, by the Security Treaty of February 28, 1952, became an alliance partner of Japan, China was thenceforth a potential enemy of America—a potentiality that became actuality in the undeclared war of the "Chinese People's Volunteer Army" versus the United States-UN "police-action" army in Korea late in 1950. Each side, however, avoided declaring war and making their alliances fully operative.

The Sino-Soviet Alliance, a product of ideological agreement and a common distrust of Japan (backed by the United States), meets only some of China's basic interests. Since Japan appears to have more or less permanently renounced mainland ambitions, the alliance is directly useful more as a weapon against the United States. The United States has remained an active enemy from the Chinese point of view (propping up a rival government on Formosa, sending forces to the approaches to China's frontiers as in Korea and Viet-Nam); thus, the alliance is compatible with certain interests of China. But the alliance has not proved helpful for China's attempts at rectifying her frontier with India, where Russia was unsympathetic. And it is potentially incompatible with China's wish to assert independence from Soviet domination and China's bid for ideological leadership, and completely incompatible with redressing her long and disputed frontier with Russia. We shall want to examine the broader implications of this later. Here we are concerned with the narrower point that the fate of the new Chinese alliance, as in the two previous examples, will be determined ultimately by whether it is really compatible with Chinese national interests.

Nothing weakens enemy strength more than detaching, or exploiting the detachment, of the enemy's allies. This is especially so when these former enemies become one's own allies—as, at least initially, in the three cases cited—for then the enemy is weakened triply: he loses the power of the ally from his own group; he sees that power now arrayed against him; and his morale is endangered by the obvious thought that the bloc is falling apart and that defeat is probable or inevitable.

5 *Undermining Enemy Strength: Destroying Hopes of New Allies*

OFTEN equally destructive of the enemy's morale is to deprive him of allies he had hoped to gain from among uncommitted, unilateralist states, by persuading these to remain neutral. This is especially effective if it is done on the brink of, or in the first stage of, a war, and particularly so if the enemy is counting fairly heavily upon obtaining these allies. But precisely because the enemy (unless fatuous) has grounds for anticipating such an alliance, it implies that there are common interests. If the enemy's plan is to be frustrated, the potential ally's counterbalancing interests must be appealed to. Germany, because she had always had the problem of avoiding simultaneous war on two or more fronts, has developed this technique in masterly fashion in modern times. It was not until Germany's first unsuccessful modern war—World War I—that this sensible rule was abandoned.

Bismarck's greatest successes owe a good deal to the use of this technique. To illustrate, his initial international relations problem as Prussian Chancellor was to loosen Austria's stranglehold on the German Confederation in order to unify the Germanies under the leadership of Prussia. To do so he had to keep France and Russia, whose interests were potentially threatened by a greater Prussia, from aiding Austria. A chance to assure Russia's friendship and neutrality came in February 1863. With a Polish insurrection against Russia in full career, Bismarck assured the tsar of his complete cooperation, and sent four Prussian army corps—half the Prussian army—to the Polish frontier. Russia, thus supported, successfully defied the intervention attempted by Britain, France, and Austria. This one action went far toward gaining Bismarck Russian benevolent neutrality in his later wars against Austria and France.

Once Bismarck was ready for war with Austria, he met Napoleon III at Biarritz, where he is supposed to have made vague promises of territorial gains for France in the Rhineland. Louis Napoleon promised in return to stay neutral, being sure that Austria would win after a long war that would conveniently exhaust both Prussia and Austria. Next Bismarck, in April 1866, with Napoleon aiding in the negotiations, made an offensive-defensive alliance with Italy who, of course, desired Venetia—at that time still a possession of Austria.

Once the way was prepared, Bismarck moved swiftly. In the Seven Weeks' War (June–August 1866) Prussia decisively defeated Austria. Bismarck now created a North German Confederation, under Prussian domination, from the German states north of the Main River; but, despite King Wilhelm's pressure, he refused to take Saxony, Austrian Silesia, and the four South German states. He took this stand not only to prevent French intervention, but also because he wished to avoid arousing the intrenched Austrian hostility that would inevitably stem from a harsh peace. Bismarck then rejected

French claims for compensation on the grounds that the areas involved were German—a position Austria would support. When Napoleon asked instead for Luxembourg and Belgium, Bismarck induced Count Benedetti, the French Ambassador, to put these claims in writing in August 1866, and filed the document carefully away.

Relations between France and Prussia grew increasingly tense. Napoleon initiated negotiations for alliances with both Italy and Austria. But Austria was unwilling to commit herself to aid France in a war against Prussia fought over German territory. Italy, for her part, was unwilling to promise aid unless the French evacuated Rome, which the Italians wanted for their capital. Napoleon shortsightedly refused, although the one counterbalancing interest far outranked the other in importance for France. He proceeded on the assumption that Austrian and Italian aid would be forthcoming.

Because Bismarck had not treated Austria very severely, and because of the situation just described, Prussia had to fear Austrian intervention only in the event of defeats. Italy's neutrality was fairly well assured, as was Russia's. England was the only additional ally France might procure. Bismarck took two steps to avoid this. On August 9, 1870, immediately after the outbreak of war, he undertook by treaty to preserve Belgian independence—as did France. The other step was to give Benedetti's written French demand for Belgium (of 1866) to the correspondent of the London *Times*, who put it in print for all the world to read. Nothing could have been more effective in ensuring British neutrality. France was crushed; at the battle of Sedan, Napoleon himself was captured; and on January 18, 1871, Wilhelm I was proclaimed German Emperor in the French palace and historical shrine of Versailles.

Hitler made use of the same technique for the same purpose—this time to deny the British and French an alliance with Russia—in 1939. The Western powers were actually in the midst of negotiations with the Soviets when the Nazi-Soviet Non-Aggression Pact was announced on August 23, 1939. It ensured Russian neutrality in the war in the West by providing in Article II that if Germany or Russia became "the object of belligerent action by a third power" (even, of course, as the text implies, if Germany started the war) the other party would "in no manner lend its support to this third power." [3]

6 *The Trend in Alignment Systems*

THESE four techniques of the balance of power are, as the illustrations indicate, perennial. They are as useful and applicable to balance-of-power manipulations today as they were in the time of Frederick the Great. What has changed, as we saw in passing in Chapter 15, is the character of alignment (especially alliance) systems today.

Where alliances were formerly concluded most frequently at or near the outset of or during wars, the contemporary trend is toward more and more

---

[3] See *Nazi-Soviet Relations*, 1939–1941, Department of State Publication 3023, pp. 76 ff., for complete text.

permanent types of arrangements concluded far in advance of war. Where once alliances were never made decades in advance of war and a fairly general European war might begin with one or more great powers uncommitted and with the others concluding hasty and temporary alliances, it is more and more the trend today for all the great nations to take part in coalitions at a time when general war has not broken out and is still fairly distant. They also tend to remain on the same side *during* a war, whereas shifts of powers to the other side were not at all rare in former times.

In the Napoleonic Wars great powers drifted in and out of the coalitions against France with a freedom and ease that seem strange to the modern observer. Back in Frederick the Great's time the shifts were even more bewildering. During the last three years of the Seven Years' War (1756–1763),[4] George II of England had been aiding Frederick of Prussia with subsidies. But following George II's death, the new king, George III, although fighting a common enemy, ceased subsidizing the Prussian armies (1760). Frederick the Great's position was greatly weakened and his back was to the wall when Tsarina Elizabeth of Russia died (January 5, 1762). The new tsar, Peter III, an admirer of Frederick's military talents, concluded peace with Prussia in March. Then in May, Prussia and Russia became *allies*. But in July Catherine II deposed Peter and recalled Russian troops from Frederick's army! Early the next year (1763) the Treaty of Paris restored peace between England and France and Spain; five days later the Treaty of Hubertsburg ended the war between Austria and Prussia.

The difference between modern or contemporary alliance systems and those of the eighteenth century is quite apparent. The sudden shifts so typical of earlier times were largely the result of policy being made by the monarch. A king's death might well be the prelude to a complete shift in alliances. Alliances were made in the king's name; when he passed away, they were not necessarily continued or honored by his successor. By contrast, the substitution of parliamentary-type regimes throughout the world has wrought a great change, mitigated only to some extent by the basic similarity of modern dictatorships to former absolute monarchies. The national interest, which has replaced dynastic interest as the criterion for policy, even in dictatorships, is a much more constant and stabilizing influence. Thus it is no accident that, beginning with 1815 and the steady decline of absolute monarchy, there has been a corresponding growth in the permanence, inclusiveness, and duration of alliances.

This trend was already apparent in the second half of the nineteenth century. By that time a system of alliances was gradually emerging that was in great contrast to the period of the Seven Years' War described above. It was much more stable; lightning changes of sides were unusual. Italy's shift was, for example, very gradual. When Britain and France settled their disputes in 1904, and Britain and Russia in 1907, neither arrangement represented an

---

[4] The conflict really involved two wars: one of Britain against France and, in 1762, Spain; and one of France, Austria, and Russia, against Prussia.

actual shift in alliance partners, but merely the subordination of local balances of power to a general balance. In the twentieth century these trends have been further accentuated, and the alliance system of the present time is both more extensive and more permanent in form than ever before. At the same time, since every alliance is made possible through the suppression of counterbalancing interests, each alliance still remains vulnerable to reappraisal and tacit or overt defection.

7 *The Contemporary Alignment Structure*

AFTER the beginning of World War II an immensely elaborate alliance structure was evolved. Because of the rapid realignments of the last decade or more, these alliances can be divided into two groups: pre-Cold War and post-Cold War.

In the first group were such twenty-year wartime treaties as the Anglo-Russian Alliance of 1942 and the Franco-Russian Alliance of 1944. Both were directed against Germany; both promised armed assistance by one party to the other in the event of a renewal of German aggression.[5] When the inability of Russia and the West to agree on common policies for all of Germany led to the creation of separate East and West German states in the first decade after the war, these treaties were robbed of any real meaning. After West Germany became a member of NATO, Russia in 1955 denounced both of them.

Following the announcement of the "Truman Doctrine" in 1947 and the "official" beginning of the Cold War, a great number of treaties were negotiated in both East and West. In 1948 Russia concluded alliances with Romania, Hungary, Bulgaria, and Finland, all directed against Germany (in this case meaning, of course, *West* Germany) and/or states allied with Germany. Typical of their provisions is Article I of the Soviet-Bulgarian Treaty in which the parties promised "to take jointly all measures within their power to set aside all threat of revival of aggression by Germany or any other state whatsoever which may unite itself with Germany directly or in any other manner whatsoever. . . ." [6] In the West the Brussels (or Western Union) Alliance was created on March 17, 1948. Signed by Belgium, the Netherlands, Luxembourg, Great Britain, and France, it entered into effect on August 25, 1948, and provided (Article IV) that "If any one of the . . . parties should be the object of an armed attack in Europe, the other . . . parties will, in accordance with the provisions of Article 51 of the Charter of the United Nations, afford the party so attacked all military and other aid and assistance in their power." [7]

The Brussels Alliance provided precedents upon which NATO, in the fol-

---

[5] For texts of these agreements see respectively *Great Britain, Treaty Series*, No. 2 (1942), Cmd. 6376, and Department of State *Bulletin*, Vol. 12, pp. 39 ff.

[6] *North Atlantic Treaty*, Senate Document No. 48, 81st Congress, 1st Session, p. 111.

[7] See *United Nations Treaty Series*, Vol. 19, No. 304 (registered), pp. 51 ff. for text.

lowing year, was erected. Not only did it contain the formula "in accordance with . . . Article 51 of the Charter" of the UN, which was repeated in the North Atlantic Pact to make it compatible with the UN, but an unprecedented peacetime military coordination was begun, with Viscount Montgomery as the Western Union Supreme Commander, with headquarters in France.

The Rio Pact (the Inter-American Treaty of Reciprocal Assistance), signed on September 2, 1947, by the Dominican Republic, Guatemala, Costa Rica, Peru, El Salvador, Panama, Paraguay, Venezuela, Chile, Honduras, Cuba, Bolivia, Colombia, Mexico, Haiti, Ecuador, Uruguay, Argentina, Brazil, and the United States, entered into effect on the heels of the Brussels Alliance (December 3, 1948). Its heart is in Article III which provides that: "an armed attack by any State against an American State shall be considered as an attack against all the American States." [8] By the terms of the Rio Pact, any threat of aggression may be dealt with by measures up to and including the use of armed force. Votes on such security matters are to be in the "Organ of Consultation" (the Meeting of Ministers of Foreign Affairs of the American Republics). Actual decisions will be by a two-thirds majority of the states ratifying the pact *except* that no state can be required to use its armed forces without its own consent (Article XX).[9] (Castro's Cuba was ousted from the pact in 1962.)

In 1949 these two treaty structures were linked together and made more elaborate by the entry of the United States and the Western Union allies into the North Atlantic Pact. Signed by the United States, along with Great Britain, France, Italy, Canada, Norway, Belgium, Denmark, the Netherlands, Luxembourg, Portugal, and Iceland on April 4, it entered into effect on August 24, 1949.

With the conclusion of these arrangements covering Latin America and Europe, the balance of power in Europe entered into a period of increasing stability. Soviet power in Europe, which had loomed so threateningly between 1947 and 1949, was being counterbalanced and contained. After 1949, in Europe, the admission of Greece and Turkey to NATO strengthened the Western coalition still more. Following West Germany's admission to NATO in 1955 the Soviets responded with the Warsaw Alliance. This grouping of Communist states in Europe (except Yugoslavia) gave a NATO-type form to the Soviet alliance system which before then had consisted of the web of bilateral treaties already noted. The Warsaw Alliance treaty was signed on May 14, 1955, within a week after West Germany joined NATO.

In Asia, however, the balance of power after World War II continued to be far from stable, and beginning with the collapse of Chinese Nationalist power in 1949, a further elaboration of the alignment system took place. In

---

[8] See for text *Inter-American Conference for the Maintenance of Continental Peace and Security*, Department of State Publication 3016, pp. 59 ff.

[9] The treaty covers not only the United States and Latin America per se but also the Aleutians, Greenland, and much of the Arctic and Antarctic regions.

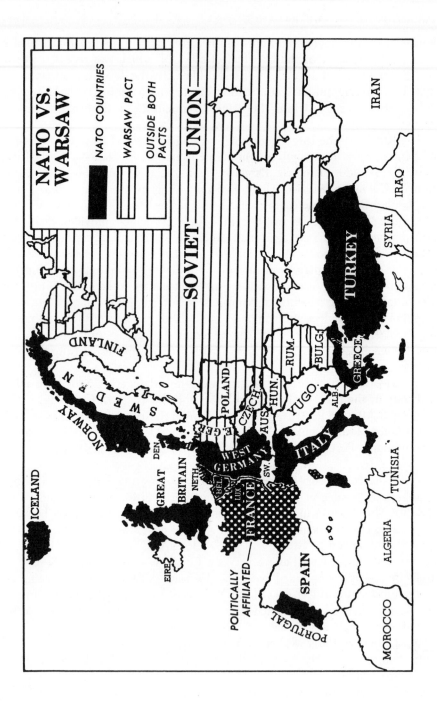

1951–1952 the United States concluded a series of treaties with Japan, the Philippines, Australia, and New Zealand. In 1953, following the American-led coalition's successful struggle to deprive North Korea and Communist China of the fruits of aggression in South Korea, the United States concluded a treaty with South Korea by which each recognized that "an armed attack in the Pacific area on either of the Parties in territories now under their respective administrative control, or hereafter recognized by one of the Parties as lawfully brought under the administrative control of the other, would be dangerous to its own peace and safety and declares that it would act to meet the common danger in accordance with its constitutional processes." [10] A treaty of alliance was also concluded between the United States and Nationalist China by which Formosa and the Pescadores were guaranteed against mainland attack. By 1954, with the formation of the SEATO alliance,[11] the balance of power in Asia too had attained a precarious stability, with Indo-China the main focus of tensions.

In the Middle East the Baghdad Pact was formed in 1955. Following Iraq's revolution and withdrawal, the alliance of Britain, Turkey, Pakistan, and Iran was renamed, in 1959, the Central Treaty Organization (CENTO).

8 The North Atlantic Treaty Organization

THE North Atlantic Treaty Organization is by far the most interesting and elaborate of these alignment developments. The Communist system, while elaborate and inclusive, has fewer novel features. Since the Soviet Union continued after 1945 to occupy most of her European satellites, so that their individual armed forces were little more than auxiliary troops for use by and with the Red Army, there was not the same high degree of multimember planning as has typified NATO. In NATO the contemporary trends toward an increasingly complex, semi-permanent, and inclusive type of alliance arrangement reached their highest development to date.

When the North Atlantic Pact first came into effect on August 24, 1949, nothing of the later elaborate structure existed. In the beginning it was merely an alliance, more inclusive than most, and covering a wide geographical area. Article V (paragraph 1), quoted at the head of this chapter, was and is the heart of the arrangement: "an armed attack against one or more . . . shall be considered an attack against them all. . . ." The parties pledged "separately and jointly, by means of continuous and effective self-help and mutual aid" to "maintain and develop their individual and collective capacity to resist armed attack." They provided for consultation "whenever, in the opinion of any of them, the territorial integrity, political independence or security of any of the Parties" was threatened. A council, on which each of

---

[10] Article III. For text see *Treaties and other International Acts Series*, No. 3097, Department of State Publication 5720.

[11] Australia, France, New Zealand, Pakistan, the Philippines, Thailand, the United Kingdom, and the United States, composed SEATO. For treaty text see *South-East Asia Treaty Organization*, Department of State Publication 6305, Far Eastern Series 72.

them was to be represented, would "set up such subsidiary bodies as may be necessary." And after the treaty had run twenty years, any party could cease to be bound one year after denouncing it.

The treaty itself was later amended. By the London Protocol to the North Atlantic Treaty, signed October 22, 1951, the original parties agreed to invite Greece and Turkey to adhere to the pact and extend the area covered by the pact correspondingly.[12] On February 18, 1952, Greece and Turkey accepted the invitation to membership in NATO. Since in 1953 the Greek army was one hundred and sixty-five thousand strong, and the Turkish army consisted of some four hundred thousand men, the net gain for NATO strength was considerable. The inclusion of West Germany in NATO in 1955 brought the membership to fifteen nations.

The organizational structure of NATO grew accordingly—perhaps too greatly for maximum military effectiveness. In part the extensive and intricate command system reflects political considerations. Prestige demands that each NATO member—in the person of its marshals, generals, and admirals—shall hold a certain number of command positions. Thus in one training exercise, such as Operation WELDFAST, which took place in a thousand-mile radius around Athens in 1953, at least fourteen separate commands were directly involved: three over-all commands—Allied Forces, Mediterranean; Allied Forces, Southern Europe; Allied Forces, Southeastern Europe; five sea commands in the Mediterranean; two Allied Ground Forces Commands; two Allied Air Forces Commands; an Allied Strike Force Headquarters at Naples; and an Advanced Allied Headquarters, Southeastern Europe. These commands were based on Malta, Naples, Izmir (Turkey), Algiers, Athens, Ankara, and Salonika, and reported variously to Paris, Naples, Malta, or Izmir. The commands were held by: five Americans—one admiral, one-vice admiral, two lieutenant-generals, one major-general; two British—both admirals; two Greeks—one a vice admiral and the other a general; two Turks —one admiral and one general; one Frenchman—a vice-admiral; and one Italian—a vice-admiral.[13] Some progress in simplification has been made more recently.

In the other command areas the situation was a little simpler since it is the Mediterranean, with its long salient stretching out eastward to the Black Sea, that represents the most complex problem from the organizational point of view.

Looking at the elaborate over-all structure, the highest NATO authority is the North Atlantic Council (which takes decisions by unanimous vote). The Council meets either at the level of ministers or of permanent representatives.[14] Normally ministerial level meetings are held two or three times a year

---

[12] See for text, British Cmd. 8489; also Royal Institute of International Affairs (hereafter cited as R.I.I.A.), *Atlantic Alliance*, London, 1952, pp. 157–158.

[13] NYHT (EE), October 6, 1953; NYT, October 1–7, 1953.

[14] Although heads of government may also represent their states, as happened for the first time in December 1957.

and involve the ministers of foreign affairs. But, since 1951, defense and economic or finance ministers may attend, too, whenever these types of questions are under discussion. Between ministerial meetings the permanent representatives, with the rank of ambassador, meet once or twice a week. The Council, which is chaired by the Secretary-General of NATO, has met an average of 80–100 times a year. The presidency of the Council is rotated among the NATO foreign ministers in alphabetical order.

NATO's secretary-general also presides over a permanent secretariat organized into a division of political affairs, a division of economics and finance, and a division of production and logistics, and a number of other offices.

The senior military authority in NATO is the Military Committee, composed of the Chiefs of Staff from each member. (Iceland, having no armed forces, may be represented by a civilian.) The Military Committee meets at least twice a year at this level. Functioning in permanent session with effective powers of decision are the permanent military representatives, and meetings of the Military Committee in Permanent Session (as the latter is called) are chaired by an officer chosen by the Chiefs of Staff for a two-year term. Until 1966 the executive agent of the Military Committee was called the Standing Group. It was composed of representatives of the Chiefs of Staff of the United States, Britain, and France and had a number of NATO military agencies (for standardization, for communications, etc.) under its control. De Gaulle's decision to cease participating in the integrated organization led to the abolition of the Standing Group. The new International Military Staff is not an executive agent but functions as a NATO committee of the whole. The plan in late 1966 was to establish it and the North Atlantic Council in Brussels.

The military command structure is not all focused under SACEUR (Supreme Allied Commander in Europe). Although SACEUR is the most important of all the commands, because of the area involved there is also a Supreme Allied Commander for the Atlantic and an English Channel–North Sea Command. Both of these report directly, along with SACEUR, to the higher headquarters.

SACEUR's headquarters, known as SHAPE (Supreme Headquarters, Allied Powers in Europe) was located at Rocquencourt, near Paris, until France's withdrawal from the integrated NATO structure. In 1966 it was decided to relocate it in Belgium. Under SHAPE are four major commands for the northern, central, southern, and Mediterranean areas. These commands are further subdivided into air, ground, and sea forces commands in an intricate fashion already indicated in reference to Operation WELDFAST above.

The growth in NATO's military strength during the Korean War was rapid; after that it was steady but slower—and with some setbacks. When General Eisenhower first activated SHAPE on January 7, 1951, he had twelve divisions in his command, and some 400 planes (few jets) and about that number of ships. By 1954 there were four to five times as many divisions (and these were combat-ready), with a total, including reserves, of "eighty odd" divisions.[15] From few jets there were many. From virtually no airfields that could take jets, the number grew in 1954 to 120 and in 1959 to 160.

Not all the progress made shows up in such figures. At the December 1953, annual meeting of the North Atlantic Council, it was announced that there had been a 40 per cent increase in military *effectiveness* during the year. This had been accomplished primarily through improving the support structure. By the beginning of 1960, as a part of the joint "infrastructure" program, over 4,600 miles of fuel supply pipelines were working, and some 26,500 miles of signals network were ready or nearly so, including well over 1,000 miles of submarine cables. Storage tanks for 528,400,000 gallons of fuel had been constructed. It is in relation to relocating many of these facilities that France's new policy toward NATO caused great concern. So much of these were constructed in France.

Progress was also made in the important field of standardization. In putting a coalition together effectively there are always two major problems—the political-prestige one: who is to command what, when, and how; and the military-logistical one: how to coordinate effectively when all the thousands of supply items are entirely different for each army. Especially in wartime the first problem becomes easier to solve, but the latter problem must be resolved largely *before* war if it is to be of most use. Since the 1953 decision on a standard, 30 caliber cartridge, and the 1954 decision to establish uniform medical treatment of battlefield casualties, standardization has not been pressed vigorously. However, the encouragement given to NATO nations to adopt each other's weapons has produced much common equipment in the aircraft and missile fields. Both the Hawk and Sidewinder missiles became all-NATO equipment.

De Gaulle's 1966 full withdrawal from the integrated structure came after several years of discussion as to NATO's future—a discussion which still continues. The debate focuses especially over the questions of how to have multiple fingers on the nuclear trigger and whether and in what form to give West Germany access to or control over nuclear weapons. But foreign policy differences, and great variations in effort, lie just behind the façade of this question. At the Council meeting in December 1965, both Secretary Rusk and Secretary McNamara stressed the growing nuclear power of China and the U.S. involvement in the Vietnamese War—questions of peripheral concern to many of NATO's members. And of some $74 billions spent for defense by the fifteen members in 1965, two-thirds was by the United States with six billions more by the United Kingdom. The financial burden and defense contribution continues to be very disproportionate. These problems did not alter NATO's unique status as the most far-reaching and intricate alliance ever entered into in peacetime.

In this chapter and the last we have focused a good deal of attention on how and why balance-of-power systems are formed; how alignments are con-

---

[15] See *NYHT* (EE) and *NYT*, January 8, 1954 for statement by General Gruenther, and *NYHT* (EE), January 6, 1954 for statement by General Collins.

cluded, and the forms they may take; how the local balance and the general balance are related; how the balance-of-power process is carried on through the use of four basic techniques; how balance-of-power systems have changed through the last several centuries; how NATO represents the ultimate development to date in this trend. We have focused little attention on the problem of what causes the balance-of-power cycle to be shorter or longer, and why general wars may vary from twenty years apart to a whole century. Insofar as these latter questions can be answered, they can best be made clear by examining the several modern balances of power in some detail. By this method we ought to be able to draw certain conclusions as to the causes and means of their collapse. This is the task of the two chapters that follow.

CHAPTER 18

Studies in the
Balance of Power: I

We talk of the *ancien régime* as though there reigned
then a divine stability. In fact Powers ran up and down
the scale with dizzy rapidity. Of the Powers indisputably
ranked among the Great at the Congress of Westphalia in
1648, three—Sweden, Holland, Spain—ceased to be Great
and one—Poland—ceased to exist, before the close of
the eighteenth century; their place was taken by Russia
and Prussia, two states hardly within notice a hundred
years before. There was no such whirligig of fortune during the nineteenth century, despite its supposedly revolutionary character. The Great Powers who launched the
First World War in 1914 were the Great Powers who had
made up the Congress of Vienna in 1814.

A. J. P. TAYLOR
The Struggle for Mastery in Europe, 1848–1918

I N examining the causes for decline and collapse in a balance-of-power system, we shall focus our efforts upon the general balance whose failure
brings general war. Local balances are relatively simple, and the reasons
for their collapse are usually fairly obvious from an examination of the foreign
policies of the two or three states typically involved. What we want to know,
if we can, is more exactly *why* local balances are swallowed up in general balances, and why general balances last or fail to last for long periods of time.
What makes one general balance "live" so much longer than another? To
what extent do particular forms of alignment manipulations *themselves* has-
ten or retard the process of collapse, irrespective of the aggressive aims of particular great powers?

Unlike the chemist who may resort to controlled and repeated experiments
at will, the international relations analyst must work with the material that
the world of nation-states provides. Since the end of the Middle Ages we can
count no more, at most, than five or six general wars. Further, as our examination of the mid-eighteenth-century balance of power in Frederick the Great's
time indicates, the functioning of the balance in monarchical days was very
different from our own. Wars were also more lightly and more frequently embarked upon two centuries ago. Consequently, although an understanding
of the pre-1815 period is useful for any complete knowledge of balance-of-
power phenomena, it is of limited direct applicability. Since 1815 the disap-

pearance of absolute monarchy, the development of the industrial revolution, and the great changes in the nature of warfare have produced circumstances that are so different from what went before that any generalizations about balances of power, covering both the ante- and post-Napoleonic eras, must be carefully formulated if they are not to mislead rather than clarify.

For these reasons we can with most profit study the events that led to those collapses of the general balance which we call World Wars I and II. Against this background we can later examine the post-World-War-II balance for clues as to whether it shows clear signs of early decline into yet a third world war.[1] In this way we can gain some insight into the type of measures that seem to prolong or shorten the life of such general balances. This understanding is highly important in a world of nation-states where war remains always *possible*, for it may indicate how, by active measures in foreign-policy formulation and implementation, general war may in certain cases be made *less probable.*

In this chapter we shall examine the balance of power that ended in World War I, and in the next, the pre-World-War-II balance. In each study we shall be looking always for lessons for today. For while the political *style* of the 1815–1914 balance may seem remote, the changing *forms* of that balance (and the counterbalancing interests behind them) have contemporary relevance.

I The Era of Repressed Nationalism and Localized Wars (1815–1871)

FOR a hundred years after the Napoleonic Wars (1815 to 1914) there was no general war simultaneously involving all the great powers in Europe. This prolonged period of general peace represents a unique condition in the history of the balance of power since Columbus discovered America. As such it merits close study. Why did it last so long?

In part the answer is to be found in the unique circumstances in which Europe found itself immediately after 1815. Monarchical Europe was determined to set the clock back and suppress the great forces of nationalism that had been unleashed by the French Revolution. That this was no imaginary danger was demonstrated by two great waves of revolution that swept across much of Europe in 1830 and most of Europe in 1848. Despite a threat of war over the (Near) Eastern Question following the Greek revolution against Turkey in 1821, the monarchs of Europe, beset by assaults upon their thrones, acted successfully to preserve peace among themselves. Their common perils drove most thoughts of wars with one another from their heads.

Beginning in 1848 this unwritten truce came to an end with the Italian kingdom of Piedmont's unsuccessful war against Austria. This conflict, whose roots lay in the same nationalist forces that had produced revolution, heralded the arrival of two related problems which were to preoccupy Europe until

---

[1] See Chapter 31.

1871: how could the congeries of Italian and German states be reformed into nation-states? The demands of nationalism within the Italian and German states could no longer be indefinitely suppressed once the banner of nationalism came to be championed by an Italian and by a German monarch (the kings of Piedmont and Prussia, respectively). Where nationalism had brought popular revolution against kings, it now brought war between kings.

Leaving apart the Crimean War (1854–1856), which was fought by Britain, France, Turkey, and Piedmont against Russia, the other five important wars that occurred in Europe between 1848 and 1870 were all concerned with either Italian or German unification, or both. Of these wars the fight of Piedmont and France against Austria in 1859, while more successful than Piedmont's earlier attempt already mentioned, gained directly only Lombardy and left Italian unification still far from complete.[2] Similarly, in the fourth struggle, the Austro-Prussian War on Denmark in 1864, little direct progress was made toward German unification. But in the fifth conflict, the Seven Weeks' War against Austria in 1866, in which for the first time the Italians and the Prussians joined forces, the results were speedy and decisive. While Venetia went to Italy, Prussia gained control of all North Germany. In the sixth war, the Franco-Prussian War of 1870–1871, Alsace and Lorraine were detached from France, all South and North Germany were joined together under Prussian leadership, and the German Empire was created.

All six wars remained local, in part because of the use of shrewd diplomatic tactics, especially in the earlier period by Italy's Cavour, and in the later period by Prussia's Bismarck.[3] But clever diplomacy and Napoleon III's bungling are by no means the whole of the explanation. The fundamental reason why the great powers did not all become involved in a general war is that in the great majority of these wars the issue at stake was the national unification of Italy and Germany—a process completely compatible with the spirit of the age.

Nothing, after all, could have so greatly altered the whole system than forming unified nation-states in Central Europe where only the weak "Germanies" and "Italies" had previously existed. Yet it was tolerated. Although the cumulative changes of these wars represented a revolutionary rearrangement of the traditional distribution of power in Europe, the main "aggressors"—Piedmont and Prussia—were engaged in a work of limited ends not itself aimed at limitless expansion and the destruction of the balance. In other words, the effects on the balance, while revolutionary, were incidental to the process of unification rather than unification a pretext to assault the traditional balance. This demonstrates a fundamental truth we shall encounter again: much disturbance of the balance can be and will be tolerated by third powers if the aim is one they consider acceptable and limited.

On the other hand, in this period two fundamental sets of relations had

---

[2] Although it set in motion a more or less spontaneous gravitation of the many Italian states toward union with Piedmont.

[3] See Chapter 17.

hardened into fixed patterns that were henceforth to endure, creating local balances that ultimately were to form together the core of the general alliance system before World War I. Franco-German hostility was symbolized by the annexation of Alsace and Lorraine to Germany and the establishment of the German Empire in the palace of the French kings at Versailles. On the other side of Europe, Austria had "repaid" the Russian tsar's aid in 1849 in suppressing the revolt against the Hapsburgs in Hungary by issuing an ultimatum to Russia at the outset of the Crimean War, requiring her to evacuate Romania—which Austria then occupied for the duration. From these beginnings a world war would yet come.

2   *The Era of Bismarck* (1871–1890)

THE pre-World-War-I balance of power entered the first of two decisive phases between 1871 and 1890. Under the careful cultivation lavished upon it by Prince Otto von Bismarck, Chancellor of Germany during this entire period, it grew into an alignment system that was as much a check on the possibility of general war as the fertile brain of man can design. Bismarck's alliance system, although it must also be said that he was extraordinarily favored by the circumstances of the time, has never been surpassed since for pure ingenuity. It is ironical that his part in making the balance of power what it was in this period has often been slighted when the credit for its smooth functioning has been apportioned. Especially because of Britain's role of "balancer" on so many occasions in modern history, "balancing" two more or less equal groups by remaining uncommitted, or providing the added weight to a weaker bloc when it was necessary to balance it against a stronger group, she has often been given the praise that in this period rightfully belongs to Bismarck. Although Britain between 1871 and 1890 did remain more or less aloof from alignments, she did *not* support the weaker side of the balance—France—for the very good reason that she was engaged in competition with France in the acquisition of colonies. She was embroiled in a similar imperialistic rivalry with Russia. As a matter of fact she flirted with a possible alliance with Germany on more than one occasion. Palmerston's famous remark that "England has no permanent friends, only permanent interests" has often been cited to indicate why Britain pursued the historic role of "balancer," but in this particular case her counterbalancing interests led her in two directions at once: toward opposition to growing German power on the continent, and toward rivalry with France and Russia in colonial areas. Germany, because of the somewhat ambiguous nature of British interests, was able to shape the mold in which the balance was cast, in large part along the lines of her own design.

Once Germany was created, as we have already remarked in passing, the whole balance-of-power situation in Europe was revolutionized. Weak disunity was replaced by organized strength in what since that day has remained the geographical center of the European balance of power. Germany was no longer a collection of pawns in the power game, at the disposal of other and stronger states.

In such circumstances it would have been very simple for Germany any time after 1870 to have aroused against herself the powerful coalition that did defeat her in 1918. That this did not occur is due to Bismarck's effort to make it clear, following 1871, that Germany's policy would be moderate and un-provocative. He realized that the Kaiser's Reich was a house whose bricks were held together by mortar that had not yet had time to dry. He proposed to give Germany that time and keep her out of war by careful diplomacy and an intricate alignment system. Bismarck made himself the architect of that system.

The heart of Bismarck's problem was to prevent a new war initiated by France to undo the defeat of 1871. It was perfectly clear that Germany had made an enemy that would not rest content without her "lost provinces" of Alsace and Lorraine. Bismarck did not so much fear being defeated in a new war with France as he wanted to prevent the war from occurring. This could be achieved by isolating France. Since England was, if anything, hostile to France, success turned upon what the Austrians and Russians did and, in a much less important way, what the Italians did. Bismarck turned his atten-tion east to resolve his problem in the west. In the long run, if he could gain both Austrian and Russian support, or the support of either without alienat-ing the other, he would have Europe in the palm of his hand. To do this he would have to handle Austrian and Russian counterbalancing interests with great care.

Bismarck developed his system in six steps. The first was the creation of the "Three Emperors' League" in 1873, binding Germany, Russia, and Austria into a loose entente. While it included a military convention whereby Ger-many and Russia pledged each other support with two hundred thousand men in the event either was attacked by another European power, develop-ments soon cast doubt upon the usefulness of this agreement for Germany. During the war scare of April–May 1875, between France and Germany, both England and Russia warned Germany against any thought of a preventive war against France. The incident demonstrated the precarious nature of the tight-rope Germany was walking, as well as the weakness of the Three Emperors' League. Revolution in the Balkans in the summer of 1875 soon made matters worse. By 1876 Bulgaria, Serbia, and Montenegro were at war with Turkey. Subsequent Turkish victories imposed a severe strain on Austro-Russian rela-tions, and when Russia inquired of Germany in September 1876, whether she could rely upon German support against Austria, Bismarck's reply—that he would not allow either to defeat the other decisively—further dampened German-Russian relations.

Early in 1877 the Austro-Russian crisis was resolved and in April Russia made war on Turkey. Russia's victories now alarmed both England and Aus-tria, who demanded the revision of the Treaty of San Stefano just imposed by Russia on Turkey. In the great-power Congress of Berlin of 1878 this was done, Russia lost many of her gains, and a fairly considerable Ottoman Empire was left in existence in Europe. But Bismarck's "honest broker" role at the Congress produced a pronounced coolness in Russo-German relations.

This led to the second step in Bismarck's alliance system: the Dual Alliance of Germany and Austria of October 7, 1879. By it Bismarck transferred his main reliance for military support from Russia to Austria. This treaty was henceforth regularly renewed and was still in force in 1914. By it each agreed to support the other if either were attacked by Russia; if either were attacked by another power, the other was at least to remain neutral; and if an attack was made by Russia plus another power, both would fight. Thus Germany was secured against the danger of fighting a two-front war alone.

Bismarck's decision to rely primarily on Austria in no way reflected a desire to alienate Russia. Accordingly, when Russia now made efforts at *rapprochement*, Bismarck responded willingly. The third step, consequently, was a new loose association of Germany, Austria, and Russia (June 1881) known as the Alliance of the Three Emperors. Strictly speaking, this was not an alliance. It provided that if one of the three parties found itself at war with a fourth power (except Turkey, and thus presumably England or France) the other two would at least maintain a benevolent neutrality.[4] The Alliance of the Three Emperors was to run three years, and in 1884 it was extended to 1887. It was kept strictly secret.

The advantages of the "alliance" were perhaps not so obvious in the case of Russia as they were for Germany and Austria. They were nonetheless real. Russia was thereby freed from much of her anxiety over Britain, with whom her relations were perennially bad but which had become worse because of war and tension between England and Afghanistan in 1878–1880. Russia wanted and got recognition of the principle that the Straits should be closed to keep out British warships from the Black Sea. She also had Bismarck's assurance that Germany would not permit Austria to inflict a decisive defeat on Russia. The only other alternative for Russia was an alliance with France—a possibility made remote, except in the extreme case of Russian isolation, by the contempt of Russia's tsars for Republican France.

In May 1882, came Bismarck's fourth step: the Triple Alliance of Germany, Austria-Hungary, and Italy. Like the Austro-German Dual Alliance of 1879, the Triple Alliance was still in effect thirty-two years later when World War I broke out. By its terms, if France attacked Italy, both Germany and Austria-Hungary would "aid . . . with all their forces." If France attacked Germany, Italy (but not Austria-Hungary) would aid. If any one or two of the three parties were attacked by two or more of the other great powers, all three alliance partners would fight. Finally, if a fourth great power were to "threaten the security of the dominions" of one of the three "and the threatened Party should find itself compelled . . . to go to war," the other two

---

[4] This did not, of course, prohibit the terms of the Austro-German Dual Alliance from being put into effect.

would "observe a benevolent neutrality" although they could, if they wanted, also give armed support to their ally.[5] The Triple Alliance was renewed and amplified in 1887, 1891, 1902, and 1912.[6]

The year 1887 marked the high-water mark of Bismarck's system. Three events indicate how successfully he had isolated France. First, in 1887 the Triple Alliance was renewed, thus preventing any possibility of a Franco-Italian *rapprochement.* Second, in the same month of February 1887, with Bismarck's encouragement, the First Mediterranean Agreement (which was really a series of bilateral notes) was reached. This constituted the fifth step in the creation of his system. By it Italy, Britain, Austria-Hungary, Spain, and Germany [7] agreed to work for the maintenance of the *status quo* in the Mediterranean (including the Aegean, Adriatic, and Black Seas) and to consult with one another beforetimes if it could not be maintained. This was obviously designed to prevent France from further imperialistic successes in the area. Third, in June 1887, the sixth step in Bismarck's system was taken with the signature of the "Reinsurance" Treaty between Germany and Russia. Its signing meant that a Franco-Russian alliance was again postponed. It replaced the Alliance of the Three Emperors, which was expiring, and which Russia did not wish to renew. Russia preferred a more direct and written guarantee that Germany would restrain Austria-Hungary. By the terms of this new treaty, if either Russia or Germany were to "find itself at war with a third great Power," the other would remain neutral, provided that the war was not brought about by a Russian attack on Austria or a German attack on France. Thus Germany would be protected against a joint Franco-Russian attack, just as Russia was reinsured against a joint Austro-German aggression. Germany also recognized Russia's "preponderant and conclusive influence in Bulgaria" and promised diplomatic support if Turkey allowed the Straits to be used "for the martial operations of a belligerent power" (England). By a "very secret protocol" it was agreed that, "In the event that His Majesty the Emperor of Russia should find himself under the necessity of assuming the task of defending the entrance of the Black Sea, . . . Germany promises . . . moral and diplomatic support to the measures which His Majesty might judge necessary to take to guard the Key of His Empire." [8] This agreement was to run three years—until 1890.

The thread of Bismarck's purpose is clearly woven into the text of all these arrangements. He wished to isolate France by balancing and reconciling Austro-Russian ambitions in the Balkans, by keeping alive and exploiting Italian rivalry with France, and by encouraging British rivalries with France and Russia. Because Britain refused to enter any firm and fast commitments, Bis-

---

[5] Articles II, III, and IV. Each of these provisions was contingent on there having been no "direct provocation" by the Triple Alliance member who was attacked.

[6] See *Die Grosse Politik der Europäischen Kabinette, 1871–1914,* Vol. 7, pp. 99 ff., for the text of the third treaty as it stood with the addition of Articles VI to XI.

[7] Germany, by adhering to the Italo-Spanish note.

[8] The text of the "Reinsurance" Treaty is taken from *Die Grosse Politik der Europäischen Kabinette, 1871–1914,* Vol. 5, pp. 253 ff.

marck's alliances were made with Italy, Austria, and Russia. Of these three the latter two were vital to his plans. At first, because of still-lingering Austrian resentment over her defeat by Prussia in 1866, Bismarck depended more upon Russia while keeping Austria integrated into the arrangements. This was the pattern of the Three Emperors' League. But the events of 1875–1878 and the coolness in German-Russian relations that followed the Congress of Berlin led him to reverse this arrangement by converting Austria into a firm alliance partner through the Dual and then the Triple Alliance, and associating Russia with the arrangements, first through the Alliance of the Three Emperors and then through the "Reinsurance" Treaty. The principle remained the same although the Russian and Austrian roles were exchanged.

These arrangements worked well because they were formulated in compatible if highly intricate terms—something quite essential if the counterbalancing interests of the three eastern powers were to be stabilized as Bismarck hoped.[9] In the "Reinsurance" Treaty, Bismarck promised neutrality *only if Austria attacked Russia*. In the Dual Alliance, Germany agreed to *support Austria if Russia attacked her* (and, in the Triple Alliance, Germany promised to do the same if Austria were attacked "without direct provocation" by two or more great powers). Bismarck was attempting to discourage an Austro-Russian break but was prepared to aid Austria if Russia actually attacked her. In turn he could depend upon Austrian help if he ever got into an unprovoked war with both France and Russia.

3   The Era of Disintegration (1890–1914)

BISMARCK, because he did not wish war, did not and could not alter the essentials of the international-relations situation in which he was to operate between 1870 and 1890. But he had the good sense to exploit it effectively by pursuing a broad concept of Germany's national interests until, on March 18, 1890, he was dismissed from office. Kaiser Wilhelm II was dissatisfied with Bismarck's policy toward Russia. From now on German policy rode off at a great pace in all directions at once: it lost subtlety, continuity, and effectiveness. It also in the end destroyed the counterbalancing interests of the great powers that Bismarck had known so well how to exploit, and made Germany at least appear as the most likely disturber of Europe's peace. After Wilhelm was through, France could no longer be called the most likely instigator of war.

Wilhelm, for example, wanted closer relations with England. To that end he sanctioned the Anglo-German Colonial Agreement of July 1, 1890, by which Germany gave up her vague claims to a vast area of East Africa, and received in return the island of Heligoland, at that time considered to be worthless. He made a great visit of state to London on July 4, 1891, and there was much talk of England's association with the Triple Alliance. But when

---

[9] For an opposing point of view see the discussion in Grant and Temperley, *op. cit.*

Lord Rosebery in the first six months of 1894 tried to work out such a connection, he found Germany unwilling to accept responsibility for any of Britain's interests, and when Lord Salisbury suggested closer relations to the Kaiser in the summer of 1895, he was rebuffed. In January 1896, the Kaiser wanted to arrange military intervention to aid President Kruger of the South African (Boer) Republic. Kruger had defeated British raiders thought by the Kaiser to have been sent by the British government. His advisers in the end dissuaded him from this action but agreed to a famous telegram of congratulations sent by Wilhelm to Kruger. This aroused a great furor in Britain. It remains a classic example of how a great power, by pursuing interests of dubious utility that are contradictory to more important ends, can pave the path to failure. While Germany had secondary interests in the South African situation, she had far more important interests in creating better relations with Britain. Wilhelm gave priority to the lesser of two counterbalancing (and in this case, contradictory) interests.

Actually, by this time, German policy was designed to irritate the British so that they would recognize how formidable Germany was and therefore wish to conclude an alliance with her—moreover, they made no secret of the fact that this was German intent! In the next years, although Anglo-German relations vacillated, they never became more than momentarily close, and more often they were antagonistic. At the end of 1897 the first extensive German naval program was announced. It was to add twelve battleships to the existing seven, ten heavy cruisers to the existing two, and twenty-three light cruisers to the existing seven. All were to be ready in 1904. On March 28, 1898, the first German Navy Law was passed by the Reichstag, and in November of the same year the preliminary concession for the Berlin-to-Baghdad Railway was obtained. Both led directly to increased friction with England; the Anglo-German alliance negotiations, attempted once more in the spring of 1901, fell through. The whole story of German relations with Britain after 1890 is a study in ineffectiveness, and of the simultaneous pursuit of incompatible policies.

With Russia, Wilhelm did even worse. By fumbling and ineptness he converted her from more or less an ally into very much an enemy. First, he allowed the "Reinsurance" Treaty to lapse on June 18, 1890, and discouraged all Russia's numerous efforts to discuss renewal. In May 1891, he prematurely renewed the Triple Alliance. Next he allowed the rumors of Britain's association with Germany and the Triple Alliance, growing out of his state visit to London of 1891, to go unchecked, and at the same time failed to obtain that association. Twenty days after that state visit a French squadron was making a visit of friendship to Kronstadt; the Tsar actually listened to the *Marseillaise* (the revolutionary hymn that had become the French national anthem) on board a French warship. Nothing could have been a clearer sign of growing Franco-Russian *rapprochement*. Even after this the Russians moved slowly, and the situation might still have been saved. In August 1891, a rather vague

Franco-Russian agreement to consult in case of aggression was concluded. A year later a military convention was drafted, but not until December 1893–January 1894, after a further delay of almost a year and a half, was the convention formally accepted and placed in effect. The convention was very much to the point in its final form. Article I specified that:

If France is attacked by Germany, or by Italy supported by Germany, Russia shall employ all her available forces in order to attack Germany.

If Russia is attacked by Germany, or by Austria supported by Germany, France shall employ all her available forces in order to fight Germany.[10]

By Article II, if the Triple Alliance powers mobilized, France and Russia were automatically to follow suit. Article III stipulated that France would furnish 1.3 million men and Russia seven to eight hundred thousand, and that these forces were to "engage fully and with all speed, *so that Germany may have to fight at the same time in the East and in the West.*" [11]

It is worth noting that the breakdown in Anglo-German alignment negotiations came in June 1894, after this Franco-Russian agreement was formally in effect. Yet instead of determined efforts to settle Anglo-German differences, Germany four years later embarked upon a naval program that could not fail to destroy any fundamental chance of Anglo-German *rapprochement*. Well within a decade of Bismarck's forced retirement, the Kaiser had undone his work: France was no longer isolated, Russia was on the opposite side, the possibility of a two-front war was confronting Germany, and Britain was being rapidly pushed into a position where, shortly after the turn of the century, she would reconsider her relations with France. The British settlement with Russia, which came in 1907, was already foreshadowed in Lord Salisbury's note of January 25, 1898, to Russia in which he proposed dividing Asia from Alexandretta to Peking into a Russian and a British sphere of influence—a proposal rejected at this time by Russia. It showed the trend of British thinking.

If the Dual Alliance of France and Russia was the first blow to the Bismarckian system, and the growing Anglo-German distrust and hostility the second, the third blow fell in April 1904, with the conclusion of the Anglo-French Entente. The outbreak of the Russo-Japanese War helped to provide the final impetus for both Britain and France to conclude an agreement, for Britain was an ally of Japan and would have to aid Japan if France aided Russia. Neither Britain nor France wished such a war. The outstanding issues were settled and, while France recognized the British position in Egypt, the British recognized French interests in Morocco.

This agreement of 1904 marks a watershed in the history of the disintegration of the Bismarckian balance of power. Although the trend since 1893–1895 had been clear, after 1904 the increase in severity and recurrence of

---

[10] Text in *Documents diplomatiques français* (1871–1914), First Series (1871–1900), Vol. 9, pp. 643 ff.

[11] *Ibid.*, italics added.

crises among Europe's great powers was most marked. There had been bilateral crises in dozens before this; now were to come multilateral crises, six of them in ten years, and ending with World War I.

The *first crisis* (the First Moroccan Crisis) began in March 1905, with the visit of the German Emperor to Tangier. For once the Kaiser had been unwilling to be provocative, but was persuaded by his advisors to make the move. His speech at Tangier, advocating the independence and territorial integrity of Morocco, immediately produced a panic in Paris. French overtures to arrange a settlement with the Germans were repulsed; Germany insisted on a conference with the idea of testing the new Anglo-French Entente.

The conference was not actually held until January 16–April 7, 1906, at Algeciras. Even before the Kaiser's speech, and again in the interim between the speech and the conference, the Germans had sought to repair in part the mistake of 1890 by attempting a German-Russian-French front against England and destroying the Anglo-French Entente. In October 1904, the Tsar accepted a German draft treaty that provided for mutual aid in the event of an attack by another European power. Russia was unwilling to sign it before consulting France; the Germans hoped that if Russia could be persuaded to sign it first, the French would be drawn in too. Negotiations fell through. They were revived in July 1905, at Björkö, where essentially the same draft was signed by the Kaiser and the Tsar during a visit to each other's yachts. The treaty again fell through due to the strong negative reaction of the Russian foreign office and the refusal of the French to consider an alliance in view of the Germans' actions at Tangier and their subsequent behavior during the Morocco crisis.

In these events the ineptness of German diplomacy was again plainly revealed. The Kaiser's speech at Tangier, followed by the brusque German reaction to French peacemaking feelers, was incompatible with the alliance Wilhelm wanted by now so much with the Russians (and thus also the French). The Kaiser, in his own words, considered this treaty "a Continental Combine" that would "block the way to the whole world becoming John Bull's private property." [12] Wilhelm had now swung over to an anti-British policy while simultaneously destroying the chances for an effective alternative. It was this kind of inept maneuvering by the Germans that ultimately alienated Russia, France, and Britain.

The Algeciras Conference (1906) revealed the weakness of the German diplomatic position. France, throughout the conference, was supported by all the great powers, including the United States, except Austria, which gave lukewarm support to Germany. The Kaiser's telegram to the Austro-Hungarian foreign minister after the conference, thanking him for having been "a brilliant second on the duelling ground," [13] is more indicative of Wilhelm's prose style than of the truth. In the Act of Algeciras, France was given con-

[12] Cited in Grant and Temperley, p. 449.
[13] *Ibid.*, p. 446.

trol of the police on the Moroccan-Algerian frontier, and a joint police control with the Spanish in the rest of Morocco. France was to have the greatest control in a state bank which was to be set up. It was quite clear which way things were tending. Further, far from destroying the Anglo-French Entente, the crisis strengthened it. The week before the conference began, Anglo-French military and naval conversations were initiated. The entente, which had begun as a settlement of dangerous points of friction between England and France, was taking on the character of a somewhat amorphous military alignment.

In August 1907, the Anglo-Russian Entente, discussed earlier, came into being. It was followed the next year by the *second crisis* (the Bosnia-Herzegovina Annexation Crisis)—just as the Anglo-French Entente had been followed by the first crisis. On October 6, 1908, Austria suddenly proclaimed the annexation of Bosnia and Herzegovina (which had been under Austrian military occupation since 1878). Serbia and Montenegro were enraged, and there was great excitement in Russia. Actually, the Russian foreign minister had given Russian consent to such a move if Austria would not oppose the opening of the Straits to Russian warships under certain conditions, but these events were to be arranged by a great-power conference; the Russian foreign minister, who was in Paris, was going on to London to lay the groundwork for the meeting when the sudden Austrian move was made. He then repudiated the agreement, which the Austrians had actually violated by their premature move. Although the French and the British both gave support, Russia's position was very weak militarily. When Germany (who had also been surprised by Austria's sudden action but who supported the Austrians to preserve the alliance) exerted some pressure (March 1909), the Russian foreign minister, glad of a pretext, yielded. Wilhelm's public comment (which stung the Russians to the quick) was that Germany had taken Austria-Hungary's side "in shining armour at a grave moment." [14]

The box score for Triple Alliance vs. Triple Entente now stood at one to one. Within the Triple Alliance itself one defeat for Germany and one victory for Austria-Hungary had been chalked up. There were four more crises left to play.

In June–November 1911, the *third crisis* occurred (the Second Moroccan Crisis). Germany was dissatisfied with the way things were developing in Morocco. France, as a follow-up to anti-foreign disorders, had entered Fez on May 21, ignoring German protests. The French, for their part, were willing to compensate Germany, in return for a really free hand in Morocco, but the Germans in conversations on June 20–21 refused to name a price. Instead, on July 1, the German warship *Panther* arrived at Agadir, Morocco, on the pretext of protecting German interests. Actually, as the Germans allowed it to be soon known, it was there to put pressure on the French. Germany was using the same type of *Machtpolitik* (power politics) that had already led to disastrous results when used on England. On July 15 the Germans finally made a

---

[14] Grant and Temperley, p. 459.

concrete demand—for the whole of the French Congo. On July 21 Lloyd George made his famous and bellicose Mansion House speech. Since he had hitherto been considered as opposed to war, this pronouncement came as a shock to the Germans. The British began preparing for an eventual war: Germany had gotten more of a reaction than she desired, and Franco-German negotiations were resumed with more modesty on the German side. On November 4 agreement was reached. France was to have a free hand in Morocco, and Germany was given a small portion of the French Congo—two strips of land which afforded her a connection between her Cameroons territory and the Congo and Ubangi rivers. Thus ended the third crisis—not a complete defeat for Germany this time but still definitely a defeat. The "score" was now: Triple Entente, 2; Triple Alliance, 1.

Like a pendulum, the focus of attention in three crises had gone from the West (Morocco) to the Balkans, and back. Now it swung back once more to the East. On October 18, 1912, the First Balkan War broke out with Turkey fighting Bulgaria, Serbia, and Greece. Montenegro had declared war on Turkey ten days earlier. Within two weeks the Turks had been soundly defeated; on November 10 the Serbs reached the Adriatic through northern Albania. On November 24 the Austrians came out flatly and finally against the incorporation of Albania into Serbia, or Serbian access to the Adriatic. (See Map 5 for the pre-World-War-I frontiers.)

Thus began the *fourth crisis* (the Balkan War Crisis). The Serbs held to their demands, with Russian backing. France in turn backed Russia. Austria was for once supported by Italy, who had no wish to see Serbia an Adriatic power. The Germans, though more hesitant, finally gave Austria support. Britain, while taking care to prevent division from her allies, worked for some solution, especially with Germany. In late November–early December the crisis was acute. Both Russia and Austria had initiated mobilization. Yet in the end war was avoided: Russia gave up, and Albania did not go to Serbia. The Second Balkan War in July 1913, was not allowed to change this verdict. Although Serbia invaded Albania late in September in retaliation for Albanian raids, she was forced to withdraw again following an Austrian ultimatum of October 18. Thus the crisis was finally over. The "score" was once more tied: 2 to 2; two German defeats in the West, two French victories; two Austrian victories in the Balkans, two Russian defeats.

The *fifth crisis* (the Liman von Sanders Crisis) came hot on the heels of the fourth in November–December 1913. Although the scene this time was laid in the East, with Russia taking the leading role for the Entente, the main protagonist on the Triple Alliance side was again Germany. Liman von Sanders, a German, was commissioned by the Turks to reorganize their army. The Russians raised no objection until they found out the extent of the powers he would have, including command of the First Army Corps at Constantinople; they then came out against the idea of the command at Constantinople. The French threw full support to the Russians although Britain took a moderate view. In January 1914, the crisis was resolved when the Germans agreed that Sanders should not hold the Constantinople command. He was made instead inspector-general of the Turkish army. In this fifth crisis the Germans had again ended up behind: the "score" was now 3 to 2 in favor of the Entente. Russia for the first time had "won."

In the spring of 1914 discussions were begun over the question of a naval convention between the English and the Russians—a tightening of the Entente. Yet on June 15 an Anglo-German agreement was reached over the troublesome question of the Baghdad Railway. The outlook seemed improved. Then on June 28 the *sixth crisis* began (the Archduke Assassination Crisis). Archduke Francis Ferdinand and his wife, on a state visit to the new realms of Bosnia and Herzegovina, were shot and killed at Sarajevo by a Bosnian acting for the Serbian Black Hand Society. The Serbian government, although aware of the plot, had done little about it. On July 5 the German government gave support to Austria, urging some action while world opinion was sympathetic to Austria. There was as yet no feeling that the situation could not be localized; the Russians were not thought to be ready to go too far. On July 23 a forty-eight-hour ultimatum was given Serbia by Austria. On the 25th the Russians, unwilling to chalk up a new humiliation by Austria, decided to go to war if Serbia were attacked. On the same day the Serbs rejected the crucial points in the Austrian demands and ordered mobilization. On July 28 Austria declared war on Serbia; the next day Bethmann-Hollweg, the German Chancellor, attempted to pressure Austria into a resumption of conversations with Russia, but Russia had already ordered general mobilization. When the Tsar heard of Germany's efforts, he changed the mobilization to be against Austria only. But the next day, because of difficulties in mobilizing on that basis, the order was again changed to general mobilization. The Germans, whose war plans depended upon defeating France in the West before the ponderous Russian mobilization could be completed, now felt forced to move. At 7 P.M. on August 1 Germany declared war on Russia. World War I had begun.

4   *The Lessons of Study I*

IN retrospect it is quite clear that after 1904 (the Anglo-French Entente), and even more so after 1907 (the Anglo-Russian Entente), an increasing and dangerous rigidity made its appearance in the balance of power. In other words, once the last important great power had made its alignments, the tension noticeably increased. There being no further allies to win (unless through defection from the opposing side), it became imperative to preserve the bloc against diplomatic inroads from the opposing group. A great power in one of these blocs might still urge moderation and use its influence to establish a compromise, as did both England and Germany occasionally, especially in the fifth and sixth crises. But if one power—and not even necessarily a great power—chose to mobilize, and refused to back down, there was little recourse for the rest in the end except to close ranks and face the enemy.

One cannot conclude that general war will necessarily follow the definitive alignment of all the great powers into two opposing blocs, but it is certain that this is the most rigid form the balance can take. When this form comes into existence, it is extremely difficult to ease tension and keep the way open for continued negotiations. Even in this most rigid form of the general balance, war may not come because no power dares to push things far enough. But, in the six crises just surveyed, Austria had gotten into the habit of expecting Russia always to yield in the end. As a result she was not very cautious about how far she went. Again, war may not come, even after this rigid form is reached, if the problems and disputes between the powers do not become themselves more pressing. The crises over Morocco could be handled, as they ultimately were, by giving Germany at least a face-saving *quid pro quo*. Unless Germany had decided she must have Morocco—all of it—and nothing else would do, war was not inevitable. In the Balkans, though, the efforts of Austria-Hungary to add more Slavs to its polyglot multinational population ran in the teeth of the whole trend of the twentieth century. Austria-Hungary was obsolete. Internal, diverse tendencies, coupled with the growing frustration of Serbian nationalism, kept building emotional and political tension ever higher. Unless Austria had been willing to sanction her own dissolution, it is difficult to see how war could ultimately have been avoided. Without the rigid division into blocs, war might still have been localized—especially if an instrument for great-power consultation had been in permanent existence. But this was before the days of the League and the United Nations.

One must conclude that the most dangerous (to general peace) situation is where this most rigid form of the general balance is inextricably centered about problems whose lack of solution, for human and emotional reasons, cannot be indefinitely postponed and where these same human and emotional factors make reasonable compromises almost impossible.

Going back to the Bismarckian era between 1870 and 1890, as one illustration, one can also conclude that the least dangerous situation (in terms of preserving general peace) is where the power that has the most grounds for desiring war is isolated by the alignments system of its most obvious opponent. To achieve such an aim successfully, it is necessary either for that opponent to create a balance-of-power system that is very complex or turn to its own purposes the complex situation resulting from the counterbalancing interests of other powers acting independently. It is due to Bismarck's actions that Russia was not cast adrift before 1890 to join in an arrangement with France. His feat is the more remarkable, even after tsarist hostility to "revolutionary" France is taken into account, when it is remembered that he did not ally himself with Russia. He merely reassured Russia that he would not ally himself with an Austria that committed aggression against Russia. This very flexible use of counterbalancing interests held Austria-Hungary, Germany, and Russia within a set of compatible alignments. On the other hand, Bismarck did not create Anglo-French and Anglo-Russian imperialistic rivalries even if he turned them to his purposes. The complexity and flexibility that characterized Bismarck's system rested upon both points. After the Kaiser threw away the first in 1890, the system retained a great deal of flexibility. It was the ineptness of German policy between 1890 and 1904 that did so much to squeeze the remaining flexibility from the system.

It is well worth exploring the reasons why the colonial rivalries of England with France and with Russia resulted in a more flexible balance until 1904–1907. Expressed in briefest terms, the *European* interests of the powers, which would have led them to one course of action, were frequently counterbalanced by their *colonial* interests, which led them toward another. The powers did not deliberately plan their colonial adventures with this result in mind, but they had that effect. At the same time that Germany and France were the contending states and the focus of a local balance in Europe (and later a focus of a general balance), they were often hand-in-glove with one another in Africa—forming a local *colonial* balance together against England. (To avoid confusion we shall speak of the balances in Europe as "primary" and those in colonial areas as "colonial" or "secondary.") While the Franco-German primary balance in Europe was founded upon direct hostility, the two states were able to cooperate at times in a secondary balance in Africa. Between 1883 and 1885 Bismarck established with Jules Ferry of France an entente which, while loose, was very real. During the London Conference on Egypt in the summer of 1884, the two powers stood together against Britain. Powers not directly hostile but also not European allies sometimes coordinated policy closely on colonial matters. In 1887, before the Franco-Russian alliance, France and Russia cooperated because of their common antagonism toward the colonial imperialism of Britain, to frustrate British proposals on the future of Egypt. Franco-German opposition to Britain was also evident after the Franco-Russian alliance in the important negotiations over the Congo and Sudan areas in 1894. Following Japan's victory over China in 1894–1895, Russia, Germany, and France intervened to prevent the Japanese taking the Liaotung Peninsula of China. This was the beginning of a loose entente of these three powers (the Far Eastern Triplice) which, in the next years, turned China's weakness to their own advantage. The very powers that were enemies in the primary balance in Europe worked together in the secondary balance in Asia. Further, even when Franco-German or Russo-German cooperation remained only potential or intermittent, it was still an active factor in the balance of power of this whole period. When the cooperation was dormant, at almost any time it might be resumed—until 1904–1907. And because European enmities were counterbalanced by need for colonial cooperation, so that the sharp hostilities in the one area were blunted in some degree by the entente in the other, rigidity and tension in the European balance remained far less than it otherwise would have been. Once the secondary balance disappeared after 1904–1907, and only the primary balance remained, rigidities and crises were quick in appearing and occurred in steadily quickening tempo.

Drawing a provisional lesson from Study I, we may conclude that the classic or external balancer form of the balance of power is not really used in this period (although it is *internalized* in the Bismarckian system in the form of deterrents to Austria-Hungary and Russia attacking one another). We may further conclude that the simple and rigid Wilhelmian form of the balance, while the most "natural," is also the most dangerous form to peace that the balance can take. Conversely, the highly complex Bismarckian form, while most "contrived" in its subtle utilization of counterbalancing interests to isolate the potential troublemaker, is the least dangerous form. It should be very clear that while the balance can take these various forms, no one of them is "inevitable." It should also be clear that certain nations have more "natural" opportunity to organize and manipulate the balance at a given time than others. They can be the decisive powers.

Keeping these tentative conclusions in mind let us now turn to the period between World War I and World War II.

CHAPTER 19

Studies in the
Balance of Power: II

Any alliance whose purpose is not the intention to wage
war is senseless and useless.

ADOLF HITLER
Mein Kampf

THE post-World-War-I balance-of-power situation was complicated by
seven factors, three of which could be readily observed from any map
showing World-War-I territorial losses, and the other four of which no
map would reveal.

| Seven Complicating Factors

ANYONE who, merely by observing the map and with no better knowledge
of the facts to the contrary, tried to decide on the losers in World War I,
would have to list Russia, Austria-Hungary, and Germany in that order. Russia lost Finland, Estonia, Latvia, Lithuania, most of what became Poland, and
Bessarabia—altogether an enormous area. Comparable in extent were the
losses of Austria-Hungary. Austria and Hungary were set up as small, independent states, and the rest of the old Hapsburg domains went to Italy (the
South Tyrol and Istria), Yugoslavia, Romania, Czechoslovakia, and Poland.
Third in losses was Germany, who had to return Alsace-Lorraine to France,
give up the Saar (although not permanently), Eupen-Malmedy, a portion of
Schleswig-Holstein, Danzig, Memel, Upper Silesia, and the famous Polish
"Corridor."

The stripping of territories from both Germany and Russia, while leaving
both sufficiently intact to exercise the role of great power, was to have tragic
consequences. As Machiavelli observed long ago, the infliction of a halfway
injury is most dangerous: it creates a lasting hatred that rules out reconciliation, without destroying the power of the enemy to retaliate at a time of his
own choosing. This is the lesson of Alsace-Lorraine, between 1871 and 1914,
all over again. With Austria-Hungary, on the other hand, the Hapsburg
domains were so thoroughly dismantled and the former centers of power
(Austria and Hungary) reduced to such weakness that it was beyond the ability of either to attempt to reconstitute the Hapsburg Empire. The danger and
complication to peace that stemmed from *this* dismantling was of another

kind: so many very small, new, and insecure units replaced the former empire that a happy hunting ground for great powers bent upon acquisitions was created, and the power structure in this important area of Europe was atomized.

All these territorial changes were made under the general heading of "self-determination." In the Austro-Hungarian case this was not too far from the truth, in Germany's case it was at times very far from the truth, and in Russia's case it represented only a half-truth. Austria and Hungary were both forced to cede, respectively, Germans and Magyars either to Italy or to the newly formed Balkan states. Even so, considering the complicated nature of the problem, the results were not too unjust in terms of the supposed standard of judgment. In Germany's case, however, where it was a question of having non-German minorities within Germany, or German minorities within the other states, the decision was given in favor of the second alternative. In the case of Russia, although the granting of independence to Finland and Poland had a great deal of justification, the case for Estonia, Latvia, and Lithuania, although one could be made, was much weaker.

In any event, "just" or not, these dispositions were ultimately to have disastrous effects. The destruction of Austria-Hungary as a Balkan power removed her as a possible restraint upon German and, especially, Russian ambitions. Concurrently, the creation in its place of a group of small powers, who were themselves prizes in, rather than deterrents to, an enlargement of the German and Russian spheres, gave Germany and Russia an opportunity to work together for mutual advantage in the area. Furthermore, as a consequence of their World-War-I territorial despoilment, both Russia and Germany had a sense of grievance. The creation of an independent Poland out of Austria, Germany, and Russia, although "just," was a standing invitation for a fourth partition between Germany and Russia.

The crowning weakness of the territorial settlements that followed World War I was that they created two "defeated" major powers, each fundamentally dissatisfied with the *status quo* distribution of power, and divided by a series of small, weak states temptingly sprawled between them. Conceivably either Germany or Russia alone might have been isolated within a balance-of-power alignment system. But to accomplish the isolation of both in any fundamental sense was impossible. An isolated Germany and an isolated Russia, even without a single formal tie between the two, meant per se an embryonic bloc. The Nazi-Soviet Pact of 1939 was implicit in the map of Europe of 1919.

The other four factors that played important roles in the development of these two decades between 1919 and 1939 are not discernible from the map.

The first of these others (the fourth factor of the seven) was Italy's feeling of frustration over her colonial position. She had expected rich rewards for her part in World War I, and although she could hardly have been treated better in Europe, her colonial ambitions went unfulfilled. For a time she had hopes of holding part of Turkey, but these in the end were frustrated. Consequently, after World War I as before, Italy found the inspiration for her moves in two conflicting interests—one colonial and one European. Her basic European interests drew her toward France and Britain, while her colonial hopes brought her into opposition to these same powers. At the same time colonial imperialism was no longer respectable after World War I. What with the new idea of collective security and resistance to aggression symbolized by the existence of the League of Nations, colonial adventures could conceivably have a disastrous balance-of-power effect if Italy was unwary enough to move against some League member in such a way as to compel Britain and France to support collective measures against her. The effect of Italy's frustrated hopes, as the fourth factor in the post-World-War-I balance-of-power situation, was potentially further to atomize the balance. It was hard enough to isolate two potential great-power troublemakers who had incentive to cooperate, but it was harder still when Italy's frustrations could so easily lead (as they were to) to a situation where Britain and France, as "keepers of the peace," were also bound by the letter and logic of the pattern of collective security to suspend the course of action that the pattern of balance-of-power alignments imperatively called for: enroll Italy in the "peace" front and keep her there at all costs.

The fifth factor was Britain's ineptitude in applying the balance-of-power principles with which historically she had been associated. It is true that Britain, in the period between the wars, attempted to act the role of "balancer" between France and Germany, and restore some power to the Germans as a balance against French hegemony on the continent. But her efforts were unfortunately either too little or too much: too little really to remove German grievances, and too much to keep the French ability to move decisively against Germany intact. Especially in the later stages of the interwar period, when France came to be pathetically dependent upon British moral and diplomatic support, the British hesitated far too long in recognizing the true character and ambitions of the Hitlerite regime. Where the dictates of the balance of power called for a strong joint Anglo-French policy, linked with Russian diplomatic support as much as possible, Britain far too often played a lone and futile hand. The Anglo-German Naval Agreement of June 18, 1935, is a perfect illustration of how Britain vacillated and ultimately misplayed her hand: on March 16 of the same year Germany had formally denounced the disarmament clauses of the Versailles Treaty. On April 11, at the Stresa Conference of England, France, and Italy, the three powers agreed on a joint policy in the face of German restiveness. Yet two months later Britain torpedoed this common front by unilaterally agreeing to allow Germany a navy, including submarines, of not more than 35 per cent of her own.

The sixth factor was America's reversion after World War I to unilateralism. She refused to enter alignments—even the generalized one of League membership. World War I was clear evidence that the United States had become a fundamental factor in the balance of power. Her aloofness had a disturbing effect upon European stability. If Britain, especially in the years after Hitler came to power, misjudged the role to which her true interests should have led her, so too did America. In the United States far too many people came to believe that America's participation in the war had been an error, and unnecessary. At the same time the great power of the United States, the unilateralist policy it pursued, taken together with the American predilection for moral stands on matters of principle, made United States action altogether too unpredictable. It encouraged the would-be disturbers of the peace while partially sapping the will of the natural opposition. In the Ethiopian sanctions episode,[1] the situation was complicated by the fact that Britain and France were acting against Italy in the name of collective security contrary to the policy clearly called for by balance-of-power principles. It was still more confused by a degree of uncertainty over whether America might insist upon freedom of the seas and trade with Italy if the members went too far. American "moral" reaction to Japan's adventures in Manchuria was obviously stronger than over Italy's move into Ethiopia, where the "good" and "evil" sides were much more sharply delineated—a factor not lost upon European observers.

The seventh factor was the Russian Revolution. The coming to power of communism there, and the dangers of its spreading, led to a pronounced gulf between East and West. Soviet suspicion of Britain and France was balanced by Western hostility toward Russia. While this factor will be examined later in detail, it needs mention here. Although it varied in importance during the period, its net effect, by introducing an ideological complication, was to further inhibit a wise handling of the balance of power.

The total effect of these seven factors, taken together, was to create a situation in which the concept of their counterbalancing interests held by the Western powers assisted the rise to power of a would-be disturber of the peace.

2 The Era of the Peace Settlements (1919–1924)

JUST as Bismarck's Germany had been the keystone of an alignment system designed to isolate France and prevent the French upsetting the power results of the Franco-Prussian War, post-World-War-I France sought to isolate Germany—and Russia. Initially she placed primary reliance vis-à-vis Germany upon the defensive treaties concluded with Britain and the United States in June 1919. The negative reaction of the United States Senate killed these agreements, for the British obligation was based upon American acceptance. France then turned to a task of fostering an alliance system, not only between herself and Germany's eastern neighbors, but also among the Balkan nations. At the same time these alliances constituted a bulwark against the spread of communism: they were a *cordon sanitaire*, sealing off the Bolshevik virus.

The main links in this chain were the Franco-Polish Treaty of February 19,

---

[1] See Chapter 20.

1921, stipulating mutual aid in the event of an attack, and the Franco-Czechoslovak Treaty of January 25, 1924, which also provided for joint opposition to unprovoked aggression. Treaties with Romania (1926), Yugoslavia (1927), and Turkey (1930) rounded out the system further. Then in 1920–1921 all these Eastern European states except Turkey linked themselves together, through a series of bilateral treaties, into what became known as the "Little Entente." It was directed against the restoration of the Hapsburgs or the resurgence of Hungarian power, and rested upon four treaties: the Czechoslovak-Yugoslav Treaty of August 1920; the offensive-defensive alliance of Poland and Romania of March 1921; the Romanian-Czechoslav Treaty of April 1921; and the Yugoslav-Romanian Treaty of June 1921.

Thus the *status quo* powers attempted to hold the line against revision of the Versailles settlement and to perpetuate the three drastic revisions of the map of Europe that we noted earlier: the territorial losses of Russia and Germany, and the dismemberment of the Austro-Hungarian monarchy. To the casual observer it might appear a strong combination; for a very short time it was. Especially as long as Russia remained torn by civil war and under foreign occupation, and Germany was economically prostrate, with the mark worthless—as was the case in the first half of the 1920's—French and Polish power by contrast was immense. The British opposition to the French occupation of the Ruhr in 1923, and British reluctance to see Germany's economy destroyed, were almost instinctive reactions to a policy that went too far. Yet as a brake upon the French it was ineffective and it left a legacy: too long after these temporary conditions of combined German-Russian weakness had passed away, Britain continued to think of Germany and France in terms of 1923. A false estimate of the situation led to a false concept of the counterbalancing interests involved.

3 The Era of Locarno (1924–1930)

THE period that began with 1924 and ended in 1930, known as the "Locarno Era," was a time of increasing stability and apparently decreasing tension. The major outlines of the alignment system elaborated by France in the early 1920's were preserved and even further undergirded. The period was marked by a *rapprochement* between France and Germany. Unfortunately this bettering of relations mostly took the shape of the French discontinuing (from the German viewpoint) what they should not have been doing in the first place. The French evacuation of Düsseldorf, Duisberg, and the Ruhr area in late August 1925, is an illustration. The unfortunate fact is that, by the time such concessions were wrung from the reluctant French, they were considered so long overdue in Germany that they failed in conciliating German public opinion.

Both Germany and Russia were still hard at work rebuilding shattered economies. Because the world in general was taking advantage of a respite from the arduous aftermath of World War I, a spirit of reconciliation was present whose roots, while extremely shallow as already indicated, might have become strong and durable if "good" times had persisted long enough. Soviet Russia re-entered the "family of nations" with her participation in 1922 in the Genoa Conference on economic problems; Germany was admitted to a permanent seat on the League Council in 1926. In October 1925, the Locarno Conference, from which this "era" gets its name, was held; and in December the Locarno Treaties were signed. The most important of these was the Locarno Pact of Mutual Guarantee (signed by Germany, Belgium, France, Great Britain, and Italy), which stipulated (Article I) that: "The high contracting parties collectively and severally guarantee . . . the maintenance of the territorial *status quo* resulting from the frontiers between Germany and Belgium and between Germany and France, and the inviolability of the said frontiers as fixed by . . . the Treaty [of] Versailles." [2] By this treaty Germany agreed to regard her western frontiers as permanent; Great Britain and Italy underwrote the guaranty by promising that, should "a flagrant violation" occur, "each of the other contracting parties hereby undertakes immediately to come to the help of the party against whom such a violation or breach has been directed as soon as the said Power has been able to satisfy itself that this violation constitutes an unprovoked act of aggression." [3]

Although the Locarno Pact in no way guaranteed the frontiers of Germany's neighbors in the East, new Franco-Polish and Franco-Czech guaranties of mutual assistance against German attack were also included in the series of agreements. Then in 1928 came the Pact of Paris, which renounced war as an instrument of national policy (other than in self-defense). It was universally accepted. The next year the Young Plan covering reparations was accepted; and in 1930 the London Naval Conference on Disarmament met with success. By the close of the year 1930 preliminary plans for the World Disarmament Conference were well advanced. For these few short years the world seemed to be progressing away from the specter of a new general war —and then came the thunder and lightning of "the gathering storm."

4   *The Era of Disintegration* (1930–1939)

THE Great Depression that began to take effect in 1930–1931 marked the passing of Locarno; it revealed the depth of the unresolved problems that confronted the great powers. It showed with almost indecent clarity how much, despite some real advances, the "spirit" of Locarno had been based upon a tacit agreement to postpone, and postpone again, issues for which there was no generally acceptable solution. The really weak point in Euorpe was not in the West so much as in the East. At the high point of cooperation during the Locarno era, the powers had been able to handle the less difficult problems of Western Europe; now in the midst of economic upheaval and waxing political

---

[2] *League of Nations Treaty Series*, Vol. 54, No. 1292, pp. 289 ff.
[3] Article IV.

extremism they found themselves totally unequipped to handle those in the East. The Polish Corridor was like an old wound in the German body politic: it throbbed when the barometer fell. Simultaneously, as capitalism faced its great crisis, hatred and distrust of communism, never far beneath the surface in Western thoughts, waxed and grew. And when the West faced its dilemma —whether to oppose the Brown Terror or the Red Peril—it fell between two stools and permitted Red and Brown, temporarily, to join forces.

The coming of the Nazis to power in Germany made the crisis acute. Once Germany openly repudiated the disarmament clauses of the Versailles Treaty on March 16, 1935, some decision had to be made. It was a difficult problem for France: not only did she distrust Communist Russia, but so did her allies, especially Poland. Nevertheless, on May 2, 1935, France concluded an alliance with Russia in which each promised aid against unprovoked aggression. The fact that it was to run for only five years was one indication of how difficult the decision had been. On May 16 this was supplemented by a Czech-Russian alliance which promised the Czechs Russian aid in the event of German attack, provided that France acted.

The proper alliances had now been concluded to restrain Germany. Yet within four years they were all allowed to crumble into dust. Fatal divisions on policy began to appear between Britain and France. The British pinned their hopes for peace basically upon reconciling Germany to a *status quo* sufficiently revised to meet Germany's minimum or "legitimate" aspirations. The French turned instead to increasing their active strength by means of a broadened alliance system. They pinned their hopes for peace upon confronting Germany with such overwhelming power that she would not dare to assault France. The basic difference in attitude is best illustrated, as we have already seen, by the almost simultaneous French alliance with Russia (May 2, 1935) and the British naval agreement with Germany (June 18, 1935).

The obvious lack of a common Anglo-French policy inspired Hitler to try for still greater diplomatic victories, for Germany had far to go to satisfy her "legitimate" aspirations. Nor was the lesson lost on Benito Mussolini. *Il Duce* had joined in the "Stresa Front" with England and France in April; yet in June the British were scuttling it and pursuing a unilateralist policy. In a world of *"sauve qui peut"* (each man for himself) Mussolini felt sure of holding his own. In September the Ethiopian crisis began. Mussolini's judgment proved correct: it was the League and Ethiopia who lost, not he. In Europe, Hitler grasped the opportunity created by the distraction over Ethiopia to reoccupy the Rhineland (March 7, 1936) in patent violation of both the Treaty of Versailles and the Locarno Pact. On March 12 the other signatories of the Locarno Pact, including Italy, denounced Germany's action. But nothing further was done, primarily because the British could not see going to war over a reoccupation of what was, after all, German territory, even if the Germans had violated treaties. It is ironic that in 1936, while Britain was leading the League's sanctions efforts to punish Italian aggression, Britain and Italy yet paused to jointly denounce Germany's aggression. The spectacle of the

Italian aggressor scolding the German aggressor (for at this time Italy was still opposed to German expansion while Britain unhappily stood opposed to both) is a measure of how great the confusion had become. It was to become still worse, with any semblance of an organized balance of power ever more difficult to resurrect.

The inability of the League and the major *status quo* powers to restrain either Mussolini or Hitler soon convinced *Il Duce* of the desirability of acting upon the old adage: "If you can't lick 'em, join 'em." When the civil war broke out in Spain in July 1936, the opportunity arose. Italy and Germany jointly supported Franco against the (Loyalist) government, which in turn was aided by Russia. Britain and France meanwhile stood on the sidelines and talked "non-intervention." The old dilemma was still acute: should they support the Fascists against the Communists, or vice versa, or neither? In October a German-Italian pact formally solemnized the coming into being of the Axis pact. Loose ties between Germany and Japan and between Italy and Japan soon followed.

The next major developments came in the terrible year of 1938. On March 12, following Austrian Chancellor von Schuschnigg's resignation (which Germany had demanded in an ultimatum the day before), the German army entered Austria. Mussolini, in his new role of partner to Hitler, and in view of his heavy commitments in Spain and the Mediterranean theater, was unwilling to take a strong hand against the occupation and incorporation of Austria into the Reich. France and Britain, harassed by a new war in China, felt unable to move. The balance of power had greatly altered since the days of July 1934, when the Nazis had staged a coup in Vienna and murdered Chancellor Dollfuss. Then Germany had been forced to disavow the action when Mussolini (and Yugoslavia) concentrated heavy troop formations on the frontier. Now Mussolini stood passively by.

The reliability of France's allies in the East was already in question before the Austrian annexation. The steady increase in German power and the continuing retreat of France were raising doubts in their minds. These doubts were not stilled by the state visit of the British king and queen to Paris in July—although this event was intended to demonstrate Anglo-French solidarity. In September came what was to shatter altogether the alliance system so painstakingly devised by France: the Munich Crisis.

In the summer of 1938 negotiations between the Sudeten Germans of Czechoslovakia and the Czechoslovakian government were conducted in an atmosphere of ever-increasing tension. On September 12 Hitler, at Nürnberg, demanded "self-determination" for the Sudetens. The following day the Czech government declared martial law, and on September 15 the Sudeten leaders fled to Germany. By this time the Czechs, Germans, and French had all mobilized large armies, and the British fleet had been ordered concentrated. On September 15 came Prime Minister Chamberlain's visit to Hitler at Berchtesgaden. Following the bald statement of Hitler's readiness to risk war, which highlighted this meeting, Britain and France decided to yield. It was they who then put pressure upon the Czechs to give in—which the Czechs, deserted, finally agreed to do on September 21. When all appeared basically resolved, Chamberlain went again to Hitler (September 22–23) at Bad Godesberg on the Rhine. Here Hitler raised his terms. Britain and France now finally took a strong stand and held discussions with Russia, who had urged such a stand from the beginning. Both Chamberlain and President Roosevelt appealed for a conference, and Hitler, evidently yielding to Mussolini's advice, agreed on September 28 to hold one. The meeting came at Munich on September 29.[4] Hitler, Mussolini, Chamberlain, and Daladier met together. Neither Czechoslovakia nor Russia was invited. In the early minutes of September 30 an agreement was signed that gave Hitler substantially all his demands. Czechoslovakia promised to evacuate the ceded areas between October 1 and October 10; England and France were to guarantee the new frontiers of Czechoslovakia against unprovoked aggression. The crisis was over.

The damage done to the allied position at Munich and the disastrous effect on the military balance of power have already been mentioned earlier. Not only did it change the military situation by giving the immensely important Skoda munitions works to Germany, disarming the fine Czech army without a shot, and removing the immediate threat of a two-front war from over Germany's head, but it destroyed the value of Anglo-French guarantees. No matter how strong the pledge, it might not be honored. Having bowed to Hitler in humiliation this time, there was no reason why anyone should believe that it might not well happen again. Russia watched and drew her own conclusions. In March 1939, Czechoslovakia was swallowed up by Nazi Germany and her Hungarian ally. Again Anglo-French pledges went unhonored and again new ones were made—to Poland on March 31, and to Romania and Greece on April 13.

On March 10, 1939, Stalin, speaking before the Eighteenth Communist Party Congress of the Soviet Union, clearly showed how deeply the Czech incidents had affected Russian thinking:

The majority of the non-aggressive countries, particularly England and France, have rejected the policy of collective security, the policy of collective resistance to the aggressors, and have taken up a position of non-intervention, a position of "neutrality." . . . The policy of non-intervention reveals an eagerness, a desire, not to hinder the aggressors in their nefarious work: not to hinder Japan, say, from embroiling herself in a war with China, or, better still, with the Soviet Union; not to hinder Germany, say from enmeshing herself in European affairs, from embroiling herself in a war with the Soviet Union. . . .

Far be it from me to moralize on the policy of non-intervention, to talk of treason, treachery, and so on. It would be naïve to preach morals to people who recog-

---

[4] In the same building which, ironically enough, was being used as an *Amerika Haus* by the United States Information Service in 1954.

nize no human morality. Politics is politics, as the old, case-hardened bourgeois diplomats say. It must be remarked, however, that the big and dangerous political game started by the supporters of the policy of non-intervention may end in a serious fiasco for them. . . .

With suspicion now so deep between Britain and France on the one hand, and Russia on the other, and with the Baltic states and Poland fearing Russia more than Germany, it proved impossible to gird Germany round with the chains of a vital East-West alliance. Russia, yielding to her suspicions of Anglo-French intentions, decided upon unilateralism and on August 23 concluded the non-aggression pact with Germany. On September 3, following Hitler's invasion of Poland and refusal to withdraw, England and France belatedly went to war.

5 *The Balance of Power: Summary Analysis*

WE are now ready to formulate as concretely as possible what we know of the workings of the balance of power.

We know that its cycle may be very short or very long—two decades or a hundred years. When it enters into a dual-coalition phase, especially when all or almost all the great powers have chosen definite sides, it is heading toward that rigidity which leads so readily to collapse. Such a two-coalition grouping may come as suddenly as the thunder on a summer's night—the product of a crisis arising out of deep-set tension whose intensity had hardly been suspected or realized. And it may disappear as quickly, if war is averted. Or such a grouping may emerge as the culmination of a trend continuing over a number of years with cold-blooded, almost mechanical deliberateness. It is this last type of development that is most likely to bring general war, for while the passion which marks the formation of the sudden coalition for the momentary crisis often expends itself short of war, this deliberate type of development is rarely in the end turned from its course. Why then does this latter phenomenon occur?

It is too pat an answer merely to say that the weak combine against the strong—sometimes they do not, as in Bismarck's time. It is also not enough to say that the *status quo* powers combine against would-be disturbers of the peace—for they may not, as in Hitler's time. There is no automatic power response by one great nation to the spectacle of power accumulation on the part of another. Insofar as a great growth in power on the part of one nation may cause the interests of another to be threatened where previously they were not, or insofar as it leads the second nation to a reappraisal of where its true interests lie, power accumulation may produce a power reaction, but it is always through the analysis of the interests involved that any reaction takes place. Expressed more simply, power changes as such do not produce counter-power moves: what happens or fails to happen in the balance of power depends upon how other states interpret the significance of those power changes.

Bismarck was successful because he revolutionized Germany's role in the balance of power in an acceptable way. Because he did not make of Germany a grave threat to the interests of other powers, or set out to establish hegemony over the others, he was allowed an opportunity to isolate France. This he could do because the other powers, not seriously threatened then by Germany's course of action, could continue to follow interests which counterbalanced or outweighed their potential interests in forming a coalition against Germany. Wilhelm, on the other hand, threw these assets away. He created alarm over Germany's peaceful intentions and diplomatic stability; he made the "German threat" a more important interest to England, France, and Russia than their mutual colonial feuds.

Between the two world wars Britain had an interest in preserving French security but also an interest in reviving, within limits, German power. She allowed the latter to outweigh the former until the situation was no longer within her control, and neither the latter nor the former was any longer feasible. This left her with the fundamental interest of preventing Hitler's dominating Europe; her fumbling grasp on how and where this had to be done led to the debacle of Munich. Again, if Hitler had been willing to impose limits upon his own gains, he would have been allowed to digest his peaceful conquests, up through the Sudetenland, in peace. It was not the great growth of German power that finally brought resistance but the refusal of the Nazis to limit their ambitions.

No one can truly understand the nature of what occurred in this period without remembering that the interest of the West in restraining Germany was counterbalanced by their interest in restraining communism (i.e., Russia). This ambivalence in the attitude and policies of the West came on top of British ambivalence over Germany and France. There being two (or with Italy, three, and with Japan, four) disturbers of the peace, it was impossible to organize an effective defense of the *status quo* without making some decision as to the relative weight to be assigned to the various threats. This paralysis of judgment, which as we have seen led to Munich, destroyed the hopes of an effective coalition against Hitler until Hitler's own errors helped to create it. It should never be forgotten that in the midst of the "phony" phase of the Second World War, in March 1940, France and Britain would have sent military aid (French troops and British bombers) to the Finns to be used against the Russians if it had proved possible. If the Scandinavian states had not balked at such an unneutral act, and if Finland had not collapsed before anything could be done, the Allies would have found themselves fighting the Germans and the Russians simultaneously.

The balance of power process, and what happens to it, is then not only the product of the power relations involved but also of the concept of interests and the foreign policies consequently followed by the great powers. Since it is merely the result of the power-problem "solutions" adopted by the various states, there is no automatic compensatory gearing in the "mechanism" of the balance that works apart from conscious policy decisions.

What keeps a balance of power from developing into two rival and mutually exclusive coalitions is the priority given by states to counterbalancing interests (i.e., interests that balance those which would otherwise cause them to join a group—permanently, wholly, and without reservations). So long as these counterbalancing interests prevail, the balance of power remains highly flexible; once they disappear, either because of the natural consequences of events or because the seeming power threat of another state causes a revision in policy, a more and more rigid form of the balance comes into being.

Thus four forms of the balance-of-power process can be identified: (1) the balancer form in which the balancer contributes flexibility to an otherwise simple, two-bloc form, restraining either bloc; (2) the Bismarckian form in which the potential troublemaker is restrained by isolating her through a complex and flexible alliance system built upon the utilization of the counterbalancing interests of the other powers; (3) the Munich-Era form in which the flexibility stems from the lack of coordination of interests upon the part of the likely victims of attack; and (4) the Wilhelmian or simple, two-bloc form such as existed in 1907–1914 and again from 1949 to 1963 or so, in which each bloc is the direct sole deterrent or restraining influence upon the other.

Flexibility, present in Forms 1 and 2 of Diagram 5 adds a desirable element from the viewpoint of prolonging peace. The flexibility of Form 3, contrariwise, is undesirable. It denotes inaction and feeble indecision on the part of the potential victims who are unable to combine their strength because their fears are too dispersed. The very lack of restraint imposed upon the potential troublemaker encourages and incites aggression. Not being isolated, the troublemaker is able to destroy his enemies piecemeal. If this potential troublemaker is gratuitously presented with allies because the potential victims treat all third states who attempt to alter their *status quo* by force or threat of force as equally dangerous, they encourage the undermining of their own security.[5] In this way the West lost both Italy and Russia at critical times between 1935 and 1940.

Peace is likely to last longest if the power with the greatest interest in upsetting the balance can be effectively isolated. If this is not done skillfully, rigidity will be the penalty. It cannot be done at all unless the state in the best position to organize this isolation is prepared to follow a very complex policy, as Bismarck did, over a sustained period of time. The crux of the matter is to find ways to reassure those who would otherwise ally themselves with the "disturber" state that they are even more secure within the complex balance that is necessarily in operation under such circumstances. In other words, *in its narrowest limits the vital task is to exploit the counterbalancing interests of the potential allies of the most likely disturber of the balance so as to induce them to refrain from that alliance.* Since the disturber state is also busily attempting to turn the counterbalancing interests to its own ends, the results may fall either way.

---

[5] The implications of this for collective security will be examined in the next chapters.

FORM 1

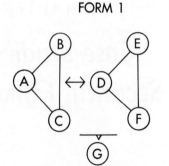

BALANCER FORM
(Semi-flexible, restraining)

FORM 2

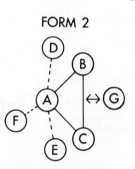

BISMARCKIAN OR
COMPLEX FORM
(Flexible, restraining)

FORM 3

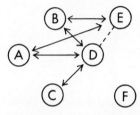

MUNICH ERA FORM
(Flexible, unrestraining)

FORM 4

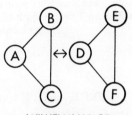

WILHELMIAN OR
COLD-WAR FORM
(Rigid, simple, two-bloc)

DIAGRAM 5
Balance of Power: Four Forms

In the end the effective manipulation of the balance-of-power mechanism depends upon wisdom and courage in foreign-policy decision. Using the materials of this chapter and the last as criteria for judgment, we shall turn in the later chapters to an appraisal of the post-World-War-II balance of power —asking ourselves in the final chapter, in the light of these standards, how wise Western policy has been toward Communist China and Soviet Russia.

CHAPTER 20

Case Studies in
Collective Security: Ethiopia

I assert that the problem . . . today . . . is the very existence of the League. It is the confidence that each State is to place in international treaties. . . . In a word, it is international morality that is at stake. . . .

Should it happen that a strong government finds that it may, with impunity, destroy a small people, then the hour strikes for that weak people to appeal to the League. . . . God and history will remember your judgment. . . .

What reply have I to take back to my people?

EMPEROR HAILE SELASSIE
To the League Assembly, June 30, 1936

NILATERALIST states are normally prepared to defend their own vital interests against aggression. Nations concluding balance-of-power alignments also enter into such obligations vis-à-vis allied and friendly states. But states following a *collective security* pattern are asked in principle to go much further: to extend the same obligation to *all* other states, regardless of *who* is attacked, and by *whom*. The reasoning behind the idea is extremely simple: if the world is to be made unsafe for aggression, all aggression must be rigorously opposed. This view holds that unopposed aggression breeds further aggression. Conversely, assuming that the world lives up to this principle fully, the opposition to aggression will be so powerful that the mere *willingness* to apply the principle will deter the aggressor.

Since the incorporation of this principle in the League Covenant, the world—for better or for worse—has never been the same. Whether or not the nations have been prepared to go through with the spirit and letter of their collective security obligations, they have no longer been able, as they could before World War I, to stand aloof from bald aggression, with a cool declaration of neutrality or a curt judgment that their own interests are not importantly involved. Whether this change is a great triumph or a bitter tragedy for the world of nation-states, whether it is progress or retrogression, it has occurred.

This represents more of a change in international relations than we often think. Those whose whole adult years have been lived under this prevailing philosophy find it hard to grasp the great differences it has made—both for "good" and "bad." In the days before World War I obvious and forthright aggression was not considered commendable, but less attention was given to who had caused or wanted to start the war than to what would come from it in terms of the national interests of the powers if the other powers did not intervene. The standards that the powers observed were more flexible in a moral sense, and where non-European aggression was involved, the limits were free indeed. In Asia and in Africa, actions were possible that might not be countenanced in the "civilized" areas of the globe. When France coveted Morocco, she did not have to consider whether her desire was "just" but only whether the other powers could be brought to agree, in return for various compensations, to France's wishes.

This old-fashioned, imperialist way seems by contemporary standards to be unjust—especially to colonial peoples. Yet one compensation it undeniably had: it provided a safety valve for pent-up, expansionist pressures, and no power felt it necessary or desirable to intervene in the aggressive actions of others on purely moral grounds. There was a freedom from the type of schizophrenia that gripped British policy during the Italian assault on Ethiopia, where national interests led in one direction and moral conscience in another. Since the creation of the League, every local war has become, at least in theory and in moral pressure, a general responsibility of the "family" of nations. It is no longer morally correct to "sit out" an aggression that involves no special national interests. When the hour of aggression strikes, no nation can with good conscience ignore it or ask for whom the bell tolls: it knows it is for itself—either as an alarm signal for action or as a mournful tribute to its inability to live up to its principles.

The bell has tolled often, but only twice under conditions where, in the absence of excuses, the withholding of sanctions would have been tantamount to a confession of hypocrisy. These two cases, one under the League and one under the United Nations, we shall examine in this chapter and the next. They are both cases in which the international organization was forced by an obvious and continued defiance to "punish" the aggressor—thus departing from its more usual and preferred role of conciliating the disputants.

It must be kept in mind that under neither the League nor the UN (although most states formally joined these organizations and nominally committed themselves to the collective security pattern) did important powers refrain from alignments. This too had an effect. Consequently, while we will now examine the collective security process, we are dealing with a mixed system.

I Italian Motivation

THE Italians entered the race for imperialist acquisitions late. In the natural area of their interest—North Africa—they were behind the French in time and strength. Then in 1919 imperialism was placed beyond the moral pale —leaving Italy still unsatiated. True she had Libya, Italian Somaliland, and

Eritrea, but elsewhere all was in British or French hands except Ethiopia. Naturally enough, the Italians coveted this land, which they already bordered in the Red Sea area, and which was the sole remaining possible colonial prize in all that part of Africa. The wish to have it antedated Mussolini. In 1895, long before "Fascist aggression" had ever been heard of, Italian forces had advanced into Ethiopia. But in 1896, some one hundred thousand Ethiopians had annihilated the Italian army of twenty-five thousand at the Battle of Adua and Italy had been forced to recognize Ethiopian independence. The rankling memory of that ignominious failure contributed to a general sense in Italy of colonial frustration.

Mussolini dreamed of reversing that defeat, of seeing Italian armies enter Addis Ababa in triumph, of converting Victor Emmanuel from mere King of Italy into Emperor of Ethiopia, just as Disraeli had made Victoria, the Queen of England, also Empress of India, and ushered in a time of national greatness. But times, as we have seen, had changed. It was not until the coming of Hitler to power in Germany on a program of destroying the "Versailles *Diktat*" that the chance arose. Mussolini was not opposed to the basic provisions of the Versailles settlement, certainly not in Europe. Italy had a vested interest in restraining German ambitions southward. Not only would an Austria in Nazi hands be dangerous for Italy, but Hitler's avowed intent to "return" all "Germans" to the Fatherland by annexing the areas where they lived could not be reconciled with Italy's retention of the South Tyrol and its Austrian (i.e., "German") minority.

On the other hand, with a sufficiently adroit and judicious policy, England and France might be brought to allow Italy to have Ethiopia as the price for doing what Italy wanted to do anyhow: help restrain Hitler. Mussolini knew that neither France nor England felt really hostile to Italy's attaining Ethiopia. No important Anglo-French national interests would thereby be threatened.

There was no doubt that England and France needed Italy to restrain Germany effectively. It had been Mussolini, after all, who had checked Hitler's first attempt on Austria in 1934.[1] Where Mussolini miscalculated was in the extent to which the nations of the world, in group assembled, could be obviously and successfully defied without setting in motion a whole train of events that might, in the end, lead Italy far astray from her original intent. If he had chosen to make it easy for the League, he might well have avoided sanctions. But by nature he was too egotistical, too bombastic, to play the shrewd politics necessitated by what he wanted. He was to write openly that he would have Ethiopia "with Geneva [i.e., the League], without Geneva, against Geneva."[2]

---

[1] See above, Chapter 19.

[2] July 31, 1935, quoted in R.I.I.A., Arnold J. Toynbee, ed., *Survey of International Affairs*, 1935, Part II, New York: Oxford, 1936, p. 173.

2   The Incident and Maneuvers in the League

AS early as 1932 Mussolini had discussed plans for the conquest of Ethiopia with Marshal de Bono. The actual incident that gave him his opportunity appears to have been fortuitous.

At Wal-Wal, in a disputed area apparently under effective Italian occupation since 1928, but claimed by Ethiopia as part of her territory, an exchange of shots occurred involving an Anglo-Ethiopian boundary commission and a native African force under Italian command. This incident took place on December 5, 1934. On December 14 Ethiopia brought the incident to League attention, charging "aggression," and on January 3, 1935, invoked Article 11 of the Covenant.

Now ensued months of intricate maneuverings. Italy, in the center of the stage, assisted from the wings by France and Britain, tried to keep the dispute from necessitating formal action by the League. Again and again Italy would show signs of agreeing to a peaceful settlement. Then when Ethiopia was willing to resume bilateral negotiations and refrain from demanding immediate Council action, Italy would raise her demands. Again and again the cycle was repeated. Ethiopia was alarmed, but in view of the obvious Franco-British desire to avoid a head-on clash with Italy, and in view of the fact that no sanctions could be effective against Italy without full Franco-British support, she did not feel able to play a completely free hand.

Aside from this consideration the Ethiopians were not in the psychological and moral position from which a European state would have benefited. Internal conditions undermined their moral claims on aid since uncivilized cruelties and barbaric practices were notoriously observed within Ethiopia. Although the Ethiopians were a Christian people, they were of the Coptic minority group, and their ways strange. Also they were dark in color and not very different from masses of Africans, throughout the continent, who were at that moment under the rule of Europe's colonial powers—including Britain and France. These intangible factors were not without importance. Although the League's standards were perfectly clear and Ethiopia as a member deserved collective help as much as the next nation, the old colonial habits were still strong in European thought, and there was some sympathy for the Italian claims that their success would represent an advance for civilization and a further suppression of barbarism in the world.

These factors help to explain why Ethiopia temporized. Yet by mid-March, Italian war preparations moved Ethiopia to place the dispute before the Council under Article 15. This article, unlike the looser and vaguer Article 11, *required* the Council to make a public assessment of the merits of the dispute if it could not effect a settlement; once a party requested and continued to insist upon the handling under Article 15 of a "dispute likely to lead to a rupture," the possibilities for delay began to evaporate.

Italy on March 22 denied she was preparing war and offered to arbitrate.

The Council, grasping at a straw and claiming an already full agenda, postponed debate on the dispute. Britain and France now strove with success to get both Italy and Ethiopia to resort to arbitration, and on May 25 the Council took cognizance of the existence of such an agreement. The dispute was now formally on the Council's agenda. The Council for the first time committed itself to eventual action if the arbitral panel was not established in sixty days or a settlement reached in ninety. This decision came five months and eleven days after Ethiopia's first appeal to the Council.

A Commission of Conciliation and Arbitration, as provided for in the Italo-Ethiopian Treaty of 1928, met in June and quickly came to an impasse over how to proceed. New Italian mobilizations moved Ethiopia to ask for (July 24) and obtain (July 31) an extraordinary Council session. The Council decided to agree to Italy's demands on how the arbitration should be carried out, in particular agreeing that the thorny question of who actually owned Wal-Wal should be excluded from the commission's investigation. On September 3 the arbitration commission reported that in the Wal-Wal incident neither Italy nor Ethiopia was particularly at fault—a conclusion that seems in accord with the known facts. There the matter could have rested—that it did not was Mussolini's doing.

3 Maneuvers by the Powers

THE spring of 1935 was not without its complications for Britain and for France. Close at hand Hitler was clearly showing every intention of tearing up the Treaty of Versailles.

On February 13 England and France suggested in a joint communiqué that they were ready to take up outstanding questions with Germany in order to reach a general settlement. Hitler welcomed such conversations—but on a bilateral basis. The British then suggested an Anglo-German meeting for early March. No sooner were the talks scheduled than Hitler proceeded openly to re-establish the *Luftwaffe* (air force) and announce the reintroduction of conscription with a goal of 36 divisions for the new German Army. On March 18 the British protested the unilateral denunciation of treaty obligations in a note which began: "His Majesty's Government feels bound to convey to the German Government their protest . . ." and ended with the statement that the British government "wish to be assured that the German Government still desire the visit to take place within the scope and for the purposes previously agreed." [3] This statement was tantamount to saying that, while a protest had to be made for the sake of the record, Britain was planning no more drastic a retaliation than participation in the bilateral talks suggested by Germany. The note, which begins like a threat of a lawsuit, ends in a manner reminiscent of asking whether or not the previous appointment for tea still

---

[3] *NYT*, March 19, 1935.

stands.[4] Although France's protests over the same actions lacked this ambiguity, Hitler could draw great comfort from the obvious fact that Britain and France were divided in their policies.

In April 1935, at the Stresa Conference, Italy, France, and England attempted to form a common front against Hitler. Here Mussolini made it clear that, in return for support of Britain and France in Europe, he expected a free hand in Africa should he wish to take action vis-à-vis Ethiopia. No objections to this intention were made by Britain or France, who were extremely anxious to avoid irritating Italy. Mussolini felt, with some reason, that he had been given a free hand with Ethiopia.

From here on matters became worse rather than better, and for the continually more disintegrating situation the British must bear a great share of the blame. The French were anxious after 1933 to conciliate Italy and form a really solid front against Hitler; this policy had the merit of being clear and unambiguous. At the same time, if Mussolini too obviously defied the League, the French, as staunch upholders of collective security (against Germany), would be placed in an embarrassing position. As early as January 1935, at the beginning of the Ethiopian incident, the French Foreign Minister, Pierre Laval, had gone to Rome to work out the terms by which Italy at last was to come into her desired heritage in Africa. He is supposed to have said later: "I have given him [Mussolini] a desert in Africa. I have given him Abyssinia." [5] Certainly the French were willing to do so in return for aid in Europe. Britain, for her part, felt that terms could be arranged both with Hitler and Mussolini. On June 18, 1935, the Anglo-German Naval Agreement, permitting Germany 35 per cent of the naval strength of the British Empire, despite the Treaty of Versailles to the contrary, was concluded. This concession further encouraged Hitler. On the very same day a British fact-finding committee on the Ethiopian situation made a report (obtained almost immediately by Italy through espionage) that said plainly: "There are no vital British interests in Abyssinia or adjoining countries such as to necessitate British resistance to an Italian conquest of Abyssinia." [6] This statement further encouraged Mussolini. It was a mistake to encourage both.

The situation was now critical. Yet none of these actions would have put fire to the tinder had it not been for two things: the first was Britain's blind persistence in her unilateral policy toward Germany—a policy that drove an ever-deeper wedge between her and France. The second was Mussolini's incurable lust for the flamboyant. The first factor led Britain and France to be at loggerheads with each other over Germany and made Italian support even more crucial to France; the second forced Britain and France into an action against Italy that neither of them wanted—and to the great joy of Hitler.

---

[4] See Dr. Paul Schmidt, *Statist auf diplomatischer Bühne, 1923–45*, p. 296, for the German reaction, which was substantially in this sense.

[5] Robert Dell, *The Geneva Racket, 1920–1939*, p. 109.

[6] R.I.I.A., Arnold J. Toynbee, ed., *Survey of International Affairs, 1935*, p. 43.

4 *The Hour of Decision*

TIME was now running out. Nine days after the Anglo-German Naval Agreement, the results of the so-called "peace ballot" in Britain were announced. British public opinion overwhelmingly favored a strong stand by the League (and Britain) against aggression. With an election to be fought in the fall, British government policy began to stiffen. Yet throughout the summer months one possible settlement after another was discussed with Mussolini, and each in turn was discarded. In September a committee of five League Council members tried and also failed. On September 26 the Council set up a Committee of Thirteen under Article 15. This committee, which embraced the Council's membership minus Italy (Ethiopia was not a Council member), proceeded to investigate the dispute with a view to making the required report. Losing patience, Mussolini on October 3 struck at Ethiopia in force. This was some ten months after the original incident, but it was only one month after the report of the arbitral commission on the Wal-Wal aspect of the dispute; and it was during the League Council's inquiry into the political aspects. Article 12 of the Covenant clearly stipulated League members would submit "any dispute likely to lead to a rupture" to a legal settlement (arbitration or adjudication) "or to inquiry by the Council, and they agreed in no case to resort to war *until three months after the award by the arbitrators . . . or the report by the Council."* [7] Mussolini could not possibly have chosen a more obvious way of declaring his contempt for the League, for the method he chose confronted the members with a deliberate breaking of the Covenant: he had not waited the stipulated three months.

With this obvious slap in the face the League members, including Britain and France, had no real choice aside from humiliation. On October 7 a League Council committee (the Committee of Six appointed October 5 to prepare recommendations) reported that "The Italian Government has resorted to war in disregard of its covenants under Article 12 of the Covenant of the League of Nations." [8] Because of the interpretative resolutions of October 1921,[9] a roll-call vote was now taken by the Council members, voting as individual states: Italy's negative vote was not considered; the other states agreed with the report. The Council then sent its records to the Assembly, where on October 9 the President of the Assembly invited the members to "express an opinion." Because of the interpretative resolutions he asked "the assent of each Government individually. We are not going to propose a vote. I shall give to those who desire to express a contrary view an opportunity to speak." Reservations or abstentions were also to be permitted. "But I shall interpret the silence of the rest as implying the currence of their Governments in the opinion already expressed by fourteen members of the Coun-

---

[7] Italics added.

[8] League of Nations, *Official Journal*, November 1935, p. 1225.

[9] See above, Chapter 9.

cil." [10] With Austria, Hungary, and Albania dissenting on economic and friendship grounds, and Switzerland holding aloof because of her neutrality, the other fifty nations agreed that Italy had committed aggression. Thus began the first sanctions experiment.

Economic sanctions were now to be applied. Beginning from scratch, an incredibly complicated effort involving fifty-two states was quickly begun. A Committee on Co-ordination (fifty-two members) was formed with a smaller "Committee of Eighteen" to bear the brunt of the work. Within eight days the Committee on Co-ordination, working without formal votes and simply reworking their proposals until all agreed, came forth with a series of recommendations to the member governments, including an embargo on all imports from Italy (except gold or silver coins or bullion) and exports to Italy of arms, ammunition, chemical warfare materials, aircraft and aircraft engines, rubber, bauxite, iron ore, scrap iron, nickel, tin, chromium, and manganese. By the middle of November these restrictions were in effect; within three months Italian exports were only somewhat more than half the year before, and Italian imports were less than half. Italy's gold reserve fell a third.

On the other side of the picture, as Litvinov, the Soviet delegate, later pointed out, the arms embargo had not been applied by seven states, financial measures by eight, cessation of exports to Italy by ten, and prohibition of imports by thirteen. He pointed out that, as a group, the Latin American states had not applied the most effective sanctions at all. Moreover, Britain and France were unable to agree to an oil embargo,[11] and the Suez Canal remained open. At the same time United States exports of oil to Italian Africa rose drastically. These were obvious weaknesses.

Even so, it is generally agreed that the most serious failure of the League was in its decision on July 2, 1936 to lift sanctions. This was within two months of Italy's entry on May 5, 1936 into the Ethiopian capital of Addis Ababa. Had sanctions been continued, Italy would almost certainly have been unable to continue its economic life. While the success of the Italian aggression encouraged a feeling of apathy on the part of the League members, it is nonetheless true that sanctions were abandoned just when their greatest effects were being felt.

5 Case Study I: The Lessons

ONE may well ask why sanctions were so quickly abandoned. One may equally well ask the even more significant question as to why the League did not go beyond economic measures and use military sanctions. In the wording of Ar-

---

[10] League of Nations, *Official Journal*, Special Supplement No. 138, 1935, pp. 100–101.

[11] Although Eden, for Britain, had proposed oil sanctions at one point—if France were willing—he knew that the French would not agree to it. Mussolini himself told Hitler on the evening of the Munich Conference in 1938 that if oil sanctions had been imposed "I would have had to order a withdrawal from Abyssinia in a week." Dr. Paul Schmidt, *Statist auf diplomatischer Bühne, 1923–45*, p. 348.

ticle 16 and the logic of the Covenant, economic sanctions were to be the forerunners of military measures. Yet at no time did the League venture near such a decision.

The answer to these questions is implied in the policies and interests of Britain and France. At no time did either the British or the French government seek war with Italy. Moreover, this was an eminently sound decision on the part of both. Nothing would have been so reckless as to have gone to war with Mussolini while Hitler cavorted in glee and proceeded to do what he wished with Europe. The most tragic act that any state can commit is to enter into a first-class war with the wrong enemy; to fight in thoroughgoing fashion a secondary enemy rather than the primary one; or to squander significant national strength upon the lesser of two threats while the other continues to wax in power untouched. Britain and France can hardly be blamed for having avoided a war with Italy from which Hitler would have drawn enormous advantage.

This conclusion may be contested, especially by those who hold that had Italy been resolutely opposed (and Japan, even earlier), Hitler would never have dared to commit aggression as he did so flagrantly following the Ethiopian crisis. Let us examine this opinion. In the first place, the Manchurian affair was, in the beginning, far from an obvious case of aggression in which there was clear intent to defy the League. There is no reason for believing that Japan's success in her Manchurian adventure inspired Mussolini's move in Ethiopia. The two situations really had little or nothing in common except for the common link of League interest in all threats to the peace anywhere in the world.

Second, if Mussolini did need inspiration from the example of others, he could find it nearer at home. Hitler had torn up the Treaty of Versailles well before Mussolini launched his full-scale attack in Africa. Nor were Hitler's defiant moves in March 1935, based upon Japan's success in defying the League. What he had to fear, League or no League, was a combination of European great powers. He had no assurance that Britain, France, and Italy would not cooperate against him, regardless of what they might or might not do in Asia. It was the British, with their naval agreement with Germany in June, who destroyed the anti-Hitler coalition for the time. Since Mussolini did not attack Ethiopia in force until October, it can hardly be claimed that Hitler moved from aggression to aggression because of any League failure in the Italian case.

Third, the evidence points to a conviction on Mussolini's part that the League per se and its power were unimportant as a source of opposition—that what mattered was the attitude of Britain and France. And certainly he had ample reason to feel from his discussions with British and French leaders that they would find a way to give him Ethiopia. Thus, if Mussolini was encouraged, it was by the promises (or lack of threats) of Britain and France, more than by the successes of Hitler. Neither Hitler nor Mussolini was ever so concerned about the League as they were about what the other great powers might do.

It has often been said that Japan's successful aggression led to Italy's, which then led to Germany's. Indeed, the general proposition that unopposed aggression breeds further aggression is rarely questioned. Yet what really caused havoc in the 1930's was the lack of effective opposition, not to aggression in general regardless of by whom and where, but to Hitler's aggression in particular. Germany's initial successes in March 1935, led on, like an endless chain, to further demands and successes, culminating in 1939 with the attack on Poland. Had Germany been effectively opposed before she engulfed Europe in war, defeated France and put England on the rim of a abyss, and invaded Russia in June 1941, Japan would hardly have been presented with the tempting situation that prevailed in December 1941.[12] The key to the whole situation lay in Europe. As we now know, if Hitler's boldness had once been resolutely opposed—even, says Churchill, as late as 1938—these disasters could have been averted or, at the very least, the war won against Germany with much less sacrifice.

The idea that any aggression is as bad as any other, while fundamental to collective security thinking, is, from a practical standpoint, very dangerous. It matters in practice, enormously, *who* is committing aggression, and where, and under what circumstances. One aggression is only as bad as another in a moral sense, just as the murder of John Doe, tramp, is as bad morally as the assassination of the President of the United States or the Premier of France. The practical consequences that flow from the morally equivalent deeds are as different in importance as day is from night. So long as Italy was prepared to aid in restraining Germany and was willing not to attack France or Britain, the all-important purpose would have been achieved. In an earlier age Italy would have been given good and sufficient territorial bribes in order to hold her true to the central and vital effort.

When one examines the logic of collective security with particular reference to this Italian case, one is led to wonder if the world did not try to establish a standard of morality far above its ability to honor, one based upon a presumption of universally shared principles, which in fact did not exist and which, when put into practice, had disastrous effects upon pre-World-War-II international relations.

It is asking a good deal of the people of one nation that they shed their blood any time a second state attacks a third, to the fortunes of which they are really indifferent. This conclusion becomes even truer when to do so they must expose their back to a very real and personally felt threat from some actual national enemy or potential enemy. Their first obligation is, after all, to themselves: Americans to America, Englishmen to England, Frenchmen to France. Their second obligation is to their allies who are willing and able to

---

[12] This is not to deny that the lack of effective opposition that Japan encountered encouraged *her* to further aggressions.

stand with them in the heat of the common battle. The whole idea of collective security is founded upon the proposition that one is not asked to turn one's back on one's own interests. One's own interests require the suppression of aggression. Otherwise there will be more aggressions, and sooner or later one is required to fight an even bigger and longer and bloodier war to defend one's own vital interests. But is this true?

If Italy could have obtained Ethiopia without running afoul of the security obligations of the League members, there is no reason to doubt, especially in view of her threat of force when Hitler first tried to gain Austria in 1934, that she would have helped restrain Hitler. It was Mussolini's pique and irritation at sanctions that led him into an alliance with Germany that was unnatural from any reasonable statement of Italian national interests. Because Mussolini chose to throw down the gauntlet in the League's face in the most insulting and obvious manner possible, something had to be done by the League. But both the British and French governments proceeded to do that something in full awareness that they were acting in opposition to all their basic interests other than the salvaging of their prestige (as League members), which Mussolini had so unnecessarily put in question.

The logic of collective security simply ignores what the other powers may actually be doing while one's own state is busy imposing sanctions on a second who has attacked a third, by assuming, in theory, that the others are making common cause and aiding with the sanctions. In practice, like Hitler, they may be beside themselves with glee, for when the police force is busy chastising the criminals inside its own ranks, it has little energy for the crimes of those outside.

It is remarkable that sanctions were imposed to the extent they were when this explanation is borne in mind. One can explain this phenomenon on moral grounds as the reaction of the outraged conscience of mankind. But one can also explain it by calling attention to the fact that Mussolini had insulted the honor and put in question the prestige of every League member by his insolent method of delivering his pointed insult. He left no way out at all with honor except sanctions, for nothing is harder to disguise in a calendar-conscious world than what day and month it is. If the formula at issue had not been "ninety days" pure and simple, if there had been the slightest straw to grasp at, sanctions would in all probability never have been imposed on the scale and in the form in which they were implemented. And even then they were never complete, and they were abandoned at the first graceful opportunity—before there was too great a danger that Italy, forced to her knees, would strike out in wrath with her armed forces.

Should the world, or the League, or Britain and France be blamed for the failure, or be commended for making the best of a dangerous and unsatisfactory predicament? That Italy would join Germany in an alliance if sanctions were imposed constituted a risk—but it was a risk that Mussolini had himself made it impossible to avoid running. Should the League have gone all-out to force Italy to her knees to demonstrate that crime does not pay? Suppose the

League, with Britain and France doing the bulk of the fighting (if it came to that), had fought Italy to defeat. All chance of Italian support against Hitler would then surely have been gone, and in the meantime Hitler would, in all probability, have exploited the rare opportunity thus presented to him. He might even have offered Mussolini an alliance before Italy had been defeated, thus producing an Axis pact sooner, with all its effects upon the European balance of power. That Hitler in 1935–1936 was not yet in a position to launch his war was not known at the time. In any event Hitler could not help being the beneficiary of a quarrel among the three powers who were most interested in containing his expansion in Central Europe. There is no logical way to avoid that conclusion.

It is ironic that, for collective security successfully to provide the protection that is its vital claim to existence, any potential aggressor, who is of second-class power per se but of primary importance to the existing balance-of-power situation, must be willing to refrain from his aggression so that the international organization will not have to take action against him while leaving a potential aggressor of first-class power unrestrained. A situation such as that is ever in danger of becoming completely unworkable, for the actions obviously necessary for balance-of-power success are contradicted by those necessary for a collective security success. The result can be, as it was in this case, chaos.

CHAPTER 21

Case Studies in
Collective Security: Korea

Korea's significance is not the final crusade. It is not
finally making valid the idea of collective security. It is
important, perhaps, for the inverse reason that in Korea we
prevented the invalidation of collective security.

SECRETARY OF STATE DEAN ACHESON
Speech of June 29, 1951

LET us examine Case Study II with this analysis in mind and see what further light is shed upon the problem.

I *The Attack—Initial Reactions*

THE United States, the United Kingdom, and Nationalist China had agreed
at Cairo in 1943 that Korea would "become free and independent"—a pledge
entered into by Russia as well at the Potsdam Conference in July 1945. When,
at the end of World War II, Russia occupied Korea north of the 38th Parallel, and America Korea south of that line, the division was to be temporary.
But the deadlocks of the Cold War were echoed in Korea too. America and
Russia could not agree on a common plan for free elections. In September
1947, the United States placed the problem before the UN. A UN Temporary
Commission on Korea subsequently observed elections in South Korea; the
Soviets refused the Commission access to North Korea. On December 12,
1948, the UN General Assembly recognized the newly elected Syngman Rhee
regime as the "lawful government" in South Korea. The North Korean "Democratic People's Republic," which had been created by Soviet-style elections,
was ignored by the UN majority although it continued to enjoy Soviet bloc
support.

There matters rested for a time—uneasily. The UN Temporary Commission was replaced by a UN Commission on Korea, charged with observing the
withdrawal of American and Soviet troops and with continuing efforts at unification. Although American and Soviet troops were withdrawn, no progress
at all was made on unification. Border incidents on the 38th Parallel continued to occur, and inflammatory speeches continued to be made on both sides
of the frontier.

Despite the known tension in Korea, the actual outbreak of hostilities in

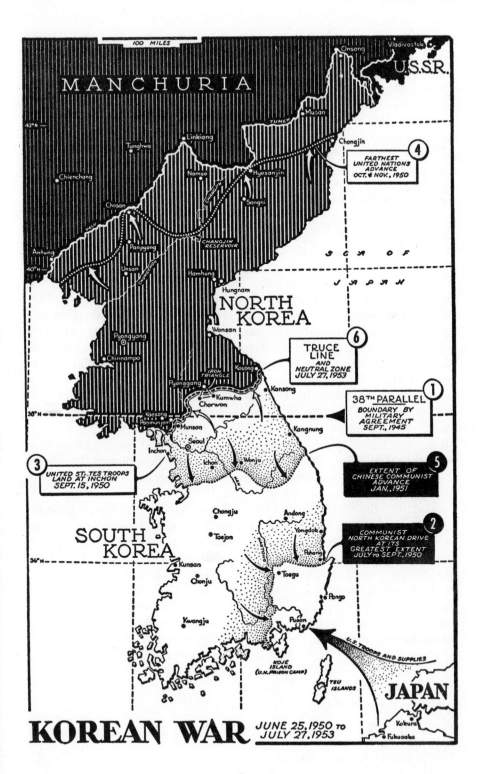

100 MILES

MANCHURIA

U.S.S.R.

Onsong • Vladivostok •

42°N —

Tunghwa • Linkiang • Musan • TUMEN

Chienchang • Chongjin

④ FARTHEST UNITED NATIONS ADVANCE OCT. & NOV., 1950

Namsa • Hyesanjin •

Chosan • Sangni •

Antung • Panpyong • CHANGJIN RESERVOIR

40°N — Unsan • Hamhung •

Hungnam •

NORTH KOREA

Wonsan •

Pyongyang • TRUCE LINE AND NEUTRAL ZONE JULY 27, 1953 ⑥

Chinnampo • Kosong

IRON TRIANGLE

Pyonggang • Kansong •

Kumwha

Chorwon

38°N — Kaesong 38TH PARALLEL BOUNDARY BY MILITARY AGREEMENT SEPT., 1945 ①

Panmunjom • Munsan •

Inchon • Seoul •

③ UNITED STATES TROOPS LAND AT INCHON SEPT. 15, 1950 Ichon • Wonju • Kangnung •

EXTENT OF CHINESE COMMUNIST ADVANCE JAN., 1951 ⑤

Chongju •

Andong •

SOUTH KOREA Taejon •

Yongdok •

COMMUNIST NORTH KOREAN DRIVE AT ITS GREATEST EXTENT JULY TO SEPT., 1950 ②

36°N — Kunsan •

Pohang •

Chonju •

Taegu •

Kwangju •

Pusan • Pango •

KOJE ISLAND (U.N. PRISON CAMP)

TSU ISLANDS

U.S. TROOPS AND SUPPLIES

JAPAN

KOREAN WAR JUNE 25, 1950 TO JULY 27, 1953

Kokura •

Fukuoka •

SEA OF JAPAN

383

June 1950, came with a distinct shock. It seems unlikely that those in the Communist world who ordered the North Korean soldiers to attack realized the emotional-psychological reaction it would produce. It brought a vivid feeling that the tragic cycle of the 1930's was repeating itself, that the steady march toward the abyss, so shortly before checked, was being resumed.

In accordance with what might be called the "time-honored" custom for sudden aggression, utilized repeatedly by Japan and Germany, the move was calculated so as to be known in the Western capitals during the week-end. The news reached Washington at 9:26 P.M., EST, on Saturday night (June 24). At 3:00 A.M. the next morning the United States requested an immediate session of the Security Council, and after much frantic telephoning and the return of delegates from week-end retreats, the Council met at 2:00 P.M. on Sunday. The first telegraphic report of the UN Commission from the scene of the crisis was already available. It spoke of a North Korean "all-out offensive" which was rapidly "assuming character of full-scale war."

Events now followed full upon one another. At its first meeting on June 25, the Security Council, by a nine to none vote, adopted with only minor modifications a United States-sponsored resolution which noted "with grave concern the armed attack upon the Republic of Korea by forces from North Korea," asserted that this action constituted a "breach of the peace," and called for "the immediate cessation of hostilities" and the withdrawal of North Korean forces. The Security Council called upon "all members to render every assistance to the United Nations in the execution of this resolution and to refrain from giving assistance to the North Korean authorities." [1] On the 26th President Truman disclosed that he had ordered General MacArthur, the United States commander in the Far East, to furnish military supplies to South Korea. Then on June 27, at noon, he announced the sending of United States air and sea forces "to give the Korean Government troops cover and support." In the meantime the UN Commission from Seoul had reported that the North Korean invasion was deliberate and on a scale designed to crush South Korean resistance quickly, and that South Korea, whose troops were not in offensive positions, had been the victim of a surprise attack. The Security Council, meeting the same afternoon (June 27), took the decisive step toward military sanctions by recommending that "the Members of the United Nations furnish such assistance to the Republic of Korea as may be necessary to repel the armed attack and to restore international peace and security in the area." [2] On July 7 this was followed by a third resolution establishing a "unified command [of UN forces] under the United States," with the President of the United States being invited to designate a Supreme Commander and the UN flag being authorized for the use of the forces fighting the North Koreans.[3]

The issue was now joined.

---

[1] *The Fight against Aggression in Korea*, Department of State Publication 3971, Washington, 1950, p. 1.

[2] *Yearbook of the United Nations*, 1950, p. 224.

[3] *Ibid.*, p. 230.

2 *Ingenuity and Adaptation in the United Nations*

THE sudden emergency of the Korean War found the UN Security Council without any more power to order sanctions into operation than its predecessor, the League Council, had at the time of the Ethiopian crisis. Although the UN was planned to have "teeth," the military agreements that were to provide those "teeth" were never concluded. As a result the Council could *recommend* measures, but it could not *decide* to order into action forces it did not possess. Any such armed action by the members, under the UN as with the League, had to be supported by "free-will offerings." For this reason, since the Security Council had no greater power than the General Assembly, and since it was essential for success that widespread support be obtained, it is not surprising that the issue was to pass basically into the hands of the Assembly. It was also reasonable to expect that nations supporting sanctions would want a direct voice in their implementation and in the control of the over-all political strategy, rather than to entrust it to the arbitrarily composed Security Council.

This is exactly what happened. What was logically necessary became practically necessary at the beginning of August, for on the first of that month the Soviet Union's delegate resumed his seat on the Security Council. This seat had been left vacant since January 1950, as a Russian protest against the continuing "illegal" representation of China on the Council by the Nationalist Government delegate instead of by a Communist Chinese spokesman. Had the Russians not been absent in June–July when the Security Council authorized sanctions, the quick Council action already described could not have occurred; Soviet vetos would have blocked any progress in that direction.[4] Even so the importance of this accidental situation or "break" for the West can easily be overrated, since exactly what happened soon after the Soviet's return would have occurred so much the sooner if there had been need: the issue would have been removed by procedural vote (a nonvetoable action) from the Security Council's agenda and placed before the Assembly.

When Jacob Malik, the Soviet representative, returned to the Council on August 1, 1950, to delay and hamstring further Western efforts to deal with Korea in the Council, nothing more remained to be done for the while in a strategic, over-all sense. The Council had already, with the resolution of July authorizing a unified command, done what was required. The rest was up to the UN members as states, to provide help on an individual basis. Trygve Lie, the Secretary-General of the UN, on July 14, 1950, had followed up the resolution of July 7, by calling for "additional effective assistance . . . including combat forces, particularly ground forces." From a tactical standpoint it remained to be seen whether the United States troops rushed from Japan could, in these critical summer weeks, retain a foothold on the Korean Peninsula.

---

[4] Russia's absence leads to interesting speculation. Was she so sure no UN action would be forthcoming? Or was the timing of North Korea's move equally a surprise for the Russians?

Any number of resolutions passed by the Security Council at this point could not have decided this critical, essentially military issue.

In the months following the Security Council's resolutions of June–July, approximately two-thirds of the sixty UN members offered aid varying from combat forces and naval and air units to medical supplies, food, money, transit facilities, clothing, and even soap. Some fourteen provided actual armed forces by February 1951, and to this number were eventually added two more.[5] A Chinese Nationalist offer of troops was declined in order to avoid inciting further Chinese Communist temptation to intervene. The Unified Command by early 1951 included two hundred fifty thousand United States troops, twenty-six thousand troops from the other thirteen states, plus the South Korean army. Coordination in policy formulation and implementation was achieved through a twice-weekly meeting in Washington of representatives of the nations doing the actual fighting. This, like the Coordination Committee of League sanctions days, was an extraorganizational body set up for the purpose. Its creation testified to the adaptability that can characterize nations acting as a group when they are agreed upon the need for doing something.

3 Chinese Intervention

AS the summer of 1950 wore along into fall, the military posture of the UN Command steadily improved. Not only had the North Koreans been held at the perimeter around Pusan, but strength had been gathered for a counterattack. Those familiar with American amphibious assault techniques could not doubt the nature of the blow that would come. Even so, its daring caught the North Koreans entirely by surprise: United States and UN forces on September 15, 1950, assaulted the beaches in the Seoul area. The tables were now reversed: from being the aggressors in occupation of a neighboring state, the North Koreans were now confronted with the necessity of defending their own soil should the UN cross the parallel.

The sudden military events outran political decisions. A decision on whether to unify Korea by force, by crossing the parallel, had to be made, and quickly: there was little time to consider all the facets of the problem without losing the military initiative and allowing the North Koreans a breathing spell to regroup. Should the UN cross the parallel after such a wait, the cost in lives would mount accordingly. Since the major expenses in blood and money, aside from South Korea, was being borne by the United States, it was natural

---

[5] The United States, Australia, Belgium, Canada, Colombia, France, Greece, the Netherlands, New Zealand, the Philippines, Thailand, Turkey, the United Kingdom, and the Union of South Africa were the fourteen, and Ethiopia and Luxembourg the two further states.

that United States desires be given great weight. When the United States urged that it be allowed freedom to pursue the enemy across the border, a resolution approving such a course by implication was jointly sponsored by Australia, Brazil, Cuba, the Netherlands, Norway, Pakistan, the Philippines, and the United Kingdom. It promised that "United Nations forces should not remain in any part of Korea otherwise than so far as necessary for achieving the objectives specified"—i.e., a united and independent Korea. By a vote of forty-seven to five, with seven abstentions, this resolution passed, despite India's strong warning (India being one of the very few non-Communist states having close diplomatic relations with Communist China) that an action such as crossing the frontier might easily enlarge the war by bringing about Chinese intervention.

By early November 1950, the North Korean armies were dispersed and fleeing, and United Nations forces had penetrated far into North Korea, soon reaching the Yalu River (the frontier with Manchuria) at one point and rapidly approaching the occupation of all North Korea. Then on November 5 the Unified Command reported "a new foe" in the form of "Chinese Communist military units." The exact scale of the intervention and Chinese intentions were at this point still unknown quantities.

China had repeatedly warned that she would not tolerate the approach of UN (especially United States) troops to her frontiers. She had also charged the United States with numerous violations of her air space over Manchuria. She viewed with fear, anger, and distaste the prospect of a United States-dominated and led anti-Communist coalition at the Yalu River gate of her house, especially since the United States had not ceased to support Chiang Kai-shek on Formosa and had not altered its unreconciled attitude toward the permanent establishment of communism on the Chinese mainland. Communist China repeatedly demanded the right to state her case against the United States before the Security Council. As events reached their climax in November, the Security Council at last agreed to hear a Communist Chinese representative late in November.

On November 10, both as a reassurance and a warning, the United States, along with Cuba, Ecuador, France, Norway, and the United Kingdom, co-sponsored a resolution before the Security Council calling upon all states to refrain from lending support to North Korean forces, guaranteeing UN intentions to keep China's frontier inviolate, and calling attention to the grave situation that continued Chinese intervention would produce. Nevertheless, the Chinese "volunteer" armed intervention was by now obviously on a large and steadily increasing scale. The only bright spot in this otherwise dismal prospect that the war was becoming enlarged was that China was refraining from a formal declaration of war. It was soon to be clear that she intended to hide behind the thin fiction that the organized bodies of regular Chinese troops were volunteers filled with a personal desire to lend aid to the North Koreans. In the UN there were last-minute proposals to establish a line south of the Yalu at which the UN forces would halt, leaving a neutral buffer zone to reassure the Chinese. It was said that the Chinese were concerned over the hydroelectric works on the Yalu; a number of them in North Korea supplied much current to South Manchurian industry.

Whether the situation could have been saved at this point is open to question. Possibly a compromise could have been reached in view of the fact that the Peking regime's delegation was en route to New York and the UN. But if the chance existed, it was lost. There had always been a danger of lack of coordination of political and military moves. The coordinating body sitting in Washington did not attempt to exercise battlefield control in Korea, and certainly the UN as such could not. Much was left to the discretion of the field commander. The control was loose. At the very moment when the UN was treading warily in New York, awaiting the Chinese delegation and a more explicit statement of China's position, the UN Commander in Korea, General Douglas MacArthur, boldly launched a general offensive (November 24) which he described as the final blow to end the war and get "the boys" out of the trenches and home by Christmas. When the strong Chinese forces struck a massive counterblow with its knife point between the two advancing UN armies, the UN defeat was so overwhelming that North Korea had to be hastily abandoned. Part of South Korea fell again into Communist hands. The UN forces fought stubbornly and courageously, but for all that it was a disaster.

On November 28 General MacArthur was forced to report to the Security Council: "We face an entirely new war." On the same day Communist China's delegation appeared before the Security Council. China bitterly castigated the United States, claimed that Chinese territory had been violated and bombed ninety times, and demanded the withdrawal of all foreign troops from Korea. The peoples of North and South Korea were to be allowed to settle their own problems. This program was rejected. On neither the part of the United States nor of China, the major protagonists, was there apparent a desire at this point to reach a settlement. In view of the UN retreat then in progress and the success of China's intervention, the Chinese were too flushed with victory to compromise; the United States, embittered and angered at having to fight the Korean War all over again on harder terms than before, pressed for the condemnation of the Peking regime as aggressors.

Twelve Arab-Asian states, led by India, now sought to find a middle ground between the United States and the Chinese demands. On December 14 they made proposals in the UN looking toward a cease-fire and a peaceful settlement of the major and unresolved issues in the Far East, which the Korean War had brought into sharp focus. A Group on Cease-Fire was created but its proposals were at first rebuffed by China (December 21) on the ground that, without Communist China's participation, all substantive proposals by the UN were illegal. The proposals were next amplified in the UN by a set of principles which, on January 13, 1951, were forwarded to Peking to make the UN position clearer. Communist China replied with a set of counterproposals. The United States, which had considered the December 21st answer of China as a complete rejection of the cease-fire idea, saw in this second answer another completely negative response, and continued to press for condemnation of Communist China as an aggressor. The United Kingdom, France, and India took more cautious positions. Further efforts by India to explore the issues with Peking again brought divided opinion in the UN. The prospects for a negotiated settlement being dim, and confronted with a feeling that something more ought to be done, the UN on February 1, 1951, passed a United States-sponsored resolution charging Communist China with having "engaged in aggression in Korea" by a vote of forty-four to seven and nine abstentions, with the Asian-Arab bloc in opposition. An "Additional Measures Committee" was created to consider new ways of bringing pressure to bear on China. On May 18 this committee was instrumental in causing a resolution to be adopted in the General Assembly calling for an embargo on the supplying of war materiel to Peking, and by September 1951, some fifty-one UN members, as well as thirteen non-members, had put such an embargo into effect.

With the coming of the new year of 1951, the Communist march southward in Korea was checked; UN forces began to advance to the north once more. Then in April a heavy counterattack by the Communists produced in effect a military stalemate at approximately the 38th Parallel. Although the fighting was to continue until the signing of the armistice in July 1953, the military position remained substantially unchanged from this time forward.

The military situation having now been stabilized and a stalemate having been created, diplomacy was once more resorted to. On June 23, 1951, the Soviet representative at the UN, Jacob Malik, speaking over the United States radio, suggested that the Korean War might be settled by the belligerents' initiating conversations on the basis of a cease-fire and an armistice allowing mutual withdrawal of armed forces from the 38th Parallel. This was essentially a proposal to restore the *status quo ante bellum*. On June 29, the new UN commander, General Ridgway, suggested a meeting aboard a Danish hospital ship in Wonsan harbor. The next day Peking radio agreed to a meeting but suggested Kaesong—a town below the 38th Parallel and one of the few there still in Communist hands. On July 10, 1951, the UN agreeing to Kaesong, conversations were begun, and they continued until August 23. A dispute over alleged UN violations of the neutral zone in which talks were proceeding then led to a two-month delay. But on October 25, 1951, conversations were resumed at Panmunjom, and there they continued intermittently for most of two years before an armistice was actually signed.

4   The Initial Stage: Failure or Success?

THE many months of negotiation at Panmunjom were a troublesome time for many people in those nations who had rallied to put down aggression. Especially in the United States, alongside great war-weariness, there was great frustration. With almost instinctive unanimity Americans had cheered President Truman's bold decision to intervene, realizing that a challenge had been laid down that could not be ignored. Nevertheless it was a strange war that was being fought there: it was neither fish nor fowl, neither a war that was to be "won" in the traditional sense (because that would have meant full-scale fighting with China in China) nor the short and relatively painless "police action" postulated by the theory of collective security. It conformed neither to traditional American ideas of warfare nor to American expectations of collective security. It was this feeling of being involved in something new, unpleasant, and seemingly unending, whose rules had to be improvised as one went along, that produced so much confusion in America. In other lands who helped to share the collective burden there were also divided counsels, but the pain did not go so deep. Having been less intimately and emotionally bound up with events in China following World War II, the other UN allies of the United States were able to see a situation involving China with more detachment. In retrospect, as the negotiations at Panmunjom continued interminably (and with "aggressors" who are according to the prevalent belief to be punished—not negotiated with), many Americans wondered whether they had erred by going into the Korean War in the first place, or whether the error lay in continuing it without making an all-out effort for victory. Almost everyone was sure that in any case a grievous error had been committed.

Yet consider the situation as it developed in late June 1950. There was not the slightest doubt that North Korean armed forces had deliberately crossed a known and defined frontier on a scale intended to destroy South Korean opposition and unify all Korea by force. No clearer case of outright aggression could be imagined, and a UN Commission on the spot left no doubt that aggression had occurred. No matter how threateningly the South Korean government had postured, no matter how ill-chosen and rash its statements, the fact remained that it was North Korea who attacked—cold-bloodedly and deliberately.

It is quite possible to contend that the idea of collective security is unworkable and even dangerous, because it can make any little war easily into a great war. But feasible or not, some sixty nations of the world, gathered in the UN, had promised that they would not allow to go unchallenged exactly that type of action in which North Korea had engaged. Not since the Italo-Ethiopian crisis had there been such a clear defiance of an international organization still capable of taking action. The UN either had to act or to lose its standing in the eyes of the world.

While it is clear that the UN had to act, was it necessary that the United States commit itself so deeply? To ask whether it was in the national interest of the United States to intervene in Korea under such circumstances is to ask a question that must be answered affirmatively. If the United States had not been a member of the UN and could have weighed the issue purely on the merits of whether South Korea was worth even a small war, the answer might still have been affirmative. The conditions under which the war broke out must be considered, as well as the Communist challenge. If the United States had not aided the South Korean state and had allowed it to be conquered by North Korea, the already precarious balance of power in Asia might have been disastrously undermined.

Whether the answer in the light of power considerations would have been yes or no remains a purely theoretical speculation. As a member of the UN, and especially as the nation that had done so much to bring the South Korean government into independent existence, United States prestige was at stake. There could, moreover, be no question of a leisurely progression through a series of economic sanctions to the use of collective force. If North Korea were to be frustrated, it had to be done by arms—and quickly. Only if that armed intervention would clearly have jeopardized other vital interests of the United States (other than prestige), would the United States have been justified in hesitating or refusing to take conclusive action. Where Britain had been in an ambiguous position in 1935–1936, the United States in 1950 was not—provided that United States involvement in the Far East did not become so thoroughgoing that Russia (the major potential enemy of the United States) was able to overthrow the existing balance of power in Europe and the rest of the world. In June 1950, the dictates of collective security and the dictates of balance of power did not lead America in opposite directions; the singleness of aims simplified the action to be taken.

The UN effort in Korea between the end of June 1950, and the beginning of November 1950, while not exactly the kind of action envisaged by collective security theorists, was at least close enough to it in essentials. Although less than a third of the UN membership sent troops to Korea, the UN force built up there was sufficient, as events proved, to destroy the enemy's power in time. The process was assisted by the fortunate availability of American troops in nearby Japan. It is conceivable, too, that more combat troops would have been forthcoming from the other UN nations had there been any widespread belief that the UN forces in Korea would not be equal to their task. Theoretically, in collective security, all other nations rally to aid the aggressed-upon to repulse the aggressor. The result is substantially the same if only ten or twenty states do so, provided the collective force mustered is of sufficient size (as in this case).

The initial stage of the Korean War, before China intervened, was clearly a success. But a degree of force easily capable of defeating North Korea is not the same as the degree of force needed to defeat Communist China. When Communist Chinese troops entered the struggle in force, an essentially collective security police action became converted into a battle between relatively evenly matched forces. The hitherto collective security problem became a balance-of-power problem due to the simple and unpleasant root fact that the UN could not muster overwhelming force against Communist China without initiating a struggle so vast that it could not in the end have been distinguished from a world war. Yet a world war fought to vindicate the principle of collective security is a contradiction in terms. Collective security rests upon the proposition that it makes the fighting of world wars unnecessary.

5 *The Final Stage: Failure or Success?*

ONCE China threw its weight into the struggle there was indeed, as Mac-Arthur said, a new war in Korea. Could this final stage have been avoided?

The answer to this question is far from clear. It is a most dangerous pastime for great powers to indulge in the luxury of not maintaining diplomatic relations with each other, especially if they have no other common forum, such as the UN. It does not follow that if the United States and Communist China had had diplomatic relations in 1950, an open break would have been avoided once United States troops were on or near the Yalu. But it is certain that the United States would have been in a far more advantageous position to assess in time the depth of Communist China's reaction to the prospect, if the two countries had been in direct communication. Marching troops toward the border of a state that one does not recognize can hardly help but create an extremely tense situation, especially where, as in this case, the United States was openly hostile to the Peking regime and publicly supporting a rival government on Formosa.

The UN decision to attempt to unify Korea by force, once the North Koreans were repulsed, was sound in itself. The aggressor would be made to pay; the tensions inherent in a divided nation would be eliminated. At the same time this goal, whether it was sound or not, could not be attained in a vacuum. It could not be achieved against the determined opposition of Communist China. What could be done in North Korea depended on Communist China's tolerance. Granted the delicate circumstances under which United States troops were approaching the Yalu in early November 1950, it remains a great mystery why, after Chinese troops had been found in North Korea, General MacArthur ordered a general offensive. The reasoning behind this move has never been persuasive. The move itself was little questioned in the United States. But among the allies it created justifiable alarm and the suspicion that United States policy was irresponsible. The proved presence of Chinese troops was an obvious indication that the Chinese Communists had not been bluffing when they threatened intervention. November 1950, was not a time for a UN general offensive: it was a time for caution—militarily and politically.

Perhaps no formula could have been found. It is quite conceivable that, if the UN Command had halted its advance and actually broken off contact with the enemy until the proper political moves had been attempted, and if there had been no general offensive, the Chinese would still have attacked in force in late November. No one can say with certainty, because the opportunity was lost. It is barely possible that the Chinese, having made up their minds to intervene, were foolhardy enough to believe that they could thrust the UN bodily out of all Korea and keep them out. If they thought so, they were equally as unrealistic as those on the UN side who argued that China could be expelled from Korea and kept out without defeating China in the citadel of its power—the Asian mainland itself.

When Churchill, a great deal later, remarked that there could be "worse situations than a stalemate in Korea—a checkmate, for instance," he aroused a number of bitter retorts in the United States. Yet he stated the truth baldly. If Communist China ever entered it in force, the Korean War was inevitably fated to become a stalemate, barring an all-out war between the United States and China. The United States was in no position to wage a full-scale war against China. Involvement in an interminable land war in Asia against a first-class military power (such as China, with Russian aid, had become in terms of that type of war) would have been disastrous for her. Dire and unavoidable circumstances would have had to be faced but inevitably the committal of United States power would have been against a secondary enemy while the primary potential enemy, Russia, went completely unchecked. As for China, lacking the means to attack the United States effectively in its wellsprings of power on the American continent, the Chinese could have ended the stalemate in Korea only by broadening the war—by attacking Japan, for example, or making an all-out effort to push United States forces out of Korea sufficient to cause the United States, in retaliation, to attack China proper. This they did not do, and even if they had done it the only kind of "victory" they could have won was seeing United States power dissipated in the attempt to conquer China. They could not hope to win a victory, in the real sense of the word, over the United States. The Chinese Communists, as their use of the "volunteer" fiction clearly shows, were anxious for reasons of their own to avoid a war between themselves and the United States. Thus both the United States and China having been unwilling or unable to fight a total war with each other, a stalemate was inescapable.

If the Chinese ever did think they could drive the UN out of Korea and somehow keep its forces from returning, they must soon have been disabused of the illusion. More probably they never entertained it in the first place. Most likely they had always in mind restoring the *status quo ante bellum* at the 38th Parallel. They, on their side, fought exactly the same type of limited war that the UN, on its side, did. The "privileged sanctuary" of Manchuria went unbombed by the UN as did the UN's "privileged sanctuary" in Japan by the Chinese. Once the front was stabilized at approximately the 38th Parallel, the war continued only because of a question of principle for the UN side and a question of prestige on the Communist side. After the stalemate reached in the spring of 1951, the continued fighting had no particular purpose other than, on each side, to demonstrate to the other that it was not defeated and could fight on if a suitable compromise for an armistice could not be found.

There can be no question as to the wisdom of a negotiated peace for both sides under the circumstances. Where a total victory is, for whatever reason, unobtainable, a negotiated peace is customary. It is also customary in such cases either to return to substantially the *status quo ante bellum* or to conclude a peace based upon what each side holds at the moment, especially if the two are (as is not unlikely) substantially the same thing. This part of the negotiations at Panmunjom, although it would be an exaggeration to say that they ran smoothly, caused at least no apparently insuperable difficulties.[6]

The issue over which the negotiations did repeatedly break down was the return of prisoners of war.[7] The UN contended that no prisoner could or would be repatriated against his will; the Communists insisted that all must be returned, regardless of their individual wishes. From a humanitarian standpoint the UN position was impeccable. The Communists had the best of the legal and traditional arguments, for it could not be denied that the procedure they advocated was customary. Still, there was no precedent for a UN military sanctions operation; it was something completely *de novo*, and if the UN chose to insist that it would not return anti-Communists to be shot or placed in "slavery," the search for a solution to the deadlock had to be delicately pursued while the fighting went on. The Communists, it seems safe to assert, were not so greatly concerned with the recovery or loss of the troops involved as such. Their vast manpower resources, which permit their habitual "human sea" military tactics (designed to counter superior weapons by sheer weight of bodies), and their historical experience with famine and war, have caused the Chinese to place small value on human lives on an individual basis. What they had in mind was avoiding at all costs a public disclosure, on a given day, that thousands of Chinese troops were unwilling, given a free choice, to return to their Communist fatherland. Prestige is a vital consideration of all nations, but in Oriental cultures its importance can hardly be overrated.

It proved very difficult to find a middle ground between the opposing demands. Negotiations dragged on and on until the Communists were finally convinced that the UN would not recede from its demands. They then set out to devise machinery (including in final form a Neutral Nations Supervisory Commission of five nations, two of which were Communist—Poland and Czechoslovakia—and one of which was not unsympathetic—India) and a time schedule for interviewing prisoners of war that would blur over the results of the choices. By stalling on a number of pretexts, by charging interminably that the rules were being violated, by carefully focusing their major interviewing efforts on groups among whom there were fewest anti-Communists and thus few failures, they succeeded not in preventing all damage to their prestige but in minimizing the results and having them published piecemeal over a long period; when the whole affair was done and the final totals known, it had largely ceased to be front-page news. Thus, although the UN won Communist China's acceptance of its principle, China through its

---

[6] A general agreement on a cease-fire settlement was reached as early March 1952, but the P.W. issue remained unsettled.

[7] The settlement of this issue took sixteen further months.

manipulation of the situation was able to avoid the worst effects of the procedure.

With the exchange of prisoners completed on September 6, 1953, the Korean War was over. Technically an armistice was in existence (from July 27, 1953) and at the Far Eastern Conference in the spring of 1954 at Geneva, attended by the United States, France, Britain, Russia, Communist China, and a number of other powers, the question of a peace treaty for Korea continued to be debated. Even so, realistic observers on both sides of the Iron Curtain understood that the chance of uniting Korea by diplomacy was infinitesimal. The *de facto* division, representing the balance of military force that each side could and would bring to bear in Korea, was almost certain to endure, barring any substantial alteration in the power of the two great worldwide blocs.

6 *Korea: A Balance Sheet*

WAS the Korean sanctions effort a success or a failure? On the whole it was a success, for it succeeded in achieving what was most essential: it prevented the overrunning and subjection of South Korea by force of arms. Like most human efforts, it was not without its flaws. Yet if South Korea had been abandoned to the fate designed for it by the Communist world, the idea of collective security would have been dead, for the challenge to the UN and its avowed principles could not have been clearer and a failure by the UN to act could not in turn have been more obvious.

The role of the UN toward Communist China raises a number of important issues. Because of the lack of agreement in the Assembly over what needed to be done, the UN condemned China as an aggressor and then, refusing to broaden the war or to institute additional sanctions, proceeded to negotiate an armistice with her rather than to "punish her for her sins." Was this right or wrong, or, more accurately, which of these opposing courses was right or wrong?

The very phrasing of the question illustrates the difficulties involved in answering it. Do we mean *morally* correct or *practically* correct? Communist China, so long as her "volunteers" remained above the 38th Parallel, was not herself technically an aggressor but rather the ally of an aggressor. Once she advanced into South Korea, she, too, became an aggressor. Her moral guilt became identical with that of North Korea, and she was denounced as such. In the end, because of UN opposition, she, like North Korea, was likewise denied the fruits of aggression. From a moral point of view, is it necessary to punish aggression further than by denying the aggressor the desired spoils? That much is morally required, but is more? To argue that more is necessary than the restoration of the *status quo ante bellum* is to assume the world community has a moral right to institute alternative arrangements on the grounds that they are better. But *morally* better, or merely *practically* better? It is unjust that South Korea be despoiled by North Korea and Communist China, but what is just once the "crime" is frustrated? There are no agreed world moral standards that can be applied in such cases. When we examine the actual tinkerings of groups of states in cases where they, by virtue of superior strength, decree alternative arrangements to replace what existed previously, we find that what is done is consummated on practical grounds of joint national interest.

It is well to ask, then, in practical terms, whether the action of the UN was right or wrong. Morally, Communist China was condemned for aggression and its fruits denied her; in practical terms it was then necessary, once the moral requirements of the situation had been met, to find some means of ending the war. Since the UN was unwilling to fight Communist China through to total defeat (a morally dubious possibility and a practical one beset with dangerous complications), it was necessary to arrange some solution *with* China's consent. This was done, and on terms not at all discreditable to the UN coalition.

That the armistice took so long to arrange was not entirely the fault of Communist China. Since the UN had not won, and was not willing to try to win, a total victory, it was inescapable that the solution, when found, would have to constitute a halfway house between the extreme demands of either side. From this point of view the UN insistence on non-forcible repatriation on terms that would inevitably humiliate Communist China meant that the war had to go on much longer than it otherwise would have. Nor was such a repatriation principle an inevitable and necessary part of a UN military sanctions procedure. It was rather an extraneous issue whose roots were not only humanitarian but also, put bluntly, political. The UN Command (especially because of American insistence) wished to show the world that communism did not have the free-will adherence of the masses of the Korean and Chinese peoples. For this a price had to be, and was, paid, for the war then continued until the Communists were able to find a way to agree to the principle and frustrate its effects as much as possible in practice.

Despite its flaws, the Korean sanctions effort must be considered successful.

7 Collective Security in Practice

WE are now in a position to weigh the results of these two experiments in collective sanctions and attempt to reach some general conclusions.

It is difficult to strike a rational balance between those who "point with pride" to the vast step forward in efficacy that the Korean sanctions present when contrasted with the Ethiopian Case, and those who, pointing to the stalemate following China's entrance into the Korean War, say collective security is unrealistic and unworkable. Before World War II a great deal of theoretical proof of collective security's inherent feasibility was in print; after

World War II a more or less equal amount proving the reverse could be found. It is not necessary to take either the one extreme position or the other. What will occur will depend in greatest measure upon the national interests and the capabilities of the states most directly involved. In circumstances where powerful nations are not led into positive opposition to the collective efforts of some or all of the rest, collective security can be successful.

The results of collective security action do not in the end depend upon the number of nations resisting aggression, nor the number of states taking a "do-nothing" attitude, nor even upon the number of states aiding the aggressor directly or indirectly. They do not even necessarily depend upon the power of the aggressor bloc as contrasted with that of the anti-aggressor group. The results do, however, depend upon the power ratio involved between the forces that the pro-aggressor group is willing and able to commit, and the forces the anti-aggressor bloc is willing and able to commit. They also depend upon how limited or unlimited the aims of the states involved are—how far the aggressor is willing to go and how far the "policemen" are determined to inflict "punishment."

Critics of collective security have frequently pointed out quite correctly that it is extremely difficult to visualize circumstances where an aggressor state will be both roundly condemned and universally opposed by all the rest. A state without friends and/or defenders from among the ranks of the other nations is difficult to visualize. Even a state without friends may be defended by third states solely because of the effect on their own national interests that would result if the first state received too drastic handling. The classical theoretical case of collective security in which *all* other states rally to the support of Y, who has been attacked by X, is thus extremely unlikely to be found in practice—and was not found in either of these two cases. At the same time the potentialities of collective security do not stand or fall upon the existence or lack of existence of these classical theoretical circumstances. If only half the states rally to the support of Y and against X, provided that X is substantially outweighed in power terms, a successful collective security action can be fought—as it was against North Korea. It was by no means inevitable that

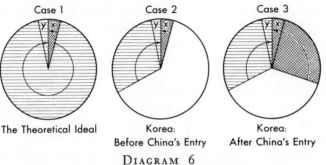

DIAGRAM 6
Collective Security: Three Possibilities.

this initial power ratio in the Korean Case had to be transformed by the addition of Communist China on the side of the aggressors. The transformation thus wrought might well have been avoided by a more modest view on the part of the UN as to the degree of punishment to be inflicted: frustration of North Korea's aggression as compared with extinction of North Korea itself. It is possible to conceive of some future collective security actions so limited in aims that a radical transformation of the power ratio involved, by the addition of another great power to the aggressor side midway in the sanctions application, does not occur.

Although there are no grounds for believing that collective security is unworkable under any and every set of conditions, it must be realistically faced that the most that can be expected in military terms from it (and assuming it does not eventuate in a third world war) is a Korean-type action without the Communist Chinese intervention overtones. In the Italian Case, Italy's small-power neighbors did not feel able to institute far-reaching economic measures without destroying their own power in far greater and faster degree than they could hope to injure and diminish that of Italy. This is true aside from their disinclination to act against Italy. Where military measures are involved, by far the greater number of states of the world are unable to contribute in any significant degree to other than purely local conflicts *even if they want to.*

From a military point of view the number of states capable of shipping overseas (or sending any great distance overland) and sustaining in battle even one division equipped and supplied in a modern and up-to-date fashion probably does not exceed twenty to twenty-five. This is, if anything, a very generous estimate, for in order to qualify for membership in this select group a state would ordinarily have to feel that it was not denuding its local defenses in sending the division overseas. Even in such great powers as the United States and Britain this kind of decision is not lightly made. This factor explains a good deal as to why, from a manpower point of view, the anti-aggressor forces in Korea were percentage-wise composed almost exclusively of South Korean and United States contingents. The South Koreans were available locally, and the United States was capable of sending its troops there in large numbers. It is also worth noting that the South Koreans were equipped with American weapons, organized along the lines of American ideas, and trained in American operational procedure. From a practical standpoint the Korean War was basically an American-supplied, equipped, and directed war. This is in no way a reflection upon United States allies in that war, for among these relatively few powers capable of shipping overseas and sustaining at least one division under battle conditions (omitting any Communist states in that category), the two most powerful were already themselves fighting wars in Asia—Britain in Malaya, and France in Indo-China.

The practical consequences of the extremely limited number of states capable of sending and maintaining a division overseas is that military sanctions imposed by the UN of necessity must be implemented only by a small number of states utilizing native manpower where possible. This unpleasant fact is too easily overlooked by extreme enthusiasts for collective security who are inclined to be overly impressed with the purely theoretical possibilities implicit in the collective power of the hundred thirty-odd sovereignties that compose the nation-state system.

To summarize briefly, there is no reason to believe that collective security is unworkable or incapable of being successfully put into practice. Even after Chinese intervention in Korea, the sanctions can be said to have been successful in that they denied to the Communist states the fruits of their aggression. Nor is it inevitable that a collective security action in the future will necessarily involve a great-power intervention in support of the aggression in the later stages—that depends in large part upon the degree of punishment which the UN is determined to administer. But, while collective security actions of this type may well occur in the future, there is no reason for believing that the necessary military burden will be or can be much more equally shared by a greater number of states unless radically new arrangements are made, such as the creation of a UN fighting force jointly supported and equipped by the UN itself. Unless some such radical innovation is introduced, the pattern of future collective military actions has already been revealed in Korea.

So far in these final observations the discussion has avoided the question that must now be faced and has run as a persistent theme through this chapter: is collective security a sound approach to the power problem? There is no doubt that collective security can be made to function as effectively as in the Korean Case's initial (pre-Communist Chinese intervention) stage. It can be smoothly and effectively put into operation with more practice. But the fundamental question is whether this approach itself is sound. It is feasible to do any number of things that may not be at all desirable.

This is a difficult question to answer in the abstract. The unique thing about collective security is that one never knows in advance what the obligation to resist aggression will amount to in practice. One never knows whom one will be expected to fight. One never knows who will be the victim of the attack. Collective security may save a small and almost friendless state from extinction; conversely, it may plunge a great power into an unwanted and undesirable war. Consequently the desirability of collective security for a particular state turns on how it is affected by an aggression.

From a general point of view, apart from its effects upon the security of particular states, the real difficulty with collective security is that it intrudes a degree of undesirable rigidity into the affairs of states. They may find themselves more or less compelled to act even where they would rather not. We have seen how they have sought with much success to "interpret" their obligations in order to restore their freedom of action (as under the League) or have refrained from hard and fast agreements to provide troops under the call of a Council (as in the UN). These trends have helped to cushion the rigidity implicit in collective security. Further, the ambiguity of many cases, the frequent impossibility of deciding where and by whom aggression has occurred, and the determined efforts of League and UN members alike to find a peaceful settlement and avoid sanctions, has prevented the collective security issue from being starkly posed very often. Yet occasions do arise, as in the two cases examined, when action of some decisive sort is necessitated by the contemptuous obviousness with which the organization's principle of "one for all and all for one" is flouted.

In such circumstances the degree of action that can be anticipated beyond mere lip service hinges upon the national interests of the great powers most directly concerned. In the Italian Case this meant that sanctions would not ever be such as to defeat Italy; in the Korean Case, conversely, the direct interest of the United States ensured an active and powerful intervention.

It might well be asked what is so rigid about a process that is in general carried out in practice only so far as the national interests of the powers most concerned dictate. The answer is that the very necessity of instituting even a relatively weak type of sanctions, as in the Italian Case, may initiate a disastrous chain of events completely inimical to the vital interests (other than prestige) of the states taking part. This happened to Britain and France in the Italian Case.

In the Korean Case, although the United States began her action against North Korea on a sound basis, she was led bit by bit, after Communist China's intervention, into a situation where, in order to administer a moral lesson, she was hovering on the brink of a full-scale war with a secondary enemy—China. As an aggressor, Communist China was to be punished according to the logic of collective security. Yet such punishment for China could not help but be punishment for the United States, too. If such an all-out war had actually occurred, the Soviet Union could either have held aloof and watched the draining of the strength of the United States in the vast reaches of China, or have joined in against the United States with the comfortable knowledge that China was on her side. While it can be argued that, UN or no UN, the United States cannot (and could not) sit idly by where and when China chooses to expand, it still remains of fundamental importance that the United States should retain full freedom of action as to where and when and *which* of China's actions should be opposed. To be committed to opposition, not where and as it is sound militarily and politically, but anywhere and any time obvious aggression is committed, are two very different things.

Of course even without a UN or League, as before World War I, forcibly wrought changes in the power relations of opposing blocs inescapably raised tension in the world. What has changed by the existence and practice of collective security sanctions is that the degree of tension is governed far too much by the nature of the action (the obviousness of the aggression) rather than from the power and interest effects of that action. This remains true despite the pronounced efforts of League and UN members (noted earlier) to regain discretion over commitments. They may still be at least nominally committed because of prestige, simply by belonging. The obverse side of the same point is that nations are not prepared to really implement collective security actions obviously contrary to their basic interests or alignments. Under these circumstances collective security obligations may lead the powers into actions that in the process undermine any hopes for a stable balance of power.[8] If a clear-cut substitution of a pure collective security power system is unobtainable, the mixed system which persists may distort the balance of power process, and neither may work effectively. In view of the great expectation for world peace that arose in the world following the birth of collective security, this condition is ironical, dangerous, and regrettable. Yet it would seem to be nonetheless true.

Seen in this perspective, the Security Council's decision in 1966 to implement economic sanctions against Rhodesia's stubborn determination to go its own way on the racial question, arouses little optimism. Not only was it unclear (at the beginning of 1967) what "threat to the peace, breach of the peace, or act of aggression" against other nations Rhodesia had committed. It was equally unclear what would happen if it became a matter of naval or military sanctions—where those nations most aroused could presumably contribute least.

Our analysis of the relations of nations has so far been directed at the functional relations of states and the organization of a power system. We have examined particular policies followed by particular nations only as illustrations of these features of the state system. Now a third perspective is both desirable and necessary: to view contemporary international relations through a systematic analysis of the interaction of the foreign policies of particular powers.

It is not possible and is not necessary to do this for all the nation-states. Each is of course vitally concerned with its own affairs, but we are concerned with their impact on the contemporary world scene. And in this feature states vary tremendously. Some few, perhaps twenty, have the resources or ability to make a serious impact in their own right. Many are important only as a bloc or group. But all have potential importance as the center of attention of the more vigorous states.

These "more vigorous" states comprise generally the super, great, and medium powers, although sometimes even small powers have had an effect, for a variety of reasons, quite out of proportion to their power. In examining these more vigorous states two cautions are again in order.

There is a temptation to divide the world into democratic, Communist, and uncommitted blocs. While useful to a point, such an approach if taken far or literally, will introduce grave distortions. The rivalry between Soviet Russia and Communist China illustrates, for it revolves around far more than an ideological disagreement within a single bloc.

There is an equal temptation to see the world outside the two super powers

---

[8] For further discussion see the excellent article by Roland N. Stromberg, "The Idea of Collective Security," *Journal of the History of Ideas*, Vol. XVII, No. 2 (April 1956), pp. 250–263. See also Stromberg's book, *Collective Security and American Foreign Policy*, New York: Praeger, 1963.

as mere reacting units to the policies of the United States and the Soviet Union who each possess destructive weapons on a scale which no other states equal. Yet the very concern of either super power over the weapons in the hands of the other, and the impossibility of resorting to nuclear weapons except as a last resort, diminishes the ability of either to act as a free agent, and increases by the very stalemate implicit in the super power relationship the possibilities of important independent action on the part of third states. France under de Gaulle illustrates. So does the sometimes extravagant wooing by both super powers of African votes in the UN.

If this were not so, the "vigorous states" would be simply the three blocs, or the two super powers, and none of the others would contribute important, essentially separate effects. Because it is so we must see the contribution of each. But it would be equally unwarranted to ignore the major roles of the super powers and visualize their policies as mere reactions to each other. Because they are the super powers we shall examine their policies first, and at greatest length. In doing so we shall give a good deal of attention to the Viet-Nam War and the Sino-Soviet dispute. Next we shall examine the major areas of the world, looking always for the effects of the actions of the more vigorous states, the interaction between non-super power policies and the policies of the super powers, and the combined effects upon those smaller powers whose role is primarily passive.

PART SIX

Contemporary International Relations

CHAPTER **22**

The United States:
The Record

But I sometimes wonder whether . . . a democracy is not uncomfortably similar to one of those prehistoric monsters with a body as long as this room and the brain the size of a pin: he lies there in his comfortable primeval mud and pays little attention to his environment; he is slow to wrath—in fact, you practically have to whack his tail off to make him aware that his interests are being disturbed; but, once he grasps this, he lays about him with such blind determination that he not only destroys his adversary but largely wrecks his native habitat.

GEORGE KENNAN [1]
American Diplomacy, 1900–1950

THE United States was born out of a balance-of-power situation that prevented England from exerting her full power to crush the colonies. But the United States happened to begin its life as an independent nation at a time when rather extraordinary conditions began to prevail in international relations. Because American views were formed and hardened into dogmas in this rather unusual period, the United States did not find it easy later to readjust to greatly altered circumstances.

I Historical Experience: Foreign Policy Effects

THE United States won her freedom through an alliance with France. Yet both Washington and Jefferson followed a sensible policy of refraining from new alignments. Jefferson warned of the dangers of "entangling alliances" that would draw the weak republic into European power politics. He knew that she could not merely by an act of will escape involvement, but he wanted the United States to refrain from looking for trouble. The powers of Europe might well check one another's ambitions, leaving the United States in peace.

So on the whole it proved to be. Britain, for reasons of her own, interposed herself between the Holy Alliance and the colonies of New Spain who had followed the example of the American Republic by casting off their kingly

---

[1] George F. Kennan, *American Diplomacy, 1900–1950*, Chicago: University of Chicago Press, 1951, pp. 45–47. Copyright, 1951, by the University of Chicago.

rulers. It was the deliberate policy of British Foreign Secretary George Canning, between 1822 and 1827, to foster the independence of the Latin American states of the New World. This British policy was already in operation in 1823 when President Monroe's message to Congress inaugurated the Monroe Doctrine. Canning had proposed a joint declaration, but the United States distrusted him and proceeded unilaterally. The Doctrine proclaimed that "the American continents . . . are henceforth not to be considered as subjects for future colonization by any European powers," that European intervention in the Western Hemisphere could not be viewed "in any other light than as the manifestation of an unfriendly disposition toward the United States," and that America, for her part, was determined to remain aloof from "the wars of the European powers in matters relating to themselves." The words and the spirit of the declaration were American; the basic policy was also British.

British policy was not adopted out of benevolence toward America. It was aimed, in Canning's famous words, at "restoring the balance of power." Confronted with the threat of Spain and France both under Bourbon rule, the British were determined "that if France had Spain it should not be Spain *'with the Indies.'* " Canning meant Spanish America. As he put it, Britain "called the New World into existence to redress the balance of the Old." [2] Thus the Americas were to be preserved in their independence to weaken Britain's enemies in Europe. Since Britain not only controlled the sea lanes but the exits and entrances from European waters into the open ocean, she could and did see that this judgment was observed by Europe so long as no world war occurred. Her own potential ambitions for further acquisitions were counterbalanced by the increasing conviction that colonies, like "ripe fruit," fell away from the mother tree once they became mature. Except during the United States Civil War when Britain was greatly tempted to intervene, and France actually sent a military expedition into Mexico, America enjoyed the benefits of this policy.

Thus the United States achieved peace and security in the nineteenth century without any positive effort on her own part. The general balance of power, for reasons discussed earlier, did not disintegrate into general war for a whole hundred years after Waterloo. Consequently, she was spared the involvement that would surely otherwise have come; no conscious important choices in international relations were demanded of her. Unilateralism sufficed. She had no reason to reflect at the time that her experience was unique or that this golden age was anything more than normal.

During this hiatus from active and precarious involvement in international relations, after 1815 and up to World War I (aside from a brief plunge into the Spanish-American War in 1898), she was able to devote her energies to the exploitation of a continent vastly rich in resources. This process she car-

---

[2] Robert Walsh, ed., *Select Speeches of the Right Honorable George Canning*, Philadelphia: Key and Biddle, 1835, pp. 466–467. Canning's speech was made in December 1826.

ried on with stupendous success. In a material sense America first caught up with and then outpaced a Europe where these conditions did not exist, and where tradition and custom impeded industrialization. Confidence came to Americans with this successful material progress—and also an underlying feeling of superiority, tempered only somewhat by the Puritanical tradition of hard work and severe moral standards. Americans came gradually to think of themselves as a people who had not only put the errors of the Old World behind them, but who had demonstrated the inherent superiority of their own ways both economically and politically. Whether this view was accurate or not, it came to influence very importantly the United States outlook on the world as a whole.

Isolated from the vicissitudes of life in an armed camp, the United States maintained only a small army (mostly for Indian warfare), and a navy which was, to say the least, nominal. Grown to maturity in an unusually peaceful century, and buoyed up by a sense of great material accomplishments, the United States held aloof from world politics and judged its activities in abstract and moral or emotional terms, like a spectator at a play. Her foreign policy was—and successfully so—almost purely negative. She wanted to prevent disturbance of her fortunate circumstances. But even in pursuit of this goal, nothing much was required of her. The coincidence of a century of unparalleled freedom from world wars (between 1815 and 1914), the desire of the British to maintain the *status quo* in the New World, and their support for their own reasons of the Open Door principle in China took most of the active burden off American shoulders. Occasional declarations of principle, such as the Monroe Doctrine and the Open Door policy, seemed to be most of what was required. The impact of international relations on the United States was remote; there was no pressing need to judge more concretely, realistically, or soberly.

2 The Tendency Toward Moral and Emotional Judgments

THE unique historical experience of the United States, and the fact that her fundamental foreign-policy circumstances have changed so recently, conspired to equip her very poorly for her present responsibility. Together, and quite naturally, they produced standards of judgment in foreign-policy matters which often left much to be desired.

In the nineteenth century the American people made moral and emotional judgments freely about what was happening in the world. The struggles of Poles to free themselves from Russian tyranny, the efforts of the Irish to win independence from Britain—movements of this type found sympathy and even private financial support in the United States. Many Americans were recent immigrants; they retained a live interest in the place of their origin. There was, however, no active intervention as a state on behalf of these movements. The United States was too weak for intervention; even more, it was the settled policy of the United States to refrain from involvement in European quarrels. The moral and abstract or emotional judgments of the American people on European events, and the essentially negative actual foreign policy of the United States toward Europe, proceeded along their separate paths. If this foreign policy had not been restricted almost exclusively to the conservative and negative function of keeping America free from foreign complications (which was, as we have said, approved by the American people), a dichotomy might have ensued. It was the absence of any intent actively to intervene with American power and aid the "good" to triumph over the "evil" which prevented this.

Once the international-relations position and foreign-policy activities of the United States in the world fundamentally altered, beginning with her involvement in World War I, the American people still continued to approach world politics on a moral and emotional basis, but with this difference: where the United States came to play an active role, she began to attempt to implement these moral-emotional judgments as the basis of foreign policy.

The major reason why this happened, aside from the by now ingrained habit of making moral-emotional judgments, was that America, although thrust suddenly into an influential role, *had as yet developed no clear ideas on what particular national interests she wished to achieve or advance.* The United States did not view her "association" (not "alliance") with Britain and France in World War I as the beginning of a permanent alignment. She did not approach the Versailles Conference with any aim of strengthening her "friends" against her "enemies," nor did she have any territorial ambitions for herself. She was thinking of a "just" peace. She had fought a war designed to end wars. She was not "for" Britain and "against" Germany. She was for peace and against war—against war in general and its recurrence. She wished to return to the happy conditions she had previously enjoyed. In order to do this, a new war had to be prevented. Since power politics, secret alliances, and the "nefarious" machinations of the balance of power were believed to have caused World War I, and since these same factors could lead to another world war, new concepts of open diplomacy and universal collective security were championed. There was no American desire that the League, once created, would serve as a defense for France against Germany any more than vice versa—it would ideally serve as a defense against the return of war.

The difficulties of making a "just" peace against the wishes and interests of the major Allied powers brought a degree of disillusionment to the American people. The idea that the United States should belong to the League and take part in Europe's quarrels, ran directly counter to traditional American policy. In the end the United States did not join the League, returned to unilateralism, and continued making moral and emotional judgments on world events without attempting to intervene. When Japan moved to swallow Manchuria, the United States announced its intention not to recognize changes wrought by force. When Japanese bombers killed defenseless Chinese women and children, Americans were enraged. But the United States did not move to undo what force had wrought. Indeed, the United States in the 1920's and 1930's was moved by a dogged, almost fanatical determination to restore "normalcy" and keep out of "foreign" wars.

3 War's Horrors vs. Aggression Unrepelled (1935–1941)

THE United States, in the mid-1930's, having participated in one world war without having understood the true reasons for her participation, was in no mood to repeat her previous "folly." World War I had been fought "to end all war," and if more war came anyhow, the United States had made her contribution; it was only appropriate that Europe's great powers, who had failed to appreciate the Wilsonian ideals, should pay for their backwardness without further United States sacrifices or involvement.

This sentiment lay behind the series of neutrality measures enacted into law between 1935 and 1939. In their first formulations these acts, although they did not prohibit trade generally with warring states, provided for an arms embargo to be extended to all belligerents indiscriminately. These embargoes were intended to remove what was then considered the most potent cause of involvement in "foreign" wars—the supply of armaments to nations at war. Yet in practice what happened was that a well-armed aggressor, attacking a poorly prepared victim, was simply gratuitously aided by the refusal of the United States to extend arms aid. In the Italo-Ethiopian conflict in 1935 the arms embargo did not hurt Italy. Oil, steel, and scrap iron could still be legally shipped; American exports of such goods to Italy and Italian Africa increased by 200 to 300 per cent in the last months of 1935 alone. When the Spanish Civil War broke out in the latter half of 1936, the Loyalist forces were penalized while the Rebels under Franco received supplies from Italy and Germany. The question was whether United States actions were not aiding those who wished to destroy the *status quo*—a *status quo* which the United States herself wished to keep essentially intact.

The Neutrality Act of 1937 did improve matters slightly by giving the President discretion to decide whether "a state of war" or "civil strife" existed. In July 1937, when war broke out between China and Japan, and each for its own reasons refrained from declaring war, the President acquiesced in the fiction in order not to cut off aid to China. Since the American people were overwhelmingly sympathetic to China, this move went unchallenged. The neutrality legislation was proving more and more difficult to square in practice with the gradually evolving concept in the United States of her national interests. Secretary of State Hull, in June 1938, also requested the United States aircraft industry to refrain from selling planes to nations—i.e., Japan—who bombed civilians from the air. In this action we see a tendency to express a semi-understood concrete American interest—opposition to Japan's spreading control in China—in terms of a generalized moral abstraction; that is, the United States showed her antagonism to those guilty of inhumane action. This emotional response is an indication of how difficult it had become for Americans to distinguish feelings from interests. Her opposition to Japan's perpetration of the act rather than the act itself became clearer when World War II broke out and Britain and the United States bombed German civilians from the air. If we consider what the effort to apply this principle would have led to in 1944, we can readily see the weakness of a foreign policy resting on abstract moral principle. This tendency to generalize abstractly recurs again and again; the United States was simply not yet in the habit of' considering concrete interests concretely. Indeed, she had hardly realized the necessity of making the effort.

In October 1937, President F. D. Roosevelt made his famous "quarantine the aggressors" speech. This "trial balloon," which seemed to herald a more positive United States policy, was quickly checked by a storm of isolationist sentiment. Roosevelt tried once more, in January 1939, in his annual message to Congress. He pointed out the rigidity of the neutrality laws that could "give aid to an aggressor and deny it to the victim," [3] but he did not recommend any concrete changes. Only in the summer did Secretary Hull belatedly request repeal of the arms embargo, a prohibition on ships of United States registry entering the war zones, and a "cash-and-carry" policy for goods exported. As Congress wrestled with these issues through the spring and early summer of 1939, the conflict in proposals was so great that no majority was found for anything. The Congress gave up, continued the 1937 act, and adjourned.

This was the situation when World War II broke out. Since it was a declared war, it left the President no loophole for discretion. This incident remains a classic historical example of how a great nation, by unwise legislation based upon a misunderstanding of its national interests, can shackle its policy and give aid and comfort to its potential enemies. On September 5, 1939, the President, bound by the law, proclaimed an arms embargo against the initial belligerents. By September 10, this embargo was in effect against Germany, Britain, France, Poland, Australia, New Zealand, India, South Africa, and Canada. Britain and France, desperately trying to close the armaments gap between themselves and Germany by drawing on United States industry, were immediately cut off from future supplies from the United States, including some $80,000,000 worth already ordered and licensed for export. On September 13, the President called a special session of Congress. Eight days later he appealed for a repeal of the arms embargo, which he described somewhat all-inclusively as "most vitally dangerous to American neutrality, American security, and American peace." Whether the embargo was really a

---

[3] R.I.I.A., Arnold J. Toynbee, ed., *Survey of International Affairs*, 1938, Vol. 1, p. 637.

threat to neutrality and peace could be argued, but that its rigidity jeopardized American security was obvious. He declared: "I regret that the Congress passed that act. I regret equally that I signed that act." The new request was for a "cash-and-carry" policy for arms and goods alike, while keeping United States shipping out of war zones.

Essentially the new Neutrality Act of 1939, passed some six weeks later, enacted these provisions into law. In the first days of November it went into effect. Britain and France could now once again buy in the United States—provided they had the money and the shipping. By the same token the United States merchant marine was barred from most of the North Atlantic, which was designated a war zone. The United States, although it had voluntarily surrendered the neutral rights for which for a century or more it had argued and fought, was at least aiding its friends—within limits.

The debate over the 1939 Neutrality Act again revealed the American tendency to argue in terms of generalized and abstract principles. Those who wanted to repeal the arms embargo based their case essentially, as the President himself had, on the proposition that it would help the United States to stay out of the war (which was very questionable) rather than that such a policy, even if it brought a risk of war, was in United States' interest; their opponents maintained with more logic that the embargo would better serve to keep the United States at peace (which was deemed a useful and desirable objective in itself). In the unreal atmosphere in which the debate unfolded, the "repealers" argued that the embargo favored the more heavily armed Axis and that it was unneutral (an argument which logically implies that neutrality means aid to the weaker side). The "stand-patters" insisted that ending the embargo after war had been declared would itself be unneutral (although it would really have been no more or less unneutral than the imposition of the embargo in the first place). Very little of the debate turned squarely on the real issues: whether a Franco-British defeat would jeopardize American security, and whether the United States could permit Hitler to attain permanent hegemony over the vast resources of industrialized Europe.

As 1939 closed and 1940 began, the main concern in the United States and Latin America was still insulation from the struggle. These twenty-one republics met together in October 1939, to declare a "zone of security" reaching out into the Atlantic and Pacific Oceans as much as 300 miles. This area was to be closed to hostile actions. The zonal limitation was ignored by all the belligerents. Indeed, the dramatic battle between three British cruisers and the German "pocket" battleship *Graf Spee* took place off Montevideo, Uruguay, in December 1939. This action demonstrated the difficulties of insulation from the struggle.

Germany's invasion of Scandinavia in the spring of 1940 destroyed any illusions that the war would not be fought out to the bitter end. The United States now began to rearm in a hurry. A goal of fifty thousand planes a year was set in May; in June came the sale of "obsolete" planes to Britain and France—a procedure that could be "justified" under an existing law but marked a definite departure from previous policy. It was unneutral in spirit. Then came the Fall of France; Congress authorized a two-ocean navy. In August, a joint defense board was created with Canada. This was tantamount to a defensive alliance with a belligerent (for Canada was, of course, at war). In September, conscription became the law of the land for the first time in peace. In September, too, came the destroyer-bases agreement with Britain by which fifty "overage" destroyers were turned over to the hard-pressed British in return for United States rights to establish naval and air bases in New-foundland, the Bermudas, the Bahamas, and other British possessions in the Caribbean. Thus was closed a dangerous gap in American defenses—the approaches to the Panama Canal.

These were steps that marked the gradual predominance of the security needs of the United States over the still-continuing abstract debate over peace and neutrality.

Following Roosevelt's unprecedented election to a third term (which constituted *de facto* an endorsement of these moves), the tempo increased. By the end of 1940, over $12 billions had been appropriated for defense. Half of the United States arms output was going to Britain—for which she still had to pay cash. As Britain's inability to pay through liquidated United States assets increased, a new solution had to be found. On March 11, 1941, the "Lend-Lease" Act (empowering the President to "lease, lend, or otherwise dispose of" arms to friendly states) became law. In the same month $7 billions was appropriated to turn the gesture into solid fact. Britain could now receive arms regardless of her ability to pay. Yet all the war materiel in the world was of no use if it did not survive the Atlantic crossing. In early 1941, British shipping losses to German submarines were approximately half a million tons monthly. If this rate held true throughout 1941, the total annual losses would be twice the tonnage of new shipping being built in the United States and Britain combined in the same period.

In April 1941, the Red Sea, which had been closed to United States shipping as a war zone under the Neutrality Act, was reclassified. Roosevelt further announced that this shipping would be protected. The Neutrality Act had become a dead letter; the United States had reached a point where people and government alike were in effect in collusion against their own too-rigid laws. By the end of the month the United States Navy was patrolling routinely as far as two thousand miles at sea; the first clash between the United States and German navies occurred.[4] On April 10, the United States announced that it had, through negotiation with the Danes, assumed responsibility for the defense of Greenland. In July, bases were acquired in Iceland (700 miles from Scotland). In rapid succession now American naval ships were ordered to "shoot first" (the USS *Greer* had been attacked off Iceland), convoys were organized, and the neutrality laws were amended to permit the arming of United States merchant shipping. Henceforth, United States ships

---

[4] The USS *Niblack*, engaged in rescuing the crew of a torpedoed Dutch ship, depth-bombed a German submarine. This was kept secret at the time.

were to be permitted to sail to belligerent ports through belligerent waters. Lend-Lease was extended to Russia in the fall. The United States—by supplying the Allies, patrolling the seas, attacking German submarines on sight, and convoying shipping through the war zone—was at war in everything but name in the Atlantic.

In the Pacific area the relations between the United States and Japan were growing tenser, although not a shot had been fired. On September 25, 1940, another $25,000,000 was loaned to China; the next day the President embargoed scrap iron and scrap steel exports, except to Britain and the Western Hemisphere, to take effect October 16. High-test aviation gasoline had already been cut off. Other forms of iron and steel continued to be sent, and American petroleum products continued to grease the wheels of the Japanese war machine into the spring of 1941. Then in July 1941, having safeguarded her rear through the conclusion of a non-aggression pact with Russia (April 1941) and knowing that the Soviets were too heavily engaged in Europe to begin a war in Asia, Japan moved to take Indo-China. Occupied and defeated, France had no choice but to give in. Japan by its move confounded those who had predicted a new Russo-Japanese war, and clearly indicated the direction that her subsequent aggressions would take. The United States and Britain, acting together, responded on July 25 by "freezing" all Japanese assets in their countries. This decision meant the end of United States trade with Japan as well as the end of United States supplies for the Japanese war effort. The issues were posed as starkly in the Pacific as they had been by the United States convoy action in the Atlantic. The United States was not going to sit idly by while Hitler defeated Britain and consolidated Europe; it was not going to supply the war materiel by which the Japanese could gobble up the rich islands of the South Pacific. Under the stark pressure of events the American people were learning that neutrality could be a two-edged sword. They realized that, where determined aggressors were at work, an abstract and dogmatic neutrality could be the means by which the United States abetted agression, including—ultimately—aggression against an isolated and friendless United States fighting by herself.

4 The Second World War (1941–1945)

AS the year 1941 opened, President Roosevelt, in his address to Congress, had said: "When the dictators, if the dictators, are ready to make war upon us, they will not wait for an act of war on our part." As the year 1941 closed, his words came true. Even as "last minute" diplomatic negotiations went on in Washington between America and Japan, the Japanese fleet, having rehearsed their Pearl Harbor attack until proficient, was already at sea. On December 7, Japan bombed Pearl Harbor. The United States was at war.

As with all moments of national crisis, the minor and the petty things, the less essential aspects, suddenly fell away. The true issues were revealed in a

way that left no doubt as to what had to be done. Like letters of fire on the
wall, the message of the Pearl Harbor attack was unmistakable: the United
States must fight—and must win. On December 8, the United States ac-
cepted the challenge and declared war on Japan. Then on December 11 came
the German and Italian declarations of war, and Congress responded. Great
Britain and Canada soon followed suit, as did a number of Latin American
states. It was now to be, as long foreshadowed, a two-ocean conflict. The
United States girded herself for a great effort in conjunction with her allies.
By January 2, 1942, on the occasion of the signing of the United Nations
Declaration pledging each government "to employ its full resources, military
or economic, against those members of the Tripartite Pact and its adherents
with which such government is at war," twenty-six governments formed the ·
grand coalition against the Axis.

The way to military victory for the United States and her allies was long
and hard. As the year 1942 began, the Allies were everywhere hard pressed.
The United States garrison on Corregidor in the Philippines, cut off from all
aid, held out until May 6. The Japanese, unhindered, swept south, taking not
only the Philippines, but the Dutch East Indies, and the "impregnable" British naval base at Singapore. All of Southeast Asia lay at their feet. Soon they
were poised for a possible attack either on India or New Zealand and Australia—if not on all three. The Pearl Harbor attack had been so successful
(from the Japanese point of view) that the once-powerful United States
Navy was hard-pressed to stop them. Even so, in May and June the battles of
the Coral Sea and Midway chalked up two important victories for the United
States. On August 7, United States marines landed at Guadalcanal, marking
the assumption of the offensive. For months their position was precarious.
Then on November 12 a three-day naval battle began in the Solomon Islands:
one Japanese battleship, five cruisers, and twelve transports were destroyed or
seriously damaged. Guadalcanal could be held; the tide was turning.

In North Africa the Germans under Rommel reached El Alamein, only
seventy miles from Alexandria, Egypt, before they were finally checked. This
was mid-1942. For a time the Suez Canal and British control of the whole
Middle East were in grave danger. Not until November 12 were Montgomery's forces able to expel Rommel from Egypt. His rear in danger from the
November 8 Anglo-American landing in French North Africa, and faced with
a determined attack in front, Rommel retreated. The first great amphibious
landing of the European theater had occurred; it was to sweep all of Africa
clean of Axis forces.

In Russia the Germans began the assault on Stalingrad on August 22, and
on September 14 they penetrated the city. Here, on November 19, 1942, they
reached their greatest penetration of Russia. After that, under the hammer
blows of a series of Soviet offensives, the Nazi tide in Russia slowly began to
recede. In November 1942, in retrospect the most critical month of the war,
in all the main theaters of action the Allied forces were passing over to the
offensive. From that time forward the attack was pressed.

In 1943 came the invasion of Sicily (July 10). On July 25 Mussolini resigned and was replaced by Marshal Badoglio, who opened negotiations for an armistice; it was signed on September 3. On September 9 United States troops landed in Italy at Salerno; the stubborn war against the German forces there began. Not until June 4, 1944, did the American army enter Rome. Two days later came the invasion of Normandy. Another ten days later came the American assault on the Marianas in the Pacific. By August the recapture of Guam was completed; the Japanese were driven back into Burma from India; Paris was liberated; and Romania surrendered to the advancing Russians. On September 12 the American First Army entered Germany. In December came the last great German offensive in the West—the Battle of the Bulge—and on April 26, 1945 the American and Russian armies met on the Elbe River at Torgau. V-E Day (victory in Europe) was proclaimed on May 8.

In Asia the bloody battle of Iwo Jima was won on March 17, 1945, giving the American air forces a base only seven hundred fifty miles from Yokohama and making fighter escort for the bombers over Japan feasible. Then on April 1 American forces invaded Okinawa, only slightly more than three hundred miles from major Japanese cities. On August 6 an atomic bomb, dropped over Hiroshima, wiped out three-fifths of the city, and two days later Russia declared war on Japan. Finally, on August 14 Tokyo accepted the Allied surrender terms, and the war in the Pacific, too, was over.

If the way to military victory for America and her allies had been hard, the way to exploit that victory in a manner satisfactory to all the Allied great powers was ultimately to prove still harder. During the war four conferences of the Big Three (the United States, Britain, and Russia) were held at irregular intervals to coordinate military strategy on the grand scale and to lay down the fundamentals along which the postwar world should be organized.

At the Moscow Conference of October 1943, at the foreign minister level, the powers agreed to the principle of no separate peace, promised punishment for German "atrocities, massacres, and executions," pledged the Allies to "continue the present close collaboration" after the war, promised to set up a free and independent Austria, and decided to create a new international organization to which they would belong. At the Cairo Conference on December 1, 1943, Roosevelt, Churchill, and Chiang Kai-shek agreed to strip Japan of her conquered territories and to return certain of these, including Formosa, to China; they also endorsed a free and independent Korea (a principle to which Russia later also agreed). Meeting in conference at Tehran, immediately after Cairo, Roosevelt, Churchill, and Stalin fixed the time for the Normandy invasion and a supporting Russian offensive, decided to support Tito's Partisans in Yugoslavia in preference to Mikhailovitch's Chetniks, and approved (unofficially) approximately the Curzon Line as Poland's eastern frontier.

In the controversial Yalta Conference of February 1945, Roosevelt, Churchill, and Stalin met again and agreed to establish a "democratic" Poland, which would receive "substantial accessions of territory in the north and west." A time and place for a conference to create the new international organization was settled: April 25, 1945, at San Francisco. Germany was to be divided into occupation zones, and the figure of $20 billions was accepted as a basis for discussion on German reparations. At Yalta it was also agreed to incorporate the veto in the organization to be established, and permit the Soviet Ukraine and Byelorussia to belong to the UN in their own right. The Soviet Union promised to enter the war against Japan within three months of Germany's defeat. In Asia, Russia was to regain essentially the status she had before her defeat in the Russo-Japanese War. The *status quo* was to be maintained in Outer Mongolia, Russia would reacquire Southern Sakhalin, Port Arthur would be leased to the Soviets as a naval base, and the Southern Manchurian and Chinese Eastern railroads would be jointly operated by Russia and the Nationalist Government of China (with whom the Soviets promised to deal as *the* government of China). In addition the Russians were to acquire the Kurile Islands. This last concession was the only significant improvement Russia gained over her pre-1904 status in Asia, aside from her steady enroachment in Mongolia between the wars.

The Potsdam Conference of July–August 1945, was the final wartime gathering. Here Churchill (replaced by Attlee after the British election), Truman, and Stalin decided to establish a Council of Foreign Ministers, representing the United Kingdom, the U.S.S.R., Nationalist China, France, and the United States. The Council, which was to be composed of high-ranking deputies in the absence of the foreign ministers, was to draw up peace treaties for Italy and the smaller European satellite countries. (For this purpose it was to meet without China, and in practice no council session of all five powers was actually held.) A set of political and economic principles for the governing of Germany was adopted. Germany was to be completely disarmed and Nazism eliminated; "for the time being, no central German Government" was to be established. The German economy was to be decentralized and cartels and trusts broken up although Germany was to be treated by the occupying powers "as a single economic unit." Reparations were to be received by Russia from its own zone plus some "industrial capital equipment" from the western zones, Russia undertaking to settle Polish reparation claims out of her own share. On Poland the Conference agreed "that the final delimitation of the western frontier of Poland shall await the peace settlement" but that, in the meantime, Poland would administer German East Prussia, Silesia, and extensive parts of Brandenburg and Pomerania. Finally, the Balkan states and Italy, following the conclusion of peace treaties, were to be jointly supported for membership in the UN.

5   *The Uneasy Peace* (1945–1967)

WHAT is impressive about these conferences from the perspective of today is how few of the long-range goals were ever implemented. The purely military obligations were honored promptly, for all had a common interest in achieving victory. But the "temporary" political arrangements tended to become more and more permanent as relations grew stiffer between Russia and the West, while many of the proposed permanent dispositions failed completely of being realized. The "temporary" division of Germany, pending the formation of an all-German government, still persisted more than twenty years later, just as did the "temporary" division of Korea at the 38th Parallel. Poland, "pending the final determination" of her western frontier at the peace settlement, was still "temporarily" administering parts of former East Germany. It was only after great difficulty that the powers were able even to agree on the composition of the conference to pass on peace treaties for Italy and the Balkan states—although such treaties were concluded in 1946. Not until December 1955, did these states achieve their promised membership in the UN. The proposed permanent disposition for a "free and independent Austria" took until mid-1955 to realize, and the "free and independent Korea" remains divided into two pieces. These pieces of unfinished business were indications of the growing disharmony among the allied great powers in the immediate postwar period.

The public discord, especially between the United States and Russia, which eventually broadened into the Cold War, grew initially out of disagreement over the future of the Balkans. In more fundamental terms, of course, the discord grew out of the obvious fact that only the United States stood in the way after 1945 of Russia's exercising unchecked power over a prostrate Europe. The great differences in outlook and philosophy between the two super powers had been deliberately soft-pedaled by common consent during the war. There had been clashes,[5] but the main issues had been kept limited and compromisable. Even as late as the San Francisco Conference in 1945 the United States–Soviet deadlock over the role of the UN General Assembly had been resolved. But after the war the incentive for adjustment on both sides was less, and the differences in outlook and interests became more apparent. The two clashed over the future of the Balkans.

Both sides were agreed that Romania, Hungary, and Bulgaria should be "democratic," but by that term they meant very different things. The United States' insistence on really free elections would almost certainly, if honored, have created anti-Communist states once more on Russia's doorstep. The United States principle—that each people should freely decide its own future—in this case dovetailed neatly with the idea of containing Russia in eastern Europe. On the other hand, because the Soviets occupied these states, the United States could do little or nothing except use words to attempt to prevent their conversion into satellites. The United States nevertheless insisted upon true self-determination. An increasing bitterness began to mark American-Russian relations. Whether the United States' insistence on Russia's honoring America's moral principle really contributed to the United States' national interests is debatable. Since it could not affect the result and

---

[5] See, for example, Gen. John R. Deane, *The Strange Alliance*, New York: Viking, 1947.

since the United States was unwilling to take any forceful action to implement her view, from a realistic (as opposed to a moral) viewpoint the actions were futile. While it kept America's record "clean," it also increased tension. And while the great differences in outlook and interests between the two super powers could not ultimately have been suppressed, their clash in this case, where Russia held all the cards, undoubtedly increased the disposition to disagree with each other, almost regardless of the interests at stake in any particular case. The promise (or lack of promise) which this clash implied for subsequent American-Russian relations was to be amply fulfilled.

On March 12, 1947, with the announcement of the Truman Doctrine, the President issued a corollary to the moral principle of self-determination of peoples: "The peoples of a number of countries of the world have recently had totalitarian regimes forced upon them against their will. The Government of the United States has made frequent protests [over] Poland, Romania, and Bulgaria." He then called upon the United States "to help free people to maintain their free institutions and their national integrity against aggressive movements that seek to impose upon them totalitarian regimes. This is no more than a frank recognition that totalitarian regimes imposed on free peoples by direct or indirect aggression, undermine the foundations of international peace and hence the security of the United States." This statement must be considered one of the most far-reaching principles ever to be announced by a major power as a guide to the conduct of its foreign policy. It would make the defense of the "free institutions" and the "national integrity" of third states threatened by totalitarian aggression a security interest of the United States; although Truman envisaged that United States "help [would] be primarily through economic and financial aid," more forceful measures were not excluded. The sweeping terms of the doctrine raised the question whether American involvement ought to depend upon the proved existence of a totalitarian threat to a state rather than upon the actual security implications for the United States in the specific case. This fundamental question was glossed over in the all-embracing general statement of policy. Yet the two things were by no means the same, even though the Truman Doctrine tended to ignore the distinction.

There were other difficulties which it raised. Truman recognized that "The world is not static, and the *status quo* is not sacred. But we cannot allow changes in the *status quo* . . . by such methods as coercion, or by such subterfuges as political infiltration." Yet since in many of the nations around the perimeter of the Soviet orbit evolutionary change was ruled out by the reactionary elements in control, in such lands the ruling out of coercion was equivalent to trying to keep the world static and the *status quo* sacred. The danger in this doctrine was that the United States would become identified with a "stand-patism" that would earn her enmity in a world undergoing social and economic revolution on an unprecedented scale. The Truman Doctrine, incautiously used, could lead to the negation of a very old American idea contained in the Declaration of Independence: "Whenever any form of government becomes destructive of those ends, it is the right of the people to alter or abolish it, and to institute new government, laying its foundations on such principles and organizing its powers in such form as to them shall seem most likely to effect their safety and happiness." [6] The lurking ambiguities and potential incompatibilities implicit in the Truman pronouncement again demonstrate the difficulty of attempting to make foreign policy in terms of moral abstractions.

The immediate purpose of the message was to secure Congressional sanction and appropriations for the strengthening and defense of Greece and Turkey. On this point the nation was almost unanimous. It was only on the possible meaning and implementation of the general principles just discussed that confusion and questions arose. There was no doubt that Truman expressed the truth of the strategic factors involved when he abandoned his moral abstractions and said: "It is necessary only to glance at a map to realize that the survival and integrity of the Greek nation are of grave importance in a much wider situation. If Greece should fall under the control of an armed minority [i.e., the Communists], the effect upon its neighbor, Turkey, would be immediate and serious. Confusion and disorder might well spread throughout the entire Middle East." The British decided on February 24 to withdraw their forces from Greece in order to economize their slender resources. This action, which had precipitated the Truman decision, also made the policy of United States' aid logical and necessary. Had the loyalist Greeks been abandoned, the Communist forces fighting in the civil war, which had begun even before the end of World War II, would have triumphed. Ultimately this particular venture of the United States was a resounding success.

The next major development in the steady deterioration of American-Soviet relations came over a proposal which seemed at first to have some potential for reversing that trend by stimulating a revival of East-West trade. On May 8, 1947, Under Secretary of State Dean Acheson, speaking of Europe's economic weakness, declared: "Without outside aid, the process of recovery in many countries would take so long as to give rise to hopelessness and despair. In these conditions freedom and democracy and the independence of nations could not long survive, for hopeless and hungry people often resort to desperate measures." Extremism of both the left and the right were possible. On June 5, 1947, Secretary of State George C. Marshall followed up this theme: "It would be neither fitting nor efficacious for this Government to undertake to draw up unilaterally a program designed to place Europe on its feet economically. That is the business of the Europeans. The initiative, I think, must come from Europe. The role of this country should consist of friendly aid in the drafting . . . and of later support of such a program. . . . The program should be a joint one, agreed to by a number of, if not all, European nations."

Whether or not Secretary Marshall intended to set on foot a program of

---

[6] See, on this point, Stuart W. Chapman, "The Right of Revolution and the Rights of Man," *The Yale Review*, Vol. 43, No. 4 (Summer 1954), pp. 576 ff.

the magnitude finally reached is not clear. In any case Britain and France reacted promptly. Bevin and Bidault met in Paris on June 17, and Molotov was
invited the next day to join them. Poland and Czechoslovakia indicated their
interest. But when Molotov came on June 27 and asked the conditions under
which United States aid would be forthcoming, no one knew. On July 2 the
meeting came to an end; Molotov expressed his belief that the aid program
would impair "the economic independence and sovereignty" of the European
states by allowing "certain strong powers" (i.e., the United States) to "make
use of some European countries against others in whatever way" proved
"profitable" in establishing their "domination." The Soviet bloc counted itself out. But on July 12, sixteen European states—all of non-Communist Europe save Spain, together with Iceland and Turkey—met together and
decided to press forward on a cooperative basis. By September 22, 1947, they
had prepared a plan for European economic recovery.

It is highly doubtful whether the United States Congress would have appropriated money for a plan in which Russia shared. Since Russia and her
bloc were strongly opposed, the plan picked up Congressional support that
might otherwise not have been forthcoming. Increasingly the program took
on the attributes of a Cold War weapon. On that basis the Economic Cooperation Act, authorizing United States participation, became law on April
3, 1948. The ECA (Economic Cooperation Administration) was established
as the American agency to work with the sixteen-nation organ, the OEEC
(Organization for European Economic Cooperation). Stop-gap aid was given
through the Reconstruction Finance Corporation until the Foreign Aid Ap-
propriation Act of June 28, 1948, provided the first $4 billions.

In February 1948, Czechoslovakia, which had sought to be a bridge between East and West, fell to an internal Communist coup. The emotional
effect of the seizure was very great even aside from the strategic implications
for the European balance of power. The Soviet Iron Curtain had advanced
still farther into the ancient citadels of the West. Then in June 1948, came
the Russian full blockade of Berlin. This double-barreled Communist threat
to the *status quo* brought an equally positive reaction. To relieve Berlin a
giant airlift was instituted. In the eleven months to May 1949 (when the Soviets lifted the blockade), 1,402,644 metric tons of food and supplies were
flown into Berlin in 277,728 flights. More long-range defenses began to take
shape on April 4, 1949, with the signing of the North Atlantic Pact (which
entered into effect on August 24, 1949).

In the Mutual Defense Assistance Act of 1949 (which became law on October 6) $1 billion was authorized for military aid. On January 27, 1950, the
President approved the plans for an "integrated defense" of the NATO area
(a procedure required under the Act), and the United States signed Mutual
Defense Agreements with eight NATO states who had requested such aid.
Yet it was the impact of the North Korean aggression in the summer of 1950
that galvanized the alliance into hurried but fruitful activity and provided the
impetus for its transformation. In July 1950, Congress appropriated a second

$1 billion and in September the North Atlantic Council agreed to "the establishment, at the earliest possible date, of an integrated force under centralized command, which shall be adequate to deter aggression and to ensure the defense of Western Europe." SHAPE (Supreme Headquarters of the Allied Powers in Europe) was activated on January 7, 1951, to implement this decision. Thereafter, as recounted elsewhere, NATO grew progressively in strength.

Asia now replaced Europe as the main theater of the Cold War. The fall of the Nationalist Chinese regime from power on the mainland in 1949 increased tensions appreciably (with major effects on internal United States politics, as we shall see in the next chapter). Then came the North Korean assault on South Korea in June 1950, and the beginning of the prolonged Korean War (discussed in Chapter 21). Hardly was this painful episode over when the crisis in the Indo-Chinese War caused by the collapse of French military power at Dien Bien Phu, threatened to involve the United States in yet a new land war in Asia. How the Geneva Conference of 1954 partitioned Indo-China and ended the conflict is told elsewhere. (See Chapters 27 and 30.)

The year 1954, coming after Stalin's death on March 5, 1953, marked a new watershed in the Cold War, for it was the year of the resumption of great-power negotiations. Since the discussions which led to the lifting of the Berlin blockade in mid-1949 the world had witnessed much shooting but no great-power discussions on the higher levels of foreign ministers or heads of state. The Berlin Conference of January 1954, and the Geneva Conference of the spring of the same year marked renewed discussions on the foreign ministers level. Although progress on Germany was nil and that on the Far East was only moderate, tension decreased appreciably. In late 1954, for the first time in more than twenty years, no significant war was going on anywhere in the world. The high point of good feeling was reached in July 1955, when Eisenhower and Bulganin, in a "meeting at the summit" in Geneva, exchanged assurances that nuclear warfare had no rational purpose and that neither the United States nor Russia intended to start such a war.

Even the failure of the Geneva Foreign Ministers Conference of October–November 1955, to follow up this statement of mutual good intentions with any concrete progress on Germany failed to diminish public optimism appreciably. But then, in mid-1956, came a fresh shock—the Aswan Dam crisis, which was followed by the blocking of the Suez Canal in the course of the short but ill-fated Suez War.[7] Simultaneously with the war came the Hungarian revolt.

The Suez crisis severely strained the bonds of NATO. It produced a great debate in the United States as to the wisdom of our actions, both in siding against our allies and in failing to aid the Hungarian rebels. But what served above all to draw the Atlantic alliance together again was Russia's spectacular

---

[7] See above, Chapter 12.

achievement in putting the *sputnik* into orbit in outer space on October 4, 1957. Not until January 31, 1958 was an American satellite (of much smaller weight) successfully placed in orbit, and not until the December 18, 1958 launching of the Atlas satellite did the U.S. more or less equal the Russian achievement of 1957.

The United States which had produced an atomic bomb four years before the Russians, and a hydrogen bomb one year before them, was now behind.

Not only that but the Russians showed new signs of a determination to upset the European *status quo*. A second Berlin crisis began in November 1958, with Khrushchev's "ultimatum" that West Berlin must be evacuated by Allied troops within six months. This led to a new foreign ministers conference (May–August 1959) and to an invitation to Khrushchev to visit the United States. Personal discussions with President Eisenhower produced the "Camp David formula": while negotiations over Berlin were not to be indefinitely prolonged, neither were they to have any precise time limit! A new summit meeting was to resume the discussion over Berlin in May 1960. But the U-2 incident washed that out completely and negotiations were suspended pending the change in administration in Washington. In early 1961, as President Kennedy took over, the Russian threat to make a separate peace with East Germany and unilaterally terminate American access to Berlin was suspended. But when Kennedy met with Khrushchev in Vienna in June he found him completely adamant. Kennedy described the experience on television: "it was a very somber two days . . ." Nine days later, also on television, Khrushchev reinstituted a deadline for the separate peace treaty—year's end. In July, Kennedy called up reserves, increased defense outlays, and placed more U.S. bombers on ground alert. Khrushchev on August 11 answered:

They [the West] declare that they will allegedly fight for the freedom of Germans in West Berlin. This is a fairy tale. . . . We shall not be the first to press the buttons at our rocket installations, we shall not start a war; but if the imperialists force a war upon us we shall meet it bravely and deal a devastating blow to the aggressor.

Khrushchev's very threats to take Berlin sent the totals for refugees fleeing to West Berlin to new heights. The climax of the Second Berlin Crisis came on August 13, 1961 with the erection of the Berlin Wall. In October, Khrushchev again suspended his deadline. But he insisted that it "must be and will be signed, with the Allied powers or without them."

How Khrushchev, flushed with the success of the Soviet space program, impatient to spread Soviet influence even further, and needled by Chinese charges of a lack of revolutionary vigor, embarked in 1962 upon the even more dangerous course of sending missiles to Cuba, has already been recounted. The confrontation of October 1962 persuaded Khrushchev of the dangers of a new ultimatum on Berlin. It was succeeded by a détente in the Cold War in the form of the Nuclear Test Ban Treaty, coupled with growing public friction between Soviet Russia and Communist China. China vehemently and simultaneously assailed Soviet "recklessness" in putting the missiles into Cuba and Soviet cowardice in removing them.

Kennedy's assassination in November 1963 and Johnson's assumption of presidential powers brought a change in American leadership paralleled in Russia in October 1964 when Khrushchev was toppled from power in a resurgence of Soviet collective rule. Alexei Kosygin and Leonid Brezhnev took over the top positions as prime minister and chairman of the party, respectively. With the stalemate over Germany tacitly recognized by both super powers, and the Cuban issue "de-fused," the stage was set for a new Cold War thaw.

That a thaw did not materialize this time had little directly to do with the Soviet Union. In the summer of 1965, the failure of the relatively minor effort by United States "observers" and training detachments in South Viet-Nam to halt Communist Viet Cong successes led to a decision by the United States to send active combat forces to the area. The escalation of American forces there in 1965 was rapid: from 23,000 troops in January to 181,329 troops in December. Systematic American bombing of military targets in North Viet-Nam was paralleled by a rise in world tension. In South Viet-Nam Americans killed in action increased in 1965 by 1,385 (for a total of 1,620 since 1961). In the United States a new "great debate" began and continued, while U.S. forces in Viet-Nam continued to rise (375,000 at the end of 1966).

While much of the debate was emotional and peripheral to the main point, some of it went to the central questions: Should the United States, which had committed land forces on the Asian continent in Korea only under special and compelling circumstances, consider South Viet-Nam an equally compelling cause for involvement? How does a great state, once involved in such a war, become again disengaged without losing the fruits of its efforts? Was the United States wise in pursuing such an active policy of involvement on the periphery of Asia—and China? What were the effects on the over-all balance of power process, especially as Russia felt bound to compete with China as a champion of revolution?

All of these questions could be put within the confines of a larger question. How adequate was an American foreign policy which had gone from a pre-World-War-II virtually total non-involvement, all the way to the opposite extreme of important involvement all over the world? Moral and emotional abstractions continued to clothe American policy pronouncements as before, although the argument that the national interests of the United States necessitated such policies was more in vogue. What the United States had done in becoming involved, was the reverse of what it used to do. Did the more frequent invocation of national interest really reflect a careful discrimination between what was necessary, and what was not? Could the United States afford to really implement the Truman Doctrine or other such general formulas virtually single-handedly, and all over the world?

CHAPTER 23

The United States:
An Analysis

It is . . . inconceivable that the government of the United States has at any time approved of all the governments with which it held diplomatic relations. . . . I hold in review the motley procession: governments liberal and governments illiberal; governments free and governments unfree; governments honest and governments corrupt; governments pacific and governments even aggressively warlike; empires, monarchies, and oligarchies; despotisms decked out as democracies, and tyrannies masquerading as republics—all representative of the motley world in which we live and with which we must do business.

JOHN BASSETT MOORE
"Candor and Common Sense,"
The Collected Papers of John Bassett Moore

Before the globalist illusion came upon us we thought it was our business to define our vital interests and defend them. As against the gross self-delusion of globalism there is the traditional realism which holds that a sound foreign policy is based on a careful and constant study of the geography of the world. This leads to the realization that American power cannot be equally effective all over the globe. . . . Globalism is the thinking of those who have not learned the facts of life. They include . . . the idealists who have overreacted from their old isolationism and expect to enforce everywhere their own views of the moral law.

WALTER LIPPMANN
Column, January 1966

THE record of the United States, just examined, raises some far-reaching questions which deserve thorough analysis. Even casual reflection indicates (1) that United States policy is frequently justified, often pursued, and normally expressed in moral and emotional formulas and doctrines permitting only very gross discriminations; and (2) that the United States finds it especially difficult to establish any strong collective support for its policies in Asia, or to see them implemented without resort to force under circumstances where American armed forces carry a very great share of the burden.

424

A habit of presenting foreign policy goals in abstract terms is not either unique or in itself an indication that these goals are unwise. Many other nations have the same habit, especially the major Communist powers and many of the new African states. The standard against which this habit must be judged is whether it enables a state to pursue a consistent and realistic policy in terms of its own professed goals, and whether those professed goals are in accord with the objective needs of the nation. But when these goals are also expressed in highly moral terms there is the danger that they will be considered absolute and uncompromisable; when they are expressed in emotional terms there is the danger that logic and reason will be crowded out. How well do these formulas achieve proper United States goals and realize objective United States national interests? To what extent can either these procedures or problems be considered "normal" even if troublesome? And are there any real alternatives?

I The Reorientation of Postwar American Policy: Psychological Dimensions

FOR a hundred years, between 1815 and 1914, United States foreign policy continued along well-cut grooves: continental expansion, no entangling alliances, the Monroe Doctrine, equal trading opportunities for all in colonial areas, freedom of the seas, and neutral rights. The commitment to other nations was minimal; the practical relationship of most of such policies to the national interests, apparent. Then in 1917 the United States left the calm shelter which the New World had become, to intervene belatedly but effectively in World War I. Having done so, she retreated to unilateralism. Between 1921 and 1941 the United States did not revert to her pre-World-War-I policy of isolation from non–New World affairs on the previous, fairly thoroughgoing scale. American interests and power were such that aloofness was no longer practical. The United States initiated the Washington Disarmament Conference of 1921, and attended the London Naval Disarmament Conference of 1930, the World Disarmament Conference at Geneva in 1932, and the London Economic Conference in 1933. She also participated to some extent in the work of the League, sending a representative to sit with the Council during the discussions on the Manchurian question. But in all of this activity the United States refrained from firm, collective obligations to use force. By the 1930's many Americans considered the involvement in World War I an aberration that should be and could be prevented.

The Neutrality Acts of 1935, 1937, and 1939 were symbols of this belief, as was the Senator Nye investigation into the part allegedly played by munitions makers in pushing the United States into war. "Cash-and-carry," the formula of the 1939 Neutrality Act, symbolized a resolution to go on trading in wartime but of escaping involvement in the conflict itself. Any belligerent could buy in America, but he must pay cash and carry the goods away in his own shipping. How such policies aided Mussolini's aggression against Ethiopia by permitting private shipments of oil, and how they led in 1939 to an embargo of arms to Britain and France, has already been told.

Between the outbreak of World War II in 1939 and participation of the United States in 1941, a gradual evolution of American opinion took place. The fall of France before the Nazi onslaught in June 1940 had a tremendous psychological effect in America. The implications for the United States of a German-dominated Europe began to sink in. The Munich Conference of 1938, with its tragic consequences for Czechoslovakia and the balance of power, made a profound impression, especially as new disasters followed. The fear that appeasement invites new aggression became deeply ingrained in American consciousness with France's defeat and America's resultant danger. The United States reacted by rearming, extending the peacetime draft, instituting Lend-Lease, and finally by convoying shipments herself. Then came Pearl Harbor, the long struggle to defeat the Axis powers, and finally the victory of 1945. Determined now to play her part, and discharge her proper responsibilities, the United States reversed policies and began an active role in world affairs continued ever since.

It was quite natural that immediate post-World-War-II United States policy centered around the prevention of a new war by Germany and Japan. Having limited experience with great-power politics, Americans also assumed, unwarrantedly, that the Allied coalition would preserve its unity to prevent such a new war. When the Soviet Union failed by its actions to conform to such a belief, the ill-prepared United States had to adjust its thinking radically. In the usual way of allied and victorious powers who have fought and won a war, the enemy having been defeated, the victors fell into hot debate over the division of the spoils and the nature of the new *status quo* to be erected. Americans came to realize that the United States and Russia, who once had a common interest in defeating the Axis, did not have a common interest in exploiting the aftermath of that defeat. The shock of that discovery was very great. Friendly, war-inspired feelings toward the Soviets evaporated, and were replaced by an ever deeper hostility. The Cold War began. The Communist *Putsch* in Czechoslovakia in 1948 seemed to show that the Soviet Union was preparing for an aggressive war; this opinion was strengthened by Soviet unwillingness to cooperate in Germany. Taking the lesson of Munich to heart, the United States determined not to appease and turned to building a "position of strength." She took the leading part in restoring Western Europe to economic health and establishing a security system coordinating the common interests of the NATO members. Because of these efforts, by 1949 the European situation, although far from tranquil, had been stabilized. After that date the Russians gained no more in Europe. Yugoslavia's defection served to counterbalance Czechoslovakia's loss. The United States, shaken by the readjustment of thinking and feeling that these events had produced, was gaining a psychological balance and an increasing conviction that danger was being met in appropriate fashion.

The new policy of active involvement and commitment was extended to other areas and other forms of activity in these first postwar years. The United States sponsored or joined in a whole range of other alliances. She furnished the most financial aid to the United Nations. She extended economic aid. She kept the armed forces deployed at stations around the world. She was determined that there would never be another Munich—anywhere in the world. In America a conviction was felt that these policies were both desirable and successful.

Into this situation of increasing confidence a bombshell was exploded as the situation in Asia disintegrated with dramatic suddenness. China, traditional friend of the United States in the Orient, embraced communism. This great blow to the world balance of power and to the Far Eastern position of the United States gave her people a renewed feeling of danger. The very foundations of the secure world previously enjoyed by the United States seemed to be disintegrating despite her new policy of commitments.

These events in Europe and in Asia had profound effects on her domestic politics. Whereas her policy toward Europe had been bipartisan and generally supported and approved by the American people, the developments in the Far East tore a great rift in bipartisanship. Of course, in 1948, while Europe was still the center of interest, there were some people in both parties who, while approving the Truman-Acheson policy of resistance to the Soviet Union, had become concerned lest it disintegrate into opposition for the sake of opposition and become a blind refusal to negotiate on the grounds that any compromise constituted appeasement. Even so, there was substantial bipartisan agreement on the fundamental policy; this was increasingly lacking in matters relating to the Far East. Extremists in the Republican Party began to adopt the position that the Democratic Party by ineptness, fumbling, and coddling of communism at home and abroad had paved the way for the Far Eastern setback. When the United States in 1950 became involved in the Korean War and shortly found herself fighting Communist Chinese "volunteers," the emotional effect was devastating. The vehemence of the United States' attitude toward China alarmed America's Western allies; the temptation to lash out at frustrations, both at home and abroad, grew geometrically. Where unilateralism as a pattern of power had been discarded, unilateralism as an emotional attitude was revived. Even the moderate Senator Taft talked of abandoning "any idea of working with the United Nations in the East" and reserving "to ourselves a completely free hand."[1] Senator Joseph McCarthy the same month said: "If there is any attempt to blackmail us into accepting a Communist peace on grounds that otherwise Britain will withdraw, then we can 'go it alone.' This nation is powerful enough, it has the guts, it has the strength to win its battle."

When the same Senator McCarthy characterized the period 1932–1952 as "twenty years of [Democratic] treason" he was not, of course, representative

---

[1] NYT, May 27, 1953.

of responsible Republican opinion, but its very voicing by a United States senator without any drastic political punishment befalling him was a symptom of the extent to which Americans, under the impact of these events, had been shaken. At the same time "communism" became an issue in every Congressional and Presidential election. It had been so in 1948; with the developments in the Far East it became a primary issue in 1950, 1952, and 1954.

Nor was the "communism issue" confined to elections. The betrayal of the secrets of the atom bomb to Russia by the Rosenbergs (who were executed in 1953) and other native American Communists, as well as earlier discoveries of Communist infiltration into positions of trust in the United States government, led to widespread concern among the American people and to a sweeping series of investigations. Alger Hiss, president of the respected Carnegie Endowment for International Peace, was sent to jail for perjury after being convicted of having lied about his connections with and aid to communism while in a relatively important post in the Department of State. There was no reasonable doubt that United States internal and external security were in jeopardy from communism. The reaction of the American people to these facts throws light on why, both under Presidents Truman and Eisenhower, a broad and exhaustive "loyalty investigation" system was instituted for government employees.

This loyalty investigation affected the conduct of American foreign policy. Whatever its intent, and however much it rooted out disloyal government servants, it also discouraged objective reporting of conditions abroad by Foreign Service personnel. The confidential reports of career officers John Paton Davies and John Carter Vincent, who in 1944 and 1945 sent information reflecting the approaching downfall of the Chinese Nationalist regime, were later used in their administrative trials, to determine whether they should be fired. After the late 1940's Congressional investigations of Communists and fellow-travelers were also extended into the universities, the ministry, labor unions, educational foundations, the movies, textbooks, and scholarly publications—in short, into most of the major opinion-making organizations in the United States. "Radical" professors (as well as labor union men) were fired, sometimes for refusing to answer the questions of Congressional investigating committees and sometimes on other grounds. Whether or not such proceedings were justified or desirable, there is no doubt that they compounded the tendency for opinion makers to take care not to express themselves too openly on controversial questions. In other words, at the very time when Americans were deeply disturbed at the development of world events already noted, the "built-in" facilities in the United States for a free discussion and analysis of alternative courses for her to pursue were drying up both inside and outside the government. So far had this process gone in early 1954 that Senator Herman Welker even suggested in a Senate speech that Congress should investigate to see if "there is at this time a thinly disguised effort to condition the American people for a radical change" in United States policy in Asia (he meant especially on the question of recognizing Communist China.) [2] This amounts to saying that individuals or groups who advocate the replacement or discarding of a given policy by an alternative should be investigated. Such a proposal implied the deification of existing policies and a presumption of disloyalty or subversion on the part of those advocating others. The implication that such advocating was conspiratorial is obvious from the phrase, "thinly disguised effort."

The debate thus stifled, but not stilled, was no longer over the great issue of the 1930's: involvement or noninvolvement. The debate of the 1950's and 1960's was over how far and under what circumstances to be involved and to what extent that involvement should take the form of resisting changes in the *status quo* (especially where communism was involved). In the next years the debate was to focus intermittently on the issue of Castro's Cuba. But it reached its greatest dimensions in the mid-1960's over the war in Viet-Nam. Involvements and commitments by the United States throughout the world were no longer being questioned. But what involvements and which commitments?

Concurrent with this major public debate over the *substance* of American involvements and commitments, a more restricted debate continued over the *manner* in which foreign policy was being conducted—the formulas and doctrines we have noted.

2   Commitments via Formulas: Manner and Substance

ONCE a super power decides on commitments, the further problem of what substantive policy to pursue is not easy to resolve. The possession of enormous physical power is a constant temptation toward over-commitment. Some might argue that a super power cannot be overcommitted, that there are no real limits to what it can achieve. But a little reflection casts doubt on this easy answer. Even the United States, although we speak of her fighting a simultaneous war in Europe and Asia in World War II, did not really do so in a full-scale sense. The Pacific War operated on a relative shoe-string until very late. Unless mere large-scale destruction via missiles can now be considered a fully effective substitute for ground warfare, the problem is no different today.

But in an age when physical destruction is likely to be mutual in any war involving nuclear nations, even the possession of great destructive power does not bring with it success or victory in the conventional sense. Because of this implicit limitation, most goals must be sought short of resort to missiles. In international relations short of war, goals are best achieved through exploitation of common interests, by creating political or alliance blocs, by amassing and coordinating psycho-political power. A nation which pursues policies which fail, after efforts, to arouse substantial support, ought to reassess those policies. The policies may subsequently still be pursued, but the failure to

---

[2] Reported in *NYHT* (EE), January 16, 1954. See also *NYT*, January 15, 1954.

arouse support is a warning signal that the policies may be too broadly conceived and contrary to the interests of other concerned but not hostile states.

The decision of the United States to become involved and accept commitments was far more laudable than not. But in the largest perspective it was essentially a simple reversal of policy rather than a systematic formulation of what was desirable, necessary, and feasible. It was obviously a better policy than the one it replaced. But that fact was not in and of itself an assurance that it was wise or the best possible. Commitments, if they are indiscriminate, are not automatically more desirable than a lack of commitments.

There is a common feature to both manner and substance in postwar American foreign policy. Each fed on the other. A pronouncement that one will oppose all aggressions anywhere in the world, or that one opposes all Communist movements wherever they come to exist, or that one is the standard-bearer of freedom for the entire "free world," has its logical consequences in actions which tend to lack discrimination. The actions become governed by answering over-simple questions affirmatively: does this constitute aggression (fight it), does this represent communism (oppose it), does this constitute something of supposed value to freedom or the free world (support it).

Now in the literal sense any such sweeping generalization as just made must be partially false in particulars. The important thing is whether it describes correctly the general thrust of United States policy. Leaving aside the first of these formulas, opposition to aggression (since we analyzed in Chapter 21 the difficulties a nation encounters in using this principle on an absolute basis), let us first examine the difficulties logically implicit in an absolute policy to defend freedom and to oppose communism. Then we shall see how well these formulas have been received in the main areas of the world where the United States has made commitments.

Questioning support for freedom sounds like questioning virtue. Certainly, it is generally true that the United States frequently benefits from the existence of freedom in other states. Free peoples are more likely to resolve their frustrations without recourse to violence. They will probably be less hostile to the United States, all other considerations being equal. And peoples wishing to be free will probably be more friendly to an America which favors such freedom in principle for all. But it is also possible for free peoples to have interests opposed to the United States. And nations not free may have interests in common with the United States. Nor is it automatically in the interests of the United States to resort to violence in order to make a people free. It may or may not be. It depends upon the costs and results.

Indeed these observations are somewhat obvious. Yet a President of the United States in January 1966 based much of the argument for prosecuting the war in Viet-Nam fairly squarely on the simple basis that a "free" peoples' freedom was at stake. The implication of his argument was that this fact in itself involved United States interests.

Let us refine the argument further. We might suppose it justifiable to generalize that the United States ought to support a people struggling for freedom whose professed or actual interests are compatible with, or common to, those of the United States. But even this more moderate generalization will not really do. If such American support entailed sacrifices of other American interests, it might not on balance be worthwhile. Suppose it led to thermonuclear war with the Soviet Union, not ultimately but directly and immediately and obviously? Suppose one free people is engaged in war with another free people? Suppose both are actual allies of the United States? Here other limitations to the validity of the generalization are apparent. At the other end of the spectrum, it might be desirable to go to war to defend the freedom of another people even if it leads to nuclear exchange. But to be accurate, we would not really be prepared to make such sacrifices to defend another's freedom as such. What would really be involved would be the consideration that the United States could not afford to allow the existing distribution of power to be fundamentally altered or see the credibility of an important American commitment destroyed. "Freedom" used in this sense is really sort of a shorthand notation to convey other, more complex propositions in succinct fashion.

It is desirable for the United States to foster freedom everywhere in the world. It is undesirable for the United States to commit itself automatically to seeing that freedom prevails. We need to reserve the right to discriminate.

The third of our formulas, anti-communism, involves similar difficulties. It was the "rule-of-thumb" standard the United States attempted most frequently to apply once the Cold War began. Once the Soviet regime, which was Communist, was deemed "bad," that which was obviously anti-Communist (at least in phraseology or professed intent) was deemed "good." One important result of the use of this standard was that it grouped together all Communists, foreign and domestic, Russian, German, Yugoslav, or Chinese. If the United States was against communism, she was against it equally strongly in any form anywhere. Conversely, all those who were also "against communism" were "good" and deserved American support. It was considered as self-evident that whatever was "anti-Communist" was good for the United States, and the more obviously "anti-Communist," the better for the United States.

In the attempt to utilize this standard in the years after 1945, we see the fruition of the tendency to marry moral judgment to foreign policy. Since communism as a system was disliked by the American people, and since Russia, the home of communism, was the chief power rival of the United States and was deemed the actual controller of all Communist movements everywhere, the marriage seemed a congenial and appropriate one. Yet it contained great pitfalls.

One of the chief pitfalls was that, if opposition to communism was official policy (as well as morally commendable), the more virulent the opposition became, the more patriotic it was called. Since every one is against sin, the way is then paved for the demagogue—as Joseph McCarthy soon discovered. If all things and persons communistic are bad, they can be harried with impunity; and if the genuine Communist article is exhausted, things "smacking of" communism and "Communist-oriented" persons form an inexhaustible reserve for attack, especially since the terms were and are so imprecise. The conditions of emotional upset in the United States made it extremely hard to deal with this type of demagogue, and yet McCarthy's investigations increasingly demoralized various important branches of the government—including the United States Army.

The second pitfall was that it prevented or seriously impeded efforts to distinguish what was actually good for the United States to do by defining the good in the purely negative terms of opposition to all things Communist. If the Russians, for example, wanted Communist China seated in the UN, an anti-Communist policy *ipso facto* called for United States opposition to that demand. Yet more careful analysis might well have led to a belief that the American interest would be better served by agreeing. By the same reasoning, if Russia wanted a great-power conference, it became difficult for the United States to agree to attend it even if she also desired one. And if Russia wanted a conference on certain terms, it was difficult to agree to accept those terms because Russia wanted them. Thus Secretary of State Dulles, on February 24, 1954, said, speaking of the decision to hold the Far Eastern Conference at Geneva: "It was agreed that the conference will be held at Geneva, as we had long ago proposed, and that the composition will be precisely that which the United States also had proposed. . . . I recognize, of course, that the Soviet Union would not have accepted, 100 per cent, our terms for the Korean political conference unless it expected to benefit thereby. But so do we." [3]

The facts were that the United States had previously insisted on a two-bloc conference (UN coalition vs. Communist aggressors) of states participating in the Korean War. This proposal meant that Russia could attend only in the capacity of a state aiding aggression; it would be seated on the "aggressor" side of the table. This status Russia refused to accept. The conference arrangements as finally concluded were very far from being "100 per cent" United States terms, as Dulles described them. The terms accepted were, however, less "anti-Communist": Russia was seated, not as an "aggressor" but as a sponsor of a four-Power meeting, which then invited other Asian states to the conference. These reasonable arrangements seemed not too obviously "anti-Communist;" Dulles defended them by painting them both as a "100 per cent" victory for the United States and by arguing that, while the Russians hoped to "benefit thereby," the United States did too.

The third pitfall was that such a policy prevented or impeded necessary distinctions being made in United States foreign policy toward Communist states, since all were equally Communist and therefore all equally bad. Yet Poland, Yugoslavia, China, and Russia, while all Communist states, by no

[3] *NYT*, February 26, 1954.

means posed an identical foreign-policy problem for the United States. This difficulty became obvious in Yugoslavia's case when Marshal Tito broke with Moscow while retaining communism as a system. Communism in Yugoslavia was not so great a threat to United States interests as was Tito's previous alliance with Moscow. Similarly, with Poland (and Hungary), as the dramatic assertion of independence in October 1956, showed, the advent of communism in a nation does not automatically mean that anti-Communist and anti-Russian feelings are terminated. Gomulka's government was a reminder to the West that the Poles, who have a long history of revolt against Russian rule, are still Poles. Again, it was unwarranted to assume that China was merely a puppet of Moscow. Because of her vast population and geographical extent, as well as her actual and potential national power, China could hardly be considered (if she ever was) as a slave to Moscow's wishes. What Communist China has been doing in the Far East since 1950 can, after all, be explained in terms of China's historic interests much more readily than on the basis of an assumption that she has been a puppet whose strings were manipulated in Russia. Ordinary prudence should lead the United States to treat with Communist states and attempt to understand their policies, not only in terms of their Communist affiliation but also in terms of their historic interests.

The fourth pitfall is that the United States, in attempting to oppose communism, may support governments and movements abroad which, while genuinely anti-Communist in their actions, may jeopardize other United States interests by United States association with their policies. Especially with the awakening of the masses in Africa and Asia—as well as in South America—to the siren's call of nationalism, and the possibilities of a better life that industrialization and mass production have brought in their wake, the United States may wittingly or unwittingly put herself in a position of supporting feudal elements that stand no chance of long retaining power. From a toughly realistic standpoint this is not an argument against support of strongly intrenched feudal elements, where it seems desirable strategically. But if the United States continually supports weak reactionaries who are subsequently overthrown, as in China, it is obvious that the new, revolutionary government will be bitterly anti-American. This question is not one of moral principle ("free the oppressed") but a question of judgment (how stable is the government concerned). It is not betting on feudal and reactionary elements which is wrong (in terms of American interests) but betting on weak and reactionary elements who then collapse. (We shall examine this question in further detail in a later chapter.)

The fifth pitfall is that the policy encourages a view of the world that is distorted and oversimplified—and one, therefore, so far from the actual truth that it must inevitably lead to disillusionment and even perhaps into danger: that for non-Communist nations, there is nothing more important than the struggle against communism. In the dramatic prose of the abstraction-burdened Truman Doctrine:

At the present moment in world history nearly every nation must choose between alternative ways of life. . . . One way of life is based upon the will of the majority, . . . freedom of speech . . . and freedom from political oppression. The second way of life is based upon the will of a minority. . . . It relies upon terror and oppression. . . .

This assumption, applied to Asia or the Middle East, where colonialism and the memory of colonialism are hated more than communism, fails to work very well. Its irrelevance to Africa is even more obvious.

These pitfalls are implicit in a policy that is "anti-Communist" because opposition to communism is "good" while communism is "bad." The basic difficulty with the approach, and the most serious of these pitfalls, is that it is essentially *negative*. It begins with the wrong thesis by defining what the Russians want, for example, as by definition bad for the United States. This, if strictly applied, means that the United States' national interests are—always and in all particulars—the reverse of Russian national interests. This is both a dangerous and a false assumption. To the extent that it is accepted as a standard of judgment, it throws a very real psychological barrier in the way of serious negotiation with the Soviet Union; at the same time it tempts the United States to take positions which, while "anti-Communist," may also be anti-American (i.e., opposed to American interests).

When an issue is argued in terms of opposed abstract ideals or formulas instead of the underlying logic of the situation, the discussion fails to increase and deepen American popular understanding of international relations. As events inevitably change the focus of American interests, new principles must be advanced to modify or replace old ones. The oft-asserted view that "The United States has no foreign policy" is an expression of exasperated frustration, because one ideal principle in this way replaces another in an endless chain. Foreign policy debates become contests in which each side argues a particular moral principle as a permanent guide for future policy. "The United States must wholeheartedly support the UN." "The United States must make it clear that she will oppose aggression with force." "The United States must oppose the further spread of communism." All these urgings, if taken literally and applied automatically, could lead the United States under certain circumstances into grave risks offering only small returns. It would be far better to ask simply: "What is best for the United States to do in this case in view of our present circumstances and our long-range objectives?" Or, even more simply: "What can the United States do that would be good for her?"

This latter type of question, although it may appear on the surface to be selfish, need not (and for best results, cannot) be asked in a narrow frame of reference. What is good for the United States cannot in the long run be achieved by disregarding the interests of others—as Hitler found out in terms of Germany's interests. Conversely, if she attempts to be morally right or to do good in the abstract, regardless of its effects on her interests, common sense will sooner or later lead to the abandonment of the attempt.

Abstract principles make sense only to the extent that they are justifications in concrete cases for foreign-policy actions that rest four-square upon the national interests of the United States. *Their usefulness or lack of it does not depend upon the moral content of the principle, but upon its concrete relationship to the national interest in the given case.* How well have these formulas actually worked in the various areas of the world?

In Europe these three policy formulas have, at least until lately, worked relatively well, particularly because the common interests of the West European powers and the United States could be largely reconciled and advanced within the confines of such propositions. These nations were concerned about possible aggression, they saw the source of such action as primarily the Soviet Union, and they collectively were, so to speak, the "original" free world. So long as the German problem could be kept in bounds (i.e., so long as German military power was not viewed with suspicion by the rest of Western Europe, and the Germans themselves were content to remain in a NATO which protected West Germany even while tending to frustrate German reunification), and important policy differences did not arise between NATO members on extra-European affairs (i.e., the Suez venture of Great Britain and France, the military involvements of the United States in Asia), the policies were largely well suited to the problems they were supposed to resolve. The more recent tendency in Europe toward less acquiescence in American proposals indicates that these earlier formulas are no longer quite suitable. De Gaulle, as one illustration, wants to exploit the diversive trends within the Soviet "bloc." Counterbalancing national interests, long suppressed through Europe's concern for potential Soviet aggression, now reassert themselves. Of which more later.

In Latin America, Africa, and the Middle East these three formulas of United States policy have aroused a variety of response. None of the states in these areas is opposed to being considered a part of the free world as a philosophical concept if tangible benefits are involved. Most of the non-Latin area is very much indisposed, however, to accept this label if it means collective obligations with the United States. All of the nations in these areas are much opposed to aggression but their definitions of aggression are much wider and more various than that which the United States entertains. To the African states there is not much of an element of aggression in the Vietnamese War (some of them even think of the United States as the aggressor), while Rhodesia's action in declaring its independence from Britain with a constitution which keeps voting rights in minority hands, is seen as a clear case of what the term means. As to communism, throughout these areas the Soviet practice of "socialism" arouses a fair degree of support and approval, for in most of these states what wealth exists is in the hands of the few.

In Asia these three formulas of United States policy arouse even less positive responses. Asian memories of Western imperialism are as live as any in Africa and the Middle East. The fact that Asia has seen the most bloodshed since World War II, and that U.S. resort to force has been almost completely restricted to that area since World War II, encourages many in these nations to conceptualize American actions as the latest form of white imperialism. In an area so much in flux as Asia essentially is, resisting aggression often sounds synonymous with attempting to buoy up a discredited *status quo*. By temperament and conviction the peoples of these areas feel only a slight response to any positive overtones in the "free world" concept. And communism offers many of the allures in Asia that it has for other parts of the "underdeveloped" (i.e., poverty-ridden) world.

Thus the success of the American formulas in Asia is the least for any of the three areas, and the problem of revolutionary Asia has been the most intractable for United States policy. Latin America's remoteness from the major Communist nations makes it relatively difficult for Russia or China to exert significant influence there. The Middle East and Africa have on the whole certain counterbalancing interests which keep them from extra-area alignments and preserve certain ties with the West. In Western Europe, whatever the calls for a revision of NATO, there is general agreement on opposing any Soviet expansion. But in Asia, mainland China is an indigenous but Communist power possessed of a dual sense of grievance and mission, and dedicated to altering the *status quo*. Not only is China a relatively strong power but neither her opposition to the United States nor her professed goals are considered altogether hostile actions by many of the nations in the area. Moreover, the traditional balance of forces which once kept China suppressed, have been gravely altered by the substantial disappearance of British and French power from Asia, the defeat and weakening of the military ambitions of Japan, and the transformation of Russia into a champion of revolution (although one with a past history and some present tendencies toward covetness of Chinese territories). For these reasons the American policy problem has been most acute in Asia.

The conclusion that the formulas of American policy do not apply well to Asia in particular, justifies a re-thinking of the basis of United States policy. But it does not automatically prove that any alternative basis for policy would be more successful. Perhaps the United States is simply the victim of historical bad luck in the Far East. A more fruitful line of inquiry, providing a sounder basis for evaluation, is to ask next the positive question of whether the policies pursued have been in the national interest of the United States.

It will help to approach the problem in two contrasting ways. First, in the next two sections, we shall inquire whether there are any fairly obvious drawbacks in our concrete policy, especially as it affects Asia. Second, we shall inquire whether the general thrust of our policy is desirable and necessary.

3 Moral Formulas vs. National Interests: Recognition Policy

WHILE it is possible to describe circumstances in which withholding of diplomatic recognition may serve the national interests of a state, one would have to be quite conservative in doing so, for such circumstances are rare. Unless the state so discriminated against is weak and its regime dependent for survival upon recognition, the most tangible results are likely to be anger on the part of the unrecognized and an impediment to the resolution of disputes. Withholding of recognition is a weapon to be wielded with discretion, for it implies that the unrecognized regime will fall; and if this does not happen, relations become embittered. The United States has used this weapon in the past against uncongenial Caribbean states with some success. She has also used it against each of the two largest Communist powers in sequence—with no success at all.

Early in its history, the United States, itself conceived in revolution, adopted the doctrine of *de facto* recognition. In 1792 Secretary of State Jefferson made it clear that the United States would recognize any government which in actual fact represented "the will of the Nation substantially declared." In 1823 President Monroe spelled this out in even simpler terms, declaring that the United States would "consider the government *de facto* as the legitimate government for us." This remained her policy on recognition until the eve of World War I (except for a short period during the Civil War, when the logic of such a policy would have aided the Confederacy to gain recognition). It was only in 1913 that the first important reversal of this policy occurred. In that year President Wilson, angered by the events then taking place in Mexico, declared: "So long as the power of recognition rests with me, the government of the United States will refuse to extend the hand of welcome to anyone who obtains power in a sister republic by treachery and violence." [4] Because, in revolutions, a government rarely obtains power without the use of treachery and violence, Wilson's statement was tantamount to refusing recognition to the results of revolutions in the Americas. Here was an attempt to govern United States policy on recognition by the standards of moral principle, although as yet the policy had not been extended beyond Latin America.

After World War I the United States did not revert completely to the Jeffersonian *de facto* doctrine. The Soviet Union, incontestably in control of Russian territories, went unrecognized until 1933; and in 1932 Secretary of State Stimson refused to recognize Japan's conquest of Manchuria.

These straws in the wind indicated what was becoming deliberate policy; non-recognition of nations whose government the people of the United States disapproved on moral grounds. In this period moral judgments became more and more the actual basis for United States policy. In the two examples cited, what harm was done to American interests was minimal. Non-recognition of the Soviet Union before 1933 and the lack of first-hand information about Russia caused no insuperable embarrassments or difficulties since neither the United States nor Russia was playing important roles in international relations, at least in terms of each other. After 1933 non-recognition would have

---

[4] Quoted in Philip C. Jessup, "The Two Chinas and U.S. Recognition," *The Reporter*, July 6, 1954, pp. 21–24.

been far more serious. The United States then would have had to deal with the increasing crisis caused by Hitler without any direct facilities for judging the reactions or power of the Soviet Union. Similarly, United States refusal to recognize Japan's rule over Manchuria did no great harm since she continued to maintain diplomatic relations with Japan proper. If diplomatic relations had been broken off with Japan instead, the situation would have become far more serious. Prior to World War II the application of moral judgments, under the stress of emotion, to concrete matters of recognition policy produced no serious difficulties.

It was not until the Communist Chinese regime came into control of mainland China in 1949 that such a policy began to be pursued more or less independently of assessments of United States interests. The beginning was on sufficiently sound grounds. Although the United States–supported Chinese Nationalist government had been driven off the mainland and had taken refuge on Formosa, it still controlled an important military force; at first the possibility could not be excluded that the Communists would be unable to retain power. If Chiang were to land on the coast, he might conceivably stage a comeback, much like Napoleon's return from Elba, gathering defecting Communist soldiers into his ranks as he advanced. But as evidence began to accumulate of the lack of popular support in China for Chiang, his return became more and more unlikely. By 1953 it was apparent that the Chinese Nationalists had no foreseeable chance of regaining power.

The United States had three major options: (1) recognize Communist China as the legitimate government of all of China, including Formosa; (2) recognize two Chinese governments as each controlling *de facto* portions of Chinese territory; (3) recognize Formosa as the sole government of China. Option 1 implied subsequent neutrality in the Chinese civil war and the abandonment of Chiang. The latter point made it unacceptable to the United States. Option 2 meant accepting the actual facts. While uncongenial to either Chinese regime, neither could argue it was not real. It did not logically imply that the United States would either necessarily endorse a further change in that *status quo* or prevent such change. Option 3 implied that the United States was determined to see Chiang's government as the sole government of China. As such it was completely unacceptable to Communist China. It is possible that Communist China would have refused to agree with the United States to Option 2. (In later years she felt strong enough to demand that third states agree to Option 1.) The possibility was not explored since the United States decided on Option 3. In the bitterness of the aftermath of the Korean War this was not surprising, but even years after, the situation continued as before. Later we shall explore the larger implications of this situation. Here we are concerned not with the outlines of any conceivable settlement but with recognition policy per se.

Assuming for the moment that Option 2 was or is actually an available choice, did the United States stand to gain more or lose more by refusing to recognize the Chinese Communist regime as the government of mainland

China? Very much the same kind of issue, although it did not involve recognition as such, was presented by the claims of Communist China to a seat in the UN.

What were the essentials of the problem? First, many Americans did not believe the almost universally accepted view and doctrine in international law, as Secretary of State Dulles expressed it in 1954, "that recognition does not imply moral approval." Any recognition action taken under circumstances of public disapproval (for the President has the sole discretion to extend recognition) could injure national unity. The public unreadiness to act was an important consideration. The morale of Chiang's government might also be so seriously undermined that it would collapse.

Other nations' responses to United States policy also had to be considered. Those holding to Jefferson's principle of de facto recognition would not see in her recognition of the Chinese Communist government a loss of prestige, if United States action appeared not to be a capitulation. Allies like Britain would feel a sense of relief in the abandonment of the negative United States policy of non-recognition, which was itself a contributing factor to Far Eastern tension. If the Chiang government could not survive without hopes for recovering the mainland, it was obviously too weak to be able to survive long in any case. Or, to argue the point differently, if Chiang's hopes rested on the possibility of United States armed aid, recognition by the United States of the mainland government would not in itself destroy that possibility.

Second, without recognition the United States could not assess at first hand Communist Chinese friction with Soviet Russia, nor could she assess the essential basis on which Chinese policy was being implemented. Yet these were matters whose importance for the United States can hardly be overstated. With diplomatic representatives in China the United States could use her own eyes. Instead of having to rely entirely on data gathered covertly through the Central Intelligence Agency, on material made public through the Chinese press and radio services, and through information acquired (and perhaps thereby distorted) second-hand from those who do maintain relations with China, the United States could make judgments first-hand and on a basis of more complete data. Coincidentally, of course, Chinese Communist diplomats would be received in the United States. The presence of one more Communist delegation would not alter the situation significantly. Considering the abundant display of military and security data in the United States press (open to China in any event through public clipping services) and the already existing Communist delegations in the United States, the disadvantage would be slight.

Considering the rational or non-emotional arguments from the viewpoint of national interest, the advantages of recognizing Communist China as the government of mainland China, while continuing to recognize National China as the de facto government of Formosa, would appear distinctly to outweigh the disadvantages. But because the United States had made such an issue of recognition and relations had been so bitter, the choosing of an appropriate occasion was itself a very important aspect of the problem. In this connection the argument that the United States could not recognize China until her attitude was different was useful as an inducement to get her to make concessions (especially if in this manner American prisoners still in China could be freed). As a proposition in itself it made little sense: until relations were resumed the mutual attitudes of the two states were very unlikely to alter. That would come, if it came at all, as a result of prolonged negotiations (i.e., after recognition).

The lack of public support for this course of action was a measure of the extent to which moral and emotional judgments had been allowed to outweigh her national interests and lead the United States down a path involving ever more unpleasant complications.

4 Moral Formulas vs. National Interests: Negotiation Policy vis-à-vis Uncongenial Governments

DIRECT negotiations between two governments, one of whom refuses to recognize the other, are not normally carried on. Direct negotiation implies recognition. Indeed, one main function of recognition is to permit negotiation to be handled on a stable and established basis. Where recognition is not extended, as with Communist China, negotiation is eventually carried on anyway if the need becomes great enough. But in such direct negotiations, because they are on so uncertain and peculiar a basis, it is very difficult to achieve satisfactory results.

Necessity forced the United States and Communist China to deal with each other in direct truce negotiations (with the fictional Chinese "People's Volunteer" army commanders at Korea's Panmunjom) and through the medium of third parties (as at the Geneva Far Eastern Conference in 1954). These kinds of negotiations tend to suffer either from the severely limited scope of the discussions, which leave a great number of vital points unresolved and undiscussed (Panmunjom), or from their indirectness, which inescapably promotes a formal and unnecessarily laborious type of negotiation (the Geneva Conference). These difficulties explain why direct, government-to-government negotiations were entered into at Geneva in 1955 and continued in following years in Warsaw between the American and Chinese Communist ambassadors. But, again, the scope of these "preliminary" discussions was necessarily limited.

Since negotiations between states with opposing national interests never run a very smooth or easy course, the unavoidable difficulties involved are unnecessarily compounded without normal diplomatic relations. It is even worse when two such states do not share the common forum of the UN.

This most difficult of diplomatic situations typified United States relations with Communist China after 1950. When Sir Winston Churchill, in an effort to prevent an Anglo-American rift over the issue, declared in July 1954 that Britain believed that "this is not the moment" to seat Communist China in the UN, Senator Wiley, chairman of the Senate Foreign Relations Committee, said, "I just can't foresee the moment" when it would ever be proper to seat the Communist Chinese. Senator Ferguson, chairman of the Senate Republican policy committee, said he was "sorry Sir Winston used the word 'moment,' because a moment isn't a very long time. I would rather he had just said he would not favor seating them." Senator William F. Knowland, Senate Republican leader, declared his intention of resigning his party leadership to wage a fight to take the United States out of the UN should Red China be seated. Secretary of State Dulles on July 8, 1954, at his news conference declared, "The record of the Chinese Communist regime is such that it is, in my opinion, clearly not qualified to be seated in the United Nations." [5] Walter H. Judd, in the House, said he would "rather suspend the UN than make it a league of gangsters, murderers, thugs, kidnapers, and completely lawless people," while Representative Kit Clardy urged withdrawal from the UN if Communist China were seated. He said: "I think the time has arrived for the representatives of the people to make it perfectly plain that this nation will not permit the butchers of our boys to sit at our table on an equality with ourselves and the rest of the world." To cite a final example of Congressional opinion, Representative Craig Hosmer supported withdrawal if Communist China were seated, unless the United States considered the UN "a common brawling ground, something like the arenas of ancient Rome, where contestants, no matter how crude, indecent or immoral, can stage their spectacles for all to see." [6] These statements were made by Republicans but at the conclusion of the debate, the House of Representatives adopted unanimously a resolution to the effect that Communist China should not be admitted to the UN.

This attitude was not restricted to the question of associating with Communist China in the UN. When Secretary of State Dulles announced at the end of the Berlin Conference in February 1954 that the United States was joining in sponsoring a great-power conference on the Far East in April 1954 at Geneva, to which Commnist China would come (although not as a sponsor), he ran into a flurry of opposition in the Senate over agreeing to this type of indirect negotiation and association with Red China. Early in the conference at Geneva, Dulles himself left, and he later recalled Under Secretary of State Bedell Smith in order to "dissociate" the United States from an Indo-Chinese partition plan. Only after the urgent plea of the French, that withdrawal left France without support, did Smith return for the final days of the conference.

Of course, these events took place in the immediate shadow of the Korean War. It was not reasonable to suppose that Americans in 1954 would feel very

---

[5] All preceding quotations in this paragraph are from *NYHT* (EE), July 13, 1954. See also *NYT*, July 9, 13, 1954.

[6] All preceding quotations in this paragraph since the last footnote are from *NYHT* (EE) and *NYT*, July 10, 1954.

friendly toward Communist China, or hold the moral quality of her actions in high regard, considering that so many American lives had been sacrificed to oppose her. But more than a decade later the feelings were very much the same. Many Americans, looking at the impending seating of Communist China in the UN, considered the action as virtually indecent, a reward for bad behavior. In October 1966, 334 members of the Congress opposed China's seating in an ad in *The New York Times*.

This general attitude raises two questions that bear on negotiation policy. One is whether the United States should negotiate with Communist (i.e., non-friendly) states. The second is whether the United States should refuse to admit or seat "immoral" states in the UN and thus automatically prevent negotiating with them there. While these two questions can be formulated and discussed separately, in practical terms they are intertwined and in logic they have the same parents.

Looking at the issues raised in the broadest of perspectives, although it is somewhat of an oversimplification, it is still basically true that the alternative to war among great powers is negotiation. It is theoretically conceivable that two great powers could remain at peace with each other and have nothing whatever to do with one another diplomatically. But this non-intercourse implies either the existence of no pressing conflicts of interests between them or a mutual willingness to refrain from any actions that would disturb their bilateral *status quo*.

It is almost impossible to conceive of two great powers, especially if they play active roles, who have no mutual interests to adjust. On the most elementary level, the very existence of each is itself an interest to which the other must adjust. Great powers, especially if their relations are quasi-hostile, must negotiate with each other or run the grave risk of sooner or later going to war with each other over their unresolved conflicts of interests.

If the United States finds it necessary to negotiate with Communist China as an alternative to war, was it in the interests of the United States to restrict negotiations to non-UN facilities and oppose the seating of Communist China in the UN?

What did the United States fear (aside from the assumed compromise of principle involved in the presumed rewarding of the evil-doer)? Could the United States really believe that the addition of the one Chinese Communist vote in the General Assembly, cast with the Communist bloc against the United States, was in itself an important consideration? How many neutral nations already do this when and as they please! Could America have feared the Chinese Communist veto in the Security Council? She after all had one herself, even if she has not needed so far to use it.

Because the Soviet Union led the fight for Communist China's seating it was easy to assume that the United States ought to continue to oppose it. But from the standpoint of United States national interests, the arguments in favor of seating Communist China in the UN and of negotiating with her as necessary would seem to outweigh those against. It is difficult to see how it would injure the United States in any important way (unless she considers herself unable to safeguard her own interests in the negotiating process). Without such action there is less chance to drive a lasting wedge into the Communist Chinese–Soviet alliance—and that is, or should be, an important strategic goal of United States Far Eastern foreign policy.

5 The United States and China: Two Decades of Friction; the Viet-Nam War

WE must now face the complex question of the extent to which American actions were automatically determined by developments as they occurred, compared against the degree to which the U.S. policy made the developments what they were. Are the disadvantages to the United States of its present situation in Asia or elsewhere the result of the policy followed, or do they persist *despite* that policy?

It has already been shown that the moral, emotional abstract formulas have often been of indifferent if not actively negative value. It has already been indicated that the U.S. policy toward recognizing and negotiating with essentially unfriendly states presents handicaps to an effective policy. But what of the core of the problem? Is Communist China the albatross predestined to be hung around the neck of the United States in Asia? One albatross, one neck, and that is that?

Suppose we inquire first who earlier determined Far Eastern destinies? Before twenty years or so ago, it was not really the United States. Later we shall see how completely ineffective the Open Door formula was, if we construe it (falsely) as a successful attempt to prevent the carving-up of China. U.S. trading interests in the Pacific, which led among other things to Commodore Perry's visit to Japan and to the "opening" of Japan, should not be classified as a political commitment of national power except in a highly limited sense. Great Britain, France, the Netherlands all played much more important roles. China survived with certain territorial losses essentially because she was too large for any one imperialist power to digest, at least without the consent of the others. China continued to exist, more particularly, because Japan and Russia were both willing to fight each other over her. Japan contained Russia, Russia contained Japan. Has this point, applied now to China's expansive tendencies, contemporary relevance or is it simply somewhat dusty history? Is the United States the sole major power in the Pacific which has an interest in keeping the Chinese within bounds? If there are other nations with such interests, what prevents them from playing more than minor roles?

A second useful inquiry is by what standards should the United States decide upon a defense perimeter in the area near China? Should the United States policy of containment, first developed for the Soviet Union in Europe, now be applied to Communist China in Asia? Important differences exist between the postwar circumstances of these two Communist powers. The Soviet Union, in the first quarter-century of its existence, controlled an area far smaller than Tsarist Russia (see Chapter 24). But after 1945 it controlled more, much more if unannexed but occupied areas are included. It had more than its "proper" share, so that its possession of part of Germany was itself a severe drain on hopes for stability and security in Europe.

What of China? The Chinese were a nominal victor nation in World War II and mainland China did benefit from the withdrawal of Japanese occupation forces and the return to China of effective control over Manchuria. But these were, so to speak, negative gains. They ended interference with "present" Chinese territories rather than restored the "rightful" China which had existed when Columbus voyaged to the New World. The disputed Chinese frontier with India is known as the "MacMahon Line," an indication in itself that the Chinese accepted it under duress. The frontier with Russia is in dispute for similar reasons. All around the periphery of China the inroads of her neighbor powers have left their mark and today's newly strong China looks forward to restoring a former greatness which includes predominance or control of the historic approaches: Mongolia, Korea, Indo-China. Containing the strong China of today within the sphere of influence of the weak and dismantled China of yesterday would be roughly equivalent in emotional stress and impact to preventing Tsarist Russia's losses at the end of World War I from being recovered by the Soviet Union at the end of World War II. A further, not unfair, comparison would be with preventing the United States from expanding to continental dimensions in the nineteenth century. Preventing such changes is not innately impossible but it is extremely difficult and involves balking what is very usual if not almost instinctive behavior by large continental powers. Nineteenth century "beachheads" near or along China's rimlands were facilitated by China's weakness and internal decay, and the lack of modern interior communications in China versus the accessibility of the coast areas to European sea power. These conditions no longer obtain. Moreover, the holding of such "beachheads" necessarily involves large troop commitments by the United States far from its own territory. Preventing Chinese expansion into the Pacific proper is a far different military problem involving essentially sea and air power.

Consider the sequence by which American obligations were extended near the Chinese mainland. She moved from a very brief neutrality in the Chinese civil war to a determination to preserve Chiang on Formosa. Next she moved into South Korea to honor her pledge to the United Nations and to prevent conquest by North Korea. Then she became involved in South Viet-Nam where the infiltration of North Vietnamese troops was an element in what can only be called civil war. Each of these moves, together with the refusal to recognize Communist China and seat her in the UN, increased tensions with China and retarded or inhibited the Sino-Soviet dispute. Most of these moves found little active support from other great powers. Although the military commitments thus assumed were quite various, they were alike justified in the name of defending freedom.

It is certainly always possible to find somewhere a people who are being forcibly subjected by another. Should the United States, especially if the subjectors are Communists, automatically intervene? An American policy dedicated to the proposition that conquest anywhere is unacceptable is or would be an extremely broad policy, one never previously implemented on a world scale by any single power. Normally, peoples retain their freedom by finding equally threatened peoples as allies. Normally, these allies tend to be geographically adjacent to the threatening power, although sometimes great power assistance is forthcoming from relatively remote areas. What is curious about the Far East today is that the United States is the sole major power offering meaningful assistance to virtually any governments or peoples threatened with intervention and subversion. Is there no other powerful nation in the Far East with an interest in inhibiting Chinese expansion? Why is Japan, for example, now so indifferent to Southeast Asia? Is not Indonesia in any realistic view more threatened by China than by the United States? Why is Indonesia apparently indifferent to Chinese aggression? Can hatred of "Western colonialism" be a more powerful and permanent factor in Indonesian foreign policy than the not unobvious threat China can constitute? Is India only capable of anger in a clash with China or Pakistan on her own frontiers? There is a curious passivity here. Can the United States, by herself and alone, save these nations from China even if the rest do not seem to comprehend a serious danger? And what of the Soviet Union? To satisfy Chinese interests means ultimately important alterations of the Soviet frontier. Why does not the Soviet Union assist the United States against China?

Too-simple but suggestive propositions are that the United States may be acting so quickly in accepting the burdens that others can gladly sit it out. Or she may be putting her finger in dikes too far away from others' croplands. She was not responding to requests from major Asian nations for assistance but was instead preventing important potential threats to their interests from materializing in any near or massive sense. Convinced that the fall of a first "dominoe" will set off a chain reaction, she prevented a first "dominoe" from falling. Thus she insulated these nations from any real fear of what the fall of the last dominoes might mean to them. Do they privately find U.S. actions useful but publicly not move to assist?

If Chinese expansionist policy constitutes a threat to the United States, it must in principle also constitute a threat to other major but much closer nations. What cannot be true is that the United States is somehow threatened but no other major power in the area is similarly threatened. If they are not equally bearing the burden of containing China, it must be because their power is inadequate, their estimate of the situation is false, the American estimate is false, or they are basing their policy (designed to achieve an equivalent end) on other tactics.

Whatever the cause, after twenty years of active but fairly unilateral involvement in Asian affairs, the United States finds herself with a variety of commitments but relatively minor support. The commitments, whether originally wise or unwise, are real. They cannot be simply ignored or wiped out. Should she go on to acquire new commitments simply as the logical extension of what has already been done? Should she cling to old commitments after the original reasons for them disappear? Once the generation of Chiang and the mainland exiles on Formosa pass from the scene should the United States, which pledged at Cairo that Formosa should be restored to China, insist on Formosa's *permanent* independence, on the grounds that the Formosans are a free people? Should the United States continue to refuse recognition and oppose a UN seat for China? Does the United States want to restrain China at every opportunity, thus ensuring that China see in the United States her principal opponent? The price to the United States may include no really meaningful Sino-Soviet split. Does she desire to pay that price? Is there no other honorable way?

The war in Viet-Nam raises every one of these issues in acute form. How one conceptualizes that war and how one thinks these issues apply, has important bearing on how one regards American policy there.

Least satisfactory from a national interest standpoint is the proposition that the U.S. is defending freedom. It is not least satisfactory because it is or is not a true description of the facts in Viet-Nam. It is least satisfactory because it raises the freedom of any people anywhere to an equal plane as an American objective regardless of the costs in American blood. No people can realistically regard the freedom of another people as worth sacrifice unless they believe that their own freedom is also at stake. But to relate in this way the grand and absolute proposition of defending freedom to the interests of the people called upon to make a policy choice, shrinks it to proportions we can more realistically appraise. Would it follow that American freedom would be threatened by the fall of South Viet-Nam?

It cannot be seriously meant that South Viet-Nam's conquest by North Viet-Nam subversion would lead to an aggression by the then united Viet-Nam against other allies of the United States. Nor can it seriously be meant that the hand of fate in some mysterious way will punish the United States by depriving it of freedom as a punishment for moral dereliction. What must be meant is that Communist China will be less restrained in her expansionist activities, or that American allies would "lose faith" in the United States willingness to carry out its commitments if the United States took a "dishonorable" way out of the Viet-Nam dilemma. These are two serious propositions, deserving serious analysis.

The second of the two is easier to dispose of. At some point prior to 1965 the United States might conceivably still have chosen (before its prestige had become massively involved) to abandon opposition to Chinese domination of the area and evacuate. Certainly by 1965 it could not simply walk out.

The first of the two propositions is more involved. Should we think of the

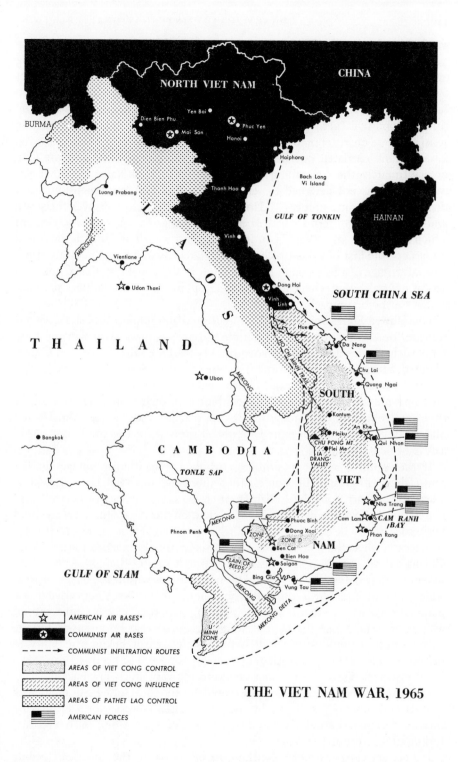

THE VIET NAM WAR, 1965

Map legend:

☆ AMERICAN AIR BASES*
⊛ COMMUNIST AIR BASES
- - - → COMMUNIST INFILTRATION ROUTES
▧ AREAS OF VIET CONG CONTROL
▨ AREAS OF VIET CONG INFLUENCE
⠿ AREAS OF PATHET LAO CONTROL
🏴 AMERICAN FORCES

war in Viet-Nam as locally initiated and controlled by the North Vietnamese with Chinese backing? Or is it the consequence of a Chinese puppet carrying out Chinese orders? If the war continues over a long time, and especially if it escalates, it will make little difference which is true. If Ho Chi Minh is attempting to unify Viet-Nam but keep it out of China's hands, then the continued bloodshed there will eventually weaken North Vietnamese ability to resist Chinese encroachment. If Ho is considered to be acting in effect for the Chinese, any escalated warfare will make Ho more dependent and the Chinese ultimately the controlling element in North Viet-Nam. Whether the war was or was not designed to serve the cause of Chinese expansionism, it does serve that cause unless (1) Ho is fairly quickly victorious over the south and wins victory on terms which keep China out or (2) there is a settlement which neutralizes all of Viet-Nam in an effective way. The United States will not accept the first of these two but has declared its support of neutralization. The advantage of this second alternative lies in the possibility that China will accept neutralization where she will not accept an American military presence on her southern approach.

The United States endorsement of neutralization implies that she does *not* want a "beachhead" on China's periphery but is content with denying militarily such an area as Viet-Nam equally to both the United States and China. (United States endorsement of "freedom" for the South Vietnamese does not discriminate: it could mean either neutralization *or* a beachhead.) The questions are whether China will be content with such partial achievement of its overall objective of dominating its approaches and whether the United States can contrive to gain more widespread support for this more limited objective of neutralization.

If the Chinese accept a limitation of their expansionist policies in the south, they will presumably (unless they alter fundamentals) press elsewhere. The choice, apart from the Indian frontier, is essentially east or north. Were it not for the Nationalist regime's existence on Formosa, the answer could fairly confidently be expected to be north—on Mongolia in particular. It is for this reason that the opportunity to unfreeze the Formosa situation after Chiang's death should not be dismissed without careful thought. While Formosa is readily defensible by sea and air-power and is within the off-shore areas which can without great difficulties be included in the American defense perimeter, its separate existence is a standing irritation, which China cannot well ignore. Since even the United States recognizes that Formosa is Chinese, its retention in non-Peking hands is the visible sign of Peking's inability to deliver on one of the most basic requirements for a self-respecting state: territorial integrity. Thus prestige considerations are very much involved.

Perhaps the most promising path would be for the United States to seek multilateral support (especially by the larger Asian powers) for a face-saving interim formula. Formosa could become a UN trusteeship, with eventual jurisdiction reverting to China.

If only stand-pat formulas continue to be followed, the American people may pay two great prices. First, they will probably continue to alienate much of Asia. What has really been most responsible for distorting the "natural" state of affairs in Far Eastern politics is that American support for Chiang has seemed to many Asians essentially unwise (and even in effect an aggressive act). Much of Asia interprets American policy as bent on a rather futile and negative task of denying the Chinese whatever they wish, irrespective of its merits. The second price is that the United States may succeed in diverting China from its grievances with Russia and monopolize the center of China's antagonisms. The Soviet Union has potentially the greatest interest of any nation on earth in containing Communist China, but so far she has been spared much effort to do so. Not that hostilities between Communist China and the Soviet Union would be to the advantage of the United States. But a degree of friction leading to mutual preoccupation of the Communist giants could hardly be undesirable.

If the foregoing analysis has validity it means that the United States program to restrain Chinese ambitions suffers, ironically, in great part because America has been so thoroughly and completely hostile to Communist Chinese interests. China has been opposed on every point and on every front, without discrimination. This relationship is, of course, reciprocal, and the Chinese have themselves played a major role in worsening relations with the United States. So Sino-American antagonisms have virtually preempted the center stage of Far Eastern politics, thus reducing the incentives for other nations to consider commitments to preserve their own interest. And since part of what China wants is generally considered legitimate by the rest (a seat in the UN, diplomatic relations as an equal, a chance to finish the Chinese civil war), the United States in addition loses support which ought otherwise in principle to be forthcoming. Most importantly, the United States foregoes the opportunity to have the Soviet Union serve American interests, whether the Russians want to or not, by keeping Chinese antagonisms unduly centered on the United States. Such tactics by the United States imply that she (1) rejects the view expressed in the first chapter of this book that the national interests of two states are never completely common or opposed, and (2) rejects the proposition most central to the manipulation of a balance of power system—namely, that all states in principle have counterbalancing interests which are suppressed under certain circumstances. The reciprocal of the U.S. suppression of a counterbalancing interest in Sino-Soviet tension (in order to follow a more negative policy toward China) is found in China's suppression of her counterbalancing interest in righting old wrongs done to her by Russia (in order to concentrate on a negative policy toward the United States).

It makes for a simple relationship, to be sure. But is it in the national interests of the United States?

6 A Needed Reform

IN this chapter we have been concerned only secondarily with the question of what concrete policies the United States has pursued, might pursue, or ought to pursue. Even where policy alternatives have been described, the primary purpose has been to contrast two methods of approach to the implementation of the basic American decision to accept involvement and commitment. The use of the national interest approach in lieu of formulas can still lead to reasonable and legitimate differences over concrete policy. The point is that it is far more suitable as a method or approach than the formulas we have discussed at such length.

The reform which is needed in American foreign policy formulation is not the abandonment of generalizations or abstractions as such. Certain interests can by their very nature not be expressed easily in any other way. But we must take care to see that such generalizations do indeed contain a content of national interests. Generalizations which have moral or emotional appeal are not automatically generalizations about the American national interest. Generalizations calling for absolute and automatic commitments should be accepted at face value least of all—and particularly where they take the form of moral formulas.

In later chapters as we examine Soviet foreign policy and the problems around which the policies of the nations in the major areas of the world find their contemporary focus, we shall continually be asking an additional question. What did and do these problems require from the viewpoint of American national interest?

CHAPTER 24

The Soviet Union: The Record

This is a hard climate, and an American finds many things to try his patience, and but few that are capable of winning his affections. One of the most disagreeable features that he has to encounter, is the secrecy with which everything is done. He can rarely obtain accurate information, until events have transpired, and he may rely upon it, that his own movements are closely observed by eyes that he never sees. The Russian mind seems naturally distrustful, and this is especially so with the government officials. . . .

Nothing is made public that is worth knowing. You will find no two individuals agreeing in the strength of the Army and Navy, in the amount of the public debt, or the annual revenue. In my opinion it is not intended that these things should be known.

NEIL S. BROWN [1]
United States Minister to Russia, 1853

I F the West is to understand the Soviet Union (and its policy), it must keep ever in mind that the basic Russian phenomena of the last several decades antedate communism. The police state under Stalin, the overbearing and multitudinous bureaucracy, and the slave labor camps had their equivalents under the tsars. Nor are Soviet attempts to extend boundaries or spheres of influence outward a new thing. Vladivostok, at the extreme eastern fringe of the Soviet Union and its window on the Pacific, was founded as a military outpost in 1860. At one time Russia not only held Alaska (subsequently sold to the United States) but had stations on the west coast of America north of San Francisco. Neither is the appearance of Russian troops in Berlin a novelty: they were even in Paris at the end of the Napoleonic Wars (although, it must be added, they did not stay).

Maps frequently appeared in the United States after World War II to show the great areas and population that have passed under Soviet direct rule as annexations since 1939. These maps are correct enough in their detail but fail to convey (what is equally important) that the 1939 boundaries of Russia

---

[1] Brown wrote this to Secretary of State Daniel Webster. See *The Christian Science Monitor*, May 27, 1952.

NOTE – BOUNDARIES ARE THOSE
OF 1914

ARCTIC OCEAN

NORWAY

FINLAND

SWEDEN

Archangel

DVINA

LAKE
LADOGA

St.
Petersburg

RUSSIAN

RUSSIAN
TERRITORIAL LOSSES
RESULTING FROM
WORLD WAR I

ESTONIA

VOLGA

DENMARK

BALTIC SEA

LATVIA

LITHUANIA

Moscow

EMPIRE

EAST
PRUSSIA

*WHITE
RUSSIA*

DON

GERMANY

POLAND

VISTULA

Kiev

DNIEPER

U K R A I N E

AUSTRIA-
HUNGARY

BESSARABIA

TRANS-
CAUCASUS

RUMANIA

DANUBE

BLACK SEA

ITALY

SERBIA

BULGARIA

KARS-
ARDAHAN

MONTE-
NEGRO

(OTT.)

ALBANIA

OTTOMAN
EMPIRE

GREECE

RUSSIA IN EUROPE, TERRITORIAL LOSSES IN WORLD WAR I

TRM

500 MILES

NOTE – BOUNDARIES ARE THOSE OF 1956

ARCTIC OCEAN

NORWAY

FINLAND

SWEDEN

Archangel

DVINA

LAKE
LADOGA

Leningrad

SOVIET

| RUSSIAN TERRITORIAL GAINS RESULTING FROM WORLD WAR II |
| GERMAN TERRITORY UNDER U.S.S.R. ADMIN. |
| GERMAN TERRITORY UNDER POLISH ADMIN. |

ESTONIA

VOLGA

Moscow

DENMARK

LATVIA

UNION

LITHUANIA

BYELO-
RUSSIA

(WEST)

EAST
PRUSSIA

DON

GERMANY

POMERANIA

FROM
POLAND

(EAST)

POLAND

SILESIA

Kiev

DNIEPER

VISTULA

U K R A I N E

CZECHOSLOVAKIA

AUSTRIA

HUNGARY

RUMANIA

TRANS-
CAUCASUS

YUGO-
SLAVIA

BLACK SEA

KARS-
ARDAHAN

ITALY

BULGARIA

(TURK.)

ALBANIA

TURKEY

GREECE

SYRIA

LEBANON

TRM

RUSSIA IN EUROPE, TERRITORIAL GAINS IN WORLD WAR II

453

represented those of a power who had lost wars in both Asia and Europe and who had consequently been stripped of many of its traditional possessions. Even today Finland, which for so long was a part of Russia, remains separate. On a net basis, comparing the Russian *frontiers* of 1900 with those after 1945, the area today directly ruled from Moscow as an integral part of Russia is substantially *smaller*.

Again, the Soviet occupation of satellites, the presence of its military units in the Balkans, and its attempts to bind these areas closely to Russia, directly and indirectly, have their parallels in tsarist times. Russian forces in these areas were as unloved then as they are now. The attitude portrayed by the joke current in Prague at the end of World War II was then, as it is now, typical of the popular reaction: the newsreel commentator asks dramatically, "What is Generalissimo Stalin saying to our President?" To this the Czech audience shouts: *"Davai casy!"* (Give me your watch!) The difference in this region today is that Russian ambitions toward permanent control of the area are more difficult to frustrate in the absence of an Austro-Hungarian Empire or of German power in the area. This important difference between yesterday and today was implicit in the disintegration of Austria-Hungary and the revival of Russian power from its low ebb in the first two decades of the present century, coupled with German postwar weakness. Yet, even so, the growth of Titoism and nationalism continues in this area, forcing some Russian concessions.

What is new, and what rightfully causes great concern in the West and in America especially, is the Soviet position in Germany and (until 1955) Austria, and, to a lesser extent, Czechoslovakia. The prolonged occupation of non-Slavic lands in the heart of Europe is new in Russian modern history. Further, the existence of large Communist parties constituting a potential fifth column behind the Western defense perimeter, are a cause of concern. Lastly, there is the extension of communism to non-Russian areas in Asia with its threat of yet greater extension, although these effects are being counterbalanced by increased fragmentation ("polycentrism") within the Communist sphere.

In this chapter we shall be concerned primarily with the record of how this came about. In the next we shall deal primarily with the meaning and implications of these developments.

I Shaped in the Crucible of Fire (1917–1933)

THE absolutism of Russia's pre-Soviet rulers found its initial justification in the successful wars to expel the Mongols; its ultimate disintegration came about as a consequence of defeat in the Far East at the hands of Japan, followed in little more than a decade by disaster in Europe and defeat by Germany.

The importance of Mongol domination and Russia's delayed unification cannot be overlooked. For almost two hundred fifty years, between 1240 and 1480, Russia lay prostrate under Asian rule. Even as late as the reign of Charles V of Austria (1519–1556), when such states as England, France, Spain, and Portugal had already reached essentially their present territorial form, great parts of European Russia were still in the hands of the Khanates of Kazan and Astrakhan (remnants of the Mongol Empire of the Golden Horde). The Crimea and a large area of the Ukraine were part of the Khanate of the Crimea (a part of the Ottoman Empire), and Russia up to Smolensk in the north, and up to Kiev and beyond in the Ukraine, was part of Poland-Lithuania. In 1684, although the Mongols had been driven out, Poland had increased her holdings in Russia as far eastward as the 35th Meridian. As a comparison, Russia in 1914 held Poland as far *west* as the 18th Meridian. Not until the First Partition of Poland (1772) did Russia acquire the areas in the West included within her post-World-War-I boundary. This delay meant that Russia was cut off from Western culture for centuries; that the great developments in Western thought, such as the Renassiance and Reformation, left her largely untouched; and that absolutist rule survived unchecked by popular movements. Tsar Peter the Great, in the early eighteenth century, introduced drastic Western-style reforms in Russia in an attempt to catch up. Yet in 1848 Russia was still behind; in that year, although revolutions swept Europe and endangered Hapsburg rule in Hungary, Russia remained quiet. The Tsar was able to dispatch Russian troops to Hungary to aid the Austrian Emperor. While the revolts in the West in the nineteenth century had a mellowing effect on monarchical absolutism (where they did not destroy it altogether) and brought constitutional reform and middle-class sharing of power, in Russia, despite the feeble efforts that followed Russia's Crimean War defeat, eighteenth-century conditions of government prevailed right into the twentieth century.

This tsarist absolutism was outmoded long before it collapsed. It was weak because it failed to retain the loyalties of the slowly-growing middle class, and because it left the peasants (through inefficiency as much as by design) in conditions that could not be allowed to worsen much if the regime was to survive. The state of military preparedness was relatively poor, and Russia's industrial base was weak. Russia's defeat in the Far East was paralleled by revolution at home (1905–1906); the creation at long last of a Duma or Parliament was more shell than substance. Her defeat in World War I brought a new revolution; Tsar Nicholas II abdicated on March 15, 1917, and Kerensky inaugurated a moderate, middle-class, parliamentary government.

Kerensky had tried to keep Russia in the war. Yet the Russian soldiers could not, or would not, continue to fight. The supply train had already disintegrated; the common soldier now joined the revolution by shooting his officers and walking east. At home the peasants seized the estates, and the city workers the factories. On November 7, 1917 (October 25 of the old Russian calendar), the Bolsheviks (or majority faction of the Social Democratic Party) took power on a program of "Peace, Land, Bread"—a slogan of irresistible appeal to the masses. Under the leadership of Lenin (a pseudonym—originally Vladimir Ulianov) the new Soviet government began to deal with a chaotic situation.

The Bolsheviks, who in 1918 reverted to calling themselves "Communists," [2] turned to the task of making peace with Germany. The Treaty of Brest-Litovsk, to which she was forced to agree, would have virtually dismembered Russia. But the treaty was soon to be nullified by Germany's defeat in the West. Shortly after its conclusion, Allied troops occupied Archangel and Murmansk in an effort to support counterrevolutionary forces who would denounce the Brest-Litovsk settlement and bring Russia once more into the war. By mid-1918 the Communists were waging a civil war against White Russian forces backed by the Allies. After these were substantially defeated, Poland attacked Russia in an effort to gain the Ukraine; a new danger confronted the Soviet state. By the summer of 1920 the Poles were driven back to Warsaw, and then the Russians in turn were forced to retreat. With the military situation now stalemated, peace was soon restored. Thus by 1921 Soviet Russia emerged from civil and foreign wars to face great internal problems. She had lost great territories in the process, including Finland, Estonia, Latvia, Lithuania (which became independent states); Western Byelorussia and the Western Ukraine (to Poland); Bessarabia (to Romania); and Kars and Ardahan (to Turkey). But she had survived. Yet the memories of her struggle were to continue to embitter her relations with the West.

In the period 1921–1933 Russia's relations with the West reflected the outcome of that struggle; they were normal in that the Soviet Union exchanged recognition (except for the United States, which refused), but they were never friendly. In 1922 she attended her first international conference at Genoa. Here Germany and Russia came as the two most important defeated states of World War I and its aftermath (for Russia's losses had been even more severe than Germany's). The Treaty of Rapallo began a *rapprochement* between them that ultimately was extended to the training of German troops and the erection of German munitions factories on Russian soil, in direct violation of the Treaty of Versailles.[3] In return the Germans aided the Soviets in their efforts to industrialize by furnishing material and technical "know-how." The bitterly anti-Communist government of Germany and the Communist regime in the citadel of Soviet revolution, Russia, while remaining ideological enemies, aided each other to achieve their common aim of restoring their former power. Since Russia had not been allowed to attend the Versailles Conference, since she had no stake in the preservation of the system created there, and since she had ultimately also fought against British and French intervention on Russian soil, this cooperation was not especially strange. But this cooperation was a warning of how easily the role of ideology in leading nations astray from the path which their national interests indicate can be

---

[2] This was the original term, used, it will be remembered, in the *Communist Manifesto*.
[3] See E. H. Carr, *German-Soviet Relations Between the Two World Wars, 1919–1939;* also Lionel Kochan, *Russia and the Weimar Republic*, Cambridge, 1954.

overvalued. With Hitler's rise to power in 1933, his open rearmament of Germany, and his scarcely veiled designs on Russia, this collaboration lost its point and came to an end. How it was resumed between 1939 and 1941, under vastly changed conditions, we shall see shortly.

2 Russia Closes Ranks with the West (1933–1939)

IN 1933 Hitler came to power, America recognized Russia, and France and the Soviet Union began negotiations for a mutual assistance pact. This new set of conditions foreshadowed the shape of things to come a decade later. On September 18, 1934, the Soviet Union, upon invitation, joined the League of Nations, and on May 2, 1935, the Franco-Soviet Pact finally materialized. It provided that (Article 2) "In the event of France or the U.S.S.R. . . . being the object . . . of an unprovoked attack on the part of a European state, the U.S.S.R. and, reciprocally, France, shall immediately give each other aid and assistance." The same month the Soviets entered into an identical pact with Czechoslovakia (except that it was made contingent on France coming to the aid of the country attacked).[4] Thus the Soviet Union, faced by new dangers, although it had lost spectacularly by the postwar *status quo*, rallied to the support of collective security to preserve what it still had. And to supplement the potential weakness of League collective security action, Russia entered into military alliances with the West directed against resurgent Germany.

The Soviet decision thus did not represent a fundamental reconciliation either with the postwar *status quo* or with their former Western enemies. Rather it represented a Soviet assessment of a situation that necessitated Soviet cooperation with the West if Russia were to escape even more drastic losses at the hands of Nazi Germany. Russia continued to hope for an eventual return to at least its 1914 frontiers in Europe and its 1904 frontiers in Asia. This underlying and not unnatural goal helps to explain some of her subsequent actions. Neither in this period of collaboration with the West (1933–1939), nor in the period of collaboration with Germany (1939–1941), any more than during the wartime alliance of Russia with the West (1941–1945), did Stalin forget the old Russian proverb: "You may always walk with the Devil till you get to the end of the bridge."

Soviet attempts to close ranks with the West in 1933–1939 were not mere gestures. The Russian national interests were best served by such a policy of genuine (even if not permanent) cooperation. Collaboration with the West rested explicitly on a coincidence of Soviet and Western interests which, like many coincidences of interests between and among great powers, was temporary.

The first real test of this new alliance system did not come until 1938. The

---

[4] France had a treaty with Czechoslovakia; Russia's honoring of *its* treaty became dependent on France honoring *hers*.

shocks it survived between 1935 and 1938 were not conclusive. During the Civil War in Spain, Mussolini's invasion of Ethiopia, and Hitler's remilitarization of the Rhineland, Russia supported the League system and urged effective action. England and France were reluctant to move, since they would obviously have had to bear the brunt of any such actions for purely geographical reasons.[5] Hitler's occupation and annexation of Austria fell into a similar category.

When in the fall of 1938 Hitler's attention was for the first time turned unmistakably and seriously eastward, German pressure on Czechoslovakia directly threatened Soviet security. Czechoslovakia's eastern frontier virtually abutted on the Russian border. In this first real test Britain and France proceeded to scuttle a Czechoslovakia willing to fight at a Munich Conference at which neither the Czechs nor the Russians were represented.

Each further development now increased Soviet alarm and distrust. On March 15, 1939, Bohemia and Moravia (parts of Czechoslovakia) became German "protectorates" in a move unopposed by the great powers; on March 23 Germany annexed Memel from Lithuania after exerting pressure. Hitler simultaneously made demands on Danzig and the Polish Corridor. On March 31 came a British pledge of aid to Poland by Britain and France; this on April 6 was converted into an actual treaty of mutual assistance. Yet the Russians, understandably enough, saw in this no great reassurance after what had happened to Czechoslovakia. When Italy on April 7 invaded Albania in violation of the Anglo-Italian *status quo* pact of the year before, Britain made no move. The extension of the Franco-British pledge of support to Romania and Greece on April 13 accordingly left the Russians skeptical. On May 22 came a military alliance between Germany and Italy. Events were moving rapidly.

As the world moved gradually closer to the outbreak of a new war, the English and the French in Moscow were attempting to negotiate the terms by which the three states would put an end to Germany's further expansion to the east. Aside from the distrust, now so great between them, the crux of the issue (which proved insoluble) was Poland's refusal to allow Russians to enter Poland in the event of imminent German aggression. To the Russians there was nothing to be gained by agreeing to go to war over Poland unless Poland could be held or at least the attempt made. The value of the agreement for the Soviets was the hope it implied of keeping Germany away from the Russian frontier. To do this, Russia believed that she had to be allowed a right of

---

[5] The resurrection of Poland following World War I, after more than a hundred years of national extinction and division among Germany, Austria-Hungary, and Russia, had a curious and unforeseen effect upon great-power relations during all these events. Because Germany and Russia, after a hundred years and more of having a common frontier, were separated by Poland in the two decades following World War I, Russia's direct restraining influence upon Germany was necessarily small so long as the Nazi regime was preoccupied with problems in the west or south, as was the case until September 1938. The military weakness of Poland as Germany's eastern neighbor and the Polish distrust of Russia consequently played a larger role both in Hitler's successive coups and in the events leading up to the startling Nazi-Soviet Pact than is sometimes recognized.

entry into Poland before it was too late, i.e., before an imminent war began. Poland would not agree; Britain and France were unwilling to include such a provision in the proposed alliance without Polish assent. There was also disagreement over the Soviet proposal for a joint guarantee of the Baltic states against internal (i.e., Nazi) revolution. The British preferred "consultation" if Germany aggressed in the Baltic. In the end the talks were to deadlock. Even as early as May there had been public signs of Soviet reconsideration of her basic policy. On the 3rd of that month Maxim Litvinov, commissar for foreign affairs and identified with the policy of cooperation with the West, was suddenly replaced. Molotov, who took over, warned at the end of the month that Russia would accept nothing less than a treaty based upon equal obligations for herself and the West. The military mission sent by the French and British, which arrived in Moscow on August 11, had no authority to meet the Russian demands. Its very composition seemed to denote its lack of primary importance in Anglo-French thinking. It brought the Soviets to a decision.[6] On August 23 the Russians, highly suspicious of Western intentions, concluded a non-aggression pact with Nazi Germany. One week later Germany unleashed her assault upon Poland.

3 The Strange Collaboration (1939–1941)

THUS began a period of strange collaboration between Nazi Germany and the Soviet Union, which was to last less than two years.

The pact with which it began and the events that led to its signature are still the subject of much controversy. The Russians were roundly condemned in the West, then and again later, after the wartime unity of Russa and the West had dissolved into the Cold War. The Soviet action helped to precipitate the war and made it possible for Hitler to concentrate his forces in the West, crush France, and drive the British off the continent at Dunkirk. Nevertheless, it is not too difficult to understand the Soviet frame of mind as they approached their decision in August 1939. They suspected England and France of intending to embroil Russia in a war with Germany while they themselves remained neutral. They suspected that the Western guarantee to Poland might not be honored at the crisis—that Poland would be allowed to go the way of Czechoslovakia and that the Baltic states, too, would be surrendered. Their conclusion was that Russia was to be tricked into declaring war against Germany but was not to be allowed to advance into Poland soon enough to establish a defensible line.

In coldly logical terms the Soviets reasoned that, if a "deal" could be made with Hitler by which Eastern Poland would be occupied by the Russians after

---

[6] As late as August 4 the German ambassador to Russia reported: "My over-all impression is that the Soviet Government is at present determined to sign with England and France if they fulfill all Soviet wishes," *Nazi-Soviet Relations, 1939–1941*, Department of State Publication 3023, p. 41.

Germany had defeated the Polish forces and was occupying Western Poland, and if Germany then turned west to attack France, both Soviet strategic objectives could be obtained: (1) a better Soviet defense line in Poland, and (2) a definitive Western involvement against Hitler. Without Russia's going to war herself, the Western guarantees of Poland would be put to their test. If Hitler moved subsequently against the Soviet Union, as they were sure he would eventually do, a defense line in Poland was still preferable to a defense line on the existing Soviet frontier. If in the end France and Britain and Russia found themselves fighting together against Hitler as a consequence of such an attack by the Nazis, the Western powers would not fight the Germans any less heartily because their own interests would be at stake until Hitler's power was broken. It would, of course, be dangerous for the Soviet Union once this last event came to pass, since the Western powers might then, in conjunction with Hitler's successors, turn a united face against the East.

This assessment was logical enough as far as it went. But it created for the Soviet Union an impressive reputation for perfidy which was in no way allayed by the circumstance that they had themselves come to this choice out of distrust of the West. It proved in Western minds that Russia could not be trusted; this opinion was a very potent factor in poisoning Soviet-Western relations at their roots after 1945.[7]

The Non-Aggression Pact itself, concluded for ten years, provided (Article II) that if either Germany or Russia became "the object of belligerent action by a third power, the other High Contracting Party shall in no manner lend its support to this third power." [8] Attached to the treaty was a "secret additional protocol" which delineated the German and Russian spheres of interest in Eastern Europe. Provision was made for the division of Poland; and Bessarabia was explicitly recognized by Germany as falling within the Russian sphere.

The next month, on September 28, following Stalin's assault on Poland from the east (September 17), these arrangements were further spelled out and somewhat modified by a "Boundary and Friendship Treaty." [9] Russia now moved rapidly to exploit the situation and consolidate her gains. Treaties were concluded with Estonia (September 29), Latvia (October 5), and Lithuania (October 10) giving Russia military bases. On November 26 the Finns refused similar demands; four days later Russian armies assaulted Finland on three fronts, beginning a war that lasted until March 12, 1940, and eventually gained Russia the Karelian Isthmus, the city of Viipuri and the shores of Lake Ladoga, and a naval base at Hangö, as well as an area near Petsamo in the north—in all some 16,173 square miles. In addition, Russia "gained" by this unprovoked attack expulsion from the League of Nations (December 14, 1939), a reputation for aggression and for military weakness (due to its slow progress in defeating a small power such as Finland), and—

---

[7] It was also a violation of the Franco-Soviet Treaty of 1935.

[8] *Nazi-Soviet Relations*, 1939–1941, Department of State Publication 3023, pp. 76 ff.

[9] *Ibid.*, p. 78.

almost—war with Britain and France (who, tempted by the lull on the Western front of the "phony war," made plans to ship troops to the Finnish front).

When Hitler's *Blitzkrieg* was unleashed against France in the spring of 1940, Moscow reacted immediately. The evidently unexpected quick collapse of France and Britain's perilous position meant that Hitler could soon be free to attack in the east. On June 4 the Dunkirk evacuation ended; on June 15–17 Russian forces took over Estonia, Latvia, and Lithuania. On June 22 came the Franco-German armistice at Compiègne; on June 26 the Soviet Union demanded the return of Bessarabia from Romania, and the cession of northern Bukovina. On June 28 these areas, too, were occupied by Soviet troops. All three were annexed on July 21. Thus Stalin attempted to gain space the whole length of Russia's western frontiers; in that same spring and summer of 1940 Hitler made the decision to prepare an attack upon her. By the end of September, German troop movements through Poland were casting the shadow of what was to come. Nazi-Soviet relations steadily deteriorated. On December 18 Hitler ordered his Wehrmacht to prepare detailed plans for "Operation Barbarossa." His order spoke of crushing Soviet Russia "in a quick campaign." On June 22, 1941, that operation began. Perhaps the most massive and large-scale military campaign in the history of Western civilization was under way.

4   *The Hot War and the Cold War* (1941–1953)

THE German assault was furious. In late November the Germans had reached within thirteen miles of Moscow. "General Winter," closing in, gave the Russians a breathing spell. In 1942, with the arrival of suitable weather, the Nazis advanced far into the Ukraine, reaching Stalingrad by late August. That same winter, culminating with the capture of von Paulus' army at Stalingrad, the tide began to turn. Through 1943 the battles continued, but the German offensives no longer gave hope of victory. By mid-1944 Russian armies were in Romania, Finland, and Poland. In 1945 came victory.

Through these years the Western powers supported Stalin to the utmost of their ability with arms, ammunition, and supplies of every kind. In 1941 and 1942 what they were able to give was very little; by 1943 their contribution reached impressive and astonishing totals. The United States alone, under Lend-Lease, ultimately sent over four hundred thousand motor vehicles and thirteen thousand three hundred planes. Of these, some one hundred thirty-eight thousand motor vehicles and forty-one hundred planes had arrived in time for use in Russia's 1943 campaigns. These supplies reached Russia by two main routes—either through Iran (one hundred thousand tons a month by July of 1943) or by convoy to Archangel—a trip that involved circumnavigating the Scandinavian Peninsula against the combined perils of winter and constant German air and submarine attack.

Despite this cooperation there were many signs indicative of trouble yet to come. But the full development of these tensions awaited the coming of V-E day in Europe and V-J day in Asia. Even without ideological dissensions, trouble between the victors would not have been abnormal; with it the Cold War became a tense struggle between East and West, waged on a number of levels—economic, psychological, political—and over a number of basically distinct issues whose exact outlines were frequently blurred in the heat of the ideological exchange.

What became known as the Cold War can be divided into four issues for purposes of analysis, even though each has a common feature: the enormous growth in power of Russia and the increasing influence of communism in the post-World-War-II world. There are, first, the questions raised by the re-establishment by Russia of her pre-1904 boundaries and position in Asia and her pre-1914 boundaries in Europe. Second, there is the issue posed by the extension of a Communist form of government to China and the events that ramify from it. Third, in Europe there is the issue brought about by Russian domination of the Balkans and Poland. And, fourth, there is the issue that Russia's position as an occupying power in Germany raises. The point is that, although these issues have the common focus already alluded to, they are problems with distinctly different implications for contemporary international relations and are, because of these differences, not susceptible of being handled by the West in terms of any one simple formula.

The existence of these four issues raised problems for the West in terms of policy formulation and implementation. The West was confronted with the need to decide whether all four of these developments constituted an equal threat to Western security, and, if not, which; it was similarly confronted with the need to develop policies adapted to coping with whichever of these issues constituted a real threat, on a basis suitable for dealing with that threat. As a response to one of these issues, for example, building a greater military force might be desirable; in terms of another the main reliance might have to be upon diplomacy or some other means. One thing was certain: no one-word formula, be it "containment" or "liberation," would suffice.

Of these four issues, the spreading of communism to China and the subsequent ramifications of this spread formed a development that owed relatively little to the foreign policy of Russia per se. It can best be examined later when we turn to a consideration of Far Eastern nations. For convenience we shall then also examine the return of Russian influence and the regaining of her pre-1904 boundaries in the area. There remain the European issues; of these, the Soviet occupation of Germany is perhaps the most important contemporary international problem involving all the great powers, and it deserves separate and detailed consideration.[10] At this point we shall touch upon it only to indicate its relation to these other European issues.

The Cold War, although it began over the Balkans and Poland, reached its greatest intensity in Europe over Germany. While the West was prepared to

[10] See Chapter 26.

see the re-establishment of Russian pre-1914 boundaries in Europe, it was far less ready to acknowledge the Balkans as a Soviet sphere of influence. Nor did it want a puppet Poland. Much less was it willing to tolerate an indefinite Red Army occupation in Germany and Austria. In other words, the degree of feeling rose steadily in direct relationship to the proximity of each of these areas to the West. The Cold War began over Poland and the Balkans, because of the rapid introduction of Soviet-type regimes there even before the end of the war in Europe. The Yalta Declaration (February 1945) on Poland had provided that the then Provisional Government would "be reorganized on a broader democratic base." By this the West meant a parliamentary regime based on free elections. Yet the only "broadening" of the base that took place in Poland was the subordination of other parties and the broadening of the Communist-dominated party to include or replace them. In the early days of March 1945, the world was confronted with the spectacle of a Romanian king, Michael, appointing (under pressure) the leader of the Romanian Communist Party as his premier. This Communist monarchy lasted some two and a half years; then Michael was forced into exile (December 1947). Throughout the Balkan states, Communist regimes came to power, backed by the ever-present threat of Soviet army bayonets. Thus came into existence, to the accompaniment of treason trials of Roman Catholic cardinals and agrarian peasant party leaders, the ring of "people's democracies," better known in the West as satellite states. By 1948 only Czechoslovakia in all the Soviet Balkan sphere had no completely Communist-dominated regime. And in February 1948, following a Communist coup, Czechoslovakia went the way of the others.

Although these developments, especially as they brought increased pressure upon Greece and Turkey, had already provoked the Truman Doctrine (March 12, 1947), it was the Communist coup in Czechoslovakia, with its extension of the Iron Curtain so far westward, and the Soviet blockade of Berlin in the summer of 1948, which so disturbed the West that a large-scale rearmament was begun and NATO created. It was here that the Cold War began to wax hot. The Allied airlift showed a willingness on the part of the West to risk war and a determination to hold Berlin. It was out of these circumstances that the West German government came into existence and the German problem assumed a new form.

The issue posed by Russia's creation of a ring of satellite Balkan states, overshadowed as it was after 1948 by the emergence of the German issue, remains to be considered. It is not new in modern history, for Russia came to blows with Austria-Hungary (as we saw earlier) over essentially this same point. With the disintegration of Austria-Hungary after World War I into splinter states of relatively small power and the disappearance of the restraining influence on Russia that Austria-Hungary had represented, the area was incorporated into the French alliance system. This endured only until German power had revived and Austria had been annexed to the Third Reich; thereafter Germany was in a position to advance her influence in the area.

This she promptly proceeded to do, although as a price for the Soviet non-aggression treaty of 1939 Germany was forced to acquiesce in Russian influence in the area as well. Had the Russians been stronger in the period between the two world wars, they would in all probability have attempted to gain then the position of dominance they achieved once Hitler had been defeated in 1945. Historically the Russians have always sought such a dominant position in the Balkans. This aim springs not alone from expansive tendencies but also from Russia's determination to hold the territorial keys to her western approaches. Because several of these states have frontiers with the Soviet Union, they constitute an area about which Russia is, understandably, especially sensitive. While this fear is no justification for Russian actions there, it does serve to explain them.

The issue of control of the Balkans was initially faced by the West in predominantly emotional terms. In particular the trial of Cardinal Mindszenty, the Roman Catholic Primate of Hungary, in February 1949, aroused a great storm of Western protest. A man of known intellectual and moral strength, he confessed abjectly and pathetically to the charges leveled against him—an obvious indication of the Communist police methods that had reduced him to such a condition. The disregard for precious human values that this trial symbolized was a blow against humanity and humaneness everywhere, and the man in the street unerringly recognized it as such. Nevertheless, the crux of the issue for the West could not, for obvious reasons, rest predominantly on a sense of moral outrage. In cold terms of their national interests the West had to face the fact that throughout modern history, with rare exceptions, the Balkans have been preserved by evenly matched great power rivalries in the area. Or they have become some great power's satellites: in earlier times, under the Ottomans; in later times, under the Austro-Hungarians, the Germans, or the Russians. To reverse this circumstance for any great period of time would not be easy; indeed, truly independent status for the Balkans may not be attainable. In facing this issue, the West had to decide not what it would like but what it was capable of achieving with or without war.

Whether Russia's domination of the area would appear such a threat if it were not also coupled with the Soviet military occupation of Germany needed to be squarely faced. It is difficult to avoid the conclusion that the central source of friction between East and West in Europe stemmed not from the Russian hegemony in the Balkans but from the continued presence of the Red Army deep in Central Europe. It should also be apparent that the Soviet position in East Germany went far toward frustrating any extension of new German influence in the Balkans as a counterweight to Soviet influence there.

By the spring of 1953, as the world approached a new turn of events in Russian affairs, East and West remained deadlocked on this and other questions.

5 *After Stalin: The Khrushchev Era* (1953–1964)

THE death of Stalin on March 5, 1953, plunged the Soviet Union overnight into a dramatic sequence of events. Was a three-cornered struggle for power among the party apparatus, the secret police, and the armed forces in the making?

The arrest and then the execution of Beria, the chief of the internal security forces, on December 23, 1953, clipped the third force off this triangle of power. Other moves seemed designed to conciliate the military: Marshal Voroshilov became president, and Marshal Zhukov (a leading Soviet hero of World War II) was restored to favor. The party apparatus under Malenkov (and Molotov) remained in control. On February 8, 1955, came Malenkov's resignation as premier and the elevation of Marshal Bulganin (a "political general") to that office. Relatively little known Nikita Khrushchev, the new party secretary, became more and more prominent; speculation in the West viewed him as Russia's new "Stalin."

But Malenkov, contrary to Soviet tradition, was not executed, and the West was soon treated to more unprecedented events. The Soviet leaders, especially Khrushchev, Bulganin, and Malenkov made themselves accessible to Western diplomats in a fashion in great contrast to practice under Stalin. Moreover, they permitted themselves to disagree with one another publicly. They then embarked on a series of visits to foreign states. Following a trip to Yugoslavia in May 1955, Khrushchev and Bulganin made a tour of India and other Asian countries, including Afghanistan. Malenkov, in his capacity of Minister for Power Stations, visited Britain in March 1956; Khrushchev and Bulganin followed his example in a state visit soon after.

These trips were not only the outward manifestation of a Soviet decision to woo the outside world; they also symbolized the relaxation of terror within the Soviet Union. In Stalin's time contact with foreigners was suspect, and much separation from fellow-leaders dangerous.

The new emphasis at home was on "collective leadership" and collective responsibility. The new leaders went to great pains to demonstrate this "return to Leninist principle." In the process they proceeded energetically to destroy the Stalin myth. At the 20th Party Congress in early 1956 Khrushchev went so far as to indict Stalin for great crimes and colossal blunders. He charged him particularly with executing old Bolsheviks and the upper command of the army in fear-crazed purges in the 1930's and after World War II. The implication that a new leaf was being turned was obvious. As a sidelight on this development an apocryphal but amusing story was circulating in Moscow in March 1956 that Khrushchev, following his denunciation of Stalin, received an anonymous note asking what he had been doing when Stalin was alive to stop the terror. Khrushchev read the note to the Congress and demanded that the author stand up. No one volunteered. "So, comrades," said

Khrushchev, "now you know what I was doing when Stalin was alive. I didn't stand up either."

As these great internal changes proceeded, the Soviet Union began also to overhaul its foreign policy. The new approach emphasized Soviet willingness to explore outstanding East-West questions diplomatically. One of the first implementations of this approach was the meeting at the summit in Geneva in July of 1955. The meeting showed new flexibility in the tactics of Soviet diplomacy but no softening on substance. Although no concrete progress was made there, either on the problem of German unification or disarmament, world tension appreciably slackened. Not even the subsequent efforts of the Russians to expand their influence in the Middle East quite reversed this trend. The new Soviet policy seemed to be increasingly oriented toward economic competition with the West in the underdeveloped countries of the world.

In Europe proper the extension of Soviet power into the heart of the continent, while it posed a threat to the West, also confronted Russia with certain dangers that grew more formidable as German power revived. These had to be weighed against the advantages for Russia in her advanced position. The decisions in 1955 to evacuate Austria and to woo Yugoslavia were apparently designed to build a neutral barrier between the opposing armies across Central Europe. But such disengagement had little point unless extended to Germany. The Soviets indeed proposed a neutral status for Germany, but at the same time showed extreme reluctance to permit free all-German elections which were the indispensable requirement for any change. Either the Soviets were hoping for easy gains or the ruling group could not agree on a policy entailing real concessions. Such a policy also entailed serious risks of renewed Titoist movements on the outer fringes of the Russian orbit. Near revolt in Poland and actual revolt in Hungary in 1956 showed these fears justified. The subsequent use of force against Hungary was not embarked upon with enthusiasm for it showed the hollowness of the Soviet claims for communism's irresistible appeal.

Khrushchev's removal of Molotov and Malenkov from positions of power (July 3, 1957), his dismissal of Zhukov (October 26, 1957), and his own assumption of the premiership, replacing Bulganin (March 27, 1958), while consolidating his power, did not return Russia to "Stalinist" rule. Russian foreign policy took, however, a new approach. Russia's tempo of diplomatic activity was still further increased in the next years. Faced with the failure of the neutral barrier concept in Central Europe, and the American decision to supply weapons with nuclear capabilities to the West German forces as well as with the increasingly untenable situation in Communist East Germany, Khrushchev resolved in late 1958 to force the West out of Berlin. For the next four years Khrushchev pursued a policy every bit as "hard" as Stalin in his hey-day.

Whether Khrushchev's initial motivation was essentially defensive is not known. Certainly the existence of free West Berlin in the heart of Soviet-occupied Germany put in ultimate question the very existence of a German satellite state—especially so long as relatively free communication and access continued between East and West Berlin. Possibly Khrushchev, by breaking Western morale over West Berlin, hoped for larger gains in Germany or elsewhere as a result of the Western defeatism which could then be anticipated. In any event, as we saw in Chapter 22, he failed in his larger object and the Berlin Wall went up in 1961 instead. In the aftermath he again threatened his separate peace (which would "end" Western rights in Berlin) and resorted to the dangerous flank maneuver which led to the Cuban Missile Crisis of 1962 (and ultimately to Khrushchev's own downfall in 1964).

By 1961–1964 Soviet policy was beset by multiple dilemmas. The German problem was only one of these. How to de-Stalinize without dismantling the Soviet bloc, or producing internal schism, continued to be another. It had important bearing not only on the political in-fighting within the Kremlin, but increasingly on relations with Communist China.

At the 22nd Party Congress in October 1961, Khrushchev continued the juggling act. The charges against Stalin were revived and were, in contrast to the 1956 "secret speech," given wide publicity within and outside Russia. Stalin's body was removed from the Lenin Tomb in Red Square and reburied. Albania was charged with clinging to one-man-rule and the "cult of the individual," and threatened with excommunication; well known Stalinists such as Molotov and former President Voroshilov were threatened with expulsion from the party.

Khrushchev's policies brought him into ever increasing friction with Communist China. Having set out to de-Stalinize, he had had to suppress the Hungarian revolt. The Chinese charges of "softness" in advancing the Communist cause may well have played a part in setting him on the dangerous course of the Second Berlin Crisis and the Cuban Missile Crisis. But in their wake the Chinese accused him of cowardice. Khrushchev's agreement to the Test Ban Treaty of 1963 (another dilemma for Russia) deteriorated relations still further, for China considered this directed primarily at her. Khrushchev's doctrinal revisions (which we shall examine in the next chapter) angered the Chinese still more. At the same time the failure of Khrushchev's policies undermined his position at home. On October 14, 1964, he was retired by his colleagues for "ill health." Quite soon thereafter it was made clear that his "adventurism" had been the real cause.

His successors were more moderate in manner. Whether they would prove more conciliatory on substance was another question. Most of the dilemmas remained as before. The policy of the Soviet Union, like that of the United States, was overdue for reappraisal in certain basic respects. Clouding the issue in 1966 was the Viet-Nam War. For the Soviets this represented a still further dilemma. They could not afford not to support a Communist "liberation movement" opposed by the "imperialists." And friction between the United States and Communist China, if kept within bounds, was not contrary to Soviet interests. But what if the situation found its fruition in World War III?

CHAPTER 25

The Soviet Union: An Analysis

We have never had and do not have now the intention of attacking anybody.

SOVIET PREMIER NIKOLAI BULGANIN
July 15, 1955

When the Chinese-Indian conflict began in 1959, the Soviet leaders frankly told the Peoples Republic of China Government that the aggravation of the dispute . . . was undesirable and fraught with negative consequences . . . for the entire international situation.

Statement of Soviet Government, September 1963

WINSTON CHURCHILL once characterized Soviet foreign policy as "a riddle wrapped in a mystery inside an enigma." This emotionally satisfying phrase is also an exaggeration. Although Soviet foreign policy is at least as complex (if not more so) as that of any other great power, it does not defy analysis—as Churchill himself contended in the very same speech. Without underrating the degree of difficulty that an analysis of Russian policy presents, it is still true that much of the confusion over the main trends of Soviet foreign relations arises from three fairly easily identifiable sources. Once we have disposed of the distortions thus introduced, we shall be able to see more clearly actual Soviet behavior.

I Sources of Confusion: Russian Policy, the Popular Preconception

THE primary source of confusion in many Western analyses of Soviet policy springs from a fixed and often oversimplified preconception as to the *strategic* aims of Soviet communism: the Soviet Union is seen as bent upon fomenting world revolution and willing and desirous of using the Red Army to precipitate war at the proper moment. It is seen as an aggressive power bent upon dominating the world. This preconception must be examined to determine to what extent it expresses the truth; that it is widely and *literally* accepted is quite evident.

Often the evidence given to buttress this view consists of the citation of various Communist pronouncements without much regard to the circumstances under which they were made. Karl Marx, himself the patron saint of

Communist theology, can be quoted to the effect that "the policy of Russia is changeless. . . . Its methods, its tactics, its maneuvers may change, but the polar star of its policy—world domination—is a fixed star." [1] Because this particular view of Russian aims fits in with Western preconceptions, it is accorded an enthusiastic reception in the most sacrosanct citadels of Western capitalism, even while other Marxist ideas are being castigated and shunned. It is rather ironical that Marx, assuming that communism would first triumph in an industrialized state (i.e., Germany), looked on Russia, the most reactionary European great power of his time, as an enemy. While it is obviously embarrasing to the Soviets that Marx should have said something for the record so indiscreet and unfriendly, this quotation also illustrates the danger of accepting statements of policy or over-all judgments without due regard to the circumstances under which they are written and the context within which the thoughts are framed.

One of Lenin's most famous statements is:

We are living not merely in a State, but in a system of States, and the existence of the Soviet Republic side by side with imperialistic States for a long time is unthinkable. One or the other must triumph in the end. And before that end supervenes, a series of frightful collisions between the Soviet Republic and the bourgeois States will be inevitable. [2]

This statement, later endorsed by Stalin, was subsequently reprinted in Lenin's and Stalin's collected works; it is often cited as evidence that Russia intends to use the Red Army to start a new and revolutionary world war at a moment of her own choosing. Actually it dates back to a time when the Red Army was incapable of any such effort and when Red Russia was fighting for survival amidst a ring of enemies. What Lenin was referring to was the bitter antagonism of a capitalist world unwilling to tolerate the existence of the Soviet state. [3]

It must be remembered that communism did not gain its foothold in Russia without struggle and bloodshed, both against foes within the tsarist frontiers and against intervening foreign (capitalist) states. Communist Russia was born in the midst of violence against the will of the "imperialistic States" (i.e., the non-Communist Powers), existed for years in an atmosphere of foreign hostility, and experienced foreign invasion aimed at stamping out the "Bolshevik virus." It is not surprising that Lenin assumed that the struggle to suppress communism in Russia by collective or individual actions of foreign

---

[1] In his "Poland's European Mission" (1867). Reprinted in Paul W. Blackstock and Bert F. Hoselitz, eds., *The Russian Menace to Europe*, Glencoe, Illinois: Free Press, 1952, p. 106.

[2] V. I. Lenin, "Report of Central Committee at 8th Party Congress" of March 18, 1919, *Selected Works*, Vol. 8, p. 33.

[3] This is even clearer in his later statement, when Russia had managed to survive and enjoyed a breathing spell of peace, that "In the end . . . a funeral requiem will be sung either over the Soviet Republic or over world capitalism. This is a respite in war." Lenin, *Collected Works*, Vol. 17 (1923), p. 398.

powers was not at an end. Soviet experience in the two decades following the Russian Revolution was not conducive to the abandoning of this view. These two decades began with foreign intervention and ended with the Munich Agreement. It was not unreasonable of Stalin (whether correct in his assumption or not) to assume that the Munich accord was the prelude to a renewal of warfare directed against the Soviet state, the citadel of communism.

Thus this quotation must be seen against a background of fear and weakness. It testifies to a Soviet conviction that "frightful collisions" were still to be expected in the future from the conflict of capitalism and communism. But it neither proves nor disproves any Soviet "warmongering" desires. Contrary to popular belief, there are no authoritative quotations from Soviet sources which unequivocably state that the Russians themselves intend to start a new war. At the same time the lack of such statements is no guarantee at all that the Russians will not. Words must be judged against circumstances and deeds.

Turning to the preconception proper, that part of it which holds that the Soviets are tirelessly fomenting world revolution is actually a simple statement of a rather complex phenomenon, as we shall soon see. The Soviets have always endorsed the view stated by Marx and Engels more than a hundred years ago in the *Communist Manifesto* of 1848: "The Communists disdain to conceal their views and aims. They openly declare that their ends can be attained only by the forcible overthrowing of all existing social conditions. Let the ruling classes tremble at a Communistic revolution. The proletarians have nothing to lose but their chains. They have a world to win. Working men of all countries, unite!" This doctrine has remained basic to communism. In Stalin's phrase, the Soviet Union has been "the base of the world revolutionary movement." He also said, "A peaceful victory over capitalism is not to be expected. In present circumstances, capitalism can only be overthrown by means of revolution which will take the form of protracted and violent struggle to the death." Yet when interviewed in 1936 by Roy Howard, president of United Press, and asked whether the Soviets had modified their plans for world revolution, Stalin replied: "We never had such plans and intentions; . . . we Marxists hold that revolution will occur in other countries too. But it will occur only when the revolutionaries of these countries find it possible or necessary. The export of revolution—that is nonsense."

It has often been maintained that Stalin was being deliberately misleading —attempting to lull the intended capitalist victims into a false sense of security. This may well have been part of his intention, for the statement was not given any publicity *within* Russia. Even so, Stalin did not deny Soviet intentions to aid revolution abroad; what he did deny was that such aid could by itself produce revolution abroad unless conditions there were ripe for revolt. "Made-in-Moscow" revolution was not exportable as a complete thing in itself; it depended upon local nourishment, care, and effort. The techniques and the apparatus could be furnished, but their operation and efficacy depended upon local labor and support. When Stalin said: "We never had such plans and intentions" (to cause and direct world revolution), he was being, probably intentionally, ambiguous. That they did have plans and intentions to further revolution piecemeal as opportunity presented is quite obvious in the light of abundant evidence in Western possession. Yet such plans remained highly elastic. The Soviets have not been politically so naïve or inexperienced as to assume that revolution will occur simultaneously throughout the world, and in accord with some absolutely rigid and detailed tactical master plan.

At the 20th Party Congress of the Soviet Communist Party in February 1956, Nikita S. Khrushchev spelled out the flexibility of the Soviet concept explicitly. He declared that communism might now be expected to come to power in some nations without a "revolutionary class struggle." The working class "in a number of capitalist and former colonial countries" might win stable parliamentary majorities in free elections. He went on: "Of course in countries where capitalism is still strong and where it controls an enormous military and police machine, the serious resistance of the reactionary forces is inevitable. There the transition to socialism (communism) will proceed amid conditions of an acute revolutionary class struggle." [4]

The most essential point, as Stalin made clear on another occasion, was to "consolidate the dictatorship of the proletariat in one country, using it as a base for the overthrow of imperialism in all countries." Once revolution spreads "beyond the limits of one country," "the epoch of world revolution" will begin.[5] This is conceived as a historical age in which progress toward world communism will be necessarily uneven both in point of time and in point of specific areas. It is again apparent that in Communist thought "world revolution" is not being discussed as a simultaneous condition to be brought into existence by a detailed master plan for subversion everywhere and at once, but rather as an "epoch." In this "epoch," which began with the spreading of Communist revolution beyond Russia, the emphasis must be on flexibility of tactics. "One of the chief conditions to which tactics must be adjusted is the ebb and flow of the forces favoring revolution. Aggressive tactics should be timed with a rising tide; tactics of defense, the assemblage of forces, and even retreat go with an ebbing tide." [6]

Thus while it is true that Soviet Russia has aided and abetted Communist movements everywhere in the hope of further preparing the ground for Communist revolutions, the consistency and degree of effort with which this process is carried on is (at least theoretically) in direct relationship to the local conditions prevailing within any given state and in accord with the "rising" or "ebbing" tide favoring or hindering the prospects for victory at any given time. In the end (except, of course, where Russians are in occupation)

---

[4] *NYT*, February 15, 1956.

[5] For a somewhat different interpretation of these familiar quotations see "Historicus," "Stalin on Revolution," *Foreign Affairs*, Vol. 27 (January 1949), especially pp. 198–206.

[6] *Ibid.*, p. 206. The quotation is again from Stalin.

the Soviet Communists place their reliance upon the strength and capacity of local Communist groups to exploit local possibilities for revolution, aiding them with funds, indoctrination, weapons, and the teaching of the techniques of subversion.

That portion of the Western preconception which holds that the Russians are tirelessly fomenting world revolution is therefore in principle correct. But where it leads to the assumption that this is being done through the vehicle of "ready-made" revolutions exported from Moscow, and is being attempted everywhere according to a detailed world plan regardless of local conditions and the "rising" or "ebbing" tide of revolution in the world, it leads to a false idea of *how* this is being attempted and an overrating of the consistency of the effort.

This makes a great deal of practical difference in understanding Soviet policy. If one merely proceeds from the simple formulation of the point that Russia is fomenting world revolution, one may easily assume that the Soviet Union at all times and places would push for local revolution. How far this can lead astray from the actual Russian policy at a given time becomes especially clear from what we have learned as a consequence of Marshal Tito's break with the Kremlin. According to Tito the conflict between himself and Stalin came to a head over Stalin's wish to see the monarchy reinstated in Yugoslavia, and to have Tito pursue a more moderate policy toward Trieste and the Greek Civil War! Tito has also revealed (and this is corroborated by others) that Stalin almost until the very end set his face against an acceleration of the Chinese civil war. Stalin himself told Tito's foreign minister, Edvard Kardelj, how he had urged Mao Tse-tung to compromise with Chiang Kai-shek and disband the Chinese Communist forces. Mao gave the impression of agreeing with Stalin, went ahead anyhow upon his return to China, and led the Chinese Communists to victory.[7] Even before this, in the years when Japan had been a danger to Russia, Stalin had pursued a policy of cooperation with Chiang Kai-shek, regardless of ideological considerations. When the Burma Road was closed by the British in the dark days of World War II, Russia was Chiang's *only* source of supplies.

The point is that while Russia has aided the spread of communism, arming satellites and giving them assistance, she has not everywhere and at all times unequivocally favored the further extension of communism. Sometimes she has favored the reverse. While this moderation is the result of tactical considerations and does not alter ultimate intentions, it is still very necessary to understand that Soviet policy is at times dedicated to immediate goals that are precisely the reverse of what is usually assumed. And where tactical considerations may lead over a period of years to a course of action diametrically opposed to the strategic aim, the tactical diversions are at least as important a factor as the strategy in evaluating Soviet policy. (One of China's main

---

[7] For a more detailed discussion of these points see Isaac Deutscher, "The Legacies and Heirs of J. V. Stalin," *The Reporter*, April 14, 1953, pp. 10–16.

charges against Russia in 1963 and after, was that Russia was not really dedi-cated to spreading revolution. See below, Section 5.)

That part of the preconception which holds that the Soviet Union is an aggressive power bent upon dominating the world through military force can-not be usefully answered on a simple open-and-shut, yes-or-no basis.

To decide whether a power is bent upon dominating the world, if such a point can be decided, still amounts to little more than an assessment of inten-tions. As such it can be important by casting light on the ultimate goals for which policy is being implemented. On the other hand, intentions have lim-ited importance unless they are linked to practice. The methods by which a state seeks to implement its goals are of crucial importance, not only as they affect whether the goal will indeed be attained but also in their effect upon other states. It is perfectly clear that the Soviet Union has in principle as an ultimate goal the triumph of communism everywhere in the world so that, in Khrushchev's famous phrase, "Your grandchildren, too, will be socialists." The outward symbol of such triumph, if accomplished, would be the erection of Communist states everywhere to replace non-Communist sovereign units. At the same time, the schisms within the Soviet bloc have destroyed Russian illusions that this would automatically ensure perfect security for the Soviet Union.

The active desire to spread communism, which is the announced goal of Soviet Russia, takes on importance, aside from the internal subversive effects it may create, to the extent that it inspires efforts to dominate the world through aggressive actions. Yet it would be very difficult indeed to prove (al-though easy to assert) that such aggressions as the Soviet Union has perpe-trated were actually inspired by ideological motivations. They are, in point of fact, readily explainable on security grounds—in terms of Russian national interests. The attack upon Finland in 1939 and the division of Poland with Nazi Germany in the same year, which are the best known illustrations, might as easily have occurred under a non-Communist form of government. Parallels for these actions in tsarist times are not hard to find.

From an over-all point of view the Russians, throughout history, have not been especially outstanding one way or the other when compared with the average tendency to aggressive actions by great powers. Their record of ag-gression since 1648 is certainly no worse than that of France or Germany (i.e., Prussia)—nor, indeed, that of Great Britain. In very recent times, under the Soviets, their record between 1917 and 1939 was practically unblemished—a condition almost certainly due to their weakness and relative vulnerability. Since 1939, apart from the two examples cited above, the greatest part of their territorial aggrandizement and their obviously improved power-bloc position stems primarily from the military results of World War II. The most impor-tant charges of aggressive activity leveled against the Soviets spring from their involvement in the Chinese Revolution, the Korean and Indo-Chinese Wars, and the Communist *coup d'état* in Czechoslovakia. In none of these cases did the Russians intervene officially or use any Red Army units as such.[8] What they were guilty of was not overt aggression in the customary sense, but what has come to be known as "indirect aggression"—i.e., aggressions perpetrated at second-hand, through the vehicle of another state or government. This method she has exploited with great success.

Although the Soviet Union's record of overt aggressive acts is not especially bad, she is undoubtedly a foremost threat to the peace, security, and stability of the world. How are we to explain this contradiction? First, one must remember that the Soviet military occupation of half of Germany and (until 1955) Austria, coming on top of their retention of Red Army units in the Balkan area and in Poland, has been a major cause of world tension. These acts prevented a satisfactory liquidation of problems arising out of the war and constituted a potential military threat to Western Europe. The unnatural conditions thus created in the very heart of Europe have constituted a continuing drain on the chances of peace whether Russia desires to commit aggression or not. Second, the Soviet use of the technique of indirect aggression, while it does not extend the territories occupied by the Red Army, has still further increased tension by altering the postwar balance of power to an extent dangerous to the security of the West. Third, Soviet aid extended to Communist parties abroad, even where such parties are in the Soviet view expected to carry the brunt and sweat of revolutionary effort using essentially native resources, continues to constitute a source of irritation and tension, especially since local conditions provide fertile soil for Communist revolutions in many areas of the world at the present time. Fourth, the Soviet drive to extend its influence in the Middle East, Africa, and Latin America makes for increased instability. The export of Soviet arms to the United Arab Republic helped cause hostilities in 1956. Soviet arms sent to Castro's Cuba precipitated the crisis of 1962.

This discussion adds up to a considerably more complicated view than the original preconception we have been examining. That the present position, actions, and policies of the Soviet Union constitute a serious threat to United States and Western security is most unfortunately true, but the nature of that threat can be better understood and better dealt with if these qualifications of the popular preconception are kept carefully in mind.

2   Sources of Confusion: The Role of Communism in Soviet Policy

ANOTHER source of confusion and argument in the West is over the degree to which Soviet actions are determined by Communist ideology versus traditional Russian national interests. Yet to pose the question in this fashion already distorts the relationship, for no nation determines national interests, or

---

[8] The use of Red Army troops to suppress the Hungarian revolt in 1956 is, of course, irrelevant in this connection. It is very relevant to what is said in the next paragraph.

pursues a foreign policy, outside the framework of a set of informal or formal values, ideas, and expectations.

An ideology is essentially a formal and systematic complex of ideas and sentiments which are assumed to have universal relevance. In this sense, as we saw in analyzing the bases of United States' actions, ideology plays a significant role in determining the content of American policy. Ideology also plays a vital role in American nationalism, providing an approach to problem-solving. While democracy means many things to many people in the United States, the essential ideas of legal equality of rights and equality of opportunity and the essential attitudes of tolerance and pragmatism that spring from it are a powerful social cement in an America composed of so many diverse peoples from all over the world who have (or had) so little else in common. Without depreciating the role of the original English culture of the thirteen colonies, and the extent to which they set the patterns of political behavior, nor the adaptability of successive waves of immigrants, it is still true that the value system which we call American democracy owes much to the obvious necessity of adjusting very different behavioral and cultural patterns into a viable whole. Lacking much of the innate unity that is the natural product of centuries of living together within a political and social community, Americans have historically relied upon developing common ideas and attitudes to a much larger extent than, for example, most Western European peoples whose indigenous nationalism is much older.

Just as Americans tend to ideological verbalization in foreign policy and tend to repair inconsistencies in action by introducing new moral abstractions to replace formulas which do not quite fit the concrete reality, so do the Soviets vary the emphasis of, or even reinterpret, basic Communist doctrines. And this in no way implies either hypocrisy or the abandonment of fundamental belief. Just as Americans are capable of supporting rather undemocratic individuals as in Spain and Portugal (in the dual name of supporting democracy and opposing communism) so too do the Russians sometimes do rather odd things in the name of furthering communism. Concrete foreign-policy situations sometimes have a drastic blunting effect upon the sword of ideology.

Communism cannot exist in a vacuum. It must be fed and housed among some people or peoples. Its advent in Russia did not thereupon eliminate all things Russian. It did not eliminate traditional Russian national interests. It meant, however, that Russian national interests would henceforth be seen in a different perspective and argued in a different "language." Both changes were important.

There is a great temptation to assess the interplay of traditional Russian interests and Communist ideology in extreme terms. At one end of the spectrum is the view that Russia is, after all, Russia, and communism has *no* real effect on policy. At the other end is the view that the coming of communism to Russia has substituted an ideological foreign policy for traditional national interests. Communist theory, incidentally, holds with the latter. National interests, according to communism, are simply the interests of the exploiting, or ruling clique. Once these elements are "liquidated," a nation has no friction-producing elements in her dealings with other similar states. Between Communist states no war can arise since all are peace-loving because of the lack of a capitalist class. Thus Soviet armed action in Hungary in 1956 was explained not as war but as fraternal aid in suppressing "counterrevolutionary" activities.

If communism (or democracy too) were so rigid and inflexible as doctrines that they could not be bent a great deal when they confront the awkwardly unyielding reality, it is probable that they would have passed away more quickly than reality could have been changed to accommodate the ideology. The point is that communism has not been pursued by the Russians at the price of traditional national interests. They have gone forward hand in hand. What basically served Russia, basically served communism. Since Soviet Russia effectively *was* communism until the last years, no great schism could develop which would have important practical consequences.

In the first years following the outbreak of the Russian Revolution, and most particularly immediately after 1917 when the cumulative effect of three years or more of intensive war had weakened the social fabric of Europe, the aims of Russian communism and the dictates of Russian national interest were substantially identical. With the collapse of Russian military power on the Eastern Front and the subsequent Allied intervention in Russia designed to bring her back into the war by restoring a pro-Allied government, the Soviets, especially under Trotsky's proddings, attempted to exploit a situation that held promise of yielding successful Red revolts in Europe and that in turn would ease the pressure upon the struggling new Soviet state. In Bavaria (in Germany) and in Hungary, Communist governments came to power for a short time. Then the situation changed with the Soviet victory over the White Russian armies and the evacuation of Russian soil by the various foreign armies in occupation. In the struggle for power, following Lenin's death in 1924, Trotsky represented the viewpoint that the fomenting of world revolution was the primary task of Russian communism, while Stalin, who triumphed, argued for the necessity of creating a Communist citadel first in one state—Russia. When the abstract goals of spreading Communist revolt abroad no longer fitted the immediate needs of the Soviet state, the preservation of Russia (or the national interests?) were given priority, and Russia turned to the task of industrialization and the mechanization (which meant as a prerequisite the collectivization) of agriculture. Without the latter the former was inevitably handicapped since, in order to free potential factory workers from the soil, productivity per agricultural worker had of necessity to be increased. These internal programs were not at all inconsistent with long-range ideological goals, but their immediate and obvious purpose was the strengthening of the gravely weakened and disrupted Soviet state.

During all of this period the Comintern (Communist International founded in 1919) functioned as the directing apparatus for Communist groups outside the Soviet Union. But it remained far more a vehicle for promoting Russian national interests (or, if one prefers, for protecting the citadel and homeland of communism) than for fomenting Communist revolt abroad per se. Its main preoccupation between 1933 and 1939, for example, was with opposing fascism—that is to say, with encouraging resistance to Hitler's efforts to strengthen his position. This action led to the formation of "Popular Front" governments in which the Communists worked to prevent the overturning and undermining of the European balance of power that was a prerequisite to Hitler's later attack upon the Soviet Union.

In May 1943, after an anti-Hitler coalition had finally come into existence and when Russian and Allied troops were engaged in fighting Germany, Stalin dissolved the Comintern. This event was hailed as a Soviet effort to reduce dissension between the Russians and their Western Allies (which it no doubt was); but, significantly, the resolution of the Presidium of the Communist International, without making this point, speaks instead of the "Deep differences in the historic paths of development of various countries, differences in their character and even contradictions in their social orders, differences in the level and the tempo of their economic and political development . . . [which] conditioned different problems affecting the working class of the various countries." This plurality of problems, different for each country, had, as the resolution goes on later to remark, led "the Seventh Congress of the Communist International, meeting in 1935" to urge the Comintern Executive Committee, "in deciding all questions of the working-class movement arising from concrete conditions and peculiarities of each country, to make a rule of avoiding interference in the internal organizational affairs of the Communist parties." Here is a fairly obvious reference to the previous Russian efforts to keep control of these parties and their growing demands for autonomy in determining how they should approach the problems unique to their state. Because of "the growth and the political maturity of Communist parties and their leading cadres in separate countries, and also having in view the fact that during the present war some sections have raised the question," the Comintern was accordingly to be dissolved.[9] In other words, because of the "maturity" of the "cadres," it was threatening to escape Moscow control. Since the Soviet Union at this time was still the only nation officially in Communist hands, it was also a harbinger of what was to come.

Not until September 1947, at a meeting in Poland, did the successor to the Comintern, the *Cominform* (Communist Information Bureau), begin operations with offices at Belgrade. It started, significantly, *after* the Truman Doctrine (March 12, 1947) of containment, the announcement of the Marshall Plan (June 5, 1947), and the June Conference of Great Britain, France, and Russia to consider the implications of Marshall's speech. It came, then, after Molotov declared that the Plan was merely a veiled instrument to extend United States domination and oppose communism. This delay of several months suggests a Soviet hesitancy over its ability to control such a movement. Doubts were overcome only by the need to unite Communist states, if possible, to oppose Western policy. The initial declaration of the Cominform

---

[9] See *NYT*, May 23, 1943, for the text.

(representing Yugoslavia, Poland, Bulgaria, Romania, Hungary, Russia, Czechoslovakia, Italy, and France) cited the efforts of the United States and Britain to "establish their dominant position." This led to the necessity for "the anti-imperialistic, democratic camp [to] close its ranks, draw up an agreed program of actions and work out its own tactics against the main forces of the imperialist camp. . . ." It was considered "that the absence of contacts among the Communist Parties . . . is a serious shortcoming in the present situation. Experience has shown that such lack of contacts among the Communist Parties is wrong and harmful. . . ." [10] On October 5, 1947, the first Cominform objective was announced as opposition to the "Truman-Marshall Plan."

Any doubts about controlling the movement were soon justified. Stalin was unsuccessful in persuading Tito to withdraw his support from the Greek Communists, and following Tito's open break with Moscow, the headquarters of the Cominform had to be shifted from Yugoslavia. Similarly, with China, Stalin was unable to make his will prevail. Apparently Stalin favored the Czechoslovak *coup d'état*, but clearly Stalin did not favor extending communism where he could not control it. It is also clear that Stalin was unable to control the actions of some Communist satellite states, such as Yugoslavia and China, where the Red Army was not in actual physical occupation. Apparently the policies followed by these states were considered by him to be opposed to Russian national interests (or, if one prefers, the ultimate interests of world communism—for in practice it amounted to substantially the same thing as far as policy was concerned) irrespective of their immediate effect upon increasing the size and the power of the Soviet bloc. Stalin's successors have not held to precisely the same policies but they have been equally agile in arguing for doctrinal interpretations consistent with their version of Soviet interests—as we shall see.

Even this short exploration indicates a consistent attempt by Soviet Russia to implement communism, internally and externally, in ways not incompatible with basic interests of the Russian state. Internally communism has served to spur the industrialization of the Soviet Union and provide a rationale and a source of morale to counteract the severe demands made upon the people.[11] Externally communism has been used to hamper the policies of antagonistic states by marshaling local Communist parties against them. In the last twenty-five years, as the non-Russian Communist parties have gained a certain measure of independence, Russia has experienced increasing difficulty in exercising control. What was already showing itself in the days of the Comintern became now explicit. Then even Communist parties in states where communism

---

[10] *North Atlantic Treaty*, Senate Document No. 48, 81st Congress, 1st Session, pp. 116 ff.

[11] This is in no way meant to deny the impact of communism on every facet of Russian life or its transformation of Soviet society. But these changes, whatever else their intent, were also made to serve the purpose of increasing Soviet power so that Soviet Russia could survive in a hostile world.

had not come to power had been restless under Moscow's direction. After World War II, in states where communism had newly taken power the resistance to Moscow's control varied from Tito's completely independent course to the semi-autonomy of Gomulka's Poland. Those who went too far, and began to oppose socialism itself, and who could be taught a lesson without enormous risks, suffered the penalty—Hungary in 1956. Communist China's ideological argument with Soviet Russia which led to the Moscow Conference of eighty-one Communist parties to restore ideological unity in November 1960, showed this process still further advanced. For both external and internal reasons communism in China and communism in Russia have become distinguishable from each other in certain respects. Which tenets of communism appear most pertinent and compelling to particular Communist states has an obvious relationship to the conditions each such state confronts. Thus the Sino-Soviet dispute and the rise of "polycentrism" in European communism is actually the latest stage of a development with a long history.

The net conclusion to be drawn is that Communist ideology in Russia has not in any obvious way been inconsistent with the attainment of traditional Russian national interests. There are no important evidences that ideological considerations have dictated the following of policy which, in the absence of communism, would obviously have been rejected as contrary to Russian national interests.

To sum up, the Soviet Union today pursues a policy both more vigorous and worldwide than that of Tsarist Russia. Some such changes would no doubt have come about simply from the substantially increased power of the Soviet Union. More significantly, traditional Russian policy objectives have not been abandoned as a consequence of Soviet communism, and the problems of attaining national security are still very much at the core of Soviet policy. But these problems and interests are conceived and evaluated through a new ideological perspective which makes them different from what they otherwise would be thought to be. We shall see how this occurs, in Section 4.

3 Sources of Confusion: Western Stereotypes and Estimates

A third source of confusion in much of the West's analysis of Soviet policy arises out of three stereotyped views that frequently encourage either overestimates or underestimates of Soviet capacities.

One such stereotype is the view that communism, as a system repugnant to Western democrats, exists in the Soviet Union and elsewhere only by virtue of the exercise of naked force and terror. Accepting this as truth, some commentators assert that the task of the West is to work toward the liberation of the oppressed (both within and outside Russia) who, in the event of war, could be expected to rise up behind Soviet lines in guerrilla and resistance movements. The "proof" offered for this contention is usually an assertion that no free man, given a free choice, would choose communism in preference to democracy.

It is demonstrably true that, behind the Iron Curtain, especially in the Russian-occupied satellite state of East Germany, in Poland, in Romania, and in Hungary, there is great unrest and discontent. The peoples of these four states have been "converted" to communism at the point of the bayonet as a consequence of Russia's advances into Europe at the end of World War II. But in the Soviet Union itself, although important nationalist separatist tendencies exist, as in the Ukraine (where Germany's conquests in World War II were greatly aided by the initial willingness of the people to be "liberated" from the Great Russian yoke), communism is not equated with foreign domination—and thus automatically damned. This is an important difference. Moreover, communism and the conservation of Russia's national interests have not been allowed to come into serious and open conflict as elements entering into Russia's foreign policy, thus engendering popular opposition on nationalist grounds within Russia. And internally communism has been the ideological vehicle by which, despite great human sacrifice, Russia has been successfully industrialized. It has provided the emotional motive power for concrete progress. Moreover, under communism, Russia fought and won a great war, emerging as a world power held in fear and/or respect by the rest of the world. In this glory the meanest peasant can find some vicarious satisfaction.

Even if enthusiasm for communism in Russia originally was far from universal, it now seems to rest upon a perfectly adequate basis of popular support. The Communists enjoyed adequate, continuing popular support during the precarious days of the Russian Revolution, when civil war and foreign intervention alike threatened the fragile Soviet state, or it could never have survived to the present day. Internal dissension and unrest within the Soviet Union over the past decades arose from the peasants' resistance to the forcible collectivization of the land; the periodic purges under Stalin were the outward manifestation of fissures in the Soviet body politic. But even at their height communism in Russia survived, and the peak of popular unrest seems well past.

In any nation, democratic or dictatorial, the prevailing system is accepted by the people unless it is so alien to their own values and has so few redeeming features that it is literally intolerable. But if a system provides sufficient employment possibilities, establishes outlets for the energies and ambitions of the young and capable, is a native rather than foreign-imposed system, and is reasonably efficient (by the standards of the people concerned), it is likely to be retained whether it calls itself democracy, fascism, or communism. Barring the stresses and disintegrative effects of war, which may make intolerable what was tolerable, the danger of popular revolution is relatively small.

In Russia the standard of living, although still low by American standards, has increased substantially over pre-Soviet days. The workers and peasants have far fewer rights than Americans; yet their condition is not bad compared to their expectations. Since Stalin's death even the arbitrariness of the secret police system, always a part of the Russian scene, has been modified. The aspiring young and capable individual in Russia can succeed regardless of his birth or social status, by joining the Communist Party and putting his talents to work for communism. This ability of an individual to be a success within the present system erodes the greatest potential source of counterrevolutionary opposition. And, finally, now that the Soviet system is five decades old, only a few have any real recollection of pre-Communist times. Thus, even if the memory of those years of tsarist weakness and collapse would exercise any particular powers of attraction, who remembers them? This analysis does not add up to a picture of a people merely awaiting the opportunity to overthrow communism in Russia. Whether the army might by a *coup d'état* attempt to seize control of the state (as Beria was accused of plotting with his police) is a very different kind of question.

A second stereotype is the view that communism as an economic system is incapable of achieving the results of democratic capitalism and that on equal terms it simply cannot, value for value, compete.

A distinction is in order here, too. Certainly communism in Russia has not (at least yet) produced a standard of living comparable to that in the United States. It has been a far less efficient system in many ways than capitalism. Again and again shortages of consumer goods, difficulties in agriculture, and the production of inferior manufactures have been revealed. But to ridicule communism, as is so frequently done in America, by comparing the real income of an American worker with a Soviet laborer, creates a misleading standard of comparison and a dangerous attitude of condescension. It ignores the fact that the Soviets have consciously and purposely withheld the greater parts of the fruits of their industrialization from the people, giving them only enough to create some feeling of improved status, and plowing back the bulk of their "profits" into an even larger industrial apparatus and into technological preparedness for war. A jet bomber or atomic missile produced under communism may be technologically the equivalent or even the superior of a similar instrument of war produced by private capitalism. To say of a system which *has* produced atomic and hydrogen bombs, as well as military (and civilian) jet planes of first-class quality, that it will not work because the inducement of private profit is missing, shows an unawareness of the efficacy of alternative incentives. Perhaps, since *sputnik* in 1957 and Yuri Gagarin's spaceship orbit in 1961, this point is more obvious and accepted than it used to be. Perhaps there is now an opposite danger: of accepting these spectacular Soviet achievements too uncritically as evidence of a general economic superiority. Soviet economic progress, while impressive, is extremely spotty. Consider the notorious lag in really good housing.

A third stereotype, which gained currency in the early 1950's, held that the Russians would never give up territory once occupied unless they were expelled by war. Where the first stereotype tends to underestimate Soviet strength in Russia by overestimating the likelihood of popular revolution, and where the second stereotype underestimates Soviet strength by discounting communism as an economic system, the third sterotype errs by overestimating Soviet power. The psychological roots of this overestimate are fairly clear. The fissures and dissensions of the Western bloc are freely advertised to the world; contrariwise, behind the Iron Curtain these are kept more from the light of day. It is easy, therefore, to fall into the habit of being aware of American difficulties in dealing with France or West Germany, and ignoring the very real problems and dangers that beset the Soviet Union in continuing to occupy advanced positions in essentially hostile territory, such as East Germany. The Soviets' maintenance of positions at the point of a bayonet can bring them into a situation of increasing tension from which they will prefer to find a satisfactory path of retreat. Russia, too, must react to situations of this sort by giving ground where it seems desirable or inevitable, just as France did in northern Indo-China in 1954 when its position proved untenable. In October 1954, in a move to avoid friction with Communist China, the Soviets agreed to evacuate Port Arthur within a year. In 1955 Russia evacuated Austria by four-power agreement. In September of the same year the Soviets agreed to evacuate their Porkkala naval base on Finnish soil.

The Soviets are not unlimited in their power. They, too, must be concerned with counterbalancing national interests, because a state that maintains military bases abroad is in a poor position to demand their elimination by others. These moves were obviously dictated by Russian national interests rather than by communism as such; they are concrete demonstrations of the over-rigidity of the stereotype we are examining.

4   Soviet Russia's View of History

IN examining what is too simple or too rigid in common Western views of the relationship between Soviet foreign policy and communism, we have also shown parts of a more complex reality. We must now delineate more positively the important interrelations which do exist. For communism distinctly affects Soviet policy in (1) establishing a particular perspective as to the meaning of world affairs—a special and distinctive view of history—and (2) providing the vocabulary for discussion of policy alternatives.

We have said that Communist ideology has not, in any important respects, led the Soviet Union to follow a policy which, in the absence of such an ideology, would obviously have been rejected as contrary to Russian national interests. This emphasis was not meant to depreciate the importance of Communist ideology, including the view of history that is an integral part of Communist theory, in providing the idea system within which concrete Soviet policy is hammered out. What was meant is that while Russian policy is decided within the framework of this idea system, the idea system itself is sufficiently flexible so that the policy best adapted to Russian needs can be supported on ideological grounds. Soviet policy, just like the foreign policy of non-Communist states, is naturally based upon certain assumptions about developments to be expected in world politics. The discussion of policy alternatives in Russia accordingly is carried on in terms of Marxist concepts and focuses upon such questions as the continuing validity of the thesis of the inevitability of wars among capitalist countries. While such a proposition is argued back and forth in the vocabulary of communism, the very fact that it is argued (as a precondition to fixing or revising policy) indicates that Communist ideology does not automatically and in a literal sense delineate a rigid policy line from which no deviation is possible even where Russia's interests would obviously lead elsewhere.

Consider Stalin's statement on a fundamental Communist doctrine, in his last important work, published in September of 1952. In his *Economic Problems of Socialism in the U.S.S.R.*, he discussed (Chapter 6) "The Question of the Inevitability of Wars Among Capitalist Countries." He wrote:

Some comrades affirm that, in consequence of the development of international conditions after the Second World War, wars among capitalist countries have ceased to be inevitable. They consider that the contradictions [sources of tensions] between the camp of socialism and the camp of capitalism are greater than the contradictions among capitalist countries, that the U.S.A. has made other capitalist countries sufficiently subservient to itself to prevent them from going to war with one another. . . .

These comrades are mistaken. They see the external appearances which glitter on the surface but they fail to see those profound forces which, though at present operating imperceptibly, will nevertheless determine the course of events.

Stalin recalled that Britain, the United States, and France, when Hitler attacked Russia, had not aided Germany, but had entered into a coalition with the U.S.S.R. This coalition had stemmed from their "desire to drown their competitors" and had proved stronger than their hostility to communism. While the United States after World War II had outwardly placed the other capitalist countries "on a dole," Stalin predicted that these states would not "tolerate without end the domination and oppression" of the United States. What guarantees were there that Germany and Japan would not "again rise to their feet . . . wrest themselves from American bondage and . . . live their own independent lives"?

I think there are no such guarantees. But it follows from this that the inevitability of wars among the capitalist countries remains.

It is said that Lenin's thesis that imperialism inevitably gives birth to wars should be considered obsolete since powerful peoples' forces have now grown up which are taking a stand in defence of peace, against a new world war. This is not correct.[12]

These views, expressed in Marxist terminology, can be put in non-Marxist phraseology quite easily. Stalin examined concrete questions: whether the West can hold together as a coalition against the Soviet Union; whether the

---

[12] Leo Gruliow, ed., *Current Soviet Policies*, New York: Praeger, 1953, pp. 7–8. Used by permission of *The Current Digest of the Soviet Press*, New York.

apparent contemporary division of a large part of the world into opposing blocs ("the camp of socialism and the camp of capitalism") is actually so solidly based upon the national interests involved as to endure; and whether Germany and Japan, in their efforts to follow an independent course, will not eventually cause a new war between themselves and the other non-Communist great powers.

From this analysis Stalin concluded that the "aim of the present movement for peace is to arouse the masses . . . for the struggle . . . to avert a new world war. Consequently it does not pursue the aim of overthrowing capitalism and establishing socialism. . . . In this respect [it] differs from the movement during the first world war to turn the imperialist war into a civil war." The "present peace movement" could, under certain circumstances, "possibly develop in one place or another into a struggle for socialism." But its "most probable" result, if successful, would be to cause the resignations of "bellicose" governments and in other ways bring about "a temporary preservation" of peace.

> This is good, of course. Even very good. But this, however, is still insufficient to eliminate altogether the inevitability of wars among capitalist countries. It is insufficient since with all these successes of the peace movement imperialism still remains and retains power, and consequently the inevitability of wars also remains.
>
> In order to eliminate the inevitability of wars imperialism must be destroyed.[13]

In other words Stalin, at the close of his long career and in the middle of the Cold War, did not himself believe that the real post-World-War-II alignment of forces was West vs. Communist bloc! He anticipated inevitable new wars among capitalist states whose disintegrative effects could be exploited for the further spread of communism. He saw the role of Communist parties abroad in non-Communist states as presently primarily concerned with fighting such warlike tendencies in an effort to preserve peace rather than with bringing about local Communist regimes through revolution. Yet the fact that "some comrades" saw the situation in other terms and considered Lenin's thesis obsolete because of the growth of "powerful people's forces" indicates that extremely dissimilar points of view—as to the nature of the foreign-policy situation confronting Russia—were held within the Soviet Union even during Stalin's years of absolute rule.

Thus the merits of very diverse tactics and strategy for Soviet Russia are argued out in Communist terminology within the framework of Communist theory. The tactics are adjusted to specific cases, and the strategy is adapted to specific decades—all within Communist theory. Where, however, the Marxist outlook makes its most telling and permanent effect upon Soviet policy is in providing what the Germans call a *Weltanschauung*: a fundamental philosophy of world affairs. This most important effect is in providing a theory to explain the nature and over-all development of the state system through the centuries.·

---

[13] *Ibid.*

In this view the causes of war are essentially economic. Since capitalism operates on the basis of a quest for profits, and since it is assumed that capitalist nations are controlled by big business, the Marxists postulate that the exhaustion of large profit possibilities within the domestic economies of capitalist states through overproduction leads them to fight over markets abroad, and, furthermore, that wars and preparations for war absorb overproduction and increase private profits for the capitalists. It is maintained that the elimination of classes, including the capitalists, and the coming to power of the masses of the people in the "dictatorship of the proletariat" will result within a Communist state in the nationalization of production, regulated in the interests of the people. Since Communist states, it is asserted, eliminate profit-seeking, they are by nature non-imperialistic and peace-loving. Yet they see themselves in danger of being attacked by capitalist states and/or of being drawn into world wars caused by conflicts and aggressions between and among capitalistic states.

Regardless of whether this view seems far-fetched or not, this fundamental philosophy of approach is an essential tenet of Communist beliefs. Although there may be disagreement over tactics and strategy on how to deal with or exploit this over-all world trend, this view is the rock upon which Communist faith rests. At the same time that this belief leaves the Soviet leaders reasonable free to decide specific tactics and strategy, it does state the essentials of how they think world politics at root operate. Bearing this in mind, it becomes clear that the inevitability of war between capitalism and communism arises, in the Marxist view, not from Soviet intentions to commit aggression but from the "inevitable" aggressions of capitalist states arising out of their own economic contradictions. When the Soviets talk of the possibilities of "coexistence," they are discussing whether or not these economic contradictions in the period they are referring to at the time will or will not produce war. Thus, at the 20th Congress of the Soviet Communist Party, meeting in the Grand Palace of the Kremlin in February 1956, Nikita S. Khrushchev declared that "there is no fatal inevitability of war" between Russia and the West, because "The Socialist (Communist) camp is invincible." He not only cited a weakening in the position of the Western powers in the East and a growing rivalry among capitalistic states, but he pointed to the decline of the postwar economic boom in the United States.

The basic orientation of the Soviet views, under both Stalin and Khrushchev is almost the reverse of the popular assumption in the West that Communist theory puts its blessing upon deliberate resort to world war as policy. It should also be clear that the further popular belief that the Communists are slaves to a rigid and completely unalterable theory is equally shallow. The basic orientation of Soviet ideas on war within this view of history is not offensive but defensive. They see themselves not as attackers but as the potential victims of attack by a capitalism faced with its own destruction because of its internal contradictions.

This view in no way guarantees the West that the Soviet Union will not use the Red Army for aggression if sufficient temptation arises or sufficient *raison d'état* exists: just as she attacked Poland for such reasons in 1939. And she would no doubt garnish her aggression with Marxist justifications even though the theory does not lean in that direction.

It is well to remember that "soft" Khrushchev also said, in early January 1961: "If the ruling classes oppose the revolution with violence and refuse to submit to the will of the people, the proletariat must crush their resistance, resort to arms and launch a resolute civil war." [14]

5 *The Transformation of the Soviet Bloc and the Sino-Soviet Dispute*

STALIN, at the height of his power, could not gain unquestioned adherence to his views except where the Red Army gave him the physical instrument to enforce obedience. His attempts to dictate the policy of other Communist states who had effective control of their own nations, failed. The insistence of foreign Communist parties upon following their own paths to "socialism," is (as we saw) not new. But so long as no Communist party outside the Soviet Union controlled an actual government, the challenge to Soviet views was largely ineffective. The Soviet Union and Communist orthodoxy were essentially synonymous.

Stalin's death left the Soviet Union with two important and connected problems to resolve. Domestically, the Stalinist terror which had transformed the Soviet state into a one-man dictatorship, had to be liquidated. Internationally, the Soviet bloc had to be changed into a group of states sharing a common ideology, who would accept the leadership of the Soviet Union as the senior partner. These problems were connected because "Stalinist" leaders held power in certain of the "satellites," and depressurizing either the Soviet Union or the bloc, could lead to the unleashing of powerful disruptive forces. Collective leadership, restored in the Soviet Union, led logically to the same sequence in the bloc. But once controls were loosened, could there be any stopping place?

The Soviets had little choice as to transforming the system, for several reasons. Tito and Mao's independent course could not very well be altered by coercion. But Yugoslav and Chinese independence set an example which the other Communist states wished to follow. The rigid program for collectivizing agriculture and for forced-draft industrialization in the bloc were building pressures higher. Once Stalin died, since no single Soviet leader had the power to rule singlehandedly, collective leadership had to be restored—even apart from the consideration that collective leadership was a more "legitimate" expression of traditional Communist views. The need to consolidate the post-Stalinist regime and conciliate opposing views at home necessarily required also introducing more flexibility in bloc relations. Preoccupation with the

---

[14] See *NYT* (Section 4), February 26, 1961.

problems of succession at home led as a natural corollary to placing Soviet relations with other Communist states on a more equal basis. There were also the long-suppressed demands of the Soviet people for some improvement in their living standard which could not be ignored. Such demands, while they could be suppressed effectively only by a Stalin now dead, could be achieved effectively only by a regime which did away with the police-terror state.

Of all the subsequent steps, therefore, one had primary importance and was necessary for all of these reasons. Stalin could not simply be succeeded by a more benevolent regime; his crimes had to be exposed as a prelude to effective reconstruction, at home and abroad.

Stalin died in March 1953. Before the year was out Beria, the secret police chief, had been executed. Malenkov became Prime Minister but Khrushchev took over the party. When, on February 8, 1955, Malenkov was ousted and replaced by Bulganin, Khrushchev continued in office, dominating Soviet politics for most of a decade—but not in a Stalinist sense. Khrushchev was henceforth to be the spokesman for Soviet views (especially after his success-ful appeal in June 1957 from a hostile Presidium to the Central Committee which backed him), but these were never solely his views.

At the crucial 20th Congress of the Communist Party of the Soviet Union in February 1956, Khrushchev made the remarks, already cited, that war be-tween the capitalist and socialist blocs was no longer inevitable—a clear break with Stalinist (and Leninist) doctrine. Mikoyan on the third day openly criti-cized Stalin: "For some twenty years we actually had no collective leader-ship." Then on February 25 came the famous "secret speech" denouncing Stalin and "the cult of the individual." [15] Khrushchev here destroyed the myth that Stalin was Lenin's chosen successor. He revealed the friction be-tween Lenin and Stalin in Lenin's last days, citing a letter from Lenin to Stalin: "I have no intention to forget so easily that which is being done against me . . . I ask you, therefore, that you weigh carefully whether you are agreeable to retracting your words and apologizing or whether you prefer the severance of relations between us." Khruschchev went on: "As later events have proven, Lenin's anxiety was justified . . . Stalin originated the concept 'enemy of the people.' This term automatically rendered it unneces-sary that the ideological errors of a man or men engaged in a controversy be proven . . . This led to glaring violations of revolutionary legality . . ." Over thirteen years elapsed between the 18th and 19th Party Congresses while Stalin ruled with an iron hand. "It was determined that of the 139 members and candidates of the Party's Central Committee who were elected at the 17th Congress [and thus predominately Old Bolsheviks who had fought the Russian Revolution], 98 persons, i.e., 70 per cent, were arrested and shot (mostly in 1937–38)." The record shows "indignation in the hall," as well it might.

---

[15] The speech was not made public within the Soviet Union although a text was made available by the Department of State on June 4. Not until late in 1961 did the Soviets dare to publicize this viewpoint widely within the Soviet Union.

While this exposé permitted the air to be cleared for a return to more collective rule within Russia and thus permit reorganization of the economy, it
also led to the stirrings within the satellites which culminated in late 1956 in
the successful Polish bid for more independence and the tragic developments
in Hungary. The new course, despite the Hungarian suppression, continued
thereafter, leading by 1965 to evacuation of Soviet troops from Romania, the
refusal of Romania to accept its role in COMECON, and to the opening of
fresh contacts on several levels between the former "satellites" and Western
Europe. Relations between Tito and Khrushchev fluctuated rather widely,
especially as all these developments gradually became linked to the growing
Sino-Soviet dispute. Albania stopped attending Warsaw Pact meetings.

Khrushchev, whose policies brought the threat of a nuclear war much nearer
over Germany in 1958–1961 and over Cuba in 1962, was simultaneously
being accused by the Chinese Communists of "softness," a lack of revolutionary vigor, and—eventually—of "adventurism." This makes for a confusing
picture since Khrushchev's actual policies toward the West were anything but
soft. Furthermore, as we shall see later, Soviet policies in Europe became
more rigid. But at the same time Khrushchev's policies toward China, coupled
with his doctrinal revisions, were antagonizing the Chinese. Specifically, the
Soviet Union cut back its aid program, refused to really assist the Chinese
in nuclear development, and finally withdrew its technicians altogether. Trade
fell 67 per cent between 1960 and 1963. These actions were resented by the
Chinese for obvious reasons of national interest. The *form* which the Chinese
attack on the Soviets took, however, was doctrinal, and was argued as we
would expect in largely doctrinal vocabulary. Specifically, the Chinese saw
grave danger in Khrushchev's proposition that capitalists might under certain
circumstances no longer foment wars against socialist states.

Khrushchev's 1956 statement rejects Leninist-Stalinist theory on two
counts: by embracing the concept of a "camp of socialism" versus a "camp of
capitalism," and by arguing that capitalists can be deterred from war by superior socialist strength. The Communist Chinese agree with the camp versus
camp interpretation. What they have been disputing is the Khrushchev thesis
that the overwhelming destructiveness of the new weapons, of which Russia
has her full share, will induce the capitalist states to refrain from all-out, open
war. The Chinese are not arguing *for* a thermonuclear war; they are arguing
that the capitalist camp will not allow its own transformation from within
without a bloody international conflict. And they are not willing to soft-pedal
the aid to revolution abroad which then automatically increases the possibility
of war. Further, they have less faith in diminishing tension through diplomatic initiatives. They are even afraid that disarmament discussions will
spread illusions among Communists which will cause them to relax more than
is safe. That the Chinese view is related to and arises out of Communist
China's foreign-policy situation and experiences is reasonably apparent.

The Russians argue that the Chinese stand is for "passive coexistence,"
which can allow a drift to war, in contrast to their own "active coexistence"

which will prevent it. In the September 1960, *Kommunist* (the Russian theoretical monthly) the point has been spelled out further: "the working class cannot conceive of the creation of a Communist civilization on the ruins of world centers of culture, on desolated land contaminated with thermonuclear fallout, which would be an inevitable consequence of such a war. For some peoples the question of socialism would in general cease to exist: they would physically vanish from the planet. It is thus clear that *a present-day nuclear war in itself can in no way be a factor that would accelerate revolution and bring the victory of socialism closer.* On the contrary, it would hurl mankind, the world revolutionary workers' movement, and the cause of the building of socialism and communism back by many decades." [16]

Khrushchev is reported to have said, at the Moscow Communist Conference of 1960, that the Chinese in indicting the "insanity of decaying imperialism" ignored the fact that "the American bourgeoisie is divided against itself" with one group seeing clearly the folly of nuclear war and wanting peace.[17] But it is here that Khrushchev's "revisionism" is most marked and the Chinese are on the "conservative" side: traditional Communist theory believes in the impossibility of coexistence over the long run because of the supposed inability of capitalist states to resolve their economic contradictions without producing new world wars.

The declaration at the end of the Moscow Conference did not really reconcile these views but rather glossed them over. While it argued "the alternative today" was "peaceful coexistence . . . or destructive war" it also said that "the aggressive nature of imperialism has not changed" and that "imperialism . . . persists in preparing a new world war." [18] The evening before returning to Peking, on December 7, 1960, President Liu Shao-chi of China, at a huge Soviet-Chinese "friendship rally" in Moscow's Lenin Stadium, kissed the cheek of President L. I. Brezhnev of Russia and said: "Russian-Chinese friendship is inviolable, eternal, indestructible, and firm as the Himalayas." What actually followed was a continuation of the bitter dispute, except that by 1963 it became open and public.

Khrushchev had been led to this revisionism by compelling reasons. Orthodox Marxism held that capitalists must cause wars. These wars in a nuclear age would destroy people by the scores (even hundreds) of millions. Consider the dilemma of orthodox Communist doctrine. Its main article of faith was its ultimate "inevitable" triumph because capitalists could not by conscious act escape the consequences which history would produce for them—their own demise. If capitalists were condemned to foment wars which would in turn lead to their own destruction, it would also in a nuclear age lead to the physical destruction of socialists as well. This made mockery of an appeal to

---

[16] As cited in Zbigniew Brzezinski, "A Book the Russians Would Like to Forget," *The Reporter*, December 22, 1960. Italics in work cited.

[17] See the interesting article by Isaac Deutscher, "The New Communist Manifesto," *The Reporter*, January 5, 1961.

[18] See NYT, December 7, 1960, for the complete text.

join the "wave of the future" by becoming Communist. While in the West some were saying, "Better Red than dead," the Communists were faced with the futility of arguing, "Better Red, then dead!" Faced with this dilemma Khrushchev and his colleagues argued that bourgeois (capitalist) elements were not foreordained to follow an inevitable path, that war was "no longer inevitable." But if capitalists could refrain from significant, previously "inevitable" actions in one respect, why not in others? The path of reasoning which did away with automatic, "scientific" cause and effect, also destroyed the inevitability of communism's triumph. It led by stages to a toleration of accommodations to the capitalist world which might still be called merely tactical but which in effect and consequence went much further. The Cuban Missile Crisis of 1962 gave way to the Test Ban Treaty of 1963. Was it only a first step?

The Chinese, embittered and frustrated by American (i.e., imperialist-capitalist) actions on their own doorstep, found it irritating to see an accommodation at their own expense. They considered the comfortable Russians to be abandoning the struggle. "Stalinist" views were exalted by the very Chinese Communists who had been callously abandoned to seek their own success by Stalin's actual policies!

The Moscow conference which led to the Test Ban agreement began on July 15. The treaty was initialed on July 25, signed August 5. It passed the U.S. Senate on September 24 and had the signatures of 99 states before that month was out. During these same months the Sino-Soviet dispute became more open and then virtually public.

The Chinese began this phase of the exchange with an open letter to the C.P.S.U. on June 14 which they next distributed in the Soviet Union illegally. (Later they also scattered it from the Trans-Siberian express as it crossed Russia!) On July 5 their delegation was received in Moscow for discussions. On July 20, they withdrew. Meanwhile, on July 14, the Soviets published the Chinese charges and their own defense. The Chinese asserted: "If the general line of the international Communist movement is one-sidedly reduced to 'peaceful co-existence,' 'peaceful competition' and 'peaceful transition,' this is to violate the revolutionary principles of the 1957 Declaration and the 1960 Statement, to discard the historical mission of proletarian world revolution and to depart from the revolutionary teachings of Marxism-Leninism." [19] The Soviets began their reply by remarking that in January they had urged "that open polemics in the Communist movement be stopped so that disputed issues could be discussed calmly and in a businesslike manner and solved on a principled Marxist-Leninist basis." [20]

The Soviet open letter put the date when the Chinese "began retreating from the general course of the world communist movement" as April 1960.

---

[19] See for virtually the full text of this letter, David Floyd, *Mao Against Khrushchev*, pp. 406–420. Floyd's book provides not only an excellent analysis but the texts of documents bearing on the dispute up through July 1963.

[20] Full text is in *Two Major Soviet Statements on China*. Crosscurrents Press, 1963.

The Soviets detailed the behind-the-scenes disagreements patched over in the 1960 Statement. They charged that the decline since in Sino-Soviet trade and delivery of industrial plant ("dropped forty times") had taken place "on the initiative of the Chinese leaders." The Soviets restated their position: ". . . there is no fatal inevitability of war between states. This conclusion is not the fruit of good intentions but the result of a realistic, strictly scientific analysis of the balance of class forces in the world arena; it is based on the gigantic might of world socialism." What did the Chinese argue? That "an end cannot be put to wars as long as imperialism exists; peaceful coexistence is an illusion. . . ." Also, "the Chinese comrades obviously underestimate all of the danger of a thermonuclear war. 'The atomic bomb is a paper tiger,' it 'is not terrible at all,' they contend. The main thing, they say, is to put an end to imperialism as quickly as possible, but how and with what losses this will be achieved seems to be a secondary question. . . . We would like to ask the Chinese comrades, who offer to build a wonderful future on the ruins of the old world destroyed by a thermonuclear war, if they have consulted the working class of the countries where imperialism dominates on this matter?" The Chinese view "may engender the well-justified suspicion that this is no longer a class approach . . . but involves some entirely different aims."

Answering the Chinese charges that the Soviets made an " 'adventurist' mistake by supplying rockets to Cuba and then, allegedly 'capitulated' to American imperialism," the Soviets explained that they had "possessed trustworthy information that an armed aggression by United States imperialism against Cuba was to start shortly." They sent missiles. In withdrawing these they got an American "commitment not to invade Cuba" which "made it possible to frustrate the plans of the extreme adventurist circles of American imperialism that were ready to go the whole hog. As a result, it was possible to defend revolutionary Cuba and save peace."

This in no way indicated softness on the class struggle: ". . . when we speak of peaceful coexistence we mean the interstate relations of the socialist countries with the countries of capitalism. The principle of peaceful coexistence, naturally, can in no way be extended to relations between the antagonistic classes in capitalist states; it is impermissible to extend it to the struggle of the working class against the bourgeoisie for its class interests, to the struggle of the oppressed peoples against the colonialists. The C.P.S.U. resolutely stands opposed to peaceful coexistence in ideology."

The Chinese reacted with a new attack on September 1 against the nuclear test ban which brought a further substantial statement from the Soviets on September 21.[21] The Soviets charged the Chinese statement was "no longer a comradely discussion between Communists but an action by people who are determined to discredit the C.P.S.U. and the Soviet Union at any cost . . ." The "unseemly stand of the Chinese Government on the nuclear test ban treaty is not supported by the peoples." Ultimately, "Imperialism props its

---

21 See for text, *Statement of the Soviet Government, Sept. 21, 1963*. New York: Crosscurrents Press, 1963.

domination by force of arms. To achieve disarmament would . . . deal a blow at the forces of imperialist aggression. . . . It is an elementary truth that as long as imperialism exists it will retain its aggressive nature, its contradictions. It is fraught with war. Proceeding from this fact the Chinese leaders contend that war is inevitable. Communists cannot take such a fatalist position." The Chinese Government has "proclaimed for all to hear that despite all its economic difficulties, it is prepared to work to create its own atomic weapons even if it takes a hundred years. Thus we see that the schemes of the Peking 'giants' are quite transparent." The Soviets went on to characterize Chinese charges of lack of U.S.S.R. support over the Formosa issue as "utter nonsense." The bitterest Soviet scorn, though, was reserved for Mao Tse-tung's "pronouncements," quoted in the Chinese letter of September 1 in (said the Soviets) altered form: ". . . If worse comes to worst, half of humanity will perish but half will remain. But imperialism will be razed off the face of the earth and the whole world will go socialist." The Soviets quoted from the "original" Chinese statement: "The words of Mao Tse-tung, expressed by him in 1957 . . . were addressed to those people who allege that in case a nuclear war is unleashed by imperialism mankind will perish. We [the Chinese] do not agree with those views, so pessimistic and full of despair. We say that if imperialism unleashes a nuclear war, it will at most bring death to half the population of the globe . . . We are confident of the bright future of mankind." The Soviet comment on this: "Monstrous talk indeed. What 'wonderful future' can one speak of in view of the prospect of the annihilation of half of mankind! There is something else no less dangerous: the Chinese leaders are making their forecasts regarding the possible consequences of war . . . because they wish to justify a definite policy. The authors of the statement themselves do not deny that. . . . they write: 'Essentially the question is what policy, after all, should be followed in the face of the nuclear blackmail and nuclear threat of American imperialism—to offer resistance or to surrender?' "

The Soviets then went on to discuss Chinese frontier revisionism, remarking that "the Chinese-Indian armed conflict was a complete surprise both for the Soviet people and the whole world public." The Soviets accused the Chinese of "more than 5,000 violations of the Soviet frontier from the Chinese side" in 1962 alone. The Soviets had offered consultations which the Chinese had evaded. "This cannot but make us wary . . ."

In the next years, after Khrushchev's fall, the dispute continued. At the end of January 1966, the official Peking *People's Daily*, for example, said: "The Soviet Union is preparing the ground to strike a new deal with U.S. imperialism just as the Lyndon Johnson administration is quickening its pace towards a wider war of aggression against Viet-Nam."

It should be abundantly clear that the Sino-Soviet argument reflects fundamental differences in the national interests of the two nations as perceived by the Soviet and Chinese governments. Communist ideology affects the views of both by providing the vocabulary of the dispute and the picture of the nature of the world's development to which each points to justify its own policy. What Communist ideology does *not* do, though, is to ensure that the policies of these states will be the same.

6 *Conclusions*

THERE are two major problems that the foreign policy of the Soviet Union presents to the West. One is a conventional problem: the overextension of Russian power in Europe due to its occupation of German-speaking lands and its links with Communist China (to the extent that these survive the friction noted). How to cope with the negative effects of these two circumstances on American interests should consequently be major strategic aims of United States and Western foreign policy. The other problem is an unconventional or ideological one that also has two aspects: understanding the influence of Communist precepts upon the tactics and strategy of Soviet foreign policy and dealing with the Russian foreign-policy implement that the existence of Communist parties in countries outside the Soviet bloc represents. We have seen that Communist ideology provides the Soviets with a *Weltanschauung,* a philosophy of approach to, and expectations from, international relations—giving them "the large picture" of what the world is like and where it is heading. It also provides the rationale or justification for doing what seems desirable per se, both internally and externally, on a day-to-day basis. Since the Russians believe in this "large-picture" Marxist view of history, Soviet foreign policy is shaped by the Communist ideology to that extent. But this Soviet picture of the future world assumes that capitalist states will come to grief by their initiation of wars; the picture postulates wars into which the Soviet Union may be drawn, rather than wars that the Soviets, in a crusade for communism, must start. As to the second aspect—the implement that non-Soviet-bloc Communist parties represent—it is evident that, as these groups have reached "maturity" (i.e., a certain power and status in their own lands), they have become correspondingly more difficult for the Soviet Union *to control in her own interests.* This does not mean that non-Soviet Communist parties are unimportant in international relations but that their importance may lie in a somewhat different direction from that ordinarily assumed.

Because Soviet Marxism includes no concept of inevitable Russian aggression does not afford the West grounds for relaxation. Basically the Russian state, like any great power, and especially so because of its actually "super" capacity to bring war and destruction upon the West, represents a threat to all other non-friendly states by the very existence of its power. In these circumstances the West would be very unwise to neglect its defenses, for power in being is a subtle temptation toward power in use; it would be the height of imprudence to proceed on the assumption that Soviet Russia is more capable of resisting such temptations than other great states have been in the past.

It should also be clear that Soviet problems have not become easier to resolve since World War II. Her policy dilemmas have no easy answers. The over-extension of the Soviets in Europe creates dangers and tensions on one flank even as friction with a newly powerful although still allied China causes concern on the other. Revisions of Marxism to retain a current appeal to potential recruits leads to a revisionism fraught with additional dangers, as the "automaticity" of a socialist triumph becomes undermined by these very revisions. Internal problems of economics and politics continue. Dealing with the underdeveloped nations creates other problems, as we shall see in later chapters. The overall picture is one of a powerful nation whose security is more difficult to attain than it was in the first "easy" years of the immediate postwar era when the West was disorganized and weak, when Germany had not revived, and when China had not yet embarked upon open rivalry.

CHAPTER 26

The European Powers: I

We do not want to put anyone in the shade, but we demand for ourselves a place in the sun.

PRINCE VON BÜLOW
December 6, 1897

The division of Germany is abnormal. It is against human and Divine law and against nature.

CHANCELLOR KONRAD ADENAUER
September 9, 1955[1]

W E have devoted greater space to an analysis of the policy of the United States and the Soviet Union than we can afford individually for the other powers. This fact in no way implies that Europe, Africa, the Middle East, Latin America, and Asia are of importance simply as the theater of interaction, the geographical scene of super power rivalries. Even in the first postwar years such a view was questionable. Today it would be obviously highly inappropriate, as we have been at pains to point out. The policies of the super powers have direct relevance to what happens in these areas, but it is equally true that the policies and problems of the nations in these regions will affect the ultimate success of super power policies. What permits us to observe this interaction in these areas as entities is the fact that European, Asian, and "third world" policies cluster about discernible major problems.

In Europe the problems are three: (1) how and if Western Europe is to work out a new and greater coordination of national interests sufficient to allow its voice to be heard effectively in a world of giant powers; (2) how and if Eastern Europe is to gain freedom to follow policies which are not automatically subservient to Soviet interests; and (3) how and if the great problem of Central Europe—the division of Germany—is to be resolved in some fashion not inconsistent with (1) and (2).

Although the popular attention is more easily taken by Western Europe's progress and then by the growing signs of Balkan independence, the resolution of the problems in this areas actually turns ultimately on some solution for the German problem. Germany is the link, geographically and politically, between the problems preoccupying either extremity of Europe.

The reasons are two: First, West Germany is the most significant economic unit in the Common Market. Membership in the Market has so far obviously

---

[1] At his first conference with Premier Bulganin in the Kremlin.

benefited Germany (in helping to restore her economic health, in gaining her a positive relationship with the West which retires the shadow of the Nazi era into the background, in providing a potential advantage as leverage in dealing with her other problems). The West Germans, if they could gain East Germany through peaceful reunification, and add it into the Community, would dominate it and benefit from it still more. But what if, on the other hand, membership in the Community and in NATO, come to be seen as impediments to German reunification? Suppose Germany envisaged the problem as one of choosing between the counterbalancing interests of coordination/union with Western Europe, *or* reunification. Would she sacrifice unity for the whole in return for the prosperity and well-being of the part? It is true that the issue has so far not been posed in stark and unavoidable fashion; but it is implicit in the present unnatural situation in the heart of Europe.

The second reason why Germany is the link is that the strivings in the former satellite states for more independence from the Soviet Union are necessarily confined within very narrow bounds so long as the German question retains its present form. This is most obvious in the case of Poland, approximately 40 per cent of whose present territory is composed of lands historically part of Germany. Of the two German states, Poland's western frontier has been accepted only by the so-called German Democratic Republic (the area we commonly call East Germany). This GDR is the only European Communist state whose adherence to the Soviet line on almost every point can be taken for granted: she has highly questionable support from her own people and the regime has relied for its existence on Soviet bayonets; it has a Soviet occupation force of roughly a quarter-million troops; it has to live side by side with a "real" Germany whose attraction for its people is greater than its own. The consequences for Poland are that Poland has no real acceptance from Germany, Poland has a Soviet puppet state on one side of her with the Soviet Union on the other, Soviet troops continue to transit Poland to and from East Germany. The advantage of having the GDR accept Polish frontiers is minor compared with the disadvantages the situation entails, except that Soviet military support for Poland is absolutely essential unless West Germany and Poland come to terms which Poland feels are really reliable. Restrictions on Polish independence are thus inevitable under present conditions.

In the Balkans the relationship to the German problem is less obvious but also critical. These states fear a resurgent Germany and this fear acts as a counterbalance in their wish for more freedom from the Soviet Union. If a stable and peaceful solution of the German problem came about, these states could use the enhanced position of Germany on their western side as a political counter to the Soviet Union. The Soviets have reason even under present circumstances to allow more freedom in the Balkans. They would have more if Germany were reunified, provided that Germany did not pursue (or appear or want to pursue) an expansionist policy outside of German territory.

Even this short survey shows that the Soviets would have much potentially to lose by agreeing to German reunification. If no other factors affected Soviet policy on Germany, we could expect no real willingness on the part of Russia to agree to reunification. Later we shall see whether other pressures and considerations might lead the Soviets to agree to reunification under certain circumstances. Here our point is much more narrow: we are not discussing the likelihood of reunification but rather the links this issue has to the mainstream of developments in both East and West.

In an age when the popular image of international relations for almost two decades of Cold War has been cast in such simplified terms, it is peculiarly difficult to argue the case for Germany's critical importance in Europe. Germany, like China, arouses strong emotions and anxieties—Germany for her past, China for her future. Any prospect of change in Germany arouses the specter of a new Nazism and violent upheaval for some, while others go to the opposite extreme and ask what difference any change in Germany makes when today only nuclear super powers really count. The error in the first reaction is that Germany today is no stronghold of extremism or adventurism, although she has a natural concern over her division. The error in the second is that if Germany really did not count, and it made no difference, neither the Soviet Union nor the United States would have thought it necessary to have two major crises over her within the space of two postwar decades.

For these reasons, in analyzing European policies, we shall focus our attention first on Germany.

I *Germany: Background Factors*

THE unification of Germany accomplished by Bismarck in 1871 revolutionized the balance of power by creating finally a strong state in the center of Europe. Until then Germany had often served as a convenient battleground for Europe—either for foreign troops or for the wars between the many German states. Both politics and geography had retarded the "inevitable" triumph of all-German nationalism. Not only were the great powers resistant to change in this strategic area, but the internal geography of Germany itself had encouraged the creation of several large states, each of them potential rivals to the rest. Saxony, Bavaria, and Prussia all contested for German leadership. So did Austria (whose Hapsburg rulers held various German territories and long presided over the outmoded Holy Roman Empire which was Germany's only form of unity until Napoleonic times).

The German Empire finally created through Bismarck's strong political leadership and through the instrumentality of the Prussian army was extensive and powerful. We have seen how Bismarck's manipulation of the balance of power kept it so. But even his success left important German areas outside the *Reich*. Austria-Hungary remained a great power with its German and Hungarian peoples in effect ruling over a heterogeneous empire of Czechs, Serbs, Slovaks, Poles, and Italians. The Germans in Austria and in the

Sudetenland of Czechoslovakia thus continued outside the frontiers of the new Germany until Hitler's time.

The accomplishment of unity by force of arms led naturally to an intimate association in German minds between armed force and national unity. Moreover, the German state thus so laboriously created through force obviously rested upon military strength for its survival. Located between the great land powers of France and Russia, without the comparative security that both of these often enjoyed on their eastern or western frontiers, and threatened by the specter of simultaneous invasion from east and west, modern Germany believed that it had to be a military state. The north European plain, allowing easy entrance into Germany from east and west, seemed like an open door that could be closed only by a large standing army and a quick mobilization schedule.

This parallel course of German nationalism and German militarism led first to a series of victories and then to a series of defeats. After World War I, Germany lost not only alien minorities in the east and west but Germans, too. Both in Alsace-Lorraine in the west, and Silesia in the east, German majorities were transferred to neighboring rule. The Saar, too, was put under the League of Nations. After a second defeat in World War II, even discounting for the moment the division of West and East Germany and the loss of Austria, this process was carried further. The ancient citadels of Prussian power in East Prussia were incorporated into Poland and Russia. The humiliation (in the German view) of the Polish Corridor, which after World War I made it necessary for Germans to cross part of Poland to reach part of Germany, was replaced by the even greater humiliation of seeing this separated area pass entirely under Slavic administration. Germans have not concluded from these experiences that one can do without armed forces. But they have seen the futility of two-front wars, with enemies on both flanks. They have not ceased to want unity, but they are less optimistic about its prospects and less disposed to equate success with force.

Neither has defeat shaken the German belief in the necessity for strong government. Given Germany's exposed location in the middle of strong neighbors it has always been obvious to the least educated of Germans that a strong hand at the helm was necessary, and internal dissensions dangerous. (It is no accident that democracy has flourished at its best within states relatively immune from attack—the United States, Great Britain, Scandinavia all illustrate.) Even after losing two world wars, Germany never experienced genuine mass revolution. Its authoritarian leaders were not overthrown from within but lost power through defeat in war. Wilhelm II abdicated for the same reason that Hitler chose suicide. But neither was executed by revolutionists. There is no parallel in German history for the execution of a Charles I, a Louis XVI, or a Tsar Nicholas. Even the assassination attempt on Hitler's life in 1944 was primarily a conspiracy of the military *élite*. Wilhelm II still commanded a loyal Wehrmacht at the end of a lost war, as did Hitler after he had executed the plotters. Each fell from power as a result of external force.

Correspondingly, the establishment of both the Weimar Republic after World War I, and the Bonn Republic after World War II, were not changes freely sought by the German people but initiated by outside pressures. The Weimar government was frequently excoriated as an imposed regime and it failed (as we shall see) to produce either a strong democratic leader able to prevail and endure, or to arouse substantial popular support. The Bonn government, led strongly and ably by the sometimes arbitrary and high-handed Chancellor Adenauer, on the other hand, aroused mass support even though Adenauer was characterized by his opponents initially as the "Chancellor of the Allies."

Germans tolerated Wilhelm's blunders although they led to defeat; they continued to support Hitler although he brought disaster; they rallied behind Adenauer who brought them recovery and prosperity. But they abandoned Weimar for its vacillation. The clue to the common feature in these actions cannot be found in a preference for democracy but in a preference for strong (and, if possible, conservative) leadership. Under Weimar they sought to compensate for the shifting and jostling of political parties for power, and express their nostalgia for a stable executive, by electing the seventy-seven year old conservative Junker, Field Marshal Paul von Hindenburg, to the presidency in 1925. Under Bonn, with greater success, they chose the seventy-three year old conservative Adenauer and re-elected him again and again with prolonged enthusiasm.

German predilection for strong government, which is so deeply rooted in German past experience, is not necessarily incompatible with democracy. But it can be expected to work well in Germany only as it continues to furnish the *Bundesrepublik* with strong, effective government. (This is not necessarily a contradiction in terms, although it could become one.) To the German, the great value of free elections lies in the possibility it may confer of choosing between alternative strong governments.

The total effect of these tendencies and attitudes is that strong German governments are allowed much more latitude by the people, and are less restricted by public opinion, than is commonly the case in America. Conversely, where they are weak, because the hand of authority is uncertain, the scorn of the people still further weakens their authority and limits their discretion. In this respect there is little resemblance to the traditional American view that strong governments are suspect in that they constitute a potential threat to popular liberties. The German today continues to want strong leadership. But he does not want any new disaster. These desires are not incompatible per se. Under certain circumstances, they might become so.

With this background in mind, let us examine the record of German policy as a preliminary to an analysis of the implications of Germany's division for international relations.

2   *The Weimar Republic* (1918–1933)

THE Weimar Republic has often been portrayed as a democratic regime which, like the lamb's fate at the hands of the wolf, was swallowed up by ruthless National Socialists. The implication is that it fell from power because of its own moderation in dealing with the extremists. Actually the government that Hitler displaced in 1933 was hardly less arbitrary than the one he substituted. How this came to be we shall see.

Although the National Assembly—elected in January 1919, to draw up a constitution—contained twice as many Social Democrats as it did members of any other political party, the Socialists controlled less than a majority. From the very first, Germany had a coalition government, with the Center and Democratic parties sharing in the power. This Weimar coalition soon lost its majority; after November 1922, it could govern only with the help of the rightists. Ministries came and went: between 1920 and 1922 there were four governments, the last of them headed by Wilhelm Cuno, an influential industrialist. In August 1923, Cuno was displaced by Gustav Stresemann, the leader of the People's Party. The coalition thus formed by the Center, Democratic, Social Democratic, and People's parties, was one resting on the right-center. For more than six years (1923–1930) this coalition held together.

With the formation of this government Stresemann assumed the leading role in German politics that he retained until his death in 1929. Although his ministry fell in late November 1923, Stresemann remained as foreign minister in the new government of Wilhelm Marx (Center Party). His foreign policy in these years we shall survey in a moment. But first we must remember that between the fall of Stresemann's ministry in late 1923 and the formation of the Brüning cabinet in the spring of 1930, and counting both of these, Germany had six governments.[2] Although this period showed some increase in stability, its rapid change and political ferment was basically uncongenial to the Germans. During this period, dominated by Stresemann more than any other German political figure, the seesaw of election returns kept political power dispersed, with now Socialists, now Center, and now Nationalists gaining. A Center government under Marx (1926) gave way to a Socialist regime under Müller (1928), and then to a new Center cabinet under Brüning (1930), in which the Socialists were replaced by parties of the right.

Stresemann's foreign-policy problem in these years was to reconcile Germany's weakness vis-à-vis France, in a context of the immoderate demands of this shifting coalition and the desires of the German masses for a return to national dignity, power, and prestige. Considering the problem involved, he had to walk a narrow tightrope. He chose a policy of cautious reconciliation with France and England, using Russia as a lever with which to pry conces-

---

[2] Including the Luther cabinet's resignation on December 5, 1925, which President von Hindenburg refused to accept.

sions from the West. The question of Germany's eastern frontiers, where Germany had suffered the most from her defeat, he left carefully open. Under the circumstances he had no other choice. His policy made sense. The only question was whether he could keep sufficient party coalition support to be able to follow this policy, while simultaneously using their restlessness as a lever to move the still reluctant French to grant a gradual improvement of Germany's position.

In February 1925, Stresemann suggested the negotiation of a Rhineland mutual guarantee treaty. This was looked on with favor by the British; the French foreign minister, Aristide Briand, accepted the idea provided Germany became a member of the League (which would imply a certain acceptance of the Versailles *status quo*). As a sign of improved relations, the French evacuated the Ruhr and Düsseldorf and Duisburg in August. In October the Locarno Conference produced the Locarno Treaty of Mutual Guarantee, underwriting the *status quo* of the German-French and German-Belgian frontiers, with Italy and Britain as guarantors. Germany remained unwilling to give a similar guarantee of her eastern frontiers, but with Locarno the climate of Western European relations improved noticeably. In September 1926, Germany took her place in the League. Then in 1929 the Young Plan marked a further easing in Germany's reparations problem. Germany's ratification of it won them evacuation of the Rhineland before the scheduled June of 1930. This was the final fruit of Stresemann's policies. After this point, with the coming of depression, little happened in foreign affairs until the convening of the ill-fated World Disarmament Conference in February 1932. There Germany, with the bulk of its attention concentrated on problems at home, continued to argue without success for equality of armaments with other great powers.

Returning to domestic events, this year of 1930 saw an increasing exercise of the presidential decree and a growing difficulty in forming new governments. In July, von Hindenburg authorized the budget by decree after the Reichstag rejected it. When the Reichstag condemned this action, von Hindenburg dissolved it and placed the budget in effect by decree. The ensuing election of September 30, 1930, came after the cessation of American loans to Germany (on which the Germans had relied for reparations payments) and after German unemployment had risen from 1,368,000 in 1929 to 3,144,000 in 1930. In the new Reichstag the National Socialists won 107 seats (compared with a previous 12), the Communists captured 77 (compared with a previous 54), and the Socialists had 143 (representing a loss of 10 seats). Almost all the moderate parties lost. The Germans in frustration and impatience had turned definitely toward the extreme parties, toward the right much more than toward the left.

In the presidential election of March 1932, von Hindenburg, the nationalist and Junker, received almost 19 million votes, Hitler got 11.3 million, the Nationalist Stahlhelm candidate polled 2.5 million, and the Communist candidate obtained just short of 5 million, out of a total of nearly 38 million.

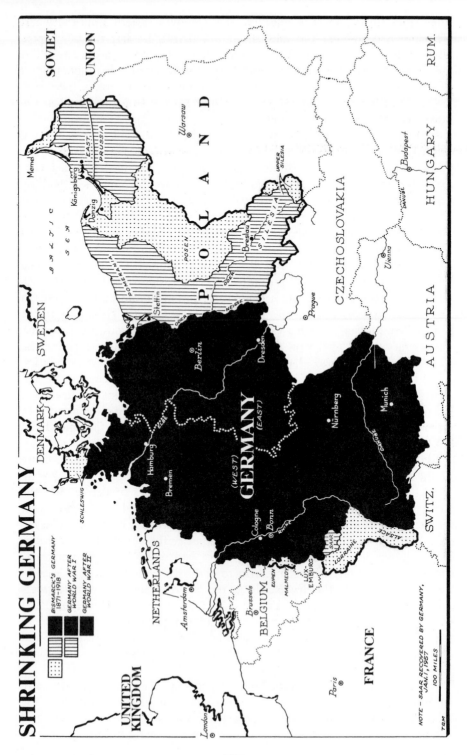

SHRINKING GERMANY

BISMARCK'S GERMANY
1871-1918

GERMANY AFTER
WORLD WAR I

GERMANY AFTER
WORLD WAR II

UNITED
KINGDOM

London ⊙

NETHERLANDS

Amsterdam ⊙

BELGIUM

Brussels ⊙

EUPEN

MALMEDY

LUX-
EMBURG

FRANCE

Paris ⊙

SWITZ.

SAAR

LORRAINE

ALSACE

RHINE

Cologne ⊙
⊙ Bonn

Nürnberg ⊙

Munich ⊙

DANUBE

AUSTRIA

Vienna ⊙

HUNGARY

Budapest ⊙

RUM.

DANUBE

CZECHOSLOVAKIA

Prague ⊙

Dresden ⊙

Berlin ⊙

(WEST)

GERMANY
(EAST)

ELBE

Bremen ⊙

Hamburg ⊙

SCHLESWIG

DENMARK

SWEDEN

B A L T I C   S E A

Memel ⊙

Königsberg ⊙

EAST
PRUSSIA

Danzig ⊙

POMERANIA

Stettin ⊙

ODER

NEISSE

ODER

P O L A N D

POSEN

SILESIA

Breslau ⊙

UPPER
SILESIA

Warsaw ⊙

SOVIET

UNION

NOTE — SAAR RECOVERED BY GERMANY,
JAN., 1957

100 MILES

T&M

This represented a clear rejection of moderate democracy as conceived in the United States. It was also a tacit endorsement of von Hindenburg's overruling of the Reichstag by decree and a renewed indication that the German people preferred a strong-willed leader.

Brüning, despite the election of 1930, remained as Chancellor even though his Center Party no longer commanded confidence in the Reichstag. The difficulties of forming a cabinet responsible to the parliament increased. Political power was spread among three major groups, each unwilling to govern in conjunction with the others. Brüning governed through emergency decrees by the president, and he continued in office only at von Hindenburg's pleasure. Brüning's ineffectiveness was publicly recognized at the end of May 1932, when he was forced to resign after von Hindenburg refused to sanction by decree the division of Junker estates among East Prussian small farmers. Franz von Papen was appointed by the president to form a "ministry of barons," responsible not to the Reichstag but to von Hindenburg himself. Von Neurath became foreign minister and von Schleicher, minister of defense. Von Papen (July 20) removed the Socialist prime minister of Prussia and placed the cities of Brandenburg and Berlin under martial law to prevent further Nazi disorders. The new Reichstag, elected on July 31 (the one chosen 22 months previously had been dissolved on June 4), gave the Nazis 230 seats; the Socialists, 133; the Center, 97; and the Communists, 89. Both extreme right and extreme left had grown in power. The government now had little relevance to the actual wishes of the electorate. Neither the Nazis nor the Communists would agree to enter a coalition. Since a majority was not attainable without one or the other, Germany's parliamentary institutions had reached full deadlock.

3 The Nazi Regime (1933–1945)

VON Hindenburg now offered Hitler the vice-chancellorship, but Hitler's answer was "all or nothing." Next von Hindenburg, by decree, dissolved the Reichstag and again ordered new elections. The November 6 election cost the Nazis some seats, but the deadlock remained. On November 17 von Papen resigned; General von Schleicher formed a new cabinet on December 2. On January 28, 1933, failing to find support from the parties, and von Hindenburg having refused a new dissolution, von Schleicher resigned. On January 30 Adolph Hitler became Chancellor; he selected a cabinet of Nazis and Nationalists and non-party members of the old ruling class. Since he, too, lacked a parliamentary majority, he decided on still another dissolution of the Reichstag. New elections were set for March 5. These facts help to clarify the picture of what happened: contrary to what is so often said, Hitler's initial grasp on the reins of power was every bit as legal as that of the preceding cabinets. But that it also represented the end of the Weimar Republic was well realized.

Hitler moved swiftly to consolidate his power. On February 27, as election time drew close, a "mysterious" fire partly destroyed the Reichstag building. Denouncing this act of arson as a Communist plot, Hitler persuaded von Hindenburg to suspend by decree the constitutional rights of free speech and free press. Nazi storm troopers were now free to "influence" the electorate. On March 5 the Nazis received 44 per cent of the vote (two hundred eighty-eight seats). Together with their Nationalist allies (the party of big business and the aristocracy, who received 8 per cent of the vote and fifty-two seats), they controlled a majority. On March 23 the Enabling Act was passed, giving the regime dictatorial powers until April 1, 1937. Since the Communist Party (eighty-one seats) had been outlawed after the Reichstag fire and since the Center Party (seventy-four seats) did not actively oppose the measure, only ninety-four Social Democratic votes were cast in opposition. Thus the Nazi dictatorship began. And by July 14, 1933, all other political parties except the Nazi had been dissolved.

These events at home soon had their repercussions abroad. In October 1933, Hitler ordered Germany's withdrawal from the Disarmament Conference and from the League of Nations. He resorted increasingly to a policy of unilateral *fait accompli*. Temperamentally he was predisposed in this direction, but from a larger point of view Hitler was in part able to pursue his policy because of Stresemann's earlier successes. Hitler would hardly have been able to remilitarize the Rhineland in March 1936, had not Stresemann achieved the evacuation of the French. Even as it was, he gave orders to retreat at the first show of armed resistance by the French. It had been only in March 1935, that Hitler had formally denounced the Versailles restrictions on armaments and reintroduced conscription. Here, too, he was aided by Stresemann's aiding and abetting of Germany's evasion of those restrictions, so that the basis for a substantial German rearmament already existed.[3] Thus Hitler built on Stresemann's foundation.

Events also played into his hands. The diversion of French and British attention from European affairs caused by Mussolini's defiance of the League and attack on Ethiopia gave him a freer hand than German military power would have permitted him. He carefully timed his Rhineland coup during the League sanctions crisis. In addition, the opposition of the League to Mussolini drove the Italians close to the Germans. Both supported Franco with arms and troops in the Spanish Civil War, which broke out in July 1936, and added one more problem for the already harassed French and British. In October 1936, this *de facto* cooperation was converted by the formation of the Berlin-Rome Axis into a formal partnership. Later in the same year Hitler moved to immobilize the Soviet Union by concluding an Anti-Comintern Pact with Japan. In March 1938, he reaped the fruit of his Italian partnership. Where in the abortive Nazi coup in Vienna in 1934 Mussolini had threatened armed intervention if German troops entered Austria, now Mussolini acquiesced in the *Anschluss* (union) of Austria with the Third

---

[3] For the part played by Stresemann see Hans W. Gatzke, *Stresemann and the Rearmament of Germany*, Baltimore: Johns Hopkins Press, 1954.

Reich. Alienated from Britain and France and heavily involved in Spain, Mussolini offered no resistance. The Munich crisis and the dismemberment of Czechoslovakia (September 1938) were quickly followed in March 1939, by the German annexation of the rump Czech state. Hitler effectively used Anglo-Saxon principles of self-determination to gather into his Reich the German-speaking peoples in Austria and Czechoslovakia; now he openly revealed, by his annexation of a Slavic people, that his ambitions were as yet far from fulfilled. On March 23 Hitler annexed Memel after exerting pressure on Lithuania, and he made demands on Poland for the return of the Polish Corridor. On April 7 Italy again diverted Anglo-French attention from Germany by embarking upon the conquest of Albania, and on the same day Spain joined the Anti-Comintern Pact. On May 22 Germany and Italy concluded a military alliance. On August 20 began the Danzig-Polish crisis over Germany's renewed demands on Poland. The next day the imminent conclusion of a Nazi-Soviet Pact was announced. On August 29 Hitler issued an ultimatum to Poland. On September 1 the attack was launched. World War II had begun.

4 German Defeat and Recovery; the First Berlin Crisis

HOW Hitler brought Germany to great success and equally great destruction and defeat is a story already recounted. With Allied armies closing in on every side, Hitler on April 30, 1945, shot himself in his underground bunker in Berlin. His last message, still breathing hate, urged "unmerciful resistance to the world poisoner of all nations—international Jewry." [4] Grand Admiral Doenitz, whom he had designated his successor, within a few days found himself an Allied prisoner awaiting trial as a major war criminal. Germany no longer had a government.

Since the days of the Russian Revolution, no great state had been reduced to the condition of Germany in 1945–1948. Not since the Thirty Years' War (1618–1648) had Germany suffered so drastically from the ravages of war and its aftermath. Part of this destruction was unavoidable—Germany had been a battlefield. Part of it was deliberate policy by the Allies—as retribution. Germany was divided into four occupation zones as a temporary measure, with France, Britain, and the United States sharing what later became West Germany, and Russia occupying what became the German Democratic Republic (GDR) in the East. Berlin, deep in the Soviet zone, was shared by all four but, unfortunately, Western rights of access to it were never reduced to writing—an oversight which was to play a significant role later.

The Yalta and Potsdam Conferences of the Allies laid down the terms of Germany's occupation. These agreements, with concealed disagreements that later made them dead letters, provided for German disarmament, the dismantling of German war industry, de-Nazification, the payment by Germany

---

[4] Quoted in Koppel S. Pinson, *Modern Germany*, p. 529.

of reparations, and the punishment of war criminals. Of all these goals, the last was most successfully and permanently achieved. Goebbels and Himmler, like Hitler, had committed suicide; the other major Nazis were delivered to the hangman's noose, so that the judgment could not later be undone. On the other points increasing dissension led to varying degrees of execution. While the West "de-Nazified" and disarmed, America taking the lead, the Russians pursued both policies less vigorously, soon creating "police" units, often led by former Nazis. The most serious friction arose, however, over economic questions. The dismantling of German heavy industry, especially in the Ruhr, together with the shipment of West German goods and factories as reparations to the east, created problems not considered carefully enough beforehand. The Russians were slow and half-hearted in discharging their counterobligation to furnish food and raw materials from their zone, partly because the Soviet army of occupation lived off the land and also because their own needs at home were so great. But also the artificial suppression of German industrial activity in the West meant that the United States and Britain, especially, were forced to divert huge sums to Germany, not only to maintain their own troops but to provide a subsistence level of living for the German masses. While the Germans sat with factories idle, the Western taxpayer had to meet and close the gap. In addition, the war-allayed suspicion between the Soviets and the West revived, and the inevitable dissension and friction arose between the allies who, having won the war, disagreed over the policies to be implemented. East and West drew further apart, and bitterness deepened.

The crux of the immediate issues was economic, although the more fundamental questions were political. With the Soviets refusing to cooperate, the immediate focus of the dissension over economics, the currency problem, soon achieved the spotlight. Since 1945 the Allies had been printing occupation marks that were used in all zones. While the West used them with comparative restraint, the Soviets poured them out in a flood of paper, using them to acquire whatever was valuable and movable from Germany. To remedy the currency crisis (for Germany, with a worthless currency, had been reduced to primitive barter and what German industry still operated was being strangled), a reform was necessary.

For the reform to be effective the Western zones would have to be merged, and for the merger to be effective some form of German government had to be restored. The logic of events led to "Bizonia" (the coupling of the British and American zones) in May 1947; and then to "Trizonia" in February 1948 when the French zone joined. On March 6, 1948, the Western powers, meeting in London, announced plans for "a federal form of government" in the now merged Western zones. Plans went forward for a new separate West German mark.

These Western actions, themselves caused by Soviet intransigence, provoked new Soviet responses. On March 20 the Allied Control Council in Berlin held its last meeting, with Marshal Sokolovsky and his delegatioi. stalking out. On March 31 came the first measures of the Berlin blockade, which were progressively extended. The new Deutsche Mark currency started to circulate in West Germany on June 20. On June 22 the Soviets announced a new currency for the Soviet zone and *all* of Berlin. To meet the new challenge the Western mark was introduced into West Berlin on June 24. That same day the Soviets cut off all Western rail traffic with Berlin. A full blockade was soon in effect. The First Berlin Crisis had begun.

Some two and a half million people now either had to depend for supply by air or surrender. Food supplies for 36 days and coal for 45 days left little margin—and winter was approaching. The Allies met the challenge with the Berlin airlift—the most sustained air supply operation in history. That airlift was to last eleven months; at its height planes were arriving or departing every thirty seconds. In all, 1,402,644 metric tons were flown into Berlin in 277,728 flights during a period of 324 days. Western economic counter pressures were also exerted. When the Soviets acknowledged the defeat of their first attempt to force the West out of Berlin, both blockade and airlift ended. But the division of Berlin into two city governments, and the division of Germany into two states, each with its own currency, remained. The blockade ended on May 12, 1949. On May 23 the new all-West German government was proclaimed. One week later the GDR "adopted" a constitution. In West Germany on September 12 a president for the new Federal Republic of Germany (FRG) was elected (and a chancellor on September 15). On October 11 the GDR elected its president.

A new economic era had begun for West Germany in 1948; a new political era began in 1949. From this time forward, progress was unimpeded. An economic transformation was wrought on the basis of the new, hard currency; the steady labor of this disciplined people produced "the German miracle," a term frequently used (especially in Germany) to describe the tremendous contrast brought about between 1948 and 1954.[5] Within five years Germany moved as a nation from poverty to prosperity, from chaos to order. In January–July 1952, West Germany alone accounted for 71.2 million tons of coal (out of the total Schuman Plan production, including Germany, of 138.6 million tons). The figures for steel were : West Germany, 8.9 million tons; Coal and Steel Community, 23.0. The comparable West German–Community figures in January–July 1955 were: coal, 75.5 against 142.6; steel, 12.0 against 30.0. These figures are also indicative of Germany's increasing industrial dominance within the new Western European economic arrangements.[6]

A prosperous economy encouraged stability in government. In the first general elections for the new Bundestag (lower house of parliament) in 1949, Dr. Konrad Adenauer's Christian Democrats (CDU) received the largest number of seats, one hundred and forty-one. Joining with the fifty-three Free Democrats (FDP) and the seventeen German Party (DP) deputies, Adenauer formed a coalition government; the Social Democrats (SPD) with one hun-

---

[5] The general index of production, 100 in 1936, was 178 in November 1953.

[6] German Press and Information Office *Bulletin*, Vol. 3, No. 33 (August 18, 1955), p. 4.

dred thirty-six seats, and the Communists (KPD) with fifteen seats, formed the opposition. When Adenauer's policies came up for endorsement or repudiation in the second general election on September 6, 1953, the Christian Democrats captured two hundred forty-four out of the four hundred eighty-seven seats: an absolute majority in its own right. A partner in the coalition, the Free Democrats, retained fifty-three seats, while the German Party declined slightly to fifteen. The opposition Social Democrats gained fourteen seats (to one hundred fifty), while the Communists failed to elect a single deputy. In the election of 1957, Adenauer gained an even greater margin of support: 270 of the 497 seats, CDU; 17 German Party seats. Germany's voters, encouraged by their prosperity and convinced of the wisdom of Adenauer's policies, including his firm ties with the West, had cast a resounding vote of approval. This was to prove the high-water mark of Adenauer's success, for the 1961 elections were to be held in the midst of the Second Berlin Crisis, immediately after the Berlin Wall.

5　The Berlin Conference and the Malenkov Era

THE ending of the Berlin blockade reduced the likelihood of an immediate armed clash between East and West in Germany. But the division of Germany, which the blockade deepened, continued to keep tensions in Europe at a high level as large armies confronted each other on either side of the Iron Curtain. And while Germany remained divided, there could be no satisfaction of fundamental German national interests: territorial integrity and unity. Yet the solution of the German problem was made difficult by the harsh reality that the power of a unified Germany, thrown on the side of either East or West, would decisively alter the European balance of power in favor of the side with which a united Germany allied herself. For more than two decades this deadlock defied resolution.

Adenauer's approach to the solution of this deadlock was clear and unambiguous: "If Russia sees that not only the Big Three powers but the rest of Europe is prepared to merge its strength, then we might hope that Russia would make concessions in a world-wide settlement." [7] In Adenauer's view, union with the West meant reunion for Germany. His foreign policy rested at root upon this fundamental proposition: Germany would use the strength represented by the coalition, of which she is a leading member, to induce the Soviets to relinquish East Germany.

The efforts of East and West after 1945 to agree diplomatically upon German reunification is a story of frustration and failure. The prospects for accord foundered repeatedly on the rock of alteration to the balance of power which any change would entail. The Soviets, first of all, have never been willing to withdraw from East Germany while Western troops remained in West Germany. Second, the Soviets have not been prepared to see a united Ger-

---

[7] Statement on February 19, 1954; NYT, February 20, 1954.

many, from which occupation troops have been withdrawn, decide to ally itself with the West. The Western position, on the other hand, has consistently rested on a refusal to evacuate West Germany merely in return for Soviet withdrawal from East Germany, and on an insistence that an unoccupied Germany must be free to ally itself as it pleases.

An impasse having been reached in the negotiations in the late 1940's, serious diplomatic efforts to achieve an East-West agreement were abandoned. Instead, the West agreed in May 1952 to the rearmament of West Germany within the proposed European Defense Community; the Soviets devoted their efforts to increasing the efficiency of their so-called "Barracks Police." Each side moved to the creation of a German army while blaming Germany's continued division on the other. In February 1954, negotiations were once more resumed in a foreign ministers meeting—the Berlin Conference. This conference, the first to really negotiate on German reunification since before the blockade, and the first after Stalin's death, did not come about because of an important alteration of position by either East or West; nor did it break the deadlock. The West wanted such a conference primarily because of fissures in the Atlantic alliance. France, deeply fearing German rearmament even with "safeguards," wanted a new attempt at negotiation. Russia, on the other hand, after the serious riots in East Berlin in June 1953 and the increasing unrest in its zone, was anxious to appear as a champion of German reunification in order to reap a propaganda harvest. The Soviets also hoped to encourage French doubts still further.

The Berlin Conference, as widely predicted, failed. The United States strove to overcome Western divisions. Anxious to show a united front to the Soviets, she insisted on the formula of neutrally supervised, all-German free elections, followed by Germany's free choice of alliances. There was, of course, no possibility that Russia would agree to this view. One of the few things connected with Germany on which East and West, as well as Germans, agree is that a united Germany, free to decide, would join the West. (Adenauer on February 19 made it explicit: "The Federal Republic has promised, and will adhere to this promise, to do everything in its power to ensure that a reunited Germany will not break away from the West. The ties of a reunited Germany to the Western camp will remain.")

From the Soviet side came a number of proposals with features equally unacceptable to the West. Thus the Soviets proposed on February 1 a draft treaty for a reunited and "neutralized" Germany which would contain the Soviet zone but not East Prussia or the former German territories now in Polish and Russian hands. This German state would "undertake not to enter into any coalition or military alliance" directed against any of the World-War-II allies. It would be "permitted such national armed forces . . . as . . . . required for the country's defense. . . ." The German government to be formed to administer this treaty was to be "all-German" (i.e., contain Communists). It is not surprising that the Soviets would insist upon Communist representation in the government. The West, after the previous experience with Communists in government as in Czechoslovakia, was naturally unen-thusiastic. This "provisional all-German government," to be formed by the two German parliaments, was to assure "democratic" elections.[8] When these proposals failed to gain approval, the Russians suggested (February 10) leaving Germany divided for the present but withdrawing all but limited occupation forces. Four-power inspection groups would supervise small "police units" in the evacuated German states, and the right to reoccupy would be maintained. Such an arrangement, establishing two weak German states would, of course, have been highly advantageous to the Soviets—relieving the pressure on their Western approaches. It had no value for Germany or the West. With an eye on wooing France, destroying NATO, and reviving the historic Franco-Russian cooperation against Germany, the Russians further proposed a general collective security treaty to include the East, the West, and the German states.[9] It, like the other Soviet proposals, was quickly rejected.

The position of the West, restated at the Berlin Conference, was easy to understand. The West (with France always approaching the problem with ambivalent feelings) was not prepared to risk the loss of West Germany to the Soviet camp by allowing an all-German government in which the Communists might seize power by a coup. Concerned with the difficult problem of military defense in the event of a Soviet assault, the West was anxious to achieve both a greater defensive forward area (especially in the age of atomic weapons and therefore the greater dispersal of forces) and an increase in the number of divisions controlled by NATO. This increase could come, in a practical sense, only from German troops. And since West Germany is by far the more important part of Germany, it is conceivable, given East German detestation of communism, that East Germany would somehow ultimately be brought to the side of the West.

Yet the position of the Soviets was also understandable. What they wanted most, they had virtually no chance of achieving: a united Germany solidly in the Soviet bloc. What they wanted most, short of all of Germany, was to continue to hold East Germany, with West Germany unarmed as before.

The advantages that the Soviets had enjoyed by holding on to East Germany are fairly obvious. They had been able to deploy their forces far inside Central Europe, where they could either carry an attack quickly to the West or parry an attack far from the Russian homeland, if the occasion arose; and as long as they remained in occupation, peaceful conquests in the form of a Soviet Germany were still conceivable. Moreover, the Communist frontier on the West remained away from Poland and the Balkans—the vital but still unreliable (for Russia) corridors into the Soviet Union.

---

[8] This proposal for an all-German government, made on February 4, envisaged the withdrawal of occupying forces *before* the elections. The West suspected this would be the prelude to a Communist coup.

[9] It would have provided that "An armed attack in Europe against any one or more of the parties . . . shall be considered an armed attack against all."

But once West German armed forces existed (and the threat of their exist-ence loomed large over the conference) the frame of reference would shift. The dangers for the Soviets implicit in holding East Germany would increase. As a way out of the dilemma the Soviets proposed a reunited Germany, armed but neutral between East and West. This idea the Soviets put forward as early as March 1952, after the EDC draft treaty was formulated; and they repeated it at the Berlin Conference. Even so, the form in which it was pre-sented to the Conference suggests either Soviet deviousness or simple indeci-sion.[10] While it would remove the frontiers of the NATO alliance westward to the Rhine, the overwhelming preference of the Germans for a Western orientation and Western ties would make German "neutrality" more a legal fiction than a real fact (certainly in the long run). While it would prevent the *integration* of German forces with NATO (an important military consid-eration for the Russians), it would not in the final analysis prevent Germany's fighting on the Western side in a World War III between East and West in which Germany, for geographic reasons, could not remain neutral if she wished. On the other hand, so long as there was no war, a band of neutral states in Central Europe would aid in the further diminution of tension—if the Soviets should continue to wish this to occur. Whether the Germans would agree to such a neutral status, of course, was something else.

Adenauer believed that the Western position of strength would induce Soviet concessions. Yet Soviet concessions could only have the effect of per-mitting the forward zone (i.e., the area from which an attack would be launched in either direction) to be that much nearer the Soviet Union. The more the Soviet Union feared war, the more disadvantage it would see in mov-ing its defenses nearer Moscow. The same logic operated in 1939 and led to an advance into Poland from the east after the Germans entered from the west. Moreover, any territorial concessions in this case that the Soviet Union made would not only move the front line further east, but by the same token Russia would be reinforcing the West by whatever she gave up.

The difficulty with the position of the Russians in Germany was that they could not go forward without war and, short of the creation of a German neutral buffer, they could not easily go back. If a neutral Germany could not be achieved and a reunited Germany in the Soviet camp was impossible, the Russians had only two major alternatives left—give back their German terri-tories (at least East Germany) or hold on to what they had at all costs. For practical purposes the choice therefore was no choice: the Russians felt they must hold what they had.

But this was easier said than done, as developments in 1954–1958 made

---

[10] They coupled it to their proposal that the unified Germany would have a government in which Communists would share power—a stipulation certain to make the West suspi-cious. They added no safeguard proposals that would mitigate the dangers for the West of a Communist coup. There was, for example, no right to be retained by the four powers to reoccupy their zones automatically, without prior East-West consultation, in certain emer-gencies. (Yet the Russians included such safeguards in their proposal of February 10, above.)

clear. The Russians continued to dominate East Germany, their puppet German Democratic Republic (the GDR). But they presided over a dwindling asset—at least so far as people were concerned. Already on September 20, 1956, the one millionth refugee from the GDR had arrived in West Berlin. Even the official statistical yearbook of the GDR admits that East Germany's population fell by over a million between 1950 and 1958.[11] And West German figures indicate that over half this continued flow of people consisted of those under 25 years of age—the very backbone of a labor, professional, and military force for the future. When the SED (the Communist "unity" party of the GDR) ran candidates in the West Berlin election of December 7, 1958, they polled 31,572 votes, or 1.9 per cent of the total—a new confirmation of how the Communists would fare in any free vote.

In these same years West German rearmament began to gain momentum. The agreement joining West Germany to NATO of October 23, 1954, went into effect following the ratification of the Paris Agreements on May 5, 1955. The Soviet campaign against these developments, waged with vigor in 1954–1955, was an utter failure. Even the Soviet decision in the early spring of 1955 to allow free elections in exchange for neutrality for Austria did not have its intended effects on German opinion. One early by-product of the failure of the Soviet campaign (although other causes were also involved) was the abrupt resignation of Malenkov as Prime Minister on February 8, 1955, only two days after the curious incident of the resolution of an "interparliamentary conference on the German question" at Warsaw.

The conference, by *unanimous* vote of its 150 members from various Communist parliaments (and including delegates from the Soviet Union), offered negotiations "on free, controlled elections in Germany, such as were proposed by Sir Anthony Eden, British Foreign Secretary, a year ago at the Berlin Conference of the Big Four. The resolution also suggested that the territorial integrity of a neutralized Germany should be guaranteed by the European states and the United States. The Warsaw resolution, voted by the Soviet delegates, went far beyond any offers made publicly by Vyacheslav M. Molotov on the reunification of Germany." [12] Soviet troops would also be withdrawn from Poland. This resolution, accepting the Eden Plan (a foolproof plan for Western-type free elections), received little publicity in the West, and most of it came three days after Malenkov's "resignation." On February 8, with Marshal Bulganin as Premier and Khrushchev in control of party

---

[11] Refugees from East Germany to West Germany then averaged over 200,000 a year. The figures are: 1949, 129,245; 1950, 197,788; 1951, 165,648; 1952, 182,393; 1953, 331,390; 1954, 184,198; 1955, 252,870; 1956, 279,189; 1957, 261,622; 1958, 204,092. See *Facts Concerning the Problem of the German Expellees and Refugees*, Fourth Edition, West German Federal Ministry for Expellees, Refugees and War Victims, Bonn, 1959. There was also some reverse flow. In 1959 about 40,000 eventually returned to the German Democratic Republic. But this figure was especially high and in early 1961 was again lower. Between 1952 and 1958 over 120,000 farmers alone fled to the West.

[12] See NYT, February 11, 1955, pp. 1 and 4 for the entire text of the dispatch.

affairs, Molotov delivered a 16,000-word foreign policy address which hardly mentioned Germany!

Whatever was going on behind the scenes in the Kremlin, the fall of Malenkov brought Khrushchev increasingly into the spotlight until, as we saw earlier, he deposed Bulganin and became the acknowledged Soviet spokes-man. Khrushchev's policy on Germany was to be anything but soft.

6 *The Second Berlin Crisis and Afterward*

THE summit meeting in July 1955 and the Geneva foreign ministers confer-ence in October–November 1955 made no progress at all toward German re-unification. At Geneva, Molotov presented the new Soviet line: there were now two German states "with different social systems." Thus, "it would be quite unrealistic to try to bring about the unification of Germany through a mechanical merger of its two parts." The problem was "primarily the affair of the Germans themselves." (In other words, a "mechanical merger" through Western-style free elections, which would liquidate "socialist achievements" in the GDR, could not be permitted; there were now two "sovereign" German states and they would have to deal with each other if progress was to be made.) The West amended the Eden Plan to provide for the supervisory commission for all-German elections to be "assisted by Germans in a consultative capac-ity," but this still remained far from Soviet views.

The Soviets, unable to gain acceptance by the West of any plan which did not envisage all-Germany in NATO, came down now on a plan to force the West to accept two Germanies indefinitely. To accomplish this, two things were necessary: the GDR must be accorded recognition by third states, and the Western position in Berlin had to be liquidated. In the opening move on the first tactical objective, Adenauer had already been invited and had gone to Moscow where the Federal Republic of Germany (FRG) had agreed to establish relations with the Soviet Union in return for the release of the re-maining German prisoners-of-war still held by the Soviets. This was accom-plished in September. The Soviet Union was now the only great power with relations with both German states.

The second tactical move was the precipitation of the Second Berlin Crisis (1958–1962). In a speech on November 10, 1958, Khrushchev unveiled the new Soviet offensive, charging the West with having violated all of the "basic provisions of the Potsdam Agreement" but one: the "so-called Four-Power status of Berlin, that is, a position in which the three Western powers . . . have the possibility of lording it in Western Berlin, turning that part of the city, which is the capital of the German Democratic Republic, into some kind of state within a state and, profiting by this, conducting subversive activities from Western Berlin . . ." It was time, said Khrushchev, to end this and "create a normal situation." Khrushchev's idea of a "normal" situation was soon set forth in a Soviet note, proposing that West Berlin become a "free city" with no armed forces permitted there. To avoid "haste and unnecessary friction" and assure "maximum possible consideration for the interests of the parties concerned" the Soviets would "make no changes in the present procedure for [Western] military traffic [to and from Berlin] for half a year." If the West did not use this time to accept, the Soviets would carry out its "planned measures," Western access rights would end, and any Western violation of the new situation would "immediately cause appropriate retaliation." This "six-months ultimatum" was to lead to the Geneva Foreign Ministers Conference of 1959 and the most prolonged crisis over Germany so far. Even before the conference the West retorted that their rights in Berlin did not stem from the Potsdam Agreement but from their conquest of Germany; they would not surrender them to a threat of force.

The Geneva Foreign Ministers Conference of 1959, like the Berlin Conference of 1954, failed. But some changes were apparent. Under the spur of Soviet demands the West showed a distinctly increased flexibility. The "Western Peace Plan" of May 14, 1959, gave up the old insistence on free elections as the very first step, proposing instead a Mixed German Committee of 25 members from West Germany and 10 from the GDR which, deciding by three-fourths votes (so that neither side could be simply outvoted), would draft an electoral law. Failing agreement on a single law within one year each side would submit a draft law to an all-German vote and any proposal receiving a majority in each part of Germany would become valid in both parts. Once this had led to an all-German government that government would be free to belong to either NATO, the Warsaw Pact, or neither, and to request the withdrawal of any or all foreign troops from its soil. If the new German state chose membership in NATO, the West was not to advance its forces east of the present Iron Curtain (and the reverse would hold too for a choice by Germany of alliance with the East).[13] The West also indicated willingness to enter into security arrangements insuring Russia against the West aiding Germany in any unprovoked aggression.

This plan, while it contained concessions to the Soviet contention that German reunification was a matter for the two German states to negotiate, was still far from acceptable to Russia. It would almost certainly in the end have cost them the loss of East Germany. Even more trouble was hidden just beneath these counterproposals. For the Soviet insistence that the two German states taken together comprise all of Germany is not accepted by West Germany which still lays claim to the areas east of Soviet Germany "under Polish and Russian administration." Part of the reason the Russians used the Berlin crisis not only to attempt to maneuver the West out of Berlin but to force acceptance "by the two German states which together comprise Germany" of a peace treaty is that they hoped in this way to force Western

---

[13] For the text of the conference meetings see *Foreign Ministers Meeting, May–August 1959, Geneva,* State Department Publication 6882. The Western Peace Plan is at pp. 55–60.

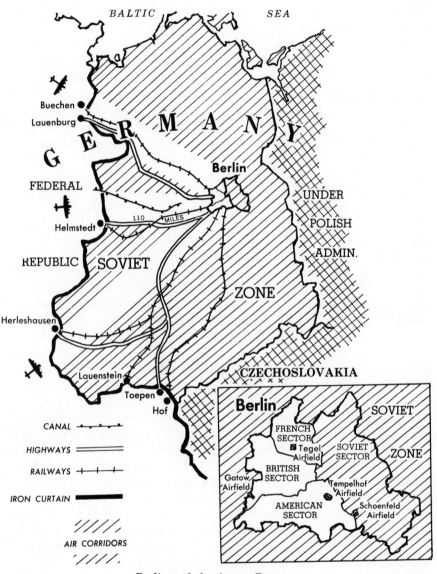

Berlin and the Access Routes

acquiescence in the permanence of the present Oder-Neisse Line. As Khrushchev said on July 17, 1959, in a speech at former Stettin in Poland: "The Western border of the socialist countries lies where the border between the GDR and the Federal Republic of Germany lies. We regard this border of the GDR as our common frontier, as a line dividing the world of socialism from the world of capitalism. This border is for each of the countries of the Warsaw Alliance and for the whole of the socialist camp as inviolable and sacred as the borders of each of our countries. We have said more than once that we shall fight for that frontier against any foe who may try to encroach against it." [14] So again, in 1959 as so often before, there was deadlock.

High tension was not immediately restored by the failure of the conference, for Khrushchev had been invited to confer with President Eisenhower at Camp David, outside Washington. At the end of September they announced the "Camp David Formula." In Khrushchev's words: "We agreed indeed that talks on the Berlin question should be resumed, that no time limit whatsoever is to be established for them, but that they also should not be dragged out for an indefinite time." By this formula, "ultimatums" were shelved—but not the issue itself. A new summit meeting was set for May 1960.

The famous U-2 incident destroyed the summit before it really began. Khrushchev announced his willingness to wait "until the dust has settled" and negotiate with the new American president, once he was elected. But when President Kennedy met Khrushchev at Vienna in June 1961, it was in the shadow of the abortive "Bay of Pigs" episode. Khrushchev on Moscow television the next week said: "We ask everyone to understand us correctly: the conclusion of a peace treaty with Germany [ending Western rights] cannot be postponed any longer. A peaceful settlement in Europe must be attained this year." In July, Kennedy announced the impending call-up of reservists. On television he said: "The solemn vow each of us gave to West Berlin in time of peace will not be broken in time of danger. If we do not meet our commitments to Berlin, where will we later stand . . . ?"

The July refugee flow from East Germany ran at about twice the monthly average; August set new records. These refugees escaped from the GDR almost solely via West Berlin (since the Iron Curtain with barbed wire and its five hundred watchtowers in a distance of only 1,381 kilometers was virtually impassable). Even before this increased flow, estimates placed 64.8 per cent of the population of the GDR as either too young or too old to work. The life-blood and the youth of the GDR was draining out through West Berlin.[15] On August 13, 1961, the Berlin Wall went up. At the end of August some 76,500 U.S. reservists were ordered to duty on October 1. In the September elections in West Germany, Adenauer lost his absolute majority: CDU, 242; SPD, 190; FDP, 67, for a total of 499. Adenauer, reelected chancellor by a slim margin, pledged retirement before the next election.

How Khrushchev maneuvered in 1962 to flank the U.S. with missiles in Cuba at the same time as he renewed the pressure on Berlin, has already been indicated earlier. The Soviet note of early 1963, following the Cuban fiasco, significantly omitted new threats on Berlin. In October–November, though, new delays of Allied military convoys on the Berlin autobahn raised tensions

---

[14] *Ibid.*, p. 516.

[15] Indicative of the GDR problem, in early 1961 the regime offered rewards to villages having no defections for a three months' period. In May the first award went to Gatow, near the Polish border. The local party secretary collected the reward. Next day he defected via West Berlin.

until the Soviets allowed the convoys to pass. When in June 1964, the Soviets finally did sign a new treaty with the GDR, it did not purport to terminate Western access rights to Berlin. The issue was tacitly shelved; on October 14, 1964, so was the man who had made it an issue: Khrushchev. Under his successors, Brezhnev and Kosygin, the German problem in 1965–1966 remained where it had been. By February 1966, the Chinese Communist Peking *People's Daily* was criticizing—without any positive foundation—the Soviet leaders for making "one concession after another on the German question and on the question of West Berlin," a policy which "frees the United States from any worry about its 'rear' so that it can shift the bulk of its military power to Asia." It *was* true that the ending of pressures had made this possible.

Ludwig Erhard, who became the second postwar chancellor of the FRG on October 16, 1963, pursued a policy of maintaining good relations with the West while undertaking careful initiatives in the East. Economic missions were sent to the Balkan satellites and overtures were made particularly to Romania and Poland. This new German interest in the East was carefully calculated to exploit the common interests of these nations with the FRG. It marked the tacit abandonment of the Adenauer contempt for these states as "puppets" of Moscow. These careful maneuvers were in no sense flamboyant, but they were highly significant. Germany began to rethink the dilemma of its self-imposed "Hallstein Doctrine" (which provided that diplomatic relations would not be permitted with any state, other than the Soviet Union, which had recognized the GDR). If it abandoned this policy, third states might recognize *both* Germanies; but if the policy was retained, it prevented diplomatic relations with the Soviet "bloc" states (who all recognized the GDR).

Even so, it was apparent that a much more sophisticated policy was being followed, one involving careful German initiatives. The FRG had come to believe that German reunification would not occur if the issue was left, as essentially in the Adenauer era, solely in the hands of the great powers. In 1965 the German electorate gave Erhard's domestic and foreign policies its endorsement: CDU, 245; SPD, 202; FDP, 49.

By the summer of 1966 the Erhard government had revised the "Hallstein Doctrine" to the extent that withholding of diplomatic recognition was no longer automatic for governments that had in effect been forced to recognize the GDR (i.e., Eastern Europe). Cautious feelers underway were interrupted by economic and political difficulties in West Germany. When the FDP resigned from the coalition over taxes, a new "grand coalition" between the CDU and the SPD was formed. On December 1, 1966 Kurt Georg Kiesinger (CDU) became Chancellor while Willy Brandt (SPD) became Vice Chancellor. This reshuffle represented an uneasy political alliance. Would it last? In the meantime the extreme right-wing National Democrats' success in state elections introduced a new and disturbing element. Unemployment was increasing.

In a speech to the Bundestag on January 18, 1967, Chancellor Kiesinger said: "It is the aim of this government to relax and remove tensions from our relations with the Eastern European countries and with the Soviet Union. This is not aimed against anyone, also not against the Russians." The expectation was for full relations with Romania and Hungary first, with Czechoslovakia next.

The German problem would not easily be resolved. Yet it was obvious that the dangers to all of a continued deployment of NATO–Warsaw Pact troops on either side of the Iron Curtain across Germany, was a permanent drain upon chances for progress on many other issues in which the West and the Soviet Union had potentially some common interests—such as preventing proliferation of nuclear weapons. It was obvious that the division of each of two much smaller nations in Asia had caused a war. Was there reason to believe that the much greater German nation could continue to be divided indefinitely without the same result? Would the FRG be willing to accept both division and no nuclear armaments? But if a peaceful solution were to be found, could it be one which entailed a Soviet retreat from the GDR and all-Germany entering NATO? Or would it have to entail an agreement on an armed, neutral Germany, guaranteed by both East and West?

CHAPTER 27

The European Powers: II

Britain will not undertake major operations of war except in cooperation with allies.

We will not accept an obligation to provide another country with military assistance unless it is prepared to provide us with the facilities we need to make such assistance effective in time. Finally, there will be no attempt to maintain defense facilities in an independent country against its wishes.

British Defense White Paper, 1966

The fact that we have again taken up our faculty of judgment and action toward all problems seems sometimes to offend a state [i.e., the United States] which could, because of its power, think that it has a supreme and universal responsibility.

PRESIDENT CHARLES DE GAULLE
April 1965

CENTRAL to the question of what will happen in Western Europe, today as before, is the problem of British-French relations. We have seen how the failure of these two nations to cooperate effectively in the 1930's helped to bring on the disaster of World War II. The problem of associating Great Britain effectively with France suffers from a number of difficulties which arise out of the experience and policies of these two nations in the last decades. Yet it is also true that some former obstacles to their close association have fallen away under the pressure of events. Let us first note the transformation in Britain's position and policies which have brought her today, although still with certain doubts, to an unprecedented willingness to be a part of "Europe." We shall then examine the developments in France which have resulted in France's coolness to the association Britain has sought.

I British Policy Before World War II

IN the time of Julius Caesar, Great Britain lay at one end of the known world, peripheral to the main area of world affairs. By the late nineteenth century, Britain still remained peripheral to the focus of great power politics on "the Continent," but she had become, geographically speaking, the center of the larger world of commerce, trade, transportation, finance. She had acquired the world-girdling British Empire—on which the sun never set. She had acquired world-wide interests, industrial leadership, formidable sea power and control of the exits and entrances of the European Continent. Her predominance in the English Channel and the North Sea as well as her hold over Gibraltar (and, later, Suez) gave her an effective veto over the ambitions of Europe's powers in Asia and the New World, for Britain was the keeper of the gates to the outside world. Overseas expeditions by European states thus became largely subject to British toleration, if not approval. British attitudes significantly affected European powers bent upon building and maintaining colonial empires. Britain thus acquired an important influence upon European affairs while essentially refraining from direct commitments on the Continent. The obverse of this same situation was that British interests became worldwide and potentially difficult to reconcile. This would be especially true if continental politics produced a threat to Britain's European interests. That is the real reason for Lord Palmerston's classic statement in 1848 that "it is a narrow policy to suppose that this country or that is to be marked out as the eternal ally or the perpetual enemies. Our interests are eternal and perpetual, and these interests it is our duty to follow." That is the real reason for the "balancer" role often ascribed to Britain.

British policy by the late nineteenth century could be conceptualized around five general principles. They included three policies toward Europe: aloofness from other than purely temporary European alliances and alignments, the maintenance of a power equilibrium on the continent, and a specific concern with the safety of the Low-Countries (the natural staging areas for an assault on the British Isles). They also included two world-wide policies: maintenance of a navy equal at least to the two next largest navies combined (to protect her lifelines) and consideration of every major event in the world in relation to its impact on British interests elsewhere. Until the turn of the twentieth century these principles served Britain well. But then the principles became in practice increasingly incompatible. British security was no longer fairly automatically assured by their implementation. A number of factors, long in the making, forced Britain first to a thorough-going rethinking of her foreign-policy problems, and then to new departures.

The first of these factors was the emergence in Asia and the New World of independent centers of power (especially of naval power) formidable enough to pose challenges to Britain's control of the seas—at least in the offshore areas adjacent to those new power centers. Japan, which had been opened to the world shortly after the mid-nineteenth-century mark, was readying herself to challenge Russia's predominant position in Manchuria and Korea. This expansion of Russia to the Far East could not be restrained by British sea power, for it took place overland across the steppes of Central Asia. At the same time the intermittent Russian moves in Afghanistan and toward India had created Anglo-Russian tension. Britain was faced by the need to formulate a policy toward a Japan which was emerging as the most effective potential barrier to further Russian expansion into China. Britain could either oppose Japan (which made no sense), allow matters to take their course, or ally herself with Japan. Britain's extensive interests in the Far East were no longer made automatically secure by British world power; hitherto no formidable naval or land power had existed or originated in Asia. Now the situation was changed.

The United States war with Spain in 1898 also created a problem of a somewhat similar kind. Britain had possessions in the Americas and in the Pacific. Now the United States emerged into the role of contender for great-power rank. She had become predominant in the Caribbean and had acquired the Philippines. A larger and more powerful United States navy to protect these areas could reasonably be expected. A legacy of Anglo-American distrust still remained from earlier, hostile days, despite the conciliating effects that had flowed from the arbitration of the Alabama Claims and the settlement of differences under the Treaty of Washington of 1871. While United States adherence to a policy of unilateralism ruled out any question of an Anglo-American alliance, it was essential that Britain consider carefully any sources of potential friction. The United States, more than most states, could dispute British naval predominance in the Atlantic under certain conditions.

Another factor Britain had to consider was the gradual weaving of a net of alliances and alignments in Europe. There was the Franco-Russian Alliance, binding together two traditional enemies of Britain in Europe. There was also the Triple Alliance of Germany, Austria-Hungary, and Italy. Although these alliances were mutually opposed, they still left Britain isolated. Moreover, in the Boer War Britain had been faced with the possibility of a European combination against her. Enmity in Europe had not prevented Franco-German cooperation against Britain in colonial matters.[1]

Complicating this situation were the German decision to build a high-seas fleet and the potential challenge of a German submarine fleet to a Britain dependent on food and other imports for its life. These developments made it inevitable that Britain would have to reconsider her policy toward Germany.

On the one hand an alliance with Germany represented a more natural grouping for Britain, who would then be aligned against her traditional French and Russian enemies. In 1901 this move was considered and rejected because, for one thing, the German price was too high: British parliamentary ratification of the Triple Alliance. The Germans put the price high because of Britain's isolation. As German Chancellor von Bülow wrote to the Kaiser on January 21, 1901: ". . . Your Majesty is quite right in perceiving that the English must come to us. They have just lost a lot of hair in Africa, America appears unsteady, Japan unreliable, France full of hate, Russia perfidious, public opinion in all countries hostile; . . . now it gradually dawns on the British consciousness that they cannot, by their own strength alone, hold their world empire against so many opponents." [2] The alliance with Japan of 1902,

---

[1] See above, Chapter 18.
[2] *Die Grosse Politik der Europäischen Kabinette, 1871–1914,* Vol. 17, pp. 20 ff.

which Britain finally decided on, fitted in well with an Anglo-German alliance.

On the other hand it was Germany who could strangle the British sea-going lifeline; and it was Germany, as the most powerful continental state, who was the potential destroyer of the European balance of power. A British alliance with Germany would lead inevitably to German control of Europe by making their victory in a war the surer.

British fears of Germany led directly to the Anglo-French Entente of 1904 and a growing Anglo-German tension. When Germany violated Belgium's neutrality in 1914, Britain's estimate of the course upon which Germany was determined to embark was confirmed. When Britain entered World War I, it was on the side of her traditional enemies, France and Russia. When Britain emerged from that war as a nominal victor (although at great costs in both blood and treasure), she had to deal with a world in which the changes which had occurred had even further complicated her problem of attaining reasonable security.

By the end of World War I the face of Europe was utterly transformed. The old Austro-Hungarian Empire had fallen apart; and the great Russian Empire, reduced in territory, was wracked by civil war. The emergence of Poland and the breaking off of Finland and the Baltic states from Russia forged a chain of weak states from the Baltic to the Mediterranean, separating Britain, France, Italy, and Germany from direct contact with the East. The temporary weakness of Germany still further made chaos out of the balance-of-power concept as it had previously applied to Europe. Outside Europe proper, great changes had also occurred. The Turkish Empire in the Middle East was gone. In its place stood a group of new, weak states—still further "Balkanizing" the balance of power. These developments did not make an effective balance impossible, but they did make it difficult to achieve. America's rise to great-power status, first signaled by the Spanish-American War, was fact; and Japan's acquisition of German colonial possessions in the Pacific, coming on top of her assumption of Russia's position in Manchuria and China after the Russo-Japanese War, transformed her into an Asian great power capable of even more important independent action.

Important changes within the British Empire were also in the making. The transformation of the Dominions into more or less independent states, owing merely a common allegiance to the British crown but free to pursue their own interests, further complicated Britain's implementation of her nineteenth-century principles. This was especially so in view of the new existence of non-European great powers. Then, too, the traditional patterns of unilateralism and the balance of power had a new rival—collective security—with a logic of behavior and action all its own. And, finally, the economic prosperity of the nineteenth century and the conditions which more or less automatically had fostered it were severely disrupted. World trade had been diverted into new and odd patterns, inflation was rampant, and the plague problem of reparations was to sap much of the effort to restore economic "normality." Passions aroused by the war were not easily stilled, and the same Lloyd George who as Prime Minister of Britain at the Versailles Peace Conference wished an "easy" solution for reparations received a telegram from three hundred seventy members of Parliament demanding that he make Germany pay. Although Lloyd George was well aware that reparations and the restoration of world trade were opposed to one another, for political reasons he felt he had to plump for severe reparations.[3]

Thus Britain's problems after World War I were immeasurably more complex. The complications and contradictions made the following of Britain's traditional principles far from easy. The question arose whether they were indeed all still appropriate principles considering the changed conditions. Problems such as reparations were not slow in demonstrating the difficulties.

There was, to begin with, Britain's traditional aloofness from permanent or semi-permanent alliances with great powers. The emotional legacy of the common Anglo-French war effort, and the French insistence on guarantees from Britain and the United States if she were to relinquish her demand for the Rhineland, induced the British to offer an alliance contingent upon assumption by the United States of the same obligation. But the United States Senate failed to ratify this treaty, and the Franco-British treaty became a dead letter. At the same time the British increasingly harbored doubts about the predominant position that the outcome of the war had brought to France. Even if France did not feel secure, it was a fact that Germany was economically and militarily impotent, that France was erecting a chain of alliances with Germany's border states on the east, and that French influence in the new League of Nations could not help being enormous. The insistence of France upon occupying the Ruhr in 1923, an act which retarded German recovery from the war, seemed to give substance to these doubts. The corresponding insistence of the French that their underlying position remained weak left the British incompletely convinced. In the British view some recovery by Germany would produce a more stable and satisfactory equilibrium. Of all her three traditional policies toward Europe only the status of the Low Countries gave Britain no concern.

Outside Europe the maintenance of the two-navy standard was in jeopardy, especially because of United States determination to create a navy surpassed by none. At the Washington Conference Britain was forced to recognize United States equality in capital ships in return for an acceptable stabilization of the Pacific area. Implicit in this arrangement was a certain dependence on American friendship, not only in the Pacific but also in the Atlantic. In a sense, because of her undeniable power as well as because of this arrangement, the United States acquired a subtle but intangible veto over British actions in a large part of the non-European world, especially in the Pacific. When the United States continued to pursue a unilateralist policy and

---

[3] In characteristic style Lloyd George asked, "Was it sensible to treat her (Germany) as a cow from which to extract milk and beef at the same time?" Quoted in Grant and Temperley, *op. cit.*, p. 537.

refused League membership (both of which actions made her policy less obvious and apparent in any world crisis), the British problem increased in difficulty. Then there were the Dominions. Not only were they affected too by United States power, but they were also newly self-conscious of their own (as distinguished from British) interests. It was Canada, for example, that sponsored the interpretative resolution of 1923 in the League to limit their collective-security obligation. It was Canada who talked of "living in a fire-proof house." The Dominions were reluctant to accept obligations vis-à-vis European continental states. Yet Britain's direct interests there were now greater than ever before, especially because of the "Balkanization" produced by the disintegration of the great European empires. With the European balance of power further than ever from maintaining itself as a "natural" product of the interrelations of five or six relatively evenly matched states (à la the pre-1914 pattern), Britain was inevitably to be forced into less aloofness toward Europe at the same time that the Dominions were obviously in favor of more.

Further, there was the built-in conflict between the dictates of the balance of power and those of collective security. This newly created problem for Britain in the 1930's sheds much light on her foreign-policy failures between the wars.

Finally, there was a factor already apparent between the two world wars that became widely recognized only after World War II. Britain was growing relatively weaker as some of the original causes for her unparalleled nineteenth-century importance disappeared. The great bloodletting on the battlefields between 1914 and 1918 had devoured most of a whole generation. In World War I Britain had lost seven hundred fifty thousand killed, while twice that number had been wounded; her foreign debt had increased tenfold. World trade, upon which British prosperity depended, was seriously disorganized. The growing industrialization of other states challenged Britain, the parent of industrialization in the world. Her lead was evaporating by the close of the nineteenth century. In the twentieth century, as such territorial giants as the United States and the Soviet Union pushed ahead, she fell relatively further behind.

Thus British policy between the wars was hampered by a relative decline in power and the introduction of many new complicating factors into the world situation. Even the domestic political party structure, with the decline of the Liberals and the rise of Labour as a third party, lost its previous stability. The Great Depression added a new blow to both the economic and political structure. A split in the Labour Party, together with the weakness in Liberal strength, delivered the Conservative Party into the hands of timid men against whom the split opposition was ineffective. Preoccupied with problems at home she was forced, after 1933 and the rise of Hitler, to face a formidable series of foreign-policy dilemmas. Foremost among these was the question whether to appease or oppose Germany, complicated as it came to be by the question of how to respond to Mussolini's Ethiopian venture.

In June 1935, new elections continued what was still technically a coalition government in power. Stanley Baldwin (Conservative) as Prime Minister moved to appease Germany, and sought again to reconcile her to the *status quo* by concluding the Anglo-German naval agreement. British willingness to assist Germany in undermining the Versailles settlement, while it failed to reconcile Germany, did alienate France. Hard on the heels of this breach in Anglo-French unity came the Ethiopian crisis. The government, seeking to avoid League sanctions, explored the situation through Foreign Secretary Sir Samuel Hoare, with the idea of appeasing Italy by partitioning Ethiopia. The Hoare-Laval plan, coming to light, led to Sir Samuel's resignation; the government, pressed by public opinion to take a stand on League principles, now turned to a consideration of League sanctions. Anthony Eden, as the new foreign secretary, took the lead at Geneva, but Baldwin knew how far he wished this policy to go. As Churchill later wrote: "The Prime Minister had declared that sanctions meant war; secondly, he was resolved there must be no war; and thirdly, he decided upon sanctions." [4] These sanctions became halfway measures as a means to avoid their consequences: both to avoid war and to preserve some semblance of the diplomatic "Stresa front" against Germany.

But the inconsistencies and failure to make choices went even deeper. Britain not only found herself unable to choose as regards Italy between the balance of power *or* collective security; she had also not been able to determine on a policy of containing German expansion in conjunction with France. British policy proved, in the end, in a sense, consistent. By keeping sanctions half-hearted she avoided war with Italy even while she continued to appease the Nazis. It is easy enough to sympathize with Britain's dilemma over Italy; it is more difficult to see what point her German policy had.

Belatedly Britain moved toward rearmament, announcing a naval construction program at the end of April 1936 of 38 warships. She sought to stabilize the Mediterranean through an agreement with Italy on January 2, 1937. The outbreak of the Spanish Civil War tore this agreement into shreds as Italy moved fifty to seventy-five thousand troops into Spain. On May 28, 1937, with Stanley Baldwin's retirement, the chancellor of the exchequer, Neville Chamberlain, became Prime Minister. Despite Baldwin's failures to reconcile Germany and Italy to a peaceful *status quo*, Chamberlain believed that the lack of success was due to too few concessions to these states. He determined to make concessions large enough to wean them away from thoughts of war.

In November of 1937, Chamberlain sent Halifax to Hitler at Berchtesgaden to find out Germany's demands. In February Anthony Eden, at odds with the policy, resigned. In March 1938, came the annexation of Austria by Germany. The British government did nothing. An April agreement with Italy to normalize relations came to naught. Mussolini, made contemptuous by Britain's very weakness toward him, moved in the opposite direction.

In September 1938 came the Munich crisis. The British, far from making a firm stand against Hitler, took the lead in advocating compromise. As the

---

[4] Winston Churchill, *The Gathering Storm*, p. 175.

crisis moved to a climax, Chamberlain flew twice to Germany to negotiate personally with Hitler. In the final hours of the crisis he went to Munich, to the conference which sacrificed Czechoslovakia and ratified the German triumph. In return Hitler gave him a "peace pact" that gratified Chamberlain enormously. "Peace in our time," he called it.

On March 31, 1939, the war clouds gathered and the full extent of Chamberlain's delusions came to be understood. Hitler threatened Poland. A stand was at last made, with Chamberlain extending a pledge, together with the French, to the Poles. Hitler's annexation of Czechoslovakia and Memel, clearly revealing the illusory nature of his demands for only Germans to be incorporated into his expanding Reich, at last brought an awakening to chilling reality. Mussolini's occupation of Albania in April 1939, showed clearly, even to the most naïve, the bankruptcy of further attempts to placate him. British guarantees were now also given to Greece and Romania. On April 27 came the too-long-delayed introduction of conscription in Britain. In late August came the Danzig-Polish crisis. On September 3 Britain declared war on Germany. Thus was brought to an end an era of British foreign-policy weakness and vacillation without parallel in modern history.

2　The Postwar Revolution in British Policies

BRITAIN emerged from World War II, like World War I, a nominal victor. But again, as with World War I, she was greatly weakened, and she faced even more serious difficulties. The consequence was to be a drastic revision in policy—the dismantling of empire, the abandonment of unilateralism, and the decision to seek much closer and more permanent economic, military and other ties with other powers. Let us first see what factors led to this reversal of historic policies and then later the problems which these new policies in turn brought about.

First, there was the economic condition of postwar Britain. Even a century ago (as the steeply rising figures between 1855 and 1880 for net food imports show) Britain was rapidly approaching a condition where she could not feed herself on domestically grown food. The disappearance of arable lands under the soot-stained walls of great factories marked Britain's transformation. As a great processing and manufacturing nation she imported raw materials and exported finished goods—and lived on the proceeds. Yet her exports in the twentieth century were less and less capable by themselves of sustaining the British people in their accustomed standard of living. The difference was made good by the profit from investments overseas and from the carrying trade of her merchant ships. But the capital drains of both world wars served to liquidate much of this investment. It had to be turned into cash, to pay for war. This process was accelerated between 1939 and the first part of 1941 by the United States "cash-and-carry" policy, under which Britain was required to pay for war goods bought there.

Since much of British industry by the 1930's was already behind the times, the British problem in the 1940's and 1950's was compounded. The British for long had had a certain competitive edge, in that British colonial possessions and the Dominions preferred many British goods. This preferential status had made perhaps for a certain complacency. Her industry, too, was far older than that of more newly industrialized nations. A state industrializing in the present decade naturally avails itself of what is newest and most efficient. While the British did modernize, they did so always in an older plant and equipment setup. This renovation frequently took a patchwork form rather than one of complete replacement; the level of comparative industrial efficiency tended to lag gradually further behind. Until World War II Britain was spared a wartime destruction of her industry; after 1945 she was forced into a wholesale replacement. The extent of British economic weakness led her to an unprecedented reliance on foreign economic aid, especially through United States loans and Marshall Plan aid. This in turn led to much more closely coordinated economic plans with the Continent (as we saw in discussing international economics).

Second, there were the economic and political effects of political forces, especially the independence movement which was so soon to give rise to many of the newly emerging Afro-Asian nations. Not only did the independence progressively given to the former British Empire in the two postwar decades disrupt old patterns of British trade. In countries such as Iran, where oil and other concessions added to London's wealth, nationalization became the mode. Britain by 1954 had had to accept an Iranian oil settlement that converted her former monopoly into an international consortium, with the nationalization of the oil industry accepted as an accomplished fact. While the settlement assured Britain of ample oil, it cut down her unilaterally-held assets in the area.

Some of the new developments toward the dismantling of empire were accepted only reluctantly by the British. The Egyptian insistence on British evacuation of the Suez Canal Zone is one illustration. On the other hand, the British moved out of Palestine, as we saw, only too gladly—tossing the problem to the UN. The British withdrawal from India was, of course, the prime example of the new British retrenchment and sharing of responsibilities. It was a remarkable example of British statesmanship at its best. Although some hailed it as a "retreat," it undoubtedly saved the British from the fate of the French in Indo-China. Moreover, it kept India out of Communist hands. In granting full self-government to India and the new Pakistan, the British succeeded in retaining these states within the British Commonwealth (or "Commonwealth of Nations" as it now came to be called to emphasize the partnership of states of both British and non-British culture). That India leaned toward a neutralism between East and West did not make the success less impressive, for in a free partnership it was inevitable that the Indians would assess the international situation in terms of India's background, attitudes, and interests. In addition Burma was permitted to sever Commonwealth bonds became a completely independent state. Ceylon, given her choice, chose like India to remain a member. The same policy, extended to Africa, was a similar success in cutting outmoded ties with a minimum of ill-feeling. Ghana and Nigeria were among the first such new African states but many more were soon added. The very conversion of the empire into the new multi-racial "Commonwealth of Nations" (for those who chose to retain ties with Britain) had the advantage of reducing drastically unilateral defensive obligations by the British—which obligations were, on the prewar scale, in any event no longer supportable in Britain's reduced power circumstances. The reduction in British commitments also led to much more flexibility for Britain in accepting commitments in Europe, as we shall see.

The third factor was the altered military situation brought about especially by the development of nuclear weapons. In World War II the airplane and guided missiles had brought the war home physically to the British civilian population. Luckily, Nazi development of the atomic bomb had not been pushed through to success before that war ended. But the dangers which these new weapons constituted for Britain were easily understood by the man-in-the-street. The later development of hydrogen bombs led the British to reckon that fifty such bombs could literally destroy Britain. From an island citadel, protected from invasion (and therefore destruction) by the English Channel and the British navy, the British Isles had been transformed by modern technological advances in armaments. She was now an area near and small enough to sustain drastic damage through the air from continental bases; she was at the mercy of an enemy able to win the battle for control of the ocean depths (and therefore its surfaces). Britain's very compactness, her very urbanization and industrialization, and her very inability to seek safety in dispersal made her civil defense problem perhaps the greatest of all the major powers.

From this development two contradictory conclusions could be drawn: (1) that Britain could no longer afford her ancient policy of aloofness from peacetime alliances, or (2) that Britain might best seek security through neutrality and (even unilateral) disarmament. Postwar British governments consistently held to the first conclusion, while a fluctuating minority public sentiment argued for the second.

Thus it was a combination of economic, political, and military factors which produced the revolutionary reversal in previous British policies in 1947 when she concluded an alliance treaty with France, directed against German aggression [5] for the unprecedented period of fifty years. This drastic change in policy aroused less public comment in the world than it deserved; it seemed such a natural move in the light of two world wars that its novelty was largely overlooked. But when one contrasts this step with the century or more before World War II, its enormity for Britain is more clearly seen.

---

[5] Actually in 1942 Britain had already signed a treaty of alliance with Soviet Russia; but the 1947 alliance was Britain's first peacetime move along these lines.

When Britain entered both world wars she had done so on the basis mainly of rather vague understandings and her interpretation of her own interests, rather than on a basis of treaty arrangements with allies. In fact, the treaties of alliance she did conclude were almost exclusively only at the very brink of war, such as the Anglo-Polish Treaty of Mutual Assistance of August 25, 1939.[6] As a policy she had refrained from alliance treaties in peacetime looking toward cooperation in war, preferring the flexibility in alliances described by Lord Palmerston. Such political-military treaties as she did become a party to were almost exclusively either general and multilateral treaties of collective guarantee, such as the Belgian neutrality agreement of 1839, and the Locarno guarantee treaty of 1925,[7] or were treaties concluded during general wars relating to the establishment of the new *status quo*, such as the Quadruple Alliance of 1815. The failure of Anglo-French efforts to negotiate a last-minute alliance with Russia in 1939 showed the dangers of making decisions at the moment of crisis. It could also be argued that the lack of a British commitment to Czechoslovakia prior to 1938 was a grave weakness in the maintenance of a stable balance of power so important to Britain. With this alliance in 1947 the British showed that they recognized that a policy which enhanced their security in the days of relative immunity from serious, sudden attack, was now a weakness. And Britain soon went even further. On March 17, 1948, along with Belgium, the Netherlands, Luxembourg, and France she signed the Brussels (Western Union) Alliance which was, in 1955, to become the vehicle through which West Germany was to associate herself with the Western bloc. This treaty also was to run fifty years, and thereafter unless denounced. It was another revolutionary step in that it set up an unprecedented peacetime military coordination among the signatory powers. While this machinery was soon absorbed into the even more inclusive North Atlantic Treaty Organization, it was also the precedent on which NATO was established, and accomplished the spadework for the foundation on which the NATO structure was subsequently built. It was ample indication that the British not only now recognized the need for alliances of long duration far in advance of wars, but also for integrated military planning and coordination of supply and training and command functions. Nor was the Western Union Treaty limited to military coordination. It also provided for economic cooperation and implied the eventual elimination of customs barriers.

The British ratification of the North Atlantic Pact of April 4, 1949, was a logical extension of these commitments. It rounded out a logical development of the original Western Union idea and added the strength of the United States and other Western or Western-oriented states to European defense. It had the additional merit of adding friendly Portugal and Canada

---

[6] The major exceptions are the Anglo-Portuguese treaties of the fourteenth century, periodically renewed, and the Anglo-Japanese Alliance of 1902.

[7] In such treaties Britain assumed not a unilateral guarantee function but a collective one. She was not obligated to take action alone.

into one over-all arrangement. Both the Western Union and the NATO treaties were worded generally,[8] but they were directed originally, of course, not only against future German aggression but also, and more immediately, against the possibility of a Soviet attack. The momentous decision in September–October 1954 to admit Germany to the Western Union and NATO, converted these treaties into instruments of defense directed solely against the Soviet Union and her satellites. At the same time Britain, to still French fears of Germany, took a further unprecedented step by pledging that she would maintain on the Continent four divisions of British troops, plus a tactical air force, and would not withdraw them against the wishes of the majority of the Brussels Treaty powers.

Britain in 1955 joined with Turkey, Iraq, and Pakistan in the Baghdad defense treaty (later CENTO), which Iran also joined; she also entered into more limited collective alliance obligations in the Pacific by joining SEATO.

Thus by 1955 the British had altered completely their pre-World-War-II alliance policy.

These moves, which increased British commitments in Europe and shifted those in the Middle and Far East to a more collective basis, did not constitute the assumption of new burdens which she otherwise would have been spared. The European arrangements represented a more efficient disposition of burdens made inescapable by the British position and British interests. It was a more effective recognition and handling of those interests. The very decentralization of the Commonwealth, while in one sense it made Great Britain's relations with all its members more complex, at the same time permitted a greater flexibility. If Britain could no longer count on unquestioned support from these nations for purely British interests, at the same time Britain was freer to pursue her own interests. It worked both ways. Where Dominion opposition had played a part in preventing Britain from safeguarding her continental interests between the world wars, Britain was now able to maintain looser Commonwealth ties (still of value in a crisis) and follow a policy in closer accord with her own needs. The corollary to India's freedom not to join a Western alliance against Russia was British freedom to join NATO.

Moreover, the ex-Dominions developed ties with the United States, such as the Australia–New Zealand–United States mutual defense arrangements, and United States–Canadian joint defense planning within and outside NATO. A close Anglo-American entente became central to British policy. These associations simplified the British foreign-policy problem in important respects. The dismantling of empire and the creation of mutual defense associations outside Europe was in better accord with British power and concerns. It enabled her to find a better basis for a more limited presence in these areas, which was the corollary to her greater commitment in Europe.

---

[8] The Western Union Treaty, Article 4, provided: "If any of the high contracting parties should be the object of an armed attack in Europe, the other high contracting parties will . . . afford the party so attacked all military and other aid and assistance in their power." For NATO's provisions, see above, Chapter 17.

On August 3, 1961, by a vote of 313–5 in the House of Commons, the British government took an equally revolutionary step in the economic-political field, by requesting admission to the European Economic Community. Britain, who had first reacted to the Coal and Steel Community by organizing the "Outer Seven" free-trade area, now made it clear that she wished to join not only the Common Market, but the Coal and Steel Community as well as Euratom. In November 1961, the actual negotiations began. They failed, at least for a time, when on January 14, 1963, de Gaulle vetoed the proposal. But even the failure emphasized the remarkable change which had come over British policy.

3 British Policies: Contemporary Developments

WE have seen the major reasons for Britain's reversal of policies. These new policies were not without their own complications. The British decision to join Europe on a more intimate basis did not in any way reflect British willingness to turn her back on the United States. Not that there initially appeared any reason to believe that the British would be asked to choose between Europe and the United States, for the American commitment to NATO was the very backbone of that alliance and the United States attitude toward the European Community was one of enthusiastic encouragement—at least through 1962.

The very reliance upon the United States as the first among Britain's allies, a policy whose positive side we have already noted, had, of course, certain dangers even if American-British-Continental interests remained firmly coordinated in Europe. For the United States was showing a tendency toward growing involvements in the Far East against China which often caused the British alarm. Having cut down much of their own commitments, the British, through their close relationship to the United States, might be called upon to assume burdens outside Europe going far beyond their own wishes. The early British recognition of Communist China made this problem especially acute during the Quemoy-Matsu crisis in 1954 when Communist China threatened to take these Nationalist Chinese-held islands which Britain, of course, recognized as belonging to Communist China. In the decade and more which followed, the difficulty implicit in contrasting China policies continued to provide Anglo-American discord.

The British position in the Far East was not without ambiguities. When the intermittent Indonesian war with Malaysia began, the British were at the same time desirous of American backing but fearful of having to reciprocate by aiding the United States who by the early 1960's was becoming more involved in the war in Viet-Nam. The situation was complicated still more by the Indian–Chinese border disputes and, in 1965, the Indian–Pakistan fighting over Kashmir. Other issues complicated Anglo-American relations, such as British trade with Castro's Cuba. But the most important difference remained that over China. The alternation of Conservative and Labour governments in Britain did not affect the British bipartisan opinion that the Far Eastern situation could be better normalized by acceptance of the fact of Chinese power, admission of Communist China to the UN, and the realization of "legitimate" Chinese Communist interests.

In the Middle East, Anglo-American policies diverged significantly only once. But that once tore a great hole in Anglo-American friendship. The British policy of retrenchment there, initiated by the Labour government of Clement Attlee after 1945, and which had led to Palestine's evacuation, had been carried further under Winston Churchill who initiated the Suez Canal arrangement of 1954 giving Egypt control over the base. When Churchill was succeeded in 1955 by Anthony Eden the area was growing tenser. How Nasser subsequently nationalized the Suez Canal Company has already been recounted. It took time before this breach was healed between Britain and the United States. The healing was helped by the patient efforts of Harold Macmillan, the new Prime Minister, plus the drawing-together of the United States and Britain in the post-*sputnik* era, when Khrushchev determined to put Western unity to the acid test. Even the shock of the United States decision in December 1962 not to complete the "Skybolt" missile to which the British had pinned their defense plans, did not destroy the restored accord. In the ensuing "Nassau Agreement," the United States offered Britain Polaris missiles for her nuclear submarines while Britain agreed that these arms would be used for NATO, except "where the supreme national interest was at stake." They were then free, if necessary, to act alone.

The British had given firm support to the United States in the Missile Crisis of 1962; they ratified the Test Ban Treaty of 1963 with particular enthusiasm. The new Labour government after October 1964 followed the same policy of close relations. Pickets, as before, continued to demonstrate for the withdrawal of United States nuclear submarines from British bases, but the majority British opinion remained firm on close association with the United States.

The British decision to rely in increasing measure on the United States while seeking closer ties with Western Europe was in part a reflection of Britain's difficulty in making her reduced economic resources stretch to cover her needs. Economic retrenchment necessitated a reduction in armed forces just as the dismantling of the Empire permitted it. Whether Britain was moving too far in this direction was a recurrent issue in British politics. By 1964 British troops totaled a mere 180,000 (as compared to 290,000 for Italy and 110,000 for Greece). In early 1966 the Labour government announced plans to purchase 50 American F111A supersonic bombers to be the spearhead of Britain's strategic strike force. The Royal Navy was to lose its naval air arm and get no new aircraft carriers, and was gradually to take over control of most strategic missiles, including those of the four Polaris submarines being built. The British base at Aden, at the tip of the Arabian peninsula, was to be phased out by 1968. The Caribbean force was to be withdrawn, and it was hoped that the 54,050 troops which had aided Malaysia against Sukarno's Indonesia could be withdrawn. The 51,000 troops in West Germany would remain but only if the West Germans would assist further in their financial support. The government made it clear that no major military operations overseas were contemplated in the future without the cooperation of allies. Both the First Sea Lord and the Navy Minister resigned in opposition. Christopher Mayhew, the Navy Minister, indicated in House debate that he wanted Britain to give up any defense role east of Suez. But if Britain would not, she must spend more. Otherwise her role became simply "an extension of United States power." This was a clear statement of one major British problem.

The question in 1966 of further British links with Europe was in abeyance. For de Gaulle continued to block British membership in the European Community and announced his intentions of dismantling the integrated command structure of NATO. It was rather ironic that Britain, so long unwilling to be in and of Europe, and now ready (with the important reservation of retained close links to the United States), was being held at arm's length by her ardent suitor of six decades—France. Labour Prime Minister Wilson's speech of November 30, 1966 was clearly addressed in de Gaulle's direction. He spoke of "building up our strength, building up an Atlantic community based on twin pillars of equal strength and power—this, so far from harming Anglo-American understanding, will give a new reality to it." As 1967 began, the prospects for British association with the European Community again increased.

4 France: Historical Experience—Political Effects

THE renaissance of French power and influence which began in 1958 with the establishment of the Fifth French Republic under the leadership of President de Gaulle marked an enormous change from the weakness and vacillation of recent decades. Whether the stability and progress would endure after de Gaulle was hotly debated, but not the fact of that progress. The Fifth French Republic marked a turning-away from a long legacy of unresolved issues.

When France emerged from defeat after 1871 she was in form once more a republic—the Third Republic. In eight decades or so she had been three times republic, twice an empire, and three times a monarchy.[9] France had known fundamental revolution, great glory, and humiliating defeat. Inevitably the many changes had left a legacy of conflicts and cleavages. Even the decision to restore and maintain a republic was due not to majority sentiment in the National Assembly but to the deadlock between two royal pretend-

---

[9] The Bourbons had reigned until 1789. Then had followed the First Republic and the First Empire. After Napoleon's fall the Bourbons had returned until 1830 when the Orléanist dynasty of Louis Philippe displaced them. In 1848 had come the Second Republic and then in 1852 the Second Empire of Louis Napoleon. After France's defeat in 1871 came the Third Republic.

ers and their adherents. The actual decision came only in 1875 and was carried by one vote.

Not only were French politics marked by a great cleavage on many questions but the new form of government served to perpetuate these divisions. France began the Third Republic with many parties, because many mutually intolerant points of view existed. And since virtually all power was centered in a Chamber of Deputies which would not dissolve itself and which could not be dissolved by the Premier,[10] these divisions were perpetuated. In the French system of government after 1870, including the Fourth Republic before de Gaulle which so resembled the Third, and excluding only Pétain's few years of rule after 1940, the executive was reduced to the plaything of the legislature.

The deliberate choice of a weak executive for the Third Republic stemmed not only from the fears of each of the contending groups of a strong executive chosen from some other group, but out of French experience between the Revolution and 1870. Both Napoleon Bonaparte and his nephew Louis Napoleon had utilized a republican executive position to seize imperial power. The French, after 1870, were weary of glory that led but to the grave. The fear of the "man on horseback" was very much in their minds.[11] The Fourth Republic continued the trend; the two strong leaders who attained power, de Gaulle and Mendes-France, were both defeated—although de Gaulle in 1958 had to be restored to avoid civil war.

Before the Fifth Republic, cabinet-making and cabinet-breaking with an endless succession of premiers was characteristic. Between 1873 and 1940, under the Third Republic, ninety-nine cabinets governed France, an average of one every eight months. During the Fourth Republic, from 1946 to 1958, there were twenty-two "governments" (i.e., cabinets) with an average tenure of just about six months. Since a premier to gain and retain power had to command a majority in the French lower house, and since majorities were continually forming and reforming as issues of domestic and foreign politics followed quickly on the heels one of the other, "governments" in France had a temporary air even when they succeeded in staying longer in power than the average. As a corollary, since governments were never easy to form, France was frequently without any government at all.

Against this picture of confusion and weakness, two long-term factors must be weighed. The first was the French habit of forming cabinets, one after the other, from basically the same individuals. The party leaders of the bloc were the natural claimants to ministerial rank, and the shift of a coalition a number of degrees to the right or to the left inevitably meant that (normally) a majority of the outgoing ministers also became incoming ministers. In the bloc and coalition system it was extremely rare for a government of the left to be replaced by one of the right, or vice versa. Since the non-Communist par-

---

[10] We are speaking here of the practice rather than the theoretical provisions of the constitution. In 1877 MacMahon did dissolve the Chamber. After that no one dared to.

[11] The term comes from General Boulanger's threatened attempts to seize power; he was the "man on horseback."

ties after 1947 refused to include the Communist left in the new cabinets, the effect was thus to reduce still further the possible extremism of any shift. In the decade after 1945 the choice in forming new governments in France was virtually confined to relying on the support of the Socialist groups on the left or the de Gaullists and others on the right. To illustrate the resulting continuity one has only to remember that, until Mendes-France came to power at the end of 1954 and assumed the office of foreign secretary as well as premier, the foreign minister of France since 1945 had been either Georges Bidault or Robert Schuman, despite almost twenty changes of government.

The second factor also offset in some degree the confusion and weakness implicit in the pre-Fifth Republic French parliamentary system: France's basic foreign-policy problems on the European continent, especially the German problem, are relatively permanent. The logic of that problem reduces France's alternatives drastically, since there are only two basic policies possible for France to follow vis-à-vis Germany. France can either treat Germany as an irreconcilable enemy or as a nation whose interests, although in many ways opposed to France, can be made compatible with French interests short of an open breach and war. Irrespective of party affiliation and because of the immediate obviousness of what is involved, deputies had little choice but to rally behind one or the other of these possibilities. Nevertheless, while France's alternatives over Germany have been relatively clear, she has not always been able to decide at critical points which to follow—as we shall see below. Paradoxically this failure cannot be laid solely at the door of the hampering effects of party politics, although these played their part. Even more basic was a reluctance to fight; a haunting sense of fear paralleled France's steadily declining power. The ability to act decisively in moments of danger was increasingly lacking.

Where the issues of foreign policy have been more complex, where the problem involved in the form it assumed was newer and further removed from the average Frenchman's direct personal experience (as in Indo-China and North Africa), the kaleidoscope of political party opinion had disastrous effects upon French interests and French prestige.

5 French Politics (1919–1954)

FRENCH politics, both at home and abroad, were marked by vacillation and weakness after World War I. This time France, with the aid of allies, had won "victory" over Germany: at a price of the lives of more than one out of every two Frenchmen, aged twenty to thirty-two when the war broke out. At the Versailles Conference she tried to dismember Germany. When this failed due to British and American opposition, she determined to dominate her enemy. France thereupon turned to an alliance system with Germany's eastern neighbors.[12]

The first French governments after World War I pursued a "hard" policy

[12] See above, Chapter 19.

toward Germany, typified by the punitive occupation of the Ruhr in January 1923, to force Germany to keep abreast of her reparations obligations. But in 1925 a new course was adopted. Aristide Briand, the new French foreign minister, who was henceforth to be closely associated with the policy of Franco-German reconciliation, concluded the Locarno Treaties (October 5–16, 1925).[13] Germany was admitted to the League in September 1926. The Briand-Kellogg Pact and the completion of the French evacuation of the Rhineland by the end of June 1930, increased good feeling.

Yet soon the clouds began to gather. Briand died on March 7, 1932. France for the next years became preoccupied with internal strife and strikes at home, while in its policy abroad it ran into the Ethiopian dilemma: alienate Italy with sanctions (and lose her support against Germany), or undermine the League (and the bulwark it represented against Germany). The in-between policy satisfied no one and dangerously lowered French prestige. So did the steady yielding to the increasing demands of Hitler. Between Briand's death and the beginning of World War II (some seven and one-half years), France had seventeen ministries.

In 1938 came the climax. The abandonment of Czechoslovakia to Hitler destroyed France's reputation for reliability as an ally in Eastern Europe; the pacts with Poland, Russia, and the others were undermined. When the final crisis came, France and England stood together, but they fought virtually alone.

Thus France entered World War II with the odds far greater against her than in World War I. Most important of all, Russia had been lost as an ally by the vacillation of Munich. France, in the last analysis, had failed to muster her courage and overcome internal divisions at the crucial times. Having been bled so severely in World War I, she was reluctant to face a new blood bath. By her dilatory tactics she merely made the ordeal worse and more certain. Her failure toward Germany was, of course, the crux of the situation. France had begun with severity to prostrate Germany (and Germany remembered this with resentment in the days of its revived power). Then followed a limited and reluctant policy of *rapprochement* in the Locarno period. But she had not offered enough concessions really to reconcile Germany to the *status quo* and avert Hitler. Nor had she brought herself to an uncompromising opposition to Germany once Hitler had attained power and compromise was no longer of any use. Until 1933 her policy was relatively unambiguous even if, as may be contended, shortsighted and inadequate. After 1933 she allowed herself to be blown about by the fury and whim of the storm.

In June 1940 disaster struck. France fell into German hands after a swift campaign, although southern France was permitted a precarious unoccupied existence until 1942. Pétain, Laval, and Darlan assumed the control of Vichy France, the French fleet was immobilized at Toulon, and French North Africa continued to be governed by Vichy. Continental France and all her territories who remained loyal to Vichy were out of the war. Intermittent

---

13 *Ibid.*

Anglo-French friction made it possible that France might re-enter the war on the Axis side.

Yet France also continued to fight on in the person of General Charles de Gaulle. Raising as his banner the Cross of Lorraine, de Gaulle rallied his "Free French" forces and contributed a powerful psychological (if not at first military) assistance to the British side. After the Allied invasion of North Africa on November 8, 1942, a confused struggle for power among the contenders for French leadership began. But in the end de Gaulle won power and became the first head of the provisional French government after Allied arms liberated France. Pétain and Laval were tried for treason and both found guilty, Laval being shot. France now faced a myriad of postwar problems.

The constitution of the Fourth French Republic, while much more elaborate than that of the Third, continued the unsatisfactory practices of 1870–1940. De Gaulle, who had hoped for a strengthened executive, was in the end disappointed and resigned from the government in 1946. New figures emerged to leadership, but the quick succession of cabinets continued as before World War II. The Vichy years, with their legacy of dissensions between those who had remained loyal to Pétain's regime and those who had not, added one more to a long list of issues dividing Frenchmen into opposed groups. The tendency in the early postwar elections toward larger and fewer political parties was balanced by their greater hostility to one another. The Communist Party became the largest single party; its ranks were fed by dissident workers and petty bourgeoisie who no longer retained faith in the Socialist Party as the party of mass reform. On the right, de Gaulle's Rally of the French People Party, as well as other conservative groups, continued to find support. The conflict deepened.

The details of the changes in political party strength in the first postwar decade are now merely of historical interest. Once the experiment of the center parties to include the Communists in the cabinets was abandoned in 1947, the general trend in France was to move the center of gravity of the government gradually to the right. The basic disagreements of the "Third Force" parties (between left and right) continued strong over such issues as nationalization of industry and the control of the inflation spiral, causing frequent crises. In the crucial first weeks of the Korean War, France had no government for over two weeks. The June 1951 (second postwar elections) cut Third Force strength drastically, and substantially increased rightist representation. With the Communists excluded from the government and the de Gaullist forces refusing cooperation except on their own terms, the total effect was to make the task of governing still more difficult.

The trend toward the right now became definite. The government of Pinay, whose coming to power in 1952 split the de Gaullists and thus in a sense resolved the immediate deadlock, was the first definitely right-wing government. In June 1954, under Mendes-France, this trend was interrupted for nine months; the government rested on the left and center so far as political complexion was concerned. In a more fundamental sense it rested upon Mendes-France (as we shall see a little later).

The political impasse to which France had been reduced by the increasing division was dramatized by the unprecedented difficulties of electing a new president in December 1954. It took seven days and thirteen ballots before René Coty was finally chosen president on December 23. Without the extra pressure of an impending Christmas, it might have taken still longer.

These weaknesses at home largely robbed France of its ability to make effective foreign-policy decisions in the postwar years. Each government was hopelessly weak. Frequently, while a new government was being formed, there was no effective government at all. Any government had to figure normally on determined Communist opposition on foreign-affairs issues; and the Communists, whether their parliamentary delegation reflected it in size or not, still represented over a quarter of the French people. The longer the impasse continued the more the feeling of hopelessness grew. It was only stark military disaster that finally enabled France to cut the Gordian knot.

What was the nature of this Gordian knot? The dilemma was this: France after World War II was militarily weak; and the supporting sources of national power out of which military strength is created had been impaired. The economy was not functioning smoothly; the currency was not sound; and industry was in large proportion destroyed, obsolescent, or obsolete. These domestic problems alone might have strained French powers of recuperation, considering the political divisions already described. But at the same time France found herself saddled with the steady drain of an increasingly hard-fought war in Indo-China, and she was under pressure in Europe to increase her contribution to NATO's forces. In addition, France was being continuously prodded by her allies (especially the United States) to make decisions on Germany that would revive German military strength. As long as French military power was being sapped in Asia, this step would have inevitably entailed a steady worsening of France's security position at home. On the other hand, if France too stubbornly refused to meet the United States point of view, it might destroy NATO and ultimately leave France even more defenseless. The French were even divided in their estimates as to where the real danger of aggression in Europe lay. They were of two minds as to whether to fear the already armed Russians more than the about-to-be-armed Germans. Finally, there was also a state of mind, not confined to any one political group or class, called "neutralism"—a sort of "plague on all your houses" unilateralist reaction. This arose partially out of war weariness and despair over France's predicament, and partially out of hopes that France could again gain a position of world leadership by holding the balance of forces steady between Soviet pressures on the one hand and United States pressures on the other.

In this situation France month after month, and even year after year, teetered on the brink of indecision. She took refuge in debate and delay. Indeed the great debate in France in 1953 and part of 1954 was over when to debate the proposed European Defense Community. And the delay over Indo-China extended to the eleventh hour, when the fall of Dien Bien Phu brought about a recognition of stark reality.

6 *The Indo-China Riddle*

IN the spring of 1954 the Indo-China War came to a climax. The government of M. Laniel had agreed to a great-power conference on Asia in Geneva. M. Laniel's Foreign Minister, Georges Bidault, represented France during the opening weeks of this conference, which began on April 26, 1954, and was designed to "settle" both the Korean problem and the Indo-China question. In the ensuing discussions Bidault took the position that the task of the conference was to arrange for the withdrawal of foreign interference in the civil war in Indo-China and to find a formula whereby the war could be brought to a close without Indo-China being lost to the French Union.

The Laniel government, like its predecessors, while not opposed to negotiations, had found itself unable to follow a consistent and feasible policy. It had not abandoned its hopes of military victory in Indo-China. Under the "Navarre Plan" it had set out to achieve this aim by occupying the fortress of Dien Bien Phu and challenging the Viet-Minh forces to a fixed battle. The reasoning of the French military was simple: the war had favored the Communist forces because their guerrilla tactics avoided Western-style warfare, in which their irregular forces could easily be destroyed. If the Communists could be lured into a fixed battle, the trained French divisions would destroy them. To bait the trap, Dien Bien Phu, in the heart of Viet-Minh territory in North Indo-China, was chosen. The temptation was made deliberately well-nigh irresistible. And the Viet-Minh forces accepted.

Even as the Geneva Conference continued its deliberations, the climactic battle of the Indo-Chinese War was under way. While Bidault refused concessions in Geneva, the military catastrophe was occurring in the East. France's political demands and her military position diverged ever further. On May 2, 1954, a new massive assault began against Dien Bien Phu. Indo-Chinese Communist troops, organized in regular divisions and fighting in just the way the French had hoped, pressed savage attacks that whittled down progressively the area at Dien Bien Phu still in French hands. The airstrip through which French supplies were being funneled (for overland reinforcement was precluded by Communist control of the surrounding areas) became increasingly untenable. A Battle of the Alamo was in the making. It became obvious that French military estimates of Viet-Minh fighting capacity had been absurdly optimistic. Even though it was reported [14] that a Communist Chinese General was at Viet-Minh headquarters, directing the attack, and

---

[14] Mr. Dulles in a press conference, reported in the NYHT (EE) and NYT, April 6, 1954.

that the Chinese Communists had assisted with communication networks and radar-controlled 37 mm. anti-aircraft guns, it was obvious that the fighting proper was in Viet-Minh hands—and that they were winning.

The disaster mounted to a climax to the accompaniment of frenzied action around the world. In Washington the United States government seemed on the brink of armed intervention. Dulles had already said on March 29 that the United States could not "passively" accept the loss of Indo-China. In the French Parliament the debate became ever fiercer, while Bidault shuttled back and forth from Geneva to Paris, trying to plug the leaks in his diplomatic dike at the conference and at the same time hold his parliamentary support. Laniel's cabinet had earlier vacillated between inviting United States intervention and refusing it; at the eleventh hour it again called for aid. The situation became desperate. On May 7 Dien Bien Phu fell, and at the last moment Washington held back from involvement in what was already a lost war. In June the French evacuated the southern part of the rich Red River Delta. In North Indo-China the French held only Hanoi and its port of Haiphong.

These events discredited Laniel's government. On June 19, 1954, he was succeeded by Pierre Mendes-France who, while a professional politician, was also a clear-sighted, vigorous speaker with great intellectual capacity. By party affiliation a Radical Socialist, he won the premiership not because of his political affiliation but by his performance in the National Assembly. Here, with incisive logic (in the best French tradition), he repeated again and again, with ever-increasing effect, that France must resolve her dilemma and that the key to the problem was the restoration of peace in Indo-China. With the drain on France in Asia once halted, France could recover her power in Europe, reform her economy, and face the inevitable and unpleasant facts of Germany's recovery. The program of Mendes-France, whatever its defects, had one great advantage: it was clear and consistent. It promised to do for France what the English Labour Government had done for Britain: cut its commitments by liquidating untenable positions in Asia and in this way permit recovery at home.

Mendes-France proceeded to put his program into effect with impressive speed. He announced that he would achieve peace in Indo-China within thirty days or resign. In the light of the Communists' reputation for endless negotiations, this promise seemed to be the height of audacity.

The task that Mendes-France undertook was most difficult. He not only had to contend with bitterness and distrust at home in a context of the sad depletion of French prestige, but he was regarded in Washington as a man dedicated to a program of appeasement. The situation was most tempting to the Communist bloc. They had won North Indo-China and already controlled great areas in the south as well. Each year since the end of World War II they had gained progressively more territory. Now there remained grave doubt that the French could for much longer resist being thrown into the sea and forced out of all Indo-China. The backbone of French military resistance had undeniably been broken at Dien Bien Phu.

Had the Communists not decided upon a policy of moderation (which must have been especially disgruntling to Ho Chi Minh, the Viet-Minh leader, who saw victory finally within his grasp), Mendes-France's program could not have been successful. It may be that the impetuosity shown in Washington, with its constant threat that the United States would intervene whether it made good military sense or not, induced the Communist moderation. Or it may have been Communist hopes that Mendes-France might be persuaded to oppose German rearmament. Or it may have been a sense that the patience of the West was wearing thin, and that the disastrous events at Dien Bien Phu had produced a blind determination not to yield further. Whatever the reason was, Russia and China, along with Viet-Minh, agreed to a solution which represented more a victory than a defeat for the West (although it was condemned nonetheless in some quarters in the United States as appeasement).

The Geneva settlement of July 1954, was a reasonable one in the light of the over-all situation. True, it divided Viet-Nam on the line of the Seventeenth Parallel.[15] But it represented a realistic recognition of the relative strength of the Communist and anti-Communist blocs in the Asian area, in view of the United States refusal to see all Indo-China gravitate into Communist control. While the Viet-Minh forces were capable of wresting the remainder of Viet-Nam from the French, it would almost certainly have meant the beginning of a third world war and the enlargement of hostilities. Communist China, subjected to a severe drain by the Korean War, was reluctant to throw down the gauntlet; and Russia, with the problems of the succession to Stalin still unresolved, also wished peace.

Mendes-France thus was able, essentially within his self-set deadline, to bring the war in Indo-China to a close. By finding a way out of what had become a nightmare, the French people regained some of their lost prestige. The cutting of the Gordian knot and the achievement of the quite respectable line of the Seventeenth Parallel enabled Mendes-France to turn his attention to problems nearer home.

7 The German Riddle

IN Europe, France's problems were equally pressing and even more complex. Here, too, Mendes-France was confronted with problems long postponed. Unless some solution to the German problem could be found, there could be no respite within which Mendes-France could devote his attention to the long-range sources of French national weakness—an economy whose heavy industry was obsolescent and whose managers preferred restricted production at high

---

[15] The terms of the settlement are given in Chapter 30.

prices to large production at low prices. Nor, in the prevailing distraction with pressing problems, could constitutional reforms be introduced that would enable the French government to become more stable.

Action on the German problem meant that some decision on the European Defense Community Treaty had to be taken. This treaty, which by the summer of 1954 had become a symbol of French governmental paralysis and instability, had been suggested by the French themselves as a counterproposal to the United States demand (in 1950, at the NATO Council's New York meeting) for a ten-division independent German army and West Germany's admission to NATO. Yet it had been repeatedly denied debate in the National Assembly, and the whole question of West Germany's affiliation with Western defense had thereby been frozen. Mendes-France now moved to press the issue and decide it one way or the other.

There was, between 1950 and 1954, hardly any issue on which the French people and the French Chamber were in so unanimous agreement as in their reluctance to see German rearmament. Across the whole range of the political spectrum, Frenchmen were able to agree that arms in the hands of the Germans, no matter under what safeguards and promises, and no matter in what form, constituted the driving of a heavy nail into the coffin of *la belle France*. At the same time, even while Frenchmen shuddered at the memories of Teutonic invasion thrice in seventy years, they were confronted with the realistic consideration that the rearmament of Germany would inescapably one day reoccur. They were also under heavy pressure from their allies who were, if Britain and the United States acted together, in a position more or less to force the issue. If Britain, the United States, and West Germany had a common policy on German rearmament, it placed French ability to delay and veto seriously in doubt over the long run. The occupation had, even by 1952 or 1953, become little more than a formality. If a test of strength were to occur, France would have to give in. Indeed, although France's great trump card appeared to be her territorial hold on a portion of West Germany, her real trump lay in her strategic location as the supply depot and deployment center for West European defense. Without France and with Germany, the NATO forces would be crammed into a very small maneuvering area and could not be dispersed in depth.

Weighing all this, and considering that the inevitable rearmament would be safest if done in a manner that France could sufficiently control, the French had originally suggested the European Defense Community. The European Army, which the proposed Community would administer, was to be composed of the armed forces of France, West Germany, the Benelux states, and Italy. They would wear a common uniform, use common equipment, and be under a common European command, the whole to be affiliated with NATO.

The EDC proposals were cast in the form of a draft treaty which was signed in May 1952 by the six states concerned. Hardly had it been signed when opposition in France became evident. This opposition was widely varied. It included at one extreme the nationalists who were against European integration on any level—economic, political, or military; but it also included many who, while supporting the idea of a European army, were concerned over what they considered defects in the treaty. Thus the opposition was a curious compound of many points of view, demonstrating once more the old political truism that it is easier to rally an opposition to a proposal than to gather a majority in its favor.

The René Mayer government in January 1953 excluded Robert Schuman, father of the European Army plan, from the foreign ministership. Only on this condition would the de Gaullists agree to allow Mayer's cabinet to take power. He also had to promise renegotiation of the treaty. Konrad Adenauer in Germany thereupon declared that Germany, too, was not completely satisfied. Mayer responded by announcing that the fate of the EDC and the solution of the Saar problem were linked.

This Saar issue was extremely troublesome—as it had been before World War II. With the Saar production in her hands, France, while not Germany's economic equal, could hope to compete; with the Saar in German hands, France would be hopelessly left behind. (French coal production at the time, *with* the Saar, was 70 million tons to West Germany's 125 million; steel was 13 million *with* the Saar, to Germany's 15 million.)

But economics was not the entire trouble. Aside from the natural temptation to keep postponing this unpleasant issue of German rearmament, and the honest doubts about the treaty provisions proper, there were also growing doubts about the ultimate feasibility of the EDC. The original French idea had been the establishment of multinational divisions, composed, for example, of a German battalion, a French battalion, and an Italian battalion. Language and other difficulties implicit in this arranagement soon led the NATO command to press for single-nation divisions, within multinational army corps, as a substitute. This proposal drained the original plan of much of its attractiveness. The step from German *divisions* to that of German *army corps* is not a long one. Once these divisions existed, what could prevent a German government from ordering such a regrouping? What then? Neither common uniform nor common equipment was proof against the loyalty of German soldiers to their government. As a European federal government became more remote in the atmosphere of renewed nationalistic claims, the value to France of the EDC became more questionable.

Therefore, while ultimately the other five signatories ratified the EDC, France, who had proposed the plan, ended by voting it down. The decisive vote, on August 30, 1954, came under Mendes-France's government. No other government in France in the many months that had elapsed since the signing of the draft treaty had even dared to bring it to a vote. When Mendes-France forced the issue, he did so without making its passage a question of confidence in his regime. He was not personally strongly in favor of the EDC.

His action was calculated to "clear the decks" for a new beginning and thus end the paralysis that the issue had produced in the French Parliament and that had brought France widespread ridicule.

The defeat of the EDC, although it was foreshadowed by preceding events, threatened to rupture allied unity. In the immediate aftermath, however, and acting with surprising speed, Britain, France, Germany, and the United States agreed upon a conference at London. This was held in October 1954 and soon produced a set of draft treaties ending the occupation of Germany, permitting German rearmament, and providing for West Germany's entry into the North Atlantic Pact. Since these, by themselves, permitted German rearmament on a divisional level with German corps commands, the problem of safeguards was approached from a new angle. The whole new arrangement was to be coordinated through the Brussels Council of Ministers (the "Western Union" Council created by the treaty of 1948 among Britain, France, and the Benelux nations), to which Germany and Italy were now to belong; and through the NATO command structure and the North Atlantic Council, in which all the Brussels states would also be represented. Germany, as an "advanced area," was not to develop or manufacture atomic, chemical, or biological weapons, long-range and guided missiles, large warships, certain kinds of mines, or strategic bombers.[16] These might fall into Russian hands in the event of an attack. This face-saving device was meant to hobble the German ability to wage independent war. The German government also promised never to have recourse to force to achieve the reunification of Germany or the modification of the present boundaries of the German Federal Republic.[17] Finally, the arrangements included an agreement by France and Germany on the "Europeanization" of the Saar,[18] and a convention between Germany, the United States, Britain, and France, "in view of the present international situation and the need to insure the defense of the free world" for the stationing of "foreign forces in the Federal Republic."

This complex set of agreements charged the Brussels Council with setting the maximum defense forces of each member state, and made the NATO Council responsible for setting the minimum contributions (which were, of course, not to exceed the maximums). These arrangements, it was hoped, would provide for European defense with German help, and yet keep German arms under control. From a psychological point of view, what, more than anything else, brought French agreement to these arrangements, was a dra-

---

16 Many other weapons and parts were to be "controlled." The full list of these restrictions, which are contained in an annex to the Brussels Protocol, appear in *NYT*, October 24, 1954.

17 See "Declaration of Bonn," *NYT*, October 24, 1954.

18 Subsequently repudiated by the Saar plebiscite of October 1955. The German-speaking Saarlanders rejected the proposal by 67.7 per cent. Further negotiations between Germany and France brought agreement in October 1956, for the return of the Saar to Germany on January 1, 1957. France will receive 90 million tons of Saar coal for 25 years, plus other rights.

matic promise by Great Britain to keep four divisions and an air force stationed on European soil for as long as a majority of the Brussels Treaty powers desired.

Mendes-France took back to his parliament this solution of the German riddle. On October 12, 1954, after a dramatic series of emotionally tense sessions in which the issue was often in doubt, the French lower chamber sustained Mendes-France's government and ratified the London Agreements. The votes on the various treaties reflected the still deep uncertainties and doubts with which many Frenchmen approached the problem, but the die had been cast. Mendes-France now turned to the third pressing problem— North Africa. But on this issue, he was not to succeed.

8 *Algeria and de Gaulle*

AFTER 1954 the African problem again and again precipitated the downfall of French governments—including that of Mendes-France in February 1955. Under his successors the policy of local autonomy for Tunisia, begun by Mendes-France, became a policy of full independence within the French Union. Morocco, too, became independent. But Algeria remained a festering sore. Unlike the other former North African territories of France, Algeria was a part of metropolitan France, with deputies in the Chamber at Paris. Where French minorities in Tunisia and Morocco were relatively small, in Algeria some one-and-a-quarter million Europeans (*colons*) confronted some eight-and-a-quarter million Moslems. Independence for Algeria meant separation from France of more than a million Frenchmen. Nor could the problem be solved by all French settlers packing up and going "home." Many of them came from families who had lived in Algeria for a hundred years or more. They knew no other home.

Even a strong government would have had trouble with this problem, let alone any of the Fourth Republic. France was in no mood simply to capitulate and withdraw, adding yet another inglorious retreat to her post-World-War-II record. There was no French leader, except possibly de Gaulle, who could conceivably propose such a course without in any event producing a revolt in Algeria. Moreover, France could (and did) send her conscripts to the Algerian front, in contrast to Indo-China, since Algeria was a part of France proper. This meant she could not easily lose the struggle militarily by self-imposed handicaps (as she had in part in Indo-China). But if she could not give up, and could not easily lose even while not giving up, could she win? Moslem longing for independence was both widespread and deep. Friendly and neighboring Tunisia offered shelter to the rebel "government." Soviet bloc arms, via Nasser, flowed in an unceasing stream to Algeria despite the most elaborate French precautions. For every rebel killed another replaced him.

By mid-February 1955, following Mendes-France's fall, France was groping towards its twenty-first post-World-War-II government. This time France had no government for nineteen days. Faure, who finally assumed the premiership, resumed the trend toward uneasy coalitions of the center and right. In October 1955, his government, too, began to encounter heavy political weather over the same North African problem that had defeated Mendes-France. In November, as a surprise move, Faure (seizing upon a technicality) dissolved the Assembly. The election returns of January 1956, in which the tax-protesting Poujade faction scored impressive victories, still further pulverized the French political system. The Communists regained the four hundred thousand votes they had previously lost, increasing their seats from ninety-six to one hundred fifty. The new minority Socialist–Radical Socialist coalition, led by Guy Mollet, represented a center-left alignment. The Fourth Republic had a little over two years of feeble life yet to live.

In May 1958, confronted with open insurrection by the *colons* in Algeria, and the establishing in obvious sympathy of a Committee of Public Safety under army leadership in Algeria, the Fourth Republic, under threat of an almost certain prospect of armed revolt, reluctantly called de Gaulle to power. On June 2, 1958, de Gaulle was granted full powers to rule France by decree for six months, during which the new constitution would be evolved. This arrangement was approved in the National Assembly by a vote of 322 to 232, and in the Council of the Republic, 260–48. Now began both constitutional reform at home and a final coming to terms with the Algerian question. On September 28, 1958, the new constitution was adopted by a vote of 31,066,502 against 5,419,749. On October 5, 1958, the Fifth Republic began. De Gaulle, with a solid majority in the Assembly, became its first president—and the first president in French history since Louis Napoleon to be legally endowed with far-reaching executive powers.

De Gaulle, who came to power through the initiative of the right, proceeded with a dexterity astounding to those who thought him motivated by dictatorial instincts, to handle the Algerian question while simultaneously shifting the sources of his political support leftwards. Disappointing the right wing he refused to insist that "Algeria is French" unless the people, in a popular referendum there, voted it so. While pushing an energetic military campaign designed to discourage rebel hopes of simple acceptance as the *de facto* government of Algeria, he also held out the olive branch to the Moslems by pledging the referendum as soon as hostilities ceased. Avoiding both extremes (a rebel-imposed government, or a French *colon*-imposed rule) he insisted upon a free vote—which he pledged would be followed whatever its results.

In May 1961, this most difficult (and yet sensible) course of action began to bear fruit with the initiation of direct conversations between the French government and the rebel leaders following de Gaulle's suppression of a new army-led coup in Algeria. In March 1962, he took the issue to the people and, in a referendum in April he received the support of 91 per cent of the votes cast by 65 per cent of the electorate. When the Algerians voted for independence, de Gaulle announced on July 3 that their decision would be honored and ties would be broken. The right-wing Secret Army organization (O.A.S.) continued attempts to assassinate him, machine-gunning the car in which he was riding on August 22 without success. The year 1962 marked a close to a shedding of French blood in military combat which had gone on steadily since 1939. A grateful French people endorsed de Gaulle's proposal to amend the constitution to permit direct presidential elections. In November 1962, his party received a clear majority. Three years later in December, de Gaulle, in the first direct presidential election won a new seven-year term, after a run-off election, with 55 per cent of the votes.

9 De Gaulle's Policies: An Assessment

ABROAD, de Gaulle's policies in the years after he had restored peace, brought mixed reactions. The keystone of Gaullist policy was the re-establishment of French power, economic health, and influence. To those ends he introduced the new "hard" franc, stabilized the currency, and halted the serious inflation, thus allowing social peace. He began the development of an independent nuclear strike force outside NATO, so that France's voice would be heard. He cooperated with Germany under Adenauer as a means of balancing American predominance in Western Europe. He vetoed British admission to the Common Market on January 29, 1963, against the wishes of the other five members, partly because of Britain's unwillingness to give up all close ties with the U.S. and the Commonwealth as admission price. He proceeded with the development of the Common External Tariff of the EEC but in July 1965 vetoed plans for proceeding to the veto-less supranational stage.

Replying on television to critics of his general approach to problems, de Gaulle in April 1965 expressed his views succinctly: "The fact that we have again taken up our faculty of judgment and action toward all problems seems sometimes to offend a state [i.e., the United States] which could, because of its power, think that it has a supreme and universal responsibility." He went on: "No matter how big the cup is that is handed to us from outside, we prefer to drink from our own, while still clinking glasses around us." And finally: "Frenchwomen, Frenchmen, you can see it. For us, for all, more than ever, France must be France."

As early as the Nassau Agreement (at which time the U.S. had offered France Polaris missiles under the same terms agreed to by Britain—at least lip-service to the idea of an integrated NATO nuclear force), de Gaulle had put his finger on the weak point in the U.S. proposals. The concept involved "a web of liaisons, transmissions and interferences within itself . . . such that, if an integral part were suddenly snatched from it [such as the British were allowed to do as an emergency measure], there would be a strong risk of paralyzing it just at the moment, perhaps, when it should act." [19] De Gaulle, who

---

[19] In his press conference of January 14, 1963. See *Major Addresses, Statements and Press Conferences of General Charles de Gaulle*, May 18, 1958–January 31, 1964 (French Embassy, Press and Information Division, 1964), p. 219.

was informed of the Nassau Agreement only after its release to the press, indicated his basic distrust of Great Britain's "special relationship" to the United States by announcing at this same press conference that he opposed British membership in the Common Market. In discussing the Nassau Agreement de Gaulle also indicated clearly his suspicions that France was to be denied a really equal voice with the Anglo-Americans: "Of course, I am only speaking of this proposal and agreement because they have been published and because their content is known." [20]

At a news conference on September 9, 1965, de Gaulle explained his opposition to supranational status for the Common Market. He said ". . . nothing which is important at present . . . and later in the operation of the Common Market of the Six, should be decided and, even more, applied, except by the responsible public authorities . . . that is, the Governments controlled by the Parliaments." He took note of the opposed and "different concept of a European federation in which . . . the countries would lose their national personalities" and "be ruled by some technocratic, stateless and irresponsible Areopagus." Such a plan, he said, "contradicts all reality." France favored "organized cooperation . . . evolving, doubtless, toward a confederation" which "could one day make possible the adherence of countries such as Britain or Spain which, like ours, could in no way accept the loss of their sovereignty. It alone would make the future entente of *all* of Europe conceivable." [21]

On January 29, 1966, it was announced from Luxembourg that the Common Market nations had agreed to de Gaulle's demand that the executive commission be stripped of much of its power, especially its supranational authority; and that each member would retain a permanent veto power over the future of the organization.

In a news conference on February 21, 1966, de Gaulle called NATO a protectorate and announced that after April 4, 1969, any foreign troops in France would have to be under French command. "It is a question of re-establishing a normal situation of sovereignty under which, whatever is French, on the ground, in the air, on the sea, and all French armed forces, and every foreign element which happens to be in France, will henceforth be subordinate only to the French authorities." Plans were going forward to produce by 1970 two nuclear-powered submarines, two large aircraft carriers, and a helicopter carrier. By 1974 the French navy was to have a squadron of nuclear-power submarines carrying 48 long-range missiles.

By 1967 much of NATO's structure in France was being liquidated. France continued, in de Gaulle's words, to be "the ally of her allies," but no longer on a fully coordinated basis.

These independent moves, and others, made de Gaulle the *enfant terrible*

[20] *Ibid.*, p. 218.

[21] "President De Gaulle Holds Twelfth Press Conference," French Embassy, Press and Information Service, Speeches and Press Conferences No. 228, September 9, 1965, pp. 4–5. Italics added.

of the Western bloc—especially in American eyes. To many Americans, in-
censed by his actions and irritated by his style, he seemed to be delaying the
natural future of Europe by opposing Western integration, and seeking to restore a vanished past. Here, precisely, was the question, for de Gaulle's actions
lend some credence to either point of view. Surely de Gaulle's style was somewhat dated although not antique. Were his actions, however, a looking backward or a looking forward? Could such ultra-sophisticated schemes as the
M.L.F. have been made to work? (We have earlier indicated skepticism on
this point.) Could the Common Market actually have proceeded to a workable supranationalism with the delicate problems of Germany's division and
Britain's association still left up in the air? Did it serve a useful purpose to coordinate most of the military power of the Atlantic Alliance states within the
NATO structure if indeed these nations did not agree to a uniform conception of the power problem and were far apart on the problem of military
commitments in Asia? Was de Gaulle's establishment of diplomatic relations
with Communist China the prerogative of a sovereign state bent upon dealing
realistically with things as they were, or a disloyal act to the United States? De
Gaulle had one incontestable merit on the world scene: he forced the West
to re-examine its problems even while they dismissed part of his efforts as mere
restoration of French *grandeur*. Kissinger remarks: "History will probably
demonstrate that de Gaulle's conceptions—as distinct from his style—were
greater than most of his critics. But a statesman must work with the material
at hand. If the sweep of his conceptions exceeds the capacity of his environment to absorb them, he will fail regardless of the validity of his insights.
. . . A structure which can be preserved only if there is a great man in each
generation is inherently fragile. . . . The irony of the Franco-American
rivalry [over the future of the Atlantic community] is that de Gaulle has conceptions greater than his strength, while United States power has been greater
than its conceptions." [22]

De Gaulle had without question brought France out of the wilderness of
chaos, confusion, and despair. Suspected by his critics of believing himself to
be France's new Joan of Arc, he had made the concept not so absurd. But
since the garments of the Fifth French Republic were so distinctly cut to the
grand measurements of de Gaulle, it also raised the question of what would
happen if a lesser man wore the cloth after him.

---

[22] Henry A. Kissinger, *The Troubled Partnership*, p. 63.

CHAPTER **28**

The Developing Nations

It is a fact too that the average daily production per well is 11 barrels in the United States, 20 barrels in Venezuela, and 4,000 barrels in the Arab area. Have I made clear how great the importance of this element of strength is? I hope so.

GAMAL ABD EL-NASSER
The Philosophy of the Revolution

It is not any particular genius which makes the Western countries richer; neither is it because of a natural disability that the other countries are poor. Colonialism is the explanation of the whole phenomenon of disparity. The peoples of Africa, Asia and Latin America, because of ages of colonialism, have been robbed of their gold, their diamonds, their cotton, their silk, their ivory, their spices, their drugs, their rubber, their oil, their animal wealth, and many times even robbed of their fabulous museums, including their dead kings and queens.

Saudi Arabian Delegate
*UN General Assembly,
Fifteenth Session*

For the first time in history the Organization of American States has created and sent to the soil of an American nation an international peacekeeping military force.

PRESIDENT LYNDON B. JOHNSON
May 28, 1965

T HE non-Western world has already bulked large in this book. We encountered it as the geographical focus in the age of empire-building. We saw it as the source of much of the membership of (and even more of the problems confronting) the UN. Events in these areas have had substantial effects on the balance of power and have led to all three sanctions ventures. UN non-fighting forces were originated to deal with disputes centering there. They have figured in the Cold War; they have a substantial place in the Sino-Soviet dispute. So the ex-colonial areas—Africa, the Middle East, Latin America, and Asia (including Southeast Asia)—have not been unnoted. What we have not yet done, and must now do, is see the problems, forces, and developments in these areas as areas. In this chapter we shall deal with

Africa, the Middle East, and Latin America. In the following two, we shall consider the vast realm which is Asia.

The areas and nations we are now about to survey have much in common; yet in some ways they are quite unlike. Latin America, for example, certainly does not consist of newly independent states with brand new names. Africa, by contrast, is scarcely recognizable today as old, colonial names have been jettisoned and new ones found. Yet both areas might legitimately be described by a term such as "the developing nations." Both areas, like the Middle East, too, are developing from one thing into another, and more quickly than the rest of the world. They all have this in common: few generalizations about them have permanent validity. Social, economic, and/or political change—and at a rapid pace—is their common hallmark.

I African Politics: An Overview

AFRICA is a vast realm, much of it still relatively unexplored. In size it is over three times as large as the continental United States. Most of its northern third is desert area, containing few natural resources so far discovered except oil. Below the Sahara, Africa has exceedingly varied terrain, from rainy tropics to highlands. As most people now know it has snow-covered mountains right on the equator. And this area contains most sought-after minerals: from diamonds; through copper, tin, and gold; to uranium and bauxite. Richest in these resources in this area by far are two states who have also furnished a disproportionate share of Africa's political problems: South Africa and the Congo.

Especially at the very north and very south of Africa are found the whites —greatest in number in South Africa, substantial in number in Kenya and Rhodesia and along the Mediterranean coast (although less now than before in Algeria). The dark Caucasoids of much of Northern Africa are related to the Caucasians of Europe; the Caucasized Negroes in the remainder of the north represent a blending, especially pronounced in the southern part of Algeria, the area to the south of it, and over by the Horn of Africa, near the Gulf of Aden. Then come the Forest Negroes of much of Central Africa, and the Bantu-speaking Southern Negroes, and the Bushmen, the Hottentots, and the rest. This is, very briefly, the Africa now so in ferment.

From a Western point of view Africa's history is ancient for north of the Sahara, reasonably old in the southern tip, and very recent for much of the rest. The history of the Roman Empire is rich with North African adventures: Carthage and Hannibal to cite an example. Cape Town, in South Africa, was a fruit of the Age of Exploration; it was founded by the Dutch in 1652. But Henry Stanley's famous greeting to David Livingstone—"Dr. Livingstone, I presume?" occurred less than a hundred years ago, at the time of the Franco-Prussian War. The great carving-up of Africa by the colonial powers (as we saw in Chapter 7) was a phenomenon of the nineteenth century, much of it of the last thirty years of that century.

So complete was Africa's exploitation that in 1914 there were only two independent states in Africa: Liberia and Ethiopia (and the Italians had tried to take the latter, and would actually conquer it a little later on). Until Ghana became independent in March 1957, the only independent states in Black Africa were Ethiopia, Liberia, the Union of South Africa, and the Sudan. Since then a flood of new states has swept over and changed the face of Africa. It is fair to say that these states, unlike the nineteenth-century norm, have no real nationalism behind them. Tribalism would describe it better. Out of this has already come trouble and unrest; out of it may come some sort of federation. So far the movement has been predominately toward more and more independent states, coupled with a still fragile regionalism in the Organization of African Unity (formed in May 1963 with 34 members by 1964 and 38 members by November 1966).

Nowhere else on the face of the globe can one find so many independent states so newly independent. Most have less than a decade of sovereign experience behind them. Their economic viability varies considerably but the standard of living is almost uniformly as low as the expectations of quick material progress are uniformly high. Malawi, the 37th independent state in Africa, becoming sovereign in 1964, began its separate existence with a per capita income of less than $20 per year. Between 1958 and 1965 the average population increase in the new sub-Sahara states was 2.5 per cent annually, while food production generally rose 1.5 per cent.

The lack of experience with independence, coupled with the lack of a stable and developed nationalism, has produced in many of these states one-party rule under the father-figure of the "liberator." Lack of pluralistic counter-pressure (other than tribal-based rivalries) has undermined stability of any other sort except for the alternative of army rule. These observations do not apply only to Black Africa although they find their most copious illustrations there. Ahmed ben Bella, leader of the fight for Algerian independence, was deposed in the summer of 1965. Joseph Kasavubu (of whom more later) fell from power in the Republic of the Congo. In late 1965–early 1966, military coups occurred (besides the Congo) in Dahomey, the Central African Republic, Upper Volta, Nigeria, and Ghana. In Ghana the coup swept Kwame Nkrumah, one of the most flamboyant and outspoken of African leaders, from the presidency. In March 1966 there was a grave crisis in Uganda, while in Nigeria the parliament remained suspended. Other nations experiencing successful coups since 1960 included Togo and the Congo Republic, while nations where coups and plots were attempted include Senegal, Guinea, the Ivory Coast, Gabon, Niger, Chad, Ethiopia, Kenya, Burundi, and Tanzania. In late 1966 the army took over Burundi.

The more flamboyant of the leaders of Black Africa have leaned heavily on Soviet or Chinese foreign aid (which between 1946 and mid-1964 amounted to $840 millions to Africa as against $2.25 billions from the United States).

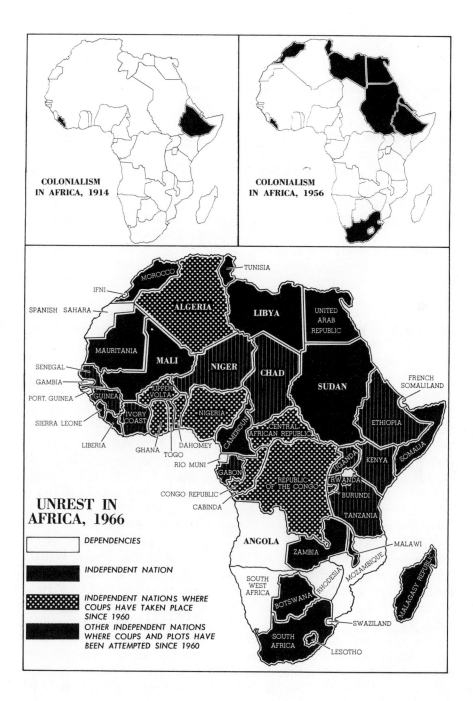

COLONIALISM
IN AFRICA, 1914

COLONIALISM
IN AFRICA, 1956

UNREST IN
AFRICA, 1966

TUNISIA
MOROCCO
IFNI
SPANISH SAHARA
ALGERIA
LIBYA
UNITED
ARAB
REPUBLIC
MAURITANIA
MALI
NIGER
CHAD
SUDAN
FRENCH
SOMALILAND
SENEGAL
GAMBIA
PORT. GUINEA
GUINEA
UPPER
VOLTA
SIERRA LEONE
IVORY
COAST
NIGERIA
ETHIOPIA
LIBERIA
GHANA
TOGO
DAHOMEY
CAMEROUN
CENTRAL
AFRICAN REPUBLIC
KENYA
SOMALIA
RIO MUNI
GABON
UGANDA
RWANDA
CONGO REPUBLIC
REPUBLIC
OF THE CONGO
BURUNDI
CABINDA
TANZANIA
ANGOLA
MALAWI
ZAMBIA
SOUTH
WEST
AFRICA
RHODESIA
MOZAMBIQUE
MALAGASY REPUBLIC
BOTSWANA
SWAZILAND
SOUTH
AFRICA
LESOTHO

DEPENDENCIES

INDEPENDENT NATION

INDEPENDENT NATIONS WHERE
COUPS HAVE TAKEN PLACE
SINCE 1960

OTHER INDEPENDENT NATIONS
WHERE COUPS AND PLOTS HAVE
BEEN ATTEMPTED SINCE 1960

553

Notable among these were Nkrumah himself, and President Sékou Touré of Guinea (who, in the aftermath of the Ghanian coup obligingly gave Nkrumah refuge). They have also tended to run up great foreign debts through the pursuit of ambitious but unrealistic plans, including a government-owned airline and shipping line for Ghana. Although Ghana began its national existence as the richest of the Black African states, Nkrumah led it to bankruptcy even while moving to ever-greater personal control. He forced the National Assembly to make him president for life in 1962, thereafter collecting titles such as "the Leader," "His Messianic Majesty," and "Osagyefo" (or "Redeemer.") Guinea and Ghana illustrate the Alice-in-Wonderland nature of some announced African moves toward federation-confederation. The unity of these two states (separated physically and by language) has never really been implemented at all.

Fairly characteristic of conditions under the less flamboyant leaders of Black African states troubled with political unrest, was Uganda. A country of 6.5 million people with 28 tribes combined in a fragile federation of five "kingdoms," its Prime Minister, Milton Obote replied to charges by five cabinet ministers of corruption by sending them to jail and taking (in his own words) "all the powers of the government." Potentially most serious was the continued crisis in Nigeria in 1966. While Lt. Col. Yakubu Gowon remained in power, the Eastern Region under rival (Ibo tribe) leadership, was virtually going its own way.

These new nations of Africa have so far developed some of the usual tendencies of newer sovereign entities more than others. They have, for example, had almost no armed clashes along or across frontiers (although there have been a number of instances where one has sheltered "resistance movements" from other states or where arms and supplies destined elsewhere have been allowed transit). Yet potential territorial disputes are available in fair supply. Africa has the largest number of incompletely agreed frontiers of any area of the world. (The only area even comparable is Asia where the officially disputed frontiers are exclusively China's except for Burma, Kashmir, and Indo-China.) Latent frontier disagreements in Africa involve at least 19 states.[1] A serious but brief armed clash occurred on the frontier between Morocco-Algeria in October 1963; it was ended through a cease-fire negotiated by Emperor Haile Selassie of Ethiopia and President Modibo Keita of Mali. The Ethiopian-Somali frontier was the scene of fighting in February 1964; the cease-fire this time resulted from direct negotiations between the parties. More such clashes can be expected once the preoccupation with internal affairs becomes less pressing and once the strong emotional post-independence legacy of hostility to colonialism or "neo-colonialism" begins to wear thinner. What is striking about the frontiers of many African (and Middle Eastern) states is their arbitrariness and artificiality. They were, after all,

---

[1] See the map in *International Boundaries and Disclaimers*, issued by The Geographer, U.S. Department of State, March 15, 1963.

for the most part not set originally as boundaries between *independent* states but as frontiers of convenience between rival (or friendly) empires. The viability of these frontiers was only a secondary consideration then, since the military or other implications of those frontiers was of only supplemental importance to the more direct relations of the imperial powers. That is, former French (or other) colonies were not essentially intended to be defended from within the colonial frontiers against more or less equal opposing forces from across the frontiers. It was the whole power of France which made them tranquil. Now that these independent states face *each other* across essentially those same frontiers, the whole effects are altered. Out of this will come many complex problems and developments. To amounts now spent on defense for largely prestige and internal security purposes, will be added other amounts spent to deal with external threats.

But for the moment such considerations have on the whole been subordinated to the movements which gain sympathetic responses in almost all the new African states: a lingering distrust of former colonial powers, opposition to "neo-colonialism" (meaning especially the still formidable economic power and tangible interests of the former empires over and in these states), "non-involvement" in the Cold War and great power antagonisms, and determination to play an important role in world politics as a bloc.

Nkrumah in the first years of African independence was probably the most fluent spokesman for such widely-held African sentiments. Two quotations will illustrate. In 1958, speaking to an Afro-Asian group, he said: "Today force is not decisive. Recent experience would indicate that all powers—great and small—are sensitive to world public opinion and take it into account in deciding their policies. We here represent a large segment of world opinion, and herein lies our strength." [2] At the Fifteenth Session of the UN General Assembly, Nkrumah also said that an African state which enters into a military alliance "with any outside power . . . not only involves the state concerned in the risk of being drawn into nuclear warfare; it also endangers the security of the neighboring African states." [3] (But Nkrumah is also a prime example of a leader who, by accepting extensive Communist aid, helped to encourage Cold War politics in Africa.)

Such statements as those of Nkrumah remind one of Woodrow Wilson's approach to peace-keeping at the end of World War I, in the sense that the Wilsonian abstractions expressed a conception of a highly undifferentiated national interest typical of new "actors" in international affairs. As time goes on, the factors which are common in the minds of Africans (centering around the colonial past) are almost certainly going to be severely counterbalanced and offset by the development of new, more nationally-oriented interests and positions. In short, there is no reason to believe that issues uniting Africans

---

[2] From *Ghana at the United Nations* (Accra: Ghana Information Service, October 1958), p. 24.

[3] UN *General Assembly, Official Records*, 15th Session, 1960–61, Part I, Vol. 1, p. 66.

against non-Africans will permanently overshadow issues dividing Africans from Africans.

The links which the former French colonies maintain with the EEC, as "associate members," already provide one source of dissension. These economic benefits are tangible: $666 million (as we saw earlier) in the Second Development Fund. In 1965 the French-speaking nations formed the African and Malagasy Common Organization (OCAM) with 13 members to improve cooperation. The Central African Economic and Customs Union (UDEAC), set up to begin in 1966, was composed of the Central African Republic, Chad, Gabon, the Congo (Brazzaville) and Cameroon—all former French colonies. Economies of many of these states are directly competitive—a factor which may inhibit any wide growth of customs unions (although in 1964, Liberia, Guinea, Sierra Leone, and the Ivory Coast, did begin a feasibility study on a free trade area). Political and military factors will also take their toll of an African "common front" in world politics in the decades ahead. These developments of differences became apparent in the early formation of loose groupings such as the Casablanca (or more pro-Communist) Group and the Monrovia (more moderate) Group (now both superseded by the OAU). They have shown up in the responses of the African states to the successive phases of the UN Congo operation. On the other hand, the fact that colonialism is still incompletely liquidated in Africa (where some Spanish and—more importantly—Portuguese colonies still exist) and the fact that the racial issue is still a factor (especially in view of Rhodesia and South Africa) remain powerful cementing forces. The *apartheid* (separatist) racial policies of South Africa are impossible for Black Africa (and the rest of the world) to ultimately accept.

The most impressive bloc actions of the African states have centered on these still unresolved racial problems, utilizing the UN as the primary vehicle for their actions. Under African pressures the UN established in late 1963 a group of experts to advise on resolving the *apartheid* problem in South Africa. When South Africa refused cooperation the Security Council appointed a new committee (June 18, 1964) to study the "feasibility, effectiveness, and implications" of economic sanctions. The vote was 8 for, none opposed, 3 abstentions (Czechoslovakia and the U.S.S.R. wanter stronger action, France wanted weaker action). The affirmative U.S. and U.K. votes were coupled to reservations that these nations did not agree in advance to accept the committee's recommendations. In December 1965 the General Assembly declared that any attempt by South Africa to annex the mandated territory of South West Africa would be an act of aggression. Rhodesia's unilateral declaration of independence from Britain (November 11, 1965) with a constitution designed to deny equal political treatment to all, brought new demands for UN actions. Colonial struggle continued, too, in the Portuguese colonies. In 1964 the Portuguese gained the upper hand in the African rebellion in Angola but lost control of large areas in Portuguese Guinea. Resistance in Portugal's east coast Mozambique colony also increased. Money and supplies for these resistance groups was coming especially from Communist China. The UN General Assembly in December 1965 characterized Portugal's attitude on these colonies as a threat to peace and urged all members to break diplomatic relations with Portugal and impose a boycott. In 1966 the failure of the Court to sustain the African point of view in the South West Africa Cases still further irritated Black Africa. At Afro-Asian prodding the General Assembly declared the mandate terminated. As the year closed the UN, upon request by Britain, decided upon mandatory economic sanctions against Rhodesia. Implementation in early 1967 was slow.

The Cold War aspect of great power relations, a serious factor already in the early Congo operation (and then even more so after the UN withdrew forces) and present also as just indicated in subversion in the Portuguese colonies, is very much an important part of African politics today. From December 1963 to early 1964, Chinese Premier Chou En-lai made an extensive African tour to ten African nations. Chinese influence grew especially strong after that visit in Zanzibar and Burundi although much of Africa was cool to the Chinese efforts. China was frustrated in her attempts to convene a second "Bandung Conference," and when the nonaligned nations did meet at Cairo in October 1964, China was not invited. Figures for Communist party membership in the new African states were virtually nonavailable. Obviously, influence in Africa is highly desirable for all the major powers, even apart from the vital raw materials which Africa supplies.

Almost every aspect of African politics so far mentioned was involved in the development of the Congo problem. In turn the experience with the Congo has had a great feedback effect on African politics.

2 The Congo

THE Democratic Republic of the Congo (not to be confused with its neighbor on the west, the Congo Republic, a former French possession) had a population of fourteen million in 1960, in an area one-third the size of the United States. It is a rich prize, well endowed with cobalt, copper, diamonds, and uranium, although its wealth is disproportionately located in the province of Katanga. In 1960 Belgium very abruptly gave it independence although it lacked virtually any native trained administrators or college graduates. Trouble developed immediately. With the native administration brand new and only nominally in control, the Congo army went on the rampage, looting, raping, even killing. Belgian paratroopers were flown in to restore order against the protest of the Congo authorities. The UN, upon the request of the Congolese government, now entered the picture. The Afro-Asian nations saw the question in colonial terms; the U.S. saw it as necessary to prevent Communist gains; the Soviets agreed to be on the African "side." On July 13, 1960, a UN African (or Congo) Force, to be drawn from contingents of African UN members was created. The ONUC, as it became known, was initially drawn from contingents from Ethiopia, Ghana, Guinea, Ireland, Liberia, Morocco, Sweden, and Tunisia. Its early strength was 11,155 men.

These forces, rushed to the Congo, had initially a relatively clear mission; they were to save white lives, control and speed evacuation, and restore a minimum of order. In this "Phase I," (from July to September), the UN did restore order and enable Belgian withdrawal. But a dilemma soon developed. For the first time in its history the UN had put troops into action, not to repel aggression (as in Korea), and not to separate belligerent armies who had agreed to the procedure (as in Suez), but to contend with an internal disequilibrium. This was unprecedented in itself. But it was not, even at that, the relatively simple task of aiding the government in power to control its own armed force. It soon came about that several "governments" existed and competed for power. This was Phase II, in which the position of the ONUC steadily deteriorated. By February 1961, there was a four-way power split: the northern and western (Leopoldville Province) areas of the Congo were under the control of President Joseph Kasavubu; the northwest (Oriental Province) followed Patrice Lumumba; the middle south was under Albert Kalonji and his Baluba tribesmen; while secessionist Katanga Province in the southwest was controlled by Moise Tshombe. Was the UN to resolve the dilemma by taking over governmental powers, setting up a UN trusteeship, and disarming the Congo army? Should it try to remain relatively inconspicuous while the contending native forces shot it out? Or what? Why send UN troops (as distinguished from UN observers as in Palestine) unless they were expected to shoot if necessary *somebody?* But who?

Lumumba, the founder of the Congolese National Movement (MNC), and a member of the fierce Mutetela tribe, had played a key role in the firecracker developments of the Congo. He was the only Congolese leader of stature who stood for a united Congo. His MNC had won 27 per cent of the vote in the elections just prior to independence, compared to President Kasavubu's party vote of 10 per cent. Lumumba had become Prime Minister on June 30, 1960; even at the independence ceremonies, in the presence of King Baudouin of the Belgians, he attacked their rule and asked for Soviet aid. Next he had invited in the UN and then attacked both the UN and the United States. To existing chaos he added more confusion. Dismissed by Kasabuvu on September 5, 1960, he was immobilized on September 14 by the army strongman, Joseph Mobutu. Taken into custody, his death—"while escaping"—was announced in February 1961.

Lumumba's death coincided with a change in the UN's mission. The UN was criticized by Lumumba's supporters, by the Casablanca Group of African states, and by the Communists for not having intervened to save Lumumba. The UN dilemma was now most acute. The ONUC was to aid the "legitimate government" of the Congo to restore order. But which "government" was "legitimate?" The ONUC was also not to use force except in self-defense, but now there was civil war. Phase III was about to begin. On February 21, 1961, the Security Council modified the ONUC's mandate. The resolution sponsored by Afro-Asian members of the Council (Liberia, the United Arab Republic, Ceylon) gave the ONUC power to take "all appropriate measures to prevent the occurrence of civil war in the Congo, including arrangements for cease-fires, the halting of all military operations, the prevention of clashes and *the use of force,* if necessary, *in the last resort.*" [4]

By April 1961 the ONUC (which had reached 19,341 in September 1960) numbered 17,941 men. Its composition had changed significantly. Now 23 nations composed the force (some with a couple of dozen men or less); but Guinea had withdrawn her 741 men while Morocco left only eight of her original 2,465; only the Sudan (one man) and Nigeria (1,678 men) had added to the African numbers, while India now had 4,016; Indonesia, 1,139; Pakistan, 551; and Canada, 284. The ONUC was becoming less African in composition exactly at the time when its mandate was broadened. In November the Secretary-General was further authorized by the Security Council to "use the requisite measure of force" to end the activities of non-UN foreign military and paramilitary personnel, and to control imports of arms. The Council declared that all secessionist activities were illegal and specifically demanded that Katanga cease and desist its resistance. This action was supported by the Afro-Asian states, the Communist states, and the Congo, as well as (with some reservations) the United States.

In July–August 1961, under UN prodding, a national parliament was convened which elected the moderate Cyrille Adoula as the Prime Minister by 200 of 221 votes. Adoula now asked UN aid to end the Katanga secession. Thus began Phase IV (August 1961—June 1964). Clashes occurred between UN units and Katanga units, followed by heavy fighting in December. (Meanwhile three African states—Ghana, Tunisia, and Liberia—withdrew units, reducing the ONUC to 15,500 troops in October.) Tshombe of Katanga now negotiated to gain time, but the negotiations, as he intended, got nowhere. By October 1962, India, alarmed at Chinese moves, spoke of wanting to withdraw her 5,500 troops. Tshombe was playing a waiting game. The UN decided to force the issue. In the fighting in December 1962—January 1963 the UN made rapid advances. By the end of January the UN controlled Katanga. By February 1963, of the ONUC's 19,798 troops, contributions of over 500 troops represented Denmark, Ethiopia, Ghana, India, Indonesia, Ireland, Malaya, Nigeria, Pakistan, Sweden, and Tunisia. India's contingent, 5,613 men, was almost a third of the whole. The ONUC was even less African.

The General Assembly ultimately established June 30, 1964 as the end of the ONUC. After that date civil war once again swept the eastern Congo, with the Chinese Communists giving support to the rebels. A temporary Belgian–U.S. rescue operation for white hostages antagonized the African nations. In July the wheel came full circle. President Joseph Kasavubu turned for support to Moise Tshombe, the former leader of Katanga's secession, who

---

[4] UN Doc. S/4741, p. 147. Italics added.

became Prime Minister on July 10. Tshombe, using Congolese units plus white mercenaries, began a vigorous and successful campaign against the rebels which restored order by 1965. But Tshombe remained anathema to many of his African neighbors, especially for his use of white mercenaries. In October 1965 he was deposed by President Kasavubu who was then ousted in November by General Joseph Mobutu. Leonard Mulamba became Prime Minister.

Such was the sequence in the UN's first serious venture into African politics. There was a clearly ironical feature to the proceedings by the UN: in appearance it disturbingly resembled the imperialism of old, but now a collective imperialism in the name of anti-imperialism—except that the UN could be expected to act more altruistically and produce more acceptable results. The Soviet Union was quick to attempt to exploit the irony in the UN. Yet the apparent alternative, in which the Soviet Union would—did—move to exploit the situation for her own benefit by gaining a foothold in central Africa, was scarcely congenial or appealing. The UN had turned a page in the book of history—but for better or for worse? If such developments recur in Africa in the still colonial areas, should the UN stage a repeat performance? The question is whether the UN is to intervene in essentially *internal* struggles because they have superficial international features or important implications—whether in the name of "anticolonialism" or in the name of insulating the scene of strife from great power interventions.

3   The Middle East: An Overview

THE Middle East (or Near East as it is often called) embraces an area whose extent is peculiarly difficult to define. Territorially and geographically its heart is in the area south of Turkey and east of Egypt; this area, the strategic crossroads of the world, provides the land bridge between Eurasia and Africa. It includes the Arab states of Saudi Arabia, Yemen, Jordan, Syria, Iraq, and Lebanon. Yet it also includes Persia (Iran), Turkey, Egypt, and Jewish Israel—states who for one reason or another are less tightly bound to this central Arab core. In addition it is the center of the Mohammedan world, and Mohammedanism as a powerful political-religious force binds the area together into something of a common world outlook far more extensive than simple enumeration suggests. Into the Balkans, across the width of North Africa, into the subcontinent of India, and even into Indonesia and the Philippines, the Moslem faith penetrates. The influence of the Middle East is thus far wider than its geographical center of gravity.

The accidents of Arab (and later Turkish) conquests at one time brought this geographical core, the Balkans, and North Africa under a common rule. From this period a legacy of distrust between Turkey and the Arab states continues. This is one of many elements of division. There is also the obvious hostility of the Arab states which surround Israel to the Jewish state. In addition there is a certain hostility between Egypt and the other Arab states which in past times were part of the Egyptian Empire. Then there is the pull of Egypt toward Africa (with which it is geographically united) and also there is the preoccupation of Turkey and Iran with the Balkans, Russia, and India (because of the nature of their location). Finally, there is antagonism between the "radical" or "socialist" republics and the "reactionary" monarchies. These complex relationships further decrease the ability of the region to act as a unit in world affairs.

These factors help to explain why the regional organization, the Arab League, has proved rather weak in practice. Even in its inception it was far from being of universal appeal to all the states of the Middle East. The original agreement to create a League of Arab States was made in October 1944, by Egypt, Syria, Trans-Jordan, Iraq, and Lebanon. On March 22, 1945, the Pact of the League of Arab States, which brought the Arab League to life, was signed by these states plus Saudi Arabia and Yemen. It provided for collective defense in the face of aggression, but unless there was unanimous agreement (excepting the vote of an aggressor) each nation was free to do what it deemed best.[5] With the Sudan, Libya, Morocco, and Tunisia joining following their independence, the League had ten members on October 1, 1958 (counting Egypt and Syria, then combined in the United Arab Republic, once). By 1964 it had thirteen members, including all independent and essentially Arabic states except Mauritania. What has held the League together has been the Palestine Question. Its main reason for being has been to oppose Israel.

The factors that unite the region, aside from religion (and here excepting Israel), are of a negative rather than of a positive form. They are also factors which, fluctuating in importance in recent years, apply unequally throughout the area. Common hostility to Western colonialism, for example, is no less meaningful in the light of the retreat of the colonial powers (especially France and Britain) from the area. Common hostility to Israel, while it continues to be important for that state's neighbors, has always been of less concern to the other Middle Eastern states. Now that Israel has demonstrated its ability to survive, the more remote Near Eastern states are even less directly interested (so long as peace is preserved). Conversely, the common fear felt by Turkey and Iran for Soviet Russia is not shared by the rest in anything like the same degree.

Apart from its strategic location, which has involved it in countless wars, the inner core of the Middle East has continued to bulk large in the affairs of the great powers because of its prodigious richness in oil. This sinew of modern war, this "black gold" as it has been called, continues to make this area of vital concern to powers far removed from it geographically. By 1951 this area alone was producing almost one-quarter of the oil in the world. Since then its

---

[5] For the text of the treaty and related documents see *Basic Documents of the League of Arab States*, New York: The Arab Information Center, 1955.

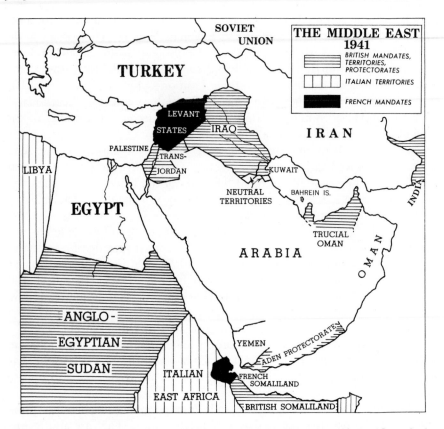

comparative production ratio has remained about the same if significantly increasing African production is figured separately. Proved reserves in the Middle East totaled 207 billion barrels in 1964 (as against 124 billions for the entire rest of the world).

Thus the Middle East in modern times has been important in world politics, not only because of the foreign policies pursued by the states within its extent but also because it is an area of weak states of great strategic and resource importance. It is an almost entirely unindustrialized area where the contrast between wealthy and poor is as great as anywhere in the world. Although the Mohammedan faith is a formidable obstacle to the expansion of communism in the area (for it teaches acquiescence—all is the "will of Allah"), the extreme poverty of the masses is an acute breeding ground of popular discontent. Feudalism is still a reality in much of the Middle East, and the rich revenues from oil royalties have poured often into the pockets of the already rich and powerful, with only a small trickle reaching the masses. Furthermore, modern ideas of nationalism are finally making headway in the area. With it is coming a greater mass awareness of the need for, and possibilities of, reform.

Sometimes this nationalist movement has been led by religious or national-

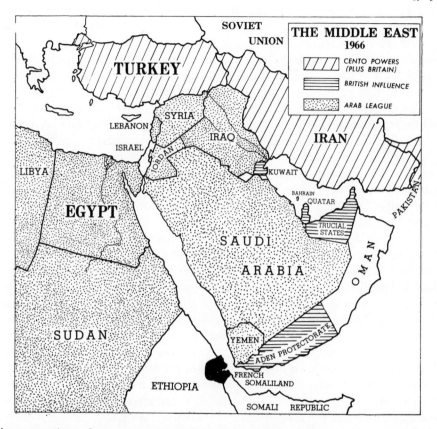

THE MIDDLE EAST
1966

CENTO POWERS (PLUS BRITAIN)

BRITISH INFLUENCE

ARAB LEAGUE

ist extremists whose very extremism led to defeat. This was the pattern in Iran where the Shah's ultimate victory over Mossadegh represented the triumph of a more moderate but still progressive nationalism. Sometimes it has been led by army officers and has resulted in the exiling of the king and the abolition of the dynasty. This was the pattern in Egypt where King Farouk's government was replaced by a military junta controlled by Lt. Col. Nasser. The pilot demonstration in the Near East of what could be done with an enlightened and moderate nationalism was provided after World War I by Turkey. The Turkish Revolution and the deposition of the sultan in 1922 have been followed since by a steady modernization and the gradual introduction of Western parliamentary methods. By his successes as the Turkish leader, Kemal Atatürk (the last name means "father of the Turks") provided precedents that the Shah of Persia and Nasser of Egypt each in his own way, followed. But even Turkey had military coups in 1960, 1962, and 1963.

In much of the remainder of the Middle East the movement is slower. It is no accident that the nationalist movement has gone furthest in the three states whose identity as separate entities goes back to ancient times. This is not surprising for the existence or independence of the other states is relatively recent (most were mandates between the two world wars), and many of their frontiers had no national significance whatsoever, but rather represented lines of administrative demarcation for the convenience of the colonial powers. Pan-Arab nationalism to such states represented something with far deeper roots than a separate Jordanian or Iraqui nationalism. Nasser, seeing (in his own words) "a role in search of a hero," offered himself as leader of a Pan-Arab movement. But a number of obstacles existed to his success.

The far greater concern of Turkey and Iraq over the Russian colossus to the north, for example, led to the formation of the Baghdad Pact in 1955 (with which Britain, Iran, and Pakistan also associated themselves). In the same year Egypt's decision to import arms from the Communist bloc to improve her military position against Israel (with whom new border incidents occurred) brought new coolness in Egyptian-Western relations. Nasser, angered over Iraq's "defection" from the Arab bloc, increased his efforts to draw the other Arab states more tightly together against Israel. He negotiated military coordination agreements with Saudi Arabia similar to his agreement with Syria. In early 1956 Jordan, under Arab pressures, threw off British control of the Arab Legion. Despite the King of Jordan's kinship with the King of Iraq, Jordan's population was two-thirds composed of Palestinians, many of them refugees, who looked to the destruction of Israel for an end to their suffering. The danger of war increased rapidly as the noose around Israel grew tighter.

As we saw in Chapter 12, the war that came in 1956 was ignited from another direction. Precipitated by Dulles' withdrawal of finances for the Aswan Dam the crisis began with Nasser's seizure of the Suez Canal Company (July 26, 1956) and led after some delays to the Suez War. In the sequel the Suez Canal was blocked by sunken ships, the UN embarked upon the first use of non-fighting forces, and the Soviet Union financed the dam.

Opinion remained divided as to the merits of America's actions. Some saw the sequence like this: Secretary Dulles slapped Nasser in the face; Nasser next slapped the British and French (who were handiest); Dulles then urged the British and French not to be too angry with Nasser; the British and French losing patience, slapped Nasser; and America ended the exchange by slapping the British and French. The winner? Soviet Russia. Others saw it as the triumph of principle over narrow interest, with the sequence something like this: "the United States will not be blackmailed over the Aswan Dam"; "the United States urges tolerance upon the parties in dispute over the Canal"; "the United States opposes the use of force to settle disputes"; "the will of the majority of the UN must be obeyed." The winner? Justice and the rule of law.

In the summer of 1958 came more developments. In Iraq both the pro-Western premier and the king were slain in a military coup. For a time it appeared that Iraq under Abdul Karim Kassem would join Nasser (which turned out not to be so). Jordan could not long stand alone in the face of such pressures. Even in half-Christian, half-Moslem Lebanon the tensions spread. The United States, heeding Lebanon's request, rushed forces to that country while Britain, invited by a fearful Jordan, did the same there. This first implementation of the Eisenhower Doctrine struck some observers as a belated attempt to prove that America had not been bluffed into the course she followed in the Suez War by Russia's threats to bombard London with missiles. Certainly it was a curiously formidable demonstration of force if it was aimed solely at seeing that Lebanon's political crisis was ended in good order. More probably it was designed to at least retard the speed with which Nasser appeared to be coordinating the Arab world for a final war with Israel. In the sequel Iraq's independent nationalist course retired for the time the specter of the powder barrel of the Middle East exploding. Iraq withdrew from the Baghdad Pact (CENTO). But the U.S. show of force had restored some stability to an area in danger of becoming a power vacuum in the wake of the undermining of Anglo-French prestige resulting from the Suez War.

4   *The Middle East: Contemporary Problems*

IN the years since 1958 tranquility has not been restored to the Middle East, but the great powers have refrained from overt interference. The U.S. landing in Lebanon had two meanings: one for Nasser, and one for the Soviet Union. In effect each was warned of the limits within which the U.S. would tolerate changes in the balance of forces there. Part of the reason for the lack of great power clashes there in the years since stem from the crises over Berlin, over Cuba, and over Viet-Nam, which diverted the U.S. and U.S.S.R. in other directions. Part of the reason came from Nasser's enforced shelving of his more ambitious plans as a consequence of Middle Eastern politics as such.

Nasser once wrote: "For some reason, it always strikes me that in this area in which we live is a role running around aimlessly looking for a hero to give it being . . . this role, exhausted by its wanderings in the vast spaces around us, has collapsed on the borders of our country and is beckoning to us to stir ourselves, to go to it, take it up, put on its costume, and give it life." [6] He attempted to fill this role. In the United Arab Republic (U.A.R.) in 1958 he linked Syria to Egypt. Iraq (perhaps Jordan) seemed within his grasp. But Iraq stayed independent, and late in 1961, Syria broke away.

The United Arab Republic continued in name, but it contained only Egypt.

Both Iraq and Syria remained the scenes of recurrent coups. In Iraq, Abdul Salam Irif became president on February 8, 1963, when Abdul Karim Kassem was overthrown. In Syria, the seventeenth military coup in seven years occurred in February 1966, replacing the more moderate Baath party leaders with a more "socialist" orientation. Developments in Algeria also dimmed Nasser's hopes. The overthrow of President Ahmed ben Bella in June 1965 by a coup led by the vice-president and army chief of staff, Houari Boumedienne, turned Algeria away from the more radical socialist path which Nasser had pioneered. In 1965 another long-time rival of Nasser, Tunisia's Habib

---

[6] Gamal Abd El-Nasser, *The Philosophy of the Revolution*, pp. 59–60.

Bourguiba, proposed Arab recognition of the existence of Israel. Consideration of this long-postponed question was sure to provide more friction in the
Arab world.

In March 1966, as the Arab premiers gathered for a conference in Cairo,
even more serious questions confronted the Arab states. The overthrow of the
monarchy in Yemen in a coup in September 1962 began a civil war in which
the republican forces were backed by the U.A.R. and the monarchical elements were supported by Saudi Arabia. After large-scale U.A.R. military
efforts in Yemen failed to bring victory, Nasser agreed with King Faisal of
Saudi Arabia in August 1965 on a Yemeni caretaker government, the withdrawal of U.A.R. troops by July 1966, and a plebiscite. Problems of Yemeni
agreement, however, soon appeared. The severe drain on the U.A.R. economy
caused by the expense of the 60,000-man Yemeni occupation would continue
until some settlement was reached. Just before the 1966 Cairo conference,
Faisal called for a meeting of Islamic states to discuss a pact which Nasser
considered a new attempt to erect a bloc more sympathetic to Western interests (and opposed to Nasser's). The granting in 1965 by West Germany of
arms aid to Israel, which caused ten Arab states to break off relations with
Bonn, was a live issue. The Kurdish revolt in northern Iraq also was a source
of trouble, with Nasser urging autonomy for the Kurds and the Kurds rejecting the subsequent Iraqi offer. Nasser's efforts to improve relations with the
West in 1965–1966 ran athwart some of these other involvements. At the end
of 1966, in the wake of an Israeli reprisal against Jordan, Syria was agitating
for King Hussein's overthrow. The Arab League was pressing Jordan to admit
Iraqi and Saudi troops.

Developments in the Middle East, where independence came earlier than
in sub-Sahara Africa, pointed the direction of what was only still implicit in
Black Africa. Although Pan-Arabism continued to command lip-service, the
hard realities of international politics and divergent national interests left it
only an ideal.

5 Latin America: An Overview

LATIN America extends as a cultural unit from the Rio Grande to Cape Horn
—from Mexico through Argentina. It spreads across two great continents
joined together by the narrow neck of land of Central America. Throughout
this area Spanish is the prevalent tongue, with the most important exception
of Brazil where the Portuguese once ruled as emperors. Here and there, clustered around the Caribbean, either on the mainland or on the scattered off-
shore islands, are still some foreign-owned possessions, remnants of colonial
days. The larger British islands such as Jamaica and Barbados are now independent, as is Guyana (former British Guiana). Barbados announced plans
in late 1966 to apply for membership in the Organization of American States
while remaining the 26th member of the Commonwealth.

Considering its vast area, Spanish America certainly ranks as the most magnificently extensive empire ever lost by a European monarchy. Between 1809 and 1825 Spain lost that empire as one by one the Latin American states gained their independence in a series of wars in which such men as Simón Bolívar led the fight for freedom. The original states thus formed through war and revolution have in the course of years divided here and there until today they number twenty. Of these twenty, three are on islands in the Caribbean —Cuba, Haiti, and the Dominican Republic. A total of six are in Central America alone, although as a unit Central America is smaller geographically than most of the separate states in South America proper.

Historically Central America has been the point at which the United States, the "Colossus of the North," has most often come into contact with Latin America. Not only is it nearer to the United States than the rest (except Mexico), but it lies athwart the Latin American point of greatest strategic interest to the United States. Here was built the Panama Canal, which affords the shortest sea route between the American East and West Coasts; even before the construction of the canal the isthmus was a natural short travel route combining sea and overland transportation.

It must be added that the very smallness and weakness of the Central American states made them an object of Yankee imperialism in the years before the Monroe Doctrine, as unilaterally interpreted by the United States, was replaced by the "good neighbor" policy. Until the early 1930's the United States considered this area more or less her private backyard, to do with as she liked. The tactics of President Theodore Roosevelt, among others, who gained the United States a Panama Canal by aiding and abetting a revolution against Colombia (which at that time included the present state of Panama), compounded a reputation for the United States in Latin America of a rather disreputable sort. On the other hand, such policies gained the United States concrete advantages. In this connection it must not be overlooked that the southwestern area of what is now the United States, including Texas, Arizona, New Mexico, Utah, Nevada, and California, was originally a part of Mexico—and these were gained as the fruits of war with Mexico in 1846–1848. This land-grab did not endear the United States to Latin America. Nor did the extension of American influence over Cuba, following the Spanish-American War, do so.

Signs of a change of policy, which had appeared even before Franklin D. Roosevelt's administration, reflected a newly awakened awareness of this reputation and a concern over it. It also reflected, especially in the next years, a larger concept of her national interests in a world where United States security was by no means to be taken for granted, and she needed allies. This change of policy was heralded in President Roosevelt's inaugural address of March 4, 1933, in these general terms: "In the field of world policy I would dedicate this nation to the policy of the good neighbor—the neighbor who resolutely respects himself and, because he does so, respects the rights of others—the neighbor who respects his obligations and respects the sanctity of his agreements in and with the world of neighbors." That the "good neighbor" policy in the sequel became primarily associated with the Latin American policy of the United States, and took on concrete meaning, was due to world developments. The European and Asian nations then dominated by militarism and dictatorship were in no mood to be good neighbors, and the United States neutrality acts severely limited possibilities vis-à-vis other European states beyond the mere intonation of general, imprecise, but laudable sentiments. As the awareness grew in the United States of the danger to herself and the Americas implicit in the world crisis, and as this view came to be shared by Latin America generally, a common will gradually developed to forge common instruments of defense. While this change in United States–Latin American relations came not suddenly but gradually, in the end it instituted a new relationship that shows every sign of being permanent.

There had long been a Pan-American Union—since 1889. Even before World War II there had been extensive cooperation between the Latin American states and the United States on questions of public health, sanitation, radio, agriculture, and a host of other subjects. What was lacking was a political-military framework for collective diplomacy and collective defense. The Inter-American Conference on Problems of War and Peace, in Mexico City in 1945, began the overhaul of the system and its expansion. These efforts came to fruition in the Rio Treaty of 1947 [7] and the Bogotá Conference of 1948, where the Charter of the Organization of American States (OAS) was approved.

Article VII of the Rio Treaty provided for the collective settlement of inter-American disputes. The Charter of the OAS, coming the next year, elaborated an over-all set of organs to assist in the implementation of these provisions, as well as to coordinate all other aspects of inter-American relations. A Council was provided to be a permanent executive body with twenty-one members (one for each state), to deal with the various problems occurring between the Inter-American Conferences normally held every five years.[8] As a third major organ there is the Meeting of Consultation of Ministers of Foreign Affairs, which is "to consider problems of an urgent nature and of common interest." This organ is not only at the heart of the collective defense coordination but also at the core of the collective diplomacy procedures for the settlement of disputes among American states. It acted in June 1954, for example, to consider the danger of Communist infiltration in Guatemala. To complete the picture of this elaborate organization, there is also an Inter-American Economic and Social Council, an Inter-American Council of Jurists, the Pan-American Union (which furnishes the general secretariat), and the Inter-American Cultural Council.

So far our discussion has focused primarily on Latin American relations with the United States. This is quite natural, since these relations are of

[7] The essential provisions of the Rio Treaty are covered above. See Chapter 17. It is worth noting that Canada is not a party to this treaty.

[8] Special conferences may be called in between.

greatest importance in their international relations. But it ignores two other sets of relations that also must be mentioned. One of these is the relations of individual Latin American states with one another, alluded to briefly above, particularly the disputes that have arisen among them. The most important of these deserve mention. One of the bitterest wars in modern history, fought by Paraguay against Brazil, Argentina, and Uruguay in 1865–1870, continued until Paraguay's population was reduced to twenty-eight thousand men and slightly over two hundred thousand women! Later, in 1879–1884, Chile fought Bolivia and Peru in the War of the Pacific in which Bolivia lost her access to the sea. The resultant bitterness still exercises some influence in Latin American relations. In 1932–1935 Paraguay and Bolivia fought a war over the Gran Chaco area which both claimed. There is today a latent dispute between Peru and Ecuador involving much of the present territory of Ecuador. Brazil, because of her relatively great power, has at times been an object of suspicion on the part of the other Latin American States. The Perón regime in Argentina in recent years awakened similar fears in her neighbors. For that matter, Argentina, so far away from the United States, has frequently been the most assertive of Latin American states toward the United States. The limited effect of these inter-American relations on the world outside the Americas does not justify their treatment here in detail, but this is not to say that they are unimportant—especially to South Americans.

The Latin American states have also had an increasing importance as a group in international relations in a way remote from their dealings with the United States per se. They were from the beginning intensely interested in the League of Nations—an interest that has carried over to the present United Nations. In an organization of some sixty nations (or even of over one hundred, as the UN became) the twenty Latin American states were bound to play a role of great importance, especially if they voted together. Whether they use this potential or not, it is still there; that fact gives them collectively a great prestige. Originally the Latin American states took up membership in the League with enthusiasm, because it offered them a certain degree of potential protection against the United States. With a world forum to speak from, Latin America gained more protection against the United States. It also gave Latin America a role in world affairs greater than their ability to exercise power outside South and Central America would otherwise have afforded them—which was naturally very welcome. It is this latter factor that continues to keep the Latin American states very much a part of the present UN even now that their fears of United States unilateralism have moderated. With the United States ever in need of votes, it gives them collectively a counterweight to her otherwise overwhelming power.

Finally, the socioeconomic situation in Latin America deserves mention. In terms of population, Latin America is increasing significantly. Even now it has a combined population of over two hundred forty millions. That these people are separated into more than twenty states diminishes the effect. On the other hand, the population is only now entering a period of sustained, rapid growth. Estimates place its population at 300 millions in 1975 and 600 millions by 2000. During 1953–1964 its annual growth of 2.8 per cent compared as follows: Western Europe, 0.8 per cent; United States, 1.67 per cent; China, 2.1 per cent. Industrialization is slowly having an impact in Latin America. Brazil's steel industry has reached significant proportions, and Venezuela is now one of the major oil-exporting nations of the world. Socially there is a continuing integration of Indians and whites. But vast numbers of Indians remain unassimiliated; they live as their forefathers did in many cases and speak their aboriginal tongues. This integration is very gradually evolving a more compact and uniform national population in these various states, and is breaking down the caste system of Spanish white supremacy that has existed alongside it. The former comic-opera nature of Latin American revolutions, as a consequence of these changes, is giving way to more fundamental reform movements and revolutions. The Perónist movement in Argentina, the Vargas dictatorship in Brazil, the Aprista movement in Peru, and the Castro revolution in Cuba, although diverse ideologically, are illustrative of a great mass ferment. The bloodless (or nearly so) palace revolutions of a colonel or general will no doubt continue but more and more they are yielding to social revolution. The true competition today in Latin America is between the democratic revolution of Mexico or Brazil and the totalitarian tendencies of latter-day Cuba.

6 *Latin America: Contemporary Problems*

QUESTIONS of social and economic progress are especially pressing today. Rapid industrialization brings with it the threat of inflation, and severe inflation is a potent cause of popular unrest. In March 1964 when a coup ousted President João Goulart, Brazil was near bankruptcy, with inflation at 7.4 per cent *a month*. President Castelo Branco's first task was to bring inflation under control. By the end of 1964 the monthly rate was down to three per cent; the announced goal for 1965 was 25 per cent for the whole year. By August the monthly rate had reached 1.1 per cent. It takes little imagination to visualize the social-political problems involved. Cuba, under a contrasting left-wing Castro government, was having severe economic problems in 1965. Castro announced in July the chaos in Cuban agriculture, saying that Cuban workers were "going at 25 per cent of their capacity 80 per cent of the time." The price of sugar, so important to the Cuban economy, dropped sharply and tight food rationing persisted.

Cuba's economy was operating under an American boycott, with Communist help. But the difficulties implicit in one-crop or one-product economies were general in Latin America. The per cent of export earnings of the nations in this area from one commodity in 1964 varied from 16 per cent (Mexico, cotton), to 94 per cent (Bolivia, tin). Eight of the twenty depended 50 per cent or more on one export commodity.

These harsh economic facts have made the prosperity of so many of these nations subject to the sometimes severe fluctuations in world commodity prices. (In 1955–1965 the price of green coffee was as high as 90 and as low as 32 cents a pound while cocoa varied from 58 to 13 cents.) Since Latin American trade continues still to be oriented primarily toward markets outside the area, progress in area economic cooperation has not been marked. Nonetheless, in 1960 the Central American Common Market (CACM) was created. Guatemala, El Salvador, Honduras, Nicaragua, and Costa Rica all belong. Although their products are frequently directly competitive they are able through the CACM to raise living standards by avoiding duplication of a great variety of facilities. It does not make sense, for example, for each of these very small nations to establish its own cement and steel or auto assembly plants. In February 1960, as a result of the Treaty of Montevideo, a much wider Latin American Free Trade Area (LAFTA) was created with all the larger and more important nations as members. It has so far enjoyed limited success.

In 1964 this region, with potentially rich agricultural possibilities, imported $1.5 billion in farm produce. The average daily diet intake hovers about 2,000 calories. Three-quarters of the farms are very small, and took up only 3.7 per cent of the land in 1950, but 1.5 per cent were 50 times larger in average area and took up 64.9 per cent of the land.[9] In 1964 per capita income in Latin America was $400 (compared to $600 in the rest of the world). Despite these facts, and despite Castro's subversive attempts to assist unrest, especially in Venezuela, free elections in Venezuela in 1948 gave the Communists only 3.64 per cent of the votes. In 1963 a new democratic leader, President Raul Leoni, was elected by 300,000 votes over his runner-up. The Communists were banned as a result of terrorist activities sparked by Cuban-supplied arms.

To this over-all situation the United States reacted in two major ways. In August 1961, with the signing of the Charter of Punta del Este, the Alliance for Progress began with a U.S. pledge of $1 billion a year to be used in conjunction with development plans prepared by the Latin American states for land and tax reform and economic growth. But progress was slow. By mid-1965 only 10 of the 19 Latin American participating states had completed their plans and only in Bolivia, Mexico, and Venezuela was significant land reform underway. (Both Bolivia's and Mexico's programs antedated the Alliance.) Chile was moving toward comprehensive land reform but all the rest lagged. Colombia, once considered a model of what could be achieved via the Alliance, lost ground under weak governmental direction and rising inflation. Nine countries had introduced some tax reforms. The ultimate results of the Alliance for Progress depended in great part on whether Latin American vested interests would consent enough to a self-imposed social revolution to avoid involuntary reforms of a violent nature on the Cuban model.

---

[9] See "Latin America, Its Problems and Possibilities," by Rómulo Betancourt (*Britannica Book of the Year, 1966*), p. 29.

The other main reliance of the United States was on the machinery of the OAS. This machinery had been used between 1948 and 1960 in a number of cases. Five uses were particularly successful: Costa Rica-Nicaragua in 1948–1949, the Caribbean situation in 1950, Costa Rica–Nicaragua again in 1955, Honduras–Nicaragua in 1957, and the Dominican Republic–Venezuela in 1960. The sanctions recommended on July 26, 1964 by the OAS against Cuba for its Venezuelan subversion (economic boycott and a collective break in diplomatic relations) represented its strongest step since its endorsement of two years before of the blockade of Cuba. It is obvious that the especially volatile situation in Central America and the Caribbean (both naturally and because of Castro) furnished a disproportionate amount of the disputes handled by the OAS. Both Communist subversion and the American CIA were involved barely beneath the surface.

The most dramatic action of the OAS since its endorsement of, and participation in, the Cuban quarantine came in the spring of 1965 following a new crisis in the Dominican Republic. Rafael Leónidas Trujillo, dictator for 31 years, had been assassinated in May 1961. In the first free elections in 38 years, Juan Bosch, a leftist, became president. In September 1963, General Elías Wessin y Wessin led a rightist coup which toppled Bosch from power. A leftist revolt came in April 1965, led by elements purporting to represent Bosch but considered by the United States to be heavily Communist-infiltrated. President Johnson said that he did not intend to sit on his hands in a rocking chair while communism extended itself further in Latin America. Even as Wessin rallied the rightest forces, the U.S. announced the sending of 400 Marines to "safeguard American lives." Next day, 3,800 more U.S. troops arrived (April 29) "to see that no Communist were to take over." By May 2, U.S. forces numbered 14,500 and the civil war continued. Both the UN and the OAS moved toward action. On May 5 a cease-fire agreement was signed by both sides in the civil war and next day the OAS Council voted an Inter-American Peace Force (OEA) by 14 to 5. By May 14 the first Latin American contingents had landed and the U.S. troops (now 30,000 strong) were being put under OAS command. Brazilian Lt. Gen. Hugo Penasco Alvin took charge of U.S. units plus contingents from Brazil, Costa Rica, El Salvador, and Nicaragua. By late 1965 the fighting was brought to a close and a new interim government under Hector Garcia-Godoy, representing elements from both sides, was attempting to restore order as a preliminary to new elections in 1966. Prominent army leaders of both factions were dispatched to "diplomatic posts" around the world. The actual election went off well, with Joaquin Balaguer, the conservative, receiving a substantial plurality. Would the new stability last?

Despite the fact that the OAS retroactively endorsed the U.S. unilateral intervention (which otherwise clearly violated Articles 15 and 17 of the OAS Charter), the whole affair unquestionably cost much of the good will so laboriously built up in prior years through the U.S. "good neighbor" policy. The OAS action made the best of a difficult situation; it came partly to extricate the U.S. from its embarrassing position and partly because the OAS nations are themselves disturbed about the prospects of an armed extension of communism. That the result in terms of a representative Dominican government was generally acceptable to Latin America, did not altogether compensate for their feelings that the precedent was also dangerous.

A far less negative impression was left by the U.S. action as a consequence of the riots in Panama in January of 1964 and 1965. Negotiations on a bilateral basis resulted in agreement in September 1965 that the old 1903 treaty would be abrogated and Panama's sovereignty over the Panama Canal Zone recognized. Plans for a new sea-level canal went forward.

It is quite clear that the contemporary Latin American scene, as in Africa and the Middle East, is full of ferment. Many of the major problems in Latin America are similar to those in these other areas. The great advantages Latin America has by comparison are its relative shelter from the storm centers of world politics, the agreed and established nature of most of its frontiers, and the greater experience of its nations in ruling their own affairs and in regional organization. The likelihood of Latin America dealing adequately with its problems was correspondingly greater.

CHAPTER 29

The Asian Powers: I

The conquest of the earth, which mostly means taking it away from those who have a different complexion or slightly flatter noses than ourselves, is not a pretty thing when you look into it.

JOSEPH CONRAD
Heart of Darkness

Communism is politically formidable to us Westerners today because it is politically attractive to anyone who is being treated as a "native." Any human being will revolt against being treated as a "native." For the millions who are still being treated as "natives" today, Communism is an obvious remedy, because they . . . know that, if they go Communist, they will not be treated as "natives" any longer.

"When is a native not a native?" "When he is a Communist," is the answer; for being a Communist and being a "native" are two statuses that are mutually exclusive. A "native" is . . . a human being to whom Western members of Parliament and Senators do not have to pay attention.

ARNOLD J. TOYNBEE
"The Revolution We Are Living Through,"
The Intercollegian, February 1955

If war breaks out, atomic and hydrogen weapons will be used. For myself I think that in the entire world there would be such suffering that half of humanity, and perhaps even more than half would perish. I had an argument about this with Nehru. . . . I told him that if half of humanity were destroyed, the other half would still remain, but that imperialism would be entirely destroyed . . . and that in half a century or in a whole century the population would again increase by even more than half.

MAO TSE-TUNG
Moscow, 1957

ASIA is a vast realm, containing more than half the peoples of the earth. In India alone there are approximately as many people as exist in the United States, West Germany, and the Soviet Union combined. But in China there are still almost three hundred millions beyond that! Especially because Asia is a vast realm, it is filled with diversity. The snow-filled empty mountains of Tibet, the sun-baked teeming plains of India—these are in enor-

574

mous contrast but geographically adjacent. From the sun-darkened white of India, through the yellow of China and Japan, to the brown-black of the Pacific Islands, there is diversity in skin color, too. In religion, Buddhism, Confucianism, Shintoism, Christianity, and Mohammedanism must be numbered among the important faiths in Asia. An enumeration of the smaller religious sects and their differences, in India or Indo-China alone, would fill a great volume. And nowhere have religious faiths continued to have greater influence on political and national affairs than in Asia.

Even these brief thoughts serve to demonstrate what everyone knows who has set foot outside his native land—that large geographical labels like "Asia" name but do not describe; that they beguile the mind into picturing what is geographically contiguous as something culturally homogeneous. This preconception is often very far from the true facts. Yet Asia is a meaningful term in delineating an area where Western ideas of punctuality, justice, and government are equally foreign importations from the one end to the other. And Asia is a most meaningful term to describe an area which, especially in the nineteenth and twentieth centuries, felt the whiplash, the cannon smoke and powder, of the West.

I The Rise and Decline of Western Imperialism in Asia

ASIA's common historical experience was subjection to white domination. From India to the Western Pacific, from Siberia to the islands of the equator, the native peoples were subordinated by the white man, "the foreign devils," the people who had superior weapons and engines of destruction, and the will to use them. In this whole vast area only Thailand (as a buffer state between French and British imperial holdings), and Japan (as a state who modernized in time) escaped substantial occupation, partition, and interference and domination by one or another of the Western powers. This is one of the most incredible facts of modern history, although repeated exposure to it has dimmed our sensitivity to the revolutionary meaning it still has for Asians today.

The parade of Western imperialism in Asia defies brief description. Every great power of the world in the last centuries except Italy and Austria-Hungary obtained its slice of Asian territory. Holland held the great "spice islands"—the East Indies; Britain held India and Burma and many islands; France held Indo-China; Spain held the Philippines—which then became a United States possession. Even Portugal had (and has) holdings; Russia took Siberia, including the Amur province of China, and Outer Mongolia; and all these powers, including Germany, held bits and pieces of China proper, in one form or another. Japan, herself an Asian nation, entered the competition late, after her modernization. She put the lessons she had learned to good effect—by Western standards; and she also had the advantage of a convenient location.

This is the picture of Asia that recent history has known. It is a picture comparable to Africa's experience. But if one goes back in history and compares Western-Asian relations, one finds them reversed. In this earlier age Genghis Khan's hordes penetrated into Europe; his followers and successors kept Russia under Tartar yoke for centuries. It was the Chinese who invented gunpowder. It was the envoy of the British king who was treated in humiliating fashion by the Chinese Emperor. It was the Chinese "Middle Kingdom" that existed in self-satisfied and self-contained power and splendor. It was this China which Marco Polo observed with awe. Africa's past has no parallel except among the Arabs who subjugated Spain.

The parts of Asia that were already divided by geography into small weak states, or consisted of detached islands, were easy prey for the superior weapons of the West. In the great Indian land mass where more difficulties might have been met, the process of conquest was fostered by the rivalries and mutual fears of India's native princes. The beginning of the subordination of China—perhaps the richest and most difficult prize—was made possible with the weakening of the imperial rule. Between 1796 and 1820 numerous revolts took place in China; the China that Britain defeated in the first of the Opium Wars (1841–1842) was no longer strong and united. Thus was ushered in Western rule. For a hundred years after the First Opium War the West was supreme, ruling over states with proud and ancient memories.

Although it was long before it was obvious, the beginning of the end of white rule came with Japan's modernization and expansion. Japan's successes, especially in the first months of World War II, dramatized a fact long in the making: as Asians learned to make and use Western weapons, the end of Western power in the Orient must follow. Japan took over from the French in Indo-China, conquered the Netherlands East Indies, humiliated the British with their capture of "impregnable" Singapore, and overwhelmed the Americans in the Philippines. These victories humbled white prestige in Asia and showed by example that Asia could win against the West. Japan's ultimate humiliation did not affect the issue; it merely proved to Asians that Japan had been overly ambitious.

Thus began one of the most far-reaching changes in the history of the nation-state system. In a single decade, where one out of every three people in the world in 1945 had been in a colonial or dependent status, by 1955 approximately one out of twelve remained so. The bulk of this change was in Asia. Yet even these figures fail to reveal the extent of the change.

2 The Asian Revolution

THESE dramatic changes represent more than the hauling down of the flags of Western powers in Asia. The influence of the West in the larger sense is not at an end because its political rule is largely terminated. The ferment introduced by Western ideas continues. Their effects have been more profound in Asia than in Africa precisely because Asia always had a more advanced culture. Just as these Western ideas ultimately served to create a great part of the intellectual hostility to the West, and were made to serve Asian needs against the West, so too Western techniques in medicine, agriculture, and industry came to be used in Asia by the Asians, and for Asian purposes.

The Asia to which these ideas were originally brought was predominantly agricultural and primitive in Western technological terms. It knew nothing of democracy in the Western sense, nor of nationalism. It was ruled by princes, kings, and emperors, wisely or unwisely, with all degrees of despotism. The social structure throughout Asia was feudal: at the top the sovereign and the aristocracy; at the foot the masses of the peasantry. Such minor "middle classes" as did exist were not thought of as such but rather as constituting the lower levels of the privileged classes. Loyalties were primarily to the family.

Into this situation came the West—a West which in the great age of Asian imperialism had left feudalism far behind; a West in which, even where emperors and kings continued to rule, the ideas of nationalism and national self-determination were all-pervasive. While predominantly the West came to gain riches and glory, and had in general no intention of doing more than harvesting the rewards, it could not prevent the introduction of Western practices and concepts as a necessary adjunct of its rule. Western concepts of individual justice could not be separated from the functioning of Western-style courts of law. Western ideas on the nature of contracts, so essential to business, could not be implemented in isolation from other, and ultimately more revolutionary, ideas. The teaching of Western tongues, so that the natives could better serve Western purposes, introduced gradually an exposure to the whole of Western thought. The training of technicians and professional men, through schools in Asia itself and through the sending of Asians abroad, while designed for a limited purpose, was ultimately to have unlimited effects. So too were the more unselfish efforts of countless missionaries who came to extend the Christian faith.

These ideas and practices were often resented; they were also absorbed. The very prestige of the conquerors drew Asian attention to them. Inevitably the first effects of this mingling of Asian and Western concepts produced enormous confusion in Asia, and a weakening of traditional methods and loyalties. But later some wedding of these concepts was achieved even though Western ideas often underwent unexpected mutations and emerged as something altogether different from previous Western practice and traditional Asian concepts.

Of all the Western ideas that of nationalism and that of an improved standard of living made the greatest impressions. Nationalism, with its corollary of self-determination, meant that each nation should govern itself—India for the Indians, China for the Chinese. Its appeal was implicit in the very circumstances of foreign domination, for it served as the rallying cry against the "oppressors." The idea of an improvement in the standard of living was even more revolutionary. Using primitive methods in an agricultural land, the masses had for endless ages been accustomed to a bare subsistence diet. There was no accumulation of surpluses against bad times, and if there was it was taxed away. Famine and pestilence were part of life—expected and inevitable. Although occasional rulers turned to flood control and other reforms from time to time, these efforts were few and often temporary. There seemed no way out of these conditions. Then came Western sanitation, medicine, agriculture, industry. While these techniques decreased the death rate in Asia and caused population increases that trod mercilessly on the heels of gradual improvements in the standard of living, they also pointed ahead to an ultimate time when their fruits could be reflected in a real and permanent and increasing improvement. It became obvious to the Asians that, once they had acquired these techniques, they could enjoy the whole of these fruits, such as they were, if the West did not drain its profits off for its own use.

It is in connection with nationalism and the standard of living that we see the especial reasons for the appeal of communism in Asia. Soviet communism, preaching anti-imperialism, could not fail on that basis alone to receive a sympathetic hearing. Soviet propaganda, emphasizing national cultural autonomy and the equality of the Asian with the Caucasian within the Soviet Union, could not fail to be contrasted with Western practice and attitude. As an Indian maharajah once pointed out, the difference between the British club in Bombay and that in Calcutta was that in the one Indians and dogs were excluded, while in the other dogs were allowed. In this atmosphere the appeal of communism to proud peoples was great. Moreover, the example of Russia in rapid industrialization appealed to peoples who remained relatively unmoved by the tales of human misery that had accompanied these achievements. Had not Asia's lot always been misery? Russia's participation in the imperialist spoils was somewhat overshadowed in Asian minds, for Russian imperialism had perforce been limited by Japan's successful war of 1904–1905. Nor did the collectivism of Russian communism seem to the Asians an evil. Had not Asia always been collectivist, both in daily family life and in general attitude? After all, the Western ideas that had always been the least comprehensible in Asia were precisely those abstractions concerning individual liberties and freedoms of which the West was and is so proud. To the Asian the idea of the individual apart from his role as a member of groups, the idea of his rights and duties as an individual rather than as a part of the group, has always seemed strange. The Asian has always found "freedom" and "justice" hard to conceive of as abstractions: he personifies these ideas in terms of human groups of which he is a part. Laotzu, the Chinese sage, when he discusses "good government" and revolution typically deals with it so:

> People starve
> If taxes eat their grain
> And the faults of starving people
> Are the fault of their rulers.
> That is why people rebel.
> Men who have to fight for their living

> And are not afraid to die for it
> Are higher men than those who, stationed high,
> Are too fat to dare to die.[1]

Here there is no cry of "taxation without representation" (American), "the king is not above the law" (British), or "liberty, equality, fraternity" (French)—here the emphasis is on humanity rather than on abstractions. A wealth of concepts is involved, but always in human terms. This helps to explain why, in an Asia in ferment, individuals as leaders of groups and group loyalties are more important than abstract programs abstractly expressed. It is something that the West finds difficult to remember, yet something that means defeat to forget.

In long-run terms, leaving aside current political issues, the economic and social changes now occurring so quickly in Asia will produce immense changes. In this field of economic-social change nothing is more important than the relatively unpublicized Colombo Plan. The Colombo Plan, which started out as a (British) Commonwealth "Marshall Plan" in 1950, had, five years later, grown to embrace, either as members or consulting associates, Australia, Burma, Cambodia, Canada, Ceylon, India, Indonesia, Laos, Nepal, New Zealand, Pakistan, the United Kingdom (including British Borneo, Malaya, etc.), the United States, and South Viet-Nam. As 1965 ended it had 22 members. The Colombo Plan has the merit of avoiding "charity" to the less well-endowed nations. Even the poorer aid in the cooperative effort, adding what they can. In this way the more advanced Asian nations are giving assistance to the less advanced, and the suspicion of disguised colonialism is avoided altogether. Although the contributions of the industrial members continued to be decisive (over $2 billion in 1963–1964), the method used avoided the colonial stigma. It was impossible to overestimate the potential value of this program in South Asia where "the average weekly food ration is about 12 ounces of grain per person, the per capita national income is well below $100 a year, and life expectancy is about half what it is in North America." [2] The Colombo Plan offers the West a chance for genuine cooperation among equals in Asia, a chance to replace the memory of imperialism with something far better. Similar in its appeal is the Asian Development Bank set up in late 1965. Of its initial $1 billion capitalization, 60 per cent would come from Asian nations.

This then is the social-ideological context within which Asia faces a continuing revolution marked by an increasing awareness by the masses of the "better" life. Bearing in mind the points made in these two introductory sections that apply to Asia generally, we can now turn to an analysis of the foreign policies of the nations that comprise this vast area.

---

[1] Witter Bynner, *The Way of Life, According to Laotzu*, New York: John Day, 1944, p. 73.
[2] "The Colombo Plan," *External Affairs*, Department of External Affairs, Ottawa, Canada, Vol. 6 (September 1954), pp. 273–285.

3 China—From Revolution to Civil War

CHINA today is again, as for long centuries before, the hub of Asia, the crucial element in Asia's destinies, the focal point of Asian politics. In important respects the foreign policies of the major Asian powers are today determined by their relations with China; it is idle to discuss developments in Pakistan, India, Indonesia, and Japan, without considering how they relate to China's frustrations, ambitions, and policies. In an Asia in the throes of revolutionary change, no change is more striking than the change in China's effects on Asia. For it was less than a handful of decades ago that China was the greatest imperialistic prize remaining in a world dominated by the search for new colonial possessions. It was only a quarter-century ago that President Roosevelt proposed to give China a position in the UN Security Council equal to the United States and the Soviet Union—a proposition which the other great powers regarded as essentially an American sentimental gesture.

This China, which in 1949 finally began to emerge from five decades of revolution and disorder, provides an enormous contrast to the China which existed between the establishment of the American Federal Union and the start of World War II. Once again a Peking government began to exercise effective control over the Chinese provinces. This revival of a strong China, coming after centuries of increasing weakness, constituted the most fundamental alteration in the balance of power that Asia has known in modern history—and this is not forgetting Japan's impact. The fact that this China was Communist and allied to the Soviet Union inevitably produced the greatest discussion and attention in the West. In perspective it was not so significant as the fact that *China* was becoming a great power. Chinese and Russian governments have allied themselves before in this century. But never since the American Declaration of Independence, never in the experience of the United States as an independent nation, has there been a strong China. It should be added that never since Russia's extension through Siberia to the Pacific and the effective beginning of modern Sino-Russian relations has China been a strong power either. A strong China is new for Russia too. This revolutionary fact of China's power is the single most important change in Asia in the twentieth century. For both the United States and Russia it implied a tremendous change in traditional policies toward China. That both countries were finding this readjustment difficult, was obvious.

China's modern humiliations began with the early nineteenth century, with the Opium Wars. Thereafter the great powers, as occasion permitted, worked industriously to carve her up into spheres and areas for exploitation. China's central government was a mockery, capable only of feeble response. So out of tune with the world of nation-states was China that she did not even possess a ministry of foreign affairs until as late as 1858. She continued officially in the dream world of former times when a ministry of tribute and capitulations was all that was really needed for dealing with "barbarians." With a curious arrogance, made even stranger by her weakness, China at first continued to refuse to accept the West on equal terms and negotiate with them as such. When ultimately she began to negotiate, her only real strength lay in playing the powers off against one another—a tactic only partially successful. Despite the spheres of influence and territorial concessions she was driven to concede, China remained a nominally independent state primarily because her very size made her difficult to digest and there were many who wished to attempt it.

America may have fondly imagined that her "Open Door" policy toward China, to which the other powers gave lip service, had stayed the process of division. But this was more or less self-delusion. In 1898 Britain, Germany, Russia, and France had forced concessions from China which, combined together, destroyed China's future as an economic unit.[3] These leases, which were to run for ninety-nine years (Russia's lease on the southern Liaotung Peninsula was for only twenty-five), provided for Chinese employment of a British inspector-general of Chinese customs, exclusive rights (to Germany) to build railroads and open mines in Shantung, the giving over of control of Port Arthur (to Russia), Kwangchow (to France), and Kowloon and Wei-hai-wei (to Britain). Italy's demand for a port in 1899 the Chinese government felt strong enough to reject. The complete colonization of China was stayed only by her great mass and by the inability of the powers to agree readily on how to divide her up.

The famous Boxer Rebellion, which broke out in 1900, was an outward sign of inward ferment in China. "Foreign devils" were put to the sword, and the Western legations in Peking were besieged. In retaliation European punitive expeditions restored order. The imperial court, which had fled, returned to Peking thoroughly discredited in Western and Chinese eyes alike. In October 1911, the long-delayed Chinese Revolution began, and in 1912 the six-year-old boy emperor abdicated. Sun Yat-sen, who had been elected president by a revolutionary provisional assembly at Nanking on December 30, 1911, resigned when Yüan Shih-k'ai was selected in mid-February as president by the national assembly. Yüan Shih-k'ai, a would-be Oriental Bonaparte, now attempted to consolidate his power. At the end of 1915 he announced his assumption of imperial powers, was forced to cancel this, and, in the middle of 1916, died. After this date the struggle for power became more and more confused. Not only were there governments at both Canton and Peking, but between 1920 and 1926 war lords fought one another in equal disregard of both.

In 1924 the first Kuomintang national congress convened at Canton. Sun Yat-sen became president; Communists were admitted, along with Russian

---

[3] The Open Door Note of September 6, 1899, proposed that, in view of China's division into British, German, and Russian spheres of influence, these three powers should promise equal treatment within their spheres for foreign goods so far as harbor and railroad duties were concerned. But the Open Door policy came eventually to have the popular meaning mentioned above, so far as American public opinion was concerned.

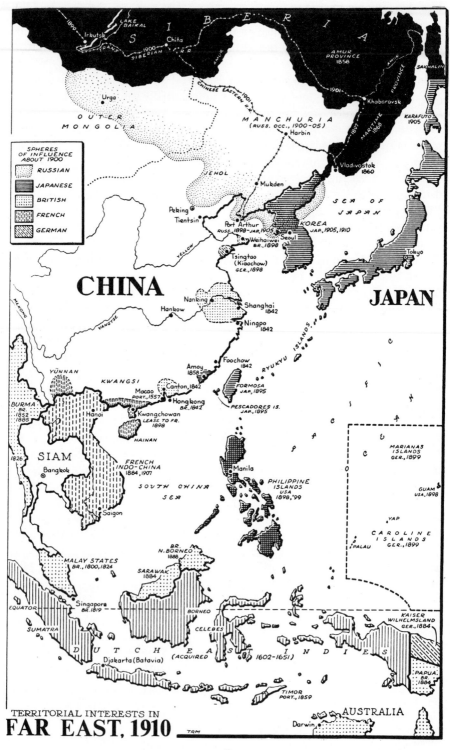

TERRITORIAL INTERESTS IN
FAR EAST, 1910

582

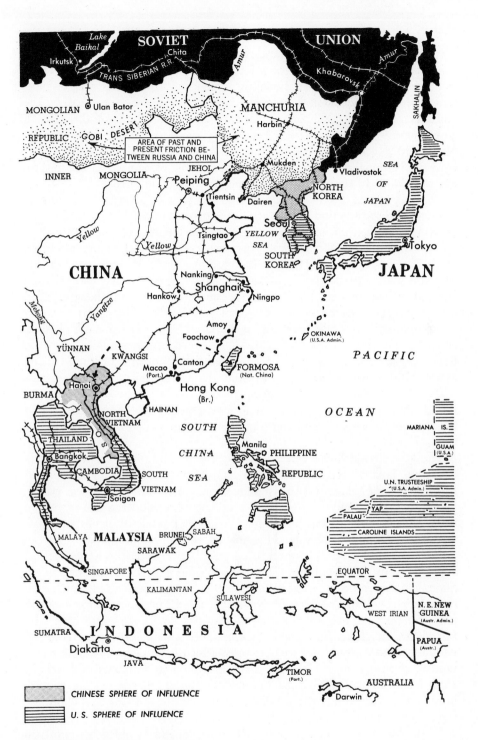

FAR EAST, 1966

advisers; and Chiang Kai-shek headed the new Whampoa Military Academy which was to train an officer corps for the new army. Sun Yat-sen's "Three Principles of the People" (nationalism, democracy, and social progress) became the official ideological program. Now began a period marked by the military campaigns of Chiang Kai-shek to assert the power of the Canton government over China. In 1928 Peking was occupied, and the same year the Nationalist government's capital was transferred to Nanking. By the end of 1928 the Nationalist government had been widely recognized as the government of China. In 1931 a provisional constitution was adopted.

China's progress toward unification and her growing strength were sources of Japanese dissatisfaction. In late 1931 the Japanese utilized the Mukden incident to begin what ultimately was revealed to be an attempt to conquer all of China. By January–March 1933, Japan had occupied Jehol and advanced south of the Great Wall. This was followed by a truce. By mid-1936 Chiang, who still wished to postpone war with Japan, was confronted with a rising demand for such a war. The Chinese Communists, who had been expelled from the Nationalist Party and who had created their own government in northern Shensi, also called for war, as did Gen. Chang Hsüeh-liang of Manchuria. In December 1936, Gen. Chang "kidnaped" Chiang Kai-shek to force him to declare war on Japan. All over China the people rallied behind Chiang as the symbol of national rebirth; even the Communists interceded with Chang. On January 28, 1937, agreement was reached between Chiang and the Communist Shensi government to fight together in the common cause: the struggle between Chiang and Mao Tse-tung since their break in 1929 was now (officially) laid aside.

The new Sino-Japanese conflict, which was to continue without interruption until Japan's 1945 defeat, began on July 7, 1937, with an incident at Luko-chiao near Peking. In August a fierce campaign for Shanghai was waged; the city fell in November. Soviet Russia in August concluded a non-aggression treaty with Nationalist China, following it up by the sale of planes and great quantities of munitions. Even earlier, in July, the United States had agreed to exchange China's large silver reserve for gold as necessary; this action helped enormously in the obtaining of credits for arms imports. Thus the United States and Russia both moved to buttress the Chinese defense, although each remained technically neutral. In November the Chinese government evacuated Nanking, the executive branch moving first to Hankow and then later inland to Chungking. Britain and America, both watching the even tenser situation in Europe, could not well act in Asia for the moment. Nanking fell at the end of 1937, Tsingtao early in 1938, Canton and Hankow in October of 1938. Japan brought one great Chinese city after another under her control; but China remained unbeaten. Where Japan held the railroads and highways, rural China remained Chinese. The war went on.

With World War II under way in Europe, Japan redoubled her efforts to win victory in China. By pressure upon the British government, which had just evacuated its forces from Dunkirk, the Japanese succeeded in having the

Burma Road closed (July 18, 1940). Since the Japanese now controlled the Chinese ports, the Burma Road had become of crucial importance. Its closing left only the long land routes across Central Asia to Russia for the importation of supplies and munitions. In October 1940, following Japan's signing of the Tripartite Pact with Germany and Italy, Britain reopened the Burma Road. Supplies again began to reach China in quantity. At the end of the next year, following Pearl Harbor, an increasing trickle of American aid reached China. Supplies were even flown in after Japan had advanced into Burma and had succeeded in cutting the Burma Road. Because of the China theater's inaccessibility and the major effort that a seaborne invasion of the China mainland would necessitate, the Pacific War largely passed it by. While Japan conquered ever more of China, she was herself ever more in danger of conquest—by the Americans, from the sea. When Japan surrendered in 1945, ironically, she had come close to the conquest of China.

Japan's surrender made the friction between the Communists and the Nationalists, already overt, really serious. In Manchuria, with Russian help, the Communist armies already were equipped with surrendered Japanese medium and heavy equipment. This armament meant they would no longer be restricted to guerrilla warfare as in the past. The Russians' slow restoration of Manchurian communications hindered any large movement of Chinese Nationalist troops into the area. Meanwhile the United States, with air and sea transport, made a considerable and successful effort to move Chiang's forces into Manchuria; and American marines were detailed to safeguard the vital communication lines behind them, between Tsingtao and Tientsin.

Already strained by the need to reoccupy most of China proper and Manchuria simultaneously, the Nationalists by 1946 had spread themselves rather thin. They found themselves further confronted with a full-scale civil war that soon spread beyond the bounds of Manchuria.

In the next three years (1946–1949) Chiang Kai-shek was beaten and driven from the continent. Why this occurred was to become perhaps the most fiercely debated issue in United States party politics between 1949 and 1953.

One reason for his defeat was military. Chiang's army of over three hundred divisions was inefficiently organized; it was larger than could be adequately trained, armed, and supported. American advisers suggested ninety divisions, but Chiang rejected this—partly because it would affect the intricate balance between the central and the provincial governments. Further, Chiang chose to try to defeat the Communists with the same tactics the Japanese had used against him (i.e., seizure of cities, control of railroads, and positional warfare). The Communists, by-passing cities, cutting railroads here and there, melting away before frontal attacks and reforming to cut at the flanks, whittled Chiang's strength down. After 1947 the military situation turned ever more in favor of the Communists.

A second reason for Chiang's defeat was the popular attitude in China. The extreme difficulties under which Chiang had fought the war, with its rampant inflation, heavy taxation, and increasing corruption had weakened the hold of the Kuomintang on the population. Chiang had come to rely upon the landlords as tax collectors—a procedure that has ended more than one dynasty in China. Moreover, the very type of government he had instituted had failed to capture the popular imagination. Chiang's support had come to him largely because he was the leader in the fight against Japan, and not because of the Kuomintang's popularity per se. In fact the Kuomintang Party governed China, through the bureaucracy, on a "paternal" rather than a democratic basis. "Real" democracy kept being postponed because of the pressing nature of immediate problems. This delay discouraged many of the young and liberal elements in China, and in the end alienated them. To the masses there was little obvious difference, in its effect on them, between the Kuomintang and the imperial regime. So long as the promises for the future, such as land reform, were taken at face value, the regime held together. But the promises of the Communists in this respect were even more alluring, as was Mao's record in the regions he controlled. Chiang felt he needed the landlords—he would at best reduce their holdings; Mao promised to liquidate them—and did.

The third reason for Mao's victory and Chiang's defeat was the greater attention paid by the Communists to political indoctrination and organization. Chiang, in control of the apparatus of state, increasingly relied upon forced conscription of unwilling draftees; Mao emphasized a voluntary cooperation of soldier and peasant, out of conviction.

Finally, Chiang lost because communism was not, despite its emphasis upon collectivism, running athwart Chinese traditions. The Kuomintang itself was collectivist in emphasis, compared with Western standards of individualism.

The efforts of the United States to aid Chiang materially could not undo the growing mass apathy. General Marshall's mission, to mediate between Chiang and Mao, ultimately failed for the reason that each distrusted the other too much, and each was convinced he could win the civil war. Thus the cease-fire agreement which Marshall managed to obtain in 1947 came to naught. When the war resumed, Chiang's troops increasingly deserted to the Communist side, taking their American equipment with them. By the end of 1948 the Nationalist Army had largely fallen apart. Between September and December of that year alone, they are reported to have lost a third of a million men—the bulk of them through desertions. In 1949 Chiang fled to Formosa. The half-century-old Chinese Revolution entered a new stage.

4 *The Two Chinas*

IN October 1949, the Chinese People's Republic was proclaimed. Its capital was the imperial capital of Peking. In his opening address to the Political Consultative Conference the month before, Mao Tse-tung flatly announced:

"Our nation will never be an insulted nation any more. . . . The era in which the Chinese were regarded as uncivilized is now over." Among the "insults" which were no longer to be tolerated was Western and foreign intervention in Chinese affairs. A treaty of friendship, alliance, and mutual assistance was signed with the Soviet Union on February 14, 1950.

Mao's definition of Chinese affairs was not limited to China's 1949 frontiers, for a cardinal part of his program was the undoing of the changes wrought by imperialism in China's traditional boundaries. Tibet was brought back under Chinese control by force in 1950–1951. Korea, historically a Chinese protectorate, also bulked importantly in these plans. So did Indo-China, which the French under Napoleon III had seized in 1862–1867. Then there were the pieces Russia now controlled—the Amur province and Mongolia. Because China was Communist, because Russia was its *de facto* ally, and because United States hostility was obvious, Mao turned his attention away from the final item to focus his efforts where the situation argued for more effective gains. He aided the Indo-Chinese rebels against the French. After North Korea had begun the Korean War and American forces had advanced toward the Chinese frontier on the Yalu, he intervened there (late 1950) with "volunteer" forces. His intervention in the face of the UN's northern advance, while it shocked the West, was hardly surprising. Any powerful Chinese government, Communist or not, would almost surely have reacted in much the same way to quasi-hostile forces advancing in Korea toward China. China had been weak for so long that its demands and warnings were brushed aside. Yet Communist China had made no secret of her intention to intervene if the northward march continued.

The West (and especially the United States as the core of the UN action) was unable to assess these warnings accurately because of the lack of American diplomats in China and the exclusion of Communist China from the UN. Sir Gladwyn Jebb, British Ambassador to the UN, commented long afterwards: "It could indeed even be argued with some force that had the government of Peking been represented in the UN at the beginning of 1950, the North Korean aggression might never have occurred at all." [4] While this opinion is questionable, there can be no doubt that the ill-fated stalemate of the Korean War, following Communist China's intervention, came about in part because China's "bluff" had to be assessed from six thousand miles away.

The final liquidation of the Korean War allowed Mao to intensify his efforts to aid Ho Chi Minh in his struggle against the French in Indo-China. It also brought Communist China once more to the brink of war with the United States, for as the position of the French forces at Dien Bien Phu [5] became more and more desperate, the United States hovered at the very brink of armed intervention. In April 1954, the world waited to see which way the decision would fall. It may well be that the surprising moderation that the Chinese and Indo-Chinese Communists displayed subsequently at

[4] *NYHT* (EE), January 15, 1954.
[5] See above, Chapter 27.

the Geneva Conference (even then in session) flowed from a realization that the United States had been provoked almost past peaceful endurance.

As 1954 blended into 1955, the spotlight shifted to the Formosan area. With Korea once again stabilized and, for the moment, partitioned, and with Indo-China also divided so that friendly forces controlled the area adjacent to Mao's southern frontier, the Chinese Communists stepped up their campaign to "recover" Formosa and the island groups still in Nationalist hands—the Pescadores, the Tachens, and Quemoy and Matsu.

Formosa and the Pescadores had been taken from China by Japan as one result of the Sino-Japanese War of 1894–1895. But in the Japanese Peace Treaty of 1951 Japan had been forced to renounce her claims to them. Sovereignty over them presumably passed into the collective hands of the Allied signers of the treaty (which included neither Russia, Communist China, nor Nationalist China). Although Roosevelt, Churchill, and Chiang Kai-shek had proclaimed (at the Cairo Conference of November 1943) "that all the territories Japan has stolen from the Chinese, such as Manchuria, Formosa, and the Pescadores," would be restored "to the Republic of China," [6] this was a mere expression of intent, and not a binding treaty commitment. Consequently, although the Nationalist Chinese government held effective control over the Formosa-Pescadores area, the legal situation remained fluid, subject to a final collective determination by the Pacific War Allies as to what to do.

At the very beginning of the Korean War, in order to keep the Formosa situation from further complicating the Far Eastern problem and hindering collective action against the Communists in Korea, President Truman had ordered the American Seventh Fleet to "neutralize" the Formosa-Pescadores area, preventing either Chinese government from attacking the other. Toward the end of the Korean War, as one of the first acts of his administration, President Eisenhower "unleashed" Chiang Kai-shek by giving orders which would permit the Nationalists to invade the mainland—if they could. At the same time he extracted a secret pledge that Chiang would undertake no such important unilateralist action without American acquiescence. A torrent of propaganda continued from Peking, the theme of which reiterated Mao's determination to "restore" these areas to his control. In the face of these threats the United States negotiated and ratified a treaty of mutual defense with the Nationalist government, which pledged American armed support for the defense of Formosa and the Pescadores.

The offshore islands of Quemoy and Matsu, of little value in themselves, became the focus of the Sino-American war of nerves in 1954 and early 1955. While Quemoy and Matsu unquestionably formed part of China, this left undecided the question of what China they were to belong to. While the Nationalists remained in *de facto* control, their nearness to the mainland (in contrast to Formosa and the Pescadores) made them very difficult to defend. The initiation of direct conversations in Geneva between the United States

---

[6] See for complete text Department of State *Bulletin*, Vol. 9, p. 393.

and Communist China in 1955 (continued in later years in Warsaw), deflated the pressure but produced no real settlement on this (or other) issues. In 1958, in a two months period, the Communists bombarded Quemoy-Matsu with 475,000 rounds of artillery. In 1960 the total for the year was 181,280.

5 Communist China: Contemporary Developments

CHINA, frustrated in these attempts to put an end to the rival government on Formosa, in the six years after 1955 concentrated primarily on pushing ahead with ambitious plans for increasing agricultural and industrial production which had been delayed by her part in the Korean War. The first five-year plan, announced in 1953, brought excellent results until 1955 when the age-old problem of floods and drought brought on a food shortage. Collectivization of agriculture and state ownership of industry was pressed, but the food shortages continued. Nonetheless a second ambitious five-year plan was promulgated for 1958–1962. This was to be the "Great Leap Forward," but it turned out disastrously. Premier Chou En-lai in early 1961 revealed that more than half of all the cultivated land had been hit by natural calamities and that crop failures had been widespread. Rationing was further tightened. (Western estimates put the Chinese diet at 600 to 1,200 calories per day.)

These internal difficulties and disappointments, coupled with continued frustration in arriving at major foreign policy goals, played their part in heaping fuel on the Sino-Soviet ideological split initially sparked by Khrushchev's condemnation of the "cult of the individual" in his "secret speech" of 1956, and Khrushchev's revisionism. China saw great advantages in breaking through the "capitalist encirclement" led by the United States, by exploiting the potentially revolutionary situation in the underdeveloped nations in the capitalists' rear. In 1960 Peking's *de jure* recognition of the rebel Algerian provisional government contrasted with Moscow's more cautious *de facto* recognition (caused by the Soviets' concern for relations with de Gaulle). When Moscow then followed the Chinese lead many African leaders drew the conclusion that each could be played against the other. In October 1961, Chou En-lai made a public gesture of laying a wreath at Stalin's bier in Red Square. The next day Stalin's body was reburied in a less conspicuous place by the Kremlin wall. The Sino-Soviet dispute, while now open, was still being conducted indirectly so far as invective went—with the Chinese condemning *Yugoslav* revisionism and the Soviets castigating *Albania's* Stalinism. Peking, in a further bid for influence at a distance, extended a $60 million loan to Cuba and agreed to buy 100,000 tons of sugar in 1961.

Border revision began to be pushed by China in 1960–1962. Discussions leading to an agreement with Nepal were concluded in 1960. In January 1961 an agreement with Burma was reached. In both cases China sweetened the arrangements with economic aid. But the Indian-Chinese border commission created in 1960 failed to reach agreement. Nehru indicted the Chinese in Parliament for its "unlawful occupation of about 12,000 square miles of Indian territory." Nehru was referring to the Chinese occupation of the Ladakh section of Kashmir (bordering Sinkiang and Tibet), but a 51,000 square mile area between Tibet and India's northeastern frontier along the "McMahon Line" was also in dispute. This line has never been recognized by any Chinese government. In September 1962 serious fighting broke out in the eastern sector which came to an end in November when Peking unilaterally announced a cease-fire and prepared to "withdraw to positions 20 km. behind the lines of actual control" as of November 7, 1959. In March 1963, China and Pakistan signed a border settlement which India refused to recognize since it involved areas of Kashmir under Pakistani control which India did not recognize as legally Pakistan's. Soviet arms continued to be sent to India.

The Soviet backdown over Cuba in late 1962, followed by the Nuclear Test Ban Treaty in 1963, led in 1963 to the public and direct phase of the Sino-Soviet dispute. Peking's reaction to the test-ban was to announce in August that it would create its own nuclear force. On August 15, 1963 the Chinese officially revealed that the Soviets who in October 1958 had agreed to assist China's nuclear effort with a sample bomb and technical data, had unilaterally broken off the agreement on June 20, 1959. In September China accused Russia of a plot to overthrow the regional government along the Sinkiang–Soviet Kazakhstan border. Moscow, which had urged India to accept China's peace proposals, confirmed in 1963 that MiG fighter planes would continue to be delivered to India and in September 1964 an Indian-Soviet agreement for military and economic aid to India was signed. Russia charged that Peking claimed 500,000 square miles of Soviet territory, with Mongolia as the point of most intense friction. In October 1964 China detonated her first nuclear device. In that same month her most prominent public adversary in the Communist world, Khrushchev, who had gained only half-hearted support from other Communist parties for a world conference to take a stand on the ideological split, fell from power.

With new Soviet leaders in power any personal antagonisms accruing from Khrushchev's tactical handling of the dispute could now be set aside. An attempt at reconciliation and a visit by Chou En-lai to Moscow (November 1964) were not followed by concrete progress; very soon both sides had resumed their public quarrel. The Chinese showed special irritation with Soviet arms aid to India, U.S.-Soviet cooperation, the Soviet attitude toward the Viet-Nam struggle and other events in Afro-Asia. When the Soviets did convene a conference of Communist parties in Moscow on March 1, 1965 no delegations came from China (or Albania, North Korea, North Viet-Nam, Japan, or Indonesia). China denounced the conference as illegal and increased her efforts to influence Afro-Asia.

China's strategy was to create unity under her leadership of the great masses of the world as a third force set over against the two super powers.

Already in 1961, the Chinese had gone on record that the "poorer nations of the world, mainly nonwhite, should unite against the richer, industrialized nations which are mainly white—including the Russians." Because this tactic proved unappealing (even to the Africans, let alone Latin American and European Communists), she dropped the racial emphasis but not the anti-Russian aspect. Chou En-lai's African tour in 1963–1964 increased Chinese prestige as did France's recognition of Peking (January 1964). Chou's comment on his tour: "an excellent revolutionary situation exists in Africa." The Zanzibar revolution of January 1964 was credited (not unnaturally, but erroneously as it turned out) to China's account, although China did make great efforts to consolidate her influence there. When Zanzibar joined Tanganyika (on the mainland) to form Tanzania the Chinese efforts were frustrated by President Julius Nyerere's moves to keep foreign influences limited. The change of government in Somalia in 1964 was a blow to Chinese plans. Burundi, from where the Chinese had been funneling aid to the Congolese rebels, broke diplomatic relations with China in January 1965 after its prime minister was assassinated. Kenya expelled the New China News Agency representative in July 1965. Ghana's Nkrumah criticized China's decision to attain nuclear arms but maintained good relations with Peking. So did Guinea. China's best relations were with Congo (Brazzaville) and Mali—who were also among the poorest.

When China sought an Afro-Asian Conference for June 1965 in Algiers (with Russia excluded), she ultimately encountered another setback. Both Premier Chou and Foreign Minister Chen Yi worked to create pro-Chinese sentiment and support for Chinese plans with good will visits to Albania, Algeria, Afghanistan, Burma, Indonesia, Pakistan, Romania, Tanzania and the United Arab Republic. The Soviets declared their wish to attend (although the U.S.S.R. had not been at the first Afro-Asian Conference in 1955). Then Ahmed ben Bella's regime was overthrown in June, removing one of China's best friends from power. Chou En-lai indicated immediate willingness to recognize the new government of Houari Boumedienne. This move, intended to salvage the chances for the conference, instead impressed many Afro-Asian nations as cynical opportunism. Sentiment to postpone the meeting increased. In Cairo on June 27, 1965 Chou conferred with Nasser (who had been generally sympathetic to China) and Indonesian President Sukarno. The conference was postponed (and later abandoned).

The difficulty with Chinese efforts to exploit the "excellent revolutionary situation" in Africa was the incompatibility between friendly relations with most of the existing governments, and cultivating unrest. Most of these governments would themselves be put in jeopardy by unrest. So long as Chinese efforts were directed at aiding the Congolese rebels or the rebel forces in the Portuguese colonies, most of Black Africa approved. But the liquidation of the Congo rebel movement worked to make China's presence less welcome even as a number of African governments came to fear for their own existence in view of Chinese operations. By the end of 1965 only 16 of Africa's independent states recognized Peking. The Soviets who emphasized good relations with most existing governments, were less suspect in Africa.

Closer to home the situation in Southeast Asia (which we shall examine more in the next chapter) grew tenser after the agreement which both Peking and Washington signed in July 1962, guaranteeing independence and neutrality for Laos, failed to work for very long. By mid-1964 the U.S. involvement there was increasing, with U.S. military planes conducting photo-reconnaisance flights over Communist-held areas at the request of the premier, Prince Suvanna Phuma. In June, pro-Communist Pathet Lao areas were raided by U.S. planes. Cambodia that same year moved closer to China, and the U.S. increased its reserve stock of military supplies in Thailand (a member of SEATO). In 1965 Laos gave further permission for bombing of the Ho Chi Minh trail, while Cambodia broke relations with the U.S. In mid-1965 came the American decision to increase U.S. forces substantially in South Viet-Nam. China increased the flow of aid to North Viet-Nam and the Viet Cong.

Further westward, fighting broke out (April 1965) between Indian and Pakistani forces in the Rann of Cutch (near West Pakistan's southern frontier). Temporarily halted, new fighting began in August in Jammu and Kashmir. Hostilities were now on a large scale. With a new cease-fire in the wind, China on September 17 gave India an ultimatum to dismantle 56 military works on what they claimed was the Tibetan side of the Chinese frontier with Sikkim. India reacted by rejecting the ultimatum and offering joint inspection. The same day that India and Pakistan agreed to a cease-fire (September 22), Peking radio claimed the installations were being dismantled and the Sino-Indian tension was allowed to slack. Quite obviously, China had moved at a time when India was fully engaged elsewhere, to demonstrate aid for Pakistan (and perhaps divert Indian forces). The Soviet Union, by contrast, invited both India and Pakistan to meet at Tashkent and resolve their immediate differences—which they did.

In 1966 China, in exploding a fourth nuclear device at the Lopnor test site, showed substantial technical gains, including a limited-range missile capability. Foreign Minister Chen Yi accused the Soviet Union of "making military deployments along the Chinese border in coordination with United States imperialist encirclement of China." Equally spectacular was the "Red Guard" movement and Mao's party purges (executed by Lin Piao, Minister of Defense). They were signs of China's frustrations, whatever else they implied.

6 *Chinese Policy: An Analysis*

IN Chapter 25, discussing Soviet foreign policy, the public phase of the Sino-Soviet dispute was examined in some detail; here we have shown this dispute more fully within the framework of Chinese policy. While some in the Western world dismiss it as an attempt to lull and deceive the non-Communist powers into relaxing their guard, the evidence is clear that friction between the two Communist giants is both deep and real. Others in the West, who consider the quarrel genuine, think it is primarily a dispute over doctrine, but it is again clear that the doctrinal disagreements spring from substantially opposed perspectives over what should be done, and that these perspectives vary because of the greatly different foreign policy problems these two nations confront. China, unlike the Soviet Union, has not succeeded in redressing her frontiers to rectify the losses in the days of weakness. China, unlike the Soviet Union, cannot point to substantial and adequate improvements in the stand-ard of living. China, unlike the Soviet Union, is not ringed round in the most vulnerable approach zones by friendly buffer states. China, unlike the Soviet Union, is substantially still a "have-not" state confronted with great opposing military forces which actively frustrate the achievement of her goals. Finally, China, to realize her ultimate ambitions for the rectification of the frontier, must tangle with her most important "ally" (the Soviet Union) while her equally formidable "enemy" (the United States) disposes of tremendous military power immediately in her rear.

The size of the Chinese problem goes far to explain the scale of the Chi-nese frustration. Chinese anger is even further compounded by the size of the Chinese pride. For hardly ever in history has a nation with such a proud past, now recovering its strength, been confronted with so many hurdles. How else account for much of Chinese behavior which reaches the irrational extremes of terming the atomic bomb "a paper tiger"?

Chinese actions, while far from moderate, have been on a much more modest scale than Chinese invective. For the Chinese have generally been prudent, avoiding full-scale commitments beyond their strength (as in the use of the fiction of "volunteers" in Korea and the careful limits they imposed on their conflict with India). The weapons used by the Chinese have been pre-dominately those of an energetic but still relatively weak nation. They have bombarded Quemoy and Matsu, but not invaded. They have sought to capitalize on "revolutionary" discontent in the Afro-Asian realm to cause trouble in the rear of their foe.

The question still frequently arises: what are the ultimate Chinese inten-tions? Within the United States, especially after the American commitment to the Viet-Nam War in 1965–1966, some argued that China had an unlim-ited program of expansion and that she should be contained wherever she tried to enlarge her position. Chinese talk and attempts to use tactics of world subversion in the less developed areas (using the "country" against the "cit-ies"), aroused much alarm. Yet, as we have seen, these tactics have aroused hostility in Africa by their very nature. In the American effort to contain China, very little effort was being expended to gain support among the great nations of Asia—or at least very little success in this effort was being achieved. Was this because the great nations of Asia did not feel threatened? (Yet In-dia at least must.) Or because these nations feel too weak? (But they could advantageously rally behind the powerful shield of American power.) Or because most of them regarded China's policies as more limited than the United States generally believed?

We have already indicated skepticism about policies based on assumptions concerning ultimate intentions. Many wars have been avoided by a simple refusal by one nation to assume a foreordained and rigid extension of another's actions to its logical ultimate. China's policies so far reveal a dogged determination to right old wrongs, to gain "acceptable" frontiers, and to be the leading nation of Asia and a power of consequence in the world at large. To accomplish these goals, even in this limited form, inevitably means increased frictions with her immediate neighbors. This is especially so when we consider what priorities the present nature of Chinese power will make unavoidable. For Chinese military power, formidable in the size of the land contingents, is still very limited in terms of ability to exert force at any great distances from China proper. The curious aspect to Far Eastern politics in the late 1960's was that the United States–Chinese hostility was tending to overshadow all the rest even though the United States was less immediately affected. How the Viet-Nam War in particular was affecting Asian politics (and the Sino-Soviet dispute) we shall observe further in the next chapter. There we shall also seek some answer to the question why Asian politics have come to be so disproportionately clustered around the Sino-American antagonism.

The Asian Powers: II

The Manila Treaty [of SEATO] represents a subtle attempt on the part of the Western Powers collectively, to force colonialism in a different guise on Southeast Asia by substituting military protection for political tutelage.

Resolution of the Steering Committee
of the Indian Congress Party, 1955[1]

We should try to create what my father [Nehru] called a climate of peace. We should encourage the spirit of Tashkent . . . and see that we have peace at home and also abroad, if possible.

MRS. INDIRA GANDHI
Prime Minister of India, January 1966

The post of Prime Minister [of Japan] is especially hazardous. Of 38 prime ministers since the 1868 Meiji Restoration, two have been hanged, three arraigned and jailed for war crimes, one forced to commit suicide prior to his arrest as a war crimes suspect, and six assassinated.

STUART GRIFFIN
"Ultranationalism in Japan,"
Eastern World, January 1961

C ONTEMPORARY Asian politics revolve above all around the question of how China will react and what China will do. That is why we have deferred considering the other nations of Asia in any detail until we first took a close look at Chinese policies. But now we turn to the rest.

I *Japan: Modernization and Expansion*

JAPAN today occupies a curious position in certain respects in Far Eastern politics, primarily because after 1945 she chose to possess a military capability far below her capacity and set her policy essentially within the framework of United States tactics and goals. Thus her impact upon the course of events has been negligible compared to her power. In the decades before that, she dominated Far Eastern politics, as China does today. Even the active role of Russia was secondary to the effects wrought by Japan, especially after the Russo-Japanese War. Before World War II Japan had (and kept) the initia-

---

[1] Quoted in a Chatham House Study Group report from the *India News* of January 22, 1955.

tive in Asia and the Soviet Union (distracted by problems in Europe) played only the lesser role in Asia as Japan steadily expanded.

Although it was Commodore M. C. Perry's visits to Japan with a U.S. squadron which finally induced Japan to abandon her self-imposed isolationism, the policy itself had been debated for several decades. Japan realized that the West and its technical progress could not be successfully ignored. After granting Perry the Treaty of Kanagawa on March 31, 1854, which opened two ports to Western commerce, Japan quickly concluded trade treaties with England, Russia, and Holland. Anti-foreign elements in Japan resisted the new course, bringing on civil war. Out of this began the Meiji Period in which the emperor became again of direct importance, displacing the *Shōgunate* of some seven hundred years' standing. Western techniques were now accepted with enthusiasm. Universal military conscription was decreed in 1872. While the Germans trained the Japanese army, the British aided in the foundation of a navy. In 1890 came the first general election (limited male suffrage). Then in 1892 a new law code was introduced, based on Western concepts. Thereafter one by one the Western powers gave up extraterritoriality. By the end of the century all Westerners in Japan were subject to Japanese courts.

The reforms being introduced at home did not cause a neglect of foreign affairs. As early as 1876 Japan had as a first step made a treaty with Korea recognizing it as independent of China. In 1894–1895 the Sino-Japanese War over Korea ended with the Treaty of Shimonoseki. In this treaty China recognized Korea's independence and ceded Formosa and the Pescadores to Japan (along with the Liaotung Peninsula). Hardly was the ink dry on this treaty before Russia, Germany, and France, acting together, forced Japan to relinquish the Liaotung Peninsula. Within fifty years Japan was to retaliate against all three—displacing Russia in Manchuria, Germany on the continent and in the Pacific Islands, and France in Indo-China. But in 1895 Japan was still too weak. At least she had Korea to exploit—provided she was able to frustrate Russian ambitions there.

Throughout the ebbing years of the nineteenth century Japan and Russia struggled for control of Korea. In 1902, with the signing of the Anglo-Japanese Alliance, Britain recognized the independence of Korea but also Japan's special interests there. The continued Russian penetration of north Korea led in 1904 to the Russo-Japanese War. Not only did the Japanese army defeat the Russian army at the Yalu River, but in the battle of Tsushima Straits the Russian thirty-two-unit fleet was annihilated. By the Treaty of Portsmouth, Russia acknowledged Japan's paramount interest in Korea, gave over her lease on the Liaotung Peninsula, and ceded the southern half of Sakhalin. Manchuria was to be returned to China, although control of the railroad to Ch'ang-ch'un was now to be Japanese instead of Russian. By mid-1907 Japan had achieved a protectorate over Korea, and in 1910 Korea was annexed. Thus ended Phase I of Japan's expansion.

Two important developments had occurred internally in the first years of the new century. In 1901 a naval and military reorganization had been adopted as a part of modernization. While Cabinet officers of these depart-ments could be civilians, these officers were to continue to be directly respon-sible to the emperor—a development quite contrary to general Western practice. Then in 1912 the Meiji reign ended with the death of Japan's strong Emperor Mutsuhito. His successor, Yoshihito (1912–1926), was weak. The combination of these events made the military forces increasingly capa-ble of being a government within a government.

With the outbreak of World War I, Phase II began. On August 23, 1914, Japan, as Britain's ally, declared war on Germany. By the end of the year she had destroyed the German forces on the Asian mainland and occupied the German island groups. The Marshalls, the Marianas, the Palaus, and the Carolines—all names to become famous in World War II—thus passed into Japanese hands. As a group they lay athwart the sea connections between America and the Philippines. Further, Japan turned successfully to an en-largement of her munitions industry, becoming a major supplier of such goods to the Allies. Finally, the shape of things to come was made known to all in the famous Twenty-One Demands on China in 1915. These were fol-lowed by further demands the next year, increasing Japanese rights in South Manchuria and Inner Mongolia. A few months earlier Japan had recognized Outer Mongolia as a Russian sphere of interest in return for Russian acquiescence in these new moves. Japan joined, too, in the Allied occupation of Siberia, but this ultimately gained them nothing. The peace settlements, however, recognized Japanese conquests in the Pacific. The islands were to be "mandates."

In 1926 Emperor Hirohito came to the throne. The next year Japan inter-vened in the Chinese civil war, blocking the northward march of Chinese Nationalist forces on the ancient capital of Peking. In 1928 came further in-tervention in Shantung; Japan's temporary seizure of the railways produced a Chinese boycott of Japanese goods in retaliation. On March 28, 1929, the incident was closed; two months later Japanese troops were withdrawn. Meanwhile population pressure was mounting at home. The 1935 population of 69.2 millions was double that of 1872, and the annual increase by 1930 was around one million. The assassination of Premier Hamaguchi in 1930 was one sign of growing unrest. Then on September 19, 1931, came the Mukden inci-dent and the beginning of the later and more serious phases of Japanese in-tervention in Manchuria and China. Premier Inukai was assassinated by militarists in May 1932; Admiral Saito became premier. What was implicit now became explicit—the armed forces were ruling. The struggle for control in Japan became one of rival military groups. In 1936 Admiral Saito was assassinated by young army officers. In 1937, after a period of some confusion, General Hayashi formed a cabinet. Then came a "national union" cabinet under Prince Konoye. Meanwhile the military and naval command both ran the war in China and dominated the government at home. Thus it continued through the 1930's.

The outbreak of World War II in Europe initiated Phase III of Japan's expansion. The continuing China war became a part of the larger war with the Japanese attack on Pearl Harbor. The period between the outbreak of World War II in 1939 and Japan's entry into it in 1941 was one of great stress and strain for Japan. Her forces were committed in China: what should now be her policy toward Russia, Germany, Britain, and America? Obviously, new opportunities beckoned. The *rapprochement* with Germany was the least complicated of her problems. Diplomatic cooperation with Germany cost nothing, and Germany had no further territory in Asia that Japan could conquer. At the same time the question of a military alliance was something else. Although Japan had joined Germany in the Anti-Comintern Pact of 1936 (which was not a military alliance),[2] she was thrown into serious confusion with the announcement of the Nazi-Soviet Pact of 1939. While the Nazi-Soviet Pact left Germany free in Europe, it also left Russia free in Asia, provided Russia felt strong enough to force the issue there. Already, in May 1939, Japan had fought an undeclared war with Russia, on a considerable scale, on the Mongolian frontier. Ostensibly this was a conflict between "independent" Manchukuo forces and "independent" Mongolian forces, but actually it was a test of strength. It convinced both sides that they were fairly evenly matched. It convinced Japan that, until Russia had become involved in war in Europe, it was safe neither to attack Russia nor turn her back on Russia while attacking the United States. Japan had learned in 1894–1895 the penalties for impatience. Japan would wait until the great powers were too preoccupied to intervene jointly against her.

2   Japan Makes the Plunge

JAPAN's patience was rewarded in the spring of 1941 when signs multiplied of a coming German attack on Russia. With France already defeated and Britain fighting for survival, only the United States among the great powers remained uninvolved. The question was whether to attack Russia in her rear while she was engaged in the West or to expand in the Pacific while Japan's own back was safe.

A war with Russia was safest. But while Japan coveted Siberia, she was already in the process of gaining a huge mainland empire in China. If a Russo-German war exhausted Russia, as seemed likely, the great strategic aim of Japan on the continent would be achieved. Russia could not then thwart the consolidation of Japan's mainland empire. Russia's far eastern territories might even be dismembered subsequently if Russia became weak enough.

---

[2] The Anti-Comintern Pact was, as made public, a treaty of cooperation against communism. It mentioned "necessary measures of defense" upon which Japan and Germany would "confer," but it contained no definite obligations. In the secret protocal annexed to it, however, it was provided that if either country were threatened or attacked by the Soviet Union without provocation, the other would not aid the Soviet Union. This was negative in emphasis and far from being a sign of close relations. See *Far Eastern Military Tribunal*, Exhibit No. 480, for the text of this secret protocol.

At the same time, with Russia forced to concentrate on Europe, the chances for enormous gains in the Pacific were unlikely ever to be again so great. To a Japan poor in raw-material resources, the riches of the East Indies beckoned alluringly. If Japan could consolidate this vast Western Pacific area under her control, while pushing ahead with the conquest of China un-hindered by fears of Russian intervention, this course would be highly de-sirable. A Pacific adventure would have the further merit of using Japanese naval forces fully. Such an enterprise was not only desirable in itself in order to make maximum conquests; it was also necessary in order to satisfy the naval high command who, it will be remembered, were in control, along with the army, of the Japanese government. The naval command had long chafed at the army's mainland successes, which gave the land forces the lion's share of prestige.

In April 1941, the decision was made. Foreign Minister Matsuoka, having visited Moscow, Berlin, and Rome, on his return home stopped again in Mos-cow and signed a five-year non-aggression pact with Russia.[3] By it the fron-tiers of Manchukuo and Outer Mongolia were mutually stabilized. The die was now cast.

The actual invasion of Russia by Germany was echoed in Tokyo by an even greater monopolization of power by the military and naval leaders. On July 18 General Tojo became Minister of War, and Vice-Admiral Toyado became foreign minister. In October, Konoye was replaced by General Tojo as premier. Japan now began the final negotiations with the United States. Kurusu was sent as a special emissary with an offer to withdraw from south Indo-China and a promise not to send further troops to any part of southeast Asia or the South Pacific other than Indo-China. In return the United States was to unfreeze Japanese assets there, resume the export to Japan of steel and oil, agree not to send further troops to the same areas, and recognize Japan's position in China. This "bargain" offered little and demanded much: it came down to being a qualified promise to behave. The United States in turn in-sisted that she would restore trade in strategic materials only if Japan with-drew from 'China and Indo-China. The impasse by late November was complete.

Determined to go on, and fearful of possible United States intervention, Japan decided to initiate a war with the United States in a manner that would cripple United States offensive power. If such a blow were successful, the Pacific would be in Japan's hands: battleships could not be replaced in less than three or four years. By then the war ought to be over. On November 27 a Japanese task force left Japanese waters and proceeded toward Pearl Har-bor. Carrier planes had already thoroughly practiced the coming strike over a Japanese island whose physical features resembled those of Pearl Harbor. On Sunday morning, December 7, 1941, they put their rehearsed skills to effective

---

[3] By it the Japanese, to demonstrate their sincerity to the Russians, agreed to give up their oil and coal concessions in northern Sakhalin.

use. The Japanese task force, undetected, launched one hundred five planes from two hundred miles north of Hawaii. When the smoke cleared away, nine American battleships, three cruisers, three destroyers, and other smaller ships had been put out of action. The war was on, with the United States fleet crippled by the first blow.

While at first Japan swept over Hong Kong, Singapore, the East Indies, the Philippines, Burma, Malaya, and Guam, her ultimate retention of this great empire was always in jeopardy if the United States could rebuild her offensive naval power. Japan could not realistically expect to conquer the United States and thus gain a complete and final victory. What she could hope for was that the United States, like Russia in similar circumstances in 1904–1905, would ultimately make peace with Japan and withdraw from the Western Pacific rather than undertake the tremendous task of advancing step by step across the Japanese Pacific islands, conquering them one by one, until finally the Japanese home islands could be attacked and subdued. Japan underestimated both the productiveness of the American war economy and United States determination to see the war through to a victorious conclusion. By March 1945, great fire raids on Japan by United States bombers were marking the first symptoms of coming invasion; on Easter Sunday the assault landing on Okinawa, virtually in the shadow of Japan's home islands, sounded a further alarm. Japan retaliated with the Kamikaze (the "divine wind" or suicide) planes, whose pilots, dressed in ceremonial robes, rode their bomb-laden planes down into cruiser, destroyer, and transport bridges and hatches, carrying Japanese and Americans alike to a flaming death. The stubbornness with which these pilots went to their target and death made it obvious that the planned assault on Japan proper in October 1945 would be extremely costly: over a million American casualties were expected.

The United States anticipated two new additions to her strength for the final assault. The first of these, Soviet Russia's entry into the war, would keep the Japanese army in Manchuria preoccupied during the critical stages of the first landings on Japan proper. At Yalta the Russian promise had been given; on April 5, 1945, Molotov denounced the Russo-Japanese non-aggression treaty of 1941, claiming that Japan had aided Germany against Russia. The second addition was the atomic bomb. In a top-secret document of December 30, 1944 (released in March 1955), Maj. Gen. Leslie R. Groves, in charge of the "Manhattan District" (the code name for the bomb project), speculated that the first test bomb would be ready in late July. So it was. On August 6, 1945, the first combat bomb was dropped over Hiroshima, exploding with the force of twenty thousand tons of TNT. Two days later Russia entered the war. On August 9 the second combat bomb laid Nagasaki waste. The next day Japan sued for peace, stipulating the retention of the emperor. The surrender was accepted, and on August 14 the war was over.

Japan had realized her defeat both before the first atom bomb dropped and before Russia entered into the war. Divided counsels in Tokyo as to the terms and timing of peace delayed decision until the destruction of Hiroshima and Nagasaki showed that useless slaughter was inevitable if there was further hesitation.

3 *Postwar Japan*

THE Occupation, in form an Allied venture, in practice an almost purely American operation, now began. An Allied Council for Japan was created in Tokyo (with the United States, Russia, Britain, and China as members) under General MacArthur as chairman; and a Far Eastern Commission was created in Washington (these same four powers, together with France, the Netherlands, India, the Philippines, Canada, Australia, and New Zealand). The real power was always in the hands of MacArthur. As Supreme Commander of the Allied Powers he governed Japan. Under his direction Japan was "democratized." The central police were decentralized, school reforms were initiated, the throne was "humanized," and the great trusts were broken up. Japan went so far as to renounce armed forces altogether in her new constitution of 1946.

In the first election after the occupation began (April 10, 1946) the Liberals (right wing conservatives) won one hundred forty-eight seats, while the only less conservative Progressives (later, "Democrats") gained one hundred ten. Out of four hundred sixty-six Diet seats, over half were in very conservative hands. The Social Democrats got only ninety-six. Shigeru Yoshida, leader of the Liberals, became Prime Minister and remained such until May 1947. In the next year-and-a-half two others took the helm and then Yoshida once more (from October 1948 until December 1954).

In 1951 came the Japanese Peace Treaty and, with it, a mutual defense agreement between Japan and the United States. By agreement United States troops were to continue to be based in Japan until such time as Japan could "assume responsibility for its own defense." During the Korean War, Japan became the main forward United States base for the fighting. Thus ended the official occupation. Japan had regained her sovereignty, renouncing as the price all her former overseas possessions. Among these were Korea and the Pescadores which passed, presumably, into the collective hands of the signers of the peace treaty.

Although India and Burma were not signatories of the Japanese Peace Treaty, separate arrangements were made with India in 1952 and with Burma in 1954. While trade agreements between Communist Chinese officials and Japanese private groups were concluded beginning in 1953, official relations were with the Formosa regime. (These agreements had an up-and-down history. In 1958 the Communist Chinese cut off all trade for a time as a political pressure. In 1961 trade stood at $43 millions.) In 1955 Japan moved to normalize relations with the Soviet Union (which had not signed the Japanese

Peace Treaty either). Diplomatic relations were restored between the two nations in 1956 and the U.S.S.R. no longer vetoed Japan's admission to the UN, in December 1956.

Foreign affairs and domestic issues continued to be fought out in Japanese politics, with the Socialists arguing for freedom from U.S. foreign policy and recognition and trade with Communist China plus retention of U.S. domestic reforms, and the conservative groups arguing the reverse. Between 1952 and 1958 the socialist strength in the house of representatives gradually increased from 111 to 166 while the conservative bloc was reduced from 325 to 287. Although the conservatives remained in power they could not make constitutional changes (which required a two-thirds majority of the 467-member house). In the reshuffling of the conservative groups which followed Yoshida's prolonged term, a Liberal-Democratic Party of conservatives emerged with a succession of leaders. Nobusuke Kishi, who took the helm in February 1958, represented a return to prewar leadership. He gave way to Hayato Ikeda after July 1960.

Kishi's resignation was triggered by the new security treaty signed by the United States and Japan on January 19, 1960. The final stages of the consideration of the treaty came in May–June 1960—in the immediate aftermath of the U-2 incident. The Communists went all-out to exploit widespread fears among the Japanese population, for it was common gossip that U-2 planes were also based on Japan, and were flying from there over the Communist mainland. Rallies were organized by the opposition parties and a part of the trade union movement. On June 15 violent student rioting broke out in the grounds outside the Diet (parliament). A visit by President Eisenhower, which was timed to coincide with the treaty's ratification, had to be abandoned when the Japanese government confessed itself unable to guarantee his safety. On June 19 the treaty was ratified: with 50,000 demonstrators assembling outside during the course of the day.

A further and gloomily reminiscent sign of trouble showed itself: on June 17 a Socialist deputy was stabbed by a right-winger outside the Diet, while on October 12, 1960, Inejiro Asanuma, leader of the Japanese Socialist Party, was assassinated while in full view of a television audience by a 17-year-old member of the ultranationalist Great Japan Patriotic Society.

Despite this unrest and later riots when U.S. nuclear submarines began to visit Japan, the conservatives continued to receive enough popular support to maintain stability and continuity. In the elections at the end of 1963, Ikeda's Liberal-Democrats got 54.8 per cent (283 seats) while the Socialists obtained 29 per cent (144 seats). The Democratic Socialists had 23 seats, the Communists only five. When Ikeda resigned because of illness in 1964, Eisaku Sato became Prime Minister. Under all of these postwar leaders Japan's policy remained essentially the same. The 1967 elections continued Sato's power.

Much depended on the economy, for Japan literally must trade or die. Japan's economic growth rate between 1953 and 1958 averaged 9.3 per cent.

But its international balance of payments which showed a surplus of $500 million in 1958 declined in the next two years and in 1961 reached a deficit of $1,085 million. In 1962 a five-year trade agreement with Peking provided for an annual total of $101 million. Next year a three-year agreement with the Soviet Union hiked the previous totals by 50 per cent. In fishery negotiations Japan obtained an expansion of the salmon catch for the first time in six years. In the decade 1955–1965 the Japanese share in world exports of manufactured goods went from 5.2 per cent to 9.8 per cent—a very healthy increase. No other major trading nation could match this growth rate except Italy (3.4 per cent to 6.9 per cent). All the other major traders except West Germany (15.6 per cent to 20.1 per cent) lost ground.[4] But imports were also large and Japan's deficit in the balance of payments still continued, although at a much reduced rate.

The issue of Japanese armed forces continued to arouse controversy. Japan, in the new constitution adopted during the Occupation, had renounced armed forces altogether. Even with U.S. protection this came to be thought unrealistic. But amending the constitution was not possible politically. Consequently Japan first created "police" units which in 1952 became "national safety" forces (110,000 in the ground forces; 8,000 in the sea forces). By 1954 these had become "self-defense forces." By 1965 military personnel totaled 246,000. Persistent reports were coming from Japan, once the Chinese began to explode nuclear devices, that military leaders were arguing behind the scenes for the development of a Japanese nuclear capability. Memories of atomic bombing were still very fresh in Japan despite more than twenty years, so this issue could cost the government its control if it was not handled very carefully. The related question of whether to increase conventional forces put the Socialists in a difficult position since they opposed expansion but also opposed the U.S. "protectorate" whose termination probably meant increasing Japanese forces.

Japan continued in her foreign policy (as in her trade policy) to straddle the great problems, leaning toward the American position as much as possible short of cutting off links to the other "camp" and offending Asian sentiments. In 1965 Japan moved gradually and carefully toward reopening the issue of the return of Okinawa and the Ryukyus to active Japanese control. Japan expressed concern over the U.S. involvement in Viet-Nam but avoided breaking with the American policy. Normal relations were established with a treaty with South Korea after 14 years of negotiations.

Although Japan remained stable it was apparent that many explosive issues were unresolved. Especially with the Chinese, the problem was becoming more acute. The combination of Chinese resentment against Japan for its continued nonrecognition and the beginning of a Chinese nuclear capability posed difficult problems. The Japanese could not help but have doubts about

---

[4] The 1965 figures, from the National Institute of Economic and Social Research, *Ecoomic Review,* are for the first half of the year adjusted to annual rates,

the increasing tensions in the Far East, seeing some of them as caused by the negative policy of the U.S. toward China. Yet China's very growth in power constituted an increasing threat to Japan's security.

4 *Indonesia—Troubled Realm*

INDONESIA is one of the largest states in population in the world. It spreads more than 3,000 miles along the equator, between the Malayan peninsula and Australia, and is comprised of hundreds of small islands and several very large ones, especially Sumatra, Java, Celebes, and (most of) Borneo. It became independent on December 27, 1949, after the Dutch ceased armed opposition to the independence movement. The new government exercised control over all of the Netherlands Indies except Netherlands New Guinea (West Irian). Indonesia's drive to acquire West Irian accelerated in 1961 when she began to receive $400 million worth of arms from the Soviet Union. President Sukarno threatened to take it by force. The Dutch, under pressure, relinquished the area to the UN on October 1, 1962, with the understanding that West Irian would go to Indonesia in May 1963.

The crisis and military preparations worked havoc with Indonesia's financial stability. The 1962–1963 budget, exclusive of spending over West Irian, showed a deficit of $822 million. By 1962 Soviet arms aid had increased a further billion dollars, and Indonesian spending on the armed forces reached 83 per cent of the revenues. In 1963 as Britain moved to establish Malaysia (a federation of Malaya, Singapore and the former British colonies of North Borneo), Indonesia stepped up her claims in Borneo and began to aid rebel groups. On September 16, Malaysia came into existence and despite a UN survey which showed that the peoples of North Borneo wished to be in Malaysia, Indonesia began to increase its pressures. Consumer prices, which had increased 420 per cent between January 1961 and November 1962, continued up in 1963. When the U.S. advanced an additional $17 millions in emergency aid, Indonesia bought three luxury airliners with the money. Disruption of trade with Singapore compounded the chaos.

In 1964 Sukarno in the name of opposing "neo-colonialism," pushed ahead with his "confrontation" policy designed to "crush" Malaysia. Indonesian guerrilla activities there continued. When Malaysia was elected to the UN Security Council at the end of the year, Indonesia announced she was leaving the UN. The U.S. finally called off its economic aid program. Soviet arms aid continued although the large Indonesian Communist Party made no secret of its pro-Peking sympathies. Sukarno pushed ahead with his programs, taking Indonesia out of the UN to the applause of Communist China.

Matters moved toward crisis in 1965. British armed support of Malaysia prevented effective Indonesian gains. Sukarno, in the face of the British build-up, thought it prudent to declare that "If Indonesia is attacked, the Indonesian people will fight back, but Indonesia will never begin the fighting."

Sukarno condemned U.S. support of South Viet-Nam and the landing in the Dominican Republic as "Nekolim" (his coined word for colonialism, neo-colonialism, and imperialism). Anti-American acts were officially encouraged, so that the U.S. finally closed out its USIA informational activities. American properties were seized although the government refrained from outright con-fiscation. The U.S. Peace Corps was withdrawn. Sukarno's comment in Feb-ruary 1965 seemed to apply to most of this: "To hell with U.S. aid." Sukarno in July announced that Indonesia would produce an atomic bomb. Singa-pore's withdrawal from Malaysia in September gave Sukarno added encour-agement.

Sukarno, a Marxist, and the hero of the Indonesian independence move-ment, despite his increasingly reckless behavior, still commanded great esteem among the masses. But his plan to continue an internal power balance of na-tionalist, religious, and Communist forces ("Nasakom") was repugnant to many influential groups. In late September 1965 the three million member Indonesian Communist Party (PKI) attempted a coup directed primarily against the army leadership. Six generals were captured and executed, includ-ing the army commander. But General Abdul Nasution, the minister of de-fense, escaped (although his daughter was killed). Sukarno, under pressure, named Major General Suharto, head of the strike command, as new army commander and ordered him to restore order. A thorough purge of the Com-munist leadership now went forward while Sukarno maneuvered to regain control. Sukarno felt strong enough by February 21, 1966 to bring Commu-nist elements back into his cabinet. This led to violent street demonstrations in early March by pro-army student groups, Kami (the university students), and Kapi (the high school students). The Communist Chinese news agency was burned on March 9 and on March 12 the army began a take-over. Sukarno and First Deputy Premier Subandrio were closely guarded as now Lt. Gen. Suharto assumed control. Purporting to act in Sukarno's still potent name, Suharto dissolved and outlawed the largest Communist party outside the Communist "bloc." On March 18 the army named a new non-Communist cabinet, arrested pro-Peking Subandrio and 14 other leftist ministers, and placed Sukarno under heavy guard.

Indonesia thus brought to an end one of the most extravagant illustrations of irresponsibility in the affairs of a significant state in the postwar era. Indo-nesia provides an excellent case study of how the pursuit of anticolonialist sentiment can jeopardize the national interests (as well as ruin the economy). What was most striking about Indonesia's policies is that they were carrying her into the waiting arms of Communist China. Out of hostility to the Dutch and the British, and determined to create a great expanded empire on a weak-ly developed material basis, Sukarno had gradually undermined his own coun-try's independence. While the Soviets furnished the arms, it was Peking who stood most to benefit, for the Indonesian Communist Party was dominated by pro-Peking sympathizers, including many Indonesian-born Chinese. (Esti-mates for 1955 placed the Chinese population at 1,600,000, concentrated mainly in the important islands of Java, Sumatra, and Borneo. The Chinese, with their usual energy and initiative control far more of Indonesian trade and commerce than these mere figures would indicate.)

It can hardly be doubted that Indonesia's great natural resources make her very attractive to the material-poor Chinese. The failure of the Communist coup represented in consequence a great defeat for Peking. From a dispassionate point of view it was obvious that China must continue to want to dominate Indonesia and that Indonesia is, in the natural order of things, more China's enemy than China's friend. But in the topsy-turvy world of Asian politics in the postwar period, these considerations only slowly began to prevail in Indonesia.

5 India and Pakistan

INDIA began her independence with far less zenophobia against colonialism because after World War II the British, unlike the Dutch, were reconciled to independence and moved toward it in an orderly way. India was spared the disruptions of wholesale armed rebellion and could proceed from the outset to cope with her many problems within the framework of Commonwealth and American aid and support.

Independence did not, however, come of its own accord. The British, who had benefited greatly in World War I from the some 1.2 million Indian combat and labor troops who took part in the European and Near Eastern campaigns, moved after the war to meet unrest through some concessions.

The first fruit of this approach, spurred by a full-scale rebellion in the Punjab, was the Government of India Act of December 1919, establishing a semi-appointive Indian legislature. The National Congress Party, still dissatisfied, heeded Gandhi's injunction and began the first non-cooperation campaign. Mohammed Ali Jinnah, leader of the Moslem League, opposing Gandhi's program, now broke with the National Congress. By 1921, despite Gandhi's efforts, violence was increasing, and the British put Gandhi in prison. A more moderate attitude on the part of the National Congress in 1923, and their decision to participate in the elections (and seek Dominion status rather than independence), led to the restoration of order. By 1924 India was quiet and Gandhi was released.

In the next six years dissatisfaction against increased, culminating in Gandhi's second civil disobedience campaign in 1930. Again Gandhi was arrested. This time the government supplemented its coercion with a round-table conference of Indian princes and liberals who favored cooperation. Again Gandhi was released; he attended the second round-table conference in London in 1931. This broke up in disagreement. Jinnah's insistence on separate voting procedures for Moslems and Hindus forced another wedge into all-Indian unity. The monotonous cycle once again repeated itself. In 1932 the National Congress was declared illegal; Gandhi was in turn arrested, released, arrested, released. In 1935 came a new Government of India Act. Burma and Aden were separated from India as crown colonies. In the ensuing elections the All-India Congress Party won the commanding position. Pandit Jawaharlal Nehru, leader of the extremist socialist-nationalist wing, was defeated by the moderates in the party who determined to cooperate with the government. In 1938 Gandhi lost control to Nehru. More vigorous measures seemed in the offing. But World War II intervened. With Japan's occupation of Burma and the obvious threat to India, the Hindus and Moslems aided in the defense of their homeland while continuing their separate demands. In 1940 Jinnah proposed the erection of a separate Moslem state once India became free. In April 1942, the Indian leaders rejected the British offer of autonomy for India after the war. Disturbances broke out; Gandhi and Nehru were arrested. At the end of the war Britain finally, under the Labour government, moved to settle the question and give freedom to the subcontinent. On August 15, 1947, this was achieved with the creation of two new independent states: India and Pakistan.

Both new states chose to remain associated with Britain. In 1949, in anticipation of the coming into force of India's republican constitution (which occurred in January 1950), a formula was agreed upon in conjunction with the other ex-Dominions by which the British monarch assumed the new title of "Head of the Commonwealth." India's allegiance to the British Crown thus became symbolic rather than formal. Pakistan, a Moslem state as Jinnah had insisted, became an "Islamic republic" in 1954 within the Commonwealth.

Just as Hindu-Moslem dissension had aided the maintenance of British imperialism for so long, so it had also delayed its ending; when the time came to liquidate the "jewel" of the British Empire, it had to be done by breaking it into smaller stones. And since the Moslems were concentrated at either extremity of the subcontinent, this meant a Pakistan which was itself two pieces—the smaller in the east and the larger in the west.

Because Pakistan existed in two pieces separated by Hindu India, the relations of India and Pakistan became of necessity delicate. The two states were bound together geographically and yet were now separate. Religious differences and a lack of sovereign experience made trouble between the two nations almost inevitable. It was made downright inescapable by the fact that the status of three of the five hundred sixty-two princely states that British rule had left in existence was still unresolved: Hyderabad, Kashmir, and Junagadh. A settlement of their fate by prior agreement, before independence, would have delayed beyond endurance the date of Indian-Pakistani freedom. Yet they represented a serious problem. Where the future of the rest of the princely states had been determined by the logic of their location or circumstances, Hyderabad and Kashmir represented far more complex issues. And of these two the Kashmir problem was to prove more troublesome. In handling both these problems the Indians, who possessed the flower of the old British Indian Army, had an initial advantage.

The Hyderabad problem arose as India put pressure on the Nizam of

Hyderabad (a Moslem), who ruled over a population containing a majority of Hindus. In August 1948, the Nizam complained to the UN Security Council, but India contended that this was a matter of Indian internal concern. The Security Council had not yet explored the issue in detail when Indian troops were sent in September into Hyderabad. The Nizam, under pressure, withdrew his complaint to the Council, and in the end India's *fait accompli* was allowed to settle the issue. On the other hand, the Kashmir dispute, beginning under similar circumstances, was not so easily disposed of. Kashmir was Hyderabad reversed, as it were: a heavily Moslem state with a Hindu maharajah. When civil disturbances broke out after the end of British rule, the maharajah requested Indian occupation and annexation. India agreed, stipulating that when order was restored a final solution of Kashmir's fate would be determined by a plebiscite. This time Pakistani irregular troops were present so that fighting occurred. The UN, appealed to, suggested a cease-fire and mutual withdrawal. In July 1949, a permanent cease-fire line was agreed upon, but the armed forces remained and the plebiscite was as far away as ever. Neither India nor Pakistan would agree to a free vote unless all forces were first withdrawn; since Pakistan would not admit to responsibility for the irregular troops, the situation remained deadlocked. It has remained so since, the new fighting in 1965 ending in the Tashkent Agreement to restore the previous line. India, in possession of the only part of Kashmir that really matters—the Vale of Kashmir—had the better of things, but at the price of continuing tension with Pakistan. Ready to capitalize on this dispute stood China—as we have seen.

It is this background of tension in the Indian subcontinent that is partly responsible for the split in foreign-policy orientation of the two states existing there. In the first postwar decade Pakistan, small and weaker (because of her initial lack of military strength and especially because of her divided territories), moved closer to the United States, while India sedulously clung to a position of neutrality in the Cold War. Pakistan accepted United States arms aid and joined the United States–sponsored South-East Asia Treaty Organization (SEATO); India avoided such commitments entirely. As one Indian official expressed it: "The whole aim of nationalization in the East has been to free the countries concerned from implicit adherence to the decisions of a foreign power." Therefore, it would be strange if, following independence, "nationalism were to consent to enter into a relationship where in the nature of things the power of ultimate and binding decision must rest with the other party." India was not going to take part "in any arrangement that might induce a sense of dependence or compromise her freedom of action." [5]

That the United States-Pakistan *rapprochement* cooled American-Indian relations is the reverse side of the same picture. Referring to President Eisenhower's March 1954 assurances that the United States would take action if anyone misused American arms sent to them, Nehru commented:

---

[5] An Indian Official, "India as a World Power," *Foreign Affairs*, Vol. 27 (July 1949), p. 548.

I have no doubt the President is opposed to aggression. But we know from past experience that aggression takes place and nothing is done about it. Aggression took place in Kashmir six-and-a-half years ago and thus far the United States has not only not condemned it, but we have been asked not to press it in the interests of peace. Aggression may well follow in spite of the best intentions of the President, and then a long argument will ensue on what exactly is aggression.

Nehru went on to cite and take exception to press reports of testimony before the United States Congress by Assistant Secretary of State Walter Robertson to the purported effect that the United States must dominate Asia for an indefinite period until Communist China has "disintegrated." Nehru declared that "the countries of Asia do not intend to be dominated by any country for any purpose." [6]

The continuance of Communist Chinese–United States tension in the Far East posed a greater problem for India than for Pakistan. India voted with the UN majority in mid-1950 to condemn North Korea as an aggressor; thenceforth she devoted her considerable talents to restoring peace. Recognizing the stalemate inevitable after Communist China's entry into the conflict, she opposed condemning China as an aggressor and instead tried to bring the two sides to common agreement. Thus she more and more tried to fill the role of Asian "honest broker" in the Asian area of the Cold War. It was India who, as a neutral supervising nation, furnished police troops to administer the prisoner-of-war agreements between the United States and North Korea (and the Chinese "volunteer" forces). She has similarly striven to gain the seating of Communist China by the UN, and aided in finding a compromise formula to end the French–Indo-Chinese war. In 1962, when the international commission on Laos was revived, India again took the chairmanship.

India's middle position is not surprising; it is not merely that she desires peace for economic progress. The background of Asian colonial development makes it natural that India should have a great deal of sympathy with mainland China's efforts to achieve a position of sovereign dignity and power (for this is the way India thinks of it). India has steadfastly insisted on the necessity of recognizing the real situation on the China mainland. Nehru likened Chiang Kai-shek's pretensions to control of the manland to a government in the Andaman Islands (off India) claiming to rule the Indian mainland. That Communist China is communist is much less important to India than that it has, in India's view, thrown out the "foreign devils"—as befits a sovereign Asian state. India is, of course, opposed to converting Asia into a battlefield. She has viewed U.S. policy in Asia with a great deal of disquiet. Her general desire to see Western strength replaced by native Asian strength in the Pacific-Asian area is not at all unnatural. Her interest in bringing this general result about has not altered although her own troubles with China, both directly and indirectly, have made her reconsider her former somewhat uncritical acceptance of China.

Both India's recurrent tensions with Pakistan and her clashes with China

[6] *NYHT* (EE) and *NYT*, March 2, 1954.

have gradually worn away the "pure model" of her early policy which was heavily and self-consciously moralistic. Although India has played a generous role in the UN, contributing substantial troops units in the Congo operation, she more lately has had to face the fact that her armed forces are needed closer to home. Although she salved her conscience in taking the Goa enclaves from Portugal in December 1961 by justifying it as the liquidation of a colonial remnant (and escaped censure in a colonial-sensitive UN) it was still, impartially considered, an act of aggression. The newly independent Asian nations are no more immune to the distortions that come from looking in the rose-colored glass of nationalism than are the nations of the West. India is in principle dedicated to peace and is antiaggressive in outlook. Yet no modern states can escape the power problem, certainly not an India with Pakistan and China as neighbors. India grew hot with resentment against Chinese frontier rectifications which had the same moral basis as her own acts against Goa: the Chinese were attempting to liquidate imperialist dispositions out of the past.

The Indians resented the Chinese claims although the Chinese argued that they had never accepted certain of the frontiers, especially the McMahon Line in Assam and the area of Ladakh in northeast Kashmir. China's refusal to continue recognizing India's special position in Bhutan and Sikkim, a heritage from British colonial days, also angered India. In 1962 fighting became frequent and severe in these areas. The removal of Indian Defense Minister Krishna Menon, who as India's representative in the UN had frequently aroused resentment in the West, was one result. With the cease-fire of November 1962 and the December Chinese withdrawal in Assam to the line of November 7, 1959 (the McMahon Line), an uneasy equilibrium was reestablished which continued in the next years without fighting. The Soviets did not hide their displeasure at the Chinese aggressiveness and India received military assistance from 11 countries (including both the U.S. and the U.S.S.R.). India refused to accept a cession of part of Kashmir under Pakistan's control to China so that the Indian-Chinese frontier was still in dispute in 1966.

Indian leadership changed twice after Nehru's death in May 1964. Lal Bahadur Shastri succeeded as Prime Minister and led India in the new fighting with Pakistan the next year. He met with Ayub Khan of Pakistan at Tashkent, at Soviet invitation in January 1966, to arrange the withdrawal to the cease-fire line. After Shastri then had a fatal heart attack, Nehru's daughter, Mrs. Indira Gandhi, was elected to the leadership of the Congress Party. In her first statement she reaffirmed the basic Indian policies.

The war with Pakistan helped India forget the humiliations of the defeat inflicted by China in 1962. Sentiment against the U.S. for its previous arms aid to Pakistan was not eliminated by America's subsequent arms aid to India. Despite record grain production, food shortages were showing up in 1965–1966 and increases in industrial production were smaller. The population of India was estimated at more than 500 million in 1966 and the great question

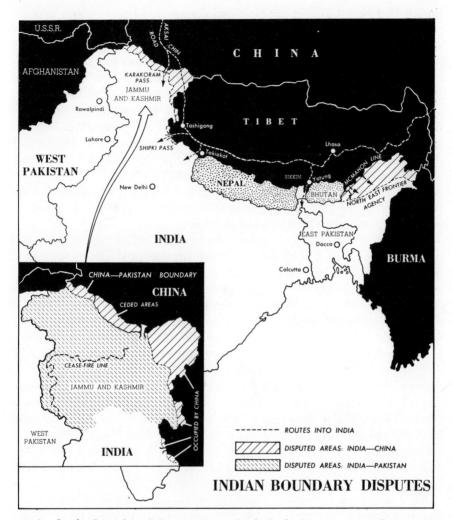

INDIAN BOUNDARY DISPUTES

remained whether this Asian nation, which had chosen a non-Communist road to industrialization, would surmount its problems.

6 Southeast Asia

SOUTHEAST Asia's importance in contemporary international relations begins with the end of the French War in Indo-China in 1954. After 172,000 casualties and a French expenditure of more than $3 billions between 1950 and 1954, the war came to an end with the "Geneva Accords" of July 1954.

The main terms of the Indo-Chinese settlement were: (1) Viet-Nam (the largest of the Indo-Chinese states) was divided into two zones, roughly along the Seventeenth Parallel; (2) Communist forces in the Southern Zone and

French Viet-Nam forces in the Northern Zone would be withdrawn within a period of approximately three hundred days following July 21, 1954; (3) prisoners were to be freed and exchanged by August 20, 1954; and (4) commissions representing both areas of Viet-Nam, and an international body composed of India, Poland, and Canada, would supervise the execution of these provisions; and (5) free elections were to take place in Laos in 1955, and in Viet-Nam proper before July 20, 1956.[7] In theory the elections would unify the country now divided into two pieces by the conference. But how this could come about was left up in the air. Not unnaturally, it did not happen. While Cambodia and Laos were both to be demilitarized, the French were to continue training Laotian troops. SEATO (Australia, France, New Zealand, Pakistan, the Philippines, Thailand, the United Kingdom, and the United States) by protocol agreed to extend military protection against aggression to these Indo-Chinese succession states.

These uneasy arrangements in an area ofttimes called "the rice bowl of Asia," were coming apart by 1961 and were virtually in shreds by the end of 1965. For purposes of clarity, let us look at Laos first.

In April 1961, as the deteriorating situation in Laos brought a flurry of diplomatic conversations and fleet movements, Communist China reaffirmed her determination to enforce her own "Monroe Doctrine" on the approaches to her frontiers. Communist China's foreign minister, Marshal Chen Yi (who had commanded the Chinese Third Army in Korea in 1950), speaking in Indonesia, referred to SEATO's warning it would take "appropriate action" to prevent Laos falling under Communist control. Chen Yi said "that up to now China has not taken part in the Laotian civil war." But if SEATO sent troops "then China will also send troops." Explaining his threat in defensive terms he compared the situation to Korea: "Remember China was compelled to participate in the Korean War only after the U.S. forces went to our border beyond the Yalu River." His solution: let Laos and Asia settle its own problems.

But Laos (even with Asia) could not settle the problem. Three factions vied for power: a rightist and pro-Western group led by Prince Boun Oum; a neutralist group led by Prince Suvanna Phuma; and a Communist group headed by Prince Suvanna Vong (Phuma's half brother). A new 14-nation conference was held at Geneva and the factions, under pressure, agreed to a coalition. In 1962 Pathet Lao (Communist) forces expanded the area under their control and Thailand requested and received a build-up of U.S. and SEATO forces. The Geneva Conference agreed in July that no foreign power would be permitted military bases in Laos. U.S. military personnel began to be withdrawn but North Vietnamese and Chinese forces evidently remained.

---

[7] It will be noted that the prisoner-of-war issue, which had proved so extremely troublesome in Korea by the introduction of the question of leaving prisoners of war who did not wish to return unrepatriated, was avoided by falling back upon the conventional device of returning all prisoners.

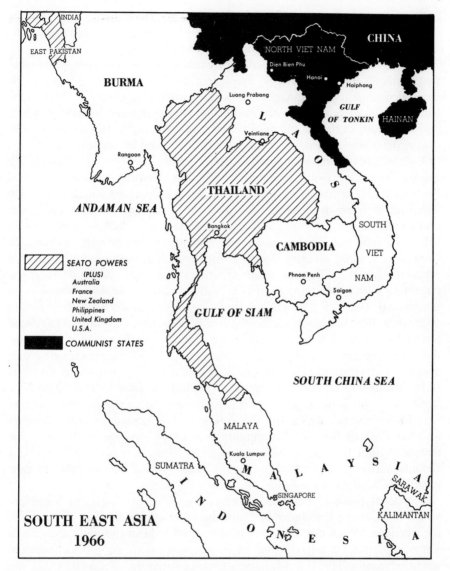

SOUTH EAST ASIA
1966

By 1963 the three different factions were each controlling separate areas of
Laos. By 1964 the cast of main characters had changed somewhat (with Gen.
Phoumi Nosavan leading the right-wing). Pathet Lao forces continued gains
in area at the expense of the others. Both Great Britain and the Soviet Union,
co-chairmen of the Geneva Conference, urged new negotiations. A coup
against Suvanna Phuma by right-wing elements was nullified by foreign pressures. In 1964 U.S. raids began on Pathet Lao positions; Suvanna Phuma continued as premier. Gen. Nosavan tried a coup in 1965 but Phuma survived.
The U.S. now got permission to bomb the Ho Chi Minh trail although the

government was reluctant to have U.S. ground troops come into Laos. Thus it is clear that the real importance of events in Laos, which are described here, was derivative from their connection to events in Viet-Nam.

This was even truer of Cambodia. In Cambodia, the dominant personality was Prince Norodom Sihanouk. Implementing his stand for neutralism, he concluded a treaty of nonagression with Communist China in May 1961. Friction marked relations with South Viet-Nam not only because of Cambodian minorities there (and South Vietnamese minorities in Cambodia) but because of a border dispute. In 1961 South Viet-Nam for its part complained of Cambodia allowing Viet Cong to utilize bases on its territory. (Thailand's similar charges led to the severance of relations.) Similar tensions continued the next year, intensified by the International Court of Justice's order to Thailand to surrender a border temple held since 1954. In 1963 Cambodia broke with South Viet-Nam and renounced U.S. aid. Ambassadors were recalled. In 1964 the Cambodians moved toward still better relations with the Communists while shooting down an American transport which had strayed across the frontier. Sihanouk spoke of "murderous raids" by South Vietnamese forces along the frontier. In May 1965 Cambodia broke relations completely with the U.S. The U.S. at the end of the year declared itself free to resort to military action in Cambodia if it became necessary in the defense of South Viet-Nam. Sihanouk's movement toward the Communist viewpoint did not imply any wish to pass under their control. But the pressure of events and the nature of Cambodia's problems on minority groups and frontiers were driving him off the dead-center of neutralism. In a letter in *The New York Times* on June 4, 1965, he conceded that "after the disappearance of the U.S.A. from our region and the victory of the Communist camp, I myself and the People's Socialist Community that I have created would inevitably disappear from the scene." Sihanouk wanted neutralism because he thought the alternative, if (as seemed to him not unlikely) the U.S. lost the struggle, would be Chinese domination.

The focal point of all these developments was, of course, in Viet-Nam where the Geneva agreement had unrealistically envisaged early all-Vietnamese elections. When elections were held in April 1961 in the south, Ngo Dinh Diem, who had become president by referendum in 1955, was re-elected overwhelmingly. The U.S. Military Assistance Advisory Group (MAAG) was expanded that same year to handle an increase in South Vietnamese armed forces. President Ho Chi Minh of North Viet-Nam was simultaneously trying to keep from taking an extreme position in the Sino-Soviet argument. In 1962 conditions in South Viet-Nam improved and the program of creating rural "strategic hamlets" as a better defense against the Viet Cong seemed to be working. But in 1963 the political situation in the south disintegrated after President Diem moved against the Buddhists. Diem in May accused the Buddhists of being penetrated by Communist and other disaffected elements. After an apparent accommodation, including a reaffirmation of religious freedom by Diem (himself a Catholic) on June 16, new riots took place. The government replied with martial law on August 21 while Buddhist priests continued spectacular protests by burning themselves to death on street corners. Military units now were raiding Buddhist pagodas and arresting monks. A new accord was reached but by this time the South Vietnamese army leaders had decided on a coup. On November 1, Diem and his brother, Ngo Dinh Nhu were overthrown and summarily executed. A military junta took over.

The war against the Viet Cong had been going well while the internal situation had been deteriorating. After the coup the Viet Cong began to gain while the South Vietnamese generals argued over how to run the government. In 1964 South Viet-Nam was governed by four different heads of states and three premiers (one of them twice). Troubles multiplied as group set itself against group. The U.S. began to withdraw some of its personnel but ended the year (after a North Viet-Nam torpedo boat attack in August on U.S. fleet units in the Gulf of Tonkin) by deciding to stick it out. By December, U.S. forces numbered 20,000 (some twenty per cent over 1963). The war continued to go badly despite South Vietnamese forces of 400,000 (compared to 150,000 in 1961). Viet Cong strength was 20,000 to 30,000 regulars, plus 60,000 to 80,000 irregulars. The "strategic hamlet" tactic went sour since the peasants were tiring of leaving their homes permanently, they got no efficient military protection from attack, and South Vietnamese troops often themselves stole peasant goods.

By 1965 some progress toward stability appeared to be occuring in the government. While there were four premiers that year, the fourth was installed by June 19 and represented the new military junta which assumed control that month. And Premier Nguyen Cao Ky (the commander of the air force) was still in office in 1967. In March 1965, 3,500 U.S. Marines were sent to protect the key air base at Da Nang. This was the first obvious departure from the "advisory" role. Air strikes at North Vietnamese targets were ordered at an accelerating rate. Ky began to move against war profiteers and tried to improve relations between the government and the independently-minded tribesmen of the mountains. U.S. troops, which in 1965 reached 185,000 (plus 15,000 South Koreans and 2,000 Australian–New Zealand combat troops), prevented any great gains. Opposed to them were now about 15,000 North Vietnamese regulars (in South Viet-Nam) plus an estimated Viet Cong strength of over 200,000 men. Obviously, the Viet Cong was making a major effort to keep pace with the expansion of the anti-Communist forces.

At SEATO'S tenth ministerial meeting in May 1965 France became only an "observer" while Pakistan, although keeping the status of full member, expressed doubts about the policies which SEATO endorsed. The other six declared that defeat of the Communist forces in South Viet-Nam was "essential . . . to the security . . . of Southeast Asia, and would provide convincing proof that Communist expansion by such tactics will not be permitted." Support for Thailand was affirmed in the light of Chinese Communist Foreign Minister Chen Yi's statement that Thailand was "the next target."

By the spring of 1966 the U.S. forces were slowly but surely gaining the upper hand on the ground in South Viet-Nam, thereby bringing Ho Chi Minh closer to a critical decision: escalate the war with greater numbers of North Vietnamese regulars and increased Chinese aid,[8] or negotiate. If Ho chose escalation he would be heavily dependent on China in particular (although the U.S.S.R., by its own claim, gave Ho $555 million in arms aid in 1965). With relations between China and Russia even worse as the 23rd Communist Party Congress of the Soviet Union began in Moscow, Ho's problem was not easy to resolve.

7 Asian Politics: An Analysis

THE mid-1960's in Asia as in Europe were marked by much greater changes than the 1950's. As the consequences of World War II receded further into the past, re-evaluation of policy was taking place all over, although at different rates. For the first time there were significant signs of some important new departures. Partly these changes were reactions to the continuing Sino-Soviet dispute and the resurgence of national differences among the Western nations. Partly these changes grew out of conditions in Asia itself, as the larger Asian nations reassessed the implications of Chinese policy and the Sino-American confrontation.

The most striking feature of the late 1950's and early 1960's in Asia had been the minor role played by the larger Asian powers (except China) in the most significant great power clashes. Not one of the three larger Asian powers, other than China, contributed forces in a combat role in Korea (although the Asian states of Australia, New Zealand, the Philippines, and Thailand—all American allies—did.) Not one of the three was involved in either of the two phases of the war in Indo-China. Japan, struggling within a reduced territorial area to maintain an adequate economic standard for its hundred million people, and ambivalent about the implication of nuclear weapons, hovered still under the protective umbrella of American power while questioning uneasily her relations (or lack of relations) with an increasingly more powerful China. Indonesia, pushing ahead with a "confrontation" with Malaysia which brought her more than a hundred million people to economic chaos and face to face with 50,000 Commonwealth troops ready to defend Malaysia, was slowly emerging from its reckless course and reflecting upon the larger problems of Asia—especially the implication of an expanding but tin and oil and rubber-poor China. India, so given to moralizing and a neutral position, was finding that power politics was not something invented and pursued only by Western nations, and that defense problems were not resolved for its five hundred million people by resort to moral formulas. Of the three nations, she was the only one who had already found herself in

---

[8] U.S. estimates in July 1966 placed the number of Chinese Communist service troops in North Viet-Nam at 40,000.

armed conflict with China and its over seven hundred seventy-five million people.

In short, these three nations, each distracted by its own peculiar problems, have not yet really played much of the role with which circumstances have ultimately confronted them. With the United States so heavily engaged in Asian affairs the shape of those affairs has been distorted, since in so many Asian eyes the Americans are "neo-colonialists." Concentration on this issue has drawn a veil over the ultimate question of the relation of these three large peripheral nations to China. The very extensiveness of the American commitments in the area, viewed so ambivalently by the Asians, has delayed an Asian appreciation of what to do about China. And yet that is the central question affecting the future of Asia—and the destinies of these larger nations.

So we find the curious circumstances that, as in Korea, the Asian contribution of forces to the fighting on the anti-Communist side in Indo-China, has come exclusively from the "white" Asian nations and the smaller and weaker Asian powers. One can argue that Japan, Indonesia, and India are too weak for any military efforts but the actual fact that weaker Asian nations have fought in Korea and/or Indo-China clearly reveals the speciousness of such a claim. The lack of participation of Japan, Indonesia, and India represented a positive policy decision rather than a course forced upon them in the absence of military power.

It is this very lack of really intimate involvement of these three larger powers in the greater affairs of Asia which makes the U.S. efforts to bring the area into stability ultimately futile if it continues. U.S. power, however great, is only imported power. It can attain decisive results in any given limited time span. But it cannot ultimately prevail without wider Asian support over the long run. SEATO itself, by its own membership list, reveals its lack of important Asian support.

In all of this we have said nothing about the Soviet Union, who must be affected by China's growing power more directly and even more immediately than the three larger Asian nations. Yet her policy, too, will have a great deal to do with the ultimate shape of things to come, for the U.S.S.R. is as much an Asian power as she is European.

The Cold War, the preoccupations of the three large peripheral, fully-Asian nations; the over-simple issue of communism versus anti-communism; and the overly involved and overly-committed role of the United States have combined to obscure the true and central issue. So, too, with the Cold War blocs now more amorphous, with the Sino-Soviet argument revealing multiple paths to communism, with the advent of Chinese nuclear power, the true nature of the central question of China's future is becoming clearer, and the signs are increasing that the larger Asian nations are thinking about it more directly and concretely. Were it not for the over-commitment of the United States, the under-commitment of the rest would be even clearer. To put the point another way, the alternative to greater U.S. involvements is greater

Asian involvements. Since the nations of Asia, precisely because they *are* Asian, must be affected more by what happens there than non-Asian nations, they cannot ultimately choose not to cope with the problem of China unless they are insulated from the problem as a consequence of the great involvement of non-Asian power.

One variable in this equation was the effect of Mao Tse-tung's "great proletarian cultural revolution." Since Mao was attempting to set the clock back, and since his solution to China's internal difficulties was inappropriate, his program will likely suffer ultimate defeat. If in the meantime the struggle seriously disrupted Chinese unity, it might retard the time sequence in which the problem of China continues to unfold. But it could only postpone, not fundamentally change it.

There were signs in the mid-1960's that the problem was becoming better understood in Asia itself—and also in the United States. China, although many of her grievances were "legitimate," cannot be permitted by Asians to run roughshod over their own interests. But the great problem of China's future in Asia, concerning limits which the interests of China's neighbors would place upon Chinese ambitions, was obscured by the sympathies of her neighbors for certain Chinese goals and the natural antipathy for a predominant Western presence in the area. To the extent that the obvious "servitudes" under which China labored (such as her lack of UN membership) disappeared, the new shape of Asian politics could be expected to emerge. As for the West, with all its power, it cannot expect that in a twentieth century in which Asia has become independent, it will really more or less determine the ultimate destinies of an area with almost half the population of the globe.

PART SEVEN

Recapitulation and Reflections

CHAPTER **31**

Prospects and Perspectives

There were two cats from Kilkenny,
Each thought there was one cat too many,
So they fought and they fit,
And they scratched and they bit,
Till, excepting their nails
　And the tips of their tails,
Instead of two cats, there weren't any.

Old Nursery Rhyme

There was once in China a great argument among mathematicians, astronomers, and other wise men. Some clung to the ancient view that the world was flat. Others held that it was spherical, and proceeded to prove their contention. "All our calculations are upon the assumption that the earth is round," they said. "If our predictions as to the movements of certain heavenly bodies prove correct, it follows that our assumption is correct also."

But there were men among them wiser than were mathematicians, who are seldom wise because of their habit of precision, which they apply to precise as well as to imprecise things. These wiser men, therefore, agreed that a formula be devised to satisfy both parties to the dispute, so that neither should lose face, and lest the dispute became too heated, which would ill become wise men. At length it was agreed among them that while the earth had a certain roundness, it was also somewhat flat in parts.

ROBERT STANDISH
Gentlemen of China

WE turn now to our final observations. We shall begin by restating in connected and concise fashion the theoretical concepts undergirding the structural parts of this book, noting the over-all conclusions to which they lead us, particularly in terms of the power problem and the balance of power. Then we shall turn to an over-all summary of the great changes occurring in contemporary international relations. These, too, have for the most part been noted in our pages where it seemed appropriate. It remains to bring these signposts to the future together; for while the way before us must remain obscure, we can discern certain trends that are already in process and which, if continued, will change the world of the next decade from that of the last. Lastly, we shall bring the discussion to a close by con-

sidering a few ideas that are highly important to us as Americans groping for
security in a world whose possibilities for evil and potental for horror are so
grimly apparent.

I *Recapitulation*

THE flesh-and-blood content of international relations is held together by a
skeleton of theoretical concepts that binds the parts in an established relation
to the whole. Theoretical concepts can no more be dismissed in the study of
international relations than the body can function without a backbone. Theory
is basic; should it prove faulty, it will need to be altered—but it can never
be eliminated. To continue our analogy, the skeleton exists—it is only our description of it that may go astray. The problem then is to identify and describe
this skeleton correctly. While the complexity of international relations does
not make this task impossible, it does make it very difficult.

In Chapter 13 we noted how international relations theory evolved through
three schools of thought. The initial emphasis stressed a presumed progress
toward strengthening "world community," especially through further institutionalization of international law and organization. This "idealist" school
emphasized the common interests of states, their common concern with overcoming tensions, their common objective in achieving an enduring peace.
Under the impact of the Nazi era and the world's downhill course toward
World War II, a second school of thought largely replaced it. This "realist"
school emphasized the opposed interests of states, the fragility and tenuous-
ness of the "world community." It pointed to the preoccupation of nations
with the "struggle for power," frequently characterizing power as the goal of
state policy.

Each of these theories pointed out much which was true, because states
have both common and opposed interests, most states do seek peace at any
given time, and each must conduct its relations with others in the full knowledge of the crucial importance of power. It was from the need to evolve a
more flexible theory, combining the insights of both earlier schools, that the
national interest school arose. The most important contribution of the new
school was to create a more operationally valid framework of analysis. It did
not deny either the factors which made states act together in accord or those
which produced opposition and conflict. It stressed that states never have interests completely opposed or completely common with other states, and that
each is subject to re-evaluation and change. It taught that states are always following policies which advance certain of their interests at the expense of certain other (counterbalancing) interests. It argued that the conception of its
interests held by a given state at a given time could be either broad or narrow,
leading to either broad or narrow foreign policies.

In stressing these points national interest theory provided a sounder ground
for generalization. All states were seen as alike in assessing interests, distin-

guishing between what was vital and what was secondary; all states were pictured as confronted with a choice of patterns of power within which they must decide, etc. But the theory allowed the necessary elasticity of analysis since states were not described as choosing identical contents of interests, as agreed upon a uniform definition of what they considered "vital," as choosing identical patterns of power, etc. Distinctions could be drawn between behavior patterns which were virtually uniform from state to state, and behavior which was substantially individual by states.

Equally important as a contribution of national interests theory was the role it ascribed to power. Where the idealists had considered power a necessary means to the end of strengthening "world community" (via, for example, collective security), and where the realists had tended to see in power the goal of state policy, the national interest theorists described the primary effect of the existence of national power in *problem* terms. National interest theory did not deny that power was an important means to foreign policy ends. It did not deny the theoretical possibility that some states at some times might seek power as an actual goal. But it emphasized that in a world of sovereign nation-states, in which each state possessed some power, the concern of each must in the first instance be with the power in the hands of potential enemies. It emphasized that calculations of national power by any one state occurred with reference to the power in the hands of opponents. Power was not seen as a universal currency sought for its own sake, irrespective of the external environment.

Here, again, national interest theory permitted more useful generalizations (as well as more precise distinctions). Since every state always fears some other states' use (or potential use) of power, each state has a power problem. But the identity of the state or states feared will vary, so that the power problem of each state is different. On this basis it becomes possible, as we saw, to erect a theory of alliances (i.e., alliances, if they have a sound basis, acquire that basis from the fact that the allying nations consider their power problems as substantially identical). It also becomes possible to theorize as to how and why alliances come apart. Still other useful theoretical applications have been noted in the course of this book.

Then, too, national interest theory permits a more complex analysis of international relations than "a search for peace" or a "struggle for power," by calling attention to the multiple facets of the problem of security in an insecure world. Disarmament agreements or negotiations rest for success upon the achievement of a condition of equivalent risks. While such agreements are obviously *concerned* with power, and affect peace, they are much more readily analyzed in the complex terms of national interest theory: such agreements are sought because of the common interest of quasi-enemy states in adjusting the effects of their opposed interests.

Finally, national interest theory does not deny but affirms that states, in choosing interests and creating policy from those choices, will do so in a way consistent with their own moral and other views. The individual variation of these views is not neglected; on the contrary, the theory is deliberately flexible enough to note the infinite variation in these internal or national viewpoints, whether it stems from unsystematic and vague sentiments on the one hand, or from highly systematic ideological convictions on the other. It does not deny but affirms that since the fundamental impact of an ideology on foreign policy is to provide a perspective through which developments are viewed, the nature of the ideology will affect the particular way in which national interests are perceived. (We saw this especially in discussing United States, Soviet, and Chinese policy.)

Thus the activities of nation-states in international affairs will be as diverse as the interaction of their moral and/or ideological concepts, their perception of their national interests, and their perception of their individual power problems. Their formulation of their national interests will vary from wise to unwise, from selfish to unselfish, from narrowly conceived to broadly conceived, depending upon the character and experience of the particular people, and the concrete nature of their power problem. All nation-states will decide upon national interests they will seek to maintain or achieve in dealing with others; but the particular formulation of those interests will vary in individual pattern and details from state to state.

The flexibility of the national-interests concept, varying in its conception from state to state and from one age to another, allows us to generalize about the nature of nation-state activities while avoiding the strait jacket of implying a universal desire for peace or power per se as a goal of all states at all times. It provides the necessary theoretical middle ground. We can study (as in Part Three) the political, legal, economic, organizational, and military relations of states as they deal with one another on the basis of their respective formulations of their national interests. We can study (as in Part Four) the attempts of states to resolve their disputes as they arise out of conflicts of interests. We can study (as in Part Five) the efforts of states to solve their power problems through the devices of the five patterns of power that are open to them: unilateralism, balance of power, collective security, world conquest, and world government. We can study (as in Part Six) the detailed conduct of the major powers as they struggle with their problem and attempt to link their aspirations in meaningful fashion to what is feasible in the light of the national interests of other states and of their own power problem.

We come in the end to the realization that world affairs defy simple solutions or permanent solutions. There is no final answer to the vital problem of war in a world of sovereign states, for what states will choose to fight about hinges on their concepts of what their vital interests are. A state whose concept of its vital interests cannot be achieved short of the impairment or destruction of the vital interests of another will, if it persists, cause war. No mechanical or organizational devices can avoid this contingency any more than the most elaborate moral code or system of law endorsement can eliminate sin and crime. While it is true that the cultivation of self-restraint on the part of nation-states, combined with an adroit manipulation of the devices of state relations and the patterns of power, can avoid wars indefinitely, the maniac who runs amok may appear on the international scene tomorrow just as his domestic equivalent may, and probably will, do likewise.

This is not a counsel of despair—it is simply realism (without quotation marks). It is the wisdom that world experience has distilled. Nor is it an advice to eat, drink, and make merry while the Rome which is our contemporary world burns under the mushroom cloud of atomic bombs. The problem of war has no foolproof solution; yet proper diplomacy and an effective response to the power problem of the state through the patterns of power can do much to enhance the security of an individual state. A state can do much to avoid war if it steers carefully between the temptation to make no concessions at all in order to avoid appeasement, and the temptation to sacrifice vital interests in return for promises of future good behavior. And while war itself is an evil, the destruction of national security by foolish, rash, or timid acts—which bring on a war that could have been avoided by firm and moderate but not adamant responses—is an even worse evil. The fact must be faced that nations do fight wars when they feel they must, rather than sacrifice their security. Even in a nuclear world, nations continue to believe that peace, however desirable for its own sake, is not so desirable as even more highly treasured values. Whether or not this should be so, it is. Those who believe that national sovereignty and national interests are obsolete in today's world have the option of attempting to transform that world—but this, too, is no simple problem.

Finally, in surveying our theoretical concepts, let us note the centrality in the power process of the balance of power. Unilateralism as a pure pattern of power (rejecting power commitments to all other states) is in decline. World government remains only a dream over the horizon. World conquest, if it is attempted again, will almost certainly come in the form of an alliance bloc that will pit its strength against the citadels of the opposition. Against such an attempt collective security under the UN would be of little avail.[1] The balance of power, consequently, is the only power pattern that holds out hope of restraining such an aggression or thwarting it if it is nevertheless attempted. Consequently, what nations do with the balance of power in the decades ahead will decide the power future of the world.

2 The Lessons of the Balance of Power

OUR experience with the balance of power in the last centuries indicates that it works best (as in Bismarck's formulation) as a restraint upon the would-be aggressor when that potential aggressor is isolated. Further, the fundamental lesson that we can derive from a study of the quick collapse of the balance

---

[1] This is per se neither an argument against collective security nor against the UN; it is rather a more precise interpretation of their possibilities in terms of the power problem. See Chapters 12 and 21.

of power between World War I and World War II is that it came about
for two reasons. First, the problem presented to the *status quo* powers (Britain
and France) was difficult, because they were confronted with two great powers (Germany and Russia) who were both fundamentally dissatisfied with
the *status quo*. Second, the problem was aggravated by the inability of the
status quo powers to come to real grips with their problem and decide finally
and conclusively, once a decision had to be made, which one of these dissatisfied powers could be rallied as a restraint against the other. The vacillation
of the *status quo* powers was their undoing. In losing Italy to the Axis camp
they strengthened Germany. By attempting to appease Germany at Munich
they lost Russia. Then, when in appearance the West had encouraged Hitler
to march east, they threw a barrier in his path. Britain and France agreed
to protect Poland, while failing to associate Russia with them. Yet it was
beyond their capabilities to do so unless Russia was associated. Alternately,
they failed to induce Germany to cooperate against Russia, or Russia to cooperate against Germany. To fail in both meant world war, since Germany
was determined on war.[2]

Putting these points together, we see that (1) it is most effective in balance-
of-power terms to isolate the potential disturber of the peace, and that (2) it
is least effective if two great powers, each dissatisfied with the *status quo*, succeed in combining against a disorganized *status quo* group.

From an analytical point of view the first of these two balance forms tends
necessarily to be extremely complex in the intricacy of the alignments necessary to frustrate the efforts of the isolated power to gain allies. It is necessarily
highly flexible to accommodate divergent interests. The second form, conversely, tends toward a marked simplicity of alignment structure, because the
dissatisfied powers link up against the *status quo* powers (simple bloc vs. simple bloc). The rigid balance thus produced, like any rigid balance, either is, as
in this case, the prelude to immediate war, or else makes war more likely in
the immediate future.

In the pre-World-War-I balance the evolution of Europe's powers into two
more or less equal and rigidly opposed blocs was delayed by Bismarck's deliberate efforts to link the non-Triple Alliance powers to the Triple Alliance
by Reinsurance Treaties, Mediterranean Pacts, etc. When this complexity became markedly more simple after 1890, the secondary or colonial balance of
power, with its strange combinations of France and Germany against Britain
in Africa, ensured that complexity would remain. Only after the secondary
balance of power had merged with the primary balance (after 1904 and 1907)
did the rigid pattern assert itself. By contrast, in the pre-World-War-II balance, the initial complexity came (unhealthily) from the amorphous nature
of the system rather than from the intricacy of the great-power align-

---

[2] While it might be objected that it could not be known with certainty whether Germany finally would fight, the fact remains that England and France failed to prepare adequately for that worst possibility.

ments. France erected an alliance group by binding the *cordon sanitaire* nations between Germany and Russia to herself, England and Italy were pursuing a unilateralist pattern, and Germany and Russia were still dealing with each other at arm's length. When Italy joined Germany and Britain moved closer to France, and when the weakness implicit in the French alliance system in Eastern Europe began to be apparent, the existing flexibility came to depend on Russia's freedom to join either bloc. Russia's commitment to the Axis produced rigidity. All Europe's great powers were now definitely aligned, and the war began almost at once.

In all these developments between 1870 and 1939 various nations played, at one time or another, the role of balancer or decisive power. Britain, the traditional balancer, played such a role hardly at all. She was not able, by shifting her weight to one camp or the other, to hold the balance between the Triple Alliance and the Dual Alliance before World War I. Nor could Britain balance the alignment of forces between World War I and World War II, for she was ultimately and fundamentally committed to the *status quo* bloc. In 1887 it was Germany who played the role of balancer between Austria-Hungary and Russia, and in 1938 Russia in turn was the decisive power. Thus the balancer or decisive power varies. Consequently, it is extremely important to grasp at any given time who the decisive power is, so that policies may be pursued with wisdom and correct judgments made as to who holds the keys to the balance of power and under what circumstances.

Let us now apply these ideas to the contemporary balance of power.

3   *The Contemporary World*

WITH fickle favor the newspapers sweep from one topic to another, bringing us a kaleidoscope of world events which in the end must leave us dizzy unless we can reduce them to perspective. For the newspaper's daily judgment is not on the lasting importance of what is reported, but on its popular interest for a moment of time. One day it is a new space probe, the next week a new development in Sino-Soviet relations, and then, perhaps, a military coup in Africa. All of these events affect the whole world, but affect it unequally, and the effects may be judged very differently depending upon *how* a people is affected.

The Soviet Union, looking out upon an Africa struggling free from the cocoon of colonial imperialism, sees it as a further proof of Marxist-Leninist "scientific" thought, and a further nail in the coffin of capitalism; the United States sees it as a step in man's slow progress toward self-rule and freedom; the Africans themselves see it in their own and varied frames of reference—and one hesitates to speculate too specifically here. When the French move to withdraw from NATO they do not do so to anger the United States; when the Chinese quarrel with the Soviet Union they do not do so to please the United States.

Without a theory (which this book has sought to provide) these events cannot be graded for importance to the world; and without a specific balance-of-power theory the emotional and transitional effects of these events cannot be distinguished from their political and lasting effects.

The balance of power after World War II was characterized by successive phases, each a subtle transformation from what had gone before. The first phase, coming at the end of hostilities, was dominated by military considerations. With much of the world in ruins and disorder, the military power of the United States and Russia was so superior to the rest as to encourage the view that they could together rule the world. But, as has happened to the victorious great-power coalition after each world war, they were not able to remain together once the object of their *de facto* alliance, the defeat of the Axis powers, had been achieved.

In any event the world quickly began to change. Old centers of power were revived, as in Britain, France, and Germany (although not necessarily to their old levels); new ones were added, as increasingly in India and China. This second phase occurred in part because of the activities (and competition) of the two super powers. But the revival of other powers would have occurred in the nature of things. Each super power now sought to become the anchor post to which the chain links of opposing alliance blocs could be fastened. NATO and the Warsaw Pact came into being. The second phase was highly political although it had its military features. For a whole host of important problems, power as such had little direct relevance. Germany, for example, could not be won or kept on the side of the East or West by bombs or the threat of bombs, for the desire was not to eliminate the Germans in an atomic cloud but to gain them as allies.

Thus the super powers, although still incomparably above all the rest in possession of means of destruction, found that power of limited direct applicability even while the developments just cited encouraged third states on a still quite circumscribed basis to speak and think for themselves.

With the erection of rival blocs completed, the super powers reached out into the greater world outside the confines of the alliances, to gain allegiance and support. Thus began the scramble for allies and influence among the "uncommitted," the third and highly political phase of the balance. Inside the UN each super power made itself as presentable as possible and wooed the rest. The United States, perhaps spurred to even greater efforts because it consistently ran ahead in the search for votes, verged on giving the impression of perennially running for first place in a popularity contest. Inside and outside the UN the two super powers jousted over Nasser's United Arab Republic, over Lumumba's Congo, over Castro's Cuba, over (whose?) Laos. But the primary response in this third area of the world to each super power's challenge of "choose your own way of life, but it must be either our's or their's," was to remain uncommitted to either bloc.

In the meantime important changes were occurring within the primary alliance blocs. Tito's independent course was an early indication of restiveness.

Nuclear power, already also in the hands of Britain, began to be developed by France (and later by Communist China). While the nuclear arsenals outside super power hands were at first unsubstantial, they began to raise serious questions in both blocs. Each super power was no longer in a position to direct what should be done, and have it done. While an atomically armed France might not be able to destroy more than a third or half of Russia before suffering virtual total destruction, what rulers of Russia want to lose a third or half of it in order to destroy all of France? The same principle applied to China. In this sense the non-super powers began to "deserve" more voice in world affairs even as the destructiveness of the weapons encouraged sober rethinking about the alliance bonds to which they were pledged. Each nuclear power had to rethink the question as to the implications of these changes. So began the fourth and present phase, which is political in a highly strategic sense.

It is clear that the balance of power, so long confined within the rigid framework of the Cold War, is now rapidly becoming more complex. The original tidiness of the Cold War concepts, "communists" here, "democrats" there, first disturbed by the emergence of "uncommitted" nations who did not wish to be classified with either "bloc," has become a shambles as France proceeds to withdraw from NATO and the Sino-Soviet cleavage deepens. Complexity reasserts itself. The question is whether we are on the verge of a flexibility of vague and amorphous relations such as encouraged Hitler, or at the beginning of a healthy flexibility utilizing hitherto neglected counterbalancing interests to isolate the greatest potential disturber of the peace. This in turn raises the question of who will be the decisive power, for each power will want to isolate its own "troublemaker."

Both super powers have witnessed these later phases in the contemporary balance with dismay.

But, however it may gall them, it is useful for the super powers to be forced to gain a new modesty in assessing the world—partly for its own sake, partly because it corresponds with operational reality, and partly because an understanding of this point could lead to other policies more broadly conceived. For it is the fact that the frozen positions of the Cold War have diverted significant attention of a positive kind from two of the most important problems of our era: the reconstitution of a united Germany within a more prosperous Europe, and the adjustment to China's dissatisfaction with the present *status quo* in Asia.

The United States and the Soviet Union have both now been forced to reassess their fundamental relationship to each other. The Cuban confrontation of 1962 led to the Test Ban Treaty of 1963. But that treaty's substance was not far-reaching. Its symbolic implications were. With the intensification of the Viet-Nam War, nothing more came of this tentative move. Yet the Soviets cannot help but be disturbed by the independent Chinese course while some Americans, viewing the prospect of a possible confrontation with China, are disposed to regard closer Soviet-American cooperation as desirable.

Some Americans even look forward to the possibility of an alliance with the Soviet Union against Communist China. This possibility is largely unreal under present circumstances for two reasons. One applies equally to both super powers: while China's destructive power is increasing, it is still highly limited; China cannot engage in far-flung war against either the United States or Russia. Second, China's increasing power is not the same threat to both since the United States finds herself so intimately involved in Asia of her own decision while the Soviet Union has no choice. Geographical fact makes China her neighbor. The present Asian situation, in the shadow of the Vietnamese War, tends to confuse appearances with deeper realities. Fundamentally, the United States and the Soviet Union are pursuing goals which are largely incompatible and each continues to possess great destructive power which remains targeted on each other. This appraisal by both super powers continued to be a realistic assessment.

The United States, in reassessing the balance, was at last moving from the fairly rigid ideological position it for so long maintained in that it was discovering the over-simplicity of a world conceptualized as democratic vs. communistic. For a long time we showed what approaches maidenly modesty at the suggestion that we might work a little harder at dismantling the Communist bloc. We tended toward accepting it as given that these states were all irrevocably committed on the opposite side. We shrank from examining whether Communist states too may not have counterbalancing interests which could be exploited. We worked hard to get all those who are non-Communist to sign up with us but left the Communist bloc without any serious threat to its integrity. It is highly ironical that anti-Communist America accepted so easily this most optimistic article of all the Communist faith —that there were no deep frictions among Communist states because the sources of such friction have been liquidated with the demise of the capitalist class. The United States, now that she has grasped the possibility of really exploiting the counterbalancing interests of Soviet bloc nations and no longer confining herself to some limited assistance to Tito and some slight flirtation with Gomulka's Poland, has an opportunity to make significant gains out of the new flexibility of the balance. She could play the role of decisive power. Whether she will is another question.

What must be seen very clearly is that the Soviet Union, although willing to entertain limited notions of *rapprochement* with the United States, is not resigned to ultimate war with Communist China or an ultimate disintegration of the Communist bloc. She had disputed China's choice of tactics toward the non-Communist world, but neither Communist giant has renounced its efforts to take apart the Western coalition. They have not ceased to hope to detach Japan from her link with the United States. They have not ceased to export arms and encourage unrest and revolution in the Middle East and undermine CENTO. They have not ceased to encourage Castro's Cuba as an entering wedge to destroy in the end the Rio Pact. They have not ceased to work on NATO. They both agree on the principle that the "citadel of reactionary capitalism," the United States, must be isolated. In short they have tried to follow the Bismarckian principle of isolating *their* troublemaker through exploiting the counterbalancing interests of America's allies. Despite Sino-Soviet dissensions which are both deep and real, both giant Communist powers continue today (quite realistically) to consider the United States as equally the main power problem of each.

This is the essential meaning of First Secretary Leonid I. Brezhnev's opening address to the Soviet Communist Party's 23rd Congress at the end of March 1966. As to the United States, he said:

As far as the U.S.S.R. is concerned, it is prepared to live at peace with all countries but will not resign itself to imperialist iniquity against other peoples.

More than once we proclaimed our readiness to develop relations with the United States, and stand by this position now. But this requires that the United States discontinue the policy of aggression.

Commenting on relations with Communist China, which "unfortunately remain unsatisfactory," Brezhnev said:

We deeply regret that the differences, which benefit only our common adversaries, have not yet been overcome. We are convinced that in the long run our parties, our peoples will overcome all difficulties . . .

Not naming China, Brezhnev also referred to deviations from Marxism-Leninism which become "particularly dangerous when combined with manifestations of nationalism, great-power chauvinism and hegemony." [3]

The United States, under these circumstances, was confronted with four important alternatives. First, she could seek to contain China *and* the Soviet Union. The disadvantage was that this alternative would serve to minimize the Sino-Soviet split. It tends to drive the Communist powers together again. Second, she could seek to organize a common Soviet-American front against China. The disadvantage was that this alternative rested upon the assumption that the Soviet Union now feared China more than the United States. Third, she could seek to improve relations with China in common opposition to the Soviets. The drawback to this program was that it had no base in the policies or attitudes of either China or the United States and was thus completely unrealistic. Fourth, she could continue to attempt to isolate the Soviet Union from great power allies by taking measures in the Far East which would increase Sino-Soviet friction and tend to make the Sino-Soviet alliance a dead letter. The disadvantage of this alternative was largely that it was complex and uncongenial from an emotional standpoint. For it involved the United States revamping its Asian policies so that the containment of China rested primarily in Asian hands, and it required the conversion of the United States role from a leading to a supporting one. Yet to the extent that China could encounter more purely Asian resistance to expansion (and here

[3] NYT, March 30, 1966.

the sympathies and policy of the Soviet Union—i.e., its counterbalancing interests—are on the Asian, non-Chinese side), the Sino-Soviet friction could be expected to grow.

The intricate questions of the present balance of power turn on how this China issue is handled as over against the withdrawal of France from NATO and Germany's still unfulfilled hopes for reunification. These questions need further discussion within the framework of the question whether their resolution can be combined with the isolation of the Soviet Union from great power allies.

4 *The Present Balance of Power: Europe*

THE "grand design" for such a new balance of power would have to be complex (in the Bismarckian sense), but its nature can be described with reasonable clarity. It is not the nature of the balance which is so complicated; rather the complexity comes (paradoxically) from the contrast to the simplicity of present United States policies.

Let us begin with the primary relationship between the United States and the Soviet Union. With these two great nations confronting one another on many fronts, with each armed and arrayed against the other, it is possible still to find ways of reducing overt tensions but it is not possible to convert the relationship to close friendship. They are each other's main power problem because their power to harm each other is enormous and their interests are substantially opposed. Again, some opposed interests can be eliminated by solutions of problems now outstanding, but the essential relation will not thereby be changed. For example, it is possible to envisage a reduction in the Soviet armed presence in Central and Eastern Europe provided this can be contrived without adding strength to the West. The Soviet Union could accept changes, provided these changes do not alter conditions to their own disadvantage. If the relationship of the Soviets to the West was not residually hostile, the U.S.S.R. would obviously care little whether changes in Europe added to Western strength; but it does care—and for that reason.

The Soviet Union's position in this whole area to the west of its frontiers is weak—not militarily but politically. Her presence is not accepted with any enthusiasm. Partly she is tolerated because she has brute force at her command; partly she is tolerated because no agreement on the future role of Germany in Eastern Europe has yet been reached. Under these circumstances active opposition to her presence is normally muted. The unrest is normally restrained and Polish and Hungarian resistance, as in 1956, is the exception. But the difference in Hungarian as against Polish behavior in 1956 is instructive. It was the smaller of the two who went further, although it had the lesser chance of success. The Poles, by contrast, agreed to limited reforms (the removal of a Red Army Marshal from command of the Polish forces, advance notification of the movement of Soviet forces across Poland, etc.) For Poland, more than Hungary (which is insulated from Germany by Austria and is off to the south of the main east-west military "corridors"), must continue as always before to exist in the shadow of two formidable neighbors, one on either flank. And since she presently has substantial former German territory without having obtained any valid title through German consent, she becomes heavily dependent upon the Soviet Union—until and unless she reaches some arrangement with Germany. (The fact that the "German Democratic Republic" recognizes the transfer of these territories to Poland can give Poland little comfort since the GDR is itself only a puppet Germany propped up in the last analysis by Soviet bayonets.) It is no accident that the Poles have been a great proponent of schemes for disengagement in Europe, for Poland must fear a Germany who at one and the same time has NATO backing and has not made peace with Poland.

The Soviet position in Eastern and Central Europe is politically vulnerable because its *political* base in these states rests much more upon fears of Germany than love of the Soviet Union or commitment to communism. With the Germans (that is, the Federal Republic) until recently dominated by an Adenauer who shelved the problem of German policy in the East until he had built a "position of strength" in the West, the fragility of the political position of the Soviets in Poland and the Balkans has been disguised. For Adenauer refused to deal with any of the states to the east (except Russia itself). He argued that the West would attain an obvious military superiority which would ultimately lead a Soviet Union confronted (he predicted) with internal economic difficulties and the growing power of China in Asia, to agree to German reunification essentially on Western terms. The difficulties Adenauer predicted have come to pass for the Soviet Union, but the West did not achieve overwhelming military superiority. Indeed, de Gaulle's removal of France from NATO command even dismantles part of the "position of strength."

Even if the Adenauer tactics in building strength had succeeded, it always remained highly doubtful that the expected results would have been achieved. A Soviet Union confronted with a potentially hostile China on one flank and a greatly superior NATO strength on the other, would much more likely have taken the risks of a "no retreat" policy than the risks of extorted concessions leading almost inevitably to even more demands and more concessions.[4] For the Soviet Union to have appeased a Germany (backed by NATO) which sought a revision of the *status quo* via an implicit threat of force, would ultimately have involved giving up much of the Soviet gains of World War II.

The Erhard government, before its fall in 1966, had already made significant departures from the earlier policy, especially through the establishment of trade missions with the "satellites." The next step involved the question of diplomatic relations and a reconsideration of the "Hallstein Doctrine" (as we saw in Chapter 26). These patient, careful German initia-

---

[4] In 1939–1941, moved by fear of attack, they thrust their frontier *westward* by incorporating part of Poland, the Baltic States, Bessarabia, etc.

tives are ultimately aimed at the weak Soviet political position in Poland and the Balkans, for all these states and Germany have a common interest which is very powerful: to end the predominent influence (or even in some cases, physical and armed presence) of the Soviet Union within their frontiers or on what can legitimately be considered (in the German case, at least for the GDR area) their own territory. Counterbalancing this common interest for Poland and the Balkans is the fear of Germany. Consequently the political effects of these initiatives will be forthcoming only if they are tied into a settlement of the German question which removes fears of a new German drive for dominance in the East.

In this intricate and involved situation, the Soviet Union's political support from virtually anywhere in Europe west of her own frontiers is tied into the German problem. So long as Western policy was content (as it still is in fundamentals) to advocate what amounted to a simple withdrawal of the Soviet Union from the GDR (as a consequence of the Communists losing the free elections), followed by the adding of the united German state to NATO's strength, the Soviet Union could continue to enjoy official and popular support from the "satellites" and unofficial popular support from many people in the West who feared a resurgent Germany even within NATO. If the West became willing to consider other alternatives, the political pressure on the Soviet Union from its own European "allies" would be substantially increased.

But what of the argument that the Soviet Union "understands" only strength, reacts only to power? Would the Soviet Union be willing to change and retrench its presently overextended position in Europe because of anything short of a confrontation with overwhelming power? The answer is that the Soviets do respond to power. But certainly the West never really meant to induce any Soviet withdrawal through an actual ultimatum. The pressures presumed to operate were in the first instance political pressures backed by sufficient military power to give the political considerations due weight. Adenauer never meant that force would be actually threatened, but only that the Soviets (in conjunction with concern over developments in China) would draw appropriate conclusions from the fact of Western power. So the Soviet decisions, when made, were to reflect calculations of prudence in terms of Soviet security. There are other ways to induce such Soviet calculations. The real questions are what advantages and disadvantages accrue to the Soviets from their present position, what effects would occur for them from the acceptance of the West's present proposals, and what effects would occur from quite different proposals? The answers to these questions will not be identical, although each will represent a calculation of interests, pressures, etc.

The advantages to the Soviets of their prolonged postwar position in Europe include an armed domination of the Western approaches, a ring of nominally "friendly" states along her frontier, a fragmentation of German power, and the existence of other socialist countries. The disadvantages are much less weighty until and unless Germany is no longer content to accept the *status quo*. Of course, there is the "satellite" discontent noted above; but it is a discontent having only limited effects so long and so far as West Germany remains passive. There is also the possibility that East Germany might be torn with new civil revolt as in 1953—with this difference now: that West Germany is rearmed and would be under grave pressure to intervene to stop the slaughter of Germans by Russians. This would be highly serious—if it happened.

The advantages the Soviets have enjoyed outweigh the disadvantages, assuming there is no war. But war is always potential in a situation where very substantial American and Soviet armed forces are deployed in the middle of Germany. And then there is the delicate problem of Berlin which has flared up in two crises so far. If the situation leads to war the disadvantages gain far the greater weight. Of course, it often seems preferable to run risks which have become familiar rather than hazard new ones. Yet the steady growth in strength and efficiency of the West German armed forces, and the recurrent discussion of nuclear armaments for the Germans in one form or another, are powerful inducements to the Soviets to keep an open mind on other possibilities, for each year increases German resentments.

The Western proposals to the Soviet Union in the postwar negotiations on Germany never had much appeal. The Soviets were aware that free elections in the Western sense would mean the end of the GDR, that a free choice of alliances for the reunited Germany would soon see All-Germany in NATO, that the Western formulas meant in practice that the Soviets must relinguish their 17 million Germans to the West and retreat. Only once, fleetingly, in Malenkov's last days in power, did the Soviets evidently seriously consider permitting free elections and only then if Germany would be made neutral, rather than be joined to NATO. The later Western amendments to the West's "Eden Plan," which still envisaged All-Germany joining NATO but (somehow) the West realizing no military advantage from the East German part, always remained rather vague and unconvincing to the Soviets.

So the postwar position of the Soviets was at least not obviously disadvantageous (assuming no war), and the Western proposals were unappealing in that they conferred no benefits on the Soviets at all equal to the losses they would face.

What, if anything, happens now, especially given the failure of the original "position of strength" policy and France's withdrawal from NATO command? It depends especially on how Germany chooses to proceed. We have already said that the political efficacy of German initiatives toward Poland and the Balkans turns on whether these states become satisfied with Germany's devotion to a modest and defined role in European affairs. Without such a conviction they will not be disposed to jump from one frying pan into another. Now we would add that such political pressures, as could be generated from the common interests of the Germans and the "satellite" states in inducing the Soviets to curtail or withdraw their presence, would be really effective only within a set of decisions which assured the Soviets that any changes would not merely replace Soviet influence in the Balkans by German influence. Any German political initiatives in the Polish-Balkan area motivated by *Machtpolitik* considerations would be unsuccessful on two counts: they would lose appeal to the "satellites" and have no appeal to the Soviets.

The withdrawal of France from NATO, de Gaulle's conviction that the line of the Iron Curtain is unreal in more than one sense, actually creates the psychological conditions for a new approach to the problem, for de Gaulle equally believes that the prolonged presence of Russians in Berlin and Central Europe is unnatural. At the same time there is a growing disillusionment in Germany with results of the policy so far followed. Germany entered NATO as a means toward unification (although the opposition argued it would prevent it). If West Germany comes to believe that alliance with the West entails the permanent division of Germany, and she is unwilling to accept that, one of two things will happen: either West Germany will ultimately move to sever the NATO ties and seek to come to terms with Russia, or will eventually seek to use NATO in a more direct way as a lever to pry the Soviet Union out of Germany. In that case the "position of strength" doctrine would undergo a subtle transformation: instead of the Soviets being expected to make concessions because of obviously superior Western strength, she would be expected to make concessions to a fairly equal bloc whose geographical spearhead takes on potentially offensive implications. Germany might herself by then have acquired nuclear weapons; but if not, NATO is well supplied with them.

Either decision on the part of West Germany has serious implications for both East and West. The second path would unite the "satellites" and the Soviet Union but could involve an unlimited war. While such a choice is highly unlikely, the West is wrong to assume that it is unlikely because the West would not be prepared to back Germany in a war. Soviet thinking on this point is more realistic, for the Soviets realize that once a war began, and for whatever reason, the question of who started it would be only of moral or historic interest. For the West would become immediately involved physically by virtue of having armed forces on German soil. Strategic considerations reinforce this conclusion, for Germany's importance to the West does not rest upon the correctness of her behavior. Thus NATO's commitment to Germany, while nominally defensive, is virtually automatic so long as NATO forces are on German soil. The Soviet realization of this point means that they would not be disposed to reject opportunities to change the *status quo* if they could do so without important losses. At present, of course, there are no signs that German policy is turning in such a dangerous direction.

The other alternative of the *quid pro quo* could be consummated either by direct West German–Russian negotiations or by great power conference.

What is possible under these circumstances is a fresh consideration of an alternative German settlement. The basis for an accord would inevitably turn upon Western evacuation of West Germany simultaneously with Soviet evacuation of East Germany. The *quid pro quo* that the Soviets would have to demand as a minimum price for withdrawal eastward would be NATO's withdrawal westward. The East-West agreement in 1955 on Austria's evacuation was based on the exact same principles for essentially the same reasons. Germany would, as part of the arrangement, be reunited through genuinely free elections, permitted arms, but required to remain aloof from alliances.

As with any solution, there are both weaknesses and strengths to such a settlement. Some argue that it is not possible for a great nation such as Germany, living in the heart of Europe, to be neutral. And without question the Germans would remain pro-Western in *sentiment*. The Soviets have few illusions in this regard. But Germany would have to remain neutral if no great power would agree to an alliance with her. It takes two to make an alliance, and all of Germany's possible allies would be parties to a public pledge not to make one. A second argument is that Germany would be exposed to Communist penetration. Internally, of course, she is now. Externally, the whole arrangement would necessarily have to include guarantees by all the powers of the frontiers of the newly reunited Germany. If the Soviets committed aggression it would not be against Germany alone.

But what of the opposite possibilities? An argument against the Soviet Union ever agreeing to a neutral Germany is that the Soviets could not trust Germany to remain peaceful. But a Germany no longer able to commit NATO to war automatically (through their becoming involved in hostilities breaking out on German soil) would presumably be a very prudent Germany. What of the fact that the West cannot allow Germany to be defeated? Could not Germany begin a war, knowing the West could not afford to see the Soviet Union defeat her? But this is a different consideration. Even if the West did intervene on the German side after Germany began a war, the lack of NATO-German joint operational plans and joint training exercises would hamper the Western military operations to a certain degree and any Western forces would have to first be sent into Germany. These considerations would afford the Soviets a certain protection against the effects of a Western contribution to a war. By the same token, however, and more realistically, the West would probably use only the *threat* of such intervention if it became necessary (in view of German setbacks) to prevent all of Germany passing into Soviet hands.

Whether the Germans themselves come to think highly of this *quid pro quo* concept cannot be known. Obviously the exact nature of the frontiers to be agreed is vital to them. But if Germany does not choose some variation of this approach to a settlement, the future in Europe will not be very bright. As to the United States, although we would lose an ally, that ally was sought as a means of restraining possible Soviet expansion. It would be difficult to conclude that the Soviets, if they agreed to these arrangements, would then attempt a further expansion westward into Europe. But if she did try, she would still face German strength—and behind it Western strength. And the initial defense line against such an assault would be much further east.

5 *The Present Balance of Power: Asia*

WE have already discussed elements of the Asian situation at considerable length, as they affect the contemporary balance of power. It remains now to draw these threads together systematically.

There can be no question that Communist China today is an anti-*status quo* power. She fully intends to see certain far-reaching revisions accomplished, particularly alterations in the frontiers imposed on her in the days of her weakness. These disputed frontiers include large areas along the Soviet border. The changes she seeks also involve the thorny question of the future of Mongolia, presently under Soviet influence. Whether China will be content with only partial changes, demand complete satisfaction on all these points, or go on to make even further assaults on the *status quo*, cannot be known. But it is certain that any of these changes inevitably range China in opposition to some of her neighbors, and the more changes China seeks, the more the number of those who will be called upon to resist in their own immediate interests. Finally, if China embarks upon a really ambitious program going beyond frontier rectification, she will threaten other Asian nations who do not share a common frontier with China. To the extent that China seeks to extend her sphere of influence more widely, and even beyond the Asian continent proper, she will encounter resistance from nations such as Japan and Indonesia.

In the efforts to contain China the United States has thus far played the leading role. It can be maintained quite rightly that setting limits to China's revisions of the *status quo* is in the national interests of the United States in principle. But even here, an unqualified endorsement of that principle would lead to the conclusion that the present Sino-Soviet frontier should be maintained intact inasmuch as it exists, a conclusion ultimately implying that the United States must support the Soviets. Here we see an excellent illustration of the importance of choosing principles carefully, for from a balance of power standpoint it would be unfortunate if the United States thus intervened instead of treating the question as one the Soviets themselves must resolve.

The point here is that the United States is not alone in having an interest in containing Chinese expansion, and that some aspects of Chinese attempts to do so might well work out to our best interests, provided no large-scale war results. The point further is that the nations much nearer to Communist China have a more obvious and immediate reason to do the containing. While it might be argued that any changes in the *status quo* which in any way strengthen China are adverse to the ultimate interests of the United States if there is finally a Sino-American armed conflict, the argument overlooks the fact that any such Chinese gains will be inevitably counterbalanced by motivating Asian resistance. Thus China's gains could also be China's losses in another sense. In any event it cannot be true that China can change the *status quo* very drastically in Asia without encountering Asian resistance; and she cannot change it greatly without encountering severe Asian resistance. It is at that point, and in a supporting role, that the United States might find it in her real interests to intervene. But if this argument has validity, it means that it is incorrect for the United States (as she presently does) to herself play the leading role.

To the extent that the United States plays the role of principal container of China, she forces the Chinese to exercise greater caution in their relations with the Soviet Union, thus potentially mitigating the Sino-Soviet dispute. If we attempt to isolate and contain the Soviet Union in Europe and China in Asia, we tend to drive them together exactly as Germany and Russia made common cause in Europe before Hitler and again in 1939. Not only does such an approach induce the Chinese to mute frictions with Russia, but the muting of those frictions removes an important part of the Soviet incentive to be concerned over Chinese territorial revisionism. From a non-Communist point of view it throws away a substantial asset.

If the United States would be content with a less obvious role in Asia, our interests there would be substantially protected, willy-nilly, by the fact that they are the interests of the other powers of Asia, including the Soviet Union. But with the United States cast in the role of a non-Asian power involved in military interventions in Asia, the Soviet Union has no real incentive to do anything but join the Chinese chorus against "neo-imperialism."

These observations must be qualified by the caveats recorded earlier in that it is impossible from the standpoint of United States honor and prestige to simply move overnight to a new position which shucks off commitments in which we are presently heavily involved. The point made above is not a tactical one as to how and when to disengage from our present commitments, but rather a strategic point that it would be wise to begin to alter our role. It is the conception of what is needed which must first be grasped.

Assuming that the United States decided upon this strategy, what tactical changes would be desirable?

First, the major tactical objective of the United States in Viet-Nam should be to disengage (at a suitable opportunity) and negotiate a settlement guaranteed by substantial Asian support. A settlement which might at first glance seem less acceptable (whatever it might be), but which enjoyed substantial Asian backing, would probably prove more lasting than a more favorable-appearing settlement without real Asian support. Over the long run the United States will, in any event, be unable to determine the future of this area unless we are prepared for a series of Vietnamese-style wars. Such wars would not only be costly but they are ultimately (if our analysis has validity) unnecessary—that is, unnecessary for the United States as virtually sole belligerent.

Second, the United States should draw a firm line of non-involvement militarily on the Asian continent, except for Korean-type aggressions if such occur. The general objective here ought to be to stay out of land warfare in Asia. This does not exclude extending arms support to continental nations such as India.

Third, the United States should terminate its opposition to China's presence in the UN and make it publicly clear that the United States is prepared to take up diplomatic relations with China (not as a token of approval but with the objective of carrying on the necessary business of ordinary international affairs). It is in this connection that difficulties will obviously occur over China's claims to Formosa. Communist China has been unwilling to accept the "two-China" solution which some third states have advocated for some years. China has been unwilling to have relations with Britain or France unless each ceased recognizing the Chinese Nationalist regime. The objective of Communist China here is two-fold. She wishes to discourage international recognition of *two* Chinas and she wishes to see Formosa returned to the control of the mainland. A possibility here is to separate the two objectives. If the Nationalist Chinese regime were terminated (at a suitable opportunity such as Chiang's death), a separate "Formosa" government might be created which could be put into UN hands as a form of "trusteeship" for a period pending final resolution of the problem. This would be especially useful if a commission of Asian powers could be chosen as trustees. Ultimately Formosa might (probably would) revert to Communist China. Such a solution would have no insurmountable military disadvantages to the United States since in any war of China against Japan or the Philippines, Chinese mainland bases are in any event still closer than Formosa.

These tactical alterations in present policy would not be undertaken to "appease" Communist China. They would be implemented to do away with important causes of Sino-American friction over issues where many Asian nations consider the United States wrong, and where any advantages the United States derives are in any event counterbalanced by considerable disadvantages. To the extent that the United States as a consequence emphasized that Asia was primarily Asia's affair, to the extent that they retained the United States in an active role in the Pacific but terminated its leading (and sometimes solitary) role in Asia, they would contribute to the strategy already described above.

If this new strategy were followed, it should destroy or neutralize any real meaning resulting from the Sino-Soviet alliance. Seen in conjunction with the European strategy already sketched, it would provide a comprehensive strategy for the isolation of the Soviet Union from great power allies in conjunction with a lessening of the tension which now is the product of the quite direct military confrontation between American power and the power of the two major Communist states. Taken as a whole these proposals constitute a plan which would utilize the national interests of the Soviet Union to bring about a lessened presence in Central Europe and a more active role against China in Asia. They are "Bismarckian" in conception for they reject the simple proposition that direct power vs. direct power, with one "camp" against another, is the only suitable arrangement for a world balance of power. They have the added merit that they would be far less costly to the United States and far more acceptable to many of the other nations of the world.

6 Reflections

ONLY a few things remain to be said; yet these few are perhaps the most important of all, for they are directed specifically to the problems of Americans living in a difficult world. Every nation approaches world affairs, as we have shown, with certain preconceptions and certain expectations. The United States, because its nationalism has been based so importantly upon a heritage of common ideas and ideals, has (not surprisingly) attempted to express these in her international relations as well. Consequently, she has encountered greater difficulties in coping with world affairs than the innate complexities of her foreign-affairs problems would seem to warrant.

We see this approach reflected in the persistent attempt to endow America's every action with the armor of moral rectitude. The United States feels compelled to put "Americanism" into action in world affairs, and to justify what it wants to do as morally good. Since American ideals are assumed to be universally shared by all peoples, or at least by all peoples who are able to express their wishes freely, it is an easy step to the assumption by Americans that what the United States wants, the world wants. American wishes may take on for Americans a presumed universal validity, and this is a very heady wine for any people to drink. As George F. Kennan has expressed it in his most provocative book, *Realities of American Foreign Policy,*

In any case . . . I think . . . international life would be quieter and more comfortable, that there would be less of misunderstanding, and that it would be easier to clear away such conflicts as do arise, if there were less of sentimentality, less eagerness to be morally impressive, a greater willingness to admit that we Americans, like everyone else, are only people, in whose lives the elements of weakness and virtue are too thoroughly and confusingly intermingled to justify us either in any claim to a special moral distinction or in any sense of shame over the fact that we do exist, that we are a great nation, and that as such we occasionally have needs we are obliged to express to other people and to ask them to respect.[5]

This caveat is not an argument (nor is Kennan's) in favor of deviation from cherished American ideals as they influence and shape American national interests; rather it is a needed reminder of the great Christian virtue of humility. We speak here not of a fawning abjectness but of true humility—a lack of self-righteousness. Moral righteousness can so easily become a cloak for something much less respectable, can so easily mask a dogmatic and uncompromising insistence that the world must agree with the United States because she alone is the designated conscience of the world. Such an approach to international relations, while it may speak in the name of "Americanism"

---
[5] P. 50.

and morality, easily degenerates into self-willfulness and immoderation, into a sort of unconscious arrogance. As an illustration, proposals were made in the United States during the Korean War that anti-Russian nationalist risings in Poland and Czechoslovakia should be encouraged in order to relieve Communist pressure on American troops in Korea. D. W. Brogan, an extremely acute British observer, pointed out that such policies, advocated on the grounds that they will "save the lives of American boys," sometimes brashly imply that only the lives of American boys really count. While saving American lives is a legitimate concern of the United States, Brogan remarks that such proposals give the impression that

. . . as an American friend of mine put it in some unpublished verses:

> Clean-limbed American boys are not like any others.
> Only clean-limbed American boys have mothers.

Their lives are of special importance to Americans, but not to the people of other lands. And there would be widespread resentment over the thoughtless implication that it is the first duty of Poles or Czechs to save American lives. These are hard sayings and they are negative sayings. But they may not be useless all the same.[6]

However painful such criticisms may be to Americans, it is much better to become aware of them. These almost ingrained attitudes are difficult to eliminate. Yet as D. W. Brogan would be happy to admit, the American tradition, while certainly filled with its share of bombast, also contains an emphasis upon its corrective. As we so often sing Katharine Lee Bates' lines:

> America! America! God mend thine ev'ry flaw:
> Confirm thy soul in self-control,
> Thy liberty in law.

These are the words of a people to whom humility is also real.

We must, finally, reflect upon the reverse side of this lack of humility, as it expresses itself in fear. We must reflect upon the ease with which self-proclaimed patriots in a distorted version of "Americanism" have in recent memory in America injured and cheapened some of the truly great values upon which this nation was built, and from which it receives its innate spiritual strength. In the struggle against communism (by definition a moral evil) many other evils were committed, in a fear-inflamed atmosphere, on the simple notion that whatever purports to fight evil is of necessity good. The problem of communism cannot be handled on this basis with success—either internally or externally. Indeed, to the extent that such fears incline us to stifle discussion and dissension, we subvert our own institutions.

As Will Herberg has said, "the upsurge of democracy, like the upsurge of nationalism, is not a simple, unmitigated good, but rather an historical development of dubious character, presenting two faces, looking in very different

---

[6] D. W. Brogan, "The Illusion of American Omnipotence," *Harper's*, Vol, 205 (December 1952), pp. 21–28.

directions." [7] The advent of mass rule, in the United States or elsewhere, carries with it an equal potential for nihilism and disaster, as well as for great advances and success. No magic endows the people with discretion and responsibility simply because they are many; rather they must develop it and cherish it against the ill winds of bigotry and ignorance and fear. A fearful people is itself an evil omen, and the practical path out of fear is not so much the elimination of the source of insecurity—for in life this is often impossible —but a recognition of reality and a sober and thoughtful assessment of the alternatives. This battle the American people have fought throughout the ages. It is the glory of their tradition that they have again and again surmounted fear with hope, and danger with courage. To make the light of reason in America shine forth ever brighter, to preserve and restore the vigorous discussion of alternatives, to confirm liberty in law even where free discussion runs athwart popular passions and prejudices, to exercise self-control even amidst the encircling dangers—this is a noble task and one to which we must rededicate ourselves as befits a free people.

---

[7] In a rebuttal to an article by Arnold Toynbee in *The Intercollegian*, February 1955, p. 10.

Bibliography

CHAPTER 1

General Introductory Readings

ARON, RAYMOND, *The Century of Total War.* New York: Doubleday, 1954.

BEARD, CHARLES A., *The Idea of National Interest.* New York: Macmillan, 1934.

BULL, HEDLEY, "International Theory: The Case for the Classical Approach," *World Politics,* Volume 18 (1966).

CARR, E. H., *The Twenty Years' Crisis, 1919–1939.* London, 1946.

HARTMANN, FREDERICK H., ed., *World in Crisis—Readings in International Relations,* Third edition. New York: Macmillan, 1967.

HERZ, JOHN, *Political Realism and Political Idealism: A Study in Theories and Realities.* Chicago: University of Chicago Press, 1951.

HOFFMANN, STANLEY, *Contemporary Theory in International Relations.* Englewood Cliffs, N.J.: Prentice-Hall, 1960.

KENNAN, GEORGE F., *American Diplomacy, 1900–1950.* Chicago: University of Chicago Press, 1951.

———, *Realities of American Foreign Policy.* Princeton: Princeton University Press, 1954.

KIRK, GRAYSON, *The Study of International Relations.* New York: Council on Foreign Relations, 1947.

MADARIAGA, SALVADOR DE, *Theory and Practice in International Relations.* Philadelphia: University of Pennsylvania Press, 1937.

MOON, PARKER T., *Syllabus on International Relations.* New York: Macmillan, 1925.

MORGENTHAU, HANS J., *In Defense of the National Interest.* New York: Knopf, 1951.

———, *Scientific Man vs. Power Politics.* Chicago: University of Chicago Press, 1946.

SPYKMAN, NICHOLAS J., *America's Strategy in World Politics.* New York: Harcourt, Brace, 1942.

WIGHT, MARTIN, *Power Politics.* New York and London: Royal Institute of International Affairs, 1949.

WOLFERS, ARNOLD, *Discord and Collaboration.* Baltimore: Johns Hopkins University Press, 1962.

CHAPTER 2

Sovereignty

DICKINSON, E. D., *The Equality of States in International Law.* Cambridge: Harvard University Press, 1920.

HAAS, ERNST B., *Beyond the Nation-State, Functionalism and International Organ-
    ization.* Stanford: Stanford University Press, 1964.
KELSEN, HANS, *General Theory of Law and State.* Cambridge: Harvard University
    Press, 1945.
————, *Das Problem der Souveränität und die Theorie des Völkerrechts.* Tü-
    bingen, 1920.
LASKI, HAROLD, *Studies in the Problem of Sovereignty.* New Haven: Yale Univer-
    sity Press, 1917.
MERRIAM, CHARLES E., *History of the Theory of Sovereignty Since Rousseau.* New
    York: Columbia University Press, 1928.

Nationalism

BARKER, ERNEST, *Christianity and Nationality.* London, 1927.
CARR, E. H., *Nationalism and After.* New York: Macmillan, 1945.
COBBAN, ALFRED, *National Self-Determination,* Revised edition. Chicago: Univer-
    sity of Chicago Press, 1948.
DEUTSCH, K. W., *Nationalism and Social Communication.* Cambridge: Massachu-
    setts Institute of Technology Press; and New York: Wiley, 1953.
FRIEDMANN, W., *The Crisis of the National State.* London, 1943.
GOOCH, GEORGE P., *Nationalism.* New York: Harcourt, Brace, 1920.
HAYES, C. J. H., *Essays on Nationalism.* New York: Macmillan, 1926.
————, *The Historical Evolution of Modern Nationalism.* New York: Macmillan,
    1948.
HERTZ, FREDERICK, *Nationality in History and Politics.* New York: Oxford, 1944.
JANOWSKY, O. I., *Nationalities and National Minorities.* New York: Macmillan,
    1945.
KOHN, HANS, *The Idea of Nationalism.* New York: Macmillan, 1944.
LASKI, HAROLD, *Nationalism and the Future of Civilization.* London, 1932.
ROYAL INSTITUTE OF INTERNATIONAL AFFAIRS, *Nationalism.* New York: Oxford,
    1946.

CHAPTER 3

Elements of National Power

BARKER, ERNEST, *National Character and the Factors of Its Formation.* London,
    1927.
BROGAN, D. W., *The American Character.* New York: Knopf, 1944.
————, *The English People.* New York: Knopf, 1943.
CORWIN, EDWARD S., *The President: Office and Powers, 1787–1948,* Third edition.
    New York: New York University Press, 1948.
————, *Total War and the Constitution.* New York: Knopf, 1947.
EMENY, BROOKS, *The Strategy of Raw Materials.* New York: Macmillan, 1934.
FAIRGRIEVE, JAMES, *Geography and World Power,* Eighth edition. London, 1941.
FIFIELD, R. H., and PEARCY, G. E., *Geopolitics in Principle and Practice.* Boston:
    Ginn, 1944.
FREEDMAN, RONALD, ed., *Population: The Vital Revolution.* Garden City, N.Y.:
    Doubleday Anchor, 1964.
GYORGY, ANDREW, *Geopolitics.* Berkeley: University of California Press, 1944.

MACKINDER, SIR HALFORD J., *Democratic Ideals and Reality*. New York: Holt, 1942.

MADARIAGA, SALVADOR DE, *Englishmen, Frenchmen, Spaniards*, Fourth edition. London, 1937.

MARKHAM, S. F., *Climate and the Energy of Nations*. London, 1944.

ORGANSKI, KATHERINE, and ORGANSKI, A. F. K., *Population and World Power*. New York: Knopf, 1961.

RATZEL, FRIEDRICH, *Politische Geographie*, Second edition. Munich, 1903.

SPYKMAN, NICHOLAS J., *The Geography of the Peace*. New York: Harcourt, Brace, 1944.

STALEY, EUGENE, *Raw Materials in Peace and War*. New York: Council on Foreign Relations, 1937.

STRAUSZ-HUPÉ, ROBERT, *Geopolitics*. New York: Putnam, 1942.

THOMPSON, WARREN S., and LEWIS, DAVID T., *Population Problems*. Fifth edition. New York: McGraw-Hill, 1965.

WEIGERT, HANS W., *Generals and Geographers*. New York: Oxford, 1942.

WHITTLESEY, DERWENT, *The Earth and the State: A Study of Political Geography*. New York: Holt, 1944.

CHAPTER 4

Foreign Policy

ALMOND, GABRIEL A., *The American People and Foreign Policy*. New York: Harcourt, Brace, 1950.

CHURCHILL, WINSTON S., *The Second World War: The Gathering Storm*. Boston: Houghton, Mifflin, 1948.

COHEN, BERNARD C., *The Political Process and Foreign Policy*. Princeton: Princeton University Press, 1957.

COOKE, ALISTAIR, *A Generation on Trial*. New York: Knopf, 1950.

HALLE, LOUIS J., *Civilization and Foreign Policy*. New York: Harper, 1952.

KENNAN, GEORGE F., *American Diplomacy, 1900–1950*. Chicago: University of Chicago Press, 1951.

LIPPMANN, WALTER, *Public Opinion*. New York: Harcourt, Brace, 1922.

LONDON, KURT, *How Foreign Policy Is Made*. New York: Van Nostrand, 1949.

MARSHALL, CHARLES B., *The Limits of Foreign Policy*. New York: Holt, 1954.

ROSENAU, JAMES N., ed., *International Politics and Foreign Policy*. New York: Free Press of Glencoe, 1961.

(SEE ALSO the listings under Chapters 22–30.)

CHAPTER 5

Diplomacy

BENDINER, R., *The Riddle of the State Department*. New York: Rinehart, 1942.

BYRNES, JAMES F., *Speaking Frankly*. New York: Harper, 1947.

CALLIÈRES, F. DE, *On the Manner of Negotiating with Princes*. Boston: Houghton, Mifflin, 1919.

CAMBON, JULES, *Le Diplomate*. Paris, 1926.

CRAIG, G. A., and GILBERT, FELIX, *The Diplomats, 1919–1939*. Princeton: Princeton University Press, 1953.

DENNETT, RAYMOND, and JOHNSON, J. E., eds., *Negotiating with the Russians*. Boston: World Peace Foundation, 1951.

FOSTER, JOHN W., *The Practice of Diplomacy*. Boston: Houghton, Mifflin, 1906.

GREY OF FALLODON, VISCOUNT, *Twenty-Five Years, 1892–1916*, Two volumes. New York: Stokes, 1925.

HANKEY, SIR MAURICE, *Diplomacy by Conference*. New York: Putnam, 1946.

HEATLEY, D. P., *Diplomacy and the Study of International Relations*. Oxford, 1919.

HENDRICK, BURTON J., *The Life and Letters of Walter Hines Page*, Three volumes. Garden City, N.Y.: Doubleday, Page, 1922–1926.

HILL, D. A., *A History of Diplomacy in the International Development of Europe*, Three volumes. New York: Longmans, Green, 1924.

JUSSERAND, J. A., *The School for Ambassadors and Other Essays*. New York: Putnam, 1925.

KERTESZ, STEPHEN D., and FITZSIMMONS, M. A., eds., *Diplomacy in a Changing World*. Notre Dame: University of Notre Dame Press, 1959.

MORLEY, VISCOUNT JOHN, *On Compromise*. London, 1923.

NICOLSON, SIR HAROLD, *The Congress of Vienna: A Study in Allied Unity, 1812–1822*. New York: Harcourt, Brace, 1946.

———, *The Evolution of Diplomatic Method*. New York: Macmillan, 1955.

PEARSON, LESTER B., *Diplomacy in the Nuclear Age*. Cambridge: Harvard University Press, 1959.

PETRIE, SIR CHARLES, *Diplomatic History, 1713–1933*. London, 1948.

POTEMKIN, VLADIMIR, *Histoire de la diplomatie*, Three volumes. Paris, 1946–1947.

REINSCH, PAUL S., *Secret Diplomacy*. New York: Harcourt, Brace, 1922.

SATOW, SIR ERNEST, *A Guide to Diplomatic Practice*, Second edition, Two volumes. London, 1922.

THAYER, CHARLES W., *Diplomat*. New York: Harper, 1959.

THOMPSON, J. W., and PADOVER, S. K., *Secret Diplomacy: A Record of Espionage and Double Dealing, 1500–1815*. London, 1937.

VANSITTART, LORD, "The Decline of Diplomacy," *Foreign Affairs*, Vol. 28, No. 2 (January 1950).

CHAPTER 6

International Law

BRIERLY, J. L., *The Law of Nations*, Sixth edition. Oxford, 1963.

———, *The Outlook for International Law*. Oxford, 1944.

BRIGGS, HERBERT W., *The Law of Nations: Cases, Documents, and Notes*, Second edition. New York: Appleton-Century-Crofts, 1952.

FENWICK, C. G., *International Law*, Third edition. New York: Appleton-Century-Crofts, 1948.

FRIEDMANN, WOLFGANG, *The Changing Structure of International Law*. New York: Columbia University Press, 1964.

GILMORE, GRANT, "The International Court of Justice," *Yale Law Journal*, Vol. 55, No. 5 (August 1946).

HUBER, MAX, *Die soziologischen Grundlagen des Völkerrechts*. Berlin, 1928.

HYDE, CHARLES C., *International Law Chiefly as Interpreted and Applied by the United States*, Second revised edition, Three volumes. Boston: Little, Brown, 1945.

KAPLAN, MORTON A., and KATZENBACH, NICHOLAS DE B., *The Political Foundations of International Law*. New York: John Wiley, 1961.

KEETON, G. W., and SCHWARZENBERGER, G., *Making International Law Work*, Second edition. London, 1946.

KELSEN, HANS, *Principles of International Law*. New York: Rinehart, 1952.

KULSKI, W. W., "The Soviet Interpretation of International Law," *American Journal of International Law*, Vol. 49 (October 1955).

LAUTERPACHT, SIR HERSH, *The Development of International Law by the International Court*, Revised edition. New York: Praeger, 1958.

LISSITZYN, O. J., *The International Court of Justice*. New York: Carnegie Endowment, 1951.

MOORE, J. B., *International Law and Some Current Illusions*. New York: Macmillan, 1924.

NUSSBAUM, ARTHUR, *A Concise History of the Law of Nations*, Revised edition. New York: Macmillan, 1954.

SCHWARZENBERGER, G., *A Manual of International Law*. London, 1947.

SVARLIEN, OSCAR, *An Introduction to the Law of Nations*. New York: McGraw-Hill, 1955.

CHAPTER 7

International Economics

BENOIT, EMILE, *Europe at Sixes and Sevens*. New York: Columbia University Press, 1961.

DIEBOLD, WILLIAM, JR., *The Schuman Plan*. New York: Praeger, 1959.

EINZIG, PAUL, *World Finance, 1914–1935*. New York: Macmillan, 1935.

GOORMAGHTIGH, JOHN, "European Coal and Steel Community," *International Conciliation*, May 1955.

HEILPERIN, M. A., *The Trade of Nations*. New York: Knopf, 1947.

HAAS, ERNEST B., *The Uniting of Europe*. Stanford: Stanford University Press, 1958.

KITZINGER, M. W., *The Politics and Economics of European Integration*, Second edition. New York: Praeger, 1964.

LISTER, LOUIS, *Europe's Coal and Steel Community*. New York: Twentieth Century Fund, 1960.

METZGER, STANLEY D., *Trade Agreements and the Kennedy Round*. Fairfax, Va.: Coiner Publications, 1964.

PENTONY, DEVERE E., *The Underdeveloped Lands: A Dilemma of the International Economy*. San Francisco: H. Chandler, 1960.

ROBBINS, LIONEL, *The Economic Causes of War*. London, 1939.

ROSTOW, W. W., *The Stages of Economic Growth*. New York: Cambridge University Press, 1960.

SCHUMPETER, J. A., *Capitalism, Socialism and Democracy*, Third edition. New York: Harper, 1950.

TRIFFIN, R. F., *Gold and the Dollar Crisis*. New Haven: Yale University Press, 1960.

The United States Balance of Payments Problem, Department of State Publication 3695, Commercial Policy Series 123 (December 1949).

VINER, JACOB, *International Economics*. Glencoe: Free Press, 1951.

Imperialism

BUKHARIN, NIKOLAI I., *Imperialism and World Economy*. New York: International Publishers, 1929.

CLARK, GROVER, *The Balance Sheet of Imperialism*. New York: Columbia University Press, 1936.

FERRY, JULES, *Le Tonkin et la Mère-Patrie*. Paris, 1890.

GROSS, LEO, *Pazifismus und Imperialismus*. Leipzig, 1931.

HOBSON, JOHN A., *Imperialism*. London, 1938.

KOEBNER, RICHARD, and SCHMIDT, H. D., *Imperialism: The Story and Significance of a Political Word, 1840–1960*. Cambridge, 1964.

LENIN, V. I., *Imperialism: The Highest Stage of Capitalism*. New York: International Publishers, 1939.

MOON, PARKER T., *Imperialism and World Politics*. New York: Macmillan, 1926.

NEARING, SCOTT, *The Tragedy of Empire*. New York: Island Press, 1945.

WINSLOW, E. M., *The Pattern of Imperialism*. New York: Columbia University Press, 1948.

WRIGHT, QUINCY, *Mandates Under the League of Nations*. Chicago: University of Chicago Press, 1930.

CHAPTER 8

War, Military Affairs

BALDWIN, HANSON W., *The Great Arms Race*. New York: Praeger, 1958.

BEARD, CHARLES A., *The Devil Theory of War*. New York: Vanguard, 1936.

BRODIE, BERNARD, "Military Demonstration and Disclosure of New Weapons," *World Politics*, Vol. 5, No. 3 (April 1953).

———, *Strategy in the Missile Age*. Princeton: Princeton University Press, 1959.

CLAUSEWITZ, KARL VON, *Principles of War*. London, 1942.

EARLE, EDWARD M., ed., *Makers of Modern Strategy*. Princeton: Princeton University Press, 1943.

GARTHOFF, RAYMOND L., *The Soviet Image of Future War*. Washington: Public Affairs Press, 1959.

HITCH, CHARLES J., and McKEAN, ROLAND N., *The Economics of Defense in the Nuclear Age*. Cambridge: Harvard University Press, 1960.

HOFFMANN, STANLEY, *The State of War: Essays in the Theory and Practice of International Politics*. New York: Praeger, 1965.

KAHN, HERMAN, *On Thermonuclear War*. Princeton: Princeton University Press, 1960.

KAUFMANN, WILLIAM W., *The McNamara Strategy*. New York: Harper and Row, 1964.

KISSINGER, HENRY A., *Nuclear Weapons and Foreign Policy*. New York: Harper, 1957.

————, ed., *Problems of National Strategy*. New York: Praeger, 1965.

LENIN, V. I., *Imperialism: The Highest Stage of Capitalism*. New York: International Publishers, 1939.

MAHAN, ALFRED T., *The Influence of Sea Power upon History, 1660–1783*. Boston: Little, Brown, 1941.

MARDER, A. J., *The Anatomy of British Sea Power*. New York: Knopf, 1940.

MILLIS, WALTER, *Arms and Men*. New York: Putnam, 1956.

OMAN, SIR CHARLES, *A History of the Art of War in the Sixteenth Century*. New York: Dutton, 1937.

OSGOOD, ROBERT E., *Limited War*. Chicago: University of Chicago Press, 1957.

RANSOM, HARRY H., *Central Intelligence and National Security*. Cambridge: Harvard University Press, 1958.

SCHELLING, THOMAS C., *The Strategy of Conflict*. Cambridge: Harvard University Press, 1960.

SAUNDERS, M. G., *The Soviet Navy*. New York: Praeger, 1958.

VAGTS, ALFRED, *A History of Militarism*. New York: Norton, 1937.

WRIGHT, QUINCY, *A Study of War*, Two volumes. Chicago: University of Chicago Press, 1942.

CHAPTERS 9, 10

International Organization

BALL, M. M., "Bloc Voting in the General Assembly," *International Organization*, Vol. 5, No. 1 (February 1951).

BURTON, M. E., *The Assembly of the League of Nations*. Chicago: University of Chicago Press, 1941.

CHASE, EUGENE, *The United Nations in Action*. New York: McGraw-Hill, 1950.

CLAUDE, INIS L., JR., *Swords into Plowshares*, Third edition. New York: Random House, 1964.

DAVIS, H. E., ed., *Pioneers in World Order*. New York: Columbia University Press, 1944.

DELL, ROBERT, *The Geneva Racket, 1920–1939*. London, 1941.

DUNN, FREDERICK S., *Practice and Procedure of International Conferences*. Baltimore: Johns Hopkins, 1929.

FINER, H., *The United Nations Economic and Social Council*. Boston: World Peace Foundation, 1946.

FLEMING, D. F., *The United States and the League of Nations*. New York: Putnam, 1932.

————, *The United States and World Organization*. New York: Columbia University Press, 1938.

GOODRICH, L. M., and HAMBRO, E., *Charter of the United Nations: Commentary and Documents*, Second edition. Boston: World Peace Foundation, 1949.

GOODSPEED, STEPHEN S., *The Nature and Function of International Organization*. New York: Oxford University Press, 1959.

HAAS, ERNST B., *Beyond the Nation-State, Functionalism and International Organization*. Stanford: Stanford University Press, 1964.

HAVILAND, HENRY F., *The Political Role of the General Assembly*. New York: Carnegie Endowment for International Peace, 1951.

HUDSON, M. O., *The Permanent Court of International Justice, 1920–1942*. New York: Macmillan, 1943.

LAWSON, RUTH C., ed., *International Regional Organizations*. New York: Praeger, 1962.

LEVI, WERNER, *Fundamentals of World Organization*. Minneapolis: University of Minnesota Press, 1950.

LIE, TRYGVE, *et al.*, *Peace on Earth*. New York: Hermitage Press, 1949.

McMURRY, R. E., and DE MUNA, L., *Cultural Approach: Another Way in International Relations*. Chapel Hill: University of North Carolina Press, 1947.

MILLER, DAVID H., *The Geneva Protocol*. New York: Macmillan, 1925.

MORLEY, FELIX, *The Society of Nations*. Washington: Brookings, 1932.

NICHOLAS, HERBERT G., *The United Nations as a Political Institution*, Second edition. New York: Oxford University Press, 1963.

PADELFORD, NORMAN J., and GOODRICH, LELAND M., eds., "The United Nations: Accomplishments and Prospects," *International Organization*, Vol. 19, No. 3 (Summer 1965).

PEASLEE, AMOS, ed., *International Governmental Organizations*, Two volumes. The Hague, 1956.

RAPPARD, WILLIAM E., *The Quest for Peace*. Cambridge: Harvard University Press, 1940.

RICHES, CROMWELL, *Majority Rule in International Organizations*. Baltimore: Johns Hopkins, 1940.

——, *The Unanimity Rule and the League of Nations*. Baltimore: Johns Hopkins, 1933.

Royal Institute of International Affairs, *International Sanctions*. London, 1938.

STOESSINGER, JOHN, *The United Nations and the Superpowers*. New York: Random House, 1965.

United Nations, *Repertory of Practice of United Nations Organs*. New York: United Nations, 1955–.

VAN WAGENEN, RICHARD W., *Research in the International Organization Field: Some Notes on a Possible Focus*. Princeton: Center for Research on World Political Institutions, 1952.

WALTERS, F. P., *A History of the League of Nations*, Two volumes. New York: Oxford, 1952.

ZIMMERN, SIR ALFRED, *The League of Nations and the Rule of Law, 1918–1935*. London, 1936.

CHAPTERS 11, 12

Conflict Resolution, the Settlement of Disputes

BORCHARD, E. M., *Distinction between Legal and Political Questions*. Washington: Government Printing Office, 1924.

CARLSTON, K. S., *The Process of International Arbitration*. New York: Columbia University Press, 1946.

DUNN, FREDERICK S., *Peaceful Change*. New York: Council on Foreign Relations, 1937.

GOODRICH, L. M., and SIMONS, A. P., *The United Nations and the Maintenance of International Peace and Security*. Washington: Brookings, 1955.

LISSITZYN, OLIVER, "The International Court of Justice: Its Role in the Maintenance of International Peace and Security," *United Nations Studies*, No. 6. New York: Carnegie Endowment, 1951.

MANNING, C. A., ed., *Peaceful Change: An International Problem*. New York: Macmillan, 1937.

PARODI, ALEXANDRE, "Pacific Settlement of Disputes," *International Conciliation*, No. 445 (November 1948).

RALSTON, J. H., *International Arbitration from Athens to Locarno*. Stanford: Stanford University Press, 1929.

SHOTWELL, J. T., and SALVIN, M., *Lessons on Security and Disarmament*. New York: King's Crown, 1949.

SMITH, S. R., *The Manchurian Crisis, 1931–1932: A Tragedy in International Relations*. New York: Columbia University Press, 1948.

TOD, MARCUS, *International Arbitration Amongst the Greeks*. New York: Oxford, 1913.

(SEE ALSO the listings under Chapters 5, 6, 9, 10.)

CHAPTERS 13, 14

Problems of Power, Security, Arms Control, and Disarmament

BLACKETT, P. M. S., *Studies of War*. New York: Hill and Wang, 1962.

BRODIE, BERNARD, ed., *The Absolute Weapon: Atomic Power and World Order*. New York: Harcourt, Brace, 1946.

BUELL, RAYMOND L., *The Washington Conference*. New York: Appleton, 1922.

CARR, E. H., *The Twenty Years' Crisis, 1919–1939*. London, 1946.

CLAUDE, INIS L., *Power and International Relations*. New York: Random House, 1962.

JESSUP, PHILIP C., *International Security*. New York: Council on Foreign Relations, 1935.

LASSWELL, HAROLD D., *World Politics and Personal Insecurity*. New York: Whittelsey, 1935.

MADARIAGA, SALVADOR DE, *Disarmament*. New York: Coward-McCann, 1929.

MERRIAM, CHARLES E., *Political Power: Its Composition and Incidence*. New York: Whittlesey, 1934.

MORGENTHAU, HANS J., *In Defense of the National Interest*. New York: Knopf, 1951.

———, *Scientific Man vs. Power Politics*. Chicago: University of Chicago Press, 1946.

NIEBUHR, REINHOLD, *Christianity and Power Politics*. New York: Scribner, 1940.

REVES, EMERY, "Why Waste Time Discussing Disarmament," *Look*, March 28, 1961.

RUSSELL, BERTRAND, *Power*. New York: Norton, 1938.

SCHELLING, THOMAS C., and HALPERN, MORTON H., *Strategy and Arms Control*. New York: Twentieth Century Fund, 1961.

SINGER, J. DAVID, *Deterrence, Arms Control, and Disarmament*. Columbus: Ohio State University Press, 1962.

SPANIER, JOHN W., and NOGEE, JOSEPH L., *The Politics of Disarmament*. New York: Praeger, 1962.

TATE, MERZE, *The Disarmament Illusion*. New York: Macmillan, 1942.

———, *The United States and Armaments*. Cambridge: Harvard University Press, 1948.

THOMPSON, KENNETH W., *Political Realism and the Crisis of World Politics*. Princeton: Princeton University Press, 1960.

WHEELER-BENNETT, JOHN, *The Pipe-Dream of Peace: The Story of the Collapse of Disarmament*. New York: Morrow, 1935.

WOODWARD, E. L., *Some Political Consequences of the Atomic Bomb*. New York: Oxford, 1946.

(SEE ALSO Department of State and United Nations document listings on disarmament, especially the Acheson-Lilienthal Report [Department of State Publication 2498, 1946], and the Atomic Energy Commission's first report to the Security Council.)

CHAPTER 15

The Patterns of Power, Unilateralism, and One World

BORGESE, G. A., *Common Cause*. New York: Duell, Sloan, Pearce, 1943.

BRINTON, C. C., *The Anatomy of Revolution*. New York: Norton, 1938.

———, *From Many One: The Process of Political Integration; the Problem of World Government*. Cambridge: Harvard University Press, 1948.

BROGAN, D. W., "The Illusion of American Omnipotence," *Harper's*, Vol. 205, No. 1231 (December 1952).

CARLETON, WILLIAM G., "What Our World Federalists Neglect," *Antioch Review*, Vol. VIII, No. 1 (Spring 1948).

CLARK, GRENVILLE, and SOHN, LOUIS B., *World Peace Through World Law*, Second edition, revised. Cambridge: Harvard University Press, 1960.

DEUTSCH, KARL W., *Political Community at the International Level*. Garden City, N.Y.: Doubleday, 1954.

GRAEBNER, NORMAN A., *The New Isolationism*. New York: Ronald Press, 1956.

HARTMANN, FREDERICK H., "Away With Unilateralism!" *Antioch Review*, Vol. 11, No. 1 (Spring 1951).

HAAS, ERNST B., "International Integration: The European and the Universal Process," *International Organization*, Volume 15 (1961).

HEMLEBEN, S. J., *Plans for World Peace through Six Centuries*. Chicago: University of Chicago Press, 1943.

HEROLD, J. CHRISTOPHER, *The Swiss Without Halos*. New York: Columbia University Press, 1948.

DE HUSZAR, GEORGE B., ed., *Persistent International Issues*. New York and London: Harper, 1947.

HUXLEY, JULIAN, *UNESCO*. Washington: Public Affairs Press, 1947.

LIPPMANN, WALTER, *Isolation and Alliances*. Boston: Atlantic–Little, Brown, 1952.

MANGONE, G. J., *The Idea and Practice of World Government*. New York: Columbia University Press, 1951.

MEYER, CORD, *Peace or Anarchy*. Boston: Little, Brown, 1947.

NIEBUHR, REINHOLD, "The Illusion of World Government," *Foreign Affairs*, Vol. 27, No. 3 (April 1949).

REVES, EMERY, *The Anatomy of Peace*. New York: Harper, 1946.

SCHUMAN, F. L., *The Commonwealth of Man: An Inquiry into Power Politics and World Government*. New York: Knopf, 1952.

STREIT, C., *Union Now*. New York: Harper, 1949.

WRIGHT, QUINCY, ed., *The World Community*. Chicago: University of Chicago Press, 1948.

CHAPTERS 16–19

The Balance of Power

BUCHAN, ALASTAIR, *NATO in the 1960's*, Revised edition. New York: Praeger, 1963.

CARLETON, WILLIAM G., "Ideology or Balance of Power?" *Yale Review*, Vol. 36, No. 4 (Summer 1947).

CHURCHILL, WINSTON S., *The Second World War: The Gathering Storm*. Boston: Houghton, Mifflin, 1948.

CLAUDE, INIS L., *Power and International Relations*. New York: Random House, 1962.

DONNADIEU, L., *Essai sur la théorie de l'équilibre*. Paris, 1900.

DUPUIS, C., *Le Principe d'équilibre et le Concert European*. Paris, 1909.

GRANT, A. J., and TEMPERLEY, H., *Europe in the Nineteenth and Twentieth Centuries, 1789–1939*. London, 1940.

GULICK, E. V., *The Balance of Power*. Philadelphia: Pacifist Research Bureau, 1943.

HAAS, E. B., "The Balance of Power: Prescription, Concept, or Propaganda," *World Politics*, Vol. 5, No. 4 (July 1953).

HOIJER, O., *La Théorie de l'équilibre*. Paris, 1917.

HUME, DAVID, "Of the Balance of Power," *Essays Moral and Political*, Third edition. London, 1748.

KAEBER, E., *Die Idee des europäischen Gleichgewichts in der publizistischen Literatur vom 16. bis zur Mitte des 18. Jahrhunderts*. Berlin, 1907.

KAPLAN, MORTON A., "Balance of Power, Bipolarity, and Other Models of International Systems," *American Political Science Review*, Volume 51 (1957).

LANGER, WILLIAM L., *The Diplomacy of Imperialism, 1890–1902*, Two volumes. New York: Knopf, 1935.

————, *European Alliances and Alignments, 1871–1890*. New York: Knopf, 1931.

LISKA, GEORGE, *Nations in Alliance*. Baltimore: Johns Hopkins Press, 1962.

OSGOOD, ROBERT E., *NATO, the Entangling Alliance*. Chicago: University of Chicago Press, 1962.

ROSECRANCE, RICHARD N., *Action and Reaction in World Politics*. Boston: Little, Brown, 1963.

SCHMITT, B. E., *Triple Alliance and Triple Entente*. New York: Holt, 1934.

SPYKMAN, N. J., *America's Strategy in World Politics*. New York: Harcourt, Brace, 1942.

TAYLOR, A. J. P., *The Struggle for Mastery in Europe, 1848–1918*. Oxford, 1954.

TEMPERLEY, HAROLD, *The Foreign Policy of Canning, 1822–1827*. London, 1925.

WEBSTER, C. K., *The Foreign Policy of Castlereagh, 1812–1815*. London, 1931.

WINDELBAND, W., *Die auswärtige Politik der Grossmächte in der Neuzeit, 1494–1919*. Stuttgart, 1925.

WOLFERS, ARNOLD, *Britain and France Between Two Wars*. New York: Harcourt, Brace, 1940.

CHAPTERS 20, 21

Collective Security

BERGER, CARL, *The Korea Knot*. Philadelphia: University of Pennsylvania Press, 1957.

BORCHARD, EDWIN, "The Impracticality of 'Enforcing' Peace," *Yale Law Journal*, Vol. 55, No. 5 (August 1946).

BUEHRIG, E. H., "The United States, the United Nations, and Bi-Polar Politics," *International Organization*, Vol. 4, No. 4 (November 1950).

GOODRICH, LELAND M., "Korea: Collective Measures Against Aggression," *International Conciliation*, No. 494 (October 1953).

HARTMANN, FREDERICK H., "The Issues in Korea," *Yale Review*, Vol. 42, No. 1 (Autumn 1952).

HULA, ERICH, "Four Years of the United Nations," *Social Research*, Vol. 16, No. 4 (December 1949).

MARTIN, A., *Collective Security: A Progress Report*. Paris, 1952.

MITRANY, DAVID, *The Problem of International Sanctions*. New York: Oxford, 1925.

SPANIER, JOHN W., *The Truman-MacArthur Controversy and the Korean War*. Cambridge: Harvard University Press, 1959.

STROMBERG, RONALD N., "The Idea of Collective Security," *Journal of the History of Ideas*, Vol. 17, No. 2 (April 1956).

WILD, PAYSON S., *Sanctions and Treaty Enforcement*. Cambridge: Harvard University Press, 1934.

WOLFERS, ARNOLD, "Collective Security and the War in Korea," *Yale Review*, Vol. 43, No. 4 (Summer 1954).

(SEE ALSO the listings for Chapters 9–12.)

CHAPTERS 22, 23

United States Foreign Policy

ALMOND, G. A., *The American People and Foreign Policy*. New York: Harcourt, Brace, 1950.

BEARD, CHARLES A., *American Foreign Policy in the Making, 1932–1940*. New Haven: Yale University Press, 1946.

————, and MARY, *The Rise of American Civilization*, Two volumes. New York: Macmillan, 1927.

CARLETON, WILLIAM G., *The Revolution in American Foreign Policy: Its Global Range*. New York: Random House, 1963.

CHEEVER, D. S., and HAVILAND, H. F., JR., *American Foreign Policy and the Separation of Powers*. Cambridge: Harvard University Press, 1952.

DAHL, R. A., *Congress and Foreign Policy*. New York: Harcourt, Brace, 1950.

DULLES, JOHN F., *War or Peace*. New York: Macmillan, 1950.

GRAEBNER, NORMAN A., *The New Isolationism*. New York: Ronald, 1956.

HARTMANNN, FREDERICK H., "Away With Unilateralism!" *Antioch Review*, Vol. 11, No. 1 (Spring 1951).

KENNAN, GEORGE F., *American Diplomacy, 1900–1950*. Chicago: University of Chicago Press, 1951.

———, *Realities of American Foreign Policy*. Princeton: Princeton University Press, 1954.

KENT, SHERMAN, *Strategic Intelligence for American Foreign Policy*. Princeton: Princeton University Press, 1949.

LANGER, W. L., and GLEASON, S. E., *The Challenge to Isolation, 1937–1940*. New York: Harper, 1952.

LEFEVER, ERNEST W., *Ethics and United States Foreign Policy*. New York: Meridian, 1957.

LIPPMANN, WALTER, *The Cold War*. New York: Harper, 1947.

———, *Isolation and Alliances*. Boston: Little, Brown, 1952.

LISKA, GEORGE, *The New Statescraft*. Chicago: University of Chicago Press, 1960.

McCAMY, JAMES L., *The Administration of American Foreign Affairs*. New York: Knopf, 1950.

MORGENTHAU, HANS J., *In Defense of the National Interest*. New York: Knopf, 1951.

NIEBUHR, REINHOLD, *The Irony of American History*. New York: Scribner, 1952.

OSGOOD, ROBERT E., *Ideals and Self-Interest in America's Foreign Relations*. Chicago: University of Chicago Press, 1953.

SPANIER, JOHN W., *American Foreign Policy Since World War II*, Second Rev. ed. New York: Praeger, 1965.

STIMSON, HENRY L., and BUNDY, McGEORGE, *On Active Service in Peace and War*. New York: Harper, 1948.

STUART, GRAHAM, *American Diplomatic and Consular Practice*, Second edition. New York: Appleton-Century-Crofts, 1952.

TANNENBAUM, FRANK, *The American Tradition in Foreign Policy*. Norman: University of Oklahoma Press, 1955.

TRUMAN, HARRY S., *Memoirs*, Two volumes. New York: Doubleday, 1955–1956.

CHAPTERS 24, 25

Soviet Russsian Foreign Policy

BAIN, LESLIE B., *The Reluctant Satellites*. New York: Macmillan, 1960.

BELOFF, MAX, *The Foreign Policy of Soviet Russia, 1929–1941*, Two volumes. New York: Oxford, 1947.

BROZ, JOSIP (TITO), "Tito Speaks," *Life*, May 12, 1952.

BRZEZINSKI, ZBIGNIEW K., *Ideology and Power in Soviet Politics*. New York: Praeger, 1962.

CARR, E. H., *German-Soviet Relations Between the Two World Wars, 1919–1939*. Baltimore: John Hopkins, 1951.

———, *The Soviet Impact on the Western World*. New York: Macmillan, 1946.

CRANKSHAW, EDWARD, *The New Cold War: Moscow versus Peking.* Baltimore: Penguin Books, 1963.

CRESSEY, G. H., *The Basis of Soviet Strength.* New York: McGraw-Hill, 1945.

DALLIN, DAVID, *The Real Soviet Russia,* Revised edition. New Haven: Yale University Press, 1947.

DEGRAS, J., *Soviet Documents on Foreign Policy.* Vol. I., 1917–1924. Vol II, 1925–1932. Vol. III, 1933–1941. New York: Oxford, 1951—.

DENNETT, RAYMOND, and JOHNSON, JOSEPH E., eds., *Negotiating with the Russians.* Boston: World Peace Foundation, 1951.

DEUTSCHER, ISAAC, *Russia—What Next?* New York: Oxford, 1953.

———, *Stalin, a Political Biography.* New York: Oxford, 1949.

FAINSOD, MERLE, *How Russia is Ruled,* Revised edition. Cambridge: Harvard University Press, 1964.

FISCHER, LOUIS, *The Soviets in World Affairs,* Two volumes. New York: Cape and Smith, 1930.

HISTORICUS, "Stalin on Revolution," *Foreign Affairs,* Vol. 27, No. 2 (January 1949).

History of the Communist Party of the Soviet Union (Bolsheviks). New York: International Publishers, 1939.

KENNAN, GEORGE F., *Russia and the West Under Lenin and Stalin.* Boston: Little, Brown, 1961.

KHRUSHCHEV, NIKITA S., *For Victory in Peaceful Competition with Capitalism.* New York: Dutton, 1960.

LENCZOWSKI, GEORGE, *Russia and the West in Iran, 1918–1948.* Ithaca: Cornell University Press, 1949.

MACKINTOSH, JOHN M., *Strategy and Tactics of Soviet Foreign Policy.* New York: Oxford University Press, 1963.

MOSELY, PHILIP E., *The Kremlin and World Politics.* New York: Vintage Books, 1960.

PENKOVSKY, OLEG, (Frank Gibney, ed.), *The Penkovsky Papers.* Garden City: Doubleday, 1965.

POPE, ARTHUR U., *Maxim Litvinoff.* New York: Fischer, 1943.

POWERS, FRANCIS G., *Trial of the U-2.* Chicago: World Publishers, 1960.

RESHETAR, JOHN S., JR., *Problems of Analyzing and Predicting Soviet Behavior.* New York: Doubleday, 1955.

RUBINSTEIN, ALVIN Z., *The Foreign Policy of the Soviet Union.* New York: Random House, 1960.

SCHAPIRO, LEONARD, *The Communist Party of the Soviet Union.* New York: Random House, 1959.

SETON-WATSON, HUGH, *From Lenin to Malenkov.* New York: Praeger, 1953.

SHULMAN, MARSHALL D., *Stalin's Foreign Policy Reappraised.* Cambridge: Harvard University Press, 1963.

SMITH, GEN. WALTER B., *My Three Years in Moscow.* Philadelphia: Lippincott, 1950.

TOWSTER, JULIAN, *Political Power in the U.S.S.R., 1917–1947.* New York: Oxford, 1948.

VERNADSKY, GEORGE, *History of Russia.* New Haven: Yale University Press, 1951.

VYSHINSKY, ANDREI Y., *The Law of the Soviet State.* New York: Macmillan, 1948.

Chapter 26

German Foreign Policy

Adenauer, Konrad, "Germany and Europe," *Foreign Affairs*, Vol. 31, No. 3 (April 1953).

Bölling, Klaus, *Republic in Suspense*. New York: Praeger, 1964.

Bullock, Alan L. C., *Hitler: A Study in Tyranny*. New York: Harper, 1952.

Butz, O., *Germany: Dilemma for American Foreign Policy*. New York: Doubleday, 1954.

Carr, E. H., *German-Soviet Relations Between the Two World Wars, 1919–1939*. Baltimore: Johns Hopkins, 1951.

Clay, Gen. Lucius D., *Decision in Germany*. New York: Doubleday, 1950.

Dulles, A. W., *Germany's Underground*. New York: Macmillan, 1947.

Ebenstein, William, *The German Record*. New York: Farrar, Rinehart, 1945.

Feld, Werner, *Reunification and West German–Soviet Relations*. The Hague: Nijoff, 1963.

Flenley, Ralph, *Modern German History*. New York: Dutton, 1953.

Freund, Gerald, *Germany Between Two Worlds*. New York: Harcourt, Brace, 1961.

Goerlitz, Walter, *History of the German General Staff, 1657–1945*. New York: Praeger, 1953.

Hartmann, Frederick H., "Settlement for Germany," *Yale Review*, Vol. 39, No. 2 (Winter 1950).

———, *Germany Between East and West: The Reunification Problem*. Englewood Cliffs, N.J.: Prentice-Hall, 1965.

Hiscocks, Richard, *Democracy in Western Germany*. New York: Oxford University Press, 1957.

Hitler, Adolf, *Mein Kampf*. New York: Reynal, Hitchcock, 1939.

Horne, Alistair, *Return to Power: A Report on the New Germany*. New York: Praeger, 1956.

Pinson, Koppel S., *Modern Germany*. New York: Macmillan, 1954.

Pollock, J. K., and Thomas, H., *Germany in Power and Eclipse*. New York: Van Nostrand, 1952.

Rauschning, Hermann, *The Revolution of Nihilism*. New York: Longmans, 1939.

Rees, Goronwy, "Talking with Germans: The Common View," *The Listener*, October 14, October 21, October 28, November 4, 1954.

Schmidt, Paul, *Statist auf diplomatischer Bühne, 1923–45*. Bonn, 1953.

Schuman, F. L., *The Nazi Dictatorship*. New York: Knopf, 1936.

Shirer, William L., *The Rise and Fall of the Third Reich*. New York: Simon and Schuster, 1960.

Snell, John L., *Dilemma Over Germany*. New Orleans: Hauser Press, 1959.

Trevor-Roper, H. R., *The Last Days of Hitler*. New York: Macmillan, 1947.

Warburg, James P., *Germany: Key to Peace*. Cambridge: Harvard University Press, 1953.

Wheeler, Bennett, J. W., *Wooden Titan*. New York: Morrow, 1936.

Chapter 27

British Foreign Policy

Bevan, Aneurin, *In Place of Fear*. New York: Simon and Schuster, 1952.
Brinton, C. C., *The United States and Britain*, Revised edition. Cambridge: Harvard University Press, 1948.
Chamberlain, Neville, *In Search of Peace*. New York: Putnam, 1939.
Churchill, Winston S., *The Second World War*, Six volumes. Boston: Houghton, Mifflin, 1948——
Crowe, Sir Eyre, "Memorandum," *British Documents on the Origins of the War*, Vol. 3, edited by Gooch and Temperley. London: 1928, pp. 397–417.
Eden, Sir Anthony, *Full Circle*. Boston: Houghton, Mifflin, 1960.
Foot, M. R. D., *British Foreign Policy Since 1898*. London, 1956.
Grey of Fallodon, Viscount, *Twenty-Five Years, 1892–1916*, Two volumes. New York: Stokes, 1925.
Halifax, Lord, *Speeches on Foreign Policy, 1934–1939*. New York: Oxford, 1940.
Henderson, Sir Nevile, *Failure of a Mission*. New York: Putnam, 1940.
McKittrick, T. E. M., *Conditions of British Foreign Policy*. London, 1951.
Mowat, Charles L., *Britain Between the Wars, 1918–1940*. Chicago: University of Chicago Press, 1955.
Rayner, Robert M., and Airey, W. T. G., *Britain and World Affairs, 1783–1946*, Second edition. London, 1948.
Seton-Watson, Robert W., *Britain in Europe, 1789–1914*. New York: Macmillan, 1937.
Sprout, Harold and Margaret, "Command of the Atlantic Ocean," *Encyclopaedia Britannica*, 1943 ed. Reprinted in their *Foundations of National Power*, Second edition. New York: Van Nostrand, 1951, pp. 482–485.
——, *Toward a New Order of Sea Power*. Princeton: Princeton University Press, 1940.
Ward, A. W., and Gooch, G. P., *Cambridge History of British Foreign Policy*, Three volumes. New York: Macmillan, 1922–1923.
Woodhouse, C. M., *British Foreign Policy Since the Second World War*. New York: Praeger, 1962.

French Foreign Policy

Brogan, D. W., *France Under the Republic*. New York: Harper, 1940.
De Gaulle, Charles, *La France n'a pas perdu la guerre*. New York: Les Editions Didier, 1944.
Furniss, Edgar S., *France, Troubled Ally*. New York: Harper, 1960.
Hammer, Ellen, *The Struggle for Indochina*. Stanford: Stanford University Press, 1954.
Kissinger, Henry A., *The Troubled Partnership*. New York: McGraw-Hill, 1965.
Luethy, Herbert, *France Against Herself*. New York: Praeger, 1955.
Osgood, Robert E., *NATO, the Entangling Alliance*. Chicago: University of Chicago Press, 1962.
Pickles, Dorothy, *The Fifth French Republic*. New York: Praeger, 1960.
Thomson, David, *Democracy in France*, Third edition. New York: Oxford, 1958.

WILCOX, FRANCIS O., and HAVILAND, H. FIELD, JR., eds., *The Atlantic Community*. New York: Praeger, 1963.

WOLFERS, ARNOLD, *Britain and France Between Two Wars*. New York: Harcourt, Brace, 1940.

CHAPTER 28

ALMOND, GABRIEL A., and COLEMAN, JAMES S., eds., *The Politics of the Developing Areas*. Princeton: Princeton University Press, 1960.

MARTIN, LAURENCE W., ed., *Neutralism and Nonalignment*. New York: Praeger, 1962.

WARD, BARBARA, *The Rich Nations and the Poor Nations*. New York: Norton, 1962.

Africa

BARTLETT, VERNON, *Struggle for Africa*. London, 1953.

CERAM, C. W., *Gods, Graves, and Scholars*. London, 1952.

DIA, MAMADOU, *The African Nations and World Solidarity*. New York: Praeger, 1961.

DEUTSCH, KARL, and FOLTZ, WILLIAM J., eds., *Nation-Building*. New York: Atherton Press, 1963.

GOLDSCHMIDT, WALTER, ed., *The United States and Africa*. New York: Praeger, 1964.

HAILEY, LORD, *An African Survey*, Second edition. London, 1945.

LEGUM, COLIN, *South Africa: Crisis for the West*. New York: Praeger, 1964.

McKAY, VERNON, *Africa in World Politics*. New York: Harper, 1963.

MARQUARD, LEO, *The Peoples and Politics of South Africa*. London, 1952.

NKRUMAH, KWAME, *Africa Must Unite*. New York: Praeger, 1963.

PADELFORD, NORMAN J., and EMERSON, RUPERT, eds., *Africa and World Order*. New York: Praeger, 1963.

PLOMER, WILLIAM, *Cecil Rhodes*. New York: Appleton, 1933.

RITNER, PETER, *The Death of Africa*. New York: Macmillan, 1960.

WALLERSTEIN, IMMANUEL, *Africa: The Politics of Independence*. New York: Vintage Books, 1961.

The Middle East

ANTONIUS, GEORGE, *The Arab Awakening*. New York: Putnam, 1946.

BERGER, MORROE, *The Arab World Today*. Garden City, N.Y.: Doubleday Anchor, 1964.

COOKE, H. V., *Challenge and Response in the Middle East*. New York: Harper, 1952.

DOUGLAS, WILLIAM O., *Strange Lands and Friendly People*. New York: Harper, 1951.

EARLE, E. M., *Turkey, The Great Powers and the Bagdad Railway*. New York: Macmillan, 1923.

LENCZOWSKI, GEORGE, *The Middle East in World Affairs*, Second edition. Ithaca: Cornell University Press, 1956.

SPEISER, E. A., *The United States and the Near East*, Revised edition. Cambridge: Harvard University Press, 1950.

WINT, GUY, and CALVOCORESSI, PETER, *Middle East Crisis*. Harmondsworth, Middlesex: Penguin, 1957.

Latin America

ADAMS, RICHARD N., *et al.*, *Social Change in Latin America Today*. New York: Harper, 1960.

ALEXANDER, ROBERT J., *Today's Latin America*. New York: Doubleday, 1962.

BERLE, ADOLPH A., *Latin America—Diplomacy and Reality*. New York: Harper and Row, 1962.

DREIER, JOHN C., *The Organization of American States and the Hemisphere Crisis*. New York: Harper and Row, 1962.

GORDON, LINCOLN, *A New Deal for Latin America, The Alliance for Progress*. Cambridge: Harvard University Press, 1963.

HARING, CLARENCE, *South America Looks at the United States*. New York: Macmillan, 1928.

MECHAM, J. LLOYD, *The United States and Inter-American Security, 1889–1960*. Austin: University of Texas Press, 1961.

PERKINS, DEXTER, *A History of the Monroe Doctrine*. Boston: Little, Brown, 1963.

———, *The United States and Latin America*. Baton Rouge: Louisiana State University Press, 1961.

QUINTANILLA, LUIS, *Pan Americanism and Democracy*. Boston: Boston University Press, 1952.

SCHMITT, KARL M., and BURKS, DAVID D., *Evolution or Chaos; Dynamics of Latin American Government and Politics*. New York: Praeger, 1963.

STUART, G. H., *Latin America and the United States*, Third edition. New York: Appleton-Century-Crofts, 1943.

TANNENBAUM, FRANK, *Ten Keys to Latin America*. New York: Knopf, 1963.

WOOD, BRYCE, *The Making of the Good Neighbor Policy*. New York: Columbia University Press, 1961.

CHAPTERS 29, 30

The Asian Powers

ASHIDA, H., and SONE, EKI, *Japan's Foreign Policy*. Tokyo, 1958.

BALL, W. M., *Nationalism and Communism in East Asia*. Melbourne, 1952.

BARNETT, A. DOAK, *Communist China and Asia*. New York: Vintage, 1961.

BENEDICT, RUTH, *The Chrysanthemum and the Sword*. Boston: Houghton, Mifflin, 1946.

BRANDT, C., SCHWARTZ, B. I., and FAIRBANK, J. K., *A Documentary History of Chinese Communism*. Cambridge: Harvard University Press, 1952.

BROWN, W. N., *The United States and India and Pakistan*. Cambridge: Harvard University Press, 1953.

BUSS, CLAUDE A., *The Far East*. New York: Macmillan, 1955.

BYAS, HUGH, *Government by Assassination*. New York: Knopf, 1942.

CHAKRAVARTI, P. C., *India's China Policy*. Bloomington: Indiana University Press, 1962.

Chinese Ministry of Information, *The Collected Wartime Messages of Generalissimo Chiang Kai-shek*. New York: John Day, 1946.

CHENG, CHU-YUAN, *Communist China's Economy, 1949–1962*. South Orange, N.J.: Seaton Hall University Press, 1963.

ELEGANT, ROBERT S., *The Centre of the World: Communism and the Mind of China*. London, 1963.

FAIRBANK, JOHN K., *The United States and China*, Second edition. Cambridge: Harvard University Press, 1958.

FEIS, HERBERT, *The Road to Pearl Harbor*. Princeton: Princeton University Press, 1950.

FITZGERALD, C. P., *Revolution in China*. New York: Praeger, 1952.

GREW, JOSEPH C., *Ten Years in Japan*. New York: Simon and Schuster, 1944.

GUPTA, KARUNAKAR, *Indian Foreign Policy*. Calcutta, 1956.

KARUNAHARAN, K. P., *India in World Affairs*. New York: Institute of Pacific Relations, 1953.

KAWAI, KAZUO, *Japan's American Interlude*. Chicago: University of Chicago Press, 1960.

KHAN, L. A., *Pakistan, the Heart of Asia*. Cambridge: Harvard University Press, 1950.

LATOURETTE, K. S., *The American Record in the Far East, 1945–1951*. New York: Macmillan, 1952.

LATTIMORE, OWEN, *Inner Asian Frontiers of China*. New York: American Geographical Society of New York, 1940.

LEVI, WERNER, *Free India in Asia*. Minneapolis: University of Minnesota Press, 1952.

——, *Modern China's Foreign Policy*. Minneapolis: University of Minnesota Press, 1953.

LINEBARGER, P. M. A., *The China of Chiang Kai-shek*. Boston: World Peace Foundation, 1941.

MARUYAMA, MASAO, *Thought and Behavior in Modern Japanese Politics*. London, 1963.

McCUNE, G. M., and GREY, A. L., JR., *Korea Today*. Cambridge: Harvard University Press, 1950.

MENDEL, DOUGLAS H., *The Japanese People and Foreign Policy*. Berkeley: University of California Press, 1961.

NEHRU, JAWAHARLAL, *Independence and After: A Collection of Speeches, 1946–1949*. New York: John Day, 1950.

OLSON, LAWRENCE, *Dimensions of Japan*. New York: American Universities Field Staff, 1963.

PANIKKAR, K. M., *Common Sense About India*. New York: Macmillan, 1960.

PATTERSON, GEORGE N., *Peking versus Delhi*. New York: Praeger, 1963.

REISCHAUER, E. O., *The United States and Japan*, Second edition. Cambridge: Harvard University Press, 1959.

SCALAPINO, ROBERT A., "The Foreign Policy of the Peoples Republic of China," in Black, J. E., and Thompson, K. W., eds., *Foreign Policies in a World of Change*. New York: Harper and Row, 1963.

VINACKE, H. M., *The United States and the Far East, 1945–1951*. Stanford: Stanford University Press, 1952.

CHAPTER 31

Prospects and Perspectives

ACHESON, DEAN, *Power and Diplomacy*. Cambridge: Harvard University Press, 1958.

BROGAN, D. W., "The Illusion of American Omnipotence," *Harper's*, Vol. 205, No. 1231 (December 1952).

BRZEZINSKI, ZBIGNIEW K., *The Soviet Bloc; Unity and Conflict*. Cambridge: Harvard University Press, 1960.

DEUTSCHER, ISAAC, *The Great Contest, Russia and the West*. New York: Oxford University Press, 1960.

FOX, WILLIAM T. R., *The Super-Powers*. New York: Harcourt, Brace, 1944.

HARTMANN, FREDERICK H., "The Renewal of Multi-Power Diplomacy," *Antioch Review*, Vol. 13, No. 4 (Winter, 1953–1954).

HOWARD, MICHAEL, *Disengagement in Europe*. Baltimore: Penguin Books, 1958.

KENNAN, GEORGE F., *Russia, the Atom and the West*. New York: Harper, 1958.

KISSINGER, HENRY A., *The Troubled Partnership: A Reappraisal of the Atlantic Alliance*. New York: McGraw-Hill, 1965.

NEUMANN, SIGMUND, *The Future in Perspective*. New York: Putnam, 1946.

NORTHROP, F. S. C., *The Meeting of East and West*. New York: Macmillan, 1946.

———, *The Taming of the Nations*. New York: Macmillan, 1952.

ROBERTS, CHALMERS, "The Day We Didn't Go to War," *The Reporter*, September 14, 1954.

STILLMAN, EDMUND, and PFAFF, WILLIAM, *The New Politics*. New York: Coward McCann, 1961.

———, *Power and Impotence*. New York: Random House, 1966.

WOLFERS, ARNOLD, ed., *Alliance Policy in the Cold War*. Baltimore: Johns Hopkins Press, 1959.

(SEE ALSO the listings under Chapters 1, 13, and 14.)

North Atlantic Treaty, April 4, 1949

Preamble

The Parties to this Treaty reaffirm their faith in the purposes and principles of the Charter of the United Nations and their desire to live in peace with all peoples and all governments.

They are determined to safeguard the freedom, common heritage and civilization of their peoples, founded on the principles of democracy, individual liberty and the rule of law.

They seek to promote stability and well-being in the North Atlantic area.

They are resolved to unite their efforts for collective defense and for the preservation of peace and security.

They therefore agree to this North Atlantic Treaty:

Article 1

The Parties undertake, as set forth in the Charter of the United Nations, to settle any international disputes in which they may be involved by peaceful means in such a manner that international peace and security, and justice, are not endangered, and to refrain in their international relations from the threat or use of force in any manner inconsistent with the purposes of the United Nations.

Article 2

The Parties will contribute toward the further development of peaceful and friendly international relations by strengthening their free institutions, by bringing about a better understanding of the principles upon which these institutions are founded, and by promoting conditions of stability and well-being. They will seek to eliminate conflict in their international economic policies and will encourage economic collaboration between any or all of them.

Article 3

In order more effectively to achieve the objectives of this Treaty, the Parties, separately and jointly, by means of continuous and effective self-help and mutual aid, will maintain and develop their individual and collective capacity to resist armed attack.

Article 4

The Parties will consult together whenever, in the opinion of any of them, the territorial integrity, political independence or security of any of the Parties is threatened.

Article 5

The Parties agree that an armed attack against one or more of them in Europe or North America shall be considered an attack against them all; and consequently they agree that, if such an armed attack occurs, each of them, in exercise of the right of individual or collective self-defense recognized by Article 51 of the Charter of the United Nations, will assist the Party or Parties so attacked by taking forthwith, individually and in concert with the other Parties, such action as it deems necessary, including the use of armed force, to restore and maintain the security of the North Atlantic area.

Any such armed attack and all measures taken as a result thereof shall immediately be reported to the Security Council. Such measures shall be terminated when the Security Council has taken the measures necessary to restore and maintain international peace and security.

Article 6

For the purpose of Article 5 an armed attack on one or more of the Parties is deemed to include an armed attack on the territory of any of the Parties in Europe or North America, on the Algerian departments of France, on the occupation forces of any Party in Europe, on the islands under the jurisdiction of any Party in the North Atlantic area north of the Tropic of Cancer or on the vessels or aircraft in this area of any of the Parties.

Article 7

This Treaty does not affect, and shall not be interpreted as affecting, in any way the rights and obligations under the Charter of the Parties which are members of the United Nations, or the primary responsibility of the Security Council for the maintenance of international peace and security.

Article 8

Each Party declares that none of the international engagements now in force between it and any other of the Parties or any third state is in conflict with the provisions of this Treaty, and undertakes not to enter into any international engagement in conflict with this Treaty.

Article 9

The Parties hereby establish a council, on which each of them shall be represented, to consider matters concerning the implementation of this Treaty. The council shall be so organized as to be able to meet promptly at any time. The council shall set up such subsidiary bodies as may be necessary; in particular it shall establish a defense committee which shall recommend measures for the implementation of Articles 3 and 5.

Article 10

The Parties may, by unanimous agreement, invite any other European state in a position to further the principles of this Treaty and to contribute to the security of the North Atlantic area to accede to this Treaty. Any state so invited may become a party to the Treaty by depositing its instrument of accession with the Government of the United States of America. The Government of the United

States of America will inform each of the Parties of the deposit of each such instrument of accession.

Article 11

This Treaty shall be ratified and its provisions carried out by Parties in accordance with their respective constitutional processes. The instruments of ratification shall be deposited as soon as possible with the Government of the United States of America, which will notify all the other signatories of each deposit. The Treaty shall enter into force between the states which have ratified it as soon as the ratifications of the majority of the signatories, including the ratifications of Belgium, Canada, France, Luxembourg, the Netherlands, the United Kingdom and the United States, have been deposited and shall come into effect with respect to other states on the date of the deposit of their ratifications.

Article 12

After the Treaty has been in force for ten years, or at any time thereafter, the Parties shall, if any of them so requests, consult together for the purpose of reviewing the Treaty, having regard for the factors then affecting peace and security in the North Atlantic area, including the development of universal as well as regional arrangements under the Charter of the United Nations for the maintenance of international peace and security.

Article 13

After the Treaty has been in force for twenty years, any Party may cease to be a Party one year after its notice of denunciation has been given to the Government of the United States of America, which will inform the Governments of the other Parties of the deposit of each notice of denunciation.

Article 14

This Treaty, of which the English and French texts are equally authentic, shall be deposited in the archives of the Government of the United States of America. Duly certified copies thereof will be transmitted by that Government to the Governments of the other signatories.

In witness whereof, the undersigned plenipotentiaries have signed this Treaty. Done at Washington, the fourth day of April, 1949.

Charter of the United Nations[*]

We the peoples of the United Nations determined

to save succeeding generations from the scourge of war, which twice in our lifetime has brought untold sorrow to mankind, and

to reaffirm faith in fundamental human rights, in the dignity and worth of the human person, in the equal rights of men and women and of nations large and small, and

to establish conditions under which justice and respect for the obligations arising from treaties and other sources of international law can be maintained, and

to promote social progress and better standards of life in larger freedom,

and for these ends

to practice tolerance and live together in peace with one another as good neighbors, and

to unite our strength to maintain international peace and security, and

to ensure, by the acceptance of principles and the institution of methods, that armed force shall not be used, save in the common interest, and

to employ international machinery for the promotion of the economic and social advancement of all peoples,

have resolved to combine our efforts to accomplish these aims.

Accordingly, our respective Governments, through representatives assembled in the city of San Francisco, who have exhibited their full powers found to be in good and due form, have agreed to the present Charter of the United Nations and do hereby establish an international organization to be known as the United Nations.

CHAPTER I
PURPOSES AND PRINCIPLES

Article 1

The Purposes of the United Nations are:

1. To maintain international peace and security, and to that end: to take effective collective measures for the prevention and removal of threats to the peace, and for the suppression of acts of aggression or other breaches of the peace, and to bring about by peaceful means, and in conformity with the principles of justice and

---

[*] Amendments are in italics.

international law, adjustment or settlement of international disputes or situations which might lead to a breach of the peace;

2. To develop friendly relations among nations based on respect for the principle of equal rights and self-determination of peoples, and to take other appropriate measures to strengthen universal peace;

3. To achieve international cooperation in solving international problems of an economic, social, cultural, or humanitarian character, and in promoting and encouraging respect for human rights and for fundamental freedoms for all without distinction as to race, sex, language, or religion; and

4. To be a center for harmonizing the actions of nations in the attainment of these common ends.

Article 2

The Organization and its Members, in pursuit of the Purposes stated in Article 1, shall act in accordance with the following Principles.

1. The Organization is based on the principle of the sovereign equality of all its Members.

2. All Members, in order to ensure to all of them the rights and benefits resulting from membership, shall fulfil in good faith the obligations assumed by them in accordance with the present Charter.

3. All Members shall settle their international disputes by peaceful means in such a manner that international peace and security, and justice, are not endangered.

4. All Members shall refrain in their international relations from the threat or use of force against the territorial integrity or political independence of any state, or in any other manner inconsistent with the Purposes of the United Nations.

5. All Members shall give the United Nations every assistance in any action it takes in accordance with the present Charter, and shall refrain from giving assistance to any state against which the United Nations is taking preventive or enforcement action.

6. The Organization shall ensure that states which are not Members of the United Nations act in accordance with these Principles so far as may be necessary for the maintenance of international peace and security.

7. Nothing contained in the present Charter shall authorize the United Nations to intervene in matters which are essentially within the domestic jurisdiction of any state or shall require the Members to submit such matters to settlement under the present Charter; but this principle shall not prejudice the application of enforcement measures under Chapter VII.

CHAPTER II
MEMBERSHIP

Article 3

The original Members of the United Nations shall be the states which, having participated in the United Nations Conference on International Organization at San Francisco, or having previously signed the Declaration by United Nations of January 1, 1942, sign the present Charter and ratify it in accordance with Article 110.

Article 4

1. Membership in the United Nations is open to all other peace-loving states which accept the obligations contained in the present Charter and, in the judgment of the Organization, are able and willing to carry out these obligations.

2. The admission of any such state to membership in the United Nations will be effected by a decision of the General Assembly upon the recommendation of the Security Council.

Article 5

A Member of the United Nations against which preventive or enforcement action has been taken by the Security Council may be suspended from the exercise of the rights and privileges of membership by the General Assembly upon the recommendation of the Security Council. The exercise of these rights and privileges may be restored by the Security Council.

Article 6

A member of the United Nations which has persistently violated the Principles contained in the present Charter may be expelled from the Organization by the General Assembly upon the recommendation of the Security Council.

CHAPTER III
ORGANS

Article 7

1. There are established as the principal organs of the United Nations: a General Assembly, a Security Council, an Economic and Social Council, a Trusteeship Council, an International Court of Justice, and a Secretariat.

2. Such subsidiary organs as may be found necessary may be established in accordance with the present Charter.

Article 8

The United Nations shall place no restrictions on the eligibility of men and women to participate in any capacity and under conditions of equality in its principal and subsidiary organs.

CHAPTER IV
THE GENERAL ASSEMBLY
Composition

Article 9

1. The General Assembly shall consist of all the Members of the United Nations.

2. Each Member shall have not more than five representatives in the General Assembly.

Functions and Powers

Article 10

The General Assembly may discuss any questions or any matters within the scope of the present Charter or relating to the powers and functions of any organs provided for in the present Charter, and except as provided in Article 12, may make recommendations to the Members of the United Nations or to the Security Council or to both on any such questions or matters.

Article 11

1. The General Assembly may consider the general principles of cooperation in the maintenance of international peace and security, including the principles governing disarmament and the regulation of armaments, and may make recommendations with regard to such principles to the Members or to the Security Council or to both.

2. The General Assembly may discuss any questions relating to the maintenance of international peace and security brought before it by any Member of the United Nations, or by the Security Council, or by a state which is not a Member of the United Nations in accordance with Article 35, paragraph 2, and, except as provided in Article 12, may make recommendations with regard to any such questions to the state or states concerned or to the Security Council or to both. Any such question on which action is necessary shall be referred to the Security Council by the General Assembly either before or after discussion.

3. The General Assembly may call the attention of the Security Council to situations which are likely to endanger international peace and security.

4. The powers of the General Assembly set forth in this Article shall not limit the general scope of Article 10.

Article 12

1. While the Security Council is exercising in respect of any dispute or situation the functions assigned to it in the present Charter, the General Assembly shall not make any recommendation with regard to that dispute or situation unless the Security Council so requests.

2. The Secretary-General, with the consent of the Security Council, shall notify the General Assembly at each session of any matters relative to the maintenance of international peace and security which are being dealt with by the Security Council and shall similarly notify the General Assembly, or the Members of the United Nations if the General Assembly is not in session, immediately the Security Council ceases to deal with such matters.

Article 13

1. The General Assembly shall initiate studies and make recommendations for the purpose of:

a. promoting international cooperation in the political field and encouraging the progressive development of international law and its codification;

b. promoting international cooperation in the economic, social, cultural, educational, and health fields, and assisting in the realization of human rights and fundamental freedoms for all without distinction as to race, sex, language, or religion.

2. The further responsibilities, functions, and powers of the General Assembly with respect to matters mentioned in paragraph 1 (b) above are set forth in Chapters IX and X.

Article 14

Subject to the provisions of Article 12, the General Assembly may recommend measures for the peaceful adjustment of any situation, regardless of origin, which it deems likely to impair the general welfare or friendly relations among nations, including situations resulting from a violation of the provisions of the present Charter setting forth the Purposes and Principles of the United Nations.

Article 15

1. The General Assembly shall receive and consider annual and special reports from the Security Council; these reports shall include an account of the measures that the Security Council has decided upon or taken to maintain international peace and security.

2. The General Assembly shall receive and consider reports from the other organs of the United Nations.

Article 16

The General Assembly shall perform such functions with respect to the international trusteeship system as are assigned to it under Chapters XII and XIII, including the approval of the trusteeship agreements for areas not designated as strategic.

Article 17

1. The General Assembly shall consider and approve the budget of the Organization.

2. The expenses of the Organization shall be borne by the Members as apportioned by the General Assembly.

3. The General Assembly shall consider and approve any financial and budgetary arrangements with specialized agencies referred to in Article 57 and shall examine the administrative budgets of such specialized agencies with a view to making recommendations to the agencies concerned.

Voting

Article 18

1. Each member of the General Assembly shall have one vote.

2. Decisions of the General Assembly on important questions shall be made by a two-thirds majority of the members present and voting. These questions shall include: recommendations with respect to the maintenance of international peace and security, the election of the non-permanent members of the Security Council, the election of the members of the Economic and Social Council, the election of members of the Trusteeship Council in accordance with paragraph 1 (c) of Article 86, the admission of new Members to the United Nations, the suspension of the rights and privileges of membership, the expulsion of Members, questions relating to the operation of the trusteeship system, and budgetary questions.

3. Decisions on other questions, including the determination of additional cate-

gories of questions to be decided by a two-thirds majority, shall be made by a majority of the members present and voting.

Article 19

A Member of the United Nations which is in arrears in the payment of its financial contributions to the Organization shall have no vote in the General Assembly if the amount of its arrears equals or exceeds the amount of the contributions due from it for the preceding two full years. The General Assembly may, nevertheless, permit such a Member to vote if it is satisfied that the failure to pay is due to conditions beyond the control of the Member.

Procedure

Article 20

The General Assembly shall meet in regular annual sessions and in such special sessions as occasion may require. Special sessions shall be convoked by the Secretary-General at the request of the Security Council or of a majority of the Members of the United Nations.

Article 21

The General Assembly shall adopt its own rules of procedure. It shall elect its President for each session.

Article 22

The General Assembly may establish such subsidiary organs as it deems necessary for the performance of its functions.

CHAPTER V
THE SECURITY COUNCIL
Composition

Article 23

1. The Security Council shall consist of *fifteen* Members of the United Nations. The Republic of China, France, the Union of Soviet Socialist Republics, the United Kingdom of Great Britain and Northern Ireland, and the United States of America shall be permanent members of the Security Council. The General Assembly shall elect *ten* other Members of the United Nations to be non-permanent members of the Security Council, due regard being specially paid, in the first instance to the contribution of Members of the United Nations to the maintenance of international peace and security and to the other purposes of the Organization, and also to equitable geographical distribution.

2. The non-permanent members of the Security Council shall be elected for a term of two years. *In the first election of the non-permanent members after the increase of the membership of the Security Council from eleven to fifteen, two of the four additional members shall be chosen for a term of one year.* A retiring member shall not be eligible for immediate re-election.

3. Each member of the Security Council shall have one representative.

Functions and Powers
Article 24

1. In order to ensure prompt and effective action by the United Nations, its Members confer on the Security Council primary responsibility for the maintenance of international peace and security, and agree that in carrying out its duties under this responsibility the Security Council acts on their behalf.

2. In discharging these duties the Security Council shall act in accordance with the Purposes and Principles of the United Nations. The specific powers granted to the Security Council for the discharge of these duties are laid down in Chapters VI, VII, VIII, and XII.

3. The Security Council shall submit annual and, when necessary, special reports to the General Assembly for its consideration.

Article 25

The Members of the United Nations agree to accept and carry out the decisions of the Security Council in accordance with the present Charter.

Article 26

In order to promote the establishment and maintenance of international peace and security with the least diversion for armaments of the world's human and economic resources, the Security Council shall be responsible for formulating, with the assistance of the Military Staff Committee referred to in Article 47, plans to be submitted to the Members of the United Nations for the establishment of a system for the regulation of armaments.

Voting
Article 27

1. Each member of the Security Council shall have one vote.

2. Decisions of the Security Council on procedural matters shall be made by an affirmative vote of *nine* members.

3. Decisions of the Security Council on all other matters shall be made by an affirmative vote of *nine* members including the concurring votes of the permanent members; provided that, in decisions under Chapter VI, and under paragraph 3 of Article 52, a party to a dispute shall abstain from voting.

Procedure
Article 28

1. The Security Council shall be so organized as to be able to function continuously. Each member of the Security Council shall for this purpose be represented at all times at the seat of the Organization.

2. The Security Council shall hold periodic meetings at which each of its members may, if it so desires, be represented by a member of the government or by some other specially designated representative.

3. The Security Council may hold meetings at such places other than the seat of the Organization as in its judgment will best facilitate its work.

Article 29

The Security Council may establish such subsidiary organs as it deems necessary for the performance of its functions.

Article 30

The Security Council shall adopt its own rules of procedure, including the method of selecting its President.

Article 31

Any Member of the United Nations which is not a member of the Security Council may participate, without vote, in the discussion of any question brought before the Security Council whenever the latter considers that the interests of that Member are specially affected.

Article 32

Any Member of the United Nations which is not a member of the Security Council or any state which is not a Member of the United Nations, if it is a party to a dispute under consideration by the Security Council, shall be invited to participate, without vote, in the discussion relating to the dispute. The Security Council shall lay down such conditions as it deems just for the participation of a state which is not a Member of the United Nations.

CHAPTER VI
PACIFIC SETTLEMENT OF DISPUTES

Article 33

1. The parties to any dispute, the continuance of which is likely to endanger the maintenance of international peace and security, shall, first of all, seek a solution by negotiation, enquiry, mediation, conciliation, arbitration, judicial settlement, resort to regional agencies or arrangements, or other peaceful means of their own choice.

2. The Security Council shall, when it deems necessary, call upon the parties to settle their dispute by such means.

Article 34

The Security Council may investigate any dispute, or any situation which might lead to international friction or give rise to a dispute, in order to determine whether the continuance of the dispute or situation is likely to endanger the maintenance of international peace and security.

Article 35

1. Any Member of the United Nations may bring any dispute, or any situation of the nature referred to in Article 34, to the attention of the Security Council or of the General Assembly.

2. A state which is not a Member of the United Nations may bring to the attention of the Security Council or of the General Assembly any dispute to which it

is a party if it accepts in advance, for the purposes of the dispute, the obligations of pacific settlement provided in the present Charter.

3. The proceedings of the General Assembly in respect of matters brought to its attention under this Article will be subject to the provisions of Articles 11 and 12.

Article 36

1. The Security Council may, at any stage of a dispute of the nature referred to in Article 33 or of a situation of like nature, recommend appropriate procedures or methods of adjustment.

2. The Security Council should take into consideration any procedures for the settlement of the dispute which have already been adopted by the parties.

3. In making recommendations under this Article the Security Council should also take into consideration that legal disputes should as a general rule be referred by the parties to the International Court of Justice in accordance with the provisions of the Statute of the Court.

Article 37

1. Should the parties to a dispute of the nature referred to in Article 33 fail to settle it by the means indicated in that Article, they shall refer it to the Security Council.

2. If the Security Council deems that the continuance of the dispute is in fact likely to endanger the maintenance of international peace and security, it shall decide whether to take action under Article 36 or to recommend such terms of settlement as it may consider appropriate.

Article 38

Without prejudice to the provisions of Articles 33 to 37, the Security Council may, if all the parties to any dispute so request, make recommendations to the parties with a view to a pacific settlement of the dispute.

Chapter VII
Action With Respect to Threats to the Peace, Breaches of the Peace, and Acts of Aggression

Article 39

The Security Council shall determine the existence of any threat to the peace, breach of the peace, or act of aggression and shall make recommendations, or decide what measures shall be taken in accordance with Articles 41 and 42, to maintain or restore international peace and security.

Article 40

In order to prevent an aggravation of the situation, the Security Council may, before making the recommendations or deciding upon the measures provided for in Article 39, call upon the parties concerned to comply with such provisional measures as it deems necessary or desirable. Such provisional measures shall be without prejudice to the rights, claims, or position of the parties concerned. The Security Council shall duly take account of failure to comply with such provisional measures.

Article 41

The Security Council may decide what measures not involving the use of armed force are to be employed to give effect to its decisions, and it may call upon the Members of the United Nations to apply such measures. These may include complete or partial interruption of economic relations and of rail, sea, air, postal, telegraphic, radio, and other means of communication, and the severance of diplomatic relations.

Article 42

Should the Security Council consider that measures provided for in Article 41 would be inadequate or have proved to be inadequate, it may take such action by air, sea, or land forces as may be necessary to maintain or restore international peace and security. Such action may include demonstrations, blockade, and other operations by air, sea, or land forces of Members of the United Nations.

Article 43

1. All Members of the United Nations, in order to contribute to the maintenance of international peace and security, undertake to make available to the Security Council, on its call and in accordance with a special agreement or agreements, armed forces, assistance, and facilities, including rights of passage, necessary for the purpose of maintaining international peace and security.

2. Such agreement or agreements shall govern the numbers and types of forces, their degree of readiness and general location, and the nature of the facilities and assistance to be provided.

3. The agreement or agreements shall be negotiated as soon as possible on the initiative of the Security Council. They shall be concluded between the Security Council and Members or between the Security Council and groups of Members and shall be subject to ratification by the signatory states in accordance with their respective constitutional processes.

Article 44

When the Security Council has decided to use force it shall, before calling upon a Member not represented on it to provide armed forces in fulfillment of the obligations assumed under Article 43, invite that Member, if the Member so desires, to participate in the decisions of the Security Council concerning the employment of contingents of that Member's armed forces.

Article 45

In order to enable the United Nations to take urgent military measures, Members shall hold immediately available national air-force contingents for combined international enforcement action. The strength and degree of readiness of these contingents and plans for their combined action shall be determined, within the limits laid down in the special agreement or agreements referred to in Article 43, by the Security Council with the assistance of the Military Staff Committee.

Article 46

Plans for the application of armed force shall be made by the Security Council with the assistance of the Military Staff Committee.

Article 47

1. There shall be established a Military Staff Committee to advise and assist the Security Council on all questions relating to the Security Council's military requirements for the maintenance of international peace and security, the employment and command of forces placed at its disposal, the regulation of armaments, and possible disarmament.

2. The Military Staff Committee shall consist of the Chiefs of Staff of the permanent members of the Security Council or their representatives. Any Member of the United Nations not permanently represented on the Committee shall be invited by the Committee to be associated with it when the efficient discharge of the Committee's responsibilities requires the participation of that Member in its work.

3. The Military Staff Committee shall be responsible under the Security Council for the strategic direction of any armed forces placed at the disposal of the Security Council. Questions relating to the command of such forces shall be worked out subsequently.

4. The Military Staff Committee, with the authorization of the Security Council and after consultation with appropriate regional agencies, may establish regional subcommittees.

Article 48

1. The action required to carry out the decisions of the Security Council for the maintenance of international peace and security shall be taken by all the Members of the United Nations or by some of them, as the Security Council may determine.

2. Such decisions shall be carried out by the Members of the United Nations directly and through their action in the appropriate international agencies of which they are members.

Article 49

The Members of the United Nations shall join in affording mutual assistance in carrying out the measures decided upon by the Security Council.

Article 50

If preventive or enforcement measures against any state are taken by the Security Council, any other state, whether a Member of the United Nations or not, which finds itself confronted with special economic problems arising from the carrying out of those measures shall have the right to consult the Security Council with regard to a solution of those problems.

Article 51

Nothing in the present Charter shall impair the inherent right of individual or collective self-defense if an armed attack occurs against a Member of the United Nations, until the Security Council has taken the measures necessary to maintain international peace and security. Measures taken by Members in the exercise of this right of self-defense shall be immediately reported to the Security Council and shall not in any way affect the authority and responsibility of the Security Council under the present Charter to take at any time such action as it deems necessary in order to maintain or restore international peace and security.

Chapter VIII
Regional Arrangements

Article 52

1. Nothing in the present Charter precludes the existence of regional arrangements or agencies for dealing with such matters relating to the maintenance of international peace and security as are appropriate for regional action, provided that such arrangements or agencies and their activities are consistent with the Purposes and Principles of the United Nations.

2. The Members of the United Nations entering into such arrangements or constituting such agencies shall make every effort to achieve pacific settlement of local disputes through such regional arrangements or by such regional agencies before referring them to the Security Council.

3. The Security Council shall encourage the development of pacific settlement of local disputes through such regional arrangements or by such regional agencies either on the initiative of the states concerned or by reference from the Security Council.

4. This Article in no way impairs the application of Articles 34 and 35.

Article 53

1. The Security Council shall, where appropriate, utilize such regional arrangements or agencies for enforcement action under its authority. But no enforcement action shall be taken under regional arrangements or by regional agencies without the authorization of the Security Council, with the exception of measures against any enemy state, as defined in paragraph 2 of this Article, provided for pursuant to Article 107 or in regional arrangements directed against renewal of aggressive policy on the part of any such state, until such time as the Organization may, on request of the Governments concerned, be charged with the responsibility for preventing further aggression by such a state.

2. The term enemy state as used in paragraph 1 of this Article applies to any state which during the Second World War has been an enemy of any signatory of the present Charter.

Article 54

The Security Council shall at all times be kept fully informed of activities undertaken or in contemplation under regional arrangements or by regional agencies for the maintenance of international peace and security.

Chapter IX
International Economic and Social Cooperation

Article 55

With a view to the creation of conditions of stability and well-being which are necessary for peaceful and friendly relations among nations based on respect for the principle of equal rights and self-determination of peoples, the United Nations shall promote:

a. higher standards of living, full employment, and conditions of economic and social progress and development;

b. solutions of international economic, social, health, and related problems; and international cultural and educational cooperation; and

c. universal respect for, and observance of, human rights and fundamental freedoms for all without distinction as to race, sex, language, or religion.

Article 56

All Members pledge themselves to take joint and separate action in cooperation with the Organization for the achievement of the purposes set forth in Article 55.

Article 57

1. The various specialized agencies, established by intergovernmental agreement and having wide international responsibilities, as defined in their basic instruments, in economic, social, cultural, educational, health, and related fields, shall be brought into relationship with the United Nations in accordance with the provisions of Article 63.

2. Such agencies thus brought into relationship with the United Nations are hereinafter referred to as specialized agencies.

Article 58

The Organization shall make recommendations for the coordination of the policies and activities of the specialized agencies.

Article 59

The Organization shall, where appropriate, initiate negotiations among the states concerned for the creation of any new specialized agencies required for the accomplishment of the purposes set forth in Article 55.

Article 60

Responsibility for the discharge of the functions of the Organization set forth in this Chapter shall be vested in the General Assembly and, under the authority of the General Assembly, in the Economic and Social Council, which shall have for this purpose the powers set forth in Chapter X.

CHAPTER X
THE ECONOMIC AND SOCIAL COUNCIL

Composition

Article 61

1. The Economic and Social Council shall consist of *twenty-seven* Members of the United Nations elected by the General Assembly.

2. Subject to the provisions of paragraph 3, *nine* members of the Economic and Social Council shall be elected each year for a term of three years. A retiring member shall be eligible for immediate re-election.

3. At the first election *after the increase in the membership of the Economic and Social Council from eighteen to twenty-seven members, in addition to the members elected in place of the six members whose term of office expires at the*

end of that year, nine additional members shall be elected. Of these nine additional members, the term of office of three members so elected shall expire at the end of one year, and of the three other members at the end of two years, in accordance with arrangements made by the General Assembly.

4. Each member of the Economic and Social Council shall have one representative.

Functions and Powers

Article 62

1. The Economic and Social Council may make or initiate studies and reports with respect to international economic, social, cultural, educational, health, and related matters and may make recommendations with respect to any such matters to the General Assembly, to the Members of the United Nations, and to the specialized agencies concerned.

2. It may make recommendations for the purpose of promoting respect for, and observance of, human rights and fundamental freedoms for all.

3. It may prepare draft conventions for submission to the General Assembly, with respect to matters falling within its competence.

4. It may call, in accordance with the rules prescribed by the United Nations, international conferences on matters falling within its competence.

Article 63

1. The Economic and Social Council may enter into agreements with any of the agencies referred to in Article 57, defining the terms on which the agency concerned shall be brought into relationship with the United Nations. Such agreements shall be subject to approval by the General Assembly.

2. It may coordinate the activities of the specialized agencies through consultation with and recommendations to such agencies and through recommendations to the General Assembly and to the Members of the United Nations.

Article 64

1. The Economic and Social Council may take appropriate steps to obtain regular reports from the specialized agencies. It may make arrangements with the Members of the United Nations and with the specialized agencies to obtain reports on the steps taken to give effect to its own recommendations and to recommendations on matters falling within its competence made by the General Assembly.

2. It may communicate its observations on these reports to the General Assembly.

Article 65

The Economic and Social Council may furnish information to the Security Council and shall assist the Security Council upon its request.

Article 66

1. The Economic and Social Council shall perform such functions as fall within its competence in connection with the carrying out of the recommendations of the General Assembly.

2. It may, with the approval of the General Assembly, perform services at the request of Members of the United Nations and at the request of specialized agencies.

3. It shall perform such other functions as are specified elsewhere in the present Charter or as may be assigned to it by the General Assembly.

Voting

Article 67

1. Each member of the Economic and Social Council shall have one vote.

2. Decisions of the Economic and Social Council shall be made by a majority of the members present and voting.

Procedure

Article 68

The Economic and Social Council shall set up commissions in economic and social fields and for the promotion of human rights, and such other commissions as may be required for the performance of its functions.

Article 69

The Economic and Social Council shall invite any Member of the United Nations to participate, without vote, in its deliberations on any matter of particular concern to that Member.

Article 70

The Economic and Social Council may make arrangements for representatives of the specialized agency to participate, without vote, in its deliberations and in those of the commissions established by it, and for its representatives to participate in the deliberations of the specialized agencies.

Article 71

The Economic and Social Council may make suitable arrangements for consultation with non-governmental organizations which are concerned with matters within its competence. Such arrangements may be made with international organizations and, where appropriate, with national organizations after consultation with the Member of the United Nations concerned.

Article 72

1. The Economic and Social Council shall adopt its own rules of procedure, including the method of selecting its President.

2. The Economic and Social Council shall meet as required in accordance with its rules, which shall include provision for the convening of meetings on the request of a majority of its members.

CHAPTER XI
DECLARATION REGARDING NON-SELF-GOVERNING TERRITORIES

Article 73

Members of the United Nations which have or assume responsibilities for the administration of territories whose peoples have not yet attained a full measure of self-government recognize the principle that the interests of the inhabitants of these territories are paramount, and accept as a sacred trust the obligation to promote to the utmost, within the system of international peace and security established by the present Charter, the well-being of the inhabitants of these territories, and, to this end:

a. to ensure, with due respect for the culture of the peoples concerned, their political, economic, social, and educational advancement, their just treatment, and their protection against abuses;

b. to develop self-government, to take due account of the political aspirations of the peoples, and to assist them in the progressive development of their free political institutions, according to the particular circumstances of each territory and its peoples and their varying stages of advancement;

c. to further international peace and security;

d. to promote constructive measures of development, to encourage research, and to cooperate with one another and, when and where appropriate, with specialized international bodies with a view to the practical achievement of the social, economic, and scientific purposes set forth in this Article; and

e. to transmit regularly to the Secretary-General for information purposes, subject to such limitation as security and constitutional considerations may require, statistical and other information of a technical nature relating to economic, social, and educational conditions in the territories for which they are respectively responsible other than those territories to which Chapters XII and XIII apply.

Article 74

Members of the United Nations also agree that their policy in respect of the territories to which this Chapter applies, no less than in respect of their metropolitan areas, must be based on the general principle of good-neighborliness, due account being taken of the interests and well-being of the rest of the world, in social, economic, and commercial matters.

CHAPTER XII
INTERNATIONAL TRUSTEESHIP SYSTEM

Article 75

The United Nations shall establish under its authority an international trusteeship system for the administration and supervision of such territories as may be placed thereunder by subsequent individual agreements. These territories are hereinafter referred to as trust territories.

Article 76

The basic objectives of the trusteeship system in accordance with the Purposes of the United Nations laid down in Article 1 of the present Charter, shall be:

a. to further international peace and security;

b. to promote the political, economic, social, and educational advancement of the inhabitants of the trust territories, and their progressive development towards self-government or independence as may be appropriate to the particular circumstances of each territory and its peoples and the freely expressed wishes of the peoples concerned, and as may be provided by the terms of each trusteeship agreement;

c. to encourage respect for human rights and for fundamental freedoms for all without distinction as to race, sex, language, or religion, and to encourage recognition of the interdependence of the peoples of the world; and

d. to ensure equal treatment in social, economic, and commercial matters for all Members of the United Nations and their nationals, and also equal treatment for the latter in the administration of justice, without prejudice to the attainment of the foregoing objectives and subject to the provisions of Article 80.

Article 77

1. The trusteeship system shall apply to such territories in the following categories as may be placed thereunder by means of trusteeship agreements:

a. territories now held under mandate;

b. territories which may be detached from enemy states as a result of the Second World War; and

c. territories voluntarily placed under the system by states responsible for their administration.

2. It will be a matter for subsequent agreement as to which territories in the foregoing categories will be brought under the trusteeship system and upon what terms.

Article 78

The trusteeship system shall not apply to territories which have become Members of the United Nations, relationship among which shall be based on respect for the principle of sovereign equality.

Article 79

The terms of trusteeship for each territory to be placed under the trusteeship system, including any alteration or amendment, shall be agreed upon by the states directly concerned, including the mandatory power in the case of territories held under mandate by a Member of the United Nations, and shall be approved as provided for in Articles 83 and 85.

Article 80

1. Except as may be agreed upon in individual trusteeship agreements, made under Articles 77, 79, and 81, placing each territory under the trusteeship system, and until such agreements have been concluded, nothing in this Chapter shall be construed in or of itself to alter in any manner the right whatsoever of any states or any peoples or the terms of existing international instruments to which Members of the United Nations may respectively be parties.

2. Paragraph 1 of this Article shall not be interpreted as giving grounds for delay or postponement of the negotiation and conclusion of agreements for placing mandated and other territories under the trusteeship system as provided for in Article 77.

Article 81

The trusteeship agreement shall in each case include the terms under which the trust territory will be administered and designate the authority which will exercise the administration of the trust territory. Such authority, hereinafter called the administering authority, may be one or more states or the Organization itself.

Article 82

There may be designated, in any trusteeship agreement, a strategic area or areas which may include part or all of the trust territory to which the agreement applies, without prejudice to any special agreement or agreements made under Article 43.

Article 83

1. All functions of the United Nations relating to strategic areas, including the approval of the terms of the trusteeship agreements and of their alteration or amendment, shall be exercised by the Security Council.

2. The basic objectives set forth in Article 76 shall be applicable to the people of each strategic area.

3. The Security Council shall, subject to the provisions of the trusteeship agreements and without prejudice to security considerations, avail itself of the assistance of the Trusteeship Council to perform those functions of the United Nations under the trusteeship system relating to political, economic, social, and educational matters in the strategic areas.

Article 84

It shall be the duty of the administering authority to ensure that the trust territory shall play its part in the maintenance of international peace and security. To this end the administering authority may make use of volunteer forces, facilities, and assistance from the trust territory in carrying out the obligations towards the Security Council undertaken in this regard by the administering authority, as well as for local defense and the maintenance of law and order within the trust territory.

Article 85

1. The functions of the United Nations with regard to trusteeship agreements for all areas not designated as strategic, including the approval of the terms of the trusteeship agreements and of their alteration or amendment, shall be exercised by the General Assembly.

2. The Trusteeship Council, operating under the authority of the General Assembly, shall assist the General Assembly in carrying out these functions.

CHAPTER XIII
THE TRUSTEESHIP COUNCIL

Composition

Article 86

1. The Trusteeship Council shall consist of the following Members of the United Nations:

a. those Members administering trust territories;

b. such of those Members mentioned by name in Article 23 as are not administering trust territories; and

c. as many other Members elected for three-year terms by the General Assembly as may be necessary to ensure that the total number of members of the Trusteeship Council is equally divided between those Members of the United Nations which administer trust territories and those which do not.

2. Each member of the Trusteeship Council shall designate one specially qualified person to represent it therein.

Functions and Powers

Article 87

The General Assembly and, under its authority, the Trusteeship Council, in carrying out their functions, may:

a. consider reports submitted by the administering authority;

b. accept petitions and examine them in consultation with the administering authority;

c. provide for periodic visits to the respective trust territories at times agreed upon with the administering authority; and

d. take these and other actions in conformity with the terms of the trusteeship agreements.

Article 88

The Trusteeship Council shall formulate a questionnaire on the political, economic, social, and educational advancement of the inhabitants of each trust territory, and the administering authority for each trust territory within the competence of the General Assembly shall make an annual report to the General Assembly upon the basis of such questionnaire.

Voting

Article 89

1. Each member of the Trusteeship Council shall have one vote.

2. Decisions of the Trusteeship Council shall be made by a majority of the members present and voting.

Procedure

Article 90

1. The Trusteeship Council shall adopt its own rules of procedure, including the method of selecting its President.

2. The Trusteeship Council shall meet as required in accordance with its rules, which shall include provision for the convening of meetings on the request of a majority of its members.

Article 91

The Trusteeship Council shall, when appropriate, avail itself of the assistance of the Economic and Social Council and of the specialized agencies in regard to matters with which they are respectively concerned.

Chapter XIV
The International Court of Justice

Article 92

The International Court of Justice shall be the principal judicial organ of the United Nations. It shall function in accordance with the annexed Statute, which is based upon the Statute of the Permanent Court of International Justice and forms an integral part of the present Charter.

Article 93

1. All Members of the United Nations are *ipso facto* parties to the Statute of the International Court of Justice.

2. A state which is not a Member of the United Nations may become a party to the Statute of the International Court of Justice on conditions to be determined in each case by the General Assembly upon the recommendation of the Security Council.

Article 94

1. Each Member of the United Nations undertakes to comply with the decision of the International Court of Justice in any case to which it is a party.

2. If any party to a case fails to perform the obligations incumbent upon it under a judgment rendered by the Court, the other party may have recourse to the Security Council, which may, if it deems necessary, make recommendations or decide upon measures to be taken to give effect to the judgment.

Article 95

Nothing in the present Charter shall prevent Members of the United Nations from entrusting the solution of their differences to other tribunals by virtue of agreements already in existence or which may be concluded in the future.

Article 96

1. The General Assembly or the Security Council may request the International Court of Justice to give an advisory opinion on any legal question.

2. Other organs of the United Nations and specialized agencies, which may at any time be so authorized by the General Assembly, may also request advisory opinions of the Court on legal questions arising within the scope of their activities.

CHAPTER XV
THE SECRETARIAT

Article 97

The Secretariat shall comprise a Secretary-General and such staff as the Organization may require. The Secretary-General shall be appointed by the General Assembly upon the recommendation of the Security Council. He shall be the chief administrative officer of the Organization.

Article 98

The Secretary-General shall act in that capacity in all meetings of the General Assembly, of the Security Council, of the Economic and Social Council, and of the Trusteeship Council, and shall perform such other functions as are entrusted to him by these organs. The Secretary-General shall make an annual report to the General Assembly on the work of the Organization.

Article 99

The Secretary-General may bring to the attention of the Security Council any matter which in his opinion may threaten the maintenance of international peace and security.

Article 100

1. In the performance of their duties the Secretary-General and the staff shall not seek or receive instructions from any government or from any other authority external to the Organization. They shall refrain from any action which might reflect on their position as international officials responsible only to the Organization.

2. Each Member of the United Nations undertakes to respect the exclusively international character of the responsibilities of the Secretary-General and the staff and not to seek to influence them in the discharge of their responsibilities.

Article 101

1. The staff shall be appointed by the Secretary-General under regulations established by the General Assembly.

2. Appropriate staffs shall be permanently assigned to the Economic and Social Council, the Trusteeship Council, and, as required, to other organs of the United Nations. These staffs shall form a part of the Secretariat.

3. The paramount consideration in the employment of the staff and in the determination of the conditions of service shall be the necessity of securing the highest standards of efficiency, competence, and integrity. Due regard shall be paid to the importance of recruiting the staff on as wide a geographical basis as possible.

CHAPTER XVI
MISCELLANEOUS PROVISIONS

Article 102

1. Every treaty and every international agreement entered into by any Member of the United Nations after the present Charter comes into force shall as soon as possible be registered with the Secretariat and published by it.

2. No party to any such treaty or international agreement which has not been registered in accordance with the provisions of paragraph 1 of this Article may invoke that treaty or agreement before any organ of the United Nations.

Article 103

In the event of a conflict between the obligations of the Members of the United Nations under the present Charter and their obligations under any other international agreement, their obligations under the present Charter shall prevail.

Article 104

The Organization shall enjoy in the territory of each of its Members such legal capacity as may be necessary for the exercise of its functions and the fulfillment of its purposes.

Article 105

1. The Organization shall enjoy in the territory of each of its Members such privileges and immunities as are necessary for the fulfillment of its purposes.

2. Representatives of the Members of the United Nations and officials of the Organization shall similarly enjoy such privileges and immunities as are necessary for the independent exercise of their functions in connection with the Organization.

3. The General Assembly may make recommendations with a view to determining the details of the application of paragraphs 1 and 2 of this Article or may propose conventions to the Members of the United Nations for this purpose.

CHAPTER XVII
TRANSITIONAL SECURITY ARRANGEMENTS

Article 106

Pending the coming into force of such special agreements referred to in Article 43 as in the opinion of the Security Council enable it to begin the exercise of its responsibilities under Article 42, the parties to the Four-Nation Declaration, signed at Moscow, October 30, 1943, and France, shall, in accordance with the provisions of paragraph 5 of that Declaration, consult with one another and as occasion requires with other Members of the United Nations with a view to such joint action on behalf of the Organization as may be necessary for the purpose of maintaining international peace and security.

Article 107

Nothing in the present Charter shall invalidate or preclude action, in relation to any state which during the Second World War has been an enemy of any signatory to the present Charter, taken or authorized as a result of that war by the Governments having responsibility for such action.

CHAPTER XVIII
AMENDMENTS

Article 108

Amendments to the present Charter shall come into force for all Members of the United Nations when they have been adopted by a vote of two-thirds of the members of the General Assembly and ratified in accordance with their respective constitutional processes by two-thirds of the Members of the United Nations, including all the permanent members of the Security Council.

Article 109

1. A General Conference of the Members of the United Nations for the purpose of reviewing the present Charter may be held at a date and place to be fixed by a two-thirds vote of the members of the General Assembly and by a vote of any seven members of the Security Council. Each Member of the United Nations shall have one vote in the conference.

2. Any alteration of the present Charter recommended by a two-thirds vote of the conference shall take effect when ratified in accordance with their respective constitutional processes by two-thirds of the Members of the United Nations including all the permanent members of the Security Council.

3. If such a conference has not been held before the tenth annual session of the

General Assembly following the coming into force of the present Charter, the proposal to call such a conference shall be placed on the agenda of that session of the General Assembly, and the conference shall be held if so decided by a majority vote of the members of the General Assembly and by a vote of any seven members of the Security Council.

Chapter XIX
Ratification and Signature

Article 110

1. The present Charter shall be ratified by the signatory states in accordance with their respective constitutional processes.

2. The ratifications shall be deposited with the Government of the United States of America, which shall notify all the signatory states of each deposit as well as the Secretary-General of the Organization when he has been appointed.

3. The present Charter shall come into force upon the deposit of ratifications by the Republic of China, France, the Union of Soviet Socialist Republics, the United Kingdom of Great Britain and Northern Ireland, and the United States of America, and by a majority of the other signatory states. A protocol of the ratifications deposited shall thereupon be drawn up by the Government of the United States of America which shall communicate copies thereof to all the signatory states.

4. The states signatory to the present Charter which ratify it after it has come into force will become original Members of the United Nations on the date of the deposit of their respective ratifications.

Article 111

The present Charter, of which the Chinese, French, Russian, English, and Spanish texts are equally authentic, shall remain deposited in the archives of the Government of the United States of America. Duly certified copies thereof shall be transmitted by that Government to the Governments of the other signatory states.

In faith whereof the representatives of the Governments of the United Nations have signed the present Charter.

Done at the city of San Francisco the twenty-sixth day of June, one thousand nine hundred and forty-five.

Index